*Number One: The Centennial Series of the
Association of Former Students*

A CENTENNIAL HISTORY OF

Texas A&M University

1876-1976

A CENTENNIAL HISTORY OF

Texas A&M University

1876-1976

BY

HENRY C. DETHLOFF

FOREWORD BY

JOSEPH MILTON NANCE

Texas A&M University Press

College Station

Library of Congress Cataloging in Publication Data

Dethloff, Henry C
    A centennial history of Texas A & M University, 1876-1976.

    (The Centennial series of the Association of Former
Students, Texas A & M University; no. 1)
        Bibliography: v.
        Includes index.
        1. Texas. A & M University, College Station —
History. I. Title. II. Series: Texas. A & M University,
College Station. Association of Former Students. The
Centennial series of the Association of Former Students,
Texas A & M University; no. 1.
    LD5309.D47   378.764'242   75-18687
    ISBN 1-58544-095-7

Manufactured in the United States of America
Single-volume Edition , 2000

To the students of Texas A&M

Table of Contents

VOLUME I

FIGURES

TABLES

Foreword

AS Texas A&M University enters its hundredth year of service to the people of Texas, to the nation, and indeed to all mankind, it is fitting that the full story of the founding, growth, and ever-widening role of this first state institution of higher learning in Texas should be told. Its history is presented here with accuracy, objectivity, and in a simple, readable style by a trained historian having a free, unhampered access to all official and institutional records, which were supplemented by a wealth of newspaper and private source materials and personal interviews.

The need for a state-supported college or university to make higher education more accessible to the masses had long been recognized in Texas, but none had actually been created until the Agricultural and Mechanical College of Texas was launched in 1876 under the aegis of the federal Morrill Act of 1862. On November 1, 1866, the Texas Legislature accepted the terms of the act and received 180,000 acres of federal land to constitute the basis of a permanent fund for "the endowment, support and maintenance of at least one college where the leading object shall be, without excluding other scientific and classical studies, and including military tactics, to teach such branches of learning as are related to agriculture and the mechanic arts . . . in order to promote the liberal and practical education of the industrial classes in the several pursuits and professions of life."

Also, the Legislature agreed to provide for the college by July 23, 1871, but the trying days of "reconstruction" and of radical Republican rule in Texas delayed enactment of the legislation necessary to create the college. As the deadline neared for doing so, the Legislature on April 17, 1871, officially established the "Agricultural and Mechanical College of Texas" and declared that it should be constituted, controlled, managed, and supervised as a part of The University of Texas. Such was the arrangement in many other states, where the land-grant college constituted an integral and subordinate part of the state university. While plans for implementing the college moved forward slowly, the state constitutional convention of 1875 called for the creation of The University of Texas and wrote into the Constitution of 1876 that the Agricultural and Mechanical College of Texas, scheduled to open in the fall of 1876, was to be a branch of The University of Texas, yet to be located, established, and organized. To expedite the opening of the College, the Legislature in 1875 created a separate Board of Directors specifically for Texas A&M.

By the time Texas A&M opened its doors on October 4, 1876, with an enrollment of 106 students, similar colleges created under the Morrill Act had been organized in no fewer than twenty-six states, but largely on paper. In fact, only two colleges of agriculture, those in Michigan and in Massachusetts, had made themselves felt in any considerable way.

As the result of the clever maneuvering of local Republican politicians and the willingness of the residents of Bryan and Brazos County to make a handsome donation of land for a site, the college was located near the center of population of the state, along the right-of-way of the Houston and Texas Central Railroad (the only significant railroad in the state) about four miles south of Bryan, upon a wild, bleak prairie, barren of trees and shrubs in its immediate vicinity — except, as an early student noted, for one small mesquite bush. The United States Post Office designated the location as College Station on February 7, 1877, with Henry D. Parsons appointed postmaster.

Although born during radical Republican rule in Texas, the College gained the support of the Democrats under the leadership of Governor Richard Coke, president of the College's Board of Directors, and commenced to grow slowly after the vicissitudes of the early years, which stemmed largely from its isolated location, financial problems, inadequate facilities, the vagaries of state politics, and factionalism within the faculty ranks and within the student body. Furthermore, the early years were marked by a struggle between the classicists and the representatives of the new science, technology, and pragmatism as efforts were made to define the role and scope of the College. The author fully explains and evaluates these and other early difficulties confronting the College and shows that, although there were yet to be problems, the reputation and popularity of Texas A&M had been established by 1902 and the twentieth century was to mark an expansion and strengthening of the institution.

From the beginning Texas A&M has been a school with a "difference," and that difference for more than three-quarters of a century stemmed largely from an interpretation of the "purposes" stated in the Morrill Act much narrower than that taken by most of the other land-grant colleges. Texas A&M elected to be an all-male school with compulsory Army ROTC and curricula confined largely to the fields of agriculture, engineering, and science. World War II brought fundamental changes in the nation and the state, which forced a re-examination of the purposes and objectives of the institution as interpreted by its Board of Directors. A broader concept was required to meet the needs of modern society. As a result of that re-examination, the school has been growing rapidly in enrollment since 1966. It has enriched the old programs and developed strong new ones in the humanities and social sciences, in marine science and transportation, in oceanography and meteorology. The ROTC training program has been made voluntary and now includes other branches of the armed services; and a Division of Continuing Education serves the people of Texas in the best traditions of the Morrill land-grant college concept. In the early 1970s Texas A&M was designated one of the first four Sea Grant Colleges in the nation. Its doors are now open to all qualified students regardless of sex, race, color, or ethnic group.

Yet, with all the changes that have come within the last two decades, Texas A&M continues to stress training for a useful vocation and to demonstrate in many ways that it cares about people. Through the years, as it has evolved into a great, complex university with a strong influence upon higher education, it has remained true to the charge given by Governor Coke at the dedicatory ceremonies opening Texas' first public institution of higher learning: namely, attention to duty, honor, and character. Fraternity, tolerance, leadership, loyalty to country, physical fitness, clean living, excellence in scholarship, and service are its watchwords. Its student body still maintains the high *esprit de corps* for which it has long been noted.

In the last quarter of a century, Texas A&M has, with remarkable swiftness, come of age; today it is meeting, within a broader spectrum, the land-grant college commitment to educate the masses in the practical arts, not to the exclusion of the liberal arts.

JOSEPH MILTON NANCE

Acknowledgments

THE author is indebted to many people at Texas A&M University for their generous advice, information, and other assistance in the preparation of this manuscript. Joseph Milton Nance, professor of history and head of the Department of History, read every chapter as it was prepared and gave invaluable assistance as to style and content. Nance, with Homer Lloyd Heaton, dean of Admissions and Records, and Edward John Romieniec, dean of the College of Architecture and Environmental Design, comprised the sponsoring *ad hoc* Centennial Celebration Committee under whose purview the preparation of this manuscript was authorized. Ernest Langford ('13), professor emeritus and former head of the Department of Architecture and Texas A&M archivist, provided much needed counseling and many insights during the preparation of the manuscript. I am very grateful for his aid and support. Mrs. Frances Evelyn Moore King, Texas A&M Special Collections librarian, and Charles R. Schultz, director of the Texas A&M Archives, and the staff of the Special Collections Library were thoughtful and helpful in every way, as was indeed the staff of Cushing Memorial Library.

Without exception those people who were interviewed were generous with their time and unstinting in their effort to provide information and direction. Charles W. Crawford, professor emeritus and former head of the Department of Mechanical Engineering and associate dean of Engineering, gave me many hours of his time both in formal interview and in informal conversation. Of those interviewed, I am also especially appreciative of the help given by Alfred D. Folweiler, director emeritus, Texas Forest Service; Marion Thomas Harrington, former president and chancellor of Texas A&M; David W. Williams, former vice-chancellor for agriculture and acting president; Eugene J. Howell, former registrar at Texas A&M and president emeritus of Tarleton State College; Ide Peebles Trotter, former director, Texas Agricultural Extension Service, and dean emeritus of the Graduate School; Edward B. Evans, president emeritus of Prairie View A&M; George R. Woolfolk, chairman, Department of History, Prairie View A&M; and Homer Lloyd Heaton, dean of Admissions at Texas A&M, who was also always available to answer questions. Other informative interviews included those with George H. Draper ('34), Mrs. Robert K. Lancaster, Mrs. Thomas D. Watts, Travis L. Smith, Jr. ('98), Josh B. Sterns ('99), Fred Robert Brison ('21), Charles W. Sherrill ('21), Elbert L. Robinson ('21), Thomas Reese Spence ('13), Clifton C. Doak ('19), and Mrs. Erma Rich. Robert G. Cherry, secretary of the Board of Directors, provided comfortable access to the Minutes of the Board of Directors. John Hutchison, director of the Texas Agricultural Extension Service, and James D. Prewit, former associate director, gave assistance relating to the Extension Service. David A. ("Andy") Anderson and Paul R. Kramer, director of the Texas Forest Service, provided materials pertaining to the Texas Forest Service. Rear Admiral James D. Craik, supervisor of the Texas Maritime Academy, provided documents, histories, and news stories about the Texas Maritime Academy. Charles J. Keese, director of the Texas Transportation Institute, offered useful information on the Institute.

President Jack K. Williams; Richard O. ("Buck") Weirus, director of the Former Students Association; Frank Wardlaw, director of the Texas A&M University Press; the Special Centennial History Editorial Committee; the Texas A&M University Centennial Committee; and Mrs. Graham Belcher Blackstock, who edited the completed study, have been instrumental in making it possible for a raw manuscript to become a book. To all of these, I am grateful.

I am especially indebted to my typists and graduate assistants, who in the course of research and preparation of a readable manuscript saved me much footwork and prevented many a pitfall. Mrs. Patricia Caruthers courageously handled the typing during the early stages of the manuscript. Mrs. Gloria Johnson, who prepared much of the preliminary and all of the final copy, gave, in addition, helpful editorial and research assistance. Earl Humphreys performed valuable research duties in the early stages, and Mrs. Barbara LeUnes can be credited with most of the research for the chapters on World War I and World War II, in addition to other research assistance. Glendon H. Weir prepared the maps and charts. Many of my colleagues in the Department of History gave encouragement and a hearing at the proper moment. My wife, Myrtle Anne, is due a very special thank you.

HENRY C. DETHLOFF

College Station, Texas

A CENTENNIAL HISTORY OF

Texas A&M University

1876-1976

CHAPTER 1

A Texas Adventure into Higher Education

O N the highest summit of the region, where it was visible for miles to passers-by on the train, the Agricultural and Mechanical College of Texas formally opened its doors on October 4, 1876, already having experienced over a decade of adventures and misadventures.

The site selected for the new college was in the rolling virgin prairies northeast of the Brazos River basin and some four miles south of the town of Bryan. One enthusiast reported that "No amateur landscape designer could have presented a more beautiful site for an institution of learning aspiring to become the central college of the State University." Of the 2,416 acres comprising the original domain of the Texas A&M College, some two thousand were open prairie and the remainder were wooded, primarily with the scrubby Texas postoak.[1] In recent years the area had served as the assembling point for cattle drives which took Texas beef to the markets at Dodge City and other points.[2] Wild longhorn cattle and mustangs, so abundant immediately after the Civil War, could still occasionally be found nearby in the brushy areas.[3] Only thirty acres of one sector, known as the Rector Farm, had ever been cultivated. Through the center of the tract ran the Houston and Texas Central Railroad, which nine years earlier had been completed to Bryan from its old northern terminus in Millican (see fig. 1).[4] The location of the new college was in a rather unsettled and wild environment for the beginning of a great institution of higher learning.

Horned toads, scorpions, rabbits, and deer vied with wolves for life. Packs of wolves challenged the intrusion and trappings of civilized man into their domain. "It was no uncommon sight at that time," reports a resident of

---

[1]Galveston *News,* July 8, 1871.

[2]Elmer Grady Marshall, "The History of Brazos County, Texas," unpublished master's thesis in history, University of Texas, 1937, p. 105 (hereinafter cited: Marshall, "Brazos County").

[3]*Ibid.,* 104.

[4]*Ibid.,* 90.

the new facility, "to see a pack of wolves leap out in front of us, at the sound of footsteps from among the tall rank weeds that encompassed the Campus grounds." One young boy who had come to enroll in the institution was

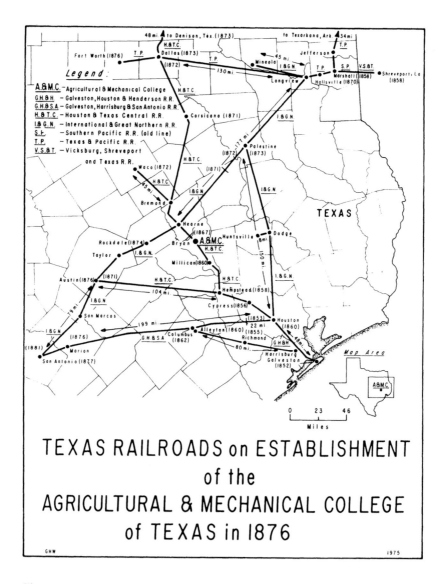

TEXAS RAILROADS on ESTABLISHMENT
of the
AGRICULTURAL & MECHANICAL COLLEGE
of TEXAS in 1876

Figure 1.

attacked by wolves during the day in full sight of the main building. One night another student finished his evening meal and on walking out on the porch slipped and fell, whereon a pack of hungry wolves jumped him. "Oh, I'm killed, I'm killed," he cried and the residents of Old Main rushed out to rescue him. Subsequently, the disappointed wolves were reported "sniffing and snorting [at the windows] as if they meant to come through." For several years the wolves refused to be intimidated by higher education and "would assemble in the small skirt of woods near the last brick residence and render that weird howl till the wee hours of the night."[5]

Conceived during the chaos of Civil War and delivered during the pain of Reconstruction, the A&M College somehow survived the wolves, the political machinations and spoilsmanship of the Radicals, and the purges of the Democratic Redeemers to become Texas' first public institution of higher learning. Its roots, however, go back far beyond the dark days of disunion, to the early days of the Texas Republic. The desire for a system of public education had contributed to Texas discontent with Mexican rule and to the outbreak of the struggle for Texas independence. That interest in public education was carried one step further when, in 1839, President Mirabeau B. Lamar addressed the Congress in Austin at some length on the necessities of establishing an institution of higher learning. "Congress," said Lamar at a time when the very survival of the Republic was in question, "is no less bound to the dissemination of knowledge than it is to attend to the physical defense of the country."[6]

But it is not the diversified and ever varying system of private instruction that are to establish the moral and political character of a people. This must be the work of those higher and more permanent institutions which shall be founded by the nation and directed by public wisdom.[7]

The Fourth Congress, meeting for the first time in the new capitol in Austin, responded magnanimously by donating three leagues of public land to each county for the support of primary schools or academies, and fifty leagues of land (221,420 acres) for the "establishment and endowment of two Colleges or Universities."[8] By July 1839 an order had been issued by the Sec-

---

[5]"College in 1876," anonymous manuscript, probably by Mrs. William A. Banks, wife of Professor Banks, University Archives, Texas A&M University, College Station, Texas (hereinafter cited: Texas A&M University Archives).

[6]Texas Cong., *Journal of the Senate: Fourth Congress*, 27.

[7]*Ibid.*, 28.

[8]H. P. N. Gammel (ed.), *The Laws of Texas, 1822-1897*, II, 134-136 (hereinafter cited: Gammel (ed.), *Laws of Texas*).

retary of State directing the location of the university lands along the Llano and San Saba or Colorado Rivers in not more than three separate tracts.[9] Subsequently, David G. Burnet, formerly *ad interim* President of the Republic and then acting Secretary of State, authorized the location of ten of the fifty leagues in Nacogdoches County.[10] Many of these lands, including those in Nacogdoches County, were then occupied by Indian tribes.

Nothing was done for some time thereafter to create the universities. On various occasions adjustments were made in the university-land surveys in order to assure the accurate location of the full fifty leagues.[11] Enabling legislation in 1856 provided for the survey of university lands in 160-acre plots to be offered for public sale at a minimum three dollars per acre in alternate sections. The sections omitted from the public offering were to be reserved by the state for future use. The proceeds from the sale of the land would constitute a University Fund.[12] Legislators in 1856 continued to use the language of the original act of 1839 calling for the establishment of two universities.[13] A somewhat different concept seemed to be indicated by the actions of the Legislature a few years later.

In 1858 the Legislature passed an act establishing "The University of Texas" and appropriated the fifty leagues of university lands to its support. The act also provided that for every ten sections of state lands donated to railroads, one section must be set aside for the state university. Had this particular provision not been set aside later, Texas' universities would have had a far greater endowment than they now enjoy. But the Legislature of 1858 was not to be satisfied with the mere grant of millions of acres of land — it also appropriated to the university $100,000 in United States bonds then in the state treasury from the boundary-adjustment money received under the Compromise of 1850.[14] The advent of Texas' first university appeared imminent, and it would not have been an agricultural and mechanical college. It would, however, even by contemporary standards, have been richly endowed. The Civil War intervened to alter substantially these bright prospects for public higher education in Texas.

From the time of the Republic throughout the ante-bellum period, nevertheless, Texas had made a firm commitment to higher education. Texas legislators had also unknowingly created confusion as to the form the facili-

[9] Texas Congress, *Fourth Congress: Reports and Relief Laws*, 33-34.

[10] *Ibid.*, 34; Texas Congress, *Journals of the House: Fourth Congress*, 235-245.

[11] Gammel (ed.), *Laws of Texas*, III, 534-535.

[12] *Ibid.*, IV, 489-492.

[13] *Ibid.*, IV, 502-503.

[14] *Ibid.*, IV, 1020-1023.

ties for higher education should assume. Would there be one, two, or even three state universities? There seemed to be some authority for either position. The grant of 1839 designated two universities; the act of 1858 established one university. Some believed that because legislation in 1856 reserved revenues from only half of the university lands for the University Fund (which would provide for the two universities specified in the act of 1839), then the remainder must be intended for a third, or even more universities. Other legislators seemed to think that the organization of "The University of Texas" in 1858 was simply the administrative vehicle for the establishment of any number of subsidiary institutions, each being simply a part of the whole university, which very nearly approaches the modern concept of The University of Texas. Opinion on these questions remained divided throughout the nineteenth century, and legislative action from time to time appeared to be based on diametrically opposite ideas.

The advent of the A&M College of Texas confused the issue even more. Was the A&M College to be a part of "The University"? The organization act of 1871 provided specifically that the A&M College be under the control of the administrators provided by the act creating The University of Texas in 1858.[15] The University of Texas Board actually served as directors of the A&M College for several years.[16] In 1875, however, the Legislature established a separate organization for the administration of the A&M College, and the following year the Constitution of 1876 specifically made the College a "branch of The University of Texas."[17] In practice, however, the College continued to function as an independent institution with a separate Board of Directors. For a while this was a genuine necessity since The University of Texas of which it was a "branch" existed only on paper. The A&M College began operation some seven years before The University of Texas opened.

Fundamental to the problem of resolving the A&M College's status as a state university, or as part of the state university, was the question of its right to revenues from designated university lands. No effective settlement was achieved until well into the twentieth century. Thus from out of Texas' past came not only a commitment and an endowment, but a number of problems to confuse and confront the developing system of public higher education in the state.

By 1860, despite the good intentions and endowments, threatening clouds of civil war and very real Indian wars promised to undo much that had

[15]*Ibid.*, VI, 938-940.
[16]Austin *Daily Journal*, May 31, 1871.
[17]*Texas Constitution of 1876*, Article VII, Section 13, Appendix G.

been done toward promoting higher education in Texas. Throughout the Civil War and the era of Reconstruction, Indian troubles on the frontier and raids across the Mexican border increased with the collapse of frontier defense.[18] In 1860 the Texas Legislature authorized the use of university funds for frontier defense, and the Confederate State Legislature later began to dip into university funds for the state's operating expenses.[19] More significantly, income from the sale of university lands, already meager, ceased to come into the treasury for many years because of the advent of hard times caused by war, reconstruction, and collapsing farm prices.[20] In addition, between 1860 and 1875 the Texas Legislature deferred payments on principal and interest for university lands that had been sold before the Civil War.[21] Thus, like many planters and farmers, Texas universities on paper were for a time genuinely "land poor." This helps to explain the long delay between the birth of the idea and the advent of a Texas university.

Although the idea had been conceived and some efforts made to develop a state university in Texas by Texans, Yankee legislation provided the immediate impetus for the establishment of Texas' first university. With Texas' secession from the Union on March 2, 1861, Texans assumed their future to be irrevocably severed from the Northern states. In this, of course, they were sorely mistaken. The Confederate world collapsed with General Robert E. Lee's surrender at Appomattox in April 1865. On May 10 President Jefferson Davis was captured and on June 2 General Kirby Smith formally signed the Canby-Buckner convention surrendering the last Confederate troops under his command and fled through Texas into Mexico. Soon afterwards Union occupation forces fanned out into Texas from Galveston. President Andrew Johnson appointed Andrew J. Hamilton provisional governor of Texas under the then lenient presidential plan for reconstruction. Voters were registered, and an elected constitutional convention framed a constitution that was approved by the people of Texas. Then Texas sought to resume her status as an operating political division of the United States. The elected Texas congressmen and senators, however, were denied seats in Congress. In 1866 the governor, James W. Throckmorton, the Legislature, and most state and local officials were of strong Confederate extraction and sympathy.[22] Congress took over the leadership in Reconstruction from the President, and

---

[18]*Governor's Messages, Coke to Ross, 1874-1891*, pp. 14-16.

[19] Gammel (ed.), *Laws of Texas*, IV, 1391-1392, 1397; V, 342-343.

[20]See Fred A. Shannon, *The Farmer's Last Frontier: Agriculture, 1860-1897*, pp. 76-97, 291-311.

[21] Gammel (ed.), *Laws of Texas*, V, 545-546, 689; VIII, 432-435.

[22] Charles W. Ramsdell, *Reconstruction in Texas*, 107, 114, 115.

the newly installed Texas state government was replaced by Radical Reconstruction with its politics, corruption, violence, hardships, and concern for establishing Texas' land-grant college to take advantage of federal support that had become available to the former Confederate states after 1865.

The inception of the land-grant-college idea is traditionally attributed to Johnathan B. Turner and Justin S. Morrill. Turner, earlier a professor of rhetoric and *belles lettres* at Illinois College, unveiled his "Plan for a State University for the Industrial Classes" at a Teachers Institute in Griggsville, Illinois, in 1850.[23] His plan had several significant implications for higher education. First, it proposed that funds from the sale of federal lands in Illinois be used to support a state university. Secondly, it argued that higher education should be made available for the "industrial classes," and thirdly, it suggested that higher education should involve teaching the "practical arts" in conjunction with the classics. In view of the fact that higher education in America had essentially been a private, as opposed to a public, concern, and in view that it had been regarded as a privilege of the "wise and well-born" rather than as a right of the common man, and since its curricula were exclusively classic in nature, Turner's proposal had revolutionary implications. His plan soon won the support of farmers in Illinois, and the Illinois Legislature petitioned Congress in 1853 for a donation of land valued at not less than $500,000 to each of the states for the endowment of a system of "industrial universities."[24]

Senator Justin S. Morrill, of Vermont, became the driving force to push the land-grant-college idea through Congress. Many attribute the original conception of the idea to Morrill, rather than to Turner. Both may have arrived at such a scheme independently; both worked ardently for its realization. Morrill, the son of a blacksmith, completed his formal education in the common schools of Vermont at the age of fifteen. He became a clerk in a general store and soon a partner in a successful mercantile business. He retired at the early age of thirty-eight and became active in Whig politics. In 1854 he won a seat in Congress on the Whig ticket, and while later changing to the Republican Party, served continuously in the House until 1866, when the Vermont Legislature elected him to the United States Senate.[25]

It should be stressed that the Republic of Texas had in many ways anticipated the land-grant-college idea of Senator Justin S. Morrill and Johnathan B. Turner. President Mirabeau B. Lamar and the Congress of the Repub-

---

[23] Edward D. Eddy, Jr., *The Land-Grant Movement: A Capsule History of the Educational Revolution Which Established Colleges for All the People,* 4-5 (hereinafter cited: Eddy, *The Land-Grant Movement*).

[24] *Ibid.,* 4-5, 8-14.

[25] *Ibid.,* 5-6.

lic of Texas clearly sought to establish in 1839 a public university funded by a national land grant which would be available to the masses rather than exclusively for the use of the "wise and well-born." They did not, however, advocate training in the "agricultural and mechanic arts," but rather sought a curriculum which would help establish the correct "moral and political character" of the people.[26]

Interest in scientific agricultural training and in the establishment of a state agricultural college, however, did exist in Texas well before the passage of the Land-Grant College Act, and prior to the introduction of Senator Morrill's bill before Congress. In 1853 the newly organized Texas State Agricultural Society included in its constitution a call for the establishment of a state-endowed agricultural college:

> One of the great objects of this Society shall be the establishment and endowment of an Agricultural College and model farm for the State, at or near the Capital, where the important business principles of Agriculture shall be scientifically taught and practically illustrated.[27]

Thus, in very significant ways, Texas anticipated the advent of the land-grant-college movement.

Morrill's plan then was unique to Texas primarily in that it called for both agricultural and industrial training. Morrill's first plan presented to Congress called for the development of "National agricultural schools" on the pattern of the military academies, where "one scholar from each Congressional district and two from each state at large" could receive a practical education at public expense. His resolution of 1856 calling for such a program failed to pass. The following years he introduced his first land-grant bill, which foundered upon the rocks of political and sectional hostilities. A revised and amended version passed in 1859 only to be vetoed by President James Buchanan. Finally, in 1862, with the sectional and political roadblock effectively removed by the secession of the Southern states, and by the dominance of the new Republican Party, Morrill's Land-Grant College Act passed and was signed into law by President Abraham Lincoln on July 2, 1862.[28]

Upon return to the Union, Texas soon became eligible for the benefits described by the Morrill Land-Grant College Act. Texas, despite its past inability to found a public university, had by no means forgotten its commitment to higher education. The Constitutional Convention of 1866, dominated by regular Democrats, former Confederates, and native Texans, made

[26] Texas Congress, *Journal of the Senate: Fourth Congress*, 28.
[27] *Transactions of the Texas State Agricultural Society*, 6.
[28] Eddy, *The Land-Grant Movement*, 15-26.

elaborate provisions for common schools and for colleges. In lieu of the grant of 1858, which would give one section of land to the university for every ten sections of land donated to railroads, the Convention called for an additional grant of one million acres of public land to the university. The new Constitution provided that "money and lands heretofore granted to, or which may hereafter be granted for the endowment and support of one or more universities, shall constitute a special fund for the maintenance of said universities." This provision also went back to the multiple-university concept, rather than retaining the single-university concept apparently envisioned in 1858. Recalling the misuse of university funds in previous years, the Constitution specified that the "Legislature shall have no power to appropriate the university fund for any other purpose than that of the maintenance of said universities," and it called upon the Legislature to make provision for the organization and operation of one state university.[29]

Subsequently, the state Legislature passed a number of acts in compliance with the constitutional mandate. Two acts amended the act of 1856 providing for the sale of university lands so as to facilitate the accrual of funds; another act "secured" the university funds by prohibiting their use for any other purpose; and still another act sought to resolve the chaotic financial situation regarding the sale of university lands by granting "relief" to purchasers.[30] On November 1, 1866, the Eleventh Legislature approved a joint resolution "to accept the provisions of the Act of Congress of the United States, approved July 2, 1862, entitled an Act to donate public land to the several States and Territories which may provide Colleges for the benefit of Agriculture and the Mechanic Arts."[31]

The Morrill Land-Grant College Act provided for the donation of public lands in a quantity equal to thirty thousand acres for each senator and representative in Congress. Such lands were to be sold and the proceeds to be invested in state or federal bonds bearing interest at not less than five percent. For those states, such as Texas, which had no vacant federal lands within their perimeters, the Secretary of the Interior would issue land scrip equal to the number of acres to which the state was entitled. The scrip entitled the purchaser to locate or claim any of the unappropriated public lands of the United States in an amount equal to the scrip held. Governors of states receiving grants were to sell the scrip and invest the proceeds in a permanent fund, from which only the interest would be available for funding the opera-

[29]*Texas Constitution of 1866*, Article X, Section 8.
[30]Gammel (ed.), *Laws of Texas*, V, 955-956, 1011-1012, 1109-1110, 1126-1127.
[31]*Ibid.*, V, 1185.

tion of the college. Neither principal nor interest could be used for building construction or maintenance. States accepting the terms of the act must provide, within five years of the date of the act, at least one college "where the leading object shall be, without excluding other scientific and classical studies and including military tactics, to teach such branches of learning as are related to agriculture and the mechanic arts." The original act provided that the states had only two years from the date of the act to accept its terms. On July 23, 1866, however, Congress had extended the deadline, giving states three years from the date for acceptance, and then five years from the date of filing their acceptance with the commissioner of the General Land office, to provide for the college — or, as specified in the original act, return any funds received from the sale of lands to the federal government. Texas, by resolution of its Legislature, November 1866, accepted an obligation to provide for the college by July 23, 1871.[32]

Acceptance of the terms of the Morrill Act by no means exhausted the efforts of the Eleventh Legislature to provide for a system of higher education in Texas. In a law entitled "An Act amendatory of an Act to establish the University of Texas, approved February 11, 1858," the Legislature again called for the establishment of "The University of Texas," and specified the branches of learning and the duties of administrators. Admission to The University would be free, and students could not follow studies in a field in opposition to the expressed wishes of parents. A special legislative committee would attend the annual examinations and "report to the Legislature thereon." Most significantly the act provided that only one-half of the lands granted by the Republic of Texas in 1839 would be reserved for the support of "The University of Texas," the remainder to be reserved for a "similar University . . . to be established in a different portion of the state."[33]

In the same session a companion piece of legislation became law, which provided for the creation of "another University, contradistinguished from the 'University of the State of Texas'." This joint resolution named specific persons to comprise a Board of Administrators of a university to be known as "East Texas University," which was to be located in a different section of the

[32]The state consistently acted upon the assumption that the deadline granted by the act of July 23, 1866, for the completion of the A&M College was July 23, 1871. The act, however, specified that the five-year extension dated from the time of filing the *acceptance* of the terms of the Morrill Act with the commissioner of the General Land Office. This would have actually made the deadline fall in November 1871, rather than in July. It is most important, of course, that they *acted* upon the July 23 date, and the school was finally opened five years after the deadline.

[33]Gammel (ed.), *Laws of Texas*, V, 1103-1105.

state from the "University of the State of Texas." The twenty-five remaining leagues of university lands were designated to the use of this institution.[34] Notably, the Legislature at the time failed to donate the one million acres of public land to higher education as called for by the Constitution of 1866. They had acted, however, to found not one state university, but three such universities, each endowed with a grant of 120,000 to 180,000 acres of land.

Yet, as in the past, much of this proved to be only a paper dream. The future of Texas' higher education was not to be determined by any single individual, legislature, or administration. Ten years were to pass before the opening of Texas' Agricultural and Mechanical College, and eighteen years before The University of Texas became a reality. The "East Texas University" as envisioned never opened. The development of higher education in Texas had been and would continue to be a continuing process of change and alteration, not always capable of being characterized as progress. Thus in 1866, just as the Texas tree of knowledge appeared about to bear fruit (as it had in 1858), the blossom failed to pollinate. Radical Reconstruction intervened either to alter or delay the inception of the universities prescribed in 1866.

The Texas Legislature of 1866, and indeed the governments and legislatures of all of the defeated Southern states, had in effect been too Confederate. The national Congress which convened in 1867 passed the Reconstruction Acts of that year, restricted the President's control over the army and removal of appointed officials, and then attempted to impeach him. Military reconstruction was imposed upon the South; the ex-Confederates were disfranchised and the Unionists and Negroes were enfranchised. General Philip Sheridan, named by the Radicals as military commander of the Fifth District, removed James W. Throckmorton as governor of Texas and appointed Elisha M. Pease in his place.[35]

Pease had served as governor of Texas from 1853 to 1857, but had strongly opposed secession and the Confederacy. Under the new registration laws established by the Reconstruction Acts, elections for a constitutional convention were held. The convention, dominated by Radicals, met in Austin in June 1868, and in effect formalized the takeover by Radical Republicans of the Texas government. A violent reaction soon developed among many white Democrats. One of the worst riots developed at Millican in July. Situated only a few miles from the future site of the Agricultural and Mechanical College, whites in Millican fought a pitched battle with Negroes. Four white

---

[34] *Ibid.*, V, 1189.
[35] Ramsdell, *Reconstruction in Texas,* 171 ff.

men and twenty Negroes were killed.[36] The riots marked a disintegration of law and order, with a marked increase in outlawry and lynchings in the east, and of Indian raids in the west. Thus again, in 1867, as in 1860, the environment became rather unfavorable for the development of institutions of higher learning.

The state elections of 1869 brought to the Governor's Office Edmund J. Davis. Described by one historian as the "most radical of the Radicals," and by a contemporary newspaper as "nothing more nor less than a devil incarnate," Davis, who came to Texas from Florida in 1838, organized a federal cavalry unit during the Civil War and obtained the rank of brigadier general in the Union army.[37] He had much to do with the advent, and some of the misadventures, of Texas A&M in its formative years.

The Twelfth Texas Legislature, controlled by the Radicals, convened in the latter part of 1870 and sat, with recesses, through June 1871, during which time it passed the necessary legislation formally organizing the agricultural and mechanical college in compliance with the terms of the Morrill Land-Grant College Act. It is interesting to note, as evidence of what must have been a popular interest in such things, that in the short session of 1870 the Twelfth Legislature chartered six county or regional agricultural and mechanical associations.[38] These associations heralded the development of a widespread farmers' movement throughout Texas which eventually united under the banner of the Grange and later the Farmers' Alliance.[39] In turn, these farm organizations had a direct impact upon the development of the agricultural and mechanical college.

The bill providing for the organization of the land-grant college originated in the Senate and was approved by that body on April 6, 1871, and by the House on April 17.[40] Thus was officially established the Texas Agricultural and Mechanical College, to be located by three commissioners appointed by the governor on not less than 1,280 acres of land. The Legislature appropriated $75,000 for the construction of academic buildings and for "suitable accommodations of the professors and their families." It was specified that work should be completed by July 23, 1871, in compliance with the

[36]Marshall, "Brazos County," 88-89.

[37]Ramsdell, *Reconstruction in Texas,* 200 ff; Austin *Tri-Weekly Statesman,* May 28, 1872.

[38]Gammel (ed.), *Laws of Texas,* VI, 515-518, 520-521, 530-531, 553-555, 637-638, 673-674.

[39]See William L. Garvin, *History of the Grand State Farmers' Alliance of Texas,* 84; William L. Garvin and S. O. Daws, *History of the National Farmers' Alliance and Cooperative Union of America,* 158; Roscoe C. Martin, *The People's Party in Texas: A Study in Third Party Politics,* 280.

[40]Gammel (ed.), *Laws of Texas,* VI, 938-940; see also Austin *Daily Journal,* March 24, April 14, 1871; Galveston *News,* April 6, 1871.

congressional Act of July 23, 1866.[41] The commissioners then had three months in which to locate and build a college. It was, of course, an impossible demand. The organization bill provided that the "control, management and supervision" of the college would be subject to the provisions of the "act to establish the University of Texas," passed February 11, 1858. It was intended, therefore, that the new facility should be a part of The University of Texas, or even, as an architect described it, the "central college of the state university."[42]

Governor Davis promptly appointed the three commissioners to locate the college. They were McDonald Lorance, John G. Bell, and F. E. Grothaus. Lorance declined the appointment and was replaced by George B. Slaughter. Slaughter, Bell, and Grothaus were all Republican members of the state Legislature.[43] Meanwhile, the state Legislature approved yet another appropriation for the new college, but Davis vetoed the bill, pointing out that ample funds were provided by the earlier bill, and that "The Commissioners who were appointed to locate the college are expected to do so without any compensation to themselves, and on the most economical basis."[44] Davis' final comments quickly assumed a certain haunting quality, for these were the days of carpetbaggery, corruption, and spoilsmanship, and the A&M College would not go untainted.

Texas had earlier received the land scrip from the Department of the Interior for 180,000 acres of federal land, the first scrip to a quarter-section of land in Colorado being issued by the U.S. Department of the Interior on February 16, 1871. By direction of the governor, the secretary of state, James P. Newcomb, sold the scrip for eighty-seven cents per acre. The $156,000 produced by the sale was invested in 7-percent gold frontier defense bonds of Texas, which, with the discount, had a face value of $174,000.[45] While funding arrangements were being made the A&M commissioners proceeded to examine proffered sites for the location of the college. Major consideration was given to sites in Grimes County, Brazos County, and Austin County.

On June 4 and 5, 1871, Bell, Grothaus, and Slaughter examined sites at Kellum Springs and Piedmont Springs, in Grimes County.[46] On June 13, the

[41] Gammel (ed.), *Laws of Texas*, VI, 1037 (amendment).

[42] Galveston *News*, July 8, 1871.

[43] J. M. Moore (secretary of state), Austin, to Louis L. McInnis, March 23, 1888, in L. L. McInnis Papers, Texas A&M University Archives.

[44] *Texas House Journal, 1871*, p. 304.

[45] *Governor's Messages, Coke to Ross, 1874-1891*, p. 137; Land Scrip No. 1 (photographic copy), George Pfeuffer Papers, Texas A&M University Archives.

[46] Clarence Ousley, *History of the Agricultural and Mechanical College of Texas, Bulletin of*

commissioners spent the day in the neighborhood of Bryan, in Brazos County. Bryan citizens eagerly sought the new college. They dined the commissioners at Mrs. Shaws' Hotel, also known as the Bowman House, and talked of contributing $20,000 or $30,000 to the proposed college should it be located at Bryan.[47] The commissioners then went to Bellville, in Austin County. A letter from Republican House member Charles W. Gardiner, of Bryan, to Governor Davis, indicates that Senator Bell, a member of the Commission, was adamant that the college be located in his home community of Bellville. Grothaus and Slaughter seemed favorable to the Bryan location. Gardiner suggested that the Governor remove Bell and appoint him, Gardiner, to the Commission so that the question would be settled in favor of Bryan, a decision he said, which would greatly improve the fortunes of the Republican Party in the area.[48] Gardiner's letter is significant, not only in detailing the controversy in the Commission, but in indicating the political nature of the decision. Bryan had powerful political support in its favor, not only from Gardiner, but from State Senator William A. Saylor, a Republican and a power in the Senate, who made his home in Brazos County.

Local effort also contributed significantly to Bryan's being named as the location for the new college. Bryan in 1871 was a relatively new, raw, but bustling community located along the Houston and Texas Central Railroad. Until 1866 Boonville, now disappeared from the map, had been the county seat and commercial center of Brazos County, but in that year the county seat was moved to Bryan in anticipation of the arrival of the railroad. The line, which since 1860 had had its terminus at Millican, was completed northwest through Bryan in 1867. Bryan then became the commercial center for the region. The cattle industry dominated the local economy, but substantial cotton production located along the Brazos River provided a yet stronger foundation. Progressive businessmen in Bryan promoted immigration by staging land give-aways. Citizens also provided a temporary home in the town for new arrivals.[49] These same progressive elements were behind the drive to secure the location of the A&M College at Bryan in 1871.

The year 1871 was a big year for Bryan. In that year the Central Texas

---

the Agricultural and Mechanical College of Texas, 4th ser., vol. 6, no. 8 (December 1, 1935), p. 39 (hereinafter cited: Ousley, *History of the A&M College*).

[47]John Rosser, "Journal of a Trip to Texas in 1871," Texas A&M University Archives; see also Ernest Langford, *Getting the College Under Way*, 13.

[48]C. W. Gardiner to E. J. Davis, July 3, 1871, photostatic copy from Governor E. J. Davis letterbook, University of Texas Archives and Manuscripts, in C. W. Gardiner Papers, Texas A&M University Archives.

[49]Marshall, "Brazos County," 90, 104-106.

Agricultural and Mechanical Association of Bryan was chartered. Indeed, there was almost an "agricultural and mechanical" association movement in Texas in the eighteen seventies — which made the advent of an A&M college a propitious occasion. In accord with those associations chartered elsewhere in the state, the Bryan association proposed to stage annual fairs with prizes, promotional activities, and various inducements to settlers and prospective farmers and businessmen. Harvey Mitchell appeared to have been the prime mover in its organization.[50]

Similarly, Mitchell figured prominently in the organization of the Bryan Male and Female Seminary in 1871.[51] Again, on the basis of legislative records, the private-academy or "university" movement in the 1870s in Texas appears to have been as great as the "agricultural and mechanical association" movement. Thus the climate was exceptionally favorable to the development of an "agricultural and mechanical college" which would combine agriculture, the mechanical arts, and education.

In addition to the organization of the Agricultural Association and the Seminary in 1871, Bryan citizens obtained a charter incorporating their town as the City of Bryan. Bryan had many of the characteristics of a raw, frontier town. Among the powers granted to the city government was the "authority to pass ordinances regulating bawdy houses, houses of ill fame or of prostitution, to license the same or abate the same."[52] Bryan experienced a degree of the lawlessness allegedly characteristic of a western town. A number of shootings and lynchings occurred in almost every year between 1869 and 1874, in or near the town. In 1874 a saloon proprietor in downtown Bryan was strung up by angry citizens for "murdering" a town favorite.[53]

Among the most active citizens of Bryan,[54] Harvey Mitchell is particularly significant because of his involvement with locating the A&M College there. Mitchell was born in "Cornersville, Middle Tennessee," on April 9, 1821. As an adventurous young man he went in 1839 to Tinnanville, Robertson County, Texas, where he entered service in the frontier forces of the Republic. In 1841 he served as a part-time school teacher in Boonville, which

[50]Gammel (ed.), *Laws of Texas*, VI, 1186-1187.

[51]*Ibid.*, VI, 1655.

[52]*Ibid.*, VII, 231-237.

[53]Marshall, "Brazos County," 92.

[54]Legislative records indicate that they would include these persons: Bennett H. Davis, C. A. Sterne, Charles F. Moore, John S. Fowlks, O. P. Bowles [probably William P. Boyles], Judge Spencer Ford, Horatio M. Moore, William B. Forman, Miller W. McGraw, Horace A. Moore, Frank M. Law, Hiram T. Downard (Mayor), William B. Eaves, Thomas D. Wilson, John W. Taber, P. R. Smith, Joseph S. Stewart, T. J. Beall, William Davis, and Harvey Mitchell.

in 1842 became the county seat of the newly organized Brazos County. Mitchell then received appointment as deputy in the county clerk's office. In 1845 he became a merchant and prospered. When the Civil War came he served as county assessor for the Confederate Texas state government.[55]

At a public meeting in Bryan during the week of June 13, 1871, after the departure of the A&M commissioners from the town, the citizens elected Harvey Mitchell, William A. Saylor, and Judge Spencer Ford to meet with the commissioners in Houston on June 20, in order to present formally the town's petition for the location of the school. Mitchell and Saylor went to Houston a few days before the meeting. Ford did not go. Saylor soon left Houston before the official meeting occurred, leaving Mitchell, according to one source, to "wrestle with powerful competitors" alone. Mitchell reportedly wired Mayor Hiram Thomas Downard for instructions, but on receiving none, on his own volition pledged 2,250 acres of land as a donation to the college in return for its location in Brazos County. The commissioners accepted Mitchell's proposal on the condition that title to the land be delivered to them within forty-eight hours.[56]

For almost a hundred years gossip has persisted in Bryan and College Station that Harvey Mitchell "won" the location of the A&M College in a poker game. This would certainly make it a "Texas style" transaction. Unfortunately, no tangible evidence proves or disproves the rumor. Nonetheless, the fact that Saylor and Mitchell were in Houston some days before the decision was made, and that Saylor left before the formal decision was made, as well as Saylor's subsequent role in A&M affairs, suggests that the location may well have been determined before the commission convened in formal session.

The negotiations for the location of the college, made in Houston, have forever remained under a cloud. Some have pointed with curiosity to the Commission's dictate that perfect title be secured for the donated lands within forty-eight hours. One may speculate that the forty-eight hours was specified so that if Bryan failed to deliver on its promises, the location would be made in Bellville. Charges of wrongdoing, however, have persisted. In part this can be explained by the fact that the location was made by a Radical, and generally unpopular, Republican administration. In 1872, for example, the Democratic *Tri-Weekly Statesman* of Austin charged that the A&M College was the front for a "grand swindle." It charged that the governor was considering moving the college to San Antonio, having been offered large

[55]John Henry Brown, *Indian Wars and Pioneers of Texas*, 593-595.
[56]*Ibid.*, 595.

sums of money toward its location, and that much of the money with which the new college had been funded had already absconded. The paper also argued, "The present location of the College is a sure guarantee that no good will ever be derived from it."[57] Almost as soon as the decision locating the college became known, criticism developed. Essentially the argument against the Bryan location was that the lands thereabout were among the poorest in the state, unfit for agriculture, and that the region was very unhealthy.[58] Even Governor Davis noted in 1873 that "some objection has been made to the selection of Bryan," but then advised the Legislature that the A&M College "had better now remain there."[59]

In regard to the location of the college, John S. Lane said in his *History of Education in Texas* that Brazos County "was then considered one of the poorest counties in the State, and its bid was the lowest made."[60] A legislative body advocating the consolidation of A&M with the State University in 1913 repeated Lane's arguments noting that much of A&M's "troubles" stemmed from its "isolated condition."[61] As late as 1932 the "isolated" location of the A&M College was pointed to in a legislative report as a distinct disadvantage.

Undoubtedly much of the controversy over the location of the college, both in the decade of the seventies and thereafter, stemmed from party conflict, factionalism, and institutional loyalties. On the other hand, it should not be overlooked that the people of Bryan energetically worked for the location of the college, that they made a substantial gift to the college, and that it was located near the population center of the state and along a railroad which provided, for the time, excellent transportation. San Antonio and Austin, for example, were still linked only by stage. Nevertheless, as the years passed new evidences of "wrong-doing" and public controversies regarding the college continued to arouse old suspicions and doubts.[62]

[57]*Statement by Members of the House of Representatives Concerning a Bill to Consolidate the Agricultural and Mechanical College and the State University,* 6-7; Austin *Tri-Weekly Statesman,* May 28, 1872.

[58]*Statement . . . (re) Consolidation of the Agricultural and Mechanical College and the State University,* 6-7; Galveston *News,* July 8, 1871; Austin *Tri-Weekly Statesman,* May 28, 1872.

[59]*Texas House Journal,* 1873, p. 37.

[60]*Statement . . . (re) Consolidation of the Agricultural and Mechanical College and the State University,* 6-7; see also J. J. Lane, *History of the University of Texas,* 6-24, 139-151.

[61]*Statement . . . (re) Consolidation of the Agricultural and Mechanical College and the State University,* 9.

[62]Joint Legislative Committee on Organization and Economy and Griffenhagen and Associates, *The Government of the State of Texas,* XI, *Education: The Agricultural and Mechanical College of Texas and Its Affiliates* (December 31, 1932), p. 8 (hereinafter cited: *The Government of the State of Texas,* XI, *Education*).

The decision having been made by the commissioners to locate the college at a point about four miles south of Bryan, Harvey Mitchell hurried back to Bryan from Houston to obtain the necessary land titles. Assisted by John N. Henderson, who later became an associate justice of the state Court of Criminal Appeals, and by Miller Woodson McGraw, a local businessman, Mitchell obtained the money for the purchase of the needed parcels of land, secured the deeds, and returned to Houston, where the lands were "granted, bargained, sold and released" to the Agricultural and Mechanical College on June 21, 1871. The transaction was witnessed by William B. Foreman (assistant U.S. Marshall) and William A. Saylor, the latter having now returned to the scene. The deeds were filed with the county clerk of Brazos County on June 23, and included the following pieces of property:

By Harvey Mitchell, one tract containing 102 acres

By Harvey Mitchell, a second tract containing 40 acres

By Harvey Mitchell, a third tract containing 838 acres

By J. Frederick Cox, one tract containing 1,226 acres

By Mrs. Rebecca Rector and her husband, Nelson W. Rector, one
    tract containing 210 acres

Thus the town made a total grant of 2,416 acres to the college.[63]

After the agreement was made, the commissioners advanced to Harvey Mitchell and William A. Saylor $12,000 from the $75,000 appropriated by the Legislature for the college. As security for the cash advance Saylor and Mitchell cosigned three notes due six months apart in the amount of $4,000 each. This money was apparently used to make partial payments for the land purchased, but may have gone to other uses.

Davis later criticized this advance as unwarranted and unnecessary, and by 1873 the notes signed by Saylor and Mitchell had not been paid. On August 28, 1871, Brazos County held a special election approving a $22,000 bond issue to cover the purchase price of the lands appropriated by the county to A&M. These bonds were authorized on May 29, 1872, and delivered to the state comptroller by the attorney general. The total cost of the 2,416 acres of land, according to the deeds recorded on June 23, 1871, in the Brazos County courthouse, was $21,130. Harvey Mitchell received $12,000 for the three tracts totaling 980 acres; J. Frederick Cox received $6,130 for 1,226 acres, and Rebecca and Nelson Rector received $3,000 for 210 acres and

[63]Brown, *Indian Wars and Pioneers of Texas*, 595; *Deed Records of Brazos County*, vol. M, 142 ff; see also Langford, *Getting the College Under Way*, 2-7, who corrects the error which dates the location of the college on June 20, 1872, *vice* June 20, 1871, which is the correct date.

[64]*Texas House Journal, 1874*, pp. 119-120.

improvements. Early newspaper reports on the transactions and on the progress of the new institution were generally favorable,[65] but within a short time the A&M project had become a political storm center.

The A&M commissioners next met at Austin on September 15. George Slaughter, who had died following a buggy accident in July, had been replaced by James W. Johnson. Grothaus, Johnson, and Bell proceeded to dispense with the services of Caleb Goldsmith Forshey, their architectural consultant for locating the institution, and retained Carl de Grote as architect. They accepted the plan for a main academic building offered by de Grote and directed him to prepare specifications. The plan was for a building of "elegant and substantial appearance." The first floor would have eighteen-foot ceilings; the second, fifteen; and the third, thirteen-foot ceilings. There were to be fifty-two rooms and fifteen-foot corridors on each story.[66] This was not, however, the building that was completed four years later, nor was de Grote the architect for the completed structure.

When the Legislature convened in November 1871, the Senate called for a report from the A&M commissioners, and from the Governor regarding A&M. The Senate wanted to know what site had been selected; what building had been purchased or erected "on or before the twenty-third of July, 1871"; what departments, curricula, tuition charges, and administration had been established by the college, and most pointedly, how the money appropriated had been spent.[67] Governor Davis then appointed an investigative committee and immediately secured a report from the comptroller on expenditures by the commissioners. His initial findings generated an angry letter to Commissioners Grothaus, Bell, and Johnson. They had spent, he declared, $16,076.80 in currency and $1,500 in gold. Of the total amount spent, Davis indicated, $12,000 was advanced for the purchase of land (unnecessarily), and $5,576.80 for "expenses." On their own personal accounts, the Governor wrote, they had drawn $3,861.75, which divided among the three of them, with exception of the time the Legislature was in session, would amount to $8.00 per day since June for each. He protested spending $150 for a clerk when he could not "perceive the necessity for a clerk, especially when you have an 'architect' drawing upwards of $200.00 per month." "I am afraid the strictest economy has not been observed," he said; and he was afraid that the whole appropriation might be exhausted without any "substantial showing

[65] *Texas House Journal, 1873*, pp. 195-198; *Brazos County Index to Commissioners Courts Minutes*, I, 25, 65. The bonds were paid in full by February 10, 1879. See also Galveston *News*, June 23, 1871; Austin *Daily Journal*, June 27, 1871, and Langford, *Getting the College Under Way*, 12.

[66] Austin *Daily Journal*, September 19, 1871.

[67] *Ibid.*, November 17, 1871.

for it."[68] Why was Davis, whose administration was notorious for the misap-propriation of public funds, concerned about the A&M money?

The anti-Davis Democratic press offered an explanation which may have had some element of accuracy, despite the fact that it always suspected the worst of the administration and could never attribute anything decent to it. The Austin *Tri-Weekly Statesman* was curious as to why Davis had person-ally exposed the possibility of scandal in the management of A&M funds, and could only believe "that villainy is at the bottom of the whole course of the administration."[69]

There was an appropriation of $60,000, or more, made by the Legislators for building the Agricultural and Mechanical College, and without other funds it would be exceedingly convenient to retain this amount for election purposes. The matter has undoubtedly been well-considered, and the idea of arresting the building of the College has been entertained for a good while, for Mr. Chalmers [one of the building contractors] informs us, that he was approached some time since, and an offer of $10,000 made him through J. W. Johnson, from W. A. Saylor, if he would abandon the contract. . . . from every appearance the matter has been worked from its incep-tion for no other purpose but to give to the administrators and its supporters a chance to work a dirty job. Money has already been withdrawn from the treasury in very large amounts [without an accounting]. . . . Saylor, we are informed, figures largely in the matter of handling these public moneys, which have been lost sight of.[70]

In other words, the A&M project was but one more example of Radical spoilsmanship in action; but, now said the Democrats, Governor Davis wanted to save the rest of the money for himself. Throughout the affair Sen-ator Saylor appears very much in the role of the "governor's man," which fact may have had much to do with the decision to locate the college in Brazos County in the first place. There is also a strong suggestion that Davis was using the A&M Commission appointment to pay off political obligations. In two years Davis made more than twelve appointments to the three-man A&M Commission with little to show for their work but money spent.

On May 16, 1872, the Board of Administrators of The University of Texas (then the legal administrative board of the A&M College under the authority of the organization act of April 17, 1871) met in Bryan at the direc-tion of Governor Davis to investigate the A&M situation. Board members

---

[68]E. J. Davis to Commissioners J. W. Johnson, F. E. Grothaus, J. G. Bell, December 23, 1871 (photostatic copy from Governor E. J. Davis letterbook, University of Texas Archives and Manuscripts), Texas A&M University Archives; see also Langford, *Getting the College Under Way*, 20.

[69]Austin *Tri-Weekly Statesman*, May 25, 1872.

[70]*Ibid.*, May 25, 28, 1872.

visited the construction at the site and reviewed contractual agreements. It reported to the Governor that "Upon investigation we find no sufficient contract, and a considerable amount of money having been expended in an unsatisfactory manner, we recommend that" the Governor invalidate all authority of the commissioners and all contractual obligations made by them. The Board attached a report of Jacob Larmour, the state's architect for the School Bureau, who accompanied the members during the inspection. Larmour noted that as of May 23 only the foundation had been laid, and that it was irregular, not level, cracked, and unsafe.[71]

Meanwhile political pressures both from within and from without Davis' party were mounting as elections drew nearer. Davis forced the resignation of Bell and Grothaus from the A&M Commission and replaced them with H. T. Downard, the mayor of Bryan, and I. M. Owens, an administration supporter.[72] At the same time, Davis came under renewed attack when it was disclosed that the state's secretary of treasury, George W. Honey, had left for "parts unknown." Democratic speculation was that either Honey had absconded with a large amount of money, or that Davis had rid himself of Honey so that he could abscond with a large amount of money.[73] With the criticism increasing and elections drawing closer, Davis apparently changed his mind, if he had ever intended it in the first place, about using A&M funds for campaign purposes. He now removed I. M. Owens and J. W. Johnson as A&M commissioners and appointed William McIntosh and Thomas McCarty.[74] In July 1872 Commissioners Downard, McCarty, and McIntosh advertised for new construction bids on the A&M main building.[75] In August they accepted the bid for one million bricks for the building and promptly withdrew $5,000 from the A&M account for the alleged payment for the bricks.[76] These bricks were never delivered or used in the construction of the main building. Davis now decided that the commissioners had taken enough for themselves, or that he wanted to share the wealth. In September he replaced McCarty and McIntosh with new men, James H. Raymond and Hamilton Stewart.[77] There certainly seemed to be some support for the Dem-

[71] Austin *Daily Journal*, May 27, 31, 1872.

[72] J. M. Moore (secretary of state), Austin, to Louis L. McInnis, March 23, 1888, L. L. McInnis Papers, Texas A&M University Archives.

[73] Austin *Tri-Weekly Statesman*, May 28, 1872.

[74] J. M. Moore (secretary of state), Austin, to Louis L. McInnis, March 23, 1888, L. L. McInnis Papers, Texas A&M University Archives.

[75] Galveston *Daily News*, July 20, 1872.

[76] *Ibid.; Texas House Journal*, 1873, pp. 195-198.

[77] J. M. Moore (secretary of state), Austin, to Louis L. McInnis, March 23, 1888, L. L. McInnis Papers, Texas A&M University Archives.

ocratic contention that "it was understood from the inception of the enterprise, that it should be managed as it now appears, not for the public good, but for private gain."[78] But in the fall elections of 1872 Davis lost control over both the House and the Senate, as Democratic "redeemers" came into power, and his influence over A&M affairs declined proportionally.

Termed the "liberators of Texas" the Thirteenth Legislature was determined to right the wrongs of Radicalism.[79] It abolished the state police, which had functioned as Davis' private army. It moved to investigate the superintendent of public instruction, Jacob C. DeGress, who was believed to have absconded with $75,000 to $100,000 of public money.[80] It also formed a special committee to investigate the A&M College situation. This committee soon reported to the Legislature that $38,023.20 of the original $75,000 appropriation remained unexpended, and there was little to show for the money that had been spent. The committee placed most of the blame on the architect, Carl de Grote, but made no specific charges against any commissioner, and it exonerated the contractors. It offered an itemized statement showing to whom $36,476.80 had been paid. It recommended that $80,000 be provided for the completion of the main building, and sponsored a bill appropriating $50,000 out of the school fund of the state for this purpose. The committee also pointed to the very large expenditures made by various other states for the support of their agricultural and mechanical colleges.[81] In effect, the committee went on record in support of the location and plan for the A&M College and charged off any "wrong-doing" to incompetency rather than to dishonesty.

Opinion in the Legislature, however, remained very divided. A stormy legislative battle over A&M developed both in the House and in the Senate. In the Senate, Senator Saylor introduced a bill which, after many amendments, would give the A&M College twenty leagues (or two-fifths) of the university lands set aside in the days of the Republic, forty of the 5-percent state bonds appropriated for the University of Texas in 1866, and an additional cash appropriation of $40,000; in all, as noted by Governor Davis, an endowment "worth more than three hundred thousand dollars in gold."[82] Opposition to Saylor's bill quickly developed in the form of a Senate resolu-

[78]Austin *Tri-Weekly Statesman*, May 28, 1872.

[79]Ramsdell, *Reconstruction in Texas*, 313 ff.

[80]*Texas House Journal*, 1872, p. 12.

[81]*Ibid.*, 195-198 (Iowa, $227,000; Missouri, $50,000 annually for ten years; Virginia, $1,044,000; Illinois, $265,544; California, $245,000).

[82]*Texas Senate Journal*, 1873, pp. 138, 919, 925, 945, 1040; *Texas House Journal*, 1873, p. 1173.

tion which proposed to remove the A&M College to another place and to launch a new examination of the situation.[83] But after many legislative maneuvers the Saylor bill passed the Senate and went to the House.

The House, meanwhile, waged its own battle over the College. Andrew S. Broaddus, a Virginia-born Democrat, former secessionist, and resident of Caldwell, in Burleson County, adjacent to Brazos, introduced a bill to endow the A&M College with two hundred sections of land out of the public lands of the state.[84] Opponents countered with an amendment of Broaddus' bill which would return the donated land to Brazos County, dispose of the building material acquired for the college, repay the money received from federal lands, and close the project down. The amendment was killed by a narrow vote of 40-30.[85] Finally, the House substituted the Senate bill for their own A&M bill and reported it back to the Senate. The bill was then presented for the Governor's signature on June 3, 1873, and Governor Davis vetoed it the following day on the grounds of extravagance and fiscal irresponsibility.[86] Davis seemingly had vetoed the new appropriations bill in order to avoid further charges of fraud and corruption in the forthcoming gubernatorial campaign.

Despite his veto, Davis appeared determined to go forward with construction of the College under existing finances. The new commissioners of the A&M College, comprising James H. Raymond, Hamilton Stewart, and Andrew S. Broaddus, met on July 30 and appointed Jacob Larmour, architect for the School Bureau, as architect for A&M construction. The commissioners accepted Larmour's plan for the main building (less the French roof) and directed that he prepare specifications for labor and materials, and that he advertise for sealed bids to be received on August 23, in Bryan.[87]

Overall the physical production of the first "redeemer legislature," insofar as the A&M College was concerned, was negative, but the Legislature had in effect gone on record as favoring continued support for the College. Thus, the A&M College could no longer be termed a "Radical" institution, but had effectually become a Democratic and Texas-supported institution, if it had not been so before. The legislative session of 1873 marked a turning point in the affairs of the College.

The contract for the new main building was let on August 23, and by mid-October a new foundation, in a slightly different location from the ear-

[83]*Texas Senate Journal, 1873,* pp. 306, 471, 566, 579.

[84]*Texas House Journal, 1873,* pp. 274, 283, 638-639, 1047-1048, 1063-1064, 1173.

[85]*Ibid.,* 1053-1054.

[86]*Ibid.,* 1204, 1207; *Texas Senate Journal, 1873,* pp. 1044, 1166-1167.

[87]Galveston *News,* July 31, 1873; see also Langford, *Getting the College Under Way,* 36.

lier de Grote foundation, had been completed.[88] Richard Coke, campaigning for governor on the Democratic ticket, visited Bryan in November and carried the county and the state in December.[89] Davis refused to accept the vote count and had a state court rule the elections void, and appealed to President Grant for troops. Grant refused his request and Davis then called on the state militia for support. The support failed to materialize. Davis made a final appeal to the President, and, failing again to receive support from Grant, he retired from his office on January 17, 1874, and Richard Coke took possession.[90] Radical reconstruction was over.

A few days after Coke took office the Galveston *News* reported that "one story of the magnificent structure [at A&M] is now completed."[91] Throughout the political turmoil construction on the College had continued without interruption. The Democrats, now in control of all offices of the state government, appropriated $40,000 for the completion of the main building, which was the first appropriation made since the original grant of $75,000 in 1871.[92] By the end of May 1874 the brick work had been completed, and by the end of June the building was almost finished.[93] Also near the end of June two hundred citizens of Bryan lynched Harry Cook, a white man and the accused murderer of James P. Farmer, inside the city jail, ignoring the forty-three guards "protecting" Cook,[94] and ignoring the omnipresence of higher learning.

On October 8 Governor Coke inspected the completed building at A&M and in his report to the Legislature in January testified:

> It is exceedingly well built, of the best material, and is a solid and most imposing and handsome structure, modeled with fine taste, and with the interior arrangements and divisions admirably suiting it for the purposes for which it is built. It is a four story building, made of brick on a foundation of hard limestone, and covered with slate, is seventy-eight feet wide by one hundred and fifty long. It is beautifully located in sight of the Central Railroad, and about four miles from Bryan. . . . it furnishes the means of supplying immediately in Texas the great want of an institution of learning of the highest grade.[95]

[88] Galveston *Daily News*, August 24, 1872, October 18, 1873.

[89] *Ibid.*, November 25, December 4, 1873.

[90] Ramsdell, *Reconstruction in Texas*, 314, 316 ff.

[91] Galveston *News*, January 31, 1874.

[92] Gammel (ed.), *Laws of Texas*, VIII, 50-51.

[93] Galveston *News*, May 28, June 21, 1874. Many sources, including official records such as *The Government of the State of Texas*, XI, *Education*, 8, mistakenly assume that Gathright Hall was the first building completed on campus. Old Main was completed in 1875, Gathright in 1876.

[94] Galveston *News*, June 17, 1874.

[95] *Governor's Messages, Coke to Ross, 1874-1891*, p. 138.

Coke then asked the Legislature for $7,000 to complete the main building, $25,000 for a boarding hall, $21,000 for three professors' homes, and $5,000 for fences, a barn, and landscaping, convinced, as he said, that the appropriations are "absolutely essential and that the appropriation heretofore made is being economically and honestly administered."[96]

After posting a reward of $4,000 for the "apprehension and delivery of the body of the notorious murderer, John Wesley Hardin," the Legislature appropriated $32,000 to A&M for the "purpose of completing the necessary buildings and enclosures."[97] Most of this money was used for the construction of a "mess hall and students quarters," later to become Gathright Hall, the second building on the campus.

In order to expedite the opening of the College, the Legislature created a separate Board of Directors, consisting of the governor, the lieutenant governor, the speaker of the House of Representatives, and six elected directors, one from each congressional district to be chosen by joint ballot of the Legislature. This Board was given authority to select a president, professors, and other officers of the College, and to impose necessary rules and regulations. The Board received authority to draw upon the fund established by the federal land grant to the A&M College.[98] Thus in 1875 the Legislature created an A&M administrative system independent of the University of Texas system, and in apparent contradiction to the organization act of 1871. The problem at the time, however, was not so abstract. The fact was that there did exist an A&M College, but there was no state university.

The first meeting of the A&M Board convened in Bryan on June 1, 1875. With Governor Coke presiding, the Board appointed a special committee (comprising Coke and Major Charles S. West) to submit a report to the Legislature describing the condition and needs of the College and recommending the necessary legislation and appropriations to put it into operation. Although there had been some desire to open the school in the fall of 1875, the Board was forced to delay the opening until the following year. There was simply too much yet to be done. The College president and faculty had not been chosen. Student resident and dining facilities did not exist. There were no residences for faculty. There was merely a huge, unequipped main building standing on a summit in the middle of the prairie, four miles from the nearest town.[99]

Negotiations for a president and the selection of faculty occupied the

[96]*Ibid.*
[97]Gammel (ed.), *Laws of Texas,* VIII, 387, 561.
[98]*Ibid.,* VIII, 444-445.
[99]Galveston *Daily News,* June 2, 3, 1875.

Board through the spring and summer of 1876.[100] Meanwhile, the organization act of 1875 creating the separate board for the A&M College had raised
anew the question of the proper relationship between this institution and the
projected state university. In an effort to resolve forever that theoretical problem the Constitutional Convention, which gathered in Austin in September
1875, sought to give the situation constitutional clarification. The Texas Constitution of 1876 declared that the new college "is hereby made, and constituted a branch of the University of Texas, for instruction in agriculture, the
mechanic arts and the natural sciences connected therewith." This provision
remains unchanged to the present. The Convention, in the Constitution,
instructed the next Legislature to appropriate not more than $40,000 to put
the College into "immediate and successful operation."[101] Thus A&M was
consigned to be a branch of The University of Texas, that did not yet exist,
with a separate board of directors whose authority over the A&M system was
exclusive, irrespective of the fact that a University of Texas board of administrators did exist.

In many physical respects the world in which the new A&M College
emerged was a primitive world. In terms of fields of knowledge and educational techniques it was perhaps more primitive still. Despite specific instruction to teach the agricultural and mechanic arts, such things had rarely if ever
been taught elsewhere and never before in Texas, and the state of knowledge
regarding them was at best very limited.[102] A&M's first faculty, as faculties
elsewhere were doing, failed to pursue vigorously the unknown and sought to
stick to the tried and true tenets of a classical education. Texas A&M became
something of a battleground between the classicists and the representatives of
the emerging new scientific, technical, vocational school. It was somewhat
the same struggle that was taking place to a greater or lesser degree in every
land-grant college and in most universities. At Texas A&M, unlike the situation in most other places, the conflict became acute.

The real challenge to the new college was not really from the outside
world, from the wolves at the door; the real challenge came from within. A
college is not legislation or buildings — it is people and ideas. Despite all the
storm and furor over legislation, contracts, and negotiations, the Agricultural
and Mechanical College of Texas did not become a reality until the students

[100]Ousley, *History of the A&M College,* 43-44.
[101]*Texas Constitution of 1876,* Article VII, Section 13.
[102]Eugene Davenport, "Agricultural Education During the Last Half Century," in *1876
. . . 1926, The Semi-Centennial Celebration of the Agricultural and Mechanical College of Texas and
the Inauguration of Thomas Otto Walton, LL.D., as President,* 35-63.

and faculty together began to give it life. This began *technically* on October 2, 1876, when the first students "matriculated." Formal opening ceremonies were held on October 4, 1876, fully a decade after Texas had accepted the terms of the Morrill Land-Grant College Act.[103]

[103]Anderson James Peeler (ed.), *Laws Relating to the Agricultural and Mechanical College of Texas and the Proceedings of the Board of Directors,* 20. Minutes of the Board name "the first Monday in October" as the date for opening the school. At the same meeting 5,000 copies of a pamphlet entitled *Announcement of the State Agricultural and Mechanical College,* which indicated October 2 as the opening date, were authorized to be published. One of the pamphlets is preserved in the Texas A&M University Archives. The "formal" opening, so often told as the opening date of the school, was exactly that, a ceremonial occasion at which Governor Richard Coke and President Thomas B. Gathright addressed the assembled visitors.

CHAPTER 2

The Gathright Era

THE official Board of Directors of the Agricultural and Mechanical College, in their first meeting in June 1875, resolved to put the school into operation at as early a day as possible. The members present included Governor Richard Coke, Lieutenant Governor Richard B. Hubbard, Speaker of the House Guy M. Bryan, Bennett H. Davis, and Charles S. West. Others elected by a joint session of the House and Senate on March 11, 1875, but not present at the first Board meeting, included Edward Bradford Pickett, Charles DeMorse, Isaac Graves, and Fletcher S. Stockdale. Coke and West were to prepare a report and make recommendations to the Legislature for needed legislation. The Board agreed to select a faculty consisting of a president and five professors, to be elected at their next regular meeting. A special committee comprising Coke, Davis, and West was to outline the courses of instruction and fix faculty salaries. Finally, the Directors agreed to offer the presidency of the College to the former President of the Confederacy, Jefferson Davis.[1]

Coke wrote to Davis on June 14, 1875, offering him the position. Most Texans at the time would have been deeply honored to have had Jefferson Davis as the head of their first college; some, however, such as the Radicals and former Unionists, who were still much in evidence, would have been mortified, as would have been many Northerners. One could speculate at great length on the efficacy of Davis' election as president of the Agricultural and Mechanical College of Texas. A very pertinent consideration is the fact that none were more outspoken in opposition to the Morrill Land-Grant Col-

[1] Anderson James Peeler (ed.), *Laws Relating to the Agricultural and Mechanical College of Texas and the Proceedings of the Board of Directors*, 17 (hereinafter cited: Peeler [ed.], *Laws Relating to A&M*). Clarence Ousley, *History of the A&M College*, 42, erroneously notes that the first Board meeting was held July 16, 1875. The Board first convened on June 1, 1875; the second meeting was held July 15-24, 1876. Contrary to reports in the Galveston *Daily News*, June 2, 3, 1875, the Board at its first meeting did not set salaries at $4,000 per year for the president and $3,000 per year for professors. For the election of the directors, see *Texas State Journal, 1875*, pp. 565-566.

lege Act in the United States Senate before the Civil War than Jefferson Davis. Davis, perhaps, could not have accepted the position in good conscience. He declined with regret, expressing business obligations and the pressure of family and friends as his reasons. He did ask, however, whether he might recommend a man for the position. The man whom he recommended, and who became A&M's first president, was Thomas S. Gathright, the recently appointed superintendent of public education in Mississippi.[2]

On July 15, 1876, one year after its initial meeting, the Board convened in Austin. The Directors approved the committee report prepared by Coke, Davis, and West, which called for the organization of the College into seven "courses" or "departments." The Commercial Department would present studies in bookkeeping, laws governing commercial transactions, and philosophy and morals of business. Modern Languages and English would offer instruction in English, German, French, and Spanish. The Agricultural and Scientific Courses would give instruction in natural history and botany to the first-year students; physical geography and an elementary course in natural philosophy and mineralogy to second-year students; chemistry and geology to third-year students; and agricultural science (including chemistry, farm tillage, horticulture, arboriculture, and the care of stock) to fourth-year students. The Department of Ancient Languages would teach Latin and Greek. The Department of Applied Mathematics offered instruction to the junior class in "surveying, descriptive geometry, mechanics and drawing (plane and projection)." Seniors studied shades, shadows and perspective, descriptive astronomy, railroad surveying, strength of materials, arches, framing, freehand drawing, mapping, sketches of tools, and designs for the commercial parts of machinery and for bridges and other structures. The Department of Pure Mathematics offered instruction in arithmetic, algebra, trigonometry, geometry, and calculus. The Department of Mental and Moral Philosophy and *Belles-Lettres* presented studies in ancient and modern history, rhetoric, logic, mental and moral philosophy, economy, and higher English. A single professor was responsible for instructing the courses in each department.[3]

The Board next chose from among the several candidates for the positions, a president and a faculty. William A. Banks of Virginia, then serving as professor of modern languages in St. John College, Little Rock, Arkansas, was chosen as professor of modern languages and English. In addition to twenty years' teaching experience in Virginia, Banks had letters of recom-

[2]Ousley, *History of the A&M College*, 43-44; Clement Eaton, *The Growth of Southern Civilization, 1790-1860*, p. 316.

[3]Peeler (ed.), *Laws Relating to A&M*, 18-19; see also *Catalogue of the State Agricultural and Mechanical College of Texas, 1876-1877*, pp. 11-18 (hereinafter cited: Texas A&M, *Catalogue*).

mendation from Governor James L. Kemper of Virginia and had the distinction of having served under Robert E. Lee when Lee's regiment captured John Brown at Harper's Ferry.[4] Although he left A&M in 1879 to found a private college in Salado, Texas, Banks returned to A&M as professor of English in 1893. Dr. (of Divinity) Carlisle P. B. Martin received appointment as professor of agriculture and science. Martin, an elderly man with a long, flowing beard, was a Presbyterian minister and part-time farmer.[5] John T. Hand received the chair of ancient languages. After leaving A&M, Hand became superintendent of schools at Brenham, Texas.[6] The Board appointed Alexander Hogg professor of pure mathematics. Hogg came to Texas A&M from the A&M College of Alabama. He was a very outgoing person who became quite popular with the people of Bryan. He later became chief of engineers for the Houston and Texas Central Railroad.[7] Robert P. W. Morris, at the age of twenty-two, headed the Department of Applied Mathematics. Because he came to A&M from the Texas Military Institute in Austin, and possibly because he was the youngest member of the faculty, Morris became responsible for organizing the students along military lines and for the administration of military discipline. Morris proved to be popular with the students and instilled a considerable degree of school spirit and respect for military discipline, which helped lay the foundation for Texas A&M's unique Corps of Cadets. After leaving A&M, Morris studied law in St. Louis at Washington University and later became a federal judge in Minnesota.[8]

The new president, Gathright, was born in Monroe County, Georgia, on January 5, 1829. His father died in 1840 shortly after the family moved to Alabama. Gathright had two years of formal schooling in Greensprings, Ala-

[4]Dallas *Morning News,* December 18, 1927; Sam W. Williams, Little Rock, Arkansas, "To whom it may concern," July 1, 1875; Judge Henry C. Caldwell, Little Rock, Arkansas, "To whom it may concern," July 1, 1875; James L. Kemper, Richmond, Virginia, to W. A. Banks, Little Rock, Arkansas, March 15, 1875; William A. Banks Biographical Papers, Texas A&M University Archives.

[5]College Station *Texas Collegian,* March 1880.

[6]John T. Hand, Brenham, Texas, to Louis L. McInnis, College Station, Texas, May 25, 1880, Louis L. McInnis Papers, Texas A&M University Archives.

[7]Bryan *Brazos Pilot,* October 31, 1879; College Station *Texas Collegian,* March 1880; Thomas S. Gathright, College Station, Texas, to George Pfeuffer, Austin, November 2, 1879, Gathright Papers, Texas A&M University Archives.

[8]Dallas *Morning News,* December 18, 1879 (interview with Aubry L. Banks); College Station *Texas Collegian,* January 1880; Thomas S. Gathright, College Station, to George Pfeuffer, Austin, November 2, 1879, Thomas Gathright Papers; Hamilton P. Bee, College Station, to George Pfeuffer, Austin, November 14, 1879, Pfeuffer Papers, Texas A&M University Archives.

bama, and began his teaching career in 1850 in Mt. Hebron, Alabama. On January 7, 1854, he opened a private school for boys called Summerville Institute in Gholson County, Mississippi, which operated until his appointment to Texas A&M in 1876. His school was subtitled A First Class Boarding School and Normal Academy, for Boys and Young Men, and apparently it was that, educating many of the sons of prominent Mississippians.[9]

President Gathright's career during the Civil War is somewhat curious. In April 1862 Gathright asked for exemption from military service (after receiving a draft call) on the grounds of poor health. He argued that he was the only male member of the family not at war and was responsible for taking care of his wife and seven children (the oldest of whom was nine), his mother-in-law, and the family of a brother-in-law. His school closed in 1861, but reopened in 1864. In that year Gathright petitioned Governor Charles Clark, of Mississippi, for exemption from the emergency draft which called all able-bodied Mississippians to arms. He noted that he had thirty-two boys enrolled in the school, many of them from out-of-state, and some the sons of parents in the army. The sons of indigent soldiers, he said, were being taught free, as was one maimed soldier from Sharpsburg. He stated that he did not question the rightness of the draft, nor did he seek to evade his duty, but there was no one to care for the boys in his absence. He indicated also that he had once volunteered for duty, but had been discharged by his regimental officer so that he might continue his professional duties.[10] In a word, Gathright succeeded in staying out of the Confederate service throughout the war.

In March 1865 Gathright announced his candidacy for the state Senate from the district comprising Winston and Noxubee Counties. The collapse of the Confederacy and the appointment of a military governor in Mississippi, however, eliminated Gathright's candidacy. Before the war ended, Gathright had publicly assumed a Conservative if not Unionist position, and in late June petitioned the Radical Governor William L. Sharkey for appointment to a position in the state government. He presumed to be "rather importunate" in his demands upon the Governor and was very critical of the

[9]S. A. Gathright, Palestine, Texas, to Louis L. McInnis, College Station, Texas, January 4, 1883, Gathright Papers, Texas A&M University Archives; Thomas S. Gathright, Gholson, Mississippi, to Governor W. L. Sharkey, Jackson, Mississippi, July 3, 1865, W. L. Sharkey Papers, Mississippi Department of Archives and History, Jackson, Mississippi, photostatic copy in Gathright Papers, Texas A&M University Archives.

[10]Thomas S. Gathright, Gholson, Mississippi, to [anonymous], April 22, 1862; Gathright, Gholson, Mississippi, to Governor Charles Clark, Jackson, Mississippi, August 18, 1864, Charles Clark Papers, Mississippi Department of Archives and History, photostatic copy in Gathright Papers, Texas A&M University Archives.

fact that many of the original "precipitators" were rushing forward and receiving the lion's share of public offices.[11] In a word, Thomas Gathright, by word and action, had been lukewarm in his support of the Confederacy.

He nonetheless remained on good terms with his neighbors, and with many prominent Mississippians, including Jefferson Davis. His dedication to education was unquestioned and respected. His school remained in operation until 1876. It opened each year on the first Monday in October, with a second term beginning on the third Monday in February. In 1876 he advertised it as the "Oldest Boarding School for Boys and Young Men in the Southwest." He charged $100.00 for each twenty-week term payable in advance, which fee included lodging, "good fare and good teaching." But the impoverishment of Mississippians during Reconstruction created continuing financial difficulties for the school. Citing "repeated misfortunes," Gathright, in March 1876, asked the newly elected Democratic governor, John M. Stone, a personal friend, for the appointment to the office of state superintendent of education. Letters from other friends to Stone and a petition signed by nineteen Mississippi legislators secured him the appointment, which was conferred by the Senate on April 3, 1876.[12] Governor Coke of Texas, meanwhile, had been in correspondence with Gathright regarding the offer of the Texas A&M presidency. According to Judge Walter Acker, Sr., when the Governor was informed that Gathright would probably not accept the A&M position, Acker was sent to Jackson, Mississippi, in the spring of 1876 to see him. Although Gathright at first demurred, he finally agreed to come to Texas.[13] His real reasons for giving up his position in Mississippi to come to Texas remain obscure. Undoubtedly the very confused state of Mississippi politics and the chaos in the Mississippi educational system had much to do with the decision.

The position of superintendent of education had become vacant only in February 1876, by reason of the impeachment of Thomas W. Cordozo, the

[11]Circular containing letters and articles reprinted from the Macon *Beacon,* one of which bears the date March 19, 1865; Thomas S. Gathright to Governor W. L. Sharkey, Jackson, Mississippi, July 3, 1865, W. L. Sharkey Papers, Mississippi Department of Archives and History, photostatic copy in Gathright Papers, Texas A&M University Archives.

[12]Thomas S. Gathright, Gholson, Mississippi, to Governor John M. Stone, Jackson, Mississippi, March 27, 1876; John R. Brice, Gholson, Mississippi, to Colonel John M. Stone, Jackson, Mississippi, March 29, 1876; petition dated March 30, 1876, Jackson, Mississippi; David E. Porter, Gholson, Mississippi, to Governor John M. Stone, Jackson, Mississippi, April 3, 1876, John M. Stone Papers, Mississippi Department of Archives and History, photostatic copies in Gathright Papers, Texas A&M University Archives.

[13]Ousley, *History of the A&M College,* 43-44.

Negro Radical superintendent. Outgoing Governor Adelbert Ames, who disputed Stone's election as governor, resigned on March 29, 1876, only after his black lieutenant governor had been impeached and impeachment proceedings were initiated against him. Thomas Gathright's appointment on April 3 was still clouded by the political contests within the state, and by the uncertainty as to what the November presidential elections would bring. Furthermore, the state was impoverished. Economy was the by-word of the "Redeemers." Legislation establishing a system of free public schools was not passed until 1878.[14] There were then good reasons for leaving Mississippi to obtain an attractive position in Texas.

On July 19, 1876, the A&M Board convened again and appointed a committee of two (Bennet H. Davis and Charles S. West) to call together such of the professors as were known to be present in Austin, and with their assistance to prepare a pamphlet for circulation announcing the general outline of studies, expenses, regulations, and procedures of the College. In a meeting on July 23 the Board ordered 5,000 copies of the pamphlet printed, and agreed that the opening date of the institution would be the first Monday in October, that is October 2, 1876.[15] Contrary to the recollections of Charles Rogan, one of the first students to enter the College, there was no plan to open the College on September 17, 1876, nor does there appear to have been any advertisement to that effect. Neither did the school open October 4, 1876, as many write; that was the date of the "formal inauguration" of the school, when Governor Coke and President Gathright, in effect, "cut the ribbon." The members of the Board of Directors and the official announcement of the College indicated that the school began enrolling students on Monday, October 2, 1876, the same time of the year when Gathright always enrolled his students.[16]

Members of the Board, in their July meeting, initiated a program to make the College available to every class of citizen. They approved a plan calling for "beneficiary scholars," or state students who would be admitted free of charge to the College. Three students were to be selected from each senatorial district, by appointment upon the completion of a competitive examination; one student could be appointed from each congressional district

---

[14]*Mississippi: A Guide to the Magnolia State*, Federal Writers' Project of the Works Progress Administration, 512.

[15]Peeler (ed.), *Laws Relating to A&M*, 20.

[16]See Ousley, *History of the A&M College*, 46; Peeler (ed.), *Laws Relating to A&M*, 20; Board of Directors, *Announcement and Circular of the State Agricultural and Mechanical College, 1876*, p. 31.

by the representative in Congress, and one student could be appointed from the state at large by each United States senator.[17] This system was dropped on January 3, 1877, but reinstated in a slightly different form in 1881. It operated until 1883, when the Legislature discontinued funding the program.[18] When the beneficiary-student system was dropped in 1877 the Board lowered student tuition fees from $250 to $200 per year for all students.[19] The announced objective of the original Board and of the first College administration was to provide a good education at the lowest possible price to the student. This has since remained a basic part of the Texas A&M philosophy.

In other business the Board named William Falconer, of Bryan, as secretary of the Board at a salary of $500.00 per year. Dr. D. Port Smythe was named surgeon of the College, to be compensated by a special $5.00 medical fee charged each student, and General Hamilton P. Bee was named steward and superintendent of the Farm, a position that later correlated to that of the business manager or agent. The Board also authorized the building of five professors' residences at a cost not to exceed $3,000 each and appointed Bennet Davis, the only Board member who resided in Bryan, Texas, to supervise the outfitting and equipping of the new mess hall, or Steward's Hall (later called Gathright Hall), and the residences as completed.[20]

The facilities, faculty, and paraphernalia of higher education having been accumulated on the Brazos prairies after so many years of effort, the "college" anxiously awaited its students. Great expectations must have been thoroughly dampened when only six students appeared for registration during the first few days of enrollment,[21] but by the end of the first term forty-eight students were in attendance, and by the end of the first year one hundred and six students had enrolled.[22]

Governor Coke gave the A&M College a brave send-off in the inaugural ceremonies of October 4, 1876:

> The magnificent college building, in which we are now assembled, with the

[17]Peeler (ed.), *Laws Relating to A&M*, 20.

[18]Gammel (ed.), *Laws of Texas*, IX, 167-178; Board of Directors, *Annual Report of the Officers and Faculty of the Agricultural and Mechanical College of Texas, 1883-1884*, p. 5 (hereinafter cited: Texas A&M, *Annual Report*).

[19]Peeler (ed.), *Laws Relating to A&M*, 26.

[20]*Ibid.*, 19-20; for information regarding construction of the Steward's Hall (or Gathright Hall) see Langford, *Getting the College Under Way*, 50-54.

[21] Charles Rogan's statement that only six students initially presented themselves for enrollment is substantiated by a report of the Board of Directors to the Legislature. See *Texas Senate Journal, 1879*, pp. 205-210. This occurred in October, and not in September, as Rogan recalled.

[22]*Texas Senate Journal, 1879*, pp. 205-210.

capacity for the accommodation of six hundred students, and around it the commodious residences for professors and a capacious steward's hall all constructed in the best style of architecture with the tract of 2400 acres of land otherwise improved, in which they stand attest to the liberality of the state as well as her earnest purpose to make this institution worthy of its grand mission.[23]

He stressed the objective of providing a good education at a low cost.[24]

President Gathright spoke briefly to the assemblage, noting that he was "a stranger to this audience and to these surroundings." He said somewhat prophetically that the faculty "may not be the proper men to work out success, and may be called to give place to others. I may not be suited to my place and may retire. Still the great work, in which all the people of this good state are interested, must go on and must succeed."[25]

Upon the completion of the inaugural ceremonies the Board began a series of business meetings, which lasted through October seventh. It selected John S. Fowlkes, of Bryan, Texas, as fiscal agent at a salary of $200.00 per year. The president and faculty of the College would constitute a subordinate board with authority to fix the rules and regulations for the government of the College. Robert Morris, professor of mathematics and commandant of cadets, received the appointment as College treasurer, responsible for receiving fees from the students, and for paying out money to the fiscal agent and steward, as required. Because the College *Announcement* made no mention of age limits for admission, the Board now specified that only boys fifteen years old and older would be admitted. The only other admission requirements were that the student be of good moral character and able to enter upon the studies prescribed.[26] In their final October session the Board gave attention to one of the primary purposes of the College, that is, the teaching of scientific agriculture.

The superintendent of the Farm was given direct responsibility for the custody and operation of the Farm. He was, however, to secure direction as to method and mode of cultivation from the professor of agriculture for "the purpose of illustrating the science of chemistry as applied to agriculture, and for this purpose only." This meant that so long as the farming had nothing to do with class instruction the professor of agriculture held no authority over the superintendent. The way was open for considerable conflict between the Department of Agriculture and the Farm. The Board did prescribe the

[23]President, *Addresses at the Inauguration of the State Agricultural and Mechanical College of Texas, Bryan, October 4, 1876*, p. 4.

[24]*Ibid.*

[25]*Ibid.*, 10-11.

[26]Peeler (ed.), *Laws Relating to A&M*, 21-22.

development of an experimental farm not to exceed thirty acres, on which student labor should be voluntary unless such labor was "necessary to a proper understanding of the principles of science." The Board also directed that an orchard be planted, and that shade and ornamental trees be placed on the campus. One thousand dollars was allowed for this purpose; another thousand was ear-marked for the purchase of a pair of mules, a wagon, and harness, and for feed and necessary farm implements.[27] Thus the Board of Directors sincerely intended to carry out the mission of the College in providing training in scientific agriculture.

A number of difficulties were encountered, however, some of which appeared within a matter of months. The greatest problem involved money. The development of a farm, with the maintenance of farm personnel, livestock, buildings, and equipment, cost money. Similarly the development of machine shops and technical and vocational training facilities, and later laboratories, to which no consideration was given in the initial planning, also proved costly. As it would be proved, training in agriculture and mechanics cost more per student than training in the arts and sciences. Many states and established universities were initially motivated to found an agricultural and mechanical college, at least partially if not wholly, in a desire to obtain the proceeds from the land grant. "They wanted the money and must organize a college of agriculture to get it,"[28] little realizing at the time the full extent of the obligation they were incurring. Texas, in part, fit the pattern. Yet, admitting the most honorable intentions in establishing an agricultural and mechanical college, no one, neither educators nor politicians, understood the full implications of such an institution. Agricultural training, the "mechanics," and engineering were still in their infancy. Textbooks, especially in agriculture, were almost nonexistent. While educators talked about the "scientific method," few understood it and most continued to lecture on the basis of "well-established authorities." In 1879, Cato's *De agricultura,* written in Rome about 300 B.C., was probably still one of the most intelligent books on practical agriculture available. Thus, even with good intentions in establishing an agricultural and mechanical school, teaching agriculture or engineering would be difficult.

Many regarded the Morrill Land-Grant College program as simply another way of obtaining sorely needed funds. Others were willing to give lip

[27] *Ibid.,* 23-24.

[28] For an excellent review of early efforts to establish the Agricultural and Mechanical College see Eugene Davenport, "Agricultural Education during the Last Half Century," *1876 . . . 1926, The Semi-Centennial Celebration of the Agricultural and Mechanical College of Texas,* 35-63, and especially pp. 49-53.

service to the objectives of the Land-Grant College Act, while continuing to function as they had always functioned in the past, in the best classical tradition. There were also those, particularly in Texas, who believed that the new Agricultural and Mechanical College necessarily had to fill the function of a public university, and therefore that its initial and primary responsibility lay in instruction in literature and the sciences, where the greater need existed. Thomas Gathright could be included among this group. Gathright opposed diverting money from classical studies to build up the agricultural and mechanical departments. He recommended supplementary appropriations to build the agricultural and mechanical departments; but he insisted on maintaining a sound academic course as the core of the institution. "We have a good academic course," he said in 1879, "the people need and demand it." He argued that this should not be sacrificed to rebuild in another direction.[29]

Yet another faction, failing to understand the concepts of scientific agriculture and desiring to carry out the mission of the College as they understood it, viewed the Agricultural and Mechanical College as an institution for training skilled labor. Included in this faction was Governor Oran Milo Roberts, who came to office in 1879. Roberts explained his position in this way:

> That it could not have been designed by Congress in furnishing to the states donations of land to found agricultural and mechanical colleges to promote the cause of literary and scientific education . . . but rather to educate skilled laborers, as they are taught in Europe, and thereby secure skilled labor at home, instead of importing it from abroad as has always been heretofore done to a very large extent . . .; that there are those who are highly educated in literature and science generally are seldom found to spend their lives between the plow handles or in the workshops or otherwise . . .; that we lack in Texas skilled laborers more than men learned in literature and science.[30]

He would make Texas A&M strictly a vocational school for training skilled labor. Problems existed even here, for most farmers had not accepted the necessity of "educating" a man to farm, and laborers similarly held little respect for a "textbook" carpenter, cabinetmaker, or brickmason. Furthermore, students who came to the new College did not come to learn to labor in the fields or even to be skilled craftsmen; they came to enter a "profession," and to use their brains rather than their brawn.

The early phases of the institution were fraught with difficulty, misdi-

[29]Thomas S. Gathright, College Station, to Governor O. M. Roberts, Austin, May 25, 1879, Gathright Papers, Texas A&M University Archives.

[30]*Governor's Messages, Coke to Ross, 1874-1891*, pp. 249-250; see also *Texas Senate Journal, 1879*, pp. 204-205.

rection, bumbling, false starts, and no starts. It incurred the enmity of politicians, the derision of the press, and the rejection of classical and religious educators; farmers called it a "humbug" and antimilitarists called it a "military peacockery." Its faculty bickered over some real and many imagined grievances. Perhaps the most remarkable thing about it all was that the school survived.

The first students, many of them young boys with little or no formal schooling, presented a "painful deficiency" and a real challenge to the faculty. Many of them likely held the attitude and values reflected in the recollections of George Baylor, a member of the first class. Baylor boarded the stage in front of the Alamo in San Antonio, caught at Seguin the first train he ever rode, and traveled all night from Houston to Bryan. Baylor never liked the College work. He did like the military training and the good food. "They certainly had good food," he said, a sentiment that seems to have been echoed throughout the early years of the College, thereby perhaps establishing another A&M "Aggie" tradition. As for his objectives, Baylor wanted nothing more than to go west and kill Indians and buffalo.[31] Not only was the philosophical environment of the new College rather raw and rugged, but so too were the students. In many respects Texas A&M students matched the stereotype of A&M students elsewhere in being "ungraded, unlettered, and unwashed."[32]

Students had the option of pursuing a field of study in agriculture, mechanics and engineering, language and literature, or military tactics. Within a chosen field students had a free choice of courses, which with six teachers probably meant they had to take what was being taught. They were required to attend at least three classes a day. Professors recorded attendance and a daily grade for each pupil and sent a weekly report on student progress to the president. Each month the school issued a grade report to parents. Upon satisfactory completion of a basic three-year course in any field students could receive a "proficiency certificate." Upon completion of the fourth year in agriculture, a student was awarded the degree of S.A. (Scientific Agriculture); after a fourth year in civil and mining engineering the C.E. degree was awarded; and the A.B. was awarded after the fourth year in language and literature.[33] The College soon found it necessary to offer a one-year preparatory course and revised the College offering to a three-year curriculum because of the general lack of preparedness of the average entering student.

[31] Florence Fenley, *Oldtimers of Southwest Texas*, 17-22.

[32] Davenport, "Agricultural Education," *The Semi-Centennial Celebration of the A&M College of Texas*, 49.

[33] *Announcement and Circular of the State A&M College*, 1876, pp. 22-27.

Upon arriving at the College each student reported immediately to President Gathright. He was introduced, interviewed, enrolled, and given a twenty-eight page set of *Rules and Regulations*, which prescribed in rather close detail his life for the academic year. The *Rules* required the student to have "two pairs of shoes, seven shirts, seven pair of socks, four handkerchiefs, six towels, one clothes brush, one comb, two pillowcases, two pair of sheets, one pair of blankets, one comfort, four pairs of drawers, four undershirts and seven collars." He was to purchase two uniforms, one including a frock of cadet gray with one row of College buttons, gray pants and a forage cap; the second a set of fatigues. Long hair, whiskers, and moustaches had to be shorn. He awoke to reveille at 6:30, answered sergeant's call, marched to breakfast, and then fell into troop formation and marched to classes. He attended compulsory study hall for thirty minutes after supper. Tattoo came at 9:30 and taps at 10:00. Every morning he attended chapel and every Sunday he attended at least one "preaching." Every Sunday morning a general inspection was held, but except for the preaching and the inspection his Sundays were free.[34]

The list of "do's" and "don'ts" in the *Rules and Regulations* for faculty and students was specific and lengthy. For example, there was to be no dueling and no fighting; no student could keep a servant, horse, or dog; in academic departments pupils were to be called "students," in the military department they were called "cadets." They must attend classes, and could not possess arms, could not drink or gamble, or hold private parties, or visit places of public amusement. No one could leave the campus without written permission of the president. Cadets were not to lie, or cheat, or steal, or damage property — all on pain of dismissal. Demerits were awarded as appropriate. If a student incurred a total of 150 demerits in any one term or 250 in any one year he was automatically dismissed.[35] Although it may seem very authoritarian, militaristic, and repressive, the regimen and rules affecting the A&M students actually changed very little from the first year of operation through World War II. But despite the rules and regulations and military discipline, good evidence indicates that the early A&M student, much like the contemporary cadet, did not feel unduly imposed upon. Good evidence indicates also that the student then, as he undoubtedly does now, successfully evaded many of the rules. In fact, the early student, rightly or wrongly, obtained a "shady" reputation in a number of quarters.

Several departing professors complained in 1879 of the "lack of disci-

[34]*Rules and Regulations of the Agricultural and Mechanical College of Texas, 1876,* pp. 5-16; Texas A&M, *Catalogue, 1877-78,* pp. 22-27.
[35]*Rules and Regulations of the A&M College, 1876,* pp. 5-16.

pline." Queries from the Board elicited allegations of instances of drunkenness by cadets, lying, and visitations to houses of ill-fame. One professor noted that it was very difficult to keep chickens near the campus. The president lost his Thanksgiving turkey in 1887. By 1884 the never too friendly Galveston *News* was repeating the "common talk" that the faculty at A&M "drank liquor and played cards." The next year a student explained his resignation from the College on grounds that the boys indulged in conduct that was not acceptable, including snow-balling the teachers, burning outhouses, and drinking in quarters. Hazing soon became a continuing and acute problem on the campus. In 1893 a former state senator felt constrained to write "he had as soon give his boy a pony, six shooter, bottle of whiskey and deck of cards and start him out to get his education as to send him to the A&MC."[36] Somewhere between the puritanical, Prussian character that might have been molded by the *Rules and Regulations* and the depraved outlaw visualized by some critics, stood the ordinary A&M College student.

By the close of the first term in January 1877, a number of financial and personnel problems had developed. There had been little or no effective development of the Farm. Owing to the "lateness of the season" and the squeeze in funds, and what must already have been a conflict between the Farm superintendent and the professor of agriculture, the Board abolished the position of superintendent of the Farm and placed farming operations under the professor of agriculture, who would receive no extra compensation for his new duties. The orchard not yet having been planted, the Board reduced the allocation for that purpose from $1,000 to $250.00. The Board also directed that no additional mules were to be purchased, and mules, wagon, and gear on hand were to be sold. Thus the Board at least temporarily suspended farming operations, undoubtedly much to the relief of most of the faculty, to President Gathright, and to the students, who generally disliked farm labor.[37] The beneficiary-student system also placed a heavy drain on College finances, and was generally thought to be unfair to the "pay" students. The Board abolished the system, but lowered tuition fees and board for the benefit of all the students. In another economy move the Board abolished the position of secretary (whose salary had been $500.00) and assigned the duties to Professor John T. Hand, without additional compensation. It also dispensed with the services of the architect, Jacob Larmour, who had been in the

---

[36]Galveston *Daily News,* November 21, 1879, September 17, 1884; H. A. Stacey, Helltown, Texas, to George Pfeuffer, New Braunfels, Texas, May 17, 1885, George Pfeuffer Papers; J. D. Reed, Sherman, Texas, to L. L. McInnis, Bryan, March 15, 1883, McInnis Papers, Texas A&M University Archives.

[37]Peeler (ed.), *Laws Relating to A&M,* 25-26.

employment of the College since 1873 at a salary of $200.00 per month. Larmour built Old Main, Steward's Hall, and the five professors' residences, the last of which was nearing completion in January 1877.[38] These economy moves were necessitated by a general "insufficiency of appropriations" for the College.[39]

Operating income for the College came from the interest accrued on the original federal land-grant fund. The original investment of $174,000 in 7-percent "frontier defense bonds of Texas" had been supplemented in 1876 by the funding of accrued interest at 6 percent, making the total investment $209,000, which yielded $14,280 per year. This interest could be used only to pay salaries and it generally proved insufficient even for that.[40] The salary deficiency, plus the other normal operating expenses of the College, including administrative salaries, supplies, and travel, could be covered, it was hoped, by tuition fees received from students.

By 1876 the Texas Legislature had appropriated a total of $187,000 to the College for capital improvements. This money was expended for the erection of the main building, Steward's Hall, and five residences for the president and professors. Ten years later state appropriations reached a total of $298,787.44. Excluding the appropriations made prior to the opening of the College, total new operating appropriations amounted to $111,787.44; thus, in the first ten years of its operation the College cost the state an average of $11,000 per year.[41] The land-grant funds continued to comprise the bulk of operating income until the late eighties.

Enrollment in January 1877 reached a total of 48, representing a rather inconspicuous beginning. By the close of the second term, however, enrollment reached 106, and facilities, especially those for housing students, had become gratifyingly crowded.[42] Anderson James Peeler, a Board member, was principal speaker during the closing or "commencement" exercises which began on June 25, 1877. Peeler reviewed the legislation and the philosophy which brought the school into being. He regarded the Land-Grant College Act as one of the "noblest things in American annals." The primary consideration behind the act lay in the fact that "the greatest warfare of the present and future centuries is industrial warfare." He compared the funding of other

[38]*Ibid.*, 26; see also Langford, *Getting the College Under Way*, 36-37, 56-58.

[39]Peeler (ed.), *Laws Relating to A&M*, 25-26.

[40]*Governor's Messages, Coke to Ross, 1874-1891*, pp. 137, 752-753; "Report of the Outgoing Directors at the January Session of the Board, 1879," *Texas Senate Journal, 1879*, pp. 205-210. Coke gives the total investment as $212,116.66; after 1885 the figure is officially cited at $209,000 and the yield at $14,280 per year.

[41]Texas A&M, *Catalogue, 1885-1886*, p. 17.

[42]"Report of the Outgoing Directors," *Texas Senate Journal, 1879*, pp. 205-210.

A&M colleges to that of Texas, and argued that Texas should do more. He reviewed the "rapid growth" of scientific and agricultural schools throughout the United States, pointing out that in 1870 there had been only 17 such schools, staffed with 144 teachers, and attended by 1,413 pupils, whereas by 1875 there were 76 schools, 758 professors, and 7,157 pupils. He championed the cause of the master mechanic, the educated businessman, and the scientific farmer. He argued the need for botanists, foresters, engineers, and architects. He worked into his address an appeal to the memory of Andrew Johnson and Stonewall Jackson, found great pride in what Texas had thus far accomplished, and finally advocated that women should be admitted to the A&M College.[43] In all, it was an effective address which omitted little.

During the several days of commencement exercises the official Board convened to conclude the business of the past year and to prepare for the next. Some minor controversy had developed among the professors over their duties and obligations. As originally constituted the faculty comprised a subordinate governing board, each member of which held equal vote and authority to the other. Each of these men, whom Gathright described as "positive men," had held some position of authority in educational circles in the past and tended to hold himself in rather high esteem. Perhaps self-esteem is a chronic disposition of the professor. In any event, it presaged trouble for the future. The Board attempted to circumvent that trouble by declaring that all differences between professors as to relative duties and powers should be promptly decided by the president, and his decision would be final unless reversed by the Board.[44]

In other action the Board approved a lease of three acres of College land on the west side of the railroad and adjacent to the Post Office, to Henry D. Parsons, providing that no intoxicating liquors be sold on the premises. Parson's Store, the Post Office, and the Railroad Station became the nucleus of College Station, the town being incorporated some seventy-five years later. The name "College Station" was already coming into usage by April 1877. At that time Gathright and other residents began to cross out "Bryan" on the letterhead of the college stationery, and insert "College Station."[45] The Board in its final action entrusted the care of the College grounds to the professor of agriculture, C. P. B. Martin, and agreed to investigate and evaluate the student mess.[46]

[43]"Address by A. J. Peeler," in Peeler (ed.), *Laws Relating to A&M*, 1-34.

[44]*Ibid.*, 28.

[45]*Ibid.*, 29; Thomas S. Gathright, College Station, Texas, to Louis L. McInnis, Lockhart, Texas, April 17, 1877, Gathright Papers, Texas A&M University Archives.

[46]Peeler (ed.), *Laws Relating to A&M*, 28-29.

The second academic year began Monday, October 1, 1877, under auspicious signs. The faculty acknowledged the "liberal support" and generous confidence given the school during its first year and expressed "profound gratitude to Almighty God for his goodness." A special academic or preparatory department had been created to raise deficient students to minimum standards for admission.[47] The faculty considered itself fully prepared and confidently faced the future. But the onslaught which struck exceeded all expectations and created a fresh new crisis. Two hundred students appeared for enrollment in the first week of the fall term; by December 1, 253 students were on campus and President Gathright refused to accept new applications throughout the remainder of the year because of the lack of facilities.[48] At best, the College could accommodate only 160 students. Housing and dining facilities were totally inadequate. No bathing facilities existed. Even first-year students had to improvise baths by borrowing tubs from the faculty. Now there was chaos. "There was considerable discomfort and not a little want of system," the annual *Catalogue* very honestly reported.[49] Gathright and Bennet Davis, the resident Board member in Bryan, ordered construction of a temporary wooden barracks to be paid for out of the student fees. By late fall one building was completed and was able to house some seventy-two students, but facilities remained crowded.[50] Many applicants returned home, and those who stayed found every inconvenience. Parents and politicians became disgruntled, and newspapers and farmer organizations became embarrassingly inquisitive. The faculty became restive.

The Directors of the College convened in an emergency session on November 15 and 19 in Austin. Expanded facilities as well as additional instructors and staff were needed to accommodate the large enrollment. The Board authorized the hiring of two "adjunct professors" at salaries of $900 each. Gathright recommended James E. Binkley and Louis L. McInnis to fill these positions and the Board approved.[51] The Board also requested and authorized Governor Hubbard, who moved to the Executive Office upon the resignation of Richard Coke on December 1, 1876, when the latter accepted a seat in the United States Senate, "to apply to the President of the United States for the assignment of an army officer to the college, as provided by act of Congress."[52] This would, it was anticipated, relieve Professor Morris of his

[47]Texas A&M, *Catalogue, 1876-1877*, p. 30.
[48]"Report of the Outgoing Directors, 1879," *Texas Senate Journal*, 1879, pp. 205-210.
[49]Texas A&M, *Catalogue, 1877-1878*, pp. 28-29; Fenley, *Oldtimers of Southwest Texas*, 17-22.
[50]Texas A&M, *Catalogue, 1877-1878*, p. 29; Peeler (ed.), *Laws Relating to A&M*, 34.
[51]Peeler (ed.), *Laws Relating to A&M*, 33-34.
[52]*Ibid.*, 32.

duties as commandant of the Corps and allow him to devote more time to mathematics, in effect providing a new position at no additional cost to the College. The Directors also limited the salary of the surgeon to a maximum of $2,000 per year. Under the original arrangements the surgeon, who resided in Bryan, received a five-dollar "incidental fee" from each student per semester. As the number of students increased, the surgeon's income increased. The steward's salary, which also had varied according to student enrollment, was fixed at $2,000 per year. Janitors had never been provided for and the faculty did their own cleaning. Now three janitorial positions were added at salaries of $300, $250, and $150 per year. An architect was also required for new construction. He was to be paid $600 for his services.[53] New personnel and new housing proved to be a heavy and unexpected expense.

The Board authorized an additional wooden barracks to be built similar to the one nearing completion, to be paid for out of the "anticipated" available fund. Another chronic and unanticipated problem which faced Texas A&M throughout its first century of operation was the lack or inadequacy of housing facilities for visitors and guests. Bennet Davis was authorized to lease ten acres of land on the west side of the tracks to anyone who would construct a "house of entertainment" to lodge and feed visitors. For the present the Board directed the steward to make available two rooms on the third floor of Steward's Hall as lodging rooms for visitors. As the decades passed the school grew much more rapidly than the surrounding town, and public and private lodging and housing facilities remained in short supply. Another problem of the past that has not been completely solved in the present was the need for adequate hospital facilities. At first there had been no provision on campus for a hospital. By the end of the first term in 1877 the need for such a facility became acute. Davis and Gathright resorted to the temporary, and subsequently unsatisfactory expediency of locating a hospital in two rooms on the upper floor of the main building.[54] All of these adjustments to meet the expanding enrollment cost money, and the College had only a fixed income.

It is true that larger enrollments would bring in more money to the "available fund," but those funds had already been pledged to the construction of the wooden barracks. Some economies would have to be made. The Board considered approving a resolution lowering the salaries of all the professors from $2,500 to $2,000 per year, arguing that the "purchasing power of the dollar" justified it, not to mention the economic necessities of the

[53]*Ibid.,* 33-34.
[54]*Ibid.,* 34-35.

moment. But caution prevailed and the resolution failed to pass. Six months later, in the January meeting, it did pass, undoubtedly much to the dissatisfaction of the faculty.[55] The administration and faculty did the best they could. By the end of the first term a sense of order and direction had returned to the campus.

The trouble of the fall term, however, had brought the school considerable public attention and unfavorable publicity. One of the chronic deficiencies of the Agricultural and Mechanical College that the public began to notice was that it made little or no effort to teach either practical agriculture or mechanics. The administration was already aware of this discontent by the fall of 1877. The Board tried to expand agricultural instruction by directing that one acre of wheat be planted for teaching purposes, and that twenty acres of new ground be broken for the Farm. It also advised the use of student labor on the Farm, and authorized allocating small tracts of land to student laborers, who would receive the profits from their assigned tract.[56] In other words, the Board advised instituting a system of share-cropping. The lack of enthusiasm among students for this plan, or for any form of agricultural labor, remained manifest for the next several decades, despite rather extreme measures taken to "shore up" the agricultural department.

By the spring of 1878 criticism of the College was more pointed and acute. The Texas State Grange met in Bryan, January 8-15, 1878, and expressed dissatisfaction with the lack of agricultural training at A&M and voted to petition the Legislature to establish an experimental farm at the college.[57] Church-supported colleges also joined in criticism of the College. In an address before the Mexia Educational Convention, William Carey Crane, president of Baylor University, located in Independence and not too distant from the new A&M College, argued that the churches should supply and control the higher education needed by the public. He argued that a "state has no right to tax people for the support" of any college which trains the citizen to do more than be a juror, voter, and soldier, for that was the full extent of the obligations of the state. He did, however, favor a system of incorporating all schools of higher learning, including church-supported institutions, under a "state university system" in which all could share in revenues from the university land funds.[58] Crane had considerable support throughout the state for the idea that taxes should not be used for the sup-

[55]*Ibid.*, 34-38.
[56]*Ibid.*, 35.
[57]Frederick Eby (ed.), *Education in Texas: Source Materials*, 705.
[58]*Who Ought to Supply and Control the Education Needed by the People?*, in Charles Judson Crane Papers, Texas A&M University Archives.

port of higher education.[59] Many Texans believed that higher education was a privilege and not a public right; in addition, hard times created considerable antipathy to new taxes. No funds for the relief of the College could be expected from the Legislature.

As public concern mounted, A&M administrators received new burdens and obligations. The Agricultural and Mechanical College for colored youths, which became Prairie View Normal School in 1879, was originally authorized by the Legislature in 1876 as a branch of the A&M College at Bryan, which was open exclusively to white students. It had been located by the commissioners at Alta Vista or Prairie View, in Waller County. In January 1878 the school was entrusted to the care of the Board of Directors of the A&M College. The Board named Gathright to be president also of Prairie View, without additional compensation, and selected Frederick W. Minor, a colored educator from Mississippi, as the resident principal of the institution.[60] Thereafter, the affairs of Prairie View remained closely intertwined in the administrative affairs of the A&M College, near Bryan. Prairie View became the first "branch" of the A&M College System.[61] Upon its opening in 1879 Prairie View confronted many of the same problems faced by its parent institution, prominently the fact that Negro youths, like their white counterparts, were not interested in going to college to learn how to farm, but to learn a profession which would get them away from the farm.

In addition to "receiving" Prairie View, the Directors relieved Robert Morris as professor of military science and replaced him with the newly assigned regular military officer, Captain George T. Olmstead. Morris remained in the chair of applied mathematics and the following year was designated professor of natural philosophy and engineering. The new adjunct professor, James E. Binkley, served as assistant commandant to Olmstead, and Louis L. McInnis was named assistant to the professor of ancient languages and literature. The Board also authorized the hiring of a professor of English language and literature for the following academic year. New economies were required to compensate for the larger faculty. In addition to lowering the salaries of professors from $2,500 to $2,000 per year, the Board dispensed with the services of Steward (whose salary was $2,000 per year) and

[59]Texas A&M, *Catalogue, 1878-1879*, p. 36.

[60]Peeler (ed.), *Laws Relating to A&M*, 37.

[61]An excellent treatment of the history of Prairie View A&M is George Ruble Woolfolk, *Prairie View: A Study in Public Conscience, 1878-1946*, 404 pp. In many respects this work might be regarded as a companion volume to the *Centennial History of Texas A&M University*. Because of the existence of this recent work, the story of Prairie View A&M has not been intensively treated in this study.

assigned his duties to President Gathright with no additional compensation. The Board concluded its business by inviting Jefferson Davis to speak at Commencement exercises in June, but he declined. The Board also directed that a photograph be taken of the campus.[62]

Course offerings and faculty remained intrinsically literary and classic in orientation. As Governor Oran M. Roberts pointed out to Gathright the following year, "Of the nine professors there is but one [C. P. B. Martin] that might not be expected to be found in any college of general learning."[63] Roberts believed that the school's efforts were being misdirected. The official catalogue of the Agricultural and Mechanical College of Texas for the third academic year, 1878-1879, reflected the concern over the increasingly bitter indictments of the school:

It has been assailed by parties who are interested to prostrate it. It has not reviled again, when it has been reviled. . . . So harsh and general were criticisms upon the College at the meeting of the Legislature, that a Committee was appointed to visit the institution and investigate its management. . . . The report of the Committee was all that the College could have asked, and all the country could have expected. We know that the press of the State will ultimately do us justice; and will commend where it now condemns. . . . One of the current rumors, industriously circulated by those who would damage us, is that the College is supported by taxation. . . . Since that time [3 years ago] not one cent has been given by the state. Nothing has been appropriated to put into operation the Agricultural and Mechanical Department. . . . [To raise the college to its full expectations] citizens, legislators, and all classes of people must cease to carp, and learn to assist.[64]

The investigation by the legislative committee should have marked a high point in the controversy over A&M. But it failed to do so. In the midst of all the tensions and agitation the faculty began bickering. "Beset by complaints growing louder every day, the faculty, with no means at hand of remedying the evils complained of, fell into dissentions [*sic*] among themselves."[65] This proved their undoing.

[62]Peeler (ed.), *Laws Relating to A&M*, 37-38.

[63]Oran M. Roberts, Austin, Texas, to Thomas S. Gathright, College Station, Texas, May 21, 1879, published in Galveston *Daily News*, November 15, 1879.

[64]Texas A&M, *Catalogue, 1878-1879*, pp. 35-36.

[65]*Ibid., 1884-1885*, p. 4.

CHAPTER 3

The Crisp Affair

T HE demise of the Gathright Administration may be attributed to an aggregation of diverse factors and events. Texas A&M began as a literary school in accord with the prevailing classical traditions of education despite its intended organization as an agricultural and mechanical institution. Even had its faculty and administrators made every effort to develop the College solely as a place for pursuing studies in scientific agriculture and practical mechanics, they likely could not have succeeded, simply for the want of knowledge of scientific and practical teaching techniques. The preferences and past experiences of A&M's faculty, like those of Southern and national educators in general, were in the classical traditions. The general public, too, remained unconvinced of the practicality of practical, scientific training. Farmers did not believe that farming could be learned in the classroom. Thus the Agricultural and Mechanical College of Texas, as its sister agricultural and mechanical institutions, faced serious obstacles. The overcrowding and disagreeable experiences of Texas A&M's second year and the limitations imposed on enrollments in that year and in the third year aroused public discontent. There were also the usual problems of a public institution — jealousy, suspicion, competition with private institutions, internal conflicts, and politics. The elections in the election year 1878 set the stage for the rather violent end of the classical era at A&M.

Governor Richard B. Hubbard, who succeeded Governor Richard Coke in 1876, strongly supported the efforts and recognized the achievements of the A&M College. In convening the Sixteenth Legislature in December 1878, Hubbard announced:

> There are now over two hundred young men receiving instruction in this school, with a corps of professors whose success has justified the expectations of the country, and with a discipline in its government and an economy in its expenditures worthy of all commendations by the people and their representatives.

Hubbard, a member of the Board of Directors since the school's organization in 1875, believed that the lack of funds alone had prevented the A&M College from expanding its agricultural features.[1] Experimental farming and machine shops cost much more than classic, literary, classroom instruction. It still does. Hubbard advised additional appropriations for the College, in order to perfect the agricultural and mechanical departments without weakening the literary features.

Hubbard, however, was a lame-duck governor. The Democratic nominating convention named Oran M. Roberts as its candidate for the governorship in the November 1878 elections, and Roberts won the election. President Gathright sensed the changing political climate as early as July 1878, after the Democratic convention had rejected Hubbard's bid for the nomination. Writing to his new Adjunct Professor Louis McInnis, Gathright said, "I greatly regret his [Hubbard's] defeat, and think our College lost its best friend."[2] Texas A&M had indeed lost a sympathetic political ally at that moment.

Governor Roberts had his own ideas about the A&M College, and was one of the most influential and powerful figures to occupy the governor's seat since secession. Oran Milo Roberts was born in South Carolina in 1815. He graduated from the University of Alabama, studied law, and served in the Alabama Legislature before moving to Texas in 1841. He was associate justice of the State Supreme Court from 1857 through 1862, and served as president of the Secession Convention of 1861. During the war he served in the Confederate infantry and achieved the rank of colonel. In August 1866 he and David G. Burnet were elected United States senators, but were refused their seats in Congress by the Radicals. When the Democrats returned to power in 1874, Coke appointed Roberts chief justice of the State Supreme Court. He was later elected to the same position, then elected governor in 1878, and re-elected in 1880. In 1883 the "Old Alcalde," as he was called, joined the law faculty at The University of Texas. He died in Austin in 1898.

In his inaugural address of January 21, 1879, Governor Roberts, somewhat ominously for A&M, promised "permanently good and efficient government, economically administered."[3] In following the tradition of the so-called Southern Bourbon, Roberts said the state should "retrench expenses from top to bottom." He also somewhat caustically pointed to one of the "burdens" of the state as being "the establishment of an agricultural and

---

[1] *Governor's Messages, Coke to Ross, 1874-1891*, pp. 752-753.

[2] Thomas S. Gathright, College Station, Texas, to Louis L. McInnis, Canton, Mississippi, July 25, 1878, Thomas S. Gathright Papers, Texas A&M University Archives.

[3] *Governor's Messages, Coke to Ross, 1874-1891*, p. 213.

mechanical college, *so styled.'*[4] Roberts announced that the institution must be made to conform to its intended function "for instruction in agriculture, the mechanic arts and natural science connected therewith." Texas' great need, he said, was for skilled laborers rather than men "learned in literature and science."[5] Roberts said that he would cheerfully recommend additional appropriations to help A&M conform to its purpose, but he did not think the existing condition of state finances could stand it. Instead he advised legislation which would make the interest from the land-grant fund available for purposes other than for salaries alone, to which it was now restricted. Those funds could then be used to expand the agricultural and mechanical facilities of the College. Roberts, however, did commend the directors, faculty, and president of the College for their extraordinary efforts in promoting the best interest of the College in pursuance of the law by which it was organized.[6] Roberts clearly intended to see that the College conformed to his conception of an agricultural and mechanical college.

Roberts and the state Legislature reviewed the report of the retiring Board of Directors of the A&M College, and found there a rather complete and detailed report of the school's progress, and a reasoned explanation for the inability of the institution to develop a strong agricultural program. A pertinent segment of that report bears repeating:

> The act of Congress, while it proposes to assist in promoting a liberal practical education of the industrial classes in the several pursuits and professions of life indicates unmistakably that a leading object shall be the teaching of such branches of learning as pertain to agriculture and the mechanic arts. This admonition has not been forgotten, but the daily expenses of the college, coupled with the erection of buildings, construction of cisterns etc., have pressed so closely upon all receipts, indeed anticipated them, that not much has been accomplished. More land should be enclosed, workshops should be erected, machinery obtained, farm implements, mules etc. Then systematic and practical instruction in agriculture and mechanics may begin on a suitable scale, and opportunity be afforded to such as desire it, to cultivate ground to pay college expenses in whole or in part. A little has been done. 160 acres have been enclosed with a substantial plank fence, 50 acres have been broken and cultivated, 1,000 apple trees have been set out and most of them are in good condition, and ornamental shrubs and trees to beautify the grounds have also been set. It is undeniable, however, that not enough has been done to carry out fully the main objects of the grant and for this short-coming the directory can only justify themselves by the positive deficiency of means, which they hope may be furnished to their

---

[4]*Ibid.*, 215, 221, 223, 249-250.
[5]*Ibid.*, 249-250.
[6]*Ibid.; Texas Senate Journal, 1879*, pp. 204-205.

successors. Could they have used for agricultural development the money put into the new dormitories, much might have been done, but without dormitories we could not have scholars and without scholars we could not build up a great State institution of learning, and those who have applied for instruction so far have not demanded instruction in agriculture or mechanics.[7]

It is not in the power of the faculty, the report continued, to make the school into what it is intended to be unless additional appropriations are made for another dormitory, a library, laboratory workshops, machinery, and agricultural implements. In conclusion, the Directors requested the Legislature to appoint a joint committee to investigate the College and verify its report.[8]

The Legislature promptly appointed an investigative committee, including two members from the Senate and three from the House; further business regarding A&M, including the election of new directors, was postponed until the investigative committee returned with its report.[9] The committee visited the College on March 3, 1879. Its members were received by the cadets in uniform and shown every courtesy. Perhaps in anticipation of the visit of the legislators it should be noted that a class in agriculture had commenced for the first time on February 14, and was conveniently in session during their tour.[10] The investigators returned to the Legislature on March 9 a generally favorable report. They found 167 students in attendance, and concluded that the directors and faculty had made every effort to achieve the objectives of the institution as a college designed to teach the branches of learning related to agriculture and the mechanic arts, without excluding scientific and classical studies and military tactics. They regarded the military discipline as beneficial to the good order and conduct of the student. They noted the inadequacy of laboratory and scientific apparatus, and the lack of adequate library materials. The school sorely needed a hospital building. Committeemen also seemed warmly disposed toward the two literary and debating societies (the Austin Society and the Calliopean Literary Society) on campus and advised making provision for a meeting hall for each. They concluded that an appropriation to A&M equal to the accumulated interest in the University Fund would remove the mentioned deficiencies.[11]

[7]"Report of the Outgoing Directors at the January Session of the Board, 1879," *Texas Senate Journal, 1879*, pp. 205-210.

[8]*Ibid.* The report on the Colored Branch at Alta Vista (Prairie View) noted that despite efforts to open the school no applications had been received from students. Governor Roberts subsequently advised renting out the property for the year.

[9]*Texas Senate Journal, 1879*, pp. 199, 348, 356, 382, 516.

[10]College Station *The Collegian*, March 1879, p. 1.

[11]"Report of the Visitation Committee," *Texas Senate Journal, 1879*, pp. 509-511.

The Visitation Committee's report was then referred to a special committee of the Legislature, which recommended that an effort be made to establish a normal school at Huntsville, Texas, and that an appropriation of $15,000 be made to the Agricultural and Mechanical College from the accumulated interest in the University Fund for the enlargement of its facilities. It also recommended making provision for a normal school at Prairie View, the A&M branch for Negroes. The Alta Vista Agricultural College for colored youths, located in Waller County, was established by the Legislature by act approved on August 14, 1876, as a branch of the State Agricultural and Mechanical College of Texas, which under prevailing Texas law admitted only whites. Twenty thousand dollars was appropriated for its founding. On January 22, 1878, the Board of Directors of the A&M College, to whom the colored branch had been entrusted, appointed Thomas Gathright as president of the colored branch, without additional salary. Professor Frederick W. Minor was then employed as principal of the school, which opened on March 11, 1878. Only eight students enrolled and those soon dropped out, the primary reason being, apparently, that Negro youths, like the white youths at College Station, did not want to go to college to learn to be sharecroppers or dirt farmers. The effort to convert Alta Vista, or Prairie View as it became known after 1879, into a normal school, as a sister colored institution to the Normal College being opened in Huntsville, was in part a plan to sustain racial segregation in Texas colleges, but also represented a sincere effort to sustain both higher and common-school education for colored Texans, and to salvage the school already founded.[12] The House approved the normal school for Prairie View.[13] Senate Bill No. 302, providing for a $15,000 appropriation to A&M, passed the Senate and went to the House, which failed to take action on the appropriation bill before adjournment on April 24, 1879.[14] Roberts promptly called a special session of the Legislature to convene on June 10.

President Gathright, who had been anticipating approval of the appropriation bill, wrote to Governor Roberts on May 17, asking him what plans he had for the College. He noted that Roberts' call of the regular session of the Legislature made references to a need for a change in policy of the College, and to its possible reorganization. Gathright wrote that he was well aware that prominence should be given to the agricultural and mechanical

---

[12]*Ibid.; Texas Senate Journal, 1879*, pp. 567-568.

[13]Gammel (ed.), *Laws of Texas*, VIII, 1482.

[14]*Ibid.; Texas Senate Journal, 1879*, pp. 567-568; "Report of the Outgoing Directors at the January Session of the Board, 1879," *Texas Senate Journal, 1879*, p. 1055.

features of the College, but there having been no appropriation to accomplish this, he wondered what kind of reorganization or rearrangement of the course of study the Governor had in mind. "The College is now in a crisis," Gathright continued, "students are unsettled and the faculty is insecure." Gathright respectfully asked for an early reply.[15]

He received the desired information a few days later. Roberts wrote a lengthy and unequivocal letter in which he argued that the College must conform to the law of Congress and to the Texas Constitution of 1876. All of the professors but one, he said, could be found in any college of general learning. Roberts explained clearly what he thought the College was all about:

> When it is found that by attending the school it would be learned how to produce two ears of wheat and corn and two bales of cotton by the same labor and capital that have been heretofore producing but one, then it will be understood that there is a new field of learning the most extensive and the most beneficial to our race that has engaged the educators of any previous age. It can and will yet be done.[16]

Roberts invited Gathright to devise a plan which could make the school conform to the law and to send it to him before June 10, when the Legislature met. He mentioned too, that the Legislature had elected a new Board of Directors without consulting him. While his letter to Gathright did not say so, Roberts did not approve of having the Legislature select the Board, but preferred to do so himself. In the special session the Administration sponsored a bill giving the Governor authority to appoint the College board.

Gathright promptly replied to the Governor, agreeing with his evaluation as to the purposes of the College; but he argued that supplementary appropriations were necessary for laboratories, an experimental farm, a library, and shops, in order to accomplish the object of the law. He did not agree with the Governor that money should be diverted from the existing classical studies and directed to agriculture and mechanical arts. The state needs both, he said: "We have a good academic course. The people need and demand it."[17] Gathright, too, of course was correct, but he was not really in accord with the Governor's point of view, for Gathright's opinion was that the A&M College must perform the services of a state university, while Rob-

[15]Thomas S. Gathright, College Station, Texas, to Oran M. Roberts, Austin, Texas, May 17, 1879, published in Galveston *Daily News,* November 15, 1879.

[16]Oran M. Roberts, Austin, Texas, to Thomas S. Gathright, College Station, Texas, May 21, 1879, published in Galveston *Daily News,* November 15, 1879.

[17]Thomas S. Gathright, College Station, Texas, to Governor Oran M. Roberts, Austin, Texas, May 24, 1879, Gathright Papers, Texas A&M University Archives.

erts believed that it was nothing more than a technical branch or adjunct of a state university that had not yet been established — but which he soon brought into being. Roberts' intentions in regard to the founding of a university could not be known to Gathright at that time.

Roberts' immediate purpose became more clear in his initial message to the special session of the Legislature on June 10, 1879. He wanted legislation to promote the more expeditious sale of university lands in order to build up the university funds, but he made no mention at the time of legislation for the organization of a new state university. That would come later. He did recommend "reasonable" appropriations for the new normal schools at Huntsville and Prairie View, and for the A&M College. He also wanted to amend the law of 1876, which allowed the interest from the A&M federal grant to be spent only for salaries. He desired, too, that the Legislature reorganize the A&M Board of Directors.[18]

Gathright seized the opportunity of the June commencement exercises at the College to win friends and influence people in the Legislature. He invited all of the state senators to attend the exercises at College Station on June 25. The senators formally wished the College well, but pleaded the urgent press of business as cause for their inability to attend the exercises as a body.[19] President Gathright became now even more pessimistic about the prospects of the school; and on July 2, he expressed doubt that any appropriation bill would pass, and believed that the "fearful drought" which gripped the region in the late spring would lower attendance in the fall. The College Farm, he believed, was an expensive burden which necessitated new appropriations. "I have never felt more depressed at the outlook than I now feel," he wrote to Louis McInnis.[20] He was overly pessimistic. The Legislature approved an appropriation of $7,500 from the interest arising out of the University Fund, but failed to pass a bill providing for the reorganization of the Board of Directors.[21]

The College meanwhile had concluded its third academic term with no outward sign of stress or strain. The faculty recommended students for graduation to the Board of Directors. Notably, none of these were completing studies in agricultural or mechanic-arts courses, but rather in languages, phi-

[18]*Governor's Messages, Coke to Ross, 1874-1891*, pp. 293-311, 312-323.

[19]*Texas Senate Journal, 1879*, pp. 106-107, 131.

[20]Thomas S. Gathright, College Station, Texas, to Louis L. McInnis, Austin, Texas, July 2, 1879, Gathright Papers, Texas A&M University Archives.

[21]*Texas Senate Journal, 1879*, pp. 221, 267; Gammel (ed.), *Laws of Texas*, VIII, 77; see also *Texas Senate Journal, 1879*, pp. 346-347, 352-353, regarding a joint resolution making specimens from the geological survey available to the A&M College.

losophy, literature, Latin, and mathematics.[22] The faculty, aware of this short-coming, soon supplemented the list of graduates by including the names of three graduates in natural science and agriculture. Each faculty member presented his final departmental report for the year 1878-1879 to the President. Generally, progress rather than problems were noted in these reports. Professor Carlisle Martin presented a very able report, which stated that things in the Agriculture Department were going well, but that apparatus, charts, maps, a microscope, and laboratory equipment were seriously needed. He stressed the importance of observation as a learning technique, but added that he necessarily had to depend on lectures, and further commented on the fact that there were no texts available for instruction in most agricultural studies. He said that more farm labor should be employed, and that purebred stock must be bought, especially dairy animals and hogs.[23] Adequate instruction clearly depended upon substantially larger appropriations, Martin thought. Yet in its June meeting the Directors authorized the firing of the superintendent of the Farm and the allocation of his duties to Professor Martin as an economy measure.[24]

July offered the prospects of a long, hot summer. "We are in *status quo*, the same hot, dry weather, and same dull prospects," Gathright wrote to Louis McInnis, who was visiting in Lockhart.[25] The National Education Association was scheduled to hold its annual meeting in Philadelphia on July 29-31, and Alexander Hogg, professor of pure mathematics, prepared to leave for that meeting. Hogg was an NEA vice-president, and chairman of the Commission of Education. He had recently published a booklet entitled "Industrial Education," which essentially described how an agricultural and mechanical college should be organized. In May he sent a copy of his study to each member of the Board and a copy to the Governor. Hogg was an ambitious, enterprising, and outgoing individual who had many friends in Bryan.[26] Hogg undoubtedly had an interest in becoming one day the president of the

[22]"Faculty to Honorable T. S. Gathright," June 22, 1879, signed by Louis L. McInnis, Secretary, George Pfeuffer Papers, Texas A&M University Archives.

[23]"Report from the Department of Chemistry, Natural Science and Agriculture, by Professor Carlisle P. B. Martin to President Thomas S. Gathright," June 23, 1879, George Pfeuffer Papers, Texas A&M University Archives.

[24]Thomas S. Gathright, College Station, Texas, to George Pfeuffer, New Braunfels, July 7, 1879, Gathright Papers, Texas A&M University Archives.

[25]Thomas S. Gathright, College Station, to Louis L. McInnis, Lockhart, Texas, July 15, 1879, Gathright Papers, Texas A&M University Archives.

[26] College Station *Texas Collegian,* March 1879, pp. 1-4; Galveston *Daily News,* November 23, 1879; Bryan *Brazos Pilot,* October 31, 1879, clipping in Louis L. McInnis Papers, Texas A&M University Archives.

A&M College. He and Gathright fell into bitter disagreement in the summer of 1879, and as they did, so did the faculty and the townspeople of Bryan.

The conflict began inauspiciously in June, when, at a meeting of the faculty, cadets were approved or disapproved for promotion as Corps officers for the following October. Captain George T. Olmstead submitted names for the different positions, recommendations which ordinarily the faculty approved. On this one occasion, however, the name of John C. Crisp came up for promotion to senior captain of Company A, the highest cadet office in the Corps. Crisp had no demerits and a good record. In the past, the captain of Company B, which Crisp had been, had automatically received the promotion. The faculty, by a vote of 4-5, now rejected Crisp's promotion. Professors Lewis, Smythe, Morris, Hogg, and Banks disapproved the promotion while Gathright, Hand, McInnis, and Olmstead supported it.[27] The reasons for rejection appeared to involve a number of old festering disputes among the faculty rather than the qualifications of Crisp.[28] Alexander Hogg was instrumental in preventing Crisp's promotion.

Subsequently, Crisp obtained permission from Gathright to remain at the College during the summer months for reading and study. Crisp took the opportunity to write letters to friends and fellow students for testimonials regarding his standing relative to that of Hogg.[29] The Board of Directors, meanwhile, scheduled a special meeting at College Station in August, for the purpose of disbursing the $7,500 recently appropriated by the Legislature to the College. Crisp now planned to lodge a formal complaint against Hogg at the Board meeting in an effort to have Hogg dismissed from the faculty. Hogg's wife received word of this from a student and telegraphed her husband to return promptly from Philadelphia. Hogg arrived in College Station on August 25, and the Board convened the following day, at which time Crisp presented his charges. He alleged (1) that Hogg was a good mathematician, but an incompetent teacher, and (2) that he had made an improper proposition to him, offering him high marks if he (Crisp) would make out some class reports.[30] Board member Anderson J. Peeler advised Crisp to drop the charges until the next regular meeting; the Board undoubtedly believed that this was a faculty affair, and that it could be best resolved at the College. Crisp agreed to do so, but did prepare a written statement of his charges, accompanied by the testimonials, and filed these with the Governor.[31]

[27]Bryan *Brazos Pilot*, October 31, 1879.

[28]"Minutes of the Board of Directors, November 20, 1879," published in Galveston *Daily News*, November 21, 1879.

[29]"A&M Investigation," Galveston *Daily News*, November 22, 1879.

[30]Galveston *Daily News*, November 23, 1879.

[31]*Ibid.*, November 22, 1879.

The Board completed most of its business on August 27. Its most significant accomplishment was another lowering of faculty salaries, argued as necessary because of the receding inflationary pressures, as well as the need for economy. The president's salary was lowered from $3,000 to $2,000; professors' salaries were lowered from $2,000 to $1,500, and adjunct professors' salaries were lowered from $900 to $800 per year. Of the $7,500 appropriation, $1,000 was allocated for purchasing farm implements, $1,550 for the development of a library facility, $2,500 for a laboratory, $500 for the English Department, $1,500 for Natural Philosophy and Agriculture, and $450 for medical supplies and equipment. Thus the small appropriation did help relieve some of the more serious deficiencies of the College. The Board also called for a monthly report from the president to the Board.[32]

On the following day, August 28, 1879, Hogg and his "faction" presented a "reply" to Crisp's charges. The letter charged that Crisp was contributing to "irregular annoyances," and that he should not be allowed to remain on campus during the summer, nor should he be admitted to the school when classes opened in October. The letter was sent to Gathright for approval and for forwarding to the Board. Gathright refused to sign the letter but did submit it to the Board.[33] The Board again took no action.

After the Board adjourned Crisp heard that Hogg sought to have him dismissed from school. Crisp again began to write letters and obtain testimonials. Hogg, in company with Morris, confronted Crisp and denied that he wanted to have Crisp dismissed. Crisp refused to believe it. Hogg then went to Gathright asking him to force Crisp to leave the campus. Gathright replied that Crisp had every right to remain on campus, but that he would ask him to stop writing the letters.[34] By now the entire faculty was involved in a full-fledged feud.

Senator George Pfeuffer asked Gathright to secure information for him regarding Hogg. Gathright was more than eager to do so. On September 13 he wrote Pfeuffer indicating that he had obtained a letter documenting Hogg's dismissal from the A&M College of Alabama. Gathright said flatly that Hogg should no longer continue on the Texas A&M faculty.[35] The controversy among the faculty flared into the open and soon involved the people of Bryan. Gathright accused Hogg of "cowardly and outrageous persecution"

[32]"Resolutions of the Board of Directors, Adopted August 27, 1879," George Pfeuffer Papers, Texas A&M University Archives.

[33]"To Honorable Board of Directors," August 28, 1879, George Pfeuffer Papers, Texas A&M University Archives.

[34]Galveston *Daily News,* November 23, 1879.

[35]Thomas S. Gathright, College Station, Texas, to George Pfeuffer, New Braunfels, Texas, September 13, 1879, Gathright Papers, Texas A&M University Archives.

of him and his family. Two-thirds of the businessmen in Bryan, he said, had turned against him.[36] In early October, William W. McGraw, a Bryan attorney, publicly accused Gathright of using Crisp to attack Hogg. Professor Martin visited Governor Roberts in Austin bearing complaints against Gathright. Gathright wrote to Pfeuffer, "The farce should not be continued. Never has Gathright had so much trouble with a faculty."[37] The opening of the fall term appeared to intensify rather than lessen the feud.

On October 20, 1879, Gathright wrote to Governor Roberts and each member of the Board, reviewing the Crisp affair and commenting on the public accusations made in Bryan against himself. He asked for an investigation. Of Hogg, he wrote, he "is unfitted, by reason of some fatal peculiarities[,] for instruction of youth." Martin, he said, "is inefficient, and for several other reasons disqualified for the position he holds in this college."[38] The following day Gathright wrote to George Pfeuffer asking his personal assistance in seeing that an investigation was held.[39] The imbroglio had passed the point of reconciliation.

Governor Roberts now addressed a letter to President Gathright and to the members of the faculty. He indicated that he had received letters from Gathright, Crisp, and others and that he had talked with Colonel Peeler.

> From all of which I learn that there is a strong feeling of antagonism arising up between members of your faculty and is spreading like a partisan struggle, broadcast over the country to the great injury of the institutions under your charge. The point of disagreement ostensibly presented, whether the real cause or not, arises out of the charges made by Mr. John C. Crisp against Professor Hogg at the late meeting of the board at the college and the subsequent conduct of the faculty in not approving Mr. Crisp's nomination as captain of cadets in the college.

He said that although the matter was held in abeyance at the last meeting of the Board, the Board had expected harmony to prevail. But that hope had not been fulfilled, said the Governor.[40]

[36]Thomas S. Gathright, College Station, Texas, to George Pfeuffer, New Braunfels, Texas, September 30, 1879; Gathright to Governor O. M. Roberts, Austin, Texas, October 20, 1879; Thomas S. Gathright Papers; see also George Olmstead to George Pfeuffer, October 3, 1879, George Pfeuffer Papers, Texas A&M University Archives.

[37]Thomas S. Gathright, College Station, to George Pfeuffer, Austin, Texas, October 15, 1879, Gathright Papers, Texas A&M University Archives.

[38]Thomas S. Gathright, College Station, Texas, to Governor O. M. Roberts, Austin, Texas, October 20, 1879, Gathright Papers, Texas A&M University Archives.

[39]Thomas S. Gathright, College Station, Texas, to George Pfeuffer, Austin, Texas, October 21, 1879, George Pfeuffer Papers, Texas A&M University Archives.

[40]Governor O. M. Roberts, Austin, Texas, to President Thomas S. Gathright and Members of the Faculty of the A. and M. College, College Station, Texas, October 21, 1879, pub-

Roberts then lectured the faculty on the responsibilities of the Board and of the faculty. The College, he said, could not be under the "direct and immediate control of the directors." The Directors were to organize and the faculty were to manage in accordance with their directions. Roberts appealed for harmony, and asked for a letter indicating that a reconciliation had been effected; or, if not, he desired a statement individually from each faculty member with his views "freely spoken."[41]

No reconciliation appeared imminent. Gathright considered resigning and rumors flew that if he left, half of the cadets would also leave.[42] He went to Austin and asked the Governor to call a meeting of the Board. Writing to Pfeuffer on November 2, Gathright bitterly assailed the "Hogg faction." "There was never such a state of things as exists here," he said. His critics were thoroughly discredited people, he believed. Morris had been fired from the Texas Military Institute, he said, and Hogg was dismissed from the A&M College of Alabama. "I would prefer a reeking corpse in the College to Banks. Old Martin is a parody on men and Professors. Lewis has been seduced by promises of the Presidency."[43]

Extreme bitterness gripped Gathright as he wrote to Pfeuffer the following week, "The College must fail and ought to fail." Then he qualified the indictment with the observation that it could be made a "grand success," and that he could make it so, but not with these men.[44] The next week Gathright was more composed and objective when he informed Pfeuffer that things were going as smoothly as could be expected, although "these scheming professors are doing heavy canvassing." As for himself, he would "observe the game."[45]

Gathright was not the only one writing letters. General Hamilton P. Bee, steward at the College, told Pfeuffer, "I felt that the inadaptability and incompetency of Gathright is the matter. He is wayward, partial, envious and mean; I profess to know him and I declare that he is not fit for his place." Gathright wanted to get rid of Hogg, said Bee, because he was a "man of mark." Bee said that Morris was well regarded by the students.[46] So, too, was

---

lished in Galveston *Daily News,* November 15, 1879.

[41]*Ibid.*

[42]Emil Kellner, College Station, Texas, to George Pfeuffer, New Braunfels, Texas, October 31, 1879, Pfeuffer Papers, Texas A&M University Archives.

[43]Thomas S. Gathright, College Station, Texas, to George Pfeuffer, Austin, Texas, November 2, 1879, Gathright Papers, Texas A&M University Archives.

[44]*Ibid.,* November 7, 1879.

[45]*Ibid.,* November 13, 1879.

[46]Hamilton P. Bee, College Station, Texas, to George Pfeuffer, Austin, Texas, November 14, 1879, Pfeuffer Papers, Texas A&M University Archives.

Gathright. On November 16, ninety-five members of the Corps of Cadets (almost two-thirds of the student body) petitioned the Governor and the Board of Directors asking that they "sustain our worthy President, Thomas S. Gathright."[47] There is no question but that at the moment Gathright's and Crisp's cause was popular with the students.

On Tuesday, November 18, 1879, Governor Roberts convened the Board of Directors in an emergency session on the campus of the Agricultural and Mechanical College. The members asked for reports and voted to investigate thoroughly the situation. On Wednesday they received a report from President Gathright relating to financial conditions, and called for oral testimony from Professors Banks, Lewis, and Morris. On Thursday, Smythe, McInnis, Olmstead, and Hogg appeared before the Board, and Gathright submitted a written statement, being at the time too ill to appear in person. Each faculty member was asked two questions: (1) Is it possible to rid the College from the present dissension and still retain the present faculty? (2) Why did you not endeavor to settle your troubles among yourselves, as suggested in the Governor's letter to the faculty? The answer to the first question was invariably *no;* a settlement among the existing faculty could not be made; and the second question "opened the floodgates of explanation."[48]

Roberts, formerly chief justice of the State Supreme Court, conducted an intensive investigation of every facet of the dispute. A few of the high points of the investigation included testimony from Hogg that the first conflict among the faculty came during the early months of the first academic year when Gathright insisted that the College catalogue be similar to that of the University of Virginia. "He flew off the handle on this matter," said Hogg, a statement which corroborated other evidence that Gathright had a hasty temper, likely kindling many controversies on the campus. Hogg also noted a problem with discipline, confirmed by other witnesses, including drinking and visitations to houses of ill-repute by cadets. Speaking of Gathright, Hogg said, he "is a good executive officer. He knows it. He has told me he was imperious."[49] Hogg's characterization of Gathright appeared fairly accurate. Banks and McInnis confirmed that a problem with discipline existed, but Banks blamed Gathright while McInnis defended him. Banks did not believe that Gathright should have given the cadets egg-nog on Christ-

[47][Petition] "To His Excellency Governor O. M. Roberts and Members of the Board of Directors, November 16, 1879," Gathright Papers, Texas A&M University Archives.

[48]"Minutes of the Board of Directors, November 18-24, 1879," George Pfeuffer Papers, Texas A&M University Archives; Galveston *Daily News,* November 21, 1879.

[49]*Ibid.*

mas day, a gesture which may help explain some of the popularity of Gathright with the cadets. He and McInnis both mentioned specific incidents in which Gathright had a disagreement with various faculty members.[50] If Gathright was intemperate, Morris must have been hot-headed. He accused the Board itself of being negligent in not having settled the Crisp affair in August.[51] Dr. Smythe had nothing but praise for President Gathright and wanted to see him vindicated, while Captain Olmstead said he had no difference with the President and called the differences among the faculty "ridiculous."[52] As the one man not on the College payroll, Olmstead remained rather aloof. Louis McInnis also remained relatively uninvolved, being rather new, young, single, an adjunct professor, and very circumspect.

Gathright's written statement to the Board expressed surprise at the bitterness of his attackers. Gathright wrote that he never lost his temper, a claim which seems to have been refuted by much of the testimony, and he found some admiration for Hogg, who always "does his best." Gathright concluded with an observation which provided a key to the entire controversy. Nowhere, he said, speaking of his faculty, could you find "six more positive men."[53]

Students as well as faculty became involved in the dispute. The Corps of Cadets by 1879 was already becoming the cohesive and spirited force on campus that it came to symbolize throughout the history of the College. During the Crisp controversy the cadet leaders presented a petition to the Board that had been unanimously adopted by the Corps demanding a hearing before the Board: "Resolved, that we are entitled to a hearing before the Board of Directors; that we desire it, and will not be satisfied until we are heard." The students charged that some among them had been "unjustly denounced" and "denied the privilege of defending themselves."[54] The petition was read by the Board on Friday, November 21, but no action was taken on it. The Board, however, did invite John C. Crisp to testify.[55]

Crisp was eloquent and ably represented himself and the Corps. He told the Board that rumors that President Gathright had encouraged him to bring charges against Hogg were false. Gathright, he said, is no coward. On the

[50]*Ibid.*
[51]*Ibid.*
[52]*Ibid.*
[53]*Ibid.*
[54]"Petition to State A&M College of Texas, November 20, 1879," George Pfeuffer Papers, Texas A&M University Archives.
[55]"Minutes of the Board of Directors, November 18-24, 1879," George Pfeuffer Papers, Texas A&M University Archives.

contrary, he noted, the people of Bryan accuse Gathright of "bulldozing and intimidating" the faculty. Reflecting the "Aggie Spirit of '79," Crisp addressed the Board as a martyr for the cause of student rights: "I am proud to be worthy to suffer for the cause of right and truth for my young and gallant comrades and my beloved Alma Mater."

"I am weak and defenseless," he said, "and for a number of years have been dependent upon my own resources. I would never have been able to go to a college," he said, "had not the fathers of Texas, in their infinite wisdom and goodness," made it possible.[56] The Directors were obviously impressed. They proclaimed Crisp an honorable young man, who in no way was at fault, and who did not lack the qualifications for the office he sought. Nonetheless, the Board ruled, the faculty had full authority over cadet promotions.[57] The real issue was no longer Crisp, but the inability of the faculty to work together.

By this time newspapers throughout the state, and especially the Galveston *News*, had made the A&M College investigations the most prominent story in the state. Because of the popular discontent with the College already manifested in the past, the current scandals generated a general condemnation of the faculty and of affairs at the College. Characteristic of the indictment is one expressed in a letter to Governor Roberts on November 20 from Rufus L. Burleson of Waco:

> But I have been badly impressed that the faculty of the A&M College are incapable of grasping the profound aims expressed by your excellency. They attach more importance to brass buttons and a little idle show and captains of cadets than to the grand aims of an A&M College as explained in your letter. . . . They are guilty of petty wranglings and unprofessional bickerings. . . . But I have well nigh despaired of its success under such men as Mssrs. Gathright, Hogg and one or two others I happen to know on the faculty. [We have become] a but[t] of ridicule to educators in other states for taking up and putting in high places 3rd rate broken down men. Men whose chief stock in trade is cheek and sharp wire pulling.[58]

Burleson advised the Governor to "go to the bottom and sweep away the rubbish."[59] Looking at the situation realistically, the Board had little option but to do as Burleson suggested.

[56]Galveston *Daily News*, November 23, 1879.
[57]"Minutes of the Board of Directors, November 18-24, 1879," George Pfeuffer Papers, Texas A&M University Archives; Galveston *Daily News*, November 23, 1879.
[58]Rufus L. Burleson, Waco, Texas, to Governor O. M. Roberts, College Station, November 20, 1879, Louis L. McInnis Papers, Texas A&M University Archives.
[59]*Ibid.*

On Saturday morning, November 22, 1879, the Board of Directors of the A&M College of Texas asked for the resignation of the entire faculty. By that afternoon most of the faculty members had submitted their formal resignations. There was some opposition to be sure. John T. Hand declared that his contract did not expire until July 1880, and that his resignation would be effective on that date. The Board summarily declared his position vacant and refused to pay him for services after November 30, 1879.[60]

Robert Morris refused to submit a resignation. "I demand to be dismissed for cause and have the record of the same placed in the minutes," he said. Morris, popular with the townspeople, received the applause of the crowd.[61] "The rattle of a crowd will not influence these proceedings," Governor Roberts, chairman of the Board, told him.[62]

"I scorn such applause," Morris replied, "this is too serious a matter."[63]

"Did you not testify that a reorganization of the college was necessary?" Roberts asked him.[64]

"I did, sir. But I hold that you should turn out those who are to blame, and not dismiss all without a hearing," Morris answered.[65] The Board, however, did not agree.

There is good evidence that the Board's decision to dismiss the faculty had been predetermined even before the hearings began. The Board had done its homework. Saturday night, after receiving faculty resignations, the members, in a relatively short session, nominated and elected a new president and faculty of the college. By Monday morning the new president and several of the faculty had already arrived at the college.[66]

Those few days in November brought a revolution in the affairs of the College. Not only was there a change in personnel, but a change in philosophy and policy. The days of a classical education at Texas A&M were over. The Directors addressed a brief message "to the People of Texas" saying,

The Directors of the A&M College respectfully state that at their recent session at Bryan they found the institution in an excellent condition except as to certain unhappy dissensions existing in the faculty. The remedy of reorganization was

[60]"Minutes of the Board of Directors, November 18-24, 1879," George Pfeuffer Papers, Texas A&M University Archives.
[61]*Ibid.*
[62]*Ibid.*
[63]*Ibid.*
[64]*Ibid.*
[65]*Ibid.*
[66]*Ibid.*

deemed indispensable and promptly applied. . . . The advantages now afforded are superior to those heretofore offered.[67]

This message constituted a serious understatement of what had happened. The next annual catalogue of the College put it more succinctly. "The instruction [now] given, both in theory and practice, has made it for the first time *in reality* a school for Agriculture and Mechanics."[68]

The Board concluded its business on Monday, November 24, 1879. Twenty-six resolutions were adopted, including approval of the statement to the "People of Texas." Other resolutions concerned a general policy agreeing to repay each faculty member for improvements to his residence. Specific resolutions named the amount to be awarded to each. Hogg, for example, claimed and received $220.33 for improvements made to his home over the past three years. Banks wanted not only payment for improvements but $50.00 for the services of his son as a drummer to the Corps. The Board disallowed the "drummer" claim.[69] Other resolutions assigned campus residences to the new faculty, declared the Department of Agriculture to be equal in importance to other departments, defined the term "faculty," and specified the various duties and the authority of the president. The Board then adjourned to resume its meetings on the campus of Prairie View A&M.[70] President Gathright and his faculty would be relieved of their duties on December 1, 1879. Meanwhile they were directed to inform and assist the new faculty and president in the assumption of their offices. It had been swift, cruel, and somewhat overzealous retribution.

The immediate cause of the ejection of the Gathright Administration and faculty was the feud among the professors. That feud undoubtedly had its roots in the character of the professors themselves — each undoubtedly a strong individualist and a "positive" man. Gathright clearly had a temper, over which he sometimes lost control. The professors and their wives and families were in a sense thrown upon each other, with little opportunity for social intercourse outside of their small, tight society. In such a situation a small sore could fester into a large wound. Aside from the personal factors involved, there were some underlying and highly impersonal situations over which Gathright and his faculty had no control.

[67]"Statement from Board," November 24, 1879, George Pfeuffer Papers, Texas A&M University Archives.

[68]Texas A&M, *Catalogue, 1880-1881*, p. 9.

[69]"Minutes of the Board of Directors, November 18-24, 1879," George Pfeuffer Papers, Texas A&M University Archives.

[70]*Ibid.*

The men had been reared and trained in the tradition of a classical education and really knew nothing else, no matter how well they meant. Even granting their understanding and full comprehension of what scientific and technical training in agriculture and the mechanics might involve, they nevertheless lacked the wherewithal to implement that kind of training. There were but few, and generally inadequate, texts; laboratory equipment was primitive; and learning by experimentation and demonstration required largely undeveloped techniques. Furthermore, the stress and indeed the real need of the moment was economy in state spending. The more expensive aspects of education at Texas A&M, invariably involving scientific and technical equipment and training, were cut back by economizing gestures, just at the time when farmers and the general public were beginning to demand such training. The growing strength of the Grange, and its objection to classical training at the A&M College also forced the issue. The too-rapid growth of the institution with the subsequent overcrowding and discontent, put the school in poor favor in many quarters. Competition with established private and parochial schools must also be considered. In view of the many obstacles that had to be overcome the Gathright era might be regarded as a time of achievement rather than of failure.

Yet, for the moment, times looked dark for the College. "The outlook for the College at present is not very bright," reported the Bryan *Brazos Pilot,* "Already a number of students have left, and others will leave."[71] Indeed, Gathright, rather than the Board, held student sympathy and support. Students chided the Board for its purge. "We are surprised that the august body did not attempt to surmount the authority of the United States government and forcibly eject our genial Commandant, Captain George T. Olmstead," reported the student newspaper, the *Texas Collegian,* in December. "They do say," gibed another memorandum "that the Board of Directors tried to displace our good old friend Mr. Minturn, the college carpenter."[72] Some students left the school. By June 1880, however, enrollment had actually risen above the November 1879 total. One hundred and forty-three students were on hand for commencement exercises as opposed to the one hundred and thirty students on campus in November.[73]

For most of the faculty who left the College, their displacement marked a new beginning rather than an end. Robert Morris went to law school and

[71]College Station *Texas Collegian,* December 1879, citing Bryan *Brazos Pilot* (undated).

[72]College Station *Texas Collegian,* December 1879.

[73]"Statement from Board," November 24, 1879, George Pfeuffer Papers, Texas A&M University Archives.

became a prominent jurist in Minnesota. Alexander Hogg became chief of the corps of engineers for the Houston and Texas Central Railway, remaining active for many years and later becoming an unsuccessful applicant for the presidency of the A&M College. Martin remained near the College on his farm. Major Banks opened a private school in Austin. Lewis became president of Marion College, in Waxahachie, Texas, and Professor Hand for many years served as the superintendent of public schools in Brenham, Texas. Louis McInnis, who submitted his resignation with the rest, was reinstated to fill the chair of mathematics when the newly appointed professor chose to resign. McInnis one day became president of the institution. Dr. Smythe remained for a time as the College surgeon, and Olmstead, over whom the Board had no authority and whom they had no reason to fire, remained as commandant until his tour was up.[74] He continued to pursue a successful military career.[75] John C. Crisp continued as a student through the first term but then left the College without completing requirements for a degree. He embarked on a successful journalism career and became the editor and manager of the *Uvalde Publishing Company*.[76] The great tragedy in the affair befell Thomas S. Gathright.

Gathright moved his family to Henderson, Texas, in December and began teaching in a small private school. "I am the saddest mortal tonight living and if I were to let out and write you a letter would give you the horrors," he wrote shortly after his arrival in Henderson.[77] Soon afterwards he described his family as living in a hut and huddled together. Mrs. Gathright cooked a little meat and bread — that is all, he said. The work was exhausting. He talked of going to Palestine to open a school. His despair was mixed with bitterness. His enemies (Lewis, Martin, Banks he named) were scoundrels or would starve.[78] He wrote a number of editorials under the pen name "Richard" which were published in the *Brazos Pilot* and which sought to tell some "wholesome truths" about Governor Roberts, Lieutenant Governor Joseph D. Sayers, and other members of the Board of Directors which deposed him.[79] He grew more and more bitter until in April he was struck by

[74]Texas A&M, *Catalogue, 1879-1880*, pp. 49-50.

[75]See College Station *Texas Collegian*, January 1880.

[76]John C. Crisp, Uvalde, Texas, to Louis L. McInnis, College Station, January 3, 1887, Louis L. McInnis Papers, Texas A&M University Archives.

[77]Thomas S. Gathright, Henderson, Texas, to Louis L. McInnis, College Station, Texas, December 31, 1879, Gathright Papers, Texas A&M University Archives.

[78]Gathright to McInnis, January 11, 1880, Gathright Papers, Texas A&M University Archives.

[79]Gathright to McInnis, March 9, 1880, Gathright Papers, Texas A&M University

a serious illness which he described as a "biliary attack, with a tendency to paralysis."[80] His health grew worse. In his last days he was bedridden and in pain. He died of an "attack of the liver,"[81] on May 24, 1880, six months after being relieved of his position at A&M. Upon his death there were many testimonials and memorials from his former students and friends in Mississippi and Texas. Through war, in adversity, and despite personal misfortune, Thomas S. Gathright remained dedicated to youth and to education.

Archives.

[80]Gathright to McInnis, April 16, 1880, Gathright Papers, Texas A&M University Archives.

[81]Gathright to McInnis, April 27, 1880; Mrs. Thomas S. Gathright, Henderson, Texas, to Louis L. McInnis, College Station, May 31, 1880, Gathright Papers, Texas A&M University Archives.

CHAPTER 4

The Agrarian Reform

ON November 22, 1879, Board Member George Pfeuffer wrote a draft of a letter to John G. James, president of Texas Military Institute, in Austin, informing James that he had been unanimously elected president of the State Agricultural and Mechanical College, "to fill the vacancy in said Faculty, declared so by the board, the day previous." Before sending it, Pfeuffer revised the letter to James to read that he was elected to fill the "vacancy in said faculty occasioned by the resignation of President Gathright," thus softening for public consumption and for the historical record the arbitrary nature of the Board's action on that fatal November day. James would assume his office on December 1, 1879, giving the departing administration one week's notice. James, a Virginian and a graduate of the Virginia Military Institute, brought to the office proven administrative abilities. He had an outstanding war record with the Army of Northern Virginia,[1] and had close connections with state officials, especially with Lieutenant Governor Joseph Draper Sayers, who had nominated him for the office. His faculty also were new to A&M.

Hardaway Hunt. Dinwiddie, the new professor of chemistry, was also a Virginian, and had served with James during the Civil War. He had completed his studies at VMI after the War ended, graduating at the head of his class. Dinwiddie, with James, was one of the founders of the Texas Military Institute, in Austin, and accompanied him to Texas A&M. James R. Cole, elected professor of English literature, came to Texas A&M from North Carolina, where he had received his education at Trinity College. He served a term in the Texas Legislature (1869-1871), and in 1876 became president of the North Texas Female College, in Sherman. Charles P. Estill, another Virginian and a graduate of Washington and Lee College, taught for a time at Washington and Lee before coming to Texas. He brought with him letters of

[1]George Pfeuffer, College Station, Texas, to Colonel John J. James, Austin, Texas, November 22, 1879, George Pfeuffer Papers, Texas A&M University Archives; Galveston *Daily News*, November 23, 1879.

recommendation from Robert E. Lee, a carte blanche for the time. He had been president of Austin College, in Huntsville, for a while, and subsequently became superintendent of schools in Brenham. Estill and John T. Hand changed jobs, Hand going to Brenham as superintendent and Estill coming to A&M to fill Hand's former position as professor of ancient languages. Dr. D. Porte Smythe, the College surgeon during the Gathright years, remained as surgeon and assumed teaching duties as professor of anatomy. This appointment perhaps marked, in a remote sense, the beginning of the College of Veterinary Medicine, which would be many years in the making.[2] Yet another native Virginian, Benjamin Allen, of Kaufman, Texas, was named to fill the chair of mathematics. Allen came to the campus in December; he apparently did not like what he saw, and returned to Kaufman, leaving the chair of mathematics vacant. The Board then appointed Louis L. McInnis to fill the position on a temporary basis. Pfeuffer wrote to McInnis that if he filled the position in a satisfactory manner he would personally support his regular appointment to the chair of mathematics.[3] In June, McInnis received the appointment on a permanent basis. George T. Olmstead continued as commandant of the Corps of Cadets.

In terms of experience, temperament, and training, the faculty which completed the academic year 1879-1880 at the A&M College was much like that which began the year. There was no tangible evidence in the spring of 1880 that the College had radically changed from a literary school into an essentially agricultural and vocational training school. As late as July 1880 no one had been hired to teach agriculture.[4] Nevertheless, President James contemplated profound changes in the faculty and curricula of the College.

During the spring term of 1880 the Gathright era was allowed to die a peaceful death. The departure of Professor of Agriculture Carlisle P. B. Martin and the failure to replace him forced the closing of the classes in agriculture, which had only recently been initiated. The loss occasioned little regret among the students. The other classes, as James stated, were "faithfully taught and successfully advanced."[5]

Nevertheless, the critics continued to raise questions about the programs of the College. The Waco *Examiner,* in commenting on the situation

[2]Galveston *Daily News,* November 23, 1879.

[3]*Ibid.;* College Station *Texas Collegian,* December 1879; George Pfeuffer, New Braunfels, Texas, to Louis L. McInnis, College Station, Texas, December 4, 1879, Louis L. McInnis Papers, Texas A&M University Archives.

[4]See "President's Report," Texas A&M, *Catalogue, 1879-1880,* pp. 48-49.

[5]*Ibid.;* see also Bryan *Brazos Pilot,* January 23, 1880, commenting on the lack of interest by the students in agricultural studies.

at A&M, said, "The whole history of the institution is a legal wrong." The Grange labeled it an "outrage" because it did not teach agriculture or anything relating to agriculture, which was perfectly true.[6] Even President James came in for his share of public rebuke. "He seems to be a hard man to become acquainted with," wrote Richard M. Smith, editor of the *Brazos Pilot,* to Louis McInnis. Although Smith did not like Governor Oran M. Roberts or A&M President James, he was sufficiently devoted to the College to overlook the *"peculiarities* of any man who may be temporarily connected with it,"[7] he said. James did not begin his administration under sunny skies.

As winter passed into spring, the weather became more miserable, if that was possible, bringing sleet, weeks of rain, an occasional freeze, and the everlasting gumbo mud which balled up on the feet of horses, dogs, students, and faculty alike.[8] Sunnier days finally came and with them spring commencement. One hundred and forty-three students completed their year's studies; most of them were enrolled in mathematics, English language and literature, ancient languages, and modern languages. Twenty-three students received diplomas for completion of work within a department, and two students, William Harrison Brown and Louis John Kopke, became the first "titled" graduates of the College, receiving the degree of Civil Engineer on June 23, 1880.[9] At commencement the students gave Governor Oran Roberts and Captain George Olmstead each three cheers.[10] Commencement exercises in 1880 marked the close of the classical era at Texas A&M. A new order of things was close at hand.

James clearly intended to fulfill his commission to make A&M into a truly agricultural and mechanical college. Following the June commencement, James prepared his first report to the governor. The College, he said, "was in spirit and in fact, as far as circumstances permitted, a strictly literary college — top-grafted with a strongly prominent military feature." The late administration, he said, "had sedulously cultivated a sentiment antagonistic" to the development of the agricultural and mechanic arts. He proposed to abolish the elective system of studies and to establish a well-defined four-year curriculum in agriculture and a companion curriculum in mechanics. The student would have to enroll in one or the other. There would be compulsory

---

[6]Waco *Examiner,* n.d., cited by Bryan *Brazos Pilot,* January 23, 1880.

[7]Richard M. Smith, Bryan, Texas, to Louis L. McInnis, College Station, Texas, May 18, 1880, Louis L. McInnis Papers, Texas A&M University Archives.

[8]College Station *Texas Collegian,* March 1880.

[9]Texas A&M, *Catalogue, 1879-1880,* pp. 17-18; and *ibid., 1884-1885,* p. 45.

[10]College Station *Texas Collegian,* June 1880.

farm work with the curriculum in agriculture, and compulsory shop work with studies in mechanics. A state experimental Farm was to be established on the campus in line with the Grange petition to the Legislature of 1878, to provide "a practical working laboratory" for testing fertilizers, seeds, plants, and methods of cultivation. James said that if people wanted a broader and more liberal education they would have to find it at a place other than the A&M College. He advised Governor Roberts that should a liberal education be the desire of the people, then it was time to found a state university.[11] Henceforth, the A&M College would abandon all studies not related to the shop and the farm.

As instruments of public sentiment and particularly of Texas farmer sentiment, Governor Roberts and President James forced the College into an extremely narrow and strict interpretation of its purposes as defined by the Morrill Land-Grant College Act. Although confusion justifiably reigned over the nature of instruction in the agricultural and mechanical college, most of the nation's agricultural and mechanical colleges seemed to follow the broader view expressed by Senator Morrill in 1887, that the land-grant colleges were to offer both a liberal and a technical education to the "broader classes" of citizens who might otherwise be unable to receive a higher education.[12] Despite the attacks, the views of President Gathright and Governor Richard Coke as to the purposes of the Texas Agricultural and Mechanical College are closer in accord with the theory and practice of the Morrill Act than is the "vocational" interpretation of James and Governor Roberts. The Gathright-Coke view is reflected in the first catalogue of the College, which states that the leading object of the school is "to afford the most thorough instruction which its means will allow in the branches of learning pertaining to the industrial arts, or necessary to the liberal and practical education of the industrial classes to the several pursuits and professions of life."[13] In de-emphasizing the classical studies and the humanities, Texas A&M developed along a unique path. As late as the 1950s, because of the singular emphasis on technical and scientific training to the almost total exclusion of liberal arts, as well as because of the compulsory military-training features, Texas A&M was somewhat out-of-phase with the broader demands of contemporary society.

[11]Texas A&M, *Catalogue, 1879-1880*, pp. 41-46; for the outline of studies see pp. 19-20.

[12]Texas A&M Land-Grant College Centennial, Sub-Committee on Historical Perspective, "The Agricultural Historical Perspective" (mimeographed), 1-11; Texas A&M Land-Grant College Centennial, "Statement of History and Purpose," 1-21.

[13]*Ibid.;* Texas A&M, *Catalogue, 1876-1877*, p. 3.

In 1880, although farm organizations clearly recognized a real need for practical agricultural training, farm boys usually attended college so that they might get away from the farm, rather than that they might become better farmers. Although Governor Roberts correctly assessed the great need of Texas for skilled laborers, college-trained youths sought something more than hiring out as skilled mechanics. College-trained Texas youths sought and more often obtained positions of leadership and responsibility in agriculture, industry, business, and public affairs. It was a question of training agricultural teachers and educators, and agri-businessmen, as opposed to plain-dirt farmers, and of the training of engineers and scientists as opposed to grease monkeys and mechanics. The advent of the James Administration, marking the agrarian reaction at A&M, was in a sense still another false start. Yet, as was true of the Gathright Administration, it provided vital building blocks upon which the College could grow.

James implemented his new program in agriculture by hiring Charles Christian Gorgeson as professor of scientific and practical agriculture and horticulture. The primary interest of Gorgeson, the first trained agricultural specialist at A&M, involved veterinary science. Gorgeson, a graduate of Michigan State College in 1878, left Texas A&M in 1883 to become for a few years professor of agriculture in the College of Agriculture of The Imperial University of Tokyo. He taught at Kansas State College from 1890 to 1897, and from 1898 to 1928 he was in charge of the work of the U.S. Department of Agriculture in Alaska. Despite the severe handicaps under which he labored, Gorgeson remained very optimistic about the future of agricultural studies at Texas A&M. He helped form the College's first beef herd, expanded acreages in cultivation on the Farm, and planted ornamental trees on the campus. In the summers he took advanced studies at Iowa State, and other schools, which were already developing competent studies in scientific agriculture.[14] Despite Gorgeson's efforts, the agricultural program initiated by James remained virtually defunct. As Gorgeson said, the agricultural studies, and particularly the compulsory farm work involved, "were unattractive to the students."[15]

Franklin Van Winkle, employed as professor of engineering, mechan-

---

[14] *Texas Agricultural and Mechanical College, Seventh Annual Report, October 1882-June 1883*, pp. 30-34 (hereinafter cited: Texas A&M, *Annual Report, 1882-1883*); Charles C. Gorgeson, Ames, Iowa, to Louis L. McInnis, College Station, Texas, August 16, 1881, Louis L. McInnis Papers, Texas A&M University Archives; S. W. Geiser, "George Washington Curtis and Frank Arthur Gulley: Two Early Agricultural Teachers in Texas," *Field and Laboratory*, XIV (January 1946), pp. 2-3, fn. 2.

[15] *Ibid.*; Texas A&M, *Catalogue, 1883-1884*, p. 5.

ics, and drawing, and superintendent of the machine shop, experienced a greater degree of success. Because of the sharp decline in enrollment following the end of the Gathright Administration, James was able to convert one of the "emergency" wooden barracks which formerly housed students into a machine shop. For this purpose $4,000 of the $7,500 allotted for 1880-1881 by the Legislature in 1879 was spent for altering and equipping the wood-frame barracks as a machine shop. Another $1,500 was spent for outfitting a Drawing Academy in the building. The remaining $2,000 of the appropriation went to the Department of Agriculture. During James' administration the $7,500 appropriation was the only money received by the College from the state for maintenance, and even that sum had been provided prior to his association with the College.[16] Yet the $5,500 which went to Van Winkle produced astonishing results, and Gorgeson's $2,000 was well spent.

Van Winkle bought wood and metal lathes, anvils, upright drills, an iron planer, wood- and metal-working tools, bellows, apparatus for constructing forges, and a steam engine for power. His classes in the Mechanics Department spent the academic year 1880-1881 doing mill-wright work and setting up the machine shop. The courses in the machine shop proved immediately attractive and interesting to the students. Even the compulsory-labor feature failed to deter their enthusiasm. While the boys in agriculture were picking and hoeing cotton or mending fences, the boys in the shop constructed tools, harness, utensils, and machinery. Small wonder then that of the ninety boys enrolled in school in the spring of 1881, eighty-six took the course in mechanics.[17] The agricultural curriculum was near collapse, and despite the better showing in mechanics, the College appeared unable to fulfill its function as a technical training school in either capacity. Most of the professors, most of the classroom instruction, and most of the student involvement continued to be in the classical fields — ancient and modern languages and literature and mental and moral philosophy. In March 1881 a special committee of the Legislature reported back after a visit to the College that the Departments of Agriculture and Mechanics still occupied a subordinate position, and that the College generally was not in a very prosperous condition.[18]

James realized that more drastic action would be required to convert the

[16]Texas A&M, *Catalogue, 1879-1880*, pp. 46-47; Texas A&M, *Catalogue, 1880-1881*, pp. 9-10. Seventy-five hundred dollars was appropriated in April 1881 for the year 1882-1883, but was reserved for paying the tuition of "state students."

[17]*Texas Legislative Record, 17th Legislature, 1881*, pp. 201-203; Texas A&M, *Annual Report, 1882-1883*, pp. 10-12.

[18]*Texas Legislative Record, 17th Legislature, 1881*, pp. 201-203.

school into a place which would stress practical training in agriculture and mechanics. He proposed to reduce or eliminate instruction in "non-essential branches," singling out metaphysics, ancient and modern languages, literature, and, interestingly enough, military science.[19] Farmers had argued that the school was nothing but a "military peacockery." James made concerted efforts to reduce the military feature of the school; and, had he remained in office for very long, he may have substantially, if not completely, altered the military features of Texas A&M. In his official report James de-emphasized the military. He said that the public had an exaggerated idea of the time spent in military instruction. Actually, instruction he said, was limited to drills which were held during only half the session and which were confined to about forty-five minutes a day, after all scholastic work was done.[20] He made the cadet dress uniform optional as an unnecessary expense, and allowed students to wear civilian clothes in doing farm and shop work.[21] He proposed, but apparently never implemented, a policy whereby students could wear uniforms only when in ranks and under arms, or for less than one hour a day.[22] The Corps persisted in spite of James' discouragement, for the military was unmistakably popular with the students, agreeable to the faculty, and quite acceptable to most political and public figures, who saw in the military a close association with the bygone glories of the Confederacy and "the Lost Cause."

James also announced that the agricultural and mechanical courses would be reduced from a four- to a three-year curriculum, to conform to the more simple requirements for vocational training. The faculty declined to grant degrees for the three-year curricula, but would grant a degree upon completion of a fourth year of advanced study. Degrees granted included the degrees of Bachelor of Science, Bachelor of Civil Engineering, and the Bachelor of Mechanical Engineering. Fourth-year students were not required to take military science, a regulation further undermining the military feature of the College.[23] Cutting more deeply into the classical "frills" of the College, at the close of the spring term in 1881 the Board of Directors released the professor of ancient languages, Charles Patrick Estill. Although Estill anticipated his discharge from the A&M faculty, his friends labeled the Board's action "trickery."[24] Conditions were still such that the press and the public retained

[19]Texas A&M, *Catalogue, 1880-1881*, pp. 9-14.

[20]*Ibid., 1879-1880*, p. 47.

[21]*Ibid.*

[22]*Ibid., 1880-1881*, p. 14.

[23]*Ibid.*, 8-9; Texas A&M, *Catalogue, 1882-1883*, pp. 28-30.

[24]Charles P. Estill, College Station, Texas, to Louis L. McInnis, College Station, Texas,

a critical view of the A&M College. Estill soon found a position at the newly organized Sam Houston Normal Institute, in Huntsville. His son, Harry F. Estill, became president of that institution in 1908 and served in that capacity through 1936.[25] President James made every effort to reorganize the College as a training school for farmers and mechanics, and to de-emphasize the military training features of the school.

Governor Roberts gave James every assistance, short of providing substantial appropriations, possibly a vital omission in assuring the success of the reorganization effort. Roberts did sponsor legislation which sought to give the governor more control over the affairs of the A&M College and thereby make it more responsive to the demands of the farmers and to the governor's constituents. Most importantly he sponsored legislation which supported the agricultural and mechanical programs by providing state tuition grants to students. The special legislative examining committee which visited the A&M College in March 1881 concluded that the faculty and staff were competent, but that the school needed patronage. The newly instituted agricultural and mechanical courses were not attracting sufficient students and the agricultural courses were in the most critical condition. The committee advised that three students be admitted from each senatorial district without charge, thereby supplementing the regular enrollment. It also advised giving the governor the authority to appoint the Board of Directors of the institution.[26]

Legislation embodying these proposals was speedily approved as "an imperative public necessity." By the end of March a single act amended the A&M College organization act of 1875 and provided that composition of the Board of Directors, instead of comprising the governor, the lieutenant governor, the speaker of the House of Representatives, and six directors elected by joint ballot of the Legislature — one from each of the six congressional districts — henceforth would consist of five men appointed by the governor from different sections of the state to serve for six-year staggered terms or during good behavior.[27] This provision, particularly the "good behavior" clause, gave the governor personal control over the Board, and made it much

---

July 15, 1881; Charles P. Estill, Huntsville, Texas, to Louis L. McInnis, College Station, Texas, April 29, 1882, Louis L. McInnis Papers, Texas A&M University Archives; Frank Carter Adams (ed.), *Texas Democracy: A Centennial History of Politics and Personalities of the Democratic Party, 1836-1936*, pp. 26-27.

[25]*Ibid.*

[26]*Texas Legislative Record, 17th Legislature, 1881*, pp. 201-203.

[27]Gammel (ed.), *Laws of Texas*, IX, 167-178. The act was later amended to include the commissioner of Agriculture, Insurance and History as ex-officio member of the Board, to fill the first vacancy, 186.

more politically responsive — which had both good and bad implications — good in that A&M policies would be immediately responsive to administrative desires and bad in that institutional independence and long-term developmental policies might be jeopardized.

A second provision of the act of 1881 was to provide free tuition to three students from each senatorial district of the state, one of whom would be appointed by the senator and the other two by the representatives in the district. The key provision of this article would *compel* one-half of these appointed students to take the agricultural course, and the other half to take the mechanical course.[28] The Roberts Administration in effect said to the state, now you have an agricultural and mechanical college and you will take advantage of it. The tuition-grant program was funded by a $7,500 grant from the University Fund.[29] The thirty-one districts in the state would produce ninety-three students, thereby virtually doubling the enrollment of the College and assuring the "success" of the agricultural and mechanical curricula. The state tuition grant saved the agricultural curriculum and helped swell enrollments in mechanics. Of the 248 students who re-enrolled in the fall term of 1881, fifty-nine were in agriculture and 199 in mechanics.[30] Despite this rather drastic action, problems, particularly in the agricultural studies, persisted to plague President James.

Nothing forced the A&M College into a shop-and-farm mold so much as the legislation sponsored by Governor Roberts to create a state university. The argument that the lack of a university in Texas compelled the Agricultural and Mechanical College to render the services of a university had some merit. The creation of a state university now rendered that argument less valid.

Governor Roberts' inaugural address of January 18, 1881, marking the beginning of his second term in the Governor's Office, by comparison to his first message of 1879, was optimistic and cheerful. "The expenses have been brought within the revenue, and our public credit has been established" he said. Farm prices and land values were rising, commerce was improving, and Texas state bonds, recovering from the debilitating influence of carpetbaggery, sold at par or better. The university endowment now included 1,302,355 acres of land, and about $425,000 in cash, bonds, and notes receivable. The time had finally come, said Roberts, for Texas to found a "university of the first class."[31]

[28]*Ibid.*
[29]*Ibid.*, 183.
[30]Texas A&M, *Catalogue, 1880-1881,* p. 17.
[31]*Governor's Messages, Coke to Ross, 1874-1891,* pp. 341-348.

"What Texan's heart does not throb with delight as he contemplates the prospects before us and, as I believe, in the near future, for the erection of a first-class state university," Lieutenant Governor L. J. Storey extolled at the inaugural ceremonies.[32] The Teachers Association of Texas memorialized the Legislature in support of The University and advised as to its organization. John G. James, president of the State Agricultural and Mechanical College, was one of the seven Teacher Association Committeemen who devised the plan of organization for The University, which soon became law. James had voiced public support for the creation of a university in 1879 and now participated in its organization.[33] In view of the subsequent years of hostility and antagonism between The University of Texas and Texas A&M, so well exemplified by John J. Lane in his *History of the University of Texas,* James' role invokes a comparison to the opening theme of a Wagnerian opera, or to the impending *hubris* in an Aeschylus trilogy.[34]

The act to establish The University of Texas became law on March 30, 1881. It provided that the location of the school should be determined by popular vote. Roberts publicly supported its location in the state capital. The election for locating The University was held on the first Tuesday of September 1881, at which time the location for a medical branch was also decided. The government of The University was to be vested in a Board of Regents, to consist of eight members selected from different portions of the state, nominated by the governor and appointed by and with the advice and consent of the Senate. The Regents reserved the power to determine the courses of instruction, to appoint professors and officers, to fix salaries, to approve the books and materials used in instruction, and to confer degrees. The Regents were given sole control over all the revenues derived from the University Fund "for the purposes herein specified, and for the *maintenance of the branches of the university."* Salaries and expenses of The University could never exceed interest derived from the University Fund, or money received from sale of University lands (soon prohibited).[35]

Governor Roberts estimated the annual income from the University Fund and from land sales to be from $20,000 to $30,000. Actual revenues almost doubled by the time The University opened in 1883 because of a new

[32]*Ibid.,* 355.
[33]Texas A&M, *Catalogue, 1879-1880,* p. 41; *Texas Senate Journal, 1881,* pp. 52-53; *Texas House Journal, 1881,* p. 67; H. Y. Benedict (ed.), *A Source Book Relating to the History of the University of Texas,* 250-251.
[34]See John J. Lane, *History of the University of Texas,* 6-19, 55-65.
[35]Gammel (ed.), *Laws of Texas,* IX, 171-174, amended, 186; *Governor's Messages, Coke to Ross, 1874-1891,* pp. 341-348.

land endowment of one million acres, new lease arrangements, and better fiscal management. The discovery of oil on University properties after 1900 produced handsome revenues in the tens of millions of dollars annually, which in time was to make the University of Texas System one of the best-endowed public institutions in the United States. Before 1900, however, the operating funds were barely sufficient to maintain The University in Austin, let alone maintain a medical school in Galveston and provide support for an agricultural and mechanical branch in College Station. Concern over the distribution of funds triggered hot debate between supporters of the A&M branch, the medical branch, and the Main University, in Austin, throughout the remainder of the century and well into the twentieth century. Initially, The University of Texas received legislative grants of $150,000 for building construction, and $40,000 for furniture and equipment, a sum somewhat comparable to initial state expenditures on Texas A&M.[36]

The election for the location of the Main University, held on September 6, 1881, produced 30,913 votes for Austin, 9,799 for Waco, 18,974 for Tyler, 3,217 for Thorp Springs, 2,829 for Lampasas, 21 for Williams Ranch, 19 for Albany, 208 for Graham, 17 for Matagorda, and 570 for Caddo Grove. Austin received the necessary one-third of the total vote cast to receive The University. In the vote for the medical branch of The University, Galveston received 29,741 votes; Houston, 12,586; Austin, 904; Waco, 199; and Tyler, 41. Galveston received the medical school.[37]

Roberts informed a special called session of the Legislature, which convened on April 6, 1882, of the progress being made in the organization of The University of Texas. The Board of Regents planned for eleven professorships at the Main University and seven at the medical branch. The Agricultural and Mechanical College, he said, under the terms of the Constitution of 1876, would serve as the agricultural and mechanical departments of The University. He recommended to the Legislature that the Board of Directors of the A&M College be dispensed with and the number of regents be enlarged "so as to incorporate in the same body the directors and regents":[38]

There is no use for two boards. A positive disadvantage might often result from a want of harmony between them. With a common control by the Board of Regents over all of the branches, and a provision of ample means to support them all, and build them up gradually together, according to the relative importance of each one, all strife for the advancement of one to the prejudice of the others would

[36]*Ibid.*
[37]Galveston *Daily News,* September 15, 1883.
[38]Benedict (ed.), *A Source Book Relating to the History of the University of Texas,* 264-271.

not be allowed to exist, and each one could have its due share of promotion, according to the means at command, and as would best forward the interests of the country.[39]

Had Roberts' proposal been implemented the conflict which developed between the Board of Directors of the A&M College and the Board of Regents of The University would have been obviated. Subsequently, a coordinating Board of Higher Education in Texas might not have been needed. An A&M College at College Station also might very well have ceased to exist, for the Regents did have considerable control over the branches by virtue of their control over the University Fund. As Governor Roberts indicated, in the early years the University Fund was actually inadequate to support the Main University, much less a medical branch and an A&M College. As a result, the Available Funds were directed by the Regents to the way of the Main University, and not to the proposed medical branch at Galveston or to the older established institution at College Station. This condition initiated complaint from the supporters of the medical branch at Galveston and from the A&M College at College Station, and set the stage for institutional rivalry and political infighting throughout the remainder of the decade.[40]

Roberts had hoped to alleviate the financial strain of supporting a "university of the first class" by calling for an additional land endowment of two million acres for The University. Roberts referred to the history of Texas university-endowment programs, pointing out that had the Constitution of 1876 not substituted a flat one-million-acre grant of land to The University for the grant of one-tenth of the alternate sections of land granted to railroads under the Act of 1858, The University would have had by 1875 an endowment of over three million acres. The Legislature, however, failed to make any additional endowment until 1883, when another one-million-acre grant was made to The University.[41] In spite of this additional grant, no matter how full the pot, there was never enough to go around.

Indicative of the coming controversy over University funds, a financial crisis struck the A&M branch at Prairie View, which had recently been converted to a normal school after the agricultural program had collapsed for lack of students.[42] In January 1882 State Comptroller William M. Brown re-

---

[39]*Ibid.*, 271-272.

[40] See Lane, *History of the University of Texas*, 56, 70-73, and Minutes of the Board of Directors of the Agricultural and Mechanical College, June 8, 1887, I, 29.

[41]Benedict (ed.), *A Source Book Relating to the History of the University of Texas*, 400-403; Gammel (ed.), *Laws of Texas*, IX, 377; *Texas House Journal, 1883*, pp. 437-438; *Governor's Messages, Coke to Ross, 1874-1891*, p. 452.

[42]Benedict (ed.), *A Source Book Relating to the History of the University of Texas*, 273-277.

fused to audit the accounts of Prairie View Normal School in the belief that legislative grants to it from the University Fund had been unconstitutional, inasmuch as Prairie View was not a branch of The University.[43] The Constitution of 1876, referring to the organization of a state university, specifically called for the creation of a colored branch to be located by a general election.[44] That branch was soon located in Austin by virtue of a statewide election for location held in November 1882.[45] Funds for the establishment of the Negro branch, however, were never provided. Prairie View was never recognized as a branch of The University, and as a normal school it was entitled to appropriations from the general revenues. Therefore, Brown thought that Prairie View should not receive appropriations from the University Fund.

Comptroller Brown's action had the effect of withholding already appropriated money from Prairie View Normal School; Principal E. H. Anderson wrote to Governor Roberts stating that the accounts for three months past had not been paid and that he had two weeks' supplies, with no credit and no money. Roberts wrote to the president of the Board of Directors of the A&M College, Edward B. Pickett, of Galveston, asking that the Board assist Prairie View. Unknown to Roberts, Pickett had just died. When news of Pickett's death reached him, Roberts wrote to another A&M Board member, in Houston, Charles C. Wiggins, to ask him to obtain private assistance for Prairie View. Wiggins succeeded in getting several Houston merchants to provide Principal Anderson, of Prairie View, some $900 worth of cash and supplies as an advance. In February the A&M Board of Directors convened, elected a new president, and agreed to provide up to $2,200 in surplus federal funds derived from the Morrill Land-Grant for the support of Prairie View.[46]

No one seriously questioned the organization and past administration of Prairie View as a branch of the A&M College, but as a branch of the A&M College was it entitled to a share in the University Fund, especially when a Negro branch of The University was specifically provided for in the Constitution, and since, as a normal school, it could be funded from the general revenues of the state. By its past actions the Legislature clearly thought that

[43]Galveston *Daily News,* January 12, 1882; Benedict (ed.), *A Source Book Relating to the History of the University of Texas,* 276.

[44]Texas Constitution of 1876, Article 7.

[45]Gammel (ed.), *Laws of Texas,* IX, 285; *Governor's Messages, Coke to Ross, 1874-1891,* p. 451.

[46]*Governor's Messages, Coke to Ross, 1874-1891,* pp. 406-410.

Prairie View could be funded from the University endowment, and Governor Roberts also thought so.[47] This situation immediately involved A&M with a competition with The University of Texas over distribution of University funds. Roberts believed that the kind of parsimony represented by withholding University funds from Prairie View would do more harm than good. "Why cripple them [the A&M College and Prairie View Normal School] in their progress, in the ineffectual effort to establish and maintain something higher?" he asked.[48]

Roberts declined to run for re-election in 1882. John Ireland succeeded him in the office. Ireland was born in Hart City, Kentucky, on January 1, 1827. He arrived at Galveston, Texas, in 1853, and moved to San Antonio, and from there to Seguin. He became mayor of Seguin in 1858, served as a member of the Secession Convention in 1861, entered the Confederate military service, and after the War became a member of the House in 1873 and of the Senate in 1874. Richard Coke appointed him associate justice of the State Supreme Court in 1875. He became governor in 1882 and was re-elected in 1884.[49] Ireland appeared to be well disposed toward the A&M College and followed Roberts' position that the school should be sustained. He told the Legislature:

> There has been from the very beginning a popular prejudice against this institution, but the foundation for a splendid institution of learning is too deeply laid to allow us to falter, and I hope this institution, as well as the normal schools, will receive at your hands all the attention that is required to make them progressive. The college will require an appropriation.[50]

President James echoed Governor Ireland's urgent plea for money for the A&M College. Writing to Senator George Pfeuffer, in Austin, James said, "Money is needed and must be gotten or the college cannot succeed." James said that one-half million acres of land should be set aside from the University lands for the exclusive use of A&M. He said that the Regents were absolutely at fault in failing to make any appropriation from the University funds to the branches. A&M should get one-fourth of the revenues, he argued. The University, he said, was making enemies by its greediness![51]

[47]*Ibid.*, 410.

[48]*Ibid.*, 408-410; see also Benedict (ed.), *A Source Book Relating to the History of the University of Texas*, 272-278.

[49]*Governor's Messages, Coke to Ross, 1874-1891*, pp. 469-470.

[50]*Ibid.*, 481-482.

[51]John G. James, College Station, Texas, to George Pfeuffer, Austin, Texas, February 14, 1883, George Pfeuffer Papers, Texas A&M University Archives.

This letter of February 14, 1883, marks the opening of what Lane refers to in his *History of the University of Texas* as the "war with University Branches."[52]

Things were not going well with James or the A&M College. Enrollment fell with the opening of the fall term in October 1882. Enrollment in agriculture declined from the fifty-nine of a year earlier to forty-five. Students in the mechanics curriculum numbered one hundred and seventy-eight, twenty-one fewer than the previous year.[53] As the months passed, more and more students dropped out, particularly those in agriculture. The chief complaint of the students involved opposition to the "forced labor" requirement of the agriculture curriculum. Work in the fields, without compensation, not only failed to intrigue or attract students, but offended them. The Board of Directors called a special meeting in February 1883 to deal with the problems and issued a ruling that agricultural labor must be instructive only, unless the student received compensation for his work.[54] Yet another aspect of the problem, confirmed by the report of a joint legislative committee investigating A&M in February 1883, was that the agricultural studies had not been adequately funded to make them informative and efficient. James had done everything possible, as the committee affirmed, to make the College an agricultural and mechanical college rather than a literary school, but he had been blocked by the failure to receive appropriations from the Legislature or from the Regents out of the University Fund to carry out his program.[55] Other than for the tuition grant, James' only resources for purchasing equipment, tools, and experimental apparatus had been the $7,500 appropriated before he ever came into office. By the spring of 1883, because of the failure of the Legislature to fund the tuition-grant program, that money was gone and many students were forced to leave school. The Board of Directors submitted a list of needs of the A&M College, which would require an appropriation in excess of $63,000.[56] Small wonder that by the spring of 1883 President James was becoming exceedingly unhappy, and that the dispute over allocation of the University Fund was crucial to A&M.

Professor Charles C. Gorgeson, head of the Department of Agriculture, defined yet another factor over which Governor Roberts, the Legislature with its tuition grant, and James with his paring of the courses to a solely agricultural and mechanics curriculum, had no control: "The Majority of students

[52]Lane, *History of the University of Texas*, 55.
[53]Texas A&M, *Catalogue, 1882-1883*, p. 12.
[54]*Ibid.*, 1883-1884, p. 6.
[55]*Texas Senate Journal*, 1883, p. 145; see also Texas A&M, *Annual Report, 1883*, pp. 30-34.
[56]*Texas Senate Journal*, 1883, p. 146.

do not come here for a technical training in agriculture or mechanics. They come for a general education, and these would always choose the course they imagine to be most pleasant."[57] Perhaps, as some already thought, an A&M College was not what the state needed and it was an experiment which should be closed down. The University of Texas officials and some legislators echoed these sentiments on various occasions throughout the years.

To compound President James' problems, the late fall of 1882 and the early spring months of 1883 brought disease and epidemic to the campus at College Station. Between November 25, 1882, and February 16, 1883, seven deaths occurred at the College, most of them from double pneumonia. Pneumonia sometimes developed from measles, which swept the campus during those months. Many of the students left the College because of the epidemics and some failed to return. Professor George Gartner became seriously ill with what James described as dysentery. He died February 15, 1883, and was buried the same day.[58]

Dr. Smythe, the College physician, attributed much of the trouble to the failure of the students to maintain proper cleanliness, noting especially the fact that they rarely bathed. There were still no bath facilities on the campus. The hospital, moved during the crises from a professor's residence to the third floor of the mess hall, was inadequate.[59] The old gossip that the College had been located in an unhealthy place cropped up around the state. The administration and legislative investigators all tried to counter the charge, by arguing that the reports of sickness had been greatly exaggerated. The location was one of the healthiest in the state, "on a high rolling beautiful prairie," College authorities reminded the public. Still students continued to depart. By late spring only 108 students were left.[60]

In March, President John G. James submitted his resignation to the Board, and without awaiting an official acceptance abruptly took his leave.[61] James had conscientiously, and energetically, and honestly endeavored to create a college devoted to the training of farmers and mechanics. It simply had not worked. Years later James recalled his experiences at A&M in a personal

[57]Galveston *Daily News,* June 25, 1883.

[58]Texas A&M, *Annual Report, 1882-1883,* pp. 44-45; John G. James, College Station, Texas, to George Pfeuffer, Austin, Texas, February 14, 1883, George Pfeuffer Papers, Texas A&M University Archives; George Gartner Funeral Notice, George Gartner Papers, Texas A&M University Archives.

[59]Texas A&M, *Annual Report, 1882-1883,* pp. 44-45.

[60]*Ibid.,* 1-2; *Texas Senate Journal, 1883,* p. 145.

[61]Texas A&M, *Catalogue, 1883-1884,* p. 6; *Catalogue, 1882-1883,* p. 3; Texas A&M, *Annual Report, 1883,* pp. 2-3.

letter to Louis L. McInnis, who was then leaving the presidency of the College: "The position was one very distasteful to *me*, as you recalled, and I left it as soon as I could. You get no thanks, and the more you do, the more stabs, and kicks, and abuse you get from those who ought to commend and support you."[62] James left A&M to become president of the Panhandle National Bank, in Wichita Falls, Texas. He remained active in banking and brokerage activities in Wichita Falls, Henrietta, and Austin for many years and died in 1930 at the age of 85.[63]

At the end of the spring term, 1883, others of the faculty also left the College.[64] The turnover in the affairs of the school in 1883 was not too unlike that of 1879. The Crisp Affair marked the end of the classical era; James' departure marked the end of the agrarian reaction; what followed was something of a leavening — an interregnum, in which the College was allowed to develop pretty much as it would, for better or for worse.

James left behind a few important legacies. On the lighter side, one of his final acts was to direct the installation of a telephone connecting Bryan and College Station. The line was installed by students under the direction of the mechanics instructor, Professor Van Winkle. It connected an office in Gathright Hall (Steward's Hall) with the telegraph office in Bryan; installation plus a year's equipment rental cost the school $453.[65] It was perhaps the school's first modern convenience. Gas lights, electric lights, bath facilities, and heating apparatus followed in the next decade.

James' departure, the strong report of the investigation committee of February 1883, and Governor Ireland's admonitions to the Legislature resulted in the first substantial appropriation to the A&M College since the school opened. On April 23, 1883, the Legislature approved a $30,000 appropriation from the General Fund for the year 1883, and a $10,000 appropriation from the University Fund for the year 1884.[66] The appropriation at that critical time probably made the difference between the life and death of the school. Governor Ireland, John James, and George Pfeuffer, who sat on the Board of Directors of the A&M College and on the Senate Finance Commit-

[62]John G. James, Henrietta, Texas, to Louis L. McInnis, College Station, Texas, June 27, 1890, Louis L. McInnis Papers, Texas A&M University Archives.

[63]John G. James, Wichita Falls, Texas, to Louis L. McInnis, College Station, Texas, December 14, 1885; and James to McInnis, June 27, 1890, McInnis Papers, Texas A&M University Archives.

[64]Texas A&M, *Catalogue, 1883-1884*, p. 6.

[65]Texas A&M, *Annual Report, 1883*, p. 5; "Frederick Giesecke Autobiography," p. 2, Giesecke Biographical Papers, Texas A&M University Archives.

[66]Gammel (ed.), *Laws of Texas*, IX, 433-434.

tee, may be regarded as primarily responsible for the passage of the appropriation bill.

The Board of Directors of the A&M College convened on April 1, 1883, and officially accepted John G. James' resignation. Members appointed James R. Cole acting president in his place.[67] In a series of meetings during the summer of 1883 the Board effected a substantial reorganization. At first glance the College appeared to have reverted to its old, classical orientation. The new academic year commenced with a fresh storm of criticism of the administration, curriculum, and management of the College. The conflict between The University of Texas and the Agricultural and Mechanical College over the distribution of University funds reached a boiling point in the newspapers and in the Legislature; yet despite the crises no resolution of the problem occurred. Despite the conflicts there would be progress, for both The University of Texas and the A&M College of Texas. The months and years which passed between November 1879, when Thomas Gathright left the College, and March 1883, when John G. James departed, mark a watershed in the affairs of the College. Problems were by no means solved, but a new and vital beginning had been made.

[67]Texas A&M, *Catalogue, 1882-1883*, p. 3; *Catalogue, 1883-1884*, p. 6.

CHAPTER 5

The Interregnum

REACTING to mounting criticism, Acting President James R. Cole publicly denied rumors of A&M's unhealthy condition. The Galveston *Daily News* quickly used Cole's published letter as one more evidence of the academic impoverishment of the College. Pointing to a number of errors in the printed letter, the *News* criticized President Cole for his mistakes and commented that this letter was good evidence that A&M was not a literary school. The *Brazos Pilot* valiantly defended Cole, saying that errors were in the typesetting, not in the letter.[1] Hostility toward the College mounted to the level of the days of the Gathright era.

The Austin *Daily News* joined the attack by charging that the A&M College had overdrawn its account by $5,000. George Pfeuffer, representing the Board of Directors, rejected the accusation. He believed that the motive behind the charges was to discredit A&M to the advantage of The University of Texas: "To an impartial observer the A&M College seems to be in bad odor with nearly all the Austin papers, and why? Is there not room enough in this broad state for a university at Austin and the A&M College at Bryan?"[2]

Several newspapers, and especially the Galveston *Daily News,* commented favorably on a "plan" to close the school at College Station and transfer it to Austin, under the auspices of The University. The buildings and grounds of the A&M College, the *News* declared, could then be converted into a "grand central lunatic asylum."[3] This proposed "plan" cropped up at various times for the next fifty years, and even appeared in the Legislature as a bill. None could miss the implication that little change would be required to make the College into a lunatic asylum.

In July the Board of Directors of the A&M College withdrew $20,000 of the $40,000 appropriation from the state comptroller and deposited it in a

---

[1]Galveston *Daily News,* June 15, 1883; Bryan *Brazos Pilot,* June 22, 1883.

[2]Austin *Daily News,* June 15, 1883.

[3]Bryan *Enterprise,* July 4, 1883, clipping from McInnis Scrapbook, Louis L. McInnis Papers, Texas A&M University Archives.

local Bryan bank. The Austin *Statesman* criticized putting the money into a "village bank," and declared that this set a bad precedent. The Galveston *News* pulled an old skeleton out of the A&M closet by comparing the action to the questionable practices of the locating committee during Reconstruction. "A portion of the fund [in 1871] was loaned to a citizen of Brazos County for private use at the very outset without the consent or knowledge of Governor Davis."[4] This time the Houston *Post* came to the defense of the A&M College, arguing that the man [Harvey Mitchell] was under bond.[5] The Houston *Post* was not always so kindly disposed toward the College and was very critical of the Board's failure to provide professors of agriculture and mechanics.[6]

As the opening of the fall term drew near, the Galveston *Daily News* became increasingly critical of affairs at the A&M College. There was no need for two state universities, said the editor; A&M should be closed down and its buildings converted into a "Central Texas Lunatic Asylum or Normal School." On another occasion the paper reported that "It is an agricultural and mechanical elephant in the hands of the state and a wayward and extravagant branch of the university." The agricultural college does not need a farm and should be moved to Austin and, furthermore, reasoned the journalist, "There is nothing to invigorate the brain in a day of sweaty toil in the crawfish lands around the college." It might, however, be different along the "flowing Colorado" in Austin.[7]

The Bryan *Enterprise* was able to put its finger on the source of Galveston discontent with the A&M College. The editors charged the Galveston *News* with wanting to merge A&M with The University in Austin in order to get for the Galveston Medical School appropriations that had been going to A&M.[8] Although Galveston had been chosen as the site for the medical school, no funds had been allocated for that school either by the Regents from the University Fund, or by the Legislature from the General Fund. Galveston and medical-school proponents blamed the A&M College for draining off revenues which they thought should be going to the medical branch. But as the years passed and neither A&M nor Galveston received funds from the Regents, a gradual accord developed between them to the point that in a dra-

[4]Galveston *Daily News*, undated clipping in McInnis Scrapbook, p. 16, Louis L. McInnis Papers, Texas A&M University Archives.

[5]Houston *Post*, August 4, 1883.

[6]*Ibid.*, July 27, 1883.

[7]Galveston *Daily News*, September 15 and 26, 1883.

[8]Bryan *Enterprise*, October 3, 1883, in McInnis Scrapbook, Louis L. McInnis Papers, Texas A&M University Archives.

matic turnabout in relationships, the Galveston Medical School and A&M College supporters were found working together. The Regents in 1887 charged: "It was an open secret that Bryan and Galveston had entered into an alliance offensive and defensive against the main branch of the university at Austin."[9] Thus many of the charges and countercharges had to do with institutional maneuvering over a division of funds.

In this acrimonious atmosphere the Board of Directors of the A&M College set about in the summer of 1883 once again to put the College back on its feet. Despite the problems of replacing faculty and improving public opinion, the Board had one distinct asset in that for the first time since its opening the school had substantial funds with which to improve accommodations and to provide equipment and staff. President Cole reported to the Board at the end of the 1883 spring session that the Department of Agriculture needed a gardener, a dairyman, and farm laborers in order to make the Farm and experimental teaching techniques functional. The mechanical shops were dilapidated, he said, and buildings needed repairs. Janitors were needed to maintain the facilities.[10] The library was reported to be *decreasing* in size because of the wear and tear upon books and periodicals and the failure to provide funds for replacement and new purchases.[11] The legislative committee which investigated the College in February received a much more detailed list of needed improvements. These included cisterns, a chemical laboratory and equipment, mules, wagons, transits, leveling rods, a hospital, dairy and beef herds, hogs and seeds, and a foreman for the Farm.[12] These "needs," at first glance, appear to be insignificant factors upon which the success or failure of a great institution of higher learning might be determined, but in a very real sense the State Agricultural and Mechanical College of Texas had been in a state of dry rot since its opening. As both Gathright and James were aware, not the best of intentions could convert a building and people into an effective technical institute. As an agricultural and mechanical institution A&M might be compared to a high-priced machine without fuel or mechanics to service it. Just as any modern institution today would soon malfunction without its usually extensive maintenance and service departments, so the A&M College by 1883 had simply run down.

Following the conclusion of the academic year in June 1883, the Directors convened to study the task of reorganization. The Board accepted the res-

[9]Minutes of the Board of Directors of the State Agricultural and Mechanical College of Texas, I, 29 (hereinafter cited: Minutes of the Board of Directors).

[10]Texas A&M, *Seventh Annual Report, 1883*, p. 609.

[11]*Ibid., Eighth Annual Report, 1884*, pp. 34-35.

[12]*Texas Senate Journal, 1883*, p. 146.

ignation of Charles C. Gorgeson, professor of agriculture, and of Franklin Van Winkle, professor of mechanics; Charles S. Miller, an assistant instructor in English, had departed in April, before the close of the term. George Gartner had died in February. Dr. D. Porte Smythe, the College physician, also submitted his resignation.[13] Of those who began with James in December 1879, only Louis McInnis, James Cole, and Hardaway Hunt Dinwiddie remained.

Upon Gartner's death in February President James hired William Lorraine Bringhurst as Gartner's replacement in the chair of ancient and modern languages. Board Member George Pfeuffer, however, regarded the appointment as temporary, and desired to hire Rudolph Wipprecht, of Pfeuffer's home town, New Braunfels, as professor of ancient and modern languages. Bringhurst protested that his had been a permanent appointment, made and accepted in good faith. But on June 25 the Board elected Rudolph Wipprecht to be professor of ancient and modern languages, without mentioning Bringhurst, who then held the position. Bringhurst's supporters, many of whom were at College Station for commencement exercises, vigorously protested the Board's action, but seemingly to no avail. Bringhurst appeared to have been replaced without having resigned or having been discharged, although the Directors may justifiably have considered the Bringhurst appointment as having been only temporary, and necessitated by virtue of Gartner's death. The problem was eventually solved by appointing Bringhurst to a different chair.[14]

The Directors hired Dr. John D. Read, M.D., to replace Dr. Smythe, and obtained Robert F. Smith to be assistant in mathematics and Walter Gillis to serve as assistant in English.[15] No applications were received by the Directors for the position of professor of agriculture to replace Gorgeson. According to press reports, people "shunned that position" because of the past unfavorable publicity, and the lack of proper equipment. As Gorgeson commented, "It is about as impossible to teach practical stock-breeding without livestock as to teach carpentry without tools and shop work."[16] James Cole argued, as did Gorgeson, that the greatest deterrent to the fulfilment of the mission of the College was not the lack of intent, or mismanagement, but the lack of money:

[13]Texas A&M, *Catalogue, 1882-1883,* p. 3; Texas A&M, *Catalogue, 1883-1884,* p. 6.

[14]W. L. Bringhurst, College Station, Texas, to George Pfeuffer, Austin, Texas, March 27, 1883, George Pfeuffer Papers, Texas A&M University Archives; Texas A&M, *Catalogue, 1882-1883,* p. 3; Galveston *Daily News,* June 27, 1883.

[15]Texas A&M, *Catalogue, 1883-1884,* p. 2.

[16]Galveston *Daily News,* June 25, 1883.

It is known to you that the college has labored under many disadvantages, the chief of which has been the want of means of carrying out the object of the institution. The public has not known of this want, or have not fully appreciated it, or we believe the college would have received more credit for what has been accomplished, and less adverse criticism.[17]

Money was critical to the improvement of the agricultural and mechanical curricula. But for the academic year 1883-1884, for the first time in its history, the A&M College could no longer argue poverty as an excuse for any failings. The school now had $40,000 in appropriated funds to spend over the next two years, exclusive of salaries. During the June sessions the Board allocated most of these funds as follows: $2,000 for a laundry and fixtures, $2,000 for a hospital and furniture, $1,500 for repairs to professors' houses, $4,000 for repairs to the mess hall, $4,000 for repairs to the Main Building, $200 for dormitory furnishings, $2,200 for a chemical laboratory and equipment, $4,500 for a metal workshop, $2,800 for tools and shop machinery, and $15,000 to the Department of Agriculture for fences, stock, and equipment. Because of the "enormous" expenditures envisioned and the constant supervision and planning regarded as essential to the expenditure of these funds, the Directors decided to select a financial manager to act as a supervisor and agent of the Board. It was reported that they might select Board member Thomas M. Scott to serve as agent, but no action was taken during the June sessions of the Board. Because of the creation of the position of business manager, which relieved the president of some of his duties, the Directors decided to reduce the president's salary from $2,400 to $2,000.[18]

The Directors, having appointed James Cole as acting president only on April 1, 1883, to replace John James, still needed to procure a permanent president for the College. Twelve applications for the position were received, including one from John J. Lane, of Austin, who later became a severe critic of A&M; one from Carlisle P. B. Martin, formerly professor of agriculture under Thomas Gathright; and one was received also from Alexander Hogg, formerly professor of mathematics under Gathright. James Cole also applied for the position. On June 26 the Board chose to retain Cole as permanent president by a vote of 4 to 1, but indicated that his duties were no longer as extensive as those of former presidents because of the creation of the position of manager.[19] While the Board was in session a new problem cropped up when Professor Van Winkle, in mechanics, submitted his resignation.[20]

[17] *Ibid.*
[18] *Ibid.*, June 25, 27, 1883.
[19] *Ibid.*, June 27, 1883.
[20] *Ibid.*, June 28, 1883.

The reason for Van Winkle's resignation did not become public until a later Board meeting. What had happened was that Van Winkle had given Board chairman James D. Thomas in June a written resignation which Thomas was to give to the Board if the Board failed to select Van Winkle as its architectural adviser and supervisor for the repair work being planned. The Board chose instead to establish the position of business manager, but did not fill the position. At this point Thomas orally advised the Directors of Van Winkle's resignation, but did not formally present the written resignation, perhaps assuming that not having filled the position of manager, the Board might later reconsider its action and employ Van Winkle in this capacity. Thomas had from the first disapproved action separating fiscal authority from the office of the president. In a meeting on July 19, 1883, in Judge Thomas' office in Bryan, the Board selected General William P. Hardemann as its business manager, and took umbrage at Van Winkle's threat of resignation if he failed to get the position. The Board ruled Van Winkle guilty of insubordination and accepted his resignation despite Thomas' protest.[21] Thus, by July, A&M had neither a professor of agriculture nor a professor of mechanics.

It also lost a president in July, much to the surprise and chagrin of Cole, who had been named permanent president only shortly before, on June 26. Cole left College Station in early July for a visit to Houston and Galveston, where he expected to promote the College and reconcile some of the opponents to the school, especially those in Galveston. Cole returned to Bryan to attend on July 19 a special meeting of the Directors, called for the purpose of selecting professors for the agricultural and mechanical departments.[22] Among those considered by the Board for the position of professor of agriculture were Carlisle P. B. Martin and William A. Banks, both formerly of the Texas A&M faculty, as well as Captain John Wharton, from Sherman, Texas, whose name had been submitted by President Cole. The Board took no action on filling the position in agriculture, but did create a Department of Physics, and named William L. Bringhurst professor of physics, and so resolved the Wipprecht-Bringhurst dispute. Then in a surprise move the Directors proceeded to abolish the position of president, and established

[21] *Ibid.*, June 28, July 22, 1883.

[22] *Ibid.*, July 22, 1883; Texas A&M, *Catalogue, 1883-1884*, p. 6; James R. Cole, *Seven Decades of My Life*, 96-97, confirms Cole's selection as permanent president of A&M and the subsequent abolition of the office of president. Cole's recollection, however, indicates that the Board abolished the position while Cole was away. Contemporary newspaper accounts indicate that Cole attended the meeting, but neither he nor the Board chairman had foreknowledge of what would happen.

instead the position of chairman of the faculty, with the chairman to be elected by the faculty. Four days later the faculty named Hardaway Hunt Dinwiddie chairman of the faculty and so effectively removed Cole from all administrative functions.[23]

The action stemmed from several factors. In June the Board recognized that the creation of the office of business manager altered the complexion of the president's authority. That action made him, in fact, if not in name, a faculty chairman. Furthermore, the Directors were influenced by the fact that The University of Texas and many "progressive" institutions of higher learning were using the manager-chairman combination, which at face value, even today, has considerable logic behind it, but which in practice proved to be an unfortunate and unwieldy arrangement. The Directors, in fact, informed Cole that they had not been at all dissatisfied with his performance as either acting or permanent president, but simply wanted to reorganize the College along the lines of The University, in Austin. Cole, however, felt that the abolition of the office of president, and his effective removal from an executive position, involved more than this. Subsequent developments would appear to support Cole's feeling that he was in "somebody's way."

The establishment of the position of business manager and the abolition of the office of president created·a rift among the Directors which ended in Judge James D. Thomas' resignation. Thomas accused the Board of trying to "drive both Cole and Professor Van Winkle away from the college." He pointed out that Cole had only recently been elected president by a vote of 4 to 1 and could not possibly be considered derelict in his duties. The vote to abolish the presidency had been 3 to 2 in favor, according to the later recollections of Cole. George Pfeuffer, who may well have been instrumental in the organizational change, and who soon came to play a very important role in A&M affairs, denied that the Board was trying to drive anyone away and especially not Van Winkle. Pfeuffer insisted that Van Winkle's written resignation be spread on the minutes to set the record straight, but Thomas refused. Thomas subsequently submitted his resignation from the Board to Governor John Ireland.[24]

Cole remained at the College, but continued to be in someone's way. In March 1885 the chairman of the faculty, Hardaway Hunt Dinwiddie, who

---

[23]Galveston *Daily News,* July 22, 1883; Texas A&M, *Catalogue, 1883-1884,* p. 6; Cole, *Seven Decades of My Life,* 96-97.

[24]*Ibid.;* Governor John Ireland, Austin, Texas, to George Pfeuffer, Austin, Texas, September 11, 1883, Pfeuffer Papers, Texas A&M University Archives.

had been elected to his position by the faculty on July 23, 1883, four days after the Board meeting in which the office of president was abolished, accused Cole of incompetency. He recommended that Bringhurst, then in physics, be assigned to Cole's duties in English, and that he (Dinwiddie) be given physics.[25] Years later, Cole briefly reviewed the situation in his autobiography as follows: "Two years passed and my work gave such satisfaction that no fault could be found; but I knew that some of the Directors were unfriendly and that I was in somebody's way."[26] Cole resigned at the close of the spring term in 1885. Bringhurst was then made professor of English and Dinwiddie added to his title and duties that of professor of chemistry and physics.[27] James Cole became superintendent of schools in Dallas. His memoirs, written in 1913, depict a pleasant, resourceful, energetic, and interesting man who lived a rich, full life.[28]

Hardaway Hunt Dinwiddie, who succeeded Cole as the first chairman of the faculty, had come to A&M with President James in 1879 from the Texas Military Institute, in Austin. He was a man of considerable tact and ability who provided a moderating but positive influence upon the school's development. Dinwiddie, a chemist, was better equipped than Gathright, James, or Cole to reconcile the classical- and technical-education conflict. He believed that scientific principles and techniques could be applied to agricultural and mechanical training. Learning to farm involved more than practicing plowing and hoeing in the time-honored techniques. Dinwiddie, furthermore, was sufficiently astute politically to know that the job of selling the Agricultural and Mechanical College involved more than having informative courses of study for the students. It involved convincing the public that what was being taught was respectable and applicable.

Dinwiddie publicly applauded the opening of The University of Texas at Austin in the fall of 1883. It would be advantageous, he said, and would for the first time allow the College to concentrate upon its primary objective of agricultural and mechanical training. Now we can show, he said, that the agricultural and mechanical courses can stand on their own, in spite of the fact that such training seemed to confront the "time-honored" educational traditions of the South. Dinwiddie recognized the necessity of educating the

[25]H. H. Dinwiddie, College Station, Texas, to George Pfeuffer, Austin, Texas, March 23, 1885, Pfeuffer Papers, Texas A&M University Archives.

[26]Cole, *Seven Decades of My Life*, 97.

[27]Texas A&M, *Catalogue, 1887-1888*, p. 13.

[28]Cole, *Seven Decades of My Life*, 1-212.

public as to the nature of this technical training and advised initiating annual "farmers institutes."[29] A farmers' institute was first inaugurated in the fifth congressional district in 1890; it became a statewide organization by 1893, and developed into the Farmers' Congresses which convened at the A&M College every year between 1898 and 1915.[30]

Dinwiddie made vigorous efforts to promote an understanding of the College's objectives with the Texas Grange. At a Grange meeting near Reagan, Texas, in the summer of 1884, Dinwiddie "struck out boldly" for one hour and ten minutes and came away convinced that the College would "be crowded next year."[31] In August 1885 he addressed the State Grange at its annual convention in Galveston and secured a Grange resolution commending the A&M College and expressing confidence in it.[32] Archibald Johnson Rose, grand master of the Grange, addressed the student body at the commencement exercises in College Station in June.[33]

Rose, who had much to do with improving the public image of the A&M College, and who became a director of the College, was one of the most influential agrarian leaders in Texas in the 1880s. Born on September 3, 1830, in Carswell County, North Carolina, Rose as a young man struck out with the "forty-niners" for the gold fields of California, where he made a sufficient stake to move his family to Texas in 1857 and to establish a ranch along the San Saba River in 1860. The Lipan-Apache and Comanche Indians drove his cattle away and terrorized his ranch in 1860 and 1861, and the outbreak of the Civil War in 1861 combined with these events to wreck his ranching career. Rose served as a major in the Confederate army and after the War sold his ranch and moved to a farm near Salado, Texas. At Salado he helped organize the first Grange of the Patrons of Husbandry in Texas, on July 6, 1873, and soon became a lecturer in the Grange, and finally grand master of the State Grange, from 1880 to 1891. Although he never became a Populist, Rose clearly helped shape agrarian-reform thought in Texas. He became a "foremost crusader for better schools and teachers, free textbooks, and vocational education." Governor Lawrence Sullivan Ross appointed Rose to the A&M Board of Directors in 1887, and later, while Ross was president of the College, Rose served as chairman of the Board during the years 1891-

[29]Texas A&M, *Eighth Annual Report, 1884*, pp. 1-4.

[30]See Chapter 11, "The Farmers."

[31]H. H. Dinwiddie, College Station, Texas, to Louis L. McInnis, Forest, Mississippi, August 8, 1884, Louis L. McInnis Papers, Texas A&M University Archives.

[32]Texas A&M, *Biennial Report, 1883-1885*, pp. 12-13.

[33]Clippings in Louis L. McInnis Scrapbook, p. 63, Louis L. McInnis Papers, Texas A&M University Archives.

1896. Finally, Governor Charles A. Culberson, who entered office in 1895, appointed Rose state commissioner of agriculture, insurance, statistics and history. Thus, in many capacities, Rose exerted a strong influence upon the development of the A&M College during the last decades of the nineteenth century.[34] Rose may be ranked with George Pfeuffer as one of the "powers" behind the College.

On July 11, 1885, following Rose's address to the A&M student body, Dinwiddie addressed the Texas State Teachers Association in their state convention on the subject of "Industrial Education in our Common Schools." Dinwiddie argued that classical education was failing the American people, but that the advent of the agricultural and mechanical colleges had inaugurated substantive educational reforms. These reforms had been slow in acceptance, he said, because "people found difficulty in associating the idea of a college education in any way with vulgar workshops and greasy machinery, with hard hands and soiled clothes." He attacked the "absurdities" of traditional educational techniques. "The world demands," he said, "direct and common-sense ways of thinking and acting." The agricultural and mechanical colleges and the new educational techniques were helping to create a "self-help citizen."[35] Dinwiddie had become very conscious of the mission of the agricultural and mechanical colleges, and of their role in reshaping American educational philosophy. His efforts substantially improved the image of the Texas A&M College in the minds of Texans and began to pay political and academic dividends.

Dinwiddie soon began to capitalize upon the improved public image of the institution. Rather than remaining silent before the critics, he rejected such ideas as having A&M merged with The University and, on the contrary, argued that the two institutions should be legally separated and that A&M should be entitled to a fair proportion of the University funds. Experience has shown, he said, that a union of literary and technical colleges has always been disastrous to the technical college. He cited the example of Louisiana, where the agricultural and mechanical system was struggling for survival under the dominance of the classic-oriented university. In Kentucky, he said, it became necessary to separate the schools which had originally been united. As for funding Texas A&M, he stated in his official biennial report in 1885, that since 67 percent of the people in Texas were farmers, to allocate one-third of the University Fund to the A&M College would be very moderate.[36]

---

[34]Walter Prescott Webb and H. Bailey Carroll (ed.), *Handbook of Texas*, II, 502-503.

[35]H. H. Dinwiddie, *Industrial Education in Our Common Schools*, 1-16.

[36]Texas A&M, *Biennial Report, 1883-1885*, pp. 14-15.

As may be recalled, an early effort to divide the lands in the University grant occurred in 1873, when Senator William A. Saylor introduced a bill to give A&M two-fifths of the University lands, and 40 percent of the bonds dedicated to The University. The approved bill was vetoed by Governor Edmund J. Davis. Subsequently, in 1887, a bill cleared the House Committee on Education to give A&M one-fifth of the University lands, but the Legislature adjourned before the bill could be put to a vote.[37] The A&M Directors in 1911 sought a constitutional amendment which would separate the schools and give A&M one-half of the land endowment, or a cash equivalent derived from a special tax.[38] Not until 1919 did such a constitutional amendment clear the Legislature. The proposal would have separated the institutions and reserved one-third of the University endowment to the Agricultural and Mechanical College.[39] This amendment was rejected by the people of Texas in the general elections in November. Finally, in 1930, a division of the endowment was agreed to by the Regents of The University and the Directors of the A&M College, which gave A&M one-third of all subsurface royalties from the University lands. This agreement became statutory law.[40] It is worthy of note that Dinwiddie's formula of one-third, which he first advanced, became the agreed-upon division forty-five years later.

In addition to his public-relations work, Dinwiddie, with the assistance of the Board and the faculty, reorganized the curricula, strengthened the faculty, and recruited a number of necessary nonacademic officers to help service the institution. The Directors made two essential and important additions to the faculty when they elected George W. Curtis, professor of agriculture, and Roger Haddock Whitlock, professor of engineering, on September 15, 1883, in time for the opening of the fall term.[41]

Whitlock came to Texas A&M at the age of twenty-three as a graduate of Stevens Institute of Technology, in Hoboken, New Jersey. When he arrived the "engineering" facilities consisted of the old wooden barracks which Van Winkle, Whitlock's predecessor, had converted into a woodworking shop. Course work had been essentially limited to practical training in woodworking, drawing, and surveying. There were no real engineering

[37]*Texas Senate Journal, 1873,* pp. 138, 919, 925, 945, 1040, 1044, 1166-1167; *Texas House Journal, 1873,* pp. 1173, 1204, 1207; Minutes of the Board of Directors, June 8, 1887, I, 27.

[38]Minutes of the Board of Directors, February 9, 1911, I, 242-245.

[39]*General Laws of Texas,* Regular Session, 1919, pp. 350-354.

[40]*Ibid.,* 1931, pp. 63-64.

[41]See Galveston *Daily News,* September 17, 1883, which erroneously reported that Whitlock had been hired in agriculture and Curtis in engineering, and Texas A&M, *Catalogue, 1883-1884,* p. 33.

courses. Over the next twenty-three years Whitlock was primarily responsible for developing solid courses of study in both mechanical and civil engineering; he also assisted in establishing a field in electrical engineering in 1903. The changes placed Texas A&M on the threshold of becoming one of the nation's most respectable schools of engineering. In 1898 (January 17-July 1) Whitlock became acting president of Texas A&M, and served again in that capacity between December 10, 1901, and July 1, 1902. He left the school in 1906. Students, who had a penchant for nicknaming professors, called him "Whitty," but not to his face. He had the reputation of being "stern," without being hard.[42] Indicative of the kind of effort made by Whitlock and his colleagues, whom he either trained, as in the case of Frederick Ernst Giesecke, or hired, as in the case of James C. Nagle, 75 percent of the graduates of Texas A&M between 1883 and 1908 were engineers; most of these were civil or mechanical engineers.[43]

George Washington Curtis, Whitlock's counterpart in agriculture, played much the same role there which Whitlock played in engineering. Basically, he modernized the agricultural curriculum.[44] Curtis did significant work in cattle feeding and stock breeding. In 1888 he published one of the earliest texts on animal husbandry for agricultural students, *Horses, Cattle, Sheep and Swine.* He assisted in development of the Agricultural Experiment Station and became director of the Station from 1890 to 1893. He developed an effective veterinary-anatomy course in his first year at A&M, and had his class prepare a horse skeleton which remained standard equipment in the class for many years. Curtis was twenty-two years old when he arrived at College Station fresh out of Iowa State College, in Ames. He remained at A&M until 1893, when he left to go into the banking business in Louisiana. Eventually he became a grain broker and miller in West Texas and Oklahoma. He died in Oklahoma City on September 18, 1945.[45] Whitlock and Curtis, by their professional ability, because of their long tenure at the A&M College, and through dedication and hard work, created reputable and permanent Departments of Engineering and Agriculture at the College.

Both men were essential ingredients in the faculty of 1884, which included Hardaway Hunt Dinwiddie as professor of chemistry and chairman of the faculty; Louis L. McInnis, professor of mathematics and vice-chairman of the faculty; James Reid Cole, professor of English literature and history;

[42]David B. Cofer (ed.), *Second Five Administrators of Texas A. and M. College*, 91-104.

[43]College Station *Longhorn, 1908*, p. 148.

[44]See Texas A&M, *Catalogue, 1883-1884*, pp. 48-49.

[45]S. W. Geiser, "George Washington Curtis and Frank Arthur Gulley: Two Early Agricultural Teachers in Texas," *Field and Laboratory*, XIV (January 1946), pp. 1-13.

Rudolph Wipprecht, professor of ancient and modern languages and librarian; Lieutenant John S. Mallory, professor of military science and commandant of Cadets; Robert F. Smith, assistant professor of mathematics; and William Lorraine Bringhurst, professor of physics and secretary of the faculty.[46] Nonacademic officers of the College included William P. Hardemann, the business manager, who approved or disapproved expenditures, and had charge of the mess hall, faculty and student housing, and staff employees. Louis McInnis served as treasurer, handling student fees and student expenditures. John D. Read was the College physician. Bernard Sbisa joined the staff as steward, in charge of the mess hall, in 1879, and remained through 1928. Sbisa became something of an institution on the campus and was extremely proficient at one of the most sensitive posts in a male college — that of chef. Emil Kellner, who also joined the staff in 1879, served as foreman of the Farm, a position which experienced frequent turnovers. Kellner left the College in 1885 after frequent controversies with the business manager. A. A. Harbers served as foreman of the Shops, and John S. Fowlkes, of Bryan, was the Board's fiscal agent or, in effect, the local banker who made disbursements upon receipt of vouchers from the agent, or later, from the president. For a time Fowlkes received a flat fee for his services, and later a percentage on expenditures and interest charges on overdrafts.[47] In contrast to its earlier status, the College by 1884 was efficiently operated by a generally competent and indispensable service staff.

The facilities of the College now included "Old Main," which served in many capacities. On the first floor were located the physical and chemical classrooms, the chemical balance room and dark room, classrooms for English languages and for mechanics, the office of the commandant, the office of the business manager, and the janitor's room. The second floor contained the library, the agricultural classroom, the office of the chairman of the faculty, the chemical laboratory, and several student quarters. The third floor included spaces for mathematics, rooms for surveying and drawing equipment, and student quarters. One-half of the fourth floor served as chapel; in the other section of the fourth floor were two halls, for the Calliopean Society and the Austin Literary Society; also on the fourth floor were an athletic hall and three small rooms. A frame building for carpentry and woodworking stood behind Main. The latter was one of Gathright's old frame dormitory structures built for the overflow of students in 1878. During the James years

[46]Texas A&M, *Catalogue, 1883-1884*, p. 33.

[47]*Ibid.*, 34; Emil Kellner, College Station, to Friend [George] Pfeuffer, New Braunfels, Texas, May 1, 1885, George Pfeuffer Papers, Texas A&M University Archives.

a blacksmith shop and boiler house had been added to this building. The Mess Hall was attached to the president's home. This frame building housed at various times the president, the chairman of the faculty, and the business manager or steward. On the second and third stories were twenty rooms for one to three students each. Until about 1890 the Mess Hall fed from one to three hundred students three times a day.[48] A brick, metal workshop was completed in 1885 north of and slightly behind Old Main. A frame barracks, completed in 1879, was capable of housing some seventy students, and remained in use throughout the eighties.

The Main Building, Steward's Hall, and outbuildings stood at the top of a rise or knoll facing the Houston and Texas Central Railway tracks, which ran parallel to the College property in a southeasterly direction. Behind the Main Building were a barn, a shed, wood piles, and fenced pastures and fields. "The Line," or row of five comfortable brick homes for faculty, were ranged southeast of the central buildings. In 1883 the railroad completed a "neat" depot building adjacent to the tracks facing Old Main, and the railroad began to make regular stops at College Station. Previously, College Station had been a flag stop. A frame general store stood some distance down the track from the depot, but seems to have been operated only intermittently through the eighties.[49]

The failure of the Legislature to fund the "state" students in 1883 caused a drop in enrollment in 1883-1884. The implementation of the tuition program in 1881 had raised enrollment to 258; in 1882 it dropped to 223, allegedly because of hard times, and the cessation of the program in 1883 brought a further marked decline. Only 108 students finished the academic year, 1883-1884. Of these, 31 were enrolled in the agriculture course and 77 in mechanics. Fourteen were in the first class, 21 in the second class, and 73 in the third class or first year of work.[50] A larger beginning class, none of whose members had been attracted by a state tuition grant, encouraged the administration to feel that the demise of the state grant was for the better.[51] Dinwiddie, at the close of the term in June 1884, looked forward to a continued, healthy growth of the College. He estimated maximum capacity of the College at 150 students. This downward revision of student "capacity" from the 250-capacity levels of earlier days may be attributed in part to the desire of

[48]Texas A&M, *Catalogue, 1883-1884*, pp. 28-29.

[49]*Ibid.*, 26-29; Galveston *Daily News*, July 19, 1883.

[50]Texas A&M, *Catalogue, 1881-1882*, p. 17; Texas A&M, *Catalogue, 1882-1883*, p. 22; Texas A&M, *Catalogue, 1883-1884*, p. 38; *Report of the Agricultural and Mechanical College, 1885*, p. 15.

[51]*Report of the Agricultural and Mechanical College, 1885*, p. 15.

A&M administrators to live with a given situation; that is, the necessity to accept a measure of defeat gracefully, the defeat being the failure to have the tuition program funded by the Legislature; at the same time Dinwiddie was giving recognition to the fact that technological training could not be engaged in on as large a scale as liberal-arts training, given the limited facilities and finances of the College. A technical education simply cost more per student than training in the humanities. The more modest estimate of the size of the A&M student body seems to have been more realistic. There would soon be more students than the College could adequately handle. As the years passed, enrollment remained steady with a small but healthy increase each year, until in the late 1890s enrollment surges began to be felt. By 1906, and until the outbreak of World War I, it was necessary to house many students in tents.

The opening of the fall session on Monday, September 1, 1884, began with 133 students enrolled. Lieutenant Mallory, with the assistance of his cadet officers, organized the students into a battalion of three companies, A, B, and C, and began the imposition of strict military discipline and training. Cadet officers were always selected from the first class (seniors) and noncommissioned officers came from the second and third classes. Cadet officers were charged with supervision of a division of the barracks, as well as with command of the ranks. Cadets marched to classes and to mess. In the Mess Hall they took their seats on command and rose and departed on command. Each cadet had an assigned seat at a certain table, presided over by a cadet officer. Cadet officers could recommend merits or demerits. Cadets could "walk off" demerits, carrying their full gear in the bull-ring on Saturday morning.[52] One student complained by 1887 that "Our commandant has turned our school into a second West Point."[53] Official publications generally continued to de-emphasize the role of the military in the life of the school, but to a very great extent student life was shaped, molded, and directed by the Corps of Cadets.

Corps life could be very rewarding. At times it could also be very arduous. New students who joined in the 1880s were greeted with the appellation "fish," a nickname which signified a new, first-semester freshman. In the eyes of the cadets the term indicated a raw, slightly odious, and distinctly questionable being who was swimming in waters over his head. All fish, of whatever former status or domicile in life, were distinctly inferior in class and

[52]Texas A&M, *Biennial Report, 1883-1885*, pp. 42-43.
[53]John E. Hill, College Station, Texas, to "Mother" [Mrs. Hill], March 13, 1887, John E. Hill Letters, Texas A&M University Archives.

status to upper classmen. New fish were sooner or later indoctrinated by a ceremonial "strapping." Joseph F. Nichols recalled his fish year in 1886:

> Strapping was done as a ceremony in presence of several students, with a leather strap or pliable wood. Being eighteen years of age it was ruled that I should receive eighteen straps when I was in position as laid over a barrel. The strapping was quite severe, and I was then given a full descriptive receipt [which exempted him from future ceremonies].[54]

It also became the tradition to strap upperclassmen when they received a promotion.[55] Although the ground work for the development of "Aggie traditions" was being prepared in the 1880s, other than for the designation "fish" there were few "traditions" such as exist today. Even the term "Aggie" was not applied to A&M College students until after World War I. The newspapers of the eighties usually referred to the students as cadets or simply as the "students of the A. & M. C." After the turn of the century the designation "Farmers" became popular, and in the 1920s and 1930s "Aggie" came into increasingly widespread use and was officially adopted as the student-body nickname in 1949, when the yearbook was changed from *The Longhorn* to *Aggieland.*

To be sure, a strong sense of school loyalty had developed by the eighties and is evidenced by the organization of an "Association of Ex-Cadets," which first convened in June 1880. The Alumni Association of the A&M College of Texas had its origins in 1886, when, according to Frederick Ernst Giesecke, who assisted in the organization, the Constitution of the Association was written. The alumni adopted the Constitution in 1887, and it was first published in 1888.[56] Not only was school loyalty developed to a high degree in the eighties, but so was "Company" and "Class" rivalry.[57] Out of these conditions came the Aggie "spirit" and traditions of later days.

Student life in the eighties, however, was characterized by an absence of

[54]"Reminiscences of Joseph F. Nichols," Texas A&M University Archives.

[55]John E. Hill, College Station, Texas, to "Mother" [Mrs. Hill], March 13, 1887, John E. Hill Letters, Texas A&M University Archives.

[56]Frederick Ernst Giesecke Biography, Giesecke Biographical Papers, Texas A&M University Archives.

[57]This is largely intuition rather than precise documentation, but see Sam A. McMillan, "Reminiscences," in David Brooks Cofer (ed.), *Fragments of Early History of Texas A. & M. College,* 78-89; Paul D. Casey, *The History of the AMC Trouble, 1908;* Texas A&M, *Biennial Report, 1883-1884,* pp. 42-43; H. H. Dinwiddie, College Station, Texas, to George Pfeuffer, New Braunfels, Texas, March 19, 1885, George Pfeuffer Papers, Texas A&M University Archives; John E. Hill, College Station, Texas, to "Mother" [Mrs. Hill], March 13, 1887, John E. Hill Letters, Texas A&M University Archives.

contemporary student mores, or "traditions." There were no bonfires, no yell practice, not even intramural or intercollegiate athletics. There was no football and no basketball and no organized baseball. There were no senior boots and no Ross Volunteers (the A&M cadet honor guard) until 1887, when the Scott Volunteers were organized in honor of Thomas M. Scott, business manager and agent of the Board. The Scott Volunteers were renamed the Ross Volunteers in 1890 in recognition of Lawrence Sullivan Ross, who had been appointed as the new president of Texas A&M.[58] The "tradition" which requires that fish polish the statue of Ross came many years after the erection of the statue in 1919.[59] The student mess was beginning to develop the rowdiness characteristic of later days, but the lack of deportment at the table could hardly be labeled a tradition.

Student activities in the eighties were largely spontaneous. There were keg-rollings, when students would haul a keg of beer in from Bryan and hide it away in the woods for a secret, and prohibited, beer-bust. In the late eighties and nineties a cane rush, actually a free-for-all brawl, became a popular pastime. This activity is described in a later chapter. Students delighted in wrecking outhouses, hiding liquor in their rooms for an occasional nip, and swiping poultry from the back yards of professors' homes.[60] A&M students in this decade were still close to the backwoods and the wild, open prairies. Their activities and interests reflected that environment. Bryan, for example, was still basically a Wild West town, and College Station, as it came to be known, was no town at all, but still a train stop in the midst of prairies. One writer noted that as late as 1900 students were required to have special permission from the president of the College to go to Bryan, which "with its fourteen or fifteen saloons, an average of two for each block, its public drunkenness, open gambling, and incidental gun play, was suspect and, therefore, forbidden to the students."[61] This very prohibition would suggest that a nefarious activity of the more daring students was to slip away to the forbidden city.

Despite the roughness of the environs, in many respects A&M students were more susceptible to the refinements of education in the latter part of the

[58]David Brooks Cofer (ed.), *Fragments of Early History of Texas A. & M. College*, 23-27.

[59]Dedication of the Statue of Lawrence Sullivan Ross, Lawrence Sullivan Ross Biographical Papers, Texas A&M University Archives.

[60]Sam A. McMillan, "Reminiscences," in Cofer (ed.), *Fragments of Early History of Texas A. & M. College*, 84-85; H. A. Stacy, Helltown, Texas, to George Pfeuffer, New Braunfels, Texas, May 17, 1885, George Pfeuffer Papers, Texas A&M University Archives; *The Olio*, 1895, p. 130; College Station *Longhorn*, 1906, pp. 154-155.

[61]Robert Eugene Byrnes, "Lafayette Lumpkin Foster: A Biography," 177.

nineteenth century than they were in the later twentieth century. Participation in the two literary societies, the Stephen F. Austin Society and the Calliopean Society, was strong and interest was keen. Periodic debates between society representatives, and particularly the annual commencement debates, were intellectual high points of the year. Sam A. McMillan, former student of A&M who finished his studies in 1909 and then became a professor at the College, believed that the World War I era witnessed a distinct change in student attitudes at A&M. The football "hysteria" began to develop; the literary societies folded their wings "for the long sleep"; "college spirit" and indoctrination surpassed and even began to smother academic interests; extra work in the labs and voluntary reading in the library became too "sissified" for the "Ruff-Tuff, Real-Stuff" A&M man.[62] It was in this later climate that contemporary Aggie traditions and student activities began to develop. It would appear to be true that, as McMillan suggested, many of these contemporary traditions "are lies that have grown whiskers."[63]

"It's really going to take a philosopher to unravel A&M's traditions and present them without bias," concluded McMillan.[64] There have been a number of attempts to describe A&M traditions, without philosophizing on them. The most prominent of these efforts include works by George Sessions Perry, *The Story of Texas A&M;* John Pasco, *Fish Sergeant;* R. Henderson Shuffler, editor of *Son, Remember . . .;* and Joseph G. Rollins, Jr., *Aggies! Y'All Caught That Dam' Ol' Rat Yet?* Aside from the specific incidents and activities of student life recorded in these books, most of them of modern vintage, they are collectively significant in testifying to the very strong identification of the students with the College and with the Corps of Cadets. What was happening in the 1880s at A&M was that while other colleges and universities in the United States were developing social clubs and fraternities characteristic of modern days, none of these were encouraged or ever developed at A&M. The Corps of Cadets instead became a single fraternity which encompassed all students at the College. Whatever student life was, it was conditioned by the Corps of Cadets; whatever Aggie traditions came to be, they were molded by the Corps of Cadets.

The Corps contributed singularly to making Texas A&M University of today a truly unique institution of higher learning. The Corps of Cadets cre-

[62]McMillan, "Reminiscences," in Cofer (ed.), *Fragments of Early History of Texas A. & M. College,* 78-89; Cofer (ed.), *Fragments of Early History of Texas A. & M. College,* 5-10.

[63]McMillan, "Reminiscences," in Cofer (ed.), *Fragments of Early History of Texas A. & M. College,* 78.

[64]*Ibid.,* 89.

ated a highly organized, responsive, cohesive, and generally well-led student body from the earliest days of the institution. This in itself marks a distinctive quality in A&M's development, in view of the fact that most student bodies have been and are disorganized, heterogeneous and usually unresponsive groupings. In the 1880s the Corps developed a respectability and stability that reflected the improved status of the College. Public regard for A&M improved measurably throughout the decade.

Governor John Ireland, addressing the Nineteenth Legislature on January 13, 1885, commented that Texas A&M College "has greatly improved in all its departments. The mechanical department is on a much larger and better scale than formerly; and so is the agricultural." Ireland advised that as a branch of The University, the College was entitled to appropriations out of the University funds. As for The University of Texas, then completing its second year of operation, Ireland had little to say, other than that he had left its management entirely up to the Board of Regents.[65]

In its early years The University of Texas experienced serious difficulties, as had the A&M College, not the least of which appeared to be a relative "coolness" from the Governor's Office. On September 15, 1883, at the opening ceremonies of The University, in Austin, while Governor Ireland had congratulated the people of Texas on the inauguration of The University and pledged his support to its success, he had at the same time charged the Regents with a "premature ceremony of bringing the university into being." The Galveston *Daily News* noted certain "misgivings in the tone of the governor's address."[66] For one thing, classes had opened in temporary quarters while the University facilities were being completed.

University faculty and officials in Austin received much the same kind of criticism that had on previous occasions been directed toward Texas A&M. Professors at The University were suspected of being infidels, drunkards, and gamblers.[67] In commenting on The University of Texas' first year of operation, H. H. Dinwiddie said: "The University people seem to be badly demoralized by the resignations of their bright men. They are down on the Governor. The [Austin] *"Statesman"* is raving mad. The name of Ireland sets it to foaming at the mouth and snapping like a mad dog."[68]

University discomfiture rose precipitously when Governor Ireland appointed Archibald J. Rose, grand master of the Texas Grange, to the Board

---

[65] *Governor's Messages, Coke to Ross, 1874-1891*, pp. 506-507.

[66] Galveston *Daily News*, September 17, 1883.

[67] *Ibid.*, September 29, 1884.

[68] H. H. Dinwiddie, Austin, Texas, to George Pfeuffer, New Braunfels, Texas, July 12, 1884, Pfeuffer Papers, Texas A&M University Archives.

of Regents of The University of Texas. Some people believed that the Grange, which had become professedly favorable to Texas A&M College, was now being arrayed against The University. While the cornerstone of The University was being laid, John J. Lane remarked, the Grange was engaged in a plan to steal the cornerstone of the University Fund.[69] Much of the so-called conflict between The University of Texas and the A&M College may have involved little more than petty bickering and professional jealousy. Yet some of it was deadly serious and much in earnest and involved allocations from the University Fund.

To be sure, Texas A&M's insistence upon appropriations from the University Fund at a time when that fund was extremely meager and when The University was struggling for survival added immeasurably to the woes of The University of Texas. From the point of view of the Regents any appropriations to A&M from the University Fund were made at the expense of the Main University.[70] Texas A&M officials, on the other hand, regarded the failure of the Regents to provide appropriations from the University Fund as destructive of an already well-established educational institution and as a flagrant violation of the constitutional mandate which made A&M a branch of The University.

None were so zealous in their efforts to promote the growth and development of the Agricultural and Mechanical College as was Senator George Pfeuffer, of New Braunfels. Pfeuffer, born October 17, 1830, in Obernbreit, Bavaria, was appointed to the A&M Board by Governor Oran M. Roberts in 1879. In 1883 he became chairman of the Board of Directors. As a director Pfeuffer played an active role in the affairs of the College and became a strong advocate of the mission of agricultural and mechanical training — and of public education generally.[71] In 1884 Pfeuffer became chairman of the important Senate Committee on Education. He hoped to devise a coordinated plan of education which would bring the common schools, the normal schools, and The University under one management with the hope of improving the efficiency and status of every aspect of education in Texas.[72] On January 20, 1885, Pfeuffer, by Senate resolution, formed the Committee on Education into an investigative committee to inspect the "conditions, affairs and wants of the State University."[73] On February 6 he introduced a bill to "Perfect the University of Texas."

[69]See John J. Lane, *History of the University of Texas,* 56, 70-71.

[70]*Ibid.*

[71]Benedict (ed.), *Source Book of the University of Texas,* 302, 318-336, 765-766.

[72]Galveston *Daily News,* January 14, 1884.

[73]Benedict (ed.), *Source Book of the University of Texas,* 318; *Texas Senate Journal, 1885,* p. 29.

In many respects the bill would formalize a somewhat nebulous situation in Texas higher education; in other respects the bill represented a substantial departure from existing procedure. The bill specified that The University of Texas, in Austin, the Agricultural and Mechanical College, in College Station, the medical branch, to be located in Galveston, and the colored branch, located in Austin, should all constitute The University of Texas. It proposed to place The University under the control of a University Board, made up of the State Board of Education, the superintendent of public instruction, and a chancellor to be chosen by the governor, with the consent of the Senate.

The existing Board of Regents comprised eight men appointed for eight-year terms. Pfeuffer and Governor Ireland argued that the Constitution limited the term of public offices to two years, unless otherwise specified. The term of office granted to the Regents was therefore unconstitutional. Pfeuffer argued that the Board which he devised, composed mostly of elected officials, would be more responsive to the public, and would be in accord with the Constitution.[74]

The proposed chancellor of The University, according to Pfeuffer's bill, would be president of the faculty; the governor of the state would be president of the University Board. The Board would have essentially the same powers that had been set forth in the original organization bill of 1881. Pfeuffer's bill prescribed a maximum tuition fee of thirty dollars for The University and prescribed the method of disbursing and accounting for University funds. Furthermore, appropriations to the different institutions from the University Fund would be specifically made by the Legislature and not by the Regents. The old law made appropriations to The University in bulk (A&M appropriations were itemized) and gave the Board of Regents authority to expend the funds in such manners as they desired, without the necessity of a detailed accounting to the Legislature. Pfueffer's bill also provided that law schools and medical schools should be self-supporting, and that tuition fees (not limited by the thirty-dollar maximum) should cover operating costs. Pfeuffer reasoned that the state had no immediate obligation to train doctors and lawyers, who were ordinarily better able to pay their own expenses, especially when the general students in the Main University were in need of greater financial support. The bill proposed to set the chancellor's salary at

---

[74]"A Bill to be Entitled an Act to Perfect the University of Texas," George Pfeuffer Papers, Texas A&M University Archives; Benedict (ed), *Source Book of the University of Texas,* 318-336; see also "An Act to Establish the University of Texas," Gammel (ed.), *Laws of Texas,* IX, 171-175; *Texas Senate Journal, 1885,* pp. 10, 93, 321.

$5,500, salaries for three professors at $2,200 each, for two professors at $2,000 each, and for one male and one female graduate assistant at $1,000 each. At the time of the proposal the thirteen faculty members of The University, consisting of seven professors, three associate professors, and three instructors, earned an average salary of $2,969. Full professors averaged $3,857 per year. Pfeuffer's bill would drastically cut University faculty salaries to a level approximating those at Texas A&M and would give control over salaries to the Legislature rather than to the Regents. As might be imagined, this provision raised loud protests from University personnel. Pfeuffer's personal dislike of the "fancy prices paid for salaries" at The University[75] seems to have been a fairly common sentiment throughout the state. There was also common objection to the fact that many of the University faculty were "imported," as indeed, had been the case with many of the A&M faculty.[76]

The most novel and interesting aspects of Pfeuffer's bill involved provisions for entrance examinations to The University, and a system of auxiliary professors to act as principals in high schools established or to be established in each of the eleven congressional districts. It was envisioned that these high schools would provide preparatory training for students planning to attend The University. Pfeuffer argued that "it is well known that the grade of scholarship established by the authorities of the University . . . is below the high school grade." The University had become, he said, "a high school in the midst of high schools." He argued that a system of preparatory schools, supervised by The University itself, would be able to help establish a high grade of scholarship in The University.[77] In many respects this aspect of Pfeuffer's proposal reflected the then very advanced educational reforms which Prince Otto von Bismark had instituted in Germany in the 1870s. Pfeuffer's proposed reforms, not coincidentally, reflected the views of Governor John Ireland.[78] While acknowledging the "close friendship" of Governor Ireland, Pfeuffer avowed that the Governor had nothing to do with the measures in his bill, and said the Governor had "neither framed them, dictated them, nor suggested them."[79]

[75]Benedict (ed.), *Source Book of the University of Texas*, 318-336.

[76]See Louis L. McInnis Scrapbook, pp. 43-49; and H. H. Dinwiddie, College Station, Texas, to Louis L. McInnis, Paterson, New Jersey, August 20, 1882, Louis L. McInnis Papers, Texas A&M University Archives.

[77]"A Bill to be Entitled an Act to Perfect the University of Texas," George Pfeuffer Papers, Texas A&M University Archives; Benedict (ed.), *Source Book of the University of Texas*, 318-336.

[78]Lane, *History of the University of Texas*, 13-14.

[79]*Ibid.*, 17-18; Benedict (ed.), *Source Book of the University of Texas*, 336.

Pfeuffer's proposals precipitated bitter attacks upon the bill, Pfeuffer, the Governor, and the A&M College. University partisans argued vehemently that Pfeuffer was trying to "destroy The University." In almost every issue of the Austin *Statesman* from February 7, 1885, through March 20, editorials attacked Pfeuffer's proposals for The University. His bill, said the *Statesman,* was a "barefaced proposal to destroy." Endorsing the management and the excellence of the University of Virginia, the editor went on to say, "But Virginia has no Pfeuffer; and it has no Ireland; no designing, sneaking pedagogues jealous of its university's greatness." Citing the Gonzales *Inquirer,* the newspaper referred to Pfeuffer as the "mouthpiece of Governor Ireland." Charging that Pfeuffer and the supporters of his bill were vandals, the editors concluded that it was fortunate that "the race of vandals in Texas is weak in number as well as in intellect." The editor of the *Statesman* said that "Evidently the authors of the Pfeuffer bill had no conception of what a first-class university is. Ignorance and opposition to higher education were the motives underlying the attempt to destroy our university." The Austin *Statesman* lamented the proposed salary cut of professors. Such reductions, it was believed, would prevent The University from attracting and holding top-quality professors. The greatness of that university should be developed. Professors at The Johns Hopkins University, reported the editors, received $5,000 each, while the president there was paid $10,000. The *Statesman* opposed placing a ceiling on tuition at thirty dollars, and favored continuing the system of free tuition. It opposed abolishing salary support for the law and medical professors and abhorred instituting the German "gymnasia" feature of the Pfeuffer bill, noting that the excellent system of sectarian colleges functioned in the capacity in which Pfeuffer's proposed high schools were to function.[80]

Why, questioned the Austin *Statesman,* should the A&M College Board be retained while the Regents were dissolved? "If A&M is really a branch why not turn it over to university management?" In commenting on the Texas A&M *Biennial Report* of 1885, the editors demanded to know why A&M thought it should be entitled to one-third of the revenues from the University Fund? It was at best, charged the *Statesman,* only one of five branches of The University. Pressing the attack, perhaps a bit too hard, the Austin journal announced that A&M had just received a windfall of $35,000 from back revenue due on United States bonds. Perhaps, chided the editors, the A&M College could now lend The University some money. Pfeuffer publicly rejected the announcement of an A&M "Bonanza," and pressed for

[80]Austin *Statesman,* February 7, 10, 11, 12, 17, 22, 26, 28, March 4, 6, 19, and 20, 1885.

an explanation. The Austin *Statesman* revealed two days later that it referred to the fact that, because the state of Texas had defaulted on payment of interest on the original bonds purchased with the funds derived from the sale of federal lands under the Morrill Act, the state had funded the interest and added it to the original $174,000 investment, making the total bonded endowment of the A&M College, $209,000; thus, said the *Statesman,* the A&M College received a $35,000 "bonanza," but for good measure the *Statesman* added that since the bonds involved were selling at a premium of twenty percent, therefore the "bonanza" really amounted to $42,000.[81]

The attack on A&M College financing stemmed in part from the introduction of a bill in the House of Representatives by House member William R. Cavitt of Bryan, whom Governor Ireland had appointed to the A&M Board of Directors in September 1883, to replace Judge James Thomas upon his resignation following Cole's removal from the presidency of the College.[82] Cavitt's bill called for the appropriation of $10,000 from the General Fund and $5,000 from the University Fund to the A&M College for each of the next two fiscal years.[83] Thus The University seemed to be under attack in the House, in the Senate, and from the Executive Office. The Galveston *News* joined in the fray by reporting from various sources that the A&M College was "the most ancient nuisance we had in the state," that none of its graduates could handle a plow or work a hoe, that its "boys were taught to curse mules in four languages," and that the College was like a pig's tail, "more ornamental than useful."[84]

Senator Rudolph Kleberg introduced a bill to give the Regents authority to regulate the lease arrangement of University lands. The bill received strong support from the Austin *Statesman* and succeeded in passing the Senate by a vote of 13-10, with four senators not voting; but it failed of passage in the House.[85] Pfeuffer's bill never got so far; it passed on the first reading in the House but was never successfully called for a final vote. It died in committee, but, according to the *Statesman,* it had already greatly damaged The University's prosperity.[86]

In a sense, perhaps, Pfeuffer's bill had been of some effect, despite its

[81]*Ibid.,* February 10, 17, 26, and 18, 1885.

[82]*Ibid.,* February 22, 1885; Governor John Ireland, Austin, Texas, to George Pfeuffer, Austin, Texas, September 11, 1883, George Pfeuffer Papers, Texas A&M University Archives.

[83]Austin *Statesman,* February 22, 1885.

[84]Clippings from Galveston *Daily News,* McInnis Scrapbook, 19, Louis L. McInnis Papers, Texas A&M University Archives.

[85]*Texas Senate Journal, 1885,* pp. 2, 202, 319; Austin *Statesman,* March 6, 1885.

[86]Austin *Statesman,* March 6, 1885.

failure to pass. The introduction of the bill, combined with the investigations of The University by the Committee on Education, plus the substantial publicity about University affairs in the newspapers around the state, made The University somewhat vulnerable. As George Pfeuffer wrote to Louis McInnis, secretary of the A&M Board of Directors, on February 20, 1885, "University fellows. are ready to make any and all concessions to A&M."[87] Perhaps one of the concessions made was an agreement to support passage of Cavitt's amended A&M appropriations bill, provided the Pfeuffer bill was allowed to die. The A&M College received $10,000 from the General Revenue Fund of the state and $5,000 from the University Fund, for each of the two fiscal years beginning March 1, 1885, and ending February 28, 1887.[88] In view of the controversy over the allocation of the University Fund, the appropriation bill set an important precedent in reinforcing the Agricultural and Mechanical College's claims to a share of the Fund. How great the share should be remained a question in great dispute.

There was yet a significant epilogue to the legislative battles between The University and the College. On March 31, 1885, in the closing days of the legislative sessions, Senator Pfeuffer rose to a question of privilege and addressed the Legislature. "The Senate knows," he said, "to what I have been subjected in the public print. . . . I desire to be heard to respond to a mischievous, selfish, and venal press that has persistently misrepresented me."[89] In remarks which consumed several hours, Pfeuffer replied to his critics, explained his bill and its intent, step by step, and rejected accusations that he had had any intention other than to build a greater University. His prefatory remarks help explain the man, his mission, and his conception of higher education and of training in the Agricultural and Mechanical College. Pfeuffer's statements and actions comprise an important aspect of the history of educational development in Texas:

I claim the right in these last hours of this session, when it may no longer be urged that I am in debate by an insidious move on questions for legislation, to reply to charges that, as stated, have been made in a thousand forms — misrepresentations that each day assume new phases.

I was made chairman of the committee of education of this session of the legislature. For some years past I have been one of the Directors of the A&M College, located at Bryan. I have felt a profound interest in the success of that institu-

[87]George Pfeuffer, Austin, Texas, to Louis L. McInnis, College Station, Texas, February 20, 1885, Louis L. McInnis Papers, Texas A&M University Archives.

[88]Gammel (ed.), *Laws of Texas,* IX, 741-742.

[89]*Texas Senate Journal, 1885,* pp. 303-308; Benedict (ed.), *Source Book of the University of Texas,* 318-336.

tion. This Legislature had scarcely met when we heard words of ridicule addressed against the A. and M. College, and derisive sneers at its efforts, and suggestions that it be abandoned as an educational institution and be converted into an asylum. These enemies of the A. and M. College thought that it was inimical to the State University at Austin. The A. and M. College had friends. There were those amongst us who believed it was an institution that should receive the first care of the State. We may have been of opinion that the class of our youth that the A. and M. College proposed to cultivate was as important to the State, and would, when leaving that institution, be worth as much for her prosperity as urbane scholars versed in the languages of Greece and Rome, or proficient in the soft tongues of Spain and Italy, the brilliant language of France, or the stately manliness of the language of my fatherland.

There were some who thought that the schools where the farmer's sons were taught the nature of soils, the chemistry of crops, were as important as the schools in which metaphysical jargon is heard in wrangling from morning to night. There were some who thought that sound instruction in the history of domestic animals, a knowledge in the capacities of their different breeds, their adaptability to our climate, their diseases and remedies and best modes of rearing, their anatomical structure, and everything necessary for their successful management, was as useful as the pleasing science of entomology that may expand itself in volumes on the anatomy of the carrion beetle, or tremendous discussions unfolding the purpose the housefly or the swamp gallinipper [may] serve as assistants in hygiene in our kitchens and around our poisonous lagoons.

There were some of us who had these thoughts relating to the relative utility of the two classes of what is termed higher education, the one looking to grain producers on our farms and ranches, the other as supplying material from which the bench and the bar, the pulpit, the medical corps, are recruited, and from which, also, come the vast herd of idlers that is too highly cultivated to work in manual labor, and too worthless to follow out in any line for which their education may fit them to be useful as members of society.

We think we may be pardoned for holding in importance the science which teaches our youth to look to the earth and inspect its soils, and discern the hidden powers of nature that, when applied, will make teeming crops and an abundant yield. We may be pardoned if we think this science equal in dignity and equally useful with the science that would consult the stars and the planets, and endeavor to determine their occult influences — influences which, if discovered, could never be controlled. It may be discovered that spots on the sun control vegetation, and the phases of the moon regulate the tides and the weather, but it is beyond the powers of man to regulate these awful influences. Metaphysical wranglers may worry their minds over innate ideas, questions of time and space, or even the calculation of number of angels that might dance upon a needle point. The practical knowledge of one's own self, as each man may discover, and an analysis of and knowledge as it grows with us, and a knowledge of things that are actual around us, are as worthy of thought as these questions of the schoolman. It is as important and dignified to know how to stretch and preserve the skins of cattle slaughtered with the knife, as to be able to kill the ephemeral butterfly with chloroform and preserve it with arsenic, packed away in a show case, with a Greek name in polysyllables pinned on its back, doing the honors of an epitaph and biography, offered as an atonement for its poor little life, that was taken for science's sake by some murderous crazy bug hunter.

There were those who thought the studies of the proper application of the pulley, the lever, the wedge and wheel and axle, to aid the powers of man's feeble muscles, and the principles of machines that assist to make work easy and redeem men, women and children from a life of toil, were quite as important and dignified as the study of the mechanics of the solar system, or as the dreams of the fanciers, who imagine in their reveries that they hear the music of spheres. There are even those who thought that the culture and development of an actual, real first-class taurus, a regular bull, that could paw the earth and bellow with no uncertain sound and whose prowess could be seen and whose future progeny could be contemplated with pride, was a study as dignified, as refined, and perhaps as useful, as the study of the prowess of the Centaur, the ferociousness of the three-headed dog Cerberus, the hideousness of the Lernean Hydra, or Jupiter, in the form of a bull, when he eloped with Europa, or the white bull that was loved by the unchaste Pasiphae, or Minotarus, their dreadful offspring. The one who has been so greatly decried as the hero of the Agricultural and Mechanical College farm is the actual bull for the farm for actual use. He is in every sense of the term fit socially to move in the society in which he belongs. The others, as the monsters and bulls of classic readings, are for the dreamers in mythology, and serve for raising ideas and images that are horrible and unchaste beyond description. But enough of these comparisons. In practical life and practical work there are no useless, senseless humbugs. In the pastimes of science, literature and art, there are thousands of things that the world were better had they never been, but being, if they were forgotten.

But, in thus contrasting much that is embraced in polite learning with the useful and practical knowledge needed in everyday life, let it not be understood that those, who gave dignity and importance to that which is useful to the masses, decried or tried to lower the proper dignity of higher education in literature, science and arts. While there is much of chaff in the ordinary so-called higher education, its aims, objects and effects on society in its enjoyments, its government, its strength and prosperity are all important. The mistake that has been made is by the zealous friends of higher education that treats of the polite branches. They have lost track of the usefulness of the branches that should be taught to the masses in agriculture and mechanics, and in kindred pursuits.

Because there were those who would not ignore the necessity that the State should endow with lavish hands the institute that looked to the enlightment of the masses in their ordinary pursuits, they were pronounced enemies of higher education — enemies of the great State University! Never was a more unjust charge uttered; never was there a party more grossly misrepresented. The importance and dignity of both classes of education were fully appreciated. It was to distribute the revenues provided for education to all these subjects, and to foster all the institutions that were to make people more enlightened, prosperous and happy, that influenced common school establishments that my name has been coupled with, much said to my detriment, and unjustly, as misunderstanding my sentiments and misrepresenting both my opinions and the measures proposed by me for legislation.[90]

Pfeuffer's address is an epilogue to the conflict between the classicists and the advocates of technical training. Though the goals and methods remained somewhat obscure, the future of educational development in Texas was more clearly defined by George Pfeuffer, whom one might characterize as "the bull of New Braunfels."

[90]*Texas Senate Journal, 1885*, pp. 303-308.

CHAPTER 6

Transition and Progress, 1885-1887

THE battle between The University of Texas and the Agricultural and Mechanical College in 1885 was productive of some good. Thoughtful individuals began to sense the futility and the danger of institutional confrontation. Moderate elements began to press for cooperation rather than conflict. By 1887 the first real attempts at coexistence were being made. Elements of discord remained, but overall a marked improvement in institutional relationships, and in the status of higher education in Texas in general, resulted. Former A&M President John G. James, who had helped frame the organizational structure of The University of Texas, wrote in April 1885, "I have been interested in the legislative fight between the College and University, and was sorry to see it, as I fear it will do neither any good."[1] James and others continued to believe that the College and The University should be operated by the same board.[2] Most importantly they deprecated the continuance of hostility between the branches of The University. This rather widespread sentiment helped promote a degree of accord, or at least of restraint, with partisans on both sides.

The various academic interests retired from the battle to dress their wounds, nurse their grievances, and attend their own special affairs. One hundred and thirteen students completed their year's studies at A&M in June 1885.[3] Students and faculty disappeared for the summer. Those who remained took refuge in their homes from the summer heat and dust, stirring about no more frequently or vigorously than the somnolent and shy horned frogs, which shaded themselves from the sun beneath a browning leaf or a hardening clod of dirt.

[1]John G. James, Wichita Falls, Texas, to Louis L. McInnis, College Station, Texas, April 18, 1885, Louis L. McInnis Papers, Texas A&M University Archives.

[2]*Ibid.*

[3]Texas A&M, *Annual Report, 1885*, p. 10.

The entire A&M faculty of eight returned to resume their teaching duties for the opening of the fall term on September 7, 1885. Student enrollment rose to a healthy 141; one student came from Mississippi.[4] By the end of the year enrollment reached 145 students, of whom 37 (25.5 percent) were enrolled in the agricultural course and 108 (74.5 percent) were enrolled in the mechanical course.[5] Students of the A&M College from 1881 to date, with the exception of a very few years, have been preponderately in the engineering curricula. The epithet "Farmers," applied to A&M students in the earlier years, and "Aggies," applied in more contemporary times, have been misnomers in that they have inaccurately identified agriculture as the normal endeavor of the Texas A&M student. But whether in agriculture or engineering, the A&M College student of 1885 followed a course of instruction unique to most American colleges and universities. Agricultural and mechanical colleges generally and the Texas Agricultural and Mechanical College had found the way to the "new idea of collegiate instruction."[6]

The educational scheme of the American agricultural and mechanical colleges ranged from the classical to the manual-labor industrial course.[7] Texas A&M had itself covered that broad spectrum in its brief existence, but now, according to the 1884-1885 catalogue, radical changes had occurred at Texas A&M in the past four years.[8] Just what changes had taken place were not clearly explained. There were allusions to "intelligent labor," "trained young men," "observation and experiment," and "pursuits by which the material development of the country is advanced." It was obvious, however, that the College officials believed that the College had now found itself, and that it was neither a classical nor an industrial school, but a school which applied scientific principles to farm and industrial production.[9]

The college year, which began auspiciously, was soon disrupted by a faculty squabble growing out of a disagreement between the professor of mathematics, Louis L. McInnis, and the chairman of the faculty, Hardaway Hunt Dinwiddie. McInnis wanted Lieutenant John S. Mallory, commandant of cadets, to be assigned as a part-time instructor in mathematics. Dinwiddie believed that Mallory's services were more urgently required in other depart-

[4]Texas A&M, *Catalogue, 1885-1886*, p. 28.

[5]Statement on "Enrollment at Texas A&M," prepared by the Institutional Self-Study Committee on Purpose of the College, 1962; see also College Station *Longhorn, 1908*, p. 148.

[6]See *1876 . . . 1926, The Semi-Centennial Celebration of the Agricultural and Mechanical College of Texas*, 15, 35-63, 81-98.

[7]Texas A&M, *Catalogue, 1884-1885*, p. 7.

[8]*Ibid.*

[9]*Ibid.*, 7-8.

ments. McInnis, familiar with the Board members by virtue of his position as secretary of the Board, appealed individually to each Board member. Without exception the members wrote to George Pfeuffer, president of the Board, supporting McInnis, rather than the chairman of the faculty. The argument soon cooled, in part because Director James G. Garrison reminded the faculty of the foolishness and danger of faculty bickering. "The fierce spirit of rivalry and disorder will soon wrench the Institution. The correspondence submitted shows the existence of this spirit and I sincerely deprecate it," Garrison wrote to Pfeuffer.[10]

The argument soon quieted and the College finished its most successful year to date, reported the Board of Directors at the commencement sessions between May 31 and June 3, 1886.

> We are gratified to be able to report that the academic session just closed has been one of the most successful and satisfactory of any since the opening of the College.
>
> The attendance was up to the limit of accommodation for students, and their scholarly deportment and manly bearing has been cause of remark and congratulations of all those having opportunity to observe and learn the facts.
>
> The Chairman of the Faculty, the several Professors and their assistants have faithfully and efficiently discharged the trust conferred upon them, as evidenced by the advancement of students under their instruction and care.[11]

Twelve students graduated; three of these completed the three-year course in agriculture and nine completed the three-year mechanical course. All were awarded certificates of completion rather than degrees. Former students of the institution met during the commencement exercises and initiated plans for the formal organization of an Alumni Association. A proposed constitution for the association was prepared at this time, and formally accepted at the first Alumni Association meeting in June 1887.[12]

The Board of Directors proposed for the faculty salary raises which would make A&M salaries commensurate with faculty salaries at The Univer-

[10]Louis L. McInnis, College Station, Texas, to Hardaway H. Dinwiddie, College Station, Texas, October 28, 1885; Hardaway H. Dinwiddie to Louis L. McInnis, College Station, Texas, October 28, 1885; Louis L. McInnis to George Pfeuffer, New Braunfels, Texas, October 19, 1885; George M. Dilly, Palestine, Texas, to George Pfeuffer, Austin, Texas, November 9, 1885; James G. Garrison, Tyler, Texas, to George Pfeuffer, New Braunfels, Texas, November 12, 1885; Thomas M. Scott, Melissa, Texas, to George Pfeuffer, New Braunfels, Texas, November 16, 1885; George Pfeuffer Papers, Texas A&M University Archives.

[11]Minutes of the Board of Directors, May 31, 1885, I, 5.

[12]*Ibid.,* 1-2; "F. E. Giesecke," F. E. Giesecke Biographical Papers, Texas A&M University Archives; Minutes of the Board of Directors, May 31, June 3, 1886, I, 5-8.

sity of Texas. While the increases fell considerably short of this goal, the new salary schedule was appreciated by the faculty. Under the new schedule the salaries of full professors at A&M were set at $2,000 for nine months (with no summer employment), plus College-provided housing, compared to average salaries of $2,969 for University of Texas professors who provided their own housing. The chairman of the faculty received an extra $400 and the secretary and College treasurer, Louis L. McInnis, an additional $200. Salaries for assistant professors ranged from $450 to $675 for nine months.[13]

George W. Curtis, for reasons unascertained, resigned as professor of agriculture on June 4. The Directors authorized the president of the Board of Directors, George Pfeuffer, personally to visit various agricultural colleges for the purpose of employing a replacement for Curtis. Dinwiddie advised Pfeuffer to go to Starkville, Mississippi, and make every effort to "steal Professor [Frank Arthur] Gulley from the A. & M. C. [there]. If he is not to be stolen, he will be most likely to advise you as to further proceedings." Although Gulley later came to Texas A&M as director of the Agriculture Experiment Station, he did not come in 1886, and the College almost began a new academic year without a professor of agriculture. George W. Curtis, however, now decided to remain with Texas A&M, and on October 6, 1886, the Board elected Curtis professor of agriculture and horticulture to fill his old seat. At this same meeting the Directors gave Curtis full control over the Farm, including the orchard.[14] It may be deduced that Curtis' original resignation was prompted by a conflict over operation of the Farm. An administrative conflict over farming operations plagued the College from the very earliest days, when Carlisle Martin served as professor of agriculture, until farming operations by the College were substantially curtailed in 1912. By then A&M sponsored an expanding system of agricultural experiment stations, which often duplicated the crop work attempted by the School of Agriculture at College Station.

The Board concluded the 1885-1886 academic year by inviting the governor to appoint a board of visitors from the Legislature to investigate the College. The Directors also recommended the development of a six-acre poultry yard on the campus, and in final action they endorsed a plan for academic reorganization submitted to them by Louis L. McInnis, professor of mathematics and secretary to the Board. In a previous meeting the Board had invited faculty members to submit suggestions for restructuring the College curricula. Of all the recommendations received only those submitted by

[13]*Ibid.*

[14]Minutes of the Board of Directors, October 6, 1886, I, 18-19.

McInnis were entered into the record.[15] His suggestions are important in several respects: (1) they indicate the prevailing academic situation; (2) they indicate the direction in which the College was moving; and (3) finally, and most significantly, Louis L. McInnis soon became chairman of the faculty, and used his position to implement such broad reforms in academic structure and policy as he had recommended in his earlier suggestions.

McInnis observed that students entering the A&M College were usually very deficient in preparation for college work. Admission standards remained low, if not virtually nonexistent. The three-year curricula then in force in the College failed to fully qualify graduates for college degrees. McInnis recommended that the course of study be changed back from three to four years, as it had been in the years of Gathright's administration. He suggested, too, that the first-year course, which was in practice a preparatory course, be recognized as such, and that the course of study for all first-year students be the same. He also advised that a fund be established for paying students for practical work in agriculture. The basic course for all first-year students, and the pay provision for farm labor, would help expand student interest and participation in the agricultural course, which still lagged far behind the mechanical course. McInnis also argued that the Departments of Agriculture and Mechanics both lacked adequate funds and that classical studies still received a preponderance of allocations. He advised expanding appropriations to Agriculture and Mechanics, even to the point of surrendering appropriations from his own Department of Mathematics. The Board took cognizance of McInnis' proposals, but no action on them.[16]

The faculty of eight was enlarged by the addition of four new assistant professors for the opening of the fall term on September 6, 1886. Frederick Ernst Giesecke joined the faculty as assistant professor of mechanics. William Bledsoe Philpott was elected as assistant professor of English; Duncan Adriance received appointment as assistant professor of agriculture and horticulture, and Walter Wipprecht, the son of Rudolph Wipprecht, the professor of ancient and modern languages, joined the faculty as assistant professor of chemistry and physics. Giesecke, Philpott, Adriance, and Wipprecht were all recent graduates of Texas A&M. Giesecke, who was to play a prominent role in the development of the College of Engineering and in the actual physical expansion of A&M, was born at Latium, Texas, near Brenham, on January 28, 1869. He was reared in New Braunfels. He served as cadet captain his senior year and graduated at the head of his class. Now seventeen years old,

---

[15]*Ibid.*, I, 9-10.
[16]*Ibid.*

he was appointed assistant professor at a salary of $50 per month plus room and board. By the time he was nineteen he had become head of his own Department of Mechanical Drawing and had authored a number of mechanical drawing texts which were used well into the twentieth century.[17] Giesecke, Philpott, Adriance, and Wipprecht all remained on the Texas A&M scene for many years and made significant contributions to the development of the College.

The fall session of 1886 opened with 134 students, of whom 39 enrolled in agriculture and 95 in the engineering courses. By the end of the second term, enrollment had risen to 176 students.[18] McInnis wrote to Pfeuffer on the first day of the fall term, noting that some of the professors were still not on hand, and that the school "would be full" by the end of the week.[19] Bernard Sbisa, the steward, also wrote to Pfeuffer on that day explaining that the poultry yard had not yet been completed because of the failure to receive lumber and supplies that had been ordered. He also reported that he had made 421 pounds of butter, and had canned fruits and jams for the mess hall during the summer. He needed $798.80 more, he said, to complete the poultry yard, and would like to have facilities for making cheese.[20] Pfeuffer never replied or visited the campus again. George Pfeuffer died suddenly in Austin on September 15, 1886.[21] Memorializing Pfeuffer, Governor John Ireland told the Legislature in January, "In the demise of such a man the country lost a valuable citizen and the college a most zealous and efficient supporter."[22]

Governor Ireland appointed Christopher C. Garrett to fill the vacancy left by Pfeuffer. The Board convened on October 5, memorialized Pfeuffer, and elected William R. Cavitt of Bryan as the new president.[23] Pfeuffer's death removed one obstacle to a reconciliation between Texas A&M and The University of Texas, for in December 1886, the Board of Directors requested

[17]Charles W. Crawford, "F. E. Giesecke, Engineer, Scholar, Gentleman," address delivered May 25, 1934, before the Texas Chapter, American Association of Heating and Ventilating Engineers, F. E. Giesecke Biographical Papers, Texas A&M University Archives.

[18]Statement on "Enrollment at Texas A&M," prepared by the Institutional Self-Study Committee on Purpose of the College, 1962; Texas A&M, *Catalogue, 1886-1887*, p. 65.

[19]Louis L. McInnis, College Station, Texas, to George Pfeuffer, Wootanville, Texas, September 6, 1886, George Pfeuffer Papers, Texas A&M University Archives.

[20]Bernard Sbisa, College Station, Texas, to George Pfeuffer, New Braunfels, Texas, September 6, 1886, George Pfeuffer Papers, Texas A&M University Archives.

[21]Texas A&M, *Catalogue, 1886-1887*, p. 12. Note: the Minutes of the Board of Directors, I, 16, give Pfeuffer's correct date of death as September 15, *vice* September 16, noted in the *Catalogue*.

[22]*Texas Senate Journal*, 1887, p. 19.

[23]Minutes of the Board of Directors, I, 16-17.

its secretary, Louis L. McInnis, to write to Alexander Penn Wooldridge, secretary of the Board of Regents of The University of Texas (and later Mayor of Austin) seeking a joint meeting of representatives of the Board of Directors with representatives of the Board of Regents to discuss mutual interests. Wooldridge replied to McInnis, suggesting a meeting of the chairman of the A&M Board, William R. Cavitt, with the Regents on January 20, 1887. Wooldridge believed that such a meeting would be "productive of much good to all parties."[24] Thus in December 1886 initial steps were being taken to end the "battle of the universities."

The new year, however, seemingly brought an intensification rather than a diminishing of the conflict between The University of Texas and the Agricultural and Mechanical College. The renewed contest was provoked by the convening of the Twentieth Legislature in Austin in January 1887. The Legislature held the financial key to the future of both institutions. The Directors of the A&M College met on January 3, in College Station, to begin planning their strategy for the legislative session. They agreed to reconvene in Austin on January 20.[25] On January 11 retiring Governor John Ireland, who had been a good friend of the A&M College, made his farewell address to the Legislature. In commenting on A&M, Ireland said, "I am glad to be able to announce that this institution is in a most flourishing condition, and that it has been brought to something like that high standard intended by its founders."[26] He recommended that a "Board of Visitors" from the Legislature visit the College and report its findings to the Legislature and to the public. "The sons of the farmers and mechanics," he said, "are reaping a rich harvest from this school."[27]

Ireland was succeeded in office by Lawrence Sullivan Ross, one of the most colorful governors in Texas history, and a man destined to play a decisive role in the affairs of the Agricultural and Mechanical College, as its president from 1891 through 1898. Ross was born at Bentonsport, Iowa, on September 27, 1838. His father became Indian agent for the Republic of Texas at Waco, in 1839. Ross received his education at Wesleyan College in Alabama and came home to Texas to fight Indians. Governor Sam Houston put the "boy captain" in command of frontier forces in 1859. Ross became one of the most famous Indian fighters in the Southwest in his battles with the Comanches.

---

[24]A. P. Wooldridge, Austin, Texas, to Louis L. McInnis, College Station, Texas, December 21, 1886, Louis L. McInnis Papers, Texas A&M University Archives.

[25]Minutes of the Board of Directors, I, 20.

[26]*Governor's Messages, Coke to Ross, 1874-1891*, pp. 544-545; *Texas Senate Journal, 1887*, p. 19.

[27]*Ibid.*

In one famous engagement Ross met Comanche Chief Peta Nocona and killed him in personal combat, and rescued Cynthia Ann Parker, a white woman who had been living as a captive of the Comanches for thirty years. Ross enlisted as a private in the Confederate army in 1862 and rose to the rank of brigadier general, distinguishing himself in battle at Corinth, Mississippi, where he won the title "Hero of Corinth." He became a planter after the War and owned a small plantation along the Brazos River. In 1881 he won election to the state Senate, and in 1886 won the Democratic Party nomination and election as governor. He was re-elected governor in 1888.[28]

Ross had his first association with the A&M College on January 20, 1887, when he met briefly with the Directors in his offices in Austin. After meeting with the Governor, the Directors withdrew and continued their meeting. There is no indication that Cavitt met with the Regents of The University of Texas on that day, as suggested by the exchange of correspondence between McInnis and Wooldridge, but on the following day the Directors appointed a special committee of three to confer with a committee representing the Regents for the purpose of agreeing upon the amount to be appropriated to Texas A&M from the University Fund. Thomas M. Scott, formerly a member of the Board of Directors who had been named agent of the Board to replace William P. Hardemann on January 3, George M. Dilley, who had been named an A&M director by Governor Ireland in 1884, and Louis L. McInnis, professor and secretary to the Board, comprised the committee. The committee went to see the chairman of the Board of Regents, Thomas Dudley Wooten, to arrange for a conference. The Regents subsequently agreed to confer with the A&M committee, with the understanding that *no* University funds would be allocated to A&M, which action effectively aborted the conference.[29]

The Directors then concluded their Austin meeting by approving the reports of the faculty, the chairman of the faculty, the agent of the Board, the secretary, and the treasurer.[30] These reports and other information were combined into the *Biennial Report* of the College covering the period from January 1885 to January 1887. The *Biennial Report* noted among other things that A&M had cost the state an average of only $14,163.04 per year for the past two years. The *Report* also contained the statement that the Regents of The University of Texas had two plans for Texas A&M. One plan was to amend

[28]*Governor's Messages, Coke to Ross, 1874-1891*, pp. 555-556.

[29]Minutes of the Board of Directors, I, 20-21; newspaper clipping signed by W. R. Cavitt, undated, Louis L. McInnis Scrapbook, Louis L. McInnis Papers, Texas A&M University Archives.

[30]Minutes of the Board of Directors, I, 21.

the Constitution so as to sever A&M from The University (and from the University Fund) and make it completely dependent upon the federal endowment and upon legislative appropriations. The second plan was to give direct control of the College to the Regents. Either plan, reported Director Cavitt, would destroy the College.[31] Recognizing what they regarded as the intractable position of the Regents regarding the University Fund, A&M College supporters began mustering public and legislative support for its claims to a share of the University Fund. By the end of January, the battle had been rejoined. Archibald J. Rose, grand master of the Texas State Grange, released a letter to the press addressed to "The Patrons of Husbandry, Farmers, Mechanics, and all interested — Greeting:"

> The [A&M College] is a branch of the University, and represents two of the most important branches of the institution, Agriculture and Mechanics. It is upon these rests the success of every other calling or vocation of man; hence the College should receive at least two-fifths of the University fund annually.[32]

Rose's communication noted that despite the efforts of the A&M Directors, the Regents refused to deal with them. There would be an effort in this legislative session, he said, to put A&M under the Regents, and to appropriate the entire University Fund to the exclusive use and benefit of The University. Rose called attention to the resolution of the Texas State Grange at Waxahachie on August 1, 1885, seeking an amendment to the Constitution which would set aside one-third of the University Fund for the exclusive use of the A&M College.[33] He also referred to a meeting of the State Grange at Marshall in August 1886, when the Grange called for a "fair and equitable division" of the University Fund. Rose cited the "five divisions" of The University as being the literary, medical, legal, agricultural, and mechanical branches. Because A&M represented two of the five departments (and the most important two, said Rose), it should receive no less than two-fifths of the state endowment for higher education. Rose urged farmers and friends of the College to write to their legislators.[34] In reply to Rose's letter, the Austin *Statesman* charged the friends of the A&M College with being "indiscreet in claiming so much for it."[35]

The Galveston *News*, frequently critical of affairs at A&M, had now

[31]Texas A&M, *Biennial Report, January 1885-January 1887*, pp. 1-7, 26-63.

[32]Published letters signed by A. J. Rose, February 2, 1887, McInnis Scrapbook, Texas A&M University Archives; see also Austin *Statesman*, February 13, 1887.

[33]*Ibid.*

[34]*Ibid.*

[35]Austin *Statesman*, February 13, 1887.

become disillusioned with The University as well, largely because of the failure of the Regents to fund the Medical Branch, to be founded in Galveston. The *News* commented:

> The usual fight between the Agricultural and Mechanical College and The University has begun. The college has opened the war by asking for one third of the University Fund. The members of the legislature are becoming tired of this continued warfare, and have come to the conclusion that the two institutions only rival each other in the extravagance of their expenditures.[36]

Pressure, in fact, began to develop from the Executive Office and within the Legislature to force an agreement between A&M and The University of Texas.[37]

Meanwhile the Legislature was busy considering a host of bills, with widely varying contents, affecting the College and The University. As usual, and pursuant to its deliberations, the Legislature sent a Joint Investigating Committee to College Station. Representative William P. Page raised a question in the Legislature regarding the recent discharge of William P. Hardemann as agent of the College and his replacement by Thomas M. Scott. The investigative committee was directed to look into the matter. Although Hardemann had protested his discharge as agent of the Board, the Joint Committee report found that the Directors had full authority to act, and that nothing in the situation reflected discredit upon either party. The Committee also found that the College had 200 acres of land under cultivation (it had been criticized in 1885 for having only 80 acres in cultivation), and it recommended construction of improved water facilities, including a deep well, and a hospital building, and the fencing of all unenclosed land.[38] Generally, the report was a favorable one.

The A&M Directors met again in Austin on March 7, and sent a delegation, including Garrett, McInnis, Cavitt, and Scott, to the Legislature in behalf of the College. These representatives first appeared before the House Committee on Finance to explain the purposes and needs of A&M. The Finance Committee had under consideration a proposed bill popularly referred to as the McGaughey Land Bill, which had some slight similarity to George Pfeuffer's earlier bill "To perfect The University of Texas." The

---

[36]Galveston *Daily News*, February 22, 1887.

[37]Board of Directors, President, *Reply to Papers Read by Dr. Thomas D. Wooten, before the State Medical Association, by the President of the Board of Directors, A&M College*, 1-10 (hereinafter cited: *Reply to Thomas D. Wooten*); Minutes of the Board of Directors, June 8, 1887, I, 27.

[38]*Texas House Journal, 1887*, pp. 258, 276-277, 740-741; Minutes of the Board of Directors, March 7, 1887, I, 22-23.

McGaughey bill would specifically designate The University of Texas as comprising the University in Austin, the A&M College, the colored branch in Austin, and the Medical Branch in Galveston. A new Board of Regents to be established would include one member from each congressional district. Each branch would be given a specific land endowment, over and above the existing University Fund, which itself would be reserved for the exclusive use of The University in Austin. One-half million acres of land reclaimed from the Texas and Pacific Railroad Company would endow the A&M College; another one-half million acres would endow the Medical Branch, and another one-half million would go to the colored branch. The University Fund, comprising some two million acres of generally more valuable land, would support the Main University.[39] The A&M representatives opposed the bill, aware that it would transfer control over the affairs of the College to a centralized and probably less sympathetic board, and that its proposed endowment would likely prove almost valueless. Overall there was generally little support for the proposal, which died in committee.[40] A&M representatives also argued for increased state appropriations before the Finance Committee, which reportedly looked favorably upon the A&M request, but for the fact that Finance committeemen believed that it was unconstitutional to make appropriations for buildings out of general revenues.[41]

The A&M people withdrew from the Finance Committee deliberations and went before the House Committee on Education. The Committee on Education was considering a bill which would place A&M under the Regents and abolish the Board of Directors. The bill cleared the House Committee by one vote, but failed to appear for a vote before the House.[42] Director Garrett and his contingent sought support for an A&M bill which would give Texas A&M one-fourth of the endowment from the University lands. Referred to as the "Buchanan Bill," it formally came before the Committee on Education on March 16, and on the eighteenth an amended version, which would give Texas A&M one-fifth of the endowment, rather than one-fourth, was favorably reported by the Committee. The bill failed to become law before the session ended.[43]

As the various institutional factions sought to muster support for their pet bills, Governor Lawrence Sullivan Ross and others began to exert their

[39]Austin *Statesman*, March 14, 15, 1887; see also Louis L. McInnis Scrapbook, 97-98, McInnis Papers, Texas A&M University Archives.

[40]*Ibid.*

[41]Minutes of the Board of Directors, June 8, 1887, I, 27; *Reply to Thomas D. Wooten*, 6.

[42]*Ibid.*

[43]*Ibid.; Texas House Journal*, 1887, pp. 690-712.

influence in behalf of a permanent reconciliation between the branches of The University. On March 10, Garrett, McInnis, Scott, and others met informally with representatives of The University, and with supporters of the Medical School from Galveston, in the parlor of the Driskill Hotel in Austin. The gathering had information that an agreement could be reached and that the Governor and the Legislature would accept any agreement that came out of the conference. After some wide-ranging and free discussion, the outlines of an accord began to emerge. The conferees then agreed to select a bipartisan committee of three to prepare a formal written agreement. Frank M. Spencer, of Galveston, represented the Galveston Medical School, Eldred James Simkins represented the Regents, and Garrett represented the A&M College on the committee.[44]

These three men withdrew and prepared a "Memorandum of Agreement between the Regents of The University of Texas, and the Directors of the Agricultural and Mechanical College." The agreement provided:

1) That The University and the Agricultural and Mechanical College shall remain under separate management, as now provided by law.

2) That the Agricultural and Mechanical College shall receive annually, after the first of March 1889, one-fifth of the available University Fund.

3) That private gifts, endowments, and federal allotments belong exclusively to each institution as provided.

4) That the Legislature shall be asked to appropriate $50,000 for the Galveston Medical School, to be accepted by The University for all claims for money against the state (such as disbursement from the University Fund to the A&M College and to Prairie View Normal).

5) That $2,500 shall be appropriated for two years beginning March 1, 1887, out of the University Fund to the Agricultural and Mechanical College and $5,000 for each of the two years from the Legislature out of general revenues.

6) That The University of Texas and the Agricultural and Mechanical College shall jointly push for an additional endowment of one million acres of land to the University Fund.

7) That the two institutions will work together to give the Regents exclusive control of University lands.

8) That the Regents will have exclusive control of the University Fund, subject to the above conditions.

9) That friends and Directors of the A&M College, the Regents of The University of Texas, and friends of The University will work together to secure the necessary legislation.[45]

[44]Minutes of the Board of Directors, June 8, 1887, I, 27-29; *Reply to Thomas D. Wooten*, 1-10.
[45]*Ibid.*

It was understood that the Regents would meet within the week to give final approval to the agreement. But that meeting never occurred.[46]

Instead, in April, Dr. Thomas D. Wooten addressed the Texas State Medical Association and publicly rejected the agreement, condemned it as a conspiracy, and attacked the A&M College. Wooten argued that although A&M claimed to represent the agricultural and mechanical class, most of its students came from towns and cities. The College, he said, sought money to pay students for labor in the fields and shops because the students have an "aversion to work." Furthermore, he said, the College required no additional funds, especially from The University, because it already received between $69,000 and $70,000 each year. The "agreement" reached in the Driskill Hotel, he said, represented a conspiracy on the part of Bryan and Galveston against The University of Texas in Austin. Galveston was giving A&M one-fifth of the University Fund in exchange for a $50,000 appropriation from the Legislature to build a medical school in Galveston. Furthermore, said Wooten, that $50,000 appropriation was to cancel out an $87,000 debt due The University by the state of Texas. Any way you look at it, Wooten argued, The University of Texas would lose.[47]

Christopher C. Garrett, soon to be elected president of the Board of Directors of the A&M College, answered Wooten's charges in a formal ten-page printed document, circulated among the members of the Legislature, the press, and interested parties. Garrett said, in part:

> It must be borne in mind that the Regents of the University, while admitting its right to a portion of the University Fund, persistently withhold and refuse their assent to any appropriation of it to be expended by the Directors of the A&M College, but demand that the control of the college shall be placed in their hands, if it must share in the University Funds.[48]

Garrett called attention to the constitutional mandate and to the vote for the location of a Medical Branch in Galveston, and to the failure of the Regents to make any effort to found the Medical School. His answer concluded with an appeal to unity:

> We rejoice that the University of Texas has an endowment, that in the course of a few years will place it above want. Men educated and trained for the learned professions and for statesmanship, are no less a necessity than skilled agriculturists and mechanics. May we not indulge the hope that the present poverty of funds will not cause dissension among the friends of a universal education, but rather

[46] *Ibid.*
[47] *Reply to Thomas D. Wooten,* 3-5.
[48] *Ibid.,* 5.

unite them in a common effort to place in the educational structure of this state a capstone worthy of a free and intelligent people.[49]

Despite overtures made in the direction of harmony and unity between The University of Texas and its branches, there had been little evidence of the occurrence of such a phenomenon in the Legislature or in the press. The Twentieth Legislature was deluged with partisan institutional measures and countermeasures. Representative William L. McGaughey, who introduced the previously mentioned McGaughey Land Bill to create a new board of management and a new endowment policy for the various institutions, also introduced a separate bill to give The University exclusive control over University lands, including lease and sale arrangements. This bill, H.B. 593, died in committee.[50]

Other bills were introduced by Representative Walter Gresham and State Senator George W. Glasscock to give the Regents control over the branches of The University and the University lands. As John J. Lane records, these bills were "pigeon-holed, adversely reported, or otherwise defeated."[51] Another bill sought to refund to The University money claimed to be owed to The University by the state.[52] University officials reckoned these funds as coming from three separate categories: (1) funds borrowed from the University Fund by the state but not repaid; (2) funds unconstitutionally granted to Prairie View Normal; and (3) warrants received from the sale of University lands, for which payments on principal and interest remained uncollected.[53] The bill for repayment of funds to The University introduced in 1887 granted $212,000 to The University of Texas, but it failed in committee.[54] In 1888 Thomas D. Wooten submitted a full University claim to Governor Ross in the amount of $431,188.85.[55] A special called session of the Legislature in 1888, "after much wrangling," reached a settlement on the debts by "loaning" The University of Texas $125,000 as a full repayment of any obligations against the state.[56]

[49]*Ibid.*, 10.

[50]H. Y. Benedict (ed.), *A Source Book Relating to the History of the University of Texas,* 342 (hereinafter cited: Benedict (ed.), *Source Book of the University of Texas*); J. J. Lane, *A History of the University of Texas,* 86-87; *Texas House Journal,* 1887, pp. 1023, 1058.

[51]Lane, *History of the University of Texas,* 86.

[52]*Ibid.,* 86; Benedict (ed.), *Source Book of the University of Texas,* 341.

[53]Lane, *History of the University of Texas,* 93-107; Benedict (ed.), *Source Book of the University of Texas,* Table XXII, 829-830.

[54]Lane, *History of the University of Texas,* 86; *Texas House Journal,* 1887, p. 1003.

[55]Lane, *History of the University of Texas,* 93-107.

[56]*Ibid.,* 93-108, 114, 115, 122-130, 262-263; Benedict (ed.), *Source Book of the University of Texas,* 352-353; *Texas House Journal,* 1887, pp. 267, 270, 278-279.

The Legislature adjourned on April 6, 1887, failing to take action on most of the University and College legislation before it. The A&M Directors, however, were satisfied with the results of the legislative session, and counted several important legislative measures as advantageous to A&M's interests. The College obtained an appropriation of $15,000 from the general revenues and of $5,000 from the University Fund for the fiscal year 1887-1888; for the fiscal year ending on February 28, 1889, it received $10,000 from the General Fund and $5,000 from the University Fund.[57] Another act accepted the federal appropriation for the development of an agricultural experiment station to be under the control of the Agricultural and Mechanical College.[58] Yet another act made the commissioner of agriculture, insurance, and statistics an ex-officio member of the Board of Directors.[59] The A&M College had failed to effect a permanent division of the University Fund, but had deterred efforts to consolidate A&M under the auspices of The University.

The Directors of the A&M College met at College Station on April 25, 1887, for a brief business session, at which time appropriations were budgeted for various projects. Christopher C. Garrett was elected president of the Board of Directors, replacing William R. Cavitt. Louis L. McInnis was re-elected secretary to the Board, and Thomas M. Scott was re-elected business agent. The Directors appointed a committee to prepare plans and solicit bids for a two-story brick dormitory, a frame hospital, and a farm house. The new dormitory was to be named Pfeuffer Hall.[60]

The Directors met again during the commencement exercises of June 6-9, at College Station. One student graduated in agriculture and nine in the engineering courses. As the legislative investigators had observed, the agricultural branch had not been raised to the level of the "expectations of the committee and the requirements of the state."[61] Despite the recent successes of Dinwiddie in winning Grange and farmer support for the College, and in spite of Grand Master Rose's personal efforts in behalf of A&M, the agricultural studies, while surviving, were not flourishing. This can be attributed to a variety of factors, which may be summed up in the phrase "the lack of popularity of the agricultural studies" among the students. Most of the A&M students, while having a rural background, did not literally come from the farm, but came from the small towns and cities of Texas, in which they were

[57]Benedict (ed.), *Source Book of the University of Texas,* 350; Gammel (ed.), *Laws of Texas,* IX, 946.

[58]Minutes of the Board of Directors, June 8, 1887, I, 27.

[59]*Ibid.*

[60]*Ibid.,* April 25, 1887, I, 23-24.

[61]*Ibid.,* June 6-9, 1887, I, 26-27; *Texas House Journal, 1887,* pp. 740-741.

exposed as much to a commercial atmosphere as to agrarian ideals. Further-more, those boys who did come from the farm often came to college to seek new opportunities outside of farming which would have been denied them without a college education. Despite the "agrarian mythology," opportunities in farming were not attractive in the last half of the nineteenth century. Farm prices slumped from the end of the Civil War until a wrenching low was reached during the depression of 1893. Only the advent of World War I in Europe decisively improved farm prosperity, and then that moment collapsed with a new farm depression beginning at the end of 1920 and lasting throughout the Great Depression that followed the Stock Market crash in 1929. In face of the unattractiveness of agriculture, the youth of the late nine-teenth century was as much absorbed with the mechanical marvels of the day — particularly the railroad — as the youth of the late twentieth century is absorbed with the scientific phenomena of his age.

The anomaly persisted that Texas A&M, like many of the agricultural and mechanical colleges throughout the nation, received most of its political and ideological support from a social and economic sector which was not directly enhanced by its services. Yet this paradox ceases to be a paradox when one considers that few Texas farmers or small-town businessmen of the late nineteenth century would object to seeing their sons become engineers. The A&M College thus was indirectly fulfilling its mission. It provided a ladder of opportunity and a relief valve for farm youths. Only with the advent of federal farm programs, initiated by the implementation of the agri-cultural experiment stations, and later by the passage of the Smith-Hughes Act, which established vocational agricultural training and a market for agri-cultural majors, and the Smith-Lever Act, which established the county-agent system and a new exciting job market for agricultural majors, did the agricul-tural studies at the A&M College reach fulfilment. With this kind of legisla-tion, amplified by the modern farm commodity programs, agriculture became a profession rather than a pursuit.

Some optimism developed immediately with the consideration and pas-sage of legislation for the Agricultural Experiment Station system, for the Board of Directors of Texas A&M believed that "the inequality between the two courses of agriculture and mechanics is growing less."[62] The Directors concluded their June deliberations by accepting bids and approving contracts for the construction of Pfeuffer Hall, the hospital, and a farm house. They allocated $12,000 for the construction of Pfeuffer Hall; $2,000 for the hospi-tal; $1,200 for the farm house; $1,800 for the construction of a creamery;

[62]Minutes of the Board of Directors, June 8, 1887, I, 29.

$500 for enlarging the machine shops; $800 for cisterns; and $300 for a chemically generated gas machine, one of the mechanical marvels of this age, to heat and light Pfeuffer Hall. Total budgeted expenditures for the forth-coming academic year were to be $33,420.[63] The Board then adjourned, and the faculty and students scattered for the summer.

Dinwiddie, who had been ailing somewhat, left to recuperate in Colo-rado Springs. He became successively weaker rather than better. Finally, in August, Mrs. Dinwiddie wrote to McInnis that her husband was very ill, "weak and prostrated," and would miss the opening of school on September 5. She asked McInnis to make arrangements for his classes.[64] Dinwiddie soon returned to the campus, but never regained his health. He died on December 11, 1887, at the age of forty-three, having been a member of the faculty at Texas A&M since 1879, and chairman of the faculty since 1883.[65] Dinwiddie had been an effective "president" at a particularly critical time in the College's history. His administration marked a turning point in the College's experiences. During the Dinwiddie years A&M made the transition from a largely experimental and controversial institution to a college of some perma-nence and respectability. While Dinwiddie never had the full powers of a president, in that he lacked the fiscal authority delegated to the agent of the Board, this had not diminished his effectiveness. In the situation where the school's income and expenditures were reasonably stable, as they were between 1885 and 1887, Dinwiddie's concern with fiscal affairs would have been a burden, rather than an asset. As it was, he could and did devote his efforts to academic affairs and public relations. Later, as the school began to expand more rapidly, the expenditure of funds became increasingly a matter of academic policy, and the separation of fiscal authority from the office of the president became cumbersome, if not intolerable.

Although Dinwiddie died on December 11, it was not until January 24, 1888, that the Directors named a replacement. On that day the Board, rather than delegating its authority to the faculty as it had in 1883, elected Professor Louis Lowrey McInnis, professor of mathematics and secretary to the Board since 1880, as chairman of the faculty. Thomas M. Scott remained as McInnis' business agent, but there is a good indication that Scott deferred to

[63]*Ibid.*, 29-32.

[64]Mrs. Hardaway Hunt Dinwiddie, Colorado Springs, Colorado, to Louis L. McInnis, College Station, Texas, August 30, 1887, Louis L. McInnis Papers, Texas A&M University Archives.

[65]Galveston *Daily News*, December 18, 21, 1887; Minutes of the Board of Directors, Janu-ary 24, 1888, I, 41.

McInnis' desires on fiscal affairs, which Hardemann had not done with Din-widdie. Thus McInnis retained greater control over the College than his predecessor.[66] The Directors also elected William L. Bringhurst as vice-chair-man of the faculty. His prime function appears to have been to substitute for the chairman in the event of his death, incapacity, or removal.[67]

McInnis, born in Jackson, Mississippi, on March 24, 1856, was attracted to Texas A&M by Thomas S. Gathright, also of Mississippi. McInnis' father, Richmond McInnis, a graduate of Oakland College, was a prominent Pres-byterian minister in Mississippi. Louis McInnis entered the University of Mississippi, at Oxford, in 1871, and graduated in June 1875. He received his Master of Arts degree from the University the following year. He then moved to Texas, where two brothers were ranching in Llano County, and in September 1876 applied to Thomas S. Gathright for a teaching position at Texas A&M, which was to open for its first session in October. Gathright indicated that the faculty positions had been filled, but that he would like to have McInnis on the faculty. McInnis then found a teaching position in Lockhart, Texas, but continued to correspond with Gathright until the Board of Directors approved his appointment in October 1877 as an associate [assistant] to the professor of English and to the professor of ancient languages.[68] McInnis, then twenty-two years old, joined the faculty at the beginning of A&M's second academic year. He survived the purge of 1879 and received a temporary appointment as professor of mathematics. That appointment was made permanent in 1880.[69] In 1882 he was made secretary to the Board, and in 1883 began to serve as treasurer of the College. He retained those functions, in addition to his teaching duties, until his appointment as chairman of the faculty.[70]

He had the reputation of having an almost infallible memory and a pre-dilection for numbers as well as for finance. He saved his money and very early began the practice of making loans to his colleagues and associates. He gave financial assistance to the Gathright family after Gathright's death, and on at least one occasion loaned money to a member of the Board of

[66]Minutes of the Board of Directors, January 24, 1888, I, 41.

[67]*Ibid.*, 42.

[68]David Brooks Cofer (ed.), *First Five Administrators of Texas A. & M. College, 1876-1890,* pp. 40-47; Thomas S. Gathright, College Station, Texas, to Louis L. McInnis, Lockhart, Texas, September 14, 1876, July 1, August 17, April 17, 1877, Thomas S. Gathright Papers, Texas A&M University Archives.

[69]George Pfeuffer, New Braunfels, Texas, to Louis L. McInnis, College Station, Texas, December 4, 1879.

[70]Cofer (ed.), *First Five Administrators of Texas A. & M. College.* 44.

Directors.[71] It was no coincidence that, upon his departure from A&M, McInnis became a banker. He never, however, became a particularly wealthy man and he always seems to have regarded his students and associates as friends rather than as customers or clients. He gave assistance to all who asked, from such things as working surveying problems for former students out in the field, to obtaining pay raises for his colleagues. He seemed to have no enemies and remained on good terms with all of his associates, and particularly with Thomas Gathright, John G. James, George Pfeuffer, Hardaway Hunt Dinwiddie, and Thomas M. Scott.[72] He was a knowledgeable, reliable, involved individual.

McInnis had been very active since 1885 in the affairs of the Directors and their dealings with the Legislature. He clearly retained the confidence of the Board, so much so that his plan for the reorganization of the College had been made a part of the official minutes.[73] He had been groomed for the job of chairman in the past years and his appointment must have been foreseen. On the day of his selection as chairman, McInnis submitted a list of recommendations to the Board which the Directors promptly accepted as policy. These recommendations called for the prompt establishment of an Agricultural Experiment Station, authorized by the Hatch Act and approved by resolution in the recent session of the Texas Legislature. He initiated an academic reorganization separating physics and chemistry. He created a new Department of Chemistry and Mineralogy, with geology under its auspices. He separated drawing from engineering to establish a new Department of Drawing. Physics was combined with a new Department of Civil Engineering, and a new Department of Veterinary Science was established. McInnis also supplied detailed plans for the organization and development of the Agricultural Experiment Station, which is described in a following chapter, and on the day after McInnis' appointment as chairman, the Directors elected Frank A. Gulley, who had recently joined the faculty as professor of experimental agriculture, to be Director of the Agricultural Experiment Station. Louis McInnis very clearly made careful and detailed plans for the development of the Col-

[71]H. G. Gathright, Palestine, Texas, to Louis L. McInnis, College Station, Texas, October 21, 1885; W. R. Cavitt, Bryan, Texas, to Louis L. McInnis, College Station, Texas, January 8, 11, 1887; G. A. Rogers, College Station, Texas, to Louis L. McInnis, Forest, Mississippi, June 19, 1888; John G. James, Henrietta, Texas, to Louis L. McInnis, College Station, Texas, June 17, 1890, in Louis L. McInnis Papers, Texas A&M University Archives.

[72]The Louis L. McInnis Papers, Texas A&M University Archives, are filled with personal correspondence from the above-named individuals.

[73]Minutes of the Board of Directors, October 6, 1886, I, 18-19.

lege prior to his official appointment as chairman.[74] His two years as chairman were packed with activity. He accomplished a sound academic consolidation and reorganization of the courses of study. Hardaway Hunt Dinwiddie provided a good foundation upon which McInnis could build, and McInnis fully exploited this happy situation. According to a former president of the Board of Directors, Christopher C. Garrett, Louis McInnis' incumbency as chairman of the faculty marked the era of the College's greatest prosperity.[75] Paradoxically, however, McInnis was dismissed from his office and from the faculty in 1890.

[74]*Ibid.*, January 25, 1888, I, 41-47.

[75]C. C. Garrett, Brenham, Texas, to Louis L. McInnis, College Station, Texas, July 5, 1890, Louis L. McInnis Papers, Texas A&M University Archives.

CHAPTER 7

The New A&M College

L OUIS LOWRY McINNIS' administration marked the era of the College's greatest prosperity up to that time, according to Christopher C. Garrett, who served as chairman of the Board of Directors between April 1887 and March 1889.[1] McInnis expanded the physical facilities of the College and modernized its academic structure and curricula. Texas A&M clearly could no longer be called a literary school, as it had functioned during the Gathright era, nor was it an industrial school, as John James would have had it be. The College had begun to live up to its commitment as described by the Morrill Land-Grant Act, its leading object being "to teach such branches of learning as are related to agriculture and the mechanical arts," and not to the exclusion of the liberal arts. The College catalogues of 1885-1890 thus interpreted the role and purpose of the College:

. . . this college is not a trade school designed to take the place of the old apprenticeship system, but an institution where young men may receive broad and liberal training in all those sciences and arts which contribute to useful citizenship in the pursuit of all productive industries.[2]

Texas A&M had become a producer of engineers, agricultural administrators, and soldiers rather than of farmers and mechanics, although the College retained facilities for vocational training for many years, facilities which were utilized most effectively during World War I.[3] This did not mean that A&M's philosophical development was at an end. As time passed, the concept of a "broad and liberal training" in the productive pursuits of life apparently became lost to the necessity of intensive training and specialization in the technology of the time. Thus in later years some argued that the educational commitment of the College had become more narrow rather than more

[1] C. C. Garrett, Brenham, Texas, to Louis L. McInnis, College Station, Texas, July 5, 1890, Louis L. McInnis Papers, Texas A&M University Archives.

[2] Texas A&M, *Catalogue, 1886-1887*. p. 25.

[3] See Chapter 11.

broad.[4] Nonetheless, by the educational standards of the nineteenth century, Texas A&M had assumed a positive role in Texas and in the nation at large as a producer of scientifically trained agriculturists and engineers.

The faculty, directors, and staff responsible for this production in 1888 and 1889 included the following:[5]

Board of Directors

William R. Cavitt, of Bryan

George M. Dilley, of Palestine

Lafayette Lumpkin Foster, ex officio, Commissioner of Insurance, Statistics, History and Agriculture, of Austin

Christopher C. Garrett, President, of Brenham

Archibald J. Rose, of Salado

Officers

Louis Lowry McInnis — Chairman of the Faculty and ex officio Secretary of the Board of Directors

William Lorraine Bringhurst — Vice-Chairman of the Faculty

Thomas M. Scott — Agent of the Board

Faculty

Duncan Adriance — Assistant Professor of Chemistry and Physics

Paul Braun, B.M.E. — Assistant Professor of Mechanical Engineering

William Lorraine Bringhurst, Ph.D. — Professor of English and History

Thomas L. Brunk, B.S. — Associate Professor of Horticulture and Botany

Lieutenant Guy Carleton, 2d Cavalry, U.S.A. — Professor of Military Science and Commandant

George Washington Curtis, M.S.A. — Professor of Agriculture

J. F. Duggar, B.S. — Assistant Professor of Agriculture

Mark Francis, V.M.D. — Associate Professor of Veterinary Science

Frederick Ernst Giesecke — Instructor in Drawing

A. M. Gunther — Instructor in Blacksmithing

Frank Arthur Gulley, M.S. — Professor of Experimental Agriculture

Henry Hill Harrington, M.S. — Professor of Chemistry and Mineralogy

John H. Kinealy, D.E. — Associate Professor of Civil Engineering and Physics

Louis Lowry McInnis, A.M. — Professor of Mathematics

[4]Statement on History and Purpose, Self-Study Committee on History and Purpose, 1962, pp. 1-21.

[5]Texas A&M, *Annual Report*, December 1889, p. xvii.

James F. McKay — Assistant Professor of Horticulture
William Bledsoe Philpott — Assistant Professor of History and English
Roger Haddock Whitlock, M.E. — Professor of Mechanical Engineering
Rudolph Wipprecht — Professor of Languages

Staff

J. H. Alsworth — Foreman of the Farm
John S. Fowlkes, of Bryan — Fiscal Agent
Charles Augustus Lewis — Foreman of the Carpenter Shop
G. A. Rogers — Clerk and Bookkeeper
Bernard Sbisa — Steward

Many of the faculty and staff served in some capacity with the Agricultural Experiment Station, established by the Hatch Act, and authorized by the Twentieth Legislature of Texas. The Directors formally organized the Agricultural Experiment Station on January 24-25, 1888, along guidelines submitted by McInnis. The Station functioned under the direction of the Agricultural Experiment Station Council, comprising the director of the Agricultural Experiment Station, Frank Arthur Gulley; the chairman of the faculty; and the agent of the Board. Texas A&M received $15,000 annually from Congress for the operation of the Station.[6]

Upon McInnis' recommendation, the Directors recognized on January 25, 1888, the establishment of eleven academic departments of the College: (1) Mathematics; (2) English and History; (3) Agriculture; (4) Mechanical Engineering; (5) Civil Engineering and Physics; (6) Horticulture and Botany; (7) Chemistry and Mineralogy; (8) Veterinary Science; (9) Drawing; (10) Languages; and (11) Military Science and Tactics.[7] This academic reorganization, along with the introduction of new courses, reflected a restructuring of the College that had been underway during the Dinwiddie years and which was essentially concluded by McInnis.

President John G. James had reduced the courses of study to a three-year program in agriculture and mechanics when he assumed the presidency in 1880. Hardaway Hunt Dinwiddie retained the three-year curricula, but changed the essentially vocational orientation of the agricultural and mechanical studies to a more scientific and theoretical approach. The three-year study program led to the award of a "diploma of the college," but not to a degree. In 1885 a fourth year of postgraduate study leading to the award of a degree was added. The earlier regulation relieving fourth-year students of participation in military drill and discipline was continued.

[6]Minutes of the Board of Directors, January 24-25, 1888, I, 44-47; see also Chapter 11.
[7]Minutes of the Board of Directors, January 24-25, 1888, I, 44-47.

In 1888 the faculty began the transition to a regular four-year, degree-granting program. New students were required to enroll in the four-year program but old students could complete their studies under either the three-year program or take the fourth year of "postgraduate" work leading to a bachelor's degree. By the 1890-1891 school year the older program had been completely supplanted by a regular four-year academic program.[8] Agricultural students could obtain a Bachelor of Science (B.S.) or a Bachelor of Scientific Agriculture (B.S.A.) degree, depending upon the option they elected in their senior year. Students in the mechanical studies could receive a Bachelor of Civil Engineering (B.C.E.) or a Bachelor of Mechanical Engineering (B.M.E.) degree, depending upon their choice of an option.[9] During McInnis' first year as chairman the College introduced the first graduate program leading to the Master of Science (M.S.) degree in either agriculture or engineering. The degree required two years of postgraduate study, a comprehensive examination, and a thesis.[10] The College also retained a program with a basic vocational orientation. Special students could enroll in a practical two-year short course in agriculture, horticulture, dairying, carpentry, blacksmithing, machinery, chemistry, drawing, or surveying. These programs led to the award of a "certificate of proficiency."[11] The retention of the special vocational program must be regarded, at least in part, as a legacy from the vocational orientation of the James era. Generally, however, under McInnis' direction, Texas A&M developed an academic structure not too unlike that of contemporary days.

Admission requirements to the College remained minimal well into the twentieth century, as they were in most colleges and universities. An applicant must be fifteen years old, must be free from contagious or infectious disease, and should have a "fair knowledge of arithmetic as far as proportion, of descriptive geography, and of elementary English grammar and composition."[12] As Sam A. McMillan, Class of 1909, recalled, the examinations for admission were administered and graded with a wide degree of latitude. A way was usually found to overcome a student's deficiency.[13] There are many indications that admission requirements to A&M in earlier years and well into the twentieth century were quite lenient.

[8]Texas A&M, *Catalogue, 1885-1886*, p. 24; *ibid., 1886-1887*, pp. 21, 22-23; *ibid., 1888-1889*, p. 22.

[9]*Ibid., 1886-1887*, p. 22.

[10]*Ibid., 1888-1889*, p. 22.

[11]*Ibid.*, 41.

[12]*Ibid.*, p. 42.

[13]"Reminiscences of Sam A. McMillan," in David Brooks Cofer (ed.), *Fragments of Early History of Texas A. and M. College*, 81.

Nonetheless, A&M students studied hard, and often proved to be more than competent engineers, agriculturists, educators, and business and professional men. Cadet Lucius Holman wrote with regularity to his mother during his years at Texas A&M between 1887 and 1889, assuring her that he was "studdying hard": "I am studdying hard as anyone can studdy. I always recite good lessons and I do not see why I do not get good marks. I never went to the blackboard, nor got up to anser [*sic*] a question yet but what I always knew it."[14] Before he left the school in February 1889 with typhoid fever, which he survived, his "studdying" and spelling had improved.[15] His handwriting remained something of a problem, but he always blamed his "stub pen" for this weakness: "You must excuse this bad hand of mine," he wrote to an aunt, "as I am writing with a stub pen and you know that is just like writing with a fence rail."[16] Holman, who was unable to complete his studies at A&M, was described as a moderately good student, majoring in architecture, who had a weakness in math.[17] During his rather brief tenure at A&M, Holman and his fellow students witnessed substantive changes in almost every aspect of the College environment.

In the autumn of 1887 Pfeuffer Hall, the new dormitory named in honor of George Pfeuffer, began service. It housed seventy-five boys. Other students lived in the upper levels of Steward's Hall and in Old Main. By the spring of 1888 contractors completed the construction of a new creamery and a residence for the Farm superintendent and the surgeon. At the same time six new forges were being added to the metal-working shop. Four new stone cisterns, just completed, helped alleviate the chronic water problem on the campus.[18] Seven more years were to pass, however, before the College developed an adequate water supply.

Lucius Holman provides from an interesting perspective a personal testimonial to the acute water deficiency on campus. "I keep a fire all the time and bathe 3 times a week regular," Cadet Holman wrote to his mother:

> The Doctor said it is healthy to bathe all over twice a week at least. He said

[14]Lucius Holman, College Station, to Mother [Mrs. P. G. Weeks], Pilots Point, Texas, November 18, 1888, Lucius Holman Papers, Texas A&M University Archives.

[15]Lucius Holman, College Station, to Mrs. P. G. Weeks, Pilots Point, Texas, November 22, 1888, and Same to Same, December 2, 1888, Lucius Holman Papers, Texas A&M University Archives.

[16]Lucius Holman, College Station, Texas, to Mrs. Rosie Yeisen, Pilots Point, Texas, November 22, 1888, Lucius Holman Papers, Texas A&M University Archives.

[17]College Station *Battalion*, October 24, 1968.

[18]Texas A&M, *Catalogue, 1886-1887*, pp. 16-17; *ibid., 1887-1888*, pp. 15-16, 22; Minutes of the Board of Directors, October 10, 1887, I, 37-39.

there was a boy that came to the Hospital and he asked him how often did he bathe and he said he had bathed twice since he had been down here and that was the first week he came two and a half months ago.[19]

McInnis did his part in trying to solve this obviously critical water problem. He requested a larger appropriation from the Legislature for drilling deep wells. Although the College eventually got water, there is no assurance that the cadets took full advantage of it.

Just as the building program neared completion in the spring of 1888 Governor Lawrence Sullivan Ross called the Legislature into special session. Preparatory to the legislative session the Board of Directors of the A&M College met to plan legislative strategy. Chairman McInnis submitted to the Directors a comprehensive report on the College, which reviewed its current status and its needs. The Directors approved the report as submitted and Board President Christopher C. Garrett forwarded a copy of it to Governor Ross. The report contained itemized requests for appropriations totalling $100,000.[20] The size of this request alone supports the conclusion that McInnis and the Directors believed that the College had not only improved in academic stature but that its political situation was also more secure. Had a similar money request been submitted only a few years earlier, such as during the legislative session of 1885, when George Pfeuffer presented his bill to "perfect the University," it may be imagined that the chairman, the Directors, and the entire institution may have been ridiculed, if not eradicated. Now in 1888 there was no ridicule and no real legislative fight. The College got much of what it sought.

McInnis' report included a request for an appropriation of $10,200 for extensive repairs to College buildings; $12,500 was asked for a new dormitory; $13,250, for an assembly hall; $2,500, for furniture; $9,500, for new residences (five of the faculty had no residence and a number of faculty families were doubling up in one house); $3,300, for employees' homes; and $18,000, for a chemical laboratory. McInnis wanted $7,000 to dig deep artesian wells. The Department of Agriculture and the Experiment Station jointly wanted a herd of improved cattle, and McInnis requested $3,500, part of which would be used to purchase a dairy herd, the remainder, to obtain beef stock. Fencing, a conservatory, barns, and equipment for the various departments completed the list.[21]

[19]Lucius Holman, College Station, Texas, to Mrs. P. G. Weeks, Pilots Point, Texas, November 18, 1888, Lucius Holman Papers, Texas A&M University Archives.

[20]Minutes of the Board of Directors, April 11, 1888, I, 48-51.

[21]*Texas House Journal, 1888*, pp. 45-46.

Governor Ross endorsed the report and submitted it to the Legislature on April 19, where it was referred to the Committee on Finance.[22] The Committee amended the appropriation request, but on May 17 the Legislature approved the general appropriation bill, which provided an appropriation of $41,500 to the Agricultural and Mechanical College.[23] This achievement alone virtually assured the success of McInnis' administration.

The itemized appropriations to the College included (1) $20,000 for a dormitory and assembly hall; (2) $2,000 for furniture; (3) $9,000 for repairs to buildings and residences; (4) $2,000 for the development of a water supply; (5) $2,500 for fencing and fence repairs; (6) $1,000 for barns; (7) $4,500 for equipment for the mechanical, civil engineering, drawing, and veterinary-science departments; and (8) $500 for work stock and farm implements.[24] Money was not obtained for new residences, a chemical laboratory, or cattle, and the water-development appropriation proved insufficient. McInnis was able, nonetheless, to stretch the appropriation to cover most of the College's real needs.

Contracts were soon let for Stephen F. Austin Hall, built on the same plan as Pfeuffer Hall, to house seventy-five students. Two frame houses for professors were constructed. Construction began on the Assembly Hall, which was also designed to serve as a chapel. Since Austin Hall cost $12,500 to build, and the Assembly Hall about $13,250, and only $20,000 was appropriated to cover the costs, rather than cut the size of the buildings, McInnis completed Austin Hall as planned; he began the Assembly Hall, and when funds ran out requested from the Legislature an additional $7,500 to complete it — which he got. Possibly he worked the two new faculty residences into the deal.[25] From the departmental appropriations and other sources the College found funds to buy a herd of Jersey grade cows.[26] Rather than build a new barn with the $1,000 appropriated for that purpose, McInnis enlarged and repaired the existing barn, which conceivably saved money used for the construction of a new stable for professors' horses.[27] Fencing, repairs, equipment purchases, and general improvements were made.

[22]*Ibid.; Messages of the Governor, Coke to Ross,* 615.

[23]Gammel (ed.), *Laws of Texas,* IX, 1016.

[24]*Ibid.*

[25]*Texas House Journal, 1888,* p. 45; Texas A&M, *Biennial Report, January 1887-December 1888,* pp. vi, xvi, xxx.

[26]G. A. Rogers, College Station, Texas, to Louis L. McInnis, Forest, Mississippi, June 29, 1888, Louis L. McInnis Papers, Texas A&M University Archives.

[27]Texas A&M, *Biennial Report, January 1887-December 1888,* pp. xvi-xxx; Minutes of the Board of Directors, October 12, 1888, I, 64.

McInnis wanted more. *The Annual Report of the College,* submitted to the Governor in December 1888, sought an appropriation for a student labor fund, justified as a self-help program for students in preference to "free scholarships." McInnis noted that the Grange supported the idea. He asked for money to establish a Farmers' Institute, so that the Department of Agriculture and the Experiment Station could promote better farming practices among farmers. The College also asked that its annual operating appropriation for the school, which during the past four years had averaged $15,000, be raised to $20,000. Ten thousand dollars was asked for a chemical laboratory and $7,500 was requested for completion of the Assembly Hall.[28] During the regular session of the Legislature the College got funds to support a Farmers' Institute, a $5,000 increase in the operating appropriation, and $7,500 for the completion of the Assembly Hall.[29]

The Bryan *Eagle* seemed to exude happiness on the College's recent good fortune, but in the same breath made some disparaging remarks about A&M's financial management. The editor remarked that it was now time to give The University to A&M (recalling recent efforts by University partisans to transfer the College to Austin). The present administrators of The University having "in a manner wrecked the Austin Branch of our university, we think it exceeding proper to consolidate it with the present institution at Bryan." The writer continued, "The College is due Ex-Governor Roberts a little settlement for the ruthless manner in which he 'busted' up the school." Obviously the old University *versus* College controversy, as well as the Gathright purge, still rankled in the hearts of A&M supporters. But the *Eagle* went on to chastise A&M too. After arguing that The University should be given to A&M, the editorial noted that A&M is good at "absorbing" things. "We have a capacious maw, into which the experimental station, fund and all, dropped and disappeared in the twinkling of an eye."[30] Reasons for the derogatory remarks about A&M and the reference to the Experiment Station emerged a little later, about 1890, in a sudden and, on the surface, almost inexplicable upheaval in the affairs of the College. Throughout 1888 and 1889, however, nothing but good things seemed to be happening on the campus.

One innovation in 1888 was the organization by Lieutenant Guy Carleton, cadet commandant, of a cadet drill team called the Scott Guards, in

---

[28]Texas A&M, *Annual Report, 1888,* pp. vi, xvi-xix.

[29]Gammel (ed.), *Laws of Texas,* IX, 1102-1103; Minutes of the Board of Directors, June 4, 1889, I, 76.

[30]Bryan *Eagle,* January 9, 1890.

honor of Thomas M. Scott, agent of the Board, and good friend of Louis McInnis. Governor Lawrence Sullivan Ross had the pleasure of viewing the first public demonstration of the Scott Guards during commencement exercises, June 3-8, 1888. Upon Ross' election as president of the A&M College in 1890, the Scott Guards were renamed the Ross Volunteers in honor of Governor Ross.[31] In yet another innovation of 1888 the Directors established the position of College chaplain and directed that daily morning chapel exercises were to be held and would be compulsory for all students.[32] This directive probably also came at McInnis' instigation, for McInnis, whose father was a Presbyterian minister, held strong religious views and throughout his life was a pillar in the Presbyterian Church in Bryan.[33] Charles Perkins Fountain became the first College chaplain, assuming his duties in 1889. He also served as librarian.[34] The College graduated sixteen students in 1888, seven of whom received degrees in agriculture and nine in civil engineering.[35] During commencement exercises the Directors held a series of business meetings, reviewed building progress, promoted several of the faculty, and authorized expenditures for the forthcoming academic year.[36]

During the spring and summer of 1888 McInnis continued Dinwiddie's program of promoting better public relations through direct contact with the public. In March, McInnis and Frank A. Gulley, director of the Agricultural Experiment Station, addressed the Texas Live Stock Association in Waco regarding mutual interests and endeavors of the A&M College, the Agricultural Experiment Station, and the Texas cattle industry. Almost as soon as it was inaugurated the Agricultural Experiment Station at A&M began a joint project with the Missouri Agricultural Experiment Station to prevent Texas cattle fever.[37] These studies eventually contributed to a successful tick-eradication program.

In the summer of 1888 McInnis attended meetings of the State Horticulture Society, the State Grange of the Patrons of Husbandry, and the State

[31]Minutes of the Board of Directors, June 3-8, 1888, I, 57-60; Bryan *Brazos Pilot*, June 8, 1888, clipping in Louis McInnis Scrapbooks, Texas A&M University Archives; see also David Brooks Cofer (ed.), *Fragments of Early History of Texas A. and M. College*, 23-27.

[32]Minutes of the Board of Directors, January 24, 1888, I, 42; June 3-6, 1888, I, 57-60; Texas A&M, *Annual Report, 1888*, p. iv.

[33]Interview with Miss Malcolm Graham (Scott) McInnis, Bryan, Texas, January 20, 1971.

[34]Minutes of the Board of Directors, June 7, 1890, I, 88; Texas A&M, *Annual Report, 1888*, p. iv.

[35]Minutes of the Board of Directors, June 3-6, 1888, p. 55.

[36]*Ibid.*, 55-60.

[37]Dallas *News*, March 20, 1888; Texas A&M, *Annual Report, 1888*, p. xxiii.

Farmers' Alliance. In each instance he invited the organizations to send a delegation to the College to inspect its facilities. The *Annual Report* of the College for 1888 indicates that in each case a delegation did visit the College and made a favorable report.[38] Out of these contacts with farmers, McInnis, Gulley, George W. Curtis, and others hit upon the idea of holding Farmers' Institutes, to teach scientific farming principles to established farmers. These institutes, first initiated by Texas A&M in 1890, anticipated in many respects the Agricultural Extension programs of a later day, and the "short courses" which became common on A&M campuses in the twentieth century.[39] In January 1889 McInnis and Gulley attended the national meeting of the newly organized Association of Agricultural Colleges and Experiment Stations. McInnis was elected vice-president of the Association. George W. Atherton, of the State College of Pennsylvania, became president.[40] Thus on both the state and the national level McInnis proved quite effective in promoting and expanding the educational role of the College.

Enrollment for the 1888-1889 school year declined slightly from that of the previous year, to 195 students. Of these, 89 were enrolled in the fourth class or first year of study. Of the remainder of the students, 33 enrolled in the agricultural courses and 73 in the mechanical studies.[41] In January 1889 Lieutenant William S. Scott, 1st Cavalry, at the request of the Directors, replaced Lieutenant Guy Carleton, who was transferred to another post by the Army. The preceding June the Directors had hired Dr. Mark Francis, of Ohio, as associate professor of veterinary science, and veterinarian of the Agricultural Experiment Station.[42] Francis' appointment marks the real beginning of the College of Veterinary Medicine.[43]

Francis was born in Shandon, Ohio, March 19, 1863. He graduated from Ohio State University with the degree of Doctor of Veterinary Medicine in 1887 and spent one year at the American Veterinary College in New York before coming to Texas A&M. As veterinarian of the Agricultural Experiment Station, Francis began a series of experiments in cooperation with the

[38]Texas A&M, *Annual Report, 1888,* pp. xviii-xix.

[39]*Ibid.; The Farmers' Institute of the Fifth Congressional District,* Henrietta, Texas, January 10-11, 1890, pp.1-4.

[40]Minutes of the Board of Directors, December 13, 1888, I, 66; George W. Atherton, State College, Centre County, Pennsylvania, to Louis L. McInnis, College Station, Texas, May 14, 1889, Louis L. McInnis Papers, Texas A&M University Archives.

[41]Texas A&M, *Annual Report, 1888,* p. xviii.

[42]Minutes of the Board of Directors, December 13, 1888, I, 67; *ibid.,* June 6, 1888, I, 59.

[43]See Herbert Schmidt, *A Brief History of the School of Veterinary Medicine, 1878-1958,* pp. 1-40.

Missouri Agricultural Experiment Station, designed to curb or prevent "Texas fever" in cattle. His experiments with inoculation of northern cattle with serum from disease-resistant southern cattle led to the successful control of Texas fever. Later Francis helped develop a systematic program of tick eradication for the state of Texas which virtually eliminated the disease and saved the Texas cattle industry hundreds of millions of dollars. For this work he became known as the "father of the Texas cattle industry." In 1903 he helped to organize the Texas State Veterinary Medical Association, and in 1917 became the first dean of the College of Veterinary Medicine at Texas A&M. Francis was known as a quiet, courteous, unassuming man.[44]

Charles Puryear also joined the A&M faculty in 1889. A Virginian, Puryear received his Master of Arts degree from Richmond College in 1881, and a bachelor's degree in civil engineering in 1885. He taught mathematics at the University of Virginia for a time before coming to Texas A&M as associate professor of civil engineering and physics. In 1890 he was made professor of mathematics and served as head of the department until 1930. At various times he served as acting president of the College.[45] In 1907 he became the first dean of the College. Along with Ernst Giesecke, James C. Nagle, Mark Francis, and others, Puryear became one of the academic workhorses of the College.

In terms of physical expansion, faculty competence, and public esteem, the administration of Louis McInnis clearly marked a high point in the affairs of Texas A&M. In June 1890, however, the upheavals of 1879 were virtually repeated. In the words of the Bryan *Eagle,* the Board of Directors made "almost a clean sweep" of the faculty and administration of the College. The cause for this reorganization was not failure; it was rather too great a success. By 1890 the office of president of the College had become a desirable position, rather than a mere academic post in some relatively fragile and insecure institution.

Shortly after McInnis took office there developed on the A&M campus the rivalry, professional jealousy, and factionalism not too unlike that of the Gathright era. Surprisingly, the academic community, while it may appear from the outside to be a passive, introverted, somnolent society, is more often

[44]*Ibid.,* 36-37. See also Mark Francis Biographical Papers, Texas A&M University Archives; Texas Agricultural Experiment Station, *Veterinary Science,* Bulletin 30 (March 1894), pp. 437-458; TAES, *Texas Fever,* Bulletin 53 (1899), pp. 53-106; TAES, *Texas Fever,* Bulletin 63 (1902), pp. 1-60.

[45]Minutes of the Board of Directors, September 25, 1889, I, 81; Cofer (ed.), *Fragments of Early History of Texas A. and M. College,* 39-41; Texas A&M, *Annual Report, January 1889-December 1890, pp. 3-4.*

a seething, highly competitive body. Because the competition occurs on other than the usual dollars-and-cents level, it is more difficult for the outsider to ascertain or to understand it. Because it happened so long ago, and witnesses of that era are no longer living, and because the internal affairs of the College rarely got into newsprint, or even into personal letters, the documentation of these events also is difficult. Yet campus politics, among other things, doubtlessly contributed to the downfall of Louis McInnis.

The first written evidence of problems during these seemingly "golden years" in A&M's affairs not surprisingly comes from a student. In this case Lucius Holman wrote his mother on October 19, 1888, the following dismal account, at a point in time when, judging by the record, things were going most satisfactorily for the College:

> Ma I am sorry to say that this school is going down faster than I ever saw a school. I would not have said this but I heard two professors talking about it yesterday. They said in two more years that it would not be worth sending to. They are not managing it rite but I think it will last long enough for me to graduate be that is I hope so.[46]

Yet another year passed and the problem or controversy never fully surfaced. The Directors' Committee on General Management reported on June 5, 1889, that the College is in a "prosperous condition." There was a need, the report continued, for plenty of fresh water, improved bathing facilities, better drainage of the grounds, and better hospital facilities.[47] But these needs were nothing new, and certainly nothing with which to foment a revolution nor with which to predict ruin.

On February 27, 1890, Thomas M. Scott, agent of the Board, and business manager of the College, resigned from his position, saying that he did so in order to allow the consolidation of the powers of the agent and of the chairman of the faculty into the hands of one person.[48] At this point there is no tangible evidence that conflict over authority had ever occurred between the chairman of the faculty and the agent of the Board. On the contrary, the greatest personal accord and amity existed between Thomas M. Scott and Louis McInnis.[49] McInnis' daughter, Malcolm Graham McInnis, was born on

[46]Lucius Holman, College Station, Texas, to Mrs. P. G. Weeks, Pilots Point, Texas, October 10, 1888, Lucius Holman Papers, Texas A&M University Archives.

[47]Minutes of the Board of Directors, June 5, 1889, I, 78.

[48]*Ibid.*, February 27, 1890, I, 84.

[49]Interview with Miss Malcolm Graham (Scott) McInnis, Bryan, Texas, January 20, 1971; Thomas M. Scott, Melissa, Texas, to Louis L. McInnis, College Station, Texas, June 27, 1890; Scott to McInnis, November 9, 1890, Louis L. McInnis Papers, Texas A&M University Archives.

the campus on January 25, 1888, and was given the middle name "Scott" by her father in honor of his good friend, Thomas Martin Scott. Miss McInnis later changed her middle name to Graham.[50] Subsequent events also fail to support the contention that there was any real concern over a possible conflict of authority between the agent and the chairman.

In March, Board President Archibald J. Rose directed McInnis to assume the duties and powers of the agent, and informed him that a replacement for the agent would soon be found.[51] Contrary to the statement attributed to Scott in the official record of the College, it soon became apparent that Scott did not ask to be relieved of his duties because of conflict with the chairman, but that he was relieved by the Board. In answer to McInnis' concern about Scott's "resignation," Rose told him that he "should in no wise be held responsible or even charged with the recent action of the Board for you had nothing whatever to do with it."[52] There was also the intimation in correspondence from Rose to McInnis that there was friction on campus and that he hoped that "harmony and cooperation may prevail."[53] Meanwhile the Bryan *Eagle*, with no word of explanation either for the resignation of Thomas M. Scott or for its rather dire prediction, foresaw "radical changes" at the A&M College.[54]

By May 1890, according to Board President Rose, things at the College seemed to be "settling down."[55] Commencement exercises were held in June. By the authority vested in them the Directors granted fourteen degrees — six Bachelor of Scientific Agriculture, one Bachelor of Scientific Horticulture, three Bachelor of Mechanical Engineering, and four Bachelor of Chemical Engineering.[56] For the first time in its history, and one of the few times such has ever occurred, the College graduated as many agriculturists as engineers. Nonetheless, a substantial disparity remained between the number of students enrolled in engineering courses and the number in agriculture courses. Still, agriculture was experiencing a better day. Thomas M. Scott attended the commencement exercises and was able to chat briefly with McInnis. Scott

[50]Interview with Miss Malcolm Graham (Scott) McInnis, Bryan, Texas, January 20, 1971.

[51]A. J. Rose, Salado, Texas, to Louis L. McInnis, College Station, Texas, March 10, 1890, Louis L. McInnis Papers, Texas A&M University Archives.

[52]*Ibid.*

[53]*Ibid.*; A. J. Rose, Salado, Texas, to Louis L. McInnis, College Station, Texas, February 29, 1890, Louis L. McInnis Papers, Texas A&M University Archives.

[54]Bryan *Eagle*, March 5, 1890.

[55]A. J. Rose, Salado, Texas, to Louis L. McInnis, College Station, Texas, May 20, 1890, Louis L. McInnis Papers, Texas A&M University Archives.

[56]Minutes of the Board of Directors, June 7-18, 1890, I, 86-91.

asked him how things were going and McInnis told him that all was going well, and that he was on quite good terms with the Directors. Scott then refrained from telling McInnis what he had come to College Station to tell him.[57] Only later, when it was too late, did McInnis find out from Scott that his optimism had been unfounded.

Following the commencement exercises, the Board of Directors, as was customary, convened in a series of business meetings, which lasted from June 7 to June 18, 1890. On June 7 the Directors elected the faculty and approved salaries for the academic year 1890-1891. Louis McInnis' name was not included. No one was elected to fill the position of professor of mathematics, McInnis' academic position since 1880. The Board also specified that the offices of agent of the Board and chairman of the faculty would be abolished effective July 1, 1890.[58] Quite suddenly, and totally without warning for McInnis, he was without both a teaching position and an administrative position. He was without a job.

The Directors selected William Lorraine Bringhurst, professor of English, to take temporary charge of the books, papers, accounts, money, and property of the College on and after July 1, 1890, and until the election of a president of the College. Over the next several weeks McInnis was to furnish Bringhurst with all information in his possession necessary to transacting the business of the College.[59] A flurry of "resignations" were accepted by the Board of Directors. C. H. Fuqua, a sugar chemist with the Agriculture Experiment Station who had been at A&M for one year, resigned. Charles Perkins Fountain, the chaplain, resigned. Frank A. Gulley, director of the Agricultural Experiment Station since its conception, resigned. T. L. Brunk, professor of horticulture and botany, resigned.[60] William S. ("Willie") Scott, commandant of the Corps of Cadets, resigned in August at the request of the Board of Directors. Scott asked A. J. Rose for an explanation as to why the Board wanted to replace him. He suggested a call for a full hearing and court martial if an explanation were not made. Rose replied simply that there was nothing in the record against Scott and that the Board had been satisfied with the manner in which he had discharged his duties.[61]

Similarly, there has never been anything in the record to the discredit of

[57]Thomas M. Scott, Melissa, Texas, to Louis L. McInnis, College Station, Texas, November 9, 1890, Louis L. McInnis Papers, Texas A&M University Archives.

[58]Minutes of the Board of Directors, June 7-18, 1890, I, 88.

[59]*Ibid.*, I, 91.

[60]*Ibid.*, I, 88-90; Texas A&M, *Biennial Report, January 1889-December 1890*, pp. 3-4.

[61]A. J. Rose, Austin, Texas, to W. S. Scott, Leavenworth, Kansas, August 24, 1890, Louis L. McInnis Papers, Texas A&M University Archives.

Louis McInnis. At first McInnis was not sure just what his status with the College was. It appeared that he might simply be relieved as chairman of the faculty, and be reappointed as professor of mathematics, since no appointment to that position had been made. He wrote to Rose about retaining a position with the College and Rose replied flatly, "I will say to you that there is no chance for you to remain at the College."[62] The following day Rose wrote again to McInnis, softening his tone considerably. He told McInnis that all the Board members thought kindly of him, and he wanted to know what he could do to release McInnis from the "false impressions in which you are placed over the state."[63] The "false impressions" to which he referred are reflected in the report of the Galveston *News* for July 12, 1890, which suggested that things were very bleak at the College: "Students were discouraged and left by the score, professors were dissatisfied, the faculty was rent into factions, discipline was lacking, scandals were rife and serious trouble apprehended."[64] This report represented a serious overstatement of the situation at A&M. McInnis wrote to Rose in August asking for a thorough examination of the business records of the College and for a public explanation of his leaving A&M.[65] McInnis did get an official examination of the business records by the Board's Committee on Finance, which found all accounts to be complete and correct.[66] But the only public and official explanation for McInnis' departure, made to the Governor and to the Legislature, was that he "retired."[67]

Meanwhile, concern and support began to develop for McInnis from many sources. Judge Christopher C. Garrett, formerly president of the Board of Directors of the College, wrote to McInnis that the Board had made a mistake: "I have always considered you especially valuable to the college from your intimate and intelligent knowledge of its affairs, and of the status of technical education throughout the United States."[68] George M. Dilley, who

[62]A. J. Rose, Salado, Texas, to Louis L. McInnis, College Station, Texas, July 18, 1890, Louis L. McInnis Papers, Texas A&M University Archives.

[63]A. J. Rose, Salado, Texas, to Louis L. McInnis, College Station, Texas, July 19, 1890, Louis L. McInnis Papers, Texas A&M University Archives.

[64]Galveston *Daily News,* July 12, 1890.

[65]Louis L. McInnis, College Station, Texas, to A. J. Rose, President, Board of Directors, August 8, 1890, Louis L. McInnis Papers, Texas A&M University Archives.

[66]Report of the Finance Committee to A. J. Rose, President, Board of Directors, August 23, 1890, Louis L. McInnis Papers, Texas A&M University Archives.

[67]Louis L. McInnis, College Station, Texas, to A. J. Rose, Salado, Texas, August 8, 1890, Louis L. McInnis Papers, Texas A&M University Archives.

[68]C. C. Garrett, Brenham, Texas, to Louis L. McInnis, College Station, Texas, June 25, 1890, Louis L. McInnis Papers, Texas A&M University Archives.

resigned from the Board of Directors of the A&M College in 1889, indicated that McInnis' trouble had been promoted by the jealousy of two certain members of the faculty. He sent McInnis a strong testimonial and letter of reference.[69] Alexander Penn Wooldridge, member of the Board of Regents of The University of Texas, wrote some time later, "you certainly were a greatly wronged man at the A&M and your friends understand it." Wooldridge added that he felt that he and McInnis were "the pioneers" in trying to bring about cordial relations between The University and the A&M College.[70]

McInnis continued to press the Directors for a resolution by the Board commending his services to the College. He asked A. J. Rose, Board president, for a testimonial. He was met in each instance by a quiet refusal.[71] Thomas M. Scott suggested a public attack on the Board.[72] Edward Benjamin Cushing, and Charles Rogan, and many of the A&M alumni began a movement to have McInnis appointed to the Board of Directors of the A&M College.[73] McInnis maintained his silence and soon went into the banking business with an established institution in Bryan, having been urged to do so by many of his friends, including Thomas M. Scott, George M. Dilley, and former A&M President John G. James.[74] According to his daughter, Malcolm Graham McInnis, her father never talked about his retirement from the College, and never held any grudge.[75] The whole affair, however, had been a strange one. Justifications and explanations simply did not readily appear. On the contrary, McInnis' administration had seemed to be tremendously successful. The College was unquestionably better off when he left it than when he became chairman.

As time passed, the explanation for McInnis' removal and for the rein-

[69]George M. Dilley, Palestine, Texas, to Louis L. McInnis, College Station, Texas, June 26, 1890, Louis L. McInnis Papers, Texas A&M University Archives.

[70]Alexander Penn Wooldridge, Austin, Texas, to Louis L. McInnis, February 24, 1891, Louis L. McInnis Papers, Texas A&M University Archives.

[71]Louis L. McInnis, Bryan, Texas, to A. J. Rose, Salado, Texas, September 8, 1890; Louis L. McInnis to A. J. Rose, Salado, Texas, October 26, 1890; A. J. Rose to Louis L. McInnis, October 28, 1890, Louis L. McInnis Papers, Texas A&M University Archives.

[72]Thomas M. Scott, Melissa, Texas, to Louis L. McInnis, Bryan, Texas, March 19, 1891, Louis L. McInnis Papers, Texas A&M University Archives.

[73]Edward N. Cushing, Houston, Texas, to Louis L. McInnis, July 12, 1890, April 2, 1891, May 4, 1891, March 27, 1891; Charles Rogan, Austin, Texas, to E. B. Cushing, Houston, Texas, April 8, 1891, Louis L. McInnis Papers, Texas A&M University Archives.

[74]Thomas M. Scott, Melissa, Texas, to Louis L. McInnis, College Station, Texas, June 17, 1890; George M. Dilley, Palestine, Texas, to Louis L. McInnis, College Station, Texas, June 26, 1890; John G. James, Henrietta, Texas, to Louis L. McInnis, College Station, Texas, June 27, 1890, Louis L. McInnis Papers, Texas A&M University Archives.

[75]Interview with Miss Malcolm Graham (Scott) McInnis, Bryan, Texas, January 21, 1971.

stitution of the office of president, as opposed to the office of chairman of the faculty, began to appear. In November 1890 Scott wrote a long letter to McInnis which revealed much that McInnis had probably never known. According to Scott there had indeed been discontent among some members of the faculty, which recalls to mind the letter of Lucius Holman written in 1888, who said he overheard two professors say "they were not managing it rite."[76] Scott named three faculty members who were the "triumvirate" behind the removal of McInnis: William Lorraine Bringhurst, George Washington Curtis, and Charles Perkins Fountain. One of these wanted to become the president, another the professor of English, and the third the director of the Agricultural Experiment Station. Scott says that the first step was his own removal as business agent. Scott says, in effect, that he did not voluntarily retire, as the record indicates, but that he was forced out. Then along with McInnis, McInnis' own closest friends were either released or resigned voluntarily.[77] They included Frank A. Gulley, William S. Scott, and Walter Wipprecht; Charles P. Fountain, whom Scott implicated in the factional controversy, resigned on his own volition; others, such as Fuqua and Brunk, presumably believed that their resignations were timely.[78] Rudolph Wipprecht, professor of languages, was removed the following year.[79] This faculty squabble, however, fails to explain fully the Board's action, which historically is seldom swayed by faculty opinion.

Most obviously, the Board of Directors removed McInnis in order to make way for the next president of the College. Between 1888 and 1890 the complexion of the Board of Directors of the A&M College had changed markedly. In 1888 Christopher C. Garrett, and in 1889 George M. Dilley, two of McInnis' strongest supporters, left the Board. Governor Lawrence Sullivan Ross appointed J. D. Fields, of Manor, and John Adriance, of Columbia, in their places. Of the remaining Directors, Lafayette Lumpkin Foster had been appointed as commissioner of agriculture by Ross, and served ex officio as a member of the Board of Directors of the College; Archibald J. Rose owed his appointment on the Board to Ross; only William R. Cavitt of Bryan was left as the possible "nonaligned" Board member.[80] This then was a "Ross" Board.

[76]Lucius Holman, College Station, Texas, to Mrs. P. G. Weeks, Pilots Point, Texas, October 10, 1888, Lucius Holman Papers, Texas A&M University Archives.

[77]Thomas M. Scott, Melissa, Texas, to Louis L. McInnis, November 9, 1890, Louis L. McInnis Papers. A letter of W. S. Scott, Fort Leavenworth, Kansas, to Louis L. McInnis, Bryan, Texas, November 4, 1890, names William L. Bringhurst and George W. Curtis as primarily responsible for the ouster of McInnis.

[78]Minutes of the Board of Directors, June 7-18, 1890, I, 89-90; July 1, 1890, I, 92.

[79]Minutes of the Board of Directors, June 19, 1891, I, 111, 117.

[80]Appendix A.

In retrospect it would appear that the Board, in removing McInnis and his associates from office, acted entirely without malice, but with the simple intent of making way for Lawrence Sullivan Ross to become president of the A&M College.

On July 1, 1890, the Board of Directors of the A&M College elected Governor Lawrence Sullivan Ross president of the College "to take effect at the end of his present term of office as Governor." The office of vice-president was created and William L. Bringhurst was elected to fill that position.[81] George W. Curtis had already been named director of the Agricultural Experiment Station.

The selection of Governor Lawrence Sullivan Ross as president of the Agricultural and Mechanical College marked a great step forward for the institution. Ross' acceptance of the presidency signaled the fact, as nothing else could, that the A&M College had become an important and respected institution, and that the office of head of that institution had also become important and prestigious. Ross was a Texas and schoolboy's hero; he was a statesman and an able and powerful administrator. He brought to the College assets that no other person could possibly bring. It came to be said that people sent their sons to "Sul" Ross, not to the College. With the coming of Ross, A&M entered a new age, but with the departure of McInnis, the College lost one of its most able and dedicated founders.

[81] Minutes of the Board of Directors, July 1, 1890, I, 92; June 7-18, 1890, I, 89-90.

CHAPTER 8

An Awakening, 1890-1898

ALMOST a living legend at the time he assumed the presidency of the Agricultural and Mechanical College of Texas, Lawrence Sullivan Ross can be understood only in terms of the immense prestige and public esteem which he brought with him to the office. Had Ross accomplished little as an administrator, his contributions to the College nonetheless would have been enormous. Fortunately, Ross not only held the public's confidence, but proved to be a very efficient and effective administrator. Even so, the overwhelming significance of Ross to the College is not what he did, but who he was.

Sul Ross, the youngest son of Shapley Prince and Katherine (Fulkerson) Ross, was born September 27, 1838, at Bentonsport, Iowa, along the Des Moines River, where his father was Indian agent. Before Sul Ross reached his first birthday, S. P. Ross loaded his family aboard a wagon and crossed the prairies alone through Indian country from Iowa to Texas. In Texas the Rosses joined friends and relatives who had preceded them and settled along the upper reaches of the Brazos River at a place they called New Nashville. Soon afterwards the family moved to a place thirty-five miles north of New Nashville, where the present town of Cameron stands. The settlement lay on the fringe of civilization. For the next twenty years the pioneer families in the region, often under the leadership of S. P. Ross, and later Sul Ross, fought the Comanche Indians in an almost unceasing struggle for survival.[1]

In 1845 S. P. Ross moved his family to Austin, where his children could be educated and learn some of the refinements of civilization. Late that year Texas was annexed to the United States, and soon after, the Mexican War broke out. S. P. Ross, who preferred Texas as an independent nation to Texas as a state in the American union, nevertheless organized a company of Texas

---

[1]Bessie Ross Clarke, "S. P. Ross and Sul Ross," 1-35, unpublished manuscript (copy) by the daughter of Lawrence Sullivan Ross, in Ross Biographical Papers, Texas A&M University Archives; original in the L. S. Ross Papers, Texas Collection, Baylor University.

Rangers and assisted in the attack upon Monterrey with the American Army under General Zachary Taylor. Soon afterwards, S. P. Ross was sent to Waco Village, on the upper Brazos, with his Rangers, to keep peace on the frontier while the Army was preoccupied with Mexico. In February 1849 the Ross family moved to Waco, near their early home, where, in addition to his occasional duties as a Ranger, S. P. Ross operated a ferry and an inn. S. P. Ross engaged in his last Indian fight in 1858, when he led a company of Rangers and Indian allies against the troublesome Comanches along the Canadian River in the Panhandle region.[2]

During that same summer of 1858 his son Sul Ross, eighteen years old and home on vacation from Wesleyan College in Florence, Alabama, organized and led a company of friendly Indians to assist a troop under Major Earl Van Dorn in an attack on the Comanches along the Wichita River. For the next several years the whole Texas frontier blazed in a fresh conflagration of Indian warfare. In the attacks on the Comanches near what is now Fort Sill, Oklahoma, Sul Ross demonstrated very clearly his fighting instincts and abilities. He was wounded by an arrow and a rifle ball and narrowly escaped the scalping knife, but succeeded in •rescuing a small white girl from the Comanches. Sul Ross named the child Lizzie Ross, and raised her with his family.[3]

The next year Governor Sam Houston commissioned Sul Ross a captain in the Texas Rangers. Indian depredations in the West had become so serious that settlers were packing up and leaving. Houston sent a whole regiment of Texas Rangers under Colonel M. T. Johnson to track down and destroy Comanche Chief Peta Nocona, who for the past several years had terrorized the frontier. Johnson failed to find Nocona and the expedition had been costly to state finances, which from the days of the Republic had never been healthy. Houston, unable to get the federal authorities to accord the protection so badly needed by the Texas frontiersmen, turned to the use of state troops. A troop of sixty men was placed under Sul Ross and equipment left from the Johnson expedition was assigned to him. He was ordered to remain in the field until Nocona had been quelled. In December 1860 Ross, "the boy captain," with his Rangers and a volunteer band of armed settlers, located Nocona's camp along the Pease River and attacked. The attack was a complete surprise and a success. Chief Nocona fled on horseback with a young

[2]Clarke, "S. P. Ross and Sul Ross," 35-53; typed manuscript, apparently written by Florine Harrington Ross, "Captain Shapley Prince Ross," L. S. Ross Papers, Texas Collection, Baylor University.

[3]Clarke, "S. P. Ross and Sul Ross," 53-58; J. W. Wilbarger, *Indian Depredations in Texas*, 333-339.

girl riding behind him and with his wife and baby on horseback at his side. Sul Ross gave pursuit, overtook the wife, who surrendered, shot at Nocona, striking the girl, who in falling pulled Nocona from his horse. Ross charged into a volley of arrows, some of which struck his horse, and shot Nocona in the elbow and then twice through the chest.[4]

Ross later recalled the affair:

> I was at such disadvantage [because of the wounded horse] that, undoubtedly, he would have killed me but for a random shot from my pistol, while I was clinging with my left hand to the pommel of my saddle. This broke his right arm at the elbow, completely disabling him. My horse, then becoming more quiet, I shot twice through the body; whereupon he deliberately walked to a small tree nearby, the only one in sight. Leaning against it, with one arm around it for support he began a wild, weird song, the death song of the savage.[5]

The woman whom he had captured, the wife of Peta Nocona, turned out to be a white woman, Cynthia Ann Parker, taken as a captive by the Comanches twenty-five years and seven months earlier in the massacre at Parker's Fort, one of the most famous Indian raids in Texas lore. Cynthia Ann and her child, Prairie Flower, lived with the Rosses until their deaths in 1864. One of the sons of Cynthia Ann, who had survived the raid on Pease River, was Quanah Parker, who became chief of the Comanches on the reservation in Indian Territory. The engagement at Pease River ended organized Comanche resistance on the frontier and earned Sul Ross everlasting fame.[6] His fame and reputation as an Indian fighter, however, were soon surpassed by his exploits as a Confederate cavalry officer.

Although Lawrence Sullivan Ross took no active part in the debates on Texas secession from the Union, he was personally sympathetic to the Unionist position of Governor Sam Houston. But when war became a reality Ross enlisted as a private in a company commanded by his eldest brother. Soon afterwards he was elected a major of the regiment to which his company was attached, the Sixth Texas Cavalry. He then became a colonel in the regular Confederate army, and in the fall of 1862, at the age of twenty-three, was commissioned brigadier general, in command of his own brigade.[7]

---

[4]Clarke, "S. P. Ross and Sul Ross," 53-58; Wilbarger, *Indian Depredations in Texas*, 333-339.

[5]Clarke, "S. P. Ross and Sul Ross," 57; Wilbarger, *Indian Depredations in Texas*, 333-337. Victor M. Rose, *Ross' Texas Brigade*, 160, gives a more romanticized version of the fight between Peta Nocona and Ross.

[6]Clarke, "S. P. Ross and Sul Ross," 59-64; see also Grace Jackson, *Cynthia Ann Parker*, 83-89.

[7]Clarke, "S. P. Ross and Sul Ross," 65-79; Rose, *Ross' Texas Brigade*, 161-170.

Ross' Texas Brigade distinguished itself in the battles of Springfield, Missouri; Corinth, Mississippi; and Atlanta, Georgia, as well as at many way stations in between. Ross was personally engaged in 135 battles, had seven horses shot from under him, and survived without a scratch. Victor M. Rose, in his book-length story of *Ross' Texas Brigade,* describes the exciting events of Sul Ross' military career.[8] Now a war hero as well as a renowned Indian fighter, Ross returned to his home in Waco, where he farmed, became sheriff of the county, served in the "Redeemer" Constitutional Convention of 1875, won election to the state Senate in 1881, and began his first term as governor of Texas on January 18, 1887.[9] Governor Ross, the first governor to occupy the new capitol building in Austin, improved the administration of the state's public lands. He also initiated efforts to establish the Railroad Commission and expanded and improved the public schools. Far ahead of his time, he went so far as to advocate free textbooks for the public schools. His achievements as governor heightened his public reputation. He completed his second term as governor on January 20, 1891, on which date he officially became president of Texas A&M.[10]

Ross' impact upon affairs at the A&M College were immediate and profound and preceded his arrival on campus. Even before his appointment as president became publicly known, the Bryan *Eagle* announced that the people were in for an "agreeable surprise" and could anticipate a "boost" for the College "far ahead of the most sanguine expectations."[11] A few days after the appointment of Ross became public a mass meeting was held in Bryan hailing his selection as a "most judicious and happy one."[12] Favorable public response to Ross' selection as president was demonstrated by the overcrowding of the school on its opening day, September 10, 1890.[13] The once hostile Galveston *News* responded warmly to Ross' election as president of the A&M College. It applauded A&M as a "great university," a "people's" university which trained young men in every profession and pursuit of life, not in the "dreamy and unconsequential inanities."[14] Acting President William L. Bringhurst's annual report of December 1890 waxed eloquent:

[8]Clarke, "S. P. Ross and Sul Ross," 79; Rose, *Ross' Texas Brigade,* entire work and 172 in particular.

[9]Clarke, "S. P. Ross and Sul Ross," 79-84; Rose, *Ross' Texas Brigade,* 161-170.

[10]Texas A&M, *Annual Report, 1899,* p. 3; Minutes of the Board of Directors, July 1, 1890, I, 92; *Handbook of Texas,* II, 506-507.

[11] Bryan *Weekly Eagle,* July 3, 1890.

[12]*Ibid.,* July 10, 1890.

[13]*Ibid.,* October 2, 1890.

[14]Cited in *Ibid.,* October 16, 1890.

I am proud to be able to say to you that the college seems to be thrilling with new life. Activity and energy and prosperity are in all its departments. We have a zealous and united faculty, and an industrious and responsive corps of students. Excellent progress is being made, and all things are, in my judgment, working together for the good of the institution, the realization of whose "high destiny" is imminent.[15]

According to Bringhurst, five hundred students would have enrolled in the College in September had there been room for them. Three hundred sixteen accepted students severely strained facilities which had been geared to accommodate a maximum of 250 students.[16]

On August 8, 1890, Governor Ross gave formal acceptance of the presidency of the A&M College, to be effective at the expiration of his term of office as governor. On August 6 the Board of Directors had raised the salary of the president of Texas A&M from $3,000, set in its June meeting, to $3,500. As chairman of the faculty, Louis L. McInnis had drawn an annual salary of $2,400.[17] Construction on a new president's home began almost immediately and the "mansion," as the student journal referred to it, was completed by February 1892.[18] Ross began and ended his administration as president of the College in an aura of munificence.

His future policies and attitudes are indicated by his past achievements, and by his letter of acceptance. Ross sounded much like a Granger when he praised agriculture as the basis of wealth. Students, he said, should be trained for the most "lucrative, honorable and important positions in every industrial enterprise." He spoke of the great need for trained labor in Texas and of the "dignity of labor." He stressed "proper moral instruction," and added that the "military feature" of the College is of "transcendental importance."[19] By all appearances he would be the most perfect president for the Agricultural and Mechanical College of Texas. As events proved, even Ross was not without his detractors and critics.

The school year 1890-1891 did indeed "thrill" with new life. The Directors approved a contract with a Bryan company to provide the College with electricity, specifying that the campus would receive 150 sixteen-candle-

[15]Texas A&M, *Annual Report, 1890*, p. 11.

[16]*Ibid.;* Texas A&M, *Biennial Report, 1893*, p. 7.

[17]Bryan *Eagle*, August 14, 1890; College Station *College Journal*, II (October 1890), 6-8.

[18]Minutes of the Board of Directors, August 20, 1890, p. 94; College Station *College Journal*, III (February 1892), 20.

[19]Minutes of the Board of Directors, August 20, 1890, I, 94-95; Bryan *Eagle* (W), August 14, 1890; College Station *College Journal, II,* (October 1890), 6-8.

power lights for five hours per day at a cost of $1,600 per year plus installation.[20] Not failing to realize the unique opportunities which the moment offered, the Directors in 1890 submitted a request for appropriations totaling $128,600 to Governor Ross, who would soon be coming to College Station as president of the College. Major items included $50,000 for new dormitories, $12,000 for a chemical laboratory, $10,000 for a carpenter shop, $10,000 for a veterinary hospital, $5,000 for enlarging facilities of the Experiment Station, $10,000 for artesian water and bath houses, $15,000 for a new mess hall, $7,500 for professors' residences, and $5,000 for a gymnasium.[21] In his final address to the Legislature, Governor Ross noted the inadequate accommodations at the A&M College and recommended strong support for the College "so vital to farming interests."[22] He also noted that the "Second Morrill Act," approved by Congress on August 30, 1890, made an annual appropriation of $15,000 to the A&M College for the benefit of agriculture, to be increased for ten years by an additional sum of $1,000 over the preceding year, and thereafter at $25,000 annually.[23] Ross had made a preliminary division of these monies, with one-third to Prairie View, the colored branch of Texas A&M, and two-thirds to the College. He asked the Legislature to approve the necessary legislation making a permanent division of these federal funds between the Negro and white branches of the A&M College as required by the act.[24] At this point, if one includes the interest from the original land-grant endowment, the Experiment Station endowment, and the Second Morrill grants, the A&M College received approximately $45,000 annually from the federal government in the 1890s, a handsome endowment for that time.

In 1891 the Legislature formed its usual visitation committee to visit the A&M College and other state institutions. Governor James Stephen Hogg, who succeeded Ross, as well as the visitation committee, recommended support for the A&M College.[25] The Legislature complied warmly but not to the extent anticipated by the Directors. The College received $19,500 for support and maintenance from general revenues, and $500 from

[20]Minutes of the Board of Directors, August 20, 1890, pp. 9-7.

[21]Texas A&M, *Annual Report, 1890*, p. 8.

[22]*Governor's Messages, Coke to Ross, 1874-1891*, p. 670.

[23]*Ibid.*, p. 671.

[24]*Ibid.*, pp. 671-672. Note: Ross also reported that a settlement had been reached on a disputed title to University lands in McLennan County by which The University of Texas received title to 6,750 acres of a 14,000-acre tract in dispute. See also *Texas House Journal, 1891*, pp. 36-37.

[25]*Texas House Journal, 1891*, pp. 39-40.

the University Fund.[26] This was still about $5,000 better than the average of the past few years. Six thousand was provided for carpenter shops (rather than $50,000), $7,500 for professors' residences, $600 for wiring and light fixtures, $10,000 for artesian wells and bath houses (as requested), and $2,000 for tools for mechanical engineering.[27] The College, in all, received some $66,400 from the state for the next two years, more than it had ever received since it opened. The Legislature also passed a measure dividing the Morrill grant of 1890 between A&M and Prairie View on a basis of one-fourth to Prairie View and three-fourths to A&M,[28] by which Prairie View received a smaller share than it had received under Ross' preliminary division.

Indicative of the new prosperity of the A&M College, the Board of Directors listed total resources of the College of the academic year 1891-1892 as being approximately $77,000, exclusive of $46,100 allocated for capital improvement.[29] Thus, in this very important material respect, Ross' presence at A&M contributed to the greater prosperity of the school. This prosperity came at a time when the country was poised on the brink of the depression of 1893, one of the more serious in the nation's history, which the College seemingly weathered very well.

As president of the College, and as an experienced public administrator, Ross gathered the reins of fiscal and administrative matters under his own control. The Board, having already abolished the position of agent of the Board, designated Ross as both president and treasurer of the College.[30] The state Legislature also designated Ross treasurer of the College and the agent to receive federal money under the Second Morrill Act.[31] Ross abolished the office of fiscal agent of the College, which office had been delegated to receive funds from the state comptroller on A&M's account and to disburse the money drawn by drafts for the treasurer or agent of the Board for which the agent was paid a commission. This office had been filled by John S. Fowlkes almost since the opening of the College. Instead, Ross now put up a personal bond of $20,000 and was authorized to place A&M funds in any bank he desired. Ross also modernized and improved the accounting system used by the College.[32] There is little question that Ross, who had appointed most of the A&M Board members, maintained during his presidency virtu-

[26]Gammel (ed.), *Laws of Texas*, IX, 125-126.

[27]*Ibid.;* see also Minutes of the Board of Directors, June 6, 1891, I, 104-105.

[28]Gammel (ed.), *Laws of Texas*, IX, 45-46; Texas A&M, *Annual Report, 1891*, p. 3.

[29]Minutes of the Board of Directors, June 6, 1891, I, 104-105.

[30]Minutes of the Board of Directors, February 10, 1891, p. 99.

[31]Gammel (ed.), *Laws of Texas*, IX, 45-46.

[32]Minutes of the Board of Directors, June 6, 1891, pp. 107-109; Texas A&M, *Annual Report, 1891*, p. 4.

ally sole and absolute control over the fiscal and administrative affairs of the College.

Numerous administrative changes and improvements were made by Ross. The Board appointed a committee comprising Ross and William R. Cavitt to revise the *Catalogue* and the rules and regulations of the College. A formal order for administrative succession provided that in the absence of the president and the vice-president of the College, or in case of their disability to discharge their duties, then the professor holding precedence by date of appointment should act as president.[33] The first official statement regarding faculty tenure provided that the tenure of faculty and the president should depend upon good behavior and efficiency of service, and that reasonable notice of dismissal should be given.[34] While this was an extremely broad statement by contemporary academic standards, it was then a liberal statement. The Department of Drawing, and the Department of Civil Engineering and Physics both received new heads. Frederick Ernst Giesecke was named head of Drawing and James C. Nagle head of Civil Engineering, each with the rank of full professor.[35] It was also provided that "faculty meetings" should be attended only by department heads. "Heads of departments" were specifically stated as being the (1) president of the College; (2) professor of English and history; (3) professor of languages; (4) professor of mechanical engineering; (5) professor of agriculture and director of the Experiment Station; (6) professor of chemistry and mineralogy; (7) professor of mathematics; (8) professor of veterinary science; (9) professor of military science and commandant of cadets; (10) professor of drawing; (11) professor of horticulture and botany; and (12) professor of civil engineering and physics.[36]

Meetings of the Board of Directors were declared to be private affairs and their proceedings were no longer for release or publication, as they had been in the past.[37] In 1892 for the first time the Directors provided formally for a system of maintaining the official minutes of the Board.[38] The Directors also provided that the Farm should be a self-sustaining operation and that separate accounts and records should be kept for it.[39] Other than for the addition and replacement of faculty, these adjustments or changes comprised most of those made by Ross during his years as president.

Ross, like McInnis, made special efforts to promote a reconciliation and

[33]Minutes of the Board of Directors, February 18, 1892, I, 125.

[34]*Ibid.*, 126.

[35]*Ibid.*, June 8, 1892, I, 135.

[36]*Ibid.*, 136.

[37]*Ibid.*

[38]*Ibid.*, July 3, 1892, I, 138.

[39]*Ibid.*, November 3, 1892, I, 143.

harmony between The University of Texas and the A&M College. Unlike McInnis, Ross was in a far better position to succeed in these efforts. In November 1892 the Directors authorized the president of the Board, Archibald Johnson Rose, to arrange a joint meeting of the A&M Directors with The University Board of Regents to discuss common interests.[40] The official report of this joint session, which took place in Austin on January 18, 1893, denotes, in view of past hostilities between the institutional directors, a completely new relationship between The University and the College.

After a short consultation the Board of Directors repaired to the office of the Board of Regents of The University of Texas in the University building. There the present condition and interests of the two institutions were fully and most pleasantly discussed by the two Boards. It was made evident that the best of feelings existed with the Boards and the two institutions generally. The Boards agreed to mutually aid each other in building up the respective educational interests, in which they are, as Directors and Regents, engaged. The Board of Directors, after more than an hour's most pleasant consultation with the Board of Regents, withdrew and returned to the Driskill Hotel, feeling that they had profited by their visit, the schools mutually benefited, that it is well for brethren to dwell together in unison, and in harmony there is success.[41]

This marked a dramatic change in the relationship as it had existed between the two institutions some years earlier. One immediate product of this situation was the creation of a Cooperative Steering Committee comprising three members of the Board of Regents and three of the Directors.[42] This Steering Committee represents the very distant ancestor of the modern Coordinating Board for Higher Education in Texas. In 1893 the A&M Directors convened in Austin to attend the commencement exercises of The University in order to "build up a closer relation and better feeling between the two institutions."[43]

The two Boards convened jointly again at College Station in 1896 and took more positive steps at cooperation. They established a Joint Committee on Revision of Curricula, which included Thomas D. Wooten, of The University Regents, as chairman, and William R. Cavitt, representing the A&M Board, as secretary. The Committee included the president of The University, George T. Winston, and two of his faculty, and President Ross and two of the A&M faculty. The Committee was directed to consider "revising the cur-

[40]*Ibid.*, November 28, 1892, I, 144.
[41]*Ibid.*, January 18, 1893, I, 146.
[42]*Ibid.*
[43]*Ibid.*, June 19, 1893, I, 150.

ricula of The University and its branches as to economize if possible, in the interests of the state and of students in the main university and its branches, and with a view of so arranging the courses in one branch that one may receive credit for the same in the other." The Committee was directed to make its report on January 1, 1897. The two Boards also recommended that the alumni of the two schools work together, and they provided that a student expelled from one branch for immoral conduct should not be admitted to the other.[44] Like the Steering Committee established in 1892, which had been more symbolic than functional, the Joint Committee on Curricula exemplified the recognition of a degree of interdependence between the College and The University. Real cooperation between the institutions never went much beyond this point during Ross' administration. Some efforts were made to maintain a liaison with The University during the administration of David F. Houston and Lafayette Lumpkin Foster, between 1898 and 1904, but by 1916 the "Battle of the Universities" was being rejoined.

Several positive products of this reconciliation, however, were manifested legislatively in the nineties. The University Regents had desired to be invested with authority to control University lands, as opposed to the commissioner of the General Land Office. Texas A&M had repeatedly opposed this. In 1895 University and College interests accepted a bill to give the Regents exclusive control over University lands, including the right to sell and lease such land, so long as the selling price was not less than that prescribed by statutes applying to the general public lands.[45] In addition, the Regents had long preferred to allocate revenues from the University Fund to the use of the Main University and had consistently opposed the legislative allocations of $5,000-$15,000 from the Fund to the A&M College. Although there was no formal written agreement to that effect, it became fairly obvious that throughout the nineties A&M supporters agreed to accept only token appropriations from the University Fund ($500) in return for larger appropriations from the General Fund, usually $19,500 annually, plus larger appropriations for capital improvements.[46] If it could not be properly called cooperation, it was at least a truce between the institutions which redounded to the advantage of both.

Despite his past reputation and his accomplishments at A&M, Lawrence Sullivan Ross was not without his critics. One of the strongest indictments of Ross was that he had developed an "imported Yankee Republican faculty."

[44]*Ibid.*, June 31, 1896, I, 185-186.
[45]Gammel (ed.), *Laws of Texas*, IX, 749.
[46]*Ibid.*, IX, 125-126, 573-576, 865-866.

One state legislator argued that "we have as good teachers in the Democratic party as in the Republican party."[47] Similar charges, it should be noted, were directed against The University in Austin.[48] In considerable measure this agitation reflected the renewed sectional hostility generated in the presidential elections of 1888 and 1892. The controversy passed without injury to either institution.

Other charges were perhaps more serious. The *Texas Farmer* argued that the College had again become a "military peacockery" and that it failed to support effectively practical training in agriculture and mechanics. Under present conditions, said the journal, Governor Ross' position is little more than a sinecure.[49] Another report said "General Ross, the President, compares it [Texas A&M] favorable with other A. and M.'s — and leans back with much self-satisfaction."[50] This unfavorable sentiment generated a fairly exhaustive legislative inquiry of the A&M College in 1893.

"The management of the College," reported a joint legislative committee in March 1893, has diverted the College "in a great measure from the plain purpose of its founding and converted it into a military and literary school":[51]

The prescribed course in military science embraces lectures, drill, guard mounting and guard duty, inspections, musters, reviews, dress parades, target practice, competitive drill, battalion drill, and as no student can graduate from the institution without a certain proficiency in the military department . . . he is confronted with the alternative of neglecting farm and shop work, or of relinquishing the hope of promotion, and the pride and pleasure excited by military display and the notice it attracts — an alternative which is generally settled in favor of the military courses.[52]

Because "all that affects the general interest and welfare of the cadets" is under the charge of the commandant of cadets, continued the report, the military feature is distinctively impressed upon the College. The committee recommended less attention to the military and unswerving devotion to the primary object of the College — "to afford a practical industrial education to

---

[47]W. A. Martin, Coleman, Texas, to Louis L. McInnis, Bryan, Texas, April 6, 1891; J. D. Read, Sherman, Texas, to McInnis, April 2, 1892; Louis L. McInnis Papers, Texas A&M University Archives; San Angelo *Standard,* April 25, 1891, clipping in Louis L. McInnis Papers, Texas A&M University Archives.

[48]H. Y. Benedict (ed.), *Source Book Relating to the History of the University of Texas,* 406-409.

[49]Dallas *Texas Farmer,* January 28, 1893, clipping in Louis L. McInnis Papers.

[50]Undated news clipping in McInnis Scrapbook, Louis L. McInnis Papers.

[51]"Joint Committee Report," *Texas House Journal,* 1893, pp. 527-528.

[52]*Ibid.*

those whose purpose is the pursuit of an industrial career."[53] Somewhat reminiscent of the agrarian protests of the Gathright era, the investigative committee advocated required manual labor for practical training in the agricultural and mechanical courses. It again distinguished between instructive and noninstructive labor and recommended the establishment of a "student labor fund" for the payment of student labor.[54] Subsequently, one result of this report was the appropriation by the Legislature of money for the payment of student labor, which had been advocated by Louis McInnis during his administration, and which helped make an A&M education available to more students.[55] Unlike that of the Gathright era, this rather critical legislative report produced very few changes in the academic or military climate of the institution. Lawrence Sullivan Ross was not one to be panicked or moved by a mere legislative report.

Ross and others were well aware that the report was in part inspired by a refreshed agrarian uprising stimulated by the depression of 1893. The new decade witnessed the rise of a new politically active farmer movement characterized by the Populist Party of America, which had become a significant, but still unmeasured factor in Texas politics. Governor James Stephen Hogg continually undermined Populism with his own Democratic brand of agrarianism, which Ross and others began to refer to as "Hoggism." The eighteen-nineties marked the culmination of the agrarian reform movements in America and in Texas.[56] Populism's impact upon Texas A&M seems to have been marginal. By 1890 the College was settled in the more conservative hands of the Alliance-Democratic-Hogg coalition — and Lawrence Sullivan Ross was above it all.

Some charges, to be sure, were brought out by the joint committee investigating A&M. They had nothing to do with agrarianism, but in other times and circumstances could have been quite serious. The committee found, for example, that cattle and hogs for the College were being bought from individual Board members. While it found nothing seriously incriminating in the purchases, the committee suggested that such transaction be scrupulously avoided.[57] The committee criticized the surgeon, the laundry work, and the cook.[58] It also found that "the Board of Directors have been advancing

[53]*Ibid.*
[54]*Ibid.*
[55]*Ibid.*
[56]See Robert F. Durden, *The Climax of Populism;* and Roscoe C. Martin, *The People's Party in Texas: A Study of "Third Party Politics."*
[57]*Texas House Journal, 1893,* p. 527.
[58]*Ibid.,* 526.

the interests of friends and relatives rather than the interests of the college in regards to the creation of positions, appointments, promotions and removals."[59] One form of nepotism which had already developed at the College and which would continue in later years was the practice of hiring large numbers of its own graduates for teaching and administrative positions.

Despite the criticism, the overall results of the investigation were positive and advantageous to the College. The committee, for example, recommended that the College withdraw from the contract with the Water, Ice and Electric Company of Bryan, for supplying the College with electricity, and that it establish its own independent electric-light plant, and institute a curriculum in electrical engineering as an adjunct of the new facility.[60] Within months the College was receiving bids for an electrical generating plant.[61] By November 1893, the facility had been installed.[62] In 1903 the Department of Physics and Electrical Engineering was created, and the College produced its first two graduates in electrical engineering in 1905. Electrical engineering was made a separate department in June 1909.[63] In 1893 the investigative committee also called for more money for the development of an adequate water supply and funds for hiring student labor, all of which were provided for by the Legislature.[64]

The critical context of the committee report was generally ignored by Ross and the Board. In a July meeting the Directors were "of the opinion" that hours at drill should be reduced, but issued no specific directions, and there is no evidence that anything changed. The Directors did request the commandant to stay in the mess hall during meals, an action which subsequently quieted the rowdy and often chaotic mealtimes.[65] Ross was himself totally unintimidated by any criticism from the Legislature. In November, Ross announced that the College was "by far, more prosperous, and in better shape, in every way, than ever before in its history." He commended the Corps of Cadets for their "obedience, studious habits and gentlemanly bearing."[66] Ross' opinion of things would prevail over that of the entire Leg-

---

[59]*Ibid.,* 527.

[60]*Ibid.*

[61]Minutes of the Board of Directors, June 7, 1893, I, 149-150.

[62]*Ibid.,* November 7, 1893, I, 157.

[63]College Station *Longhorn, 1908,* pp. 43-44, 148; Minutes of the Board of Directors, June 7, 1909, II, 158.

[64]"Joint Committee Report," *Texas House Journal, 1893,* pp. 526-527; Gammel (ed.), *Laws of Texas,* X, 537-576.

[65]Minutes of the Board of Directors, July 7, 1893, I, 156.

[66]*Ibid.,* November 7, 1893, I, 157.

islature — there would be no de-emphasis of the military features of the College.

Ross' good opinion of things, it is worth noting, was not simply a statement for public consumption but was a reflection of his private thoughts. He wrote to his former secretary, Major Holmes, in December 1893 that "I am getting along very smoothly here and the young men seem devoted to me. I have made great improvements and people coming here hardly recognize the place."[67] Ross admitted soon after his arrival at the College that he found things that "made me turn grey fast," but these things were straightened out. Ross found great personal pleasure in the fact that sons of the "best families" of the state were sent to A&M because he was at its head.[68]

The cadets also took great pride and pleasure in having Ross as their president. He was their leader, their inspiration, and their hero. The first student annual, the *Olio,* published in 1895, proudly recounted Ross' exploits.[69] Ross has subsequently become an integral part of Aggie "traditions," further indication of the impact which he had on the students at the time.

While to a considerable extent Texas A&M reached a degree of academic maturity during the administration of Louis L. McInnis, it reached a high degree of psychological maturity during the years of Lawrence Sullivan Ross. These are the years which reaffirmed and reconstituted the strong military orientation of the College, and these are the years which gave conception to the "Aggie Spirit" and "Aggie traditions," for which the College gained repute in later years. Ross announced upon assuming the office of president that the military feature was of "transcendental importance." It was so when the investigating committee visited in 1893, and it appeared so in 1958, when compulsory military training was reinstituted on campus after a brief experiment with voluntary ROTC.[70]

Under Ross the Corps of Cadets became synonymous with an A&M student; there was no longer any differentiation, as in the Gathright days, between a "cadet" and a "student." The "student" effectively ceased to exist, and in his place for several decades was to stand the "cadet." As the *Olio* put it in 1895, "sons of the rich and poor, high and low are treated as equals. . . . We all dress alike, eat alike and sleep alike."[71] Over fifty years later the senti-

[67]Lawrence Sullivan Ross, College Station, Texas, to Major Holmes, Austin, Texas, December 30, 1893, L. S. Ross Papers, Texas Collection, Baylor University.

[68]*Ibid.;* L. S. Ross to Major Holmes, August 9, 1891, L. S. Ross Correspondence, Texas Collection, Baylor University.

[69]College Station *The Olio,* 1895, p. 32.

[70]Texas A&M, *A Report on Faculty-Staff-Student Aspirations,* 1962, p. 25.

[71]College Station *The Olio,* 1895, p. 32.

ment was closely paraphrased in an official brochure published upon the celebration of the seventy-fifth anniversary of the College, which added, the school is "simply a dormitory school for men in which today, as in the days of the Texas frontier, each man is expected to 'win his spurs,' to stand solely on his own merits as a man."[72]

The cadets' day usually began at 6:00 A.M. with morning reveille and roll call. Calls, which had been made by drum from the opening of the College through the 1891-1892 academic years, were apparently made by bugle beginning in 1892-1893, although the exact date has not been ascertained.[73] After roll call cadets returned to their rooms to dress, sweep out, pile their bunks, and police their rooms, whereupon breakfast call was sounded. Cadets then formed up and marched to breakfast, where they made a hearty meal of bacon, eggs, pancakes, or sausage, and such things as "reg" (syrup), "axle-grease" (butter), "sawdust" (sugar), and "shot-gun" (applesauce). The cadets then rose on command, formed up, and marched to morning chapel. After chapel services, guard duty was called; then followed sick call.[74]

Guard-duty assignments usually ran in one-hour to two-hour watches twenty-four hours a day. The guards were almost invariably "fish," or first-year cadets, particularly those holding the late watches. On the hour sentinels called out the hours, their post number, and "all is well." James Bedford ("Josh") Sterns recalls that one fish sentinel, fed-up with the harassment and night duty, yelled out upon the appointed hour, "Post Number 6, one o'clock, all's well, kiss my foot, and go to hell, you sons of bitches." Whereupon he threw down his gun, went to his room, packed his clothes and left on the 2 A.M. train.[75]

The first study call came at 8:00 A.M. and on the hour thereafter until 4:00 or 4:30 P.M.[76] By 1908 the calls had been refined to give a five-minute "break" between the end of one class and the beginning of the next.[77] In 1896 marching to and from recitations was abolished.[78]

The time after the close of classes, between 5:00 and 6:00 P.M., was usually occupied by drill exercises, or various other military duties. Supper came

[72]Texas A&M, *1876 . . . 1951, 75th Anniversary* [10].

[73]The last official mention of a "drummer" is in the Minutes of the Board of Directors, November 5, 1891, I, 122, in which the directors authorize the payment of $30 per month to "Major Fish as drummer."

[74]College Station *Battalion*, December 1, 1893.

[75]J. B. Sterns Reminiscences, "Sentinel Duty," Texas A&M University Archives.

[76]College Station *Battalion*, December 1, 1893.

[77]Paul D. Casey, *The History of the A. & M. College Trouble, 1908*, pp. 11-12.

[78]Texas A&M, *Annual Report, 1896*, pp. 21-22.

at 6:00 study call at 7:30, tattoo at 9:45, and taps at 10:00 P.M.[79] The student's life was highly regimented, occupied, and organized, and as one "nemo" opined in the student paper, there really was very little time for study.

There were diversions from the military, of course, as well as from studies. Perhaps most of these activities occurred "after the lights went out," for one of the reasons given for the establishment of the College's own electric power plant and lighting system in 1893 was that the authorities would be better able to "detect absences."[81] Similar arguments had been given for the installation of gas lighting in 1887.[82]

By the 1890s numerous extracurricular activities had come to the campus. The Austin Literary Society and the Calliopean Literary Society, founded during the Gathright years, still flourished. In 1889 the two societies joined in the publication of the *College Journal,* a literary magazine containing small excerpts of student news and views.[83] The *Journal* continued in publication until 1893, when it was replaced by the *Battalion,* which had more of a newspaper format, but retained a strong literary flavor for many years. The first issue of the *Battalion,* which continues in print today as the A&M student newspaper, appeared on October 1, 1893. Its editor was Ernest L. Bruce, and it continued to be sponsored by the Austin and Calliopean Literary Societies until the demise of these organizations early in the next century.[84]

The nature of the *Battalion* in the nineties is indicated by the leading "story" in the first issue, which was an essay on Shakespeare's interpretation of King Lear. A feature on "life in the U.S. Army" composed a prominent portion of six issues of the *Battalion.* Mention of sports activities appeared with increasing frequency, but the journal remained essentially literary until 1904, when the Austin and Calliopean Societies turned sponsorship of the organ over to the Association of Former Students. In that year it became a weekly newspaper. Both the *College Journal* and the *Battalion* owed much to the direction and guidance provided by William Bledsoe Philpott, associate and then full professor of English. Philpott, born in Brenham, Texas, in 1865, attended John G. James' Texas Military Academy in Austin. Upon James' move to A&M, Philpott followed in 1881, graduating in 1884, with a

[79]College Station *Battalion,* December 1, 1893.

[80]*Ibid.*

[81]"Joint Committee Report," *Texas House Journal, 1893,* pp. 526-527.

[82]Minutes of the Board of Directors, June 8, 1887, I, 29-32.

[83]College Station *College Journal* (microfilm, 1889-1893), Texas A&M University Library. Some issues of the *Journal* are missing. See also Vick Lindley, *The Battalion: Seventy Years of Student Publications at the A&M College of Texas,* 1-7.

[84]College Station *Battalion,* October 1, 1893; see also Lindley, *The Battalion,* 1-7.

degree in mechanical engineering. He became principal of Bethel Academy and then turned to journalism as editor of the short-lived *Brazos Blade*. In 1887 he returned to A&M as associate professor of English. Philpott was promoted to full professor and became head of the Department of English in 1900. He left the school in 1902, a few years before his death in 1908.[85]

The two literary societies on campus held monthly meetings, at which a debate was usually staged on some popular question, such as free silver, prohibition, and the division of Texas into five separate states. The societies, faculty, and individual students also participated in what were called the "Friday night exercises." In one typical Friday-night exercise in November 1891, the College Quartet sang "Come Where the Lilies Bloom," and several young ladies from Bryan and the faculty read poetry; there was a lecture by one of the professors, and students and adults played a number of orchestral arrangements. The Friday-night exercises, however, appear to have been short-lived. They soon came only once a month and seem to have disappeared after a short time.[86]

The Young Men's Christian Association, which came on campus in 1889, struggled for existence during its first few years. The organization seems to have picked up steam in 1891, and by 1893 was reported to be in a "flourishing condition." The YMCA joined the College in the construction of a small gymnasium in 1893.[87] It sponsored lectures, athletic activities, and various social events. Soon after the turn of the century, and essentially through World War II, the YMCA was the dominant student social organization on campus. In 1910 the association of former students, largely through the inspiration and leadership of Edward B. Cushing, began a drive to obtain funds for a permanent YMCA structure on campus. Although sufficient funds were not on hand at the time, construction on a YMCA building began in June 1912, and the building was completed the following year.[88]

Cushing, with former A&M College students in Houston, also sponsored the organization of an association of former students, or, as it was first named, Alpha Phi. Cushing pointed out in 1896 that at the time there were 3,000 former students of the College, but only about 150 graduates eligible for alumni status. Alpha Phi, or the association of former students, first elected officers in 1896.[89] It soon absorbed the existing Alumni Association,

[85]Lindley, *The Battalion*, 2-3.

[86]College Station *College Journal*, III (November 1891), 18-19.

[87]College Station *College Journal*, III (February 1891), 20, and *ibid.*, IV (February 1893), 16.

[88]Minutes of the Board of Directors, September 5, 1910, II, 218, 220; March 8, 1912, III, 6; June 11, 1912, III, 16.

[89]College Station *Battalion*, October 1896, p. 23, and June 1897, p. 39.

organized in 1886, and the Association of Ex-Cadets, which had been created in 1880, and which provided the broad structure characteristic of the very active and involved Association of Former Students as it exists today.

Organized sports appeared on campus and made ˙considerable advances during the nineties. Baseball came on campus several years prior to football. While it would be presumptuous to say when the first competitive baseball game was played by A&M, an early game was played between A&M and Navasota on April 1, 1891. The game evoked considerable excitement among the spectators and a dispute in the sixth inning, when the score stood 6-5 in favor of A&M. Apparently the dispute ended the game, for the referees finally declared A&M the victor by a score of 9-0.[90] The following year the two teams met again and the College beat Navasota 21-12.[91]

The next year, 1893, the seniors challenged the faculty to a baseball game, but there is no report on the results.[92] That same year the first issue of the *Battalion* announced that baseball was on the decline. The reason for the decline seems to have been the advent of football on campus. The *College Journal* of February 1893 announced that A&M College now "boasts a crack football team," thus indicating that the initial efforts to organize a football team must have been made in the fall of 1892. The first football game of record occurred on November 29, 1894, when A&M defeated Ball High School in Galveston 14-6.[93] In 1896 two professors, A. M. Soule and Horace W. South, served as coaches. The students hired C. W. Taylor as a regular coach in 1897.[94] In 1901 the College obtained its first "physical director," whose duties were to take charge of the "gymnasium and natatorium at the college and direct the athletic sports of every character among the students," and who was to receive a salary of $1,000 for nine months.[95] The first director was George S. Whitney, who was relieved a year later. Whitney became a victim of increasing faculty hostility to competitive football. The A&M faculty passed a ruling in 1902 refusing to allow A&M football teams to meet other Texas educational institutions in competitive games. The students reacted by sending a petition to the Board of Directors and to the president asking that the faculty "rescind their actions." While the prohibition against competitive games was rescinded, the control over athletics remained for a

[90]College Station *College Journal*, III (April 1891), pp. 14-15.

[91]*Ibid.*, IV (April 1892), 15. Note: The volume numbers on the *College Journal* are erratic.

[92]*Ibid.*, III.

[93]Bryan *Eagle*, December 6, 1894, p. 4; see also George Sessions Perry, *The Story of A. & M.*, 74, 128, 246-248.

[94]Perry, *The Story of A. & M.*, 74, 128.

[95]Minutes of the Board of Directors, July 23, 1901, I, 242.

time under the direct auspices of the faculty.[96] Organized sports, particularly football, struggled along in the early years with a lack of facilities, equipment, and knowhow and professional direction, and with some faculty discouragement and hostility.

A social high point in the cadet's year during the nineties came on San Jacinto Day. Celebrations were varied in character, but were invariably exciting, and marked that day as something very special with A&M, an importance which it maintains to this day, as Aggies around the world stage their famous annual Musters on the anniversary of the Texas victory over Santa Anna's army at San Jacinto. On April 21, 1892, San Jacinto Day, the cadets enjoyed an outing on the Navasota River.[97] In the 1894 festivities the Austin Literary Society held a "celebration" on campus, including speeches, debates, and "readings" pertaining to Texas.[98] In 1897 the faculty and Corps of Cadets attended San Jacinto Day celebrations in Houston.[99] Thus, while celebrated in different ways, San Jacinto Day observance became a "tradition" with Aggies.

Other extracurricular activities of the cadets are suggested by the poetic prose of the *Olio:* "Behind the great dam of the lake, cozily nestling in a corner of the wide ravine, is Lover's Retreat . . . a charming grotto."[100] Cadets, unfortunately, were plagued by a shortage of female companions, and had to import their dates from Bryan and from their home towns, as has been customary throughout the College's history. There was then no women's college available as a "sister school," as there later came to be. Daughters of faculty members, particularly the Hutson twins, received constant attention from the cadets.[101] Out of this initial deficiency of female companionship developed one of the most novel aspects of social life at the College — the "stag dance." As had been the case in earlier frontier days in the West, stag dances developed spontaneously and soon became a regular thing. The first record of a stag dance appears in 1893, but such dances likely existed much earlier.[102] Charles B. Campbell, who came to the College as a professor of modern languages in 1903, mentions the stag dances, and Ernest Langford, a student between 1909 and 1913, recalls them vividly as a regular Saturday-night occurrence. The "girls" at these affairs were identified by handkerchieves tied to

---

[96]Minutes of the Board of Directors, June 10, 1902, I, 261; Minutes, March 26, 1902, I, 257.

[97]College Station *College Journal*, IV (April 1892), 15.

[98]College Station *Battalion*, May 1894.

[99]Bryan *Eagle*, April 22, 1897, p. 6.

[100]College Station *The Olio, 1895*, p. 49.

[101]*Ibid.*

[102]College Station *College Journal*, IV (February 1893), 15.

their arms.[103] Undoubtedly the advent of the automobile, the "interurban," and improved transportation had much to do with the demise of the stag dance.

Other notable events in the life of the cadets in the nineties included the organization of a "Fat Man's Club" and a "Bowlegged Men's Club."[104] After the turn of the century the number of frivolous social organizations mushroomed. In October 1894 the Corps went to the circus in Bryan on a specially chartered train.[105] Following the visitation to the circus an epidemic of measles swept the campus, but fortunately there were no fatalities.[106] In 1895 the cadets attended the Confederate Reunion in Houston and in 1896 the Corps Band, so very evident at A&M sports events today, was organized.[107] In 1897 a College Bicycle Club, including students and faculty, was organized.[108] That same year the Corps visited the State Fair in Dallas in special "cars."[109] Admittedly, occasionally time did hang heavy on the hands of the cadets, who frequently sought relief from boredom by staging a contest between "fighting tarantulas." The sport of fighting tarantulas apparently ceased abruptly one night when two "champions" got out of their box in a dormitory room, and, perhaps fortunately, were never found again.[110] Other activities seem to have included occasional fistfights between cadets, hunting, horseback riding, and pranks.

Ross was justifiably proud of his boys. In 1896 he reported that A&M graduates had found positions of leadership in all walks of life:

A large number are employed as surveyors and engineers in the U.S. geological survey, Mississippi levees, railway construction, and machine shops and mines of Mexico; as draughtsmen, architects, superintendents of dairy and stock farms. Some are physicians and lawyers, prominent in their professions. One is at this time worthily filling a place on the district bench [William M. Sleeper]. Another has recently . . . been appointed [to the chair of veterinary science] in the Oklahoma University [*sic*] [L. L. Lewis], in which young prosperous institution another of our graduates is regent [F. Caruthers]. Nine are employed as teachers in their Alma Mater. Many of the most prominent officers of the state militia received their training here. . . . Not one has ever proved a gambler, drunkard, or idler in the great hive of industry.[111]

[103]C. B. Campbell, "My Recollections of the College," Texas A&M University Archives.
[104]College Station *Battalion*, November 1, 1893.
[105]College Station *The Olio, 1895*, p. 130.
[106]Minutes of the Board of Directors, November 1, 1893.
[107]Texas A&M, *Annual Report, 1896*, pp. 21-22; Minutes of the Board of Directors, I, 174.
[108]Bryan *Eagle*, October 7, 1897, p. 3.
[109]Bryan *Eagle*, November 4, 1897, p. 6.
[110]J. B. Sterns Reminiscences, "Fighting Tarantulas," Texas A&M University Archives.
[111]Texas A&M, *Biennial Report, 1894-1896*, p. 5.

During Ross' years as president of the College numerous changes in faculty personnel occurred and many new faculty members were added to accommodate the increasing enrollment. The most significant and interesting changes in faculty occurred with the resignations in 1893 of George W. Curtis, professor of agriculture and director of the Experiment Station, and of William Lorraine Bringhurst, professor of English and vice-president of the College. Curtis followed in the footsteps of President John James, Thomas M. Scott, and Louis McInnis to become a banker. He accepted a position with a bank in Washington, Louisiana. He later pursued a variety of endeavors including that of railroad auditor, secretary-treasurer of a wholesale grocery, and special agent for the United States Department of Agriculture, and, finally, he served as a partner and manager of a number of grain-milling and elevator companies in Oklahoma and Texas.[112] Bringhurst became a public-school teacher in Bryan and later in San Antonio.[113] Both presumably left for personal reasons, including financial reasons in the case of Curtis, and for reasons of health in the case of Bringhurst, but one can also conjecture that the departure of the two most important and influential men on campus, next to President Ross, may have involved some conflict over authority between Ross and these two men. Ross was not the kind of man to permit anyone to usurp his authority.

James H. Connell, from the A&M College of Mississippi, at Starkville, replaced Curtis as professor of agriculture and director of the Agricultural Experiment Station. George W. Hutson of Cuthbert, Georgia, father of two attractive twin daughters (Sophie and Mary) who became such a sensation on campus, replaced Bringhurst as professor of English and history.[114]

Other important additions or changes in faculty included the appointment in 1890 of Helge Ness, who had been serving as foreman of the garden and greenhouse, as assistant professor of horticulture and botany.[115] In the same year Phineas S. Tilson was named assistant professor of chemistry at a salary of $750 plus board for twelve months.[116] Reverend Thomas C. Bittle, of Manor, Texas, came to A&M as chaplain and librarian, replacing Charles P. Fountain.[117] Charles Puryear, who arrived in 1889, as associate professor of civil engineering and physics, was named professor of mathematics to replace

[112]S. W. Geiser, "George Washington Curtis and Frank Arthur Gulley: Two Early Agricultural Teachers in Texas," *Field and Laboratory*, XIV (January 1946), pp. 7-8.

[113]Interview with Ernest Langford, College Station, Texas, February 24, 1971.

[114]Minutes of the Board of Directors, June 3, 1893, I, 148.

[115]*Ibid.*, July 1, 1890, I, 92.

[116]*Ibid.*, 93.

[117]*Ibid.*, August 6, 1890, I, 94.

Louis L. McInnis.[118] Samuel A. Beach became associate professor of horticulture and botany,[119] and Robert H. Price, of Blackstrong, Virginia, became head of the Department of Horticulture in 1892, at a salary of $1,500 per year.[120] Also in 1892 Thomas C. Bittle, the chaplain, was made associate professor of English and history, and soon thereafter was named professor of languages.[121] The Reverend W. S. Red, a Presbyterian minister, then came to serve as chaplain, librarian, and assistant professor of languages.[122]

David W. Spence was employed as assistant professor of civil engineering and drawing in November 1892.[123] Lieutenant Benjamin C. Morse, who replaced Lieutenant William S. Scott in 1890, served as commandant through 1894 and was replaced by Lieutenant George L. Bartlett.[124] R. T. Bray, of Blacksburg, Virginia, became assistant professor of mechanical engineering in 1893.[125] William A. Banks, once professor of modern languages as a member of the first faculty of the College, returned to A&M in 1894 to serve two years as assistant professor of English until his retirement in June 1896.[126] Duncan Adriance, a former student and for many years a member of the faculty, died in 1897.[127] Others who served on the faculty or staff for varying periods of time during Ross' administration included James Clayton, associate professor of agriculture (1894-1896); Charles E. Burgoon, assistant professor of mechanical engineering (1897-1901); Eugene Wycliffe Kerr, assistant professor of mechanical engineering (1897-1903); H. C. Kyle, foreman of the Farm (1896-1900); William Charles Martin, assistant chemist, Texas Experiment Station (1898-1901); and Buel C. Pittuck, agriculturist, Texas Experiment Station (1897). Many of the "old hands," of course, were still around and would be for many years to come. These included such individuals as James C. Nagle, Frederick Ernst Giesecke, Robert Franklin Smith, Mark Francis, Henry Hill Harrington, and Roger Haddock Whitlock.[128]

During Ross' administration the Agricultural Experiment Station added many new services and substations, which will be examined in a later chapter.

[118]*Ibid.*, August 20, 1890, I, 95.

[119]*Ibid.*

[120]*Ibid.*, June 8, 1892, I, 130.

[121]*Ibid.*, 136; July 2, 1892, I, 137.

[122]*Ibid.*, November 2, 1892, I, 141.

[123]*Ibid.*

[124]*Ibid.*, January 18, 1893, I, 146; June 2, 1894, I, 164.

[125]*Ibid.*, July 4, 1893, I, 152.

[126]*Ibid.*, June 27, 1894, I, 166; June 31, 1896, I, 189.

[127]Bryan *Eagle*, February 11, 1897, p. 3.

[128]See David Brooks Cofer (ed.), *Early History of Texas A. and M. College through Letters and Papers*, 140-143; and Texas A&M, *Catalogue, 1891-1898* through 1897-1898.

The College acquired its first adequate bathing facility, the Natatorium, which included a swimming pool 51 × 26 feet, with bathing tubs along enclosures on the side of the building.[129] Construction of a new mess hall began in 1897, and Ross Hall, a new brick dormitory, was completed in 1892.[130] Ross "modernized" the College by converting to electric lighting, improving water supplies and bathing facilities, building a new mess hall, dormitories, laboratories, and classroom buildings. By his emphasis upon the Corps of Cadets, military training, and esprit de corps, and by his own personal example and prestige, he became the founder of the modern "Aggie tradition." He made A&M a more attractive place in which to live, study, and work.

He loved his school and was in turn loved and respected by the students and faculty, as innumerable personal testimonials indicate. On one occasion, in 1894, Sul Ross seriously considered leaving A&M, to accept an appointment as railroad commissioner, and in fact submitted his resignation as president of the College. On January 1, 1895, he withdrew his resignation, saying he had no idea "such an estimate was placed in his services as president." Students at the College reportedly "celebrated far into the night" upon hearing he would stay. The faculty gave a banquet in his honor and presented him a gold watch. William Bledsoe Philpott gave a long speech at the affair, comparing Ross favorably to Robert E. Lee, Jefferson Davis, and others.[131] Ross stayed on until his sudden death, on January 3, 1898, at the age of sixty, of pneumonia after a cold, wet, hunting trip on the Navasota bottoms.[132] Lawrence Sullivan Ross fought the good fight; he left behind a college and a state which, because of his life, would never be the same again.

[129]Texas A&M, *Biennial Report, 1892-1894*, p. 5; see also George Sessions Perry, *The Story of A&M*, 72-73.

[130]Bryan *Eagle*, July 3, 1897, and August 26, 1897; Minutes of the Board of Directors, July 2, 1891, I, 138.

[131]Bryan *Eagle*, December 20, 1894, and January 3, 10, 17, 24, 1895.

[132]Minutes of the Board of Directors, January 17, 1898, I, 199-201.

CHAPTER 9

Foster and Houston: Two Progressives

T EXANS everywhere were stunned by the death of Lawrence Sullivan Ross. Ross was buried in Waco on January 4, 1898. He was mourned and memorialized by A&M cadets, former students, and faculty.[1] Roger Haddock Whitlock became acting president of the College, and life and academics moved on. While national attention centered on such things as the prospect of war with Spain, gold strikes in the Klondike, labor strikes in the Northeast, and lynchings in the South, the Directors of the A&M College began the search for a new president. Among those considered as a possible replacement for Ross were such notables as Joseph D. Sayers, lieutenant governor of Texas; Thomas V. Munson, horticulturist in Denison, Texas, and founder of the Texas Horticultural Society; Fred W. Mally, an entomologist and in 1898 proprietor of a nursery in Dickinson, Texas; Colonel Woodford H. Mabry, Texas state adjutant general; Frank P. Holland, former mayor of Dallas and editor of the *Texas Farm and Home* magazine; Henry Hill Harrington, A&M professor of chemistry and mineralogy and son-in-law of Lawrence Sullivan Ross; and Lafayette Lumpkin Foster, former speaker of the Texas House of Representatives, ex-railroad commissioner, and businessman.[2]

According to the official minutes for June 7, 1898, "After several ineffectual ballots the Honorable L. L. Foster, of Velasco, Texas, was unanimously elected president of the A&M College of Texas." Foster accepted the position effective July 1, 1898, and formally assumed his duties on that day.[3]

Foster, then forty-six years old, had behind him a rather remarkable and active career in politics, journalism, and business. He came to Texas from

[1]Bryan *Eagle,* January 13, 1898. (Citations to Bryan *Eagle* are to the weekly edition. The Bryan *Daily Eagle* ran concurrently with the weekly for a time.)

[2]Robert Eugene Byrns, "Lafayette Lumpkin Foster: A Biography," unpublished Master's thesis, Texas A&M University, 1964, pp. 146, 153, 155-156, 188.

[3]Minutes of the Board of Directors, June 7, 1898, I, 207.

Forsythe County, Georgia, at the age of eighteen and settled at Horn Hill, in Limestone County. He attended Waco University for a time and in 1873 began to publish the *Limestone New Era* at Groesbeck, Texas. He married Laura Pender of Groesbeck in 1875, and in 1880 won election to the Texas House of Representatives. He was re-elected to the Legislature in 1882 and again in 1884. Upon taking his seat in 1885, he was elected speaker of the House, at the age of thirty-four, the youngest Texan at the time to have achieved that position. In November 1886 Governor Ross appointed Foster commissioner of insurance, statistics, and history (to which agriculture was added in 1887), and Governor James S. Hogg reappointed him commissioner in 1890. The next year Hogg appointed Foster to the newly created Texas Railroad Commission. Foster completed his term on the Railroad Commission in June 1895, and in July accepted the position of vice-president and general manager of the Velasco Terminal Company.[4]

In January 1898 Foster became campaign manager for Joseph Draper Sayers, then lieutenant governor, who sought the governor's office. In June, Foster was elected president of Texas A&M College,[5] and in August, Sayers won the Democratic Party nomination for governor. Foster's association with higher education had been tenuous, but probably no more so than that of Lawrence Sullivan Ross. Foster, a lay minister of the Baptist Church and a founder of the First Baptist Church of Groesbeck, presided at the joint meeting of the Baptist General Association and the State Convention at Temple, Texas, on December 9, 1885, when the two state Baptist associations merged to form the Baptist General Convention of Texas. Foster played a major role in this consolidation and in the organization of Baylor Female College (Mary Hardin-Baylor) by the General Convention. From 1887 until 1891 Foster sat on the Board of Directors of the Agricultural and Mechanical College in his capacity as commissioner of agriculture, insurance, statistics, and history.[6] Nonetheless, Foster was attacked in some quarters for being a "political appointee" rather than an educator. The Bryan *Eagle* rejoined candidly to the charges and argued that Foster's political qualifications would be an asset and that the Directors could have found a qualified educator had they wanted one.[7]

Foster proved to be an effective and "compassionate" leader of the A&M College. The junior class, in their annual banquet of April 7, 1900,

---

[4]Walter Prescott Webb and H. Bailey Carroll (eds.), *The Handbook of Texas*, I, 636-637.
[5]Quoted in Byrns, "Lafayette Lumpkin Foster," 157-158.
[6]*Ibid.*, 28-30, 62-65, 179.
[7]Galveston *Daily News*, June 14, 1898; Bryan *Eagle*, June 23, 1898.

toasted Foster with the salute, "Here's to him who is a father to us, while our Fathers are not here — Our President," which suggests the genial character of the man who went out of his way on the campus to greet his "boys" individually and pleasantly.[8] During his brief tenure as president, he was confronted with some unusual problems and situations.

Shortly after Foster assumed office he and James H. Connell, A&M's professor of agriculture and director of the Experiment Station, hosted a Farmers' Camp Meeting on the campus from July 13 to July 15, 1898. Farmers who attended were allowed reduced railroad fares. While on the campus they attended instructive programs in stock breeding and crop management, and were addressed by both Foster and Connell. Connell succeeded in organizing the farmers into a Farmers' Congress, of which he became the first president, and which met on the A&M campus regularly until the outbreak of World War I. Foster, in the tried and true tradition of past A&M presidents, urged the Congress to work for larger legislative appropriations for the College.[9]

By the time Foster entered upon his duties as president most Americans, as well as the cadets at A&M, were preoccupied with war news from Cuba and the Pacific. The United States had declared war against Spain on April 25, 1898, following a series of crises in February, including the sinking of the battleship *Maine* in Havana Harbor and the publication of a letter by Dupuy Enrique de Lôme, the Spanish Minister in Washington, critical of President William McKinley. The American "yellow press" had meanwhile fanned American sentiment against the Spanish "tyrants," "maddogs," and "butchers." War fever first struck the campus in March, as a result of which the cadets petitioned President Foster for permission to organize a regiment "in case of war with Spain,"[10] although most of the cadets were underage for military service.

During the spring and summer some of the older cadets volunteered for service, as did many of the former students. After the commandant of cadets and regular-army personnel left the College for the duration of the war, Harry B. Martin, professor of military science, performed the duties of commandant in their absence.[11] The *Biennial Report* of the College for December 1898 contained the following classified listing of A&M participants in the Spanish-American War:

[8]Byrns, "Lafayette Lumpkin Foster," 173.
[9]Bryan *Eagle*, June 23, July 14, and August 18, 1898.
[10]*Ibid.*, March 24, 1898.
[11]Texas A&M, *Biennial Report*, December 1898, p. 31.

One Lieutenant-Colonel, one Major, one Regimental Sergeant-Major, fifteen Captains, ten First Lieutenants, eight Second Lieutenants, six First Sergeants, thirteen Sergeants, five Corporals, twenty-two privates. One Sergeant and one private in the hospital corps, one trumpeter; one man in the Rough Riders, one in Missouri Regulars, one in Santiago as chief civilian clerk and Major [George T.] Bartlette who was the preceding Commandant of this place, and one alumni has received the rank of 2nd Lieutenant in the regular army. In all we had *89 men* in the army — 63 of which are officers or NCOs.[12]

While not all of the Spanish-American War participants can be individually listed, among those referred to, but not named in the *Official Report* of 1898, can be found the names of Major Robert Allan Rogers (student, 1877-1879), Regimental Sergeant-Major C. Guy Robson (Class of '98), Captains George McCormick, Jr. ('91), E. G. Rees Fowler ('94), Joseph F. Nichols ('89), James Richard Holman ('95), Wilton F. Rose ('94), William D. Anderson ('90), and Mark Sims Swain ('88). First lieutenants included Elisha G. Abbott ('94), Hugh F. McDonald ('95), William Ferguson Hutson ('95), Willie E. Perlitz ('93), and Edgar A. Cook ('92). Sergeants included Wesley P. Cottingham ('92), Alfred Wainneright Bloor ('95), Robert Moore Middlebrook ('91), and Henry M. Rollins ('97). E. M. Moursund ('97), H. L. Hutson ('96), and Dan Cushing served as Corporals. The regular-army officer referred to in the report was Second Lieutenant Charles C. Todd ('97); Alex M. Ferguson ('94) held regular sergeant's stripes in the 5th Artillery.[13] Texas A&M students made a substantial showing during the War, which foreshadowed the impressive participation of A&M students in World Wars I and II.

The War, however, made little impression on student enrollment at the College. Foster reported in December 1898, that the school was overcrowded (391 matriculated) and that many prospective students were being turned away.[14] In June 1898 the College awarded its first Master of Science degree (in horticulture). From this time on through World War I, although enrollment increased slowly but steadily, accommodations for students remained deficient and inadequate. From 1906 through 1918 large numbers of students were housed in tents.

The unusually hard winter of 1898-1899 brought more severe problems to A&M than the recently concluded war. Cases of smallpox occurred

---

[12] *Ibid.*, 31.

[13] Bryan *Eagle*, January 25, 1898; Texas A&M, *Catalogue, 1898-1899*, p. 87, and *1899-1900*, pp. 93-94.

[14] Texas A&M, *Biennial Report, 1898*, p. 6; Bryan *Eagle*, January 12, 1899; Texas A&M, *Catalogue, 1898-1899*, pp. 79, 87.

throughout the state and a near panic seems to have followed. President Foster placed the College under a "strict quarantine against the world until further notice."[15] No deaths were reported at the College. Then in January and February temperatures fell as low as $-11°$ in Dallas and $-4°$ in Bryan. Galveston Bay froze over to the extent that it was possible to drive a team and wagon from Galveston over this ice to Point Bolivar. The weather brought a personal sorrow to the Foster family when word came that Drew Pender, Mrs. Foster's brother, "had frozen to death aboard ship in the Gulf of Mexico." A&M students consumed 3,000 cords of wood in their efforts to keep warm. President Foster felt "continually uneasy" about the threat of fire, while wood smoke cast a pall over the campus.[16]

Despite advances made on the campus during the McInnis and Ross years, sanitary and living conditions remained somewhat primitive as late as 1900. There was no modern sewage system, and drinking water still came from cisterns. The well water was sulfurous and corrosive, and dormitories and homes were still heated by wood stoves.[17] Foster continually pressed for larger appropriations for the College in order to modernize its facilities. He particularly pressed the Legislature to levy a regular tax, the proceeds from which would provide a permanent maintenance and operating fund for A&M. He deplored the necessity of constantly having to beg the Legislature for new appropriations.[18]

The Board of Directors, in support of Foster, in January 1899 asked the Legislature for $38,000 for a dormitory; $31,000 for an agricultural and horticultural building; $12,000 for four new subexperiment stations (plus $10,000 for each successive year); $15,000 for a steam heating plant; $10,000 for a sewage system; $8,000 for five new professors' residences, and $10,000 for a new electrical and ice plant, plus a few other necessary items, totalling, in all, $165,000.[19]

In the meantime the visitation committee from the Legislature came to the College, witnessed drills by the Corps of Cadets, and seemed pleased with what it found. They went away supporting A&M's request for appropriations.[20] The legislative session of 1899 promised to have many

[15]Corpus Christi *Caller,* February 3, 1899, cited by Byrns, "Lafayette Lumpkin Foster," 191.

[16]Byrns, "Lafayette Lumpkin Foster," 192.

[17]Texas A&M, *Biennial Report, 1898,* pp. 8-9.

[18]John J. Lane, *History of Education in Texas,* 190, cited by Byrns, "Lafayette Lumpkin Foster," 196; Bryan *Eagle,* February 16, 1899.

[19]Bryan *Eagle,* January 12, 1899.

[20]*Ibid.,* March 23, 1899.

direct and indirect effects upon the A&M College, over and above fiscal appropriations.

On February 25 the Legislature approved an "emergency" act directing the A&M College to employ an "expert entomologist" whose duty would be to devise means of destroying the Mexican boll weevil, which was creating havoc throughout the cotton industry. In April the Directors of the College appointed Frederick William Mally to fill the position of entomologist, but years were to pass before effective controls for the "boll weevil" could be devised.[21] On March 9 the Legislature reorganized the Board of Directors of the College by providing for the governor's appointment of eight rather than five directors, to hold office for eight years, rather than for six years, as provided in the Act of 1881. It was stipulated that the directors must reside in different portions of the state and were to serve without compensation, other than for actual expenses incurred.[22] The Twenty-sixth Legislature also established two new colleges in Texas, North Texas State Normal, in Denton, and Southwest Texas Normal, on Chatauqua Hill, in San Marcos.[23] The Legislature also considered, but failed to pass in that session, a bill providing for a Girls' Industrial School.

An industrial school for women had been under consideration during President Ross' administration. Ross favored annexing such an institution to Texas A&M, in College Station. The University of Texas supporters in 1899 wanted to establish it as an adjunct of The University of Texas in Austin, arguing that the locale was better suited for girls; A&M supporters argued to the contrary that College Station provided a more moral environment for women. Bryan and A&M officials made strong and public efforts to obtain the girls' school for College Station. Louis L. McInnis, Mayor Cliff Adams, William R. Cavitt, and General Henry Bates Stoddard played a major role in the local efforts, but the bill failed in the House. A bill supporting the College Station location squeezed out of the Senate by a vote of 11-10 but the bill failed of passage in the House. Finally, in 1901, a law created the Texas Industrial Institute and College for the Education of White Girls of the State of Texas in the Arts and Sciences, known today as Texas Woman's University, to be located by a special commission appointed by the governor.[24] The school was to have its own independent Board of Regents, but was nonetheless adopted by Texas A&M as its "sister school."

[21]*General Laws of Texas, 1897-1902*, p. 9; Minutes of the Board of Directors, April 11, 1899, I, 220.

[22]*General Laws of Texas, 1897-1902*, p. 21.

[23]*Ibid.*, 74-75.

[24]Bryan *Eagle* (W), May 11, 18, 1899; *General Laws of Texas, 1897-1902*, pp. 306-309.

While the Legislature was in session Governor Sayers invited the entire A&M student body to Austin to attend the Governor's reception. The cadets departed on the noon train on Friday, May 26, 1899, and returned the following day. The *Battalion* reported that

the weather was propitious, the track clear, everyone knew his neighbor, our college band was along so that with bunting flying, singing, joking, eating, dozing, no indecorum to mar our glee we reached Austin at 6 o'clock P.M. . . . The Governor's reception from 8 to 11 o'clock that evening was an elegant function; the youngest Cadet felt as much at home in those handsomely decorated parlors as he does in Mr. Sbisa's mess hall.[25]

A good time was had by all.

While the cadets were in Austin the Legislature approved A&M's appropriation bill totalling $104,000, over and above the Morrill and other federal funds.[26] It was the largest appropriation to date, and can in part be attributed to Lafayette Lumpkin Foster's close association with the Governor and the legislators. As the Bryan *Eagle* had observed upon Foster's appointment to the College, his political qualifications would be a definite asset. In June, Governor Sayers attended the A&M commencement exercises. The College graduated twenty-three students, including two with a Master of Engineering degree.[27]

During the summer, construction began on a new agricultural building, several professors' dwellings, a new dormitory (to be named Foster Hall), and a sewage system.[28] In prohibiting the use of any lights other than electric on the campus, the Directors gave testimony to the fact that the modern age was indeed arising at A&M.[29] During the summer also heavy floods caused extensive damage along the Brazos River.[30] The school year 1899-1900 commenced with the usual two days for entrance examinations, starting on September 11. Again Texas A&M was forced to turn students away for the lack of accommodations. Enrollment for the year was reported to be 443.[31]

A highlight of the fall term was a trip by the A&M Band to the San Antonio Fair, where the cadets won third prize of $50 in band competition.[32]

[25]College Station *Battalion*, May-June, 1899, cited by Byrns, "Lafayette Lumpkin Foster," 197.

[26]*General Laws of Texas, 1897-1902*, pp. 292-293.

[27]Byrns, "Lafayette Lumpkin Foster," 199; Texas A&M, *Catalogue, 1899-1900*, p. 79.

[28]Minutes of the Board of Directors, June 12, 1899, I, 220, 222, 225, 230.

[29]*Ibid.*, July 19, 1899, I, 227.

[30]Byrns, "Lafayette Lumpkin Foster," 200.

[31]Bryan *Eagle*, September 28, 1899; Texas A&M, *Biennial Report, 1900*, p. 45.

[32]Bryan *Eagle*, November 9, 1899.

The Band, organized in 1893 by Joseph F. Holick, A&M bugler and a Czechoslovakian cobbler by trade, by 1899 had sixteen members under the direction of F. H. Miller, and was on the way to becoming the 325-man-strong Texas Aggie Marching Band of today.[33]

During the academic year 1899-1900 several new professors joined the faculty, including Alex M. Ferguson, assistant professor of horticulture, and C. H. Alvord, assistant professor of agriculture. The name of the Horticulture Department was changed to the Department of Horticulture and Mycology, to reflect the recent current botanical interest in fungi.[34] The Department of History and English was divided in the summer of 1900 to create the Department of History, headed by Charles W. Hutson, and the Department of English, headed by William B. Philpott, formerly head of the combined Department of History and English.[35] In late October, Governor Sayers wrote that he had received reports that the College was "in excellent condition"; however, the Governor, known on the national scene while in Congress as the "Watchdog of the Treasury," and in Texas, while governor, as "Honest Joe," took exception to a contract that the Board of Directors of A&M had awarded to one of its own members for furnishing certain supplies to "either the college or to the Prairie View Normal. . . . I have forgotten which. This it occurs to me [wrote the Governor] is a gross irregularity and should not be permitted. It will at least lead to unfavorable criticism."[36]

Two days before students returned to classes in the fall of 1900 a terrible hurricane devastated the island and City of Galveston, Texas. Thousands of lives were lost in Galveston and property damage was estimated to be in the millions. College Station reported slight wind damage. Cadets raised $163 for the aid of the Galveston storm victims.[37]

Unlike the preceding year, the academic year 1900-1901 passed without natural catastrophe, epidemic, or epic event. Affairs proceeded quite peacefully and normally. Foster reported in October that "the college is among the most successful of its class in the United States. It never was in its history in greater popular favor."[38]

Foster was well on the way to establishing himself as one of the most

[33]Bryan *Daily Eagle*, March 29, 1971; see Texas A&M, *Catalogue, 1899-1900*, plate facing p. 81.

[34]Minutes of the Board of Directors, October 16, 1899, I, 228-229.

[35]*Ibid.*, July 4, 1900, I, 233.

[36]Joseph D. Sayers to L. L. Foster, October 28, 1899, in Joseph D. Sayers Papers, Texas State Archives.

[37]Byrns, "Lafayette Lumpkin Foster," 222.

[38]Texas A&M, *Biennial Report, 1900*, p. 16.

competent and progressive A&M presidents when he died suddenly in Dallas on December 2, 1901. Foster had suffered an attack of pneumonia some weeks before but seemingly had recovered fully and was traveling in northern Texas when stricken. He was buried on the Texas A&M Campus in a cemetery set aside by Foster only a year earlier for the use of the College community. In 1938 the site became the location for Duncan Dining Hall and the cemetery was moved to a new place 1.2 miles south of the West Gate. The College was stunned by Foster's death.

Roger Haddock Whitlock was appointed to serve as *ad interim* president, pending the selection of Foster's replacement.[39]

Candidates considered for president of the A&M College by the Directors at their meeting in the New State House in Waco on April 7, 1902, included General Henry Bates Stoddard, of Bryan; General Felix Robertson, of Waco; Professor T. R. Day, of Henderson; Professor S. H. Flake, of Navasota; Professor A. C. Easley, of Waco; Clarence Ousley, of Galveston; James M. Skinner, from West Virginia; Professor E. F. Comegyo, of Gainsville; Judge Charles Rogan, of Austin; Judge John H. Cochran, Nolan County; Judge A. J. Boaty, Fort Worth; Professor R. S. Abbott, Waco; Wells Thompson, Columbus; Professor John F. Anderson, Whitewright; Professor Wilbur Colvin, Dahlonega, Georgia; Professor David F. Houston, Austin; and Professor Henry Carr Pritchett, of Huntsville. After four hours of balloting the Directors settled upon an academic man for president, rather than upon a political figure.[40]

The man selected to take charge of the institution, effective July 1, 1902, was David Franklin Houston, dean of the faculty of The University of Texas. Houston was born in Monroe County, North Carolina, and graduated from South Carolina College in 1887. He served as superintendent of schools in Spartanburg from 1888 to 1891 and then, from 1891 to 1894, he was enrolled in Harvard, where he received a Masters of Arts (M.A.) degree in political science in 1892. He later received honorary degrees from Yale, Rutgers, Brown, Tulane, University of Wisconsin, Missouri, and North Carolina. He came to The University of Texas as an adjunct professor of political science in 1894 and served as dean of the faculty of that institution from 1899 to 1902.[41]

In 1897 Houston almost ran afoul of the state Legislature on a charge of having sympathies unbecoming a Southerner. A legislative committee inves-

[39]Minutes of the Board of Directors, December 10, 1901, I, 251-253.
[40]*Ibid.*, April 7, 1902, I, 260.
[41]Webb and Carroll (eds.), *The Handbook of Texas.* I, 844-845.

tigated members of The University of Texas faculty who were suspected of holding Southern institutions and traditions in contempt. Specifically questioned were President George T. Winston; David F. Houston, professor of political science; and George T. Garrison, professor of history. The investigating committee appeared to be most concerned with a book written by Houston, entitled *A Critical Study of Nullification in South Carolina*, which was the published version of his doctoral dissertation. The committee reported that it had not had time to make a critical examination of the book, but that from a casual reading it "would pronounce it to be unacceptable from a Southern standpoint as setting forth principles contrary to Southern teachings." Upon questioning Professor Houston, the committee determined that he had written the book before coming to Texas, and that he did not refer to it in his teaching. The committee apparently decided ultimately that the motives of all involved, even by Southern standards, were honorable.[42]

Certainly the affair did nothing to injure Houston's academic career. He became dean of the faculty at The University of Texas in 1899, president of Texas A&M in 1902, president of The University of Texas in 1905, and chancellor of Washington University, in St. Louis, in 1908.[43] The affair does suggest, however, a strong resurgence of sectionalism in the nineties which substantially declined with the outbreak of the Spanish-American War in 1898. In part, the resurgence of "Southernism" can be attributed to the "bloody shirt" campaign tactics of northern Republicans in the preceding several presidential elections.

Houston was himself a dedicated progressive Democrat. Although his study of nullification in South Carolina may have been mildly critical in that he referred to the "backwardness" of South Carolina, and called the Civil War a "victory for the general government," the investigating committee of the Legislature would have had to be very sensitive to find anti-Southern sentiments in his book.[44] Houston was a great admirer of Grover Cleveland and cast his first vote for Cleveland in 1888. He did not like, however, William Jennings Bryan, but did admire Theodore Roosevelt.[45] Although it is not on record, it is quite conceivable that Houston may have voted for Roosevelt in 1904, for Houston became a follower of the Progressive idea which advocated social reform in order to ease the inequities of the capitalist system. In 1912

---

[42]H. Y. Benedict (ed.), *A Source Book Relating to the History of the University of Texas*, 406-409.

[43]Webb and Carroll (eds.), *The Handbook of Texas*, I, 844-845.

[44]See Houston, *A Critical Study of Nullification in South Carolina*, 1-169.

[45]Houston, *Eight Years with Wilson's Cabinet, 1913-1920*, pp. 1-8.

he became a strong supporter of Woodrow Wilson and maintained close connections with Wilson's nomination and campaign through his associations
with Wilson's close personal advisor, Colonel Edward M. House, who is
sometimes referred to as the "Warwick" of Texas politics. Houston referred
to the Democratic Convention of 1912 as a struggle between Wilson and the
bosses, "the enlightened element of the party against the machine." In
December 1912, while Houston was in New York, Colonel House, whom
Houston had known for many years, asked him whether he would consider
serving in Wilson's Cabinet. Houston says that at first he did not take the
offer seriously; and that, finally, when pressed to accept the position of Secretary of Agriculture, held strong misgivings, largely because he believed that
he could not afford the expense of the office on the very meager savings
from his academic posts.[46] His salary, for example, as president of Texas
A&M was set at $4,000 per year.[47]

Houston finally accepted the appointment as United States Secretary of
Agriculture. He presided over the great expansion in federal agricultural programs caused by implementation of the Smith-Hughes Act, which established vocational agricultural training, and the Smith-Lever Act, which established the county-agent system. During the World War I years he aided in
the expansion of farm production, which added some 26 million acres of crop
lands to the nation's farms and increased yields and total farm production in
the United States to the highest levels in the nation's history at that time.
Houston recalls the years with Wilson's Cabinet in a two-volume work entitled *Eight Years with Wilson's Cabinet, 1913-1920.*[48]

Houston's term as president of the A&M College marked a period of
sustained growth of that institution. Houston gave more attention to the academic structure of the College than had his two predecessors, and did less
building. With his approval, the Board of Directors elected James G. Harrison treasurer of the College, and separated the fiscal office from that of the
president. James H. Connell, professor of agriculture and director of the
Experiment Station, resigned in June 1902 to accept the position of assistant
general manager of *Farm and Ranch*,[49] a periodical which had begun publication in 1887. Houston scoured the United States for a successor to Connell
and, upon his recommendation, the Board offered the position of dean of the

[46]*Ibid.*, 1-14.

[47]Minutes of the Board of Directors, February 11, 1903, I, 274.

[48]See also Murray R. Benedict, *Farm Policies of the United States, 1790-1950: A Study of Their Origins and Development;* Alfred C. True, *A History of Agricultural Extension Work in the United States, 1785-1923.*

[49]Minutes of the Board of Directors, June 10, 1902, I, 263-264.

Agricultural Department and director of the Experiment Station to William D. Gibbs, of New Hampshire Agriculture College, and the position of professor of agriculture to Frederick S. Johnston, of the University of Indiana. These appointments marked the beginning of the move to establish formally a College of Agriculture. Gibbs remained at A&M only one year before returning to New Hampshire as president of his former college. He was replaced by John A. Craig, reported to be one of the "foremost authorities of the country on livestock."[50] Beginning in 1903, a uniform degree of Bachelor of Science was awarded for the completion of all undergraduate courses in both engineering and agriculture, and a substantially enlarged offering of courses was subsequently made available in every field. At the same time the age limit for admission to the College was raised to sixteen years, and entrance requirements were stiffened, although it remained possible to take special entrance exams in lieu of the presentation of a satisfactory high-school diploma.[51]

Houston created a chair of botany and mycology, a chair of animal husbandry, and an instructorship in dairying. N. H. Brown of Chattanooga, Tennessee, a graduate of Ohio State, came to A&M as professor of physics and electrical engineering. Charles Boyle Campbell, a Phi Beta Kappa from De Pauw University, came as instructor in modern languages; Davis K. Doyle, of Stephenville, Texas, was hired as the College's first full-time librarian. Albert Frederick Conradi filled a new position as assistant professor of entomology, and T. P. Junkin, formerly superintendent of schools in Cuero, Texas, became assistant professor of mathematics.[52] Houston brought in F. R. Marshall, a graduate of the University of Ontario, Canada, and a former student of Iowa State University, as associate professor of dairying and animal husbandry.[53]

In 1903 the state Legislature provided for the establishment of a Department of Textile Engineering at A&M and appropriated $50,000 for that purpose. Characteristically a thorough planner, Houston soon left for a tour of textile schools in the East in order to determine exactly what would be needed at A&M. He again looked all over the United States for an effective head for the textile school. The man he finally selected was James S. Wier, professor of textile engineering at the A&M College of Mississippi. In

[50]*Ibid.*, August 4, 1902, I, 264-265; Bryan *Eagle*, August 6, 1903, and September 24, 1903; Texas A&M, *Biennial Report, 1903-1904*, p. 17.

[51]See Clarence Ousley, *History of the Agricultural and Mechanical College of Texas*, 89, 63-65; Texas A&M, *Catalogue, 1903-1904*, pp. 22-82; *1904-1905*, pp. 22-95; *1905-1906*, pp. 22-98.

[52]Bryan *Eagle*, June 18, 1903, p. 2, and August 13, 1903, p. 8.

[53]*Ibid.*, October 22, 1903, p. 4.

1904 Wier and Houston ordered the necessary machinery for the textile school and were able to secure such excellent terms from the manufacturers that an estimated $20,000 worth of machinery was purchased for $8,000. Students who enrolled in the textile course were to assemble the machinery as it arrived as part of their instruction.[54] Houston proved to be one of the best-qualified academic heads and most proficient administrators in the history of Texas A&M.

Cotton specialist R. L. Bennett, former director of the Arkansas Agriculture Experiment Station, and Houston conferred with Secretary of Agriculture James Wilson in February 1904 in regard to the boll-weevil problem, which was causing serious economic losses in the Texas and Southern cotton industry. As a result of the conference a train tour was made by "specialists" through the cotton regions of Texas to discuss methods of controlling the boll weevil and of solving various other farm problems. The tour, sponsored by the Department of Agriculture, included Seaman A. Knapp, who drafted the plan for the establishment of agricultural experiment stations in the 1880s (The Hatch Act) and was a leader in the development of farm-demonstration work, and was presently serving as special agent of the Department of Agriculture. Also included were George W. Curtis, former professor of agriculture at Texas A&M, and A&M professors Edwin Jackson Kyle, professor of plant husbandry, Edward C. Green, associate professor of plant husbandry, Frederick S. Johnston, professor of farm husbandry, and F. R. Marshall, professor of animal husbandry.[55] The tour suggests a very close liaison of Texas A&M with the Department of Agriculture in developing a strong farm-extension and farm-demonstration program in Texas.

Texas A&M also sponsored the annual Farmers' Congress, which in July 1904 was attended by 1,200 farmers. According to an editorial in the Bryan *Eagle*, the Congress seemed to emphasize a new look in American agriculture. Farming, commented the editor rather bluntly, required a combination of both "muscle and mind," which reflects with some accuracy the objectives of the Land-Grant College Act.[56] In a similar vein John A. Craig of A&M addressed the Texas Cattle Raisers' Association, in March 1904, and gave them a comprehensive report of how Texas A&M taught scientific farming. He referred to the course work offered at the College, to the activities of the Farmers' Congress, to the nearly one hundred Farm Institutes, or short courses, sponsored by A&M each year throughout the state, and to the

[54]Bryan *Eagle*, September 24, 1903, p. 4; October 15, 1903, p. 6; July 21, 1904, p. 4, and September 29, 1904, p. 1; *General Laws of Texas, 1903-1907*, p. 74.

[55]Bryan *Eagle*, February 18, 1904, p. 1, and February 25, 1904, p. 3.

[56]*Ibid.*, July 21, 1904, p. 4, and July 27, 1905, p. 1.

Agricultural Experiment Stations in operation at Beeville, Hearne, and College Station.[57] In the field of agricultural education Texas A&M had become a nationally recognized leader.

A&M's reputation in engineering was older and well established. President Houston concentrated on providing the Engineering Department with the equipment and personnel necessary for the most modern and efficient instruction in engineering theory and practice. In addition to establishing the Textile Department, Houston aided Roger H. Whitlock, professor of mechanical engineering, to modernize and enlarge the machine and blacksmith shops, and furthered the development of plans to build a new "mechanical laboratory."[58] A&M graduates in engineering, reported the Bryan *Eagle* in 1904, were receiving lucrative and honorable positions in their profession, as were the trained agriculturalists.[59]

On yet another level of activity Houston had much to do with promoting the construction of an interurban railway linking College Station and Bryan. He addressed a meeting of the Business League in Bryan in September 1904, and argued strongly and convincingly that an interurban line would prove to be a tremendous economic asset to Bryan. Houston was supported by Louis L. McInnis, former president of A&M and now a Bryan banker, as well as by James C. Nagle, professor of civil engineering.[60] It was not until June 1910, however, that a gasoline interurban, financed by businessmen from Shreveport, Louisiana, began operation between Bryan and College Station, making scheduled runs on the hour between the two places on a route which is now substantially Cavitt Avenue in Bryan. The gasoline car proved primitive and troublesome, but represented a substantial improvement over the horse and buggy. In 1915 an electric trolley replaced the gasoline car and continued to operate until the automobile in turn made the trolley obsolete.[61]

Other aspects of campus life during Houston's administration included the enforcement of a Board of Directors rule against smoking on the campus and the establishment of an athletic field for the students.[62] San Jacinto Day of 1904 was marked by the 6th Annual Field Day, which included track and field events and a game of baseball. Edwin Jackson Kyle, head of the Department of Horticulture, managed the affair.[63] Commencement exercises in 1904

[57] *Ibid.*, March 24, 1904, p. 3.

[58] *Ibid.*, May 12, 1904, p. 1.

[59] *Ibid.*, June 9, 1904, p. 4.

[60] *Ibid.*, September 29, 1904, p. 6, and April 13, 1905, p. 4.

[61] David W. Cofer (ed.), *Fragments of Early History of Texas A&M College*, 10-13.

[62] Minutes of the Board of Directors, July 19, 1904, I, 282-288.

[63] Bryan *Eagle*, April 28, 1904, p. 1.

included a lengthy address by the Reverend Sam R. Hay, who spoke on "Life" and emphasized that the world was crowded with "unprepared people." He advised the students to utilize their opportunities for education to the fullest. Individual competitive drills, orations, battalion drill, a sham battle, and a dress parade filled out the agenda of commencement exercises, as had been true in past years, and would be for some time in the future.[64] The faculty apparently enjoyed tennis as their favorite pastime.[65]

Texas A&M's "salad years," which began with the inauguration of Lawrence Sullivan Ross, lasted through the administrations of Lafayette Lumpkin Foster and David Franklin Houston. The achievements of these years can obviously not be solely attributed to any single individual or administrator. A&M had become too complex an institution for that, but at the same time, the achievements and contributions of these very able presidents cannot be overestimated. For example, although Houston's real achievements lay in his academic work, in stressing quality and achievement in instruction, he appeared to obtain, almost without effort, munificent financial support from the Legislature. In 1903 the Legislature provided an average of $150,000 for A&M for the next two academic years, far in excess of any funding the College had received previously. The situation became so offensive to some critics that even certain state legislators were saying that A&M had "become too powerful and was running the state." One legislator, after failing to limit the A&M appropriations bill, facetiously introduced a bill to appropriate all money "now or hereafter in the treasury not otherwise appropriated" to A&M.[66]

Although obviously biased in his appraisal, the editor of the Bryan *Eagle* summarized with considerable accuracy the character and contributions of David F. Houston to Texas A&M. The College, said the editor, "was in the hands of a master." He had given the institution a "re-creation" and a "rebirth." While working quietly and efficiently he had created a "quality faculty" and earned the support of the people of the state.[67] Too soon, perhaps, Houston left A&M.

He submitted his resignation to the Board of Directors on August 24, 1905, to be effective September 1, on which date he assumed the position of president of The University of Texas. The Directors commended him highly.[68] He remained with The University until 1908, when he accepted

[64]*Ibid.*, June 9, 1904, p. 1.

[65]*Ibid.*, May 28, 1903, p. 1.

[66]*Ibid.*, April 23, 1903, p. 4; May 7, 1903, p. 5, and May 21, 1903, p. 1.

[67]*Ibid.*, November 25, 1904, p. 4.

[68]Minutes of the Board of Directors, August 24, 1905, I, 300-301.

appointment as chancellor of Washington University, in St. Louis. President Woodrow Wilson appointed him Secretary of Agriculture, in which capacity he served most effectively from March 1913 until February 1920. From February 1920 to March 1921 Houston was Secretary of the Treasury and chairman of the Federal Reserve Board and of the Federal Farm Loan Board.[69]

He left public office in 1921 to become vice-president of the American Telephone and Telegraph Company and president of Bell Telephone Securities Company. In 1930 he became president of Mutual Life Insurance Company and in 1940 chairman of the Board of Trustees of that Company. At various times he was a member of the Boards of Directors of AT&T Guaranty Trust Company, United States Steel, and North British and Mercantile Insurance Company. During his life he published numerous professional articles and a number of books. He married Helen Beall, of Austin, Texas, in 1895, and had five children. He died of a heart attack in New York City on September 2, 1940, and is buried in Memorial Cemetery, Cold Spring Harbor, Long Island, New York.[70]

During the two decades from 1885 to 1905 Texas A&M made tremendous strides in becoming what it was meant to become, a reputable and established college for teaching the "branches of learning as are related to agriculture and the mechanic arts . . . in order to promote the liberal and practical education of the industrial classes in the several pursuits and professions in life." After 1905 the A&M College in some respects began to settle into a more narrow construction of the Morrill Land-Grant College Act in that its efforts became more specialized in the training of engineers, agriculturists, and soldiers somewhat to the exclusion of the broader fields of business, education, and the humanities. But, after all, between 1905 and 1940 America needed and demanded scientifically and specially trained engineers and agriculturists. Only after World War II did the College begin to turn again to that broader construction characteristic of earlier days.

Houston's presidency marked a high point in the affairs of the College thus far. Few anticipated that the next few years would be more difficult and would end with "The Great Trouble."

[69]Webb and Carroll (eds.), *The Handbook of Texas*, I, 844-845.
[70]*Ibid.*

CHAPTER 10

The Great Trouble

HERBERT SPENCER JENNINGS came to Texas A&M in 1889 as assistant professor of horticulture, and left one year later, the "last and the least" to be pitched out by the Board of Directors in the purge which ended the administration of Louis L. McInnis. Years later Jennings saw a library volume entitled *The Trouble at the A. and M. College,* and, thinking that it must be about those times in 1889, seized upon it. He found instead that it referred to the "trouble" in 1908. He got the impression, he said, that "volcanic eruptions were rather regular occurrences in the life of A. and M."[1] Of all these eruptions, the "great trouble" of 1908 was the most serious.

Internal disharmony indeed had occurred in the past, and would recur in the future. The College had been conceived in the alleged corruption of the carpetbag governments. The end of the Gathright era had brought problems of cataclysmic proportions. The McInnis years ended in factional bickering and finally in wholesale dismissals. Most of the earlier episodes involved faculty and administrative squabbles, but in 1908 the students became involved in a very decisive way.

Henry Hill Harrington, who succeeded David Franklin Houston as president of Texas A&M in 1905, joined the A&M faculty in 1887, as professor of chemistry. Unlike Herbert Jennings, he survived the purge of 1889. Harrington went on to become head of the Department of Chemistry, and in 1892 married Florine Ross, a daughter of Lawrence Sullivan Ross. Harrington was born in Buena Vista, Mississippi, December 14, 1859. He attended the University of Mississippi and then entered Mississippi A&M (now Mississippi State University) when it opened in 1880. He received the degree of B.S. in physics in 1883 and an M.S. in 1885 from Mississippi A&M, and accepted a teaching position as assistant professor of chemistry and physics at his alma mater before coming to Texas.[2]

[1] Herbert Spencer Jennings, "Stirring Days at A. and M.," *Southwest Review,* XXXI (1946), 341-343.

[2] B. M. Walker, "Henry Hill Harrington," *Journal of Mississippi History,* II (July 1940), 156-158.

The A&M Directors elected Harrington president of the College on September 8, 1905.[3] Harrington pledged himself to a program of consolidation rather than expansion.[4] He noted the overcrowded conditions of the College and lamented the necessity of students having to live in tents. Admission requirements, he said, were being enforced more stringently than in the past, in part to discourage enrollment, but the College resolved to take everyone who could qualify, and who was willing to accept the cramped conditions in order to pursue an education. He rejected the "old notions" that the College was unfavorably located, pointing out that the old apprehension that the College was located in a malarial district had been disproved by the mosquito. He contended that the old notion that the soil around College Station was infertile and unsuited to agricultural purposes had been overcome by scientific cultivation, and by the practice of locating subexperiment stations in a variety of soils and locations about the state.[5]

Harrington rejected the accusation that the isolation of the College bred unrest and disharmony among students and faculty — a charge, incidentally, to be raised again by A&M critics in 1913. He argued that, on the contrary, its relative isolation gave the College a tremendous advantage in that "its boys are in large measure removed from those temptations which beset young men; bad company and the evils which follow in its wake; idleness, saloons, gambling halls, disreputable resorts." A&M, he said, cultivated that great secondary objective of an industrial college, the *spirit* and *habit* of *industry*.[6]

The students of the College warmly welcomed their new leader by dedicating the 1906 student annual to Henry Hill Harrington:

A True Friend of the Student Body,
OUR NEW PRESIDENT
Whose sterling qualities as a Southern Gentleman,
and Rare Ability as an Executive,
Have Won for Him the Love and Admiration
of the class of
Nineteen Hundred and Six.[7]

Harrington and the Directors asked for special appropriations for A&M totaling $258,000 for 1908, and $102,500 for 1909, to improve the buildings and facilities of the College. Harrington's report to the governor observed

[3]Minutes of the Board of Directors, September 8, 1905, I, 302-304.
[4]College Station *Longhorn*, 1906, p. 9.
[5]Texas A&M, *Biennial Report*, 1905-1906, pp. 13-14.
[6]*Ibid.*, 14.
[7]College Station *Longhorn*, 1906, p. 4.

that "technological education is far more expensive . . . than is any other kind of college or university training. Applied science," he said, "is developing so rapidly that the appliances of one year are displaced by the inventions of the next."[8] Specifically, in 1907, the College requested of the Legislature $75,000 for an engineering building and $25,000 for laboratory and shop equipment.

In seeking improved accommodations and facilities for faculty and students, Harrington sought $50,000 for a steam-heating plant, $5,000 to improve campus roads, $3,000 to extend the sewer system, $50,000 for a new dormitory, $6,000 for faculty residences, $10,000 for a veterinary hospital, and $10,000 for a natatorium and bathing facility for the cadets, plus other funds for sheds, tools, and laborers' cottages.[9]

A&M received much of what it desired from the Legislature, which appropriated $79,500 for operating funds for each of the two years, 1908 and 1909. The Legislature appropriated also $188,200 for permanent construction, including $50,000 for a dormitory "to be known as Goodwin Hall." Naming a building in an appropriation bill was a rather unusual act for the Legislature. In this instance "Goodwin Hall" was named in honor of George Iverson Goodwin, of Bryan.[10] Upon his death Goodwin was further memorialized by the Directors of the A&M College, who approved a resolution stating: "As a member of the twelfth legislature of Texas he [George Iverson Goodwin] was the author of the act accepting the land grant of the federal government and establishing the A. and M. College."[11] Although Goodwin very likely played an important role in getting the A&M College established, and may very well have written the bill accepting the land grant of the federal government in 1866, he did not introduce that bill into the Legislature and was not a member of the Eleventh or the Twelfth Legislature.[12] The resolution approving the terms of the Morrill Land Grant, recommended in the message of Governor James W. Throckmorton on September 3, 1866, received final approval by the Legislature on November 1.[13]

In addition to the appropriation for the dormitory, A&M received $5,000 for a veterinary hospital, $10,000 for a natatorium, $3,000 for improvement of its sewerage system, $7,500 for building repairs, $65,000 for an engi-

[8]Texas A&M, *Biennial Report, 1905-1906*, pp. 6, 9-12.

[9]*Ibid.*, 9-12.

[10]*General Laws of Texas, 1903-1907*, pp. 373-375.

[11]Minutes of the Board of Directors, October 28, 1916, III, 203.

[12]George Iverson Goodwin was a member of the House of Representatives of the 14th Legislature.

[13]Gammel (ed.), *Laws of Texas*, V, 1185; *Texas Senate Journal, 1866*, pp. 106, 457.

neering building, and $30,000 for stock and equipment. In a word, the College had a very good year in the Legislature in 1907.[14] The state Legislature also approved several other important acts in the interest of the College. One bill authorized the Directors to lease thirty acres of College property for use as a brick yard; another bill accepted the federal grant to the Agricultural Experiment Station supplied by the Adams Act of March 16, 1906. The federal appropriation initially provided $10,000 per year for agricultural research, which was to be increased to $25,000 per year.[15] A Stock Feed Law named the Texas Agricultural Experiment Station as the inspector for all stock feed sold in Texas and required such feeds to meet certain minimum specifications. An inspection tax of 10 cents per ton of feedstuff sold, or offered for sale in Texas, was payable to the general fund of the College, to be used to meet expenses of the act, with excess to be used by the College for building construction. Harrington estimated that this bill would produce some $50,000 for College construction purposes.[16] Harrington summarized the work of the Thirtieth Legislature as giving "the Institution the most liberal appropriation that it has ever acquired. . . . The total appropriation amounted to almost one-third of the total amount given the Institution during its previous thirty years' existence."[17] In a material and political sense Harrington's administration had already been a great success.

Harrington made an important administrative change at the College in 1907 when the Board of Directors created the office of dean of the College, whose duties were to be prescribed by the president of the College and by the president of the Board. Charles Puryear, then head of the Department of Mathematics, was appointed the first dean of the College at a salary of $2,700 for twelve months. Puryear, in effect, became the academic vice-president of Texas A&M.[18] He is credited with having been one of "the most capable men ever to be connected in any capacity" with A&M.[19] Puryear was primarily responsible for maintaining and raising the academic standards of the school.

He was born at Boydton, Virginia, on October 21, 1860, and received his M.A. from Richmond College, and the C.E. from the University of Virginia. Puryear joined the Texas A&M faculty as associate professor of civil engineering and physics in 1889, and in 1890 he replaced Louis L. McInnis as

[14]*General Laws of Texas, 1903-1907*, pp. 373-375.

[15]*Ibid.*, 433; Minutes of the Board of Directors, August 3, 1907, II, 43.

[16]*General Laws of Texas, 1903-1907*, pp. 243-244; Texas A&M, *Biennial Report, 1907-1908*, p. 14.

[17]Texas A&M, *Biennial Report, 1907-1908*, p. 14.

[18]Minutes of the Board of Directors, June 27, 1907, II, 31.

[19]David Brooks Cofer (ed.), *Fragments of Early History of Texas A. and M. College*, 39-41.

head of the Department of Mathematics, a position which he retained after his appointment as dean. He retired from the College in 1932, and died in Bryan on July 11, 1940.[20] Mrs. Erma Munson Rich, who served as Dean Puryear's secretary for a number of years in the twenties, recalls him as a real Southern gentleman, and a very precise administrator. Puryear had the habit, she recalls, of mailing himself a copy of all circular letters sent to the faculty.[21]

A number of key faculty members left the campus in 1906, not the least of whom was Roger Haddock Whitlock, head of the Department of Mechanical Engineering. Whitlock was replaced by Emil Jerome Fermier.[22] John A. Craig, director of the Agricultural Experiment Station, resigned, as did Dr. Howard M. Lanham, the College physician and health officer.[23] Buel C. Pittuck, state feed inspector, left to take a position at Louisiana State University.[24] Cadet Commandant Herbert H. Sargent left for other duties after four years at Texas A&M.[25] Sargent had been much admired by the cadets as a thirty-year man who had fought the Sioux, the Spaniards in Cuba, and the "Bolomen" of the Philippine Islands.[26] He was replaced by Captain Andrew "Bull" Moses, a native of Burnet County, Texas, and a '97 West Point graduate. The cadets wanted to "find him out," and upon doing so came to regard him with so much esteem that they dedicated the 1907 *Longhorn* to Moses.[27] Apparently being unable to find a replacement for John A. Craig, past director of the Agricultural Experiment Station, the Board appointed President Harrington ex officio director of the Station on June 21, 1907, and created the position of vice-director of the Station, to which position it named W. C. Welborn.[28] The change gave Harrington more direct control over Station activities. Dr. Joe Gilbert replaced Dr. Lanham as the College physician.[29]

James C. Blake filled Harrington's former position as head of chemistry. Frederick S. Johnston, professor of agriculture, was replaced by Charles H. Alvord, who had been assistant professor of agriculture. John M. Carson,

---

[20]*Ibid.*

[21]Interview with Mrs. Erma Munson Rich, College Station, Texas, May 14, 1971.

[22]Minutes of the Board of Directors, June 12, 1906, II, 6-17.

[23]*Ibid.*

[24]Texas A&M, *Biennial Report, 1905-1906*, p. 36.

[25]Minutes of the Board of Directors, June 27, 1907, II, 30.

[26]Paul D. Casey, *The History of the A. and M. Trouble, 1908*, xiv-xvi.

[27]*Ibid.*, College Station *Longhorn, 1907*, dedication.

[28]Minutes of the Board of Directors, June 27, 1907, II, 31-32, and August 3, 1907, II, 43.

[29]Texas A&M, *Biennial Report, 1905-1906*, p. 19.

a graduate of A&M, and the brother of James W. Carson, the Farm superintendent, was elected treasurer of the College.[30] There were many faculty changes in the lower positions. From the students' point of view the faculty changes appeared to be excessive and unsettling. While they may have been unsettling, they were no more frequent between 1906 and 1908 than they had been in the years between 1902 and 1906. The causes of the great trouble in 1908 were almost intangible.

Perhaps the numerous faculty changes over the past years, the rapid growth of the student body, and the continuing inadequacy of housing and sanitation facilities contributed to some unrest. Over a hundred cadets lived in thirty-six tents in 1907-1908. The College physician and the commandant of cadets repeatedly called attention to the unsanitary, unhealthy, and inadequate bathing facilities on campus. Dormitories were still heated by wood stoves. The old natatorium, where students bathed, remained in use until the new one was completed in 1908. It had no heat at all. The hospital, too, was considered inadequate.[31] Most important, during the 1906-1907 academic year the students developed a strong and almost personal dislike for President Harrington.

There are few precise events in the record which pinpoint any real controversy between President Harrington and the students prior to the development of an outright student revolt in February 1908. Certainly the cadets had most cordially received Harrington into the president's office, and his achievements with the Legislature during the spring of 1907 were most beneficial to the College. A large part of the appropriations obtained in 1907 went to the improvement of student accommodations and facilities. The explanation for the unanimity of student disaffection with the President of the College lies partly in the unique characteristics of the A&M student body itself — in a word in the composition and character of the Corps of Cadets.

All undergraduate students at Texas A&M College from the time of its founding through World War II were required to enroll in the Corps of Cadets and were subject to military discipline and regulations as defined in the College "Blue Book." The one exception occurred in 1886, when, upon adding a fourth-year degree program to the then existing three-year curricula, the Directors exempted fourth-year students from participation in the military regimen. The College student body existed primarily as a military organization.

[30]*Ibid.*, pp. 80-81; Minutes of the Board of Directors, August 2, 1906, II, 19, and March 4, 1907, II, 20.

[31]Texas A&M, *Biennial Report, 1903-1904*, pp. 152-156; *Biennial Report, 1905-1906*, pp. 75-79.

The A&M student of the 1930s would have had little, if any, difficulty in understanding and embracing the cadet life of the 1890s. Indeed, his activities in the 1930s were largely built upon the customs and traditions of the past, of which the A&M student, unlike the students of most other institutions, is so uniquely aware. Because of the basic continuity and identity of cadet life in one time with that of another time, custom and tradition have become powerful guidelines or mores in the life of the A&M cadet. These customs and traditions have been perpetuated by conscious "enforcement" by the Corps of Cadets, a situation very similar to that at West Point, Annapolis, the Citadel, and similar institutions. But while militarily oriented, Texas A&M has been substantially dissimilar from these named academies in that it is a land-grant college, and in that its overriding purpose has been to train for civil employment rather than for the military. Indeed, education at Texas A&M, as in other land-grant institutions, emphasized teaching one how to make a living, rather than the more classic-oriented educational philosophy of teaching one how to live.

To be sure, the A&M student of the first decade of the twentieth century had fewer customs and traditions than the cadet in the twenties, thirties, and forties. During the earlier years there were no bonfires or yell practices, and "school spirit" in the modern sense was still in its infancy. Football and organized athletics were just beginning and there was no hysteria about them. Unfortunately, some of the traditions of a later day were indeed "lies that had grown whiskers." In time school indoctrination seemed to become more important for the cadet than intellectual curiosity. But this is a story of later days, not of the early 1900s. Custom and traditions had little to do with what happened in the spring of 1908, but the thing upon which that custom and tradition is founded had much to do with the "great trouble."

The cadets of 1908 had already acquired a characteristic that the cadets of 1938 possessed, an intensive *esprit de corps,* or group loyalty, without all the garnishment of real or imagined "customs and traditions." Perhaps the overriding factors contributing to the A&M spirit included the democratic nature of the student society, the fraternal bonds of the student society, and the influence of the senior class. A&M student society became a unique compound of seemingly conflicting values. Its military organization created a hierarchy in one sense, while in another sense A&M students lived a highly democratic existence — democratic if one stresses the equalitarian as opposed to the libertarian aspects of democracy. As official publications, and the A&M students themselves, liked to put it around the turn of the century:

The poor man's son and the rich man's son stand on precisely the same footing at the Agricultural and Mechanical College. . . . All students dress alike, all eat the same kind of food at the same table, all have to get up at the same time in the morning, and make their own fires, bring the water, clean their rooms, and during the day all have to do the same kind of work. And there are no social or other occasions when the poorest boys in the corps are placed at any disadvantage on account of their poverty. . . . Each student is judged by what he is and what he does, rather than by his wealth, social position, or family connections.[32]

Of equality there was much, of personal liberty and freedom of choice, there was little. The cadet came to consider duty, the class, the Corps, and the school, ahead of self. The seamy side of this kind of selflessness was "blind class loyalty."[33] As Sam A. McMillan, a student who participated in the strike of 1908, reflected years later, "A&M students maintain a fine democratic attitude to those who need to work, but they lack the democratic ideal of open and free discussion by which to shape class decisions."[34] The A&M student, in a word, was more susceptible than most students to both "good" and "bad" leadership.

Leadership at Texas A&M has always had a "class" orientation, because class standing determines one's rank and privileges. Cadet officers invariably came from the senior class; seniors framed and directed "the policies and movements that are of importance to the whole Corps of Cadets in all college movements like athletics, clubs, publication, etc."[35] While seniors in any college or university, or in any high school for that matter, have a certain influence by nature of their age, tenure, and experience, the A&M cadet senior was something very special, because he had not only the influence but also the real authority, derived from his military rank, to back him up. The key ingredient in the 1908 student strike was the senior class; weak senior participation in a similar movement in 1913 marked that movement for failure. When one or a few cadets came to have grievances against the President, the entire Corps of Cadets came to share those grievances. Unfortunately for Harrington, he seems almost deliberately to have antagonized the entire student body. The difficulties of 1908 became almost a personal quarrel between Harrington and the student body, although the ramifications of that quarrel seemed to be much broader than mere personal antagonism. Many of the grievances of the student body against the President were as much imagined as real. Some of the student hostility was derived from faculty contentions.

[32]Casey, *The History of the A. and M. Trouble,* 12.
[33]Sam A. McMillan, "Reminiscences," in Cofer (ed.), *Fragments of Early History of Texas A. and M. College,* 88.
[34]*Ibid.*
[35]Casey, *The History of the A. and M. Trouble,* 9.

The first tangible incident which contributed to the rift between the student body and the President came about in a very indirect way. On April Fool's Day, Sunday, April 1, 1906, a number of cadets "cut" chapel, and the remainder of the Corps gave pursuit in what became a game of "fox and hare," or chase. The delinquents were rounded up and placed in the guard-house under orders of Commandant Herbert H. Sargent. President Harring-ton came upon the scene and, perhaps feeling the somewhat jovial mood of the occasion, ordered the cadets released from the guardhouse, over the objec-tions of Captain Sargent. Sprung from their confinement the students ran out of the guardhouse shouting "to Hell with Sargent." Harrington, for the moment, was a very popular fellow. Then a reaction began to set in, perhaps stimulated somewhat by the Commandant, who felt a bit miffed because President Harrington had humiliated him by overriding his authority in front of the boys. The boys, said Cadet Richard P. Beauregard, "had waked up."[36]

Another event following close upon the April 1st incident involved the assembling of the sophomore class by President Harrington for a lecture on hazing. Instead of appealing to their higher motives, Harrington chastised the sophomores as "sneaks" and "cowards" and thoroughly offended the entire class, who, from their point of view, believed they were only doing what others had done unto them, and were carrying on a custom of the school. Each of them had been hazed when he entered the College.[37] They had either to accept Harrington's humiliation or react to it, and they reacted, taking this episode as one more evidence of President Harrington's "mean-ness."

When the cadets returned to school for the 1906-1907 sessions, the prej-udices which had built up against Harrington returned with them. The open-ing of the school term brought renewed "hazing" or initiations of "fish" into the student body, and fresh, personal rebukes from the President. The cadets became increasingly convinced that he was maliciously interfering in the ordinary and accepted practices of student life.[38]

Soon after the session opened, the student newspaper, the *Battalion*, reproduced an article from *World's Work* magazine, praising former A&M president David Franklin Houston as one of the leading educators in the South:

> For two years Dr. Houston left the university and served as president of the

---

[36]*Ibid.*, p. 163; Hatton W. Sumners [Dallas, Texas] to James Cravens, Houston, Texas [undated], in William Daniel Roseborough Papers, Texas A&M University Archives.

[37]Sumners to Cravens, W. D. Roseborough Papers, Texas A&M University Archives.

[38]Casey, *The History of the A. and M. Trouble*, 16.

Texan [*sic*] Agricultural and Mechanical College, which he completely reorganized and vivified. Called back to the university as its president, at the age of forty, he is the real and wise leader of public education in the whole wide empire of Texas, as well as the head of the most vigorous of all the Southern State universities. For Texas has generously provided for public education of every grade; and her foremost citizen and man of best judgment and best equipped economist is at the head of the whole system.[39]

Henry Hill Harrington, quite understandably, took offense at the article, which inferred that whatever Texas A&M had become must be credited to Houston. It suggested the inferiority of A&M to The University, and the intellectual and professional inferiority of other Texas educators and of the current A&M College president to David Franklin Houston. While most of the A&M faculty might have felt some uneasiness with the article, Harrington, who by past and future measures can be judged only as a most sensitive man, reacted strongly to the publication of the article in the *Battalion*. He called the responsible student reporter, Thomas E. Holloway, to his office and berated the student's judgment, suggesting to Holloway that a man "of ordinary intelligence" could not accept such statements as were contained in the article.[40] Within hours, the entire Corps of Cadets had digested the incident as one more example of President Harrington's unwarranted and petty interferences. By the end of the school year a considerable estrangement had developed between the cadets and the President, so much so that the senior class considered petitioning the Directors for the removal of President Harrington at the annual June Board meeting following commencement.[41]

The regular commencement exercises were not held in June 1907, because of a typhoid epidemic which had swept the state and which led to the dismissal of classes seventeen days earlier than scheduled.[42] Whatever might have happened was averted by the early closing.

During the typhoid quarantine and closure of the school, Marion Sansom, former director of the College, issued a public statement saying that the A&M College was located at the wrong place. "Youth jeopardize their health . . . when they attend the A&M College at College Station. . . . The surroundings are calculated to produce oppression. The environments are con-

[39]*World's Work*, XII (July 1906), p. 7728; The article was published in the *Battalion*, October 10, 1906.

[40]Sumners to Cravens, W. D. Roseborough Papers, Texas A&M University Archives; Casey, *The History of the A. and M. Trouble*, 16-17.

[41]Casey, *The History of the A. and M. Trouble*, 17-18.

[42]*Ibid.*, 155; Minutes of the Board of Directors, February 12, 1908, II, 74.

ductive of mental inertia and the chance one runs while attending the college are enough to brand the student man brave indeed":[43]

> During my connection with the college we practically buried two presidents of that institution. Governor Ross died a few weeks before I took up the work and President Foster never recovered from the move to Bryan. Dr. Harrington, the present president, has buried all of his children, save one, and he himself is now at the point of death.[44]

Sansom recommended using the facilities at College Station for Prairie View Normal and Industrial Institute and moving A&M to a point between Dallas and Fort Worth.

During the summer Captain Herbert H. Sargent, who had grown in stature in the eyes of the boys in proportion to the decrease in their esteem for Harrington, left the College upon completing a four-year tour of duty.[45] Sargent's departure left the cadets for a time without a hero, but with their continuing antipathy toward the President, which in itself may have heightened the tension on the campus in the fall of 1907.

Sargent, as it turned out, was replaced by one of the most able and popular commandants of that era, Captain Andrew ("Bull") Moses. Moses, a native of Burnet County, in West Texas, and an 1897 graduate of West Point, walked into a very sticky situation in his new assignment at the A&M College. As usual, the boys wanted to "find him out," and during the year they found, to their complete satisfaction, that Moses was every bit the man, the commander, and the gentleman.[46] But in those few months while Moses was getting adjusted to the new position, affairs deteriorated in part because of the simple change in a key administrator — the commandant.

As might be surmised, the tensions and discontent had come to include the faculty, and indeed the dissensions among faculty fed the student unrest, which in turn precipitated greater friction among faculty. The waves of tension began sucking up the ill currents of discontent to generate a maelstrom which became in total force much more powerful than the bits and pieces which created it. The setting had all the makings of a Greek tragedy in which *hubris,* or pride, provoked nemesis, or retribution.

The school year 1907-1908 began with the storm flags flying from the turrets of Old Main. In August and September 1907 several disagreements

[43]Undated clipping in McInnis Scrapbook, Louis L. McInnis Papers, Texas A&M University Archives.

[44]*Ibid.*

[45]Minutes of the Board of Directors, June 27, 1907, II, 30.

[46]Casey, *The History of the A. and M. Trouble,* xiv-xvii.

between Harrington and the campus chaplain, Nathan Powell, provoked new tensions on campus. Powell believed that Harrington had "broken confidence" with him when, upon Powell's appearance before the Board of Directors in behalf of a fund-raising campaign to obtain a pipe organ for the chapel, Harrington suddenly opposed Powell, arguing that other things were more vitally needed for the campus than a pipe organ. Earlier, Harrington had encouraged Powell and had invited him to appear before the Board. Powell now felt that he had been embarrassed and mistreated by Harrington. In August, Harrington dismissed Powell from the faculty, on the grounds that Powell kept on College grounds horses that were used for hire, but Harrington then relented to the point that he would let Powell stay until December 1.[47] On November 9, 1907, Powell's resignation was officially presented to the Board.[48] By December then, the cadets lost a "spiritual" leader, and blamed Harrington for their loss.

Subsequently, Powell wrote James H. Connell, former director of the Agricultural Experiment Station, who had resigned in June 1906, and Albert Frederick Conradi, entomologist, who left in August 1907, telling them of the situation at A&M and asking them to contact their friends in Austin to urge an investigation. He wrote in a similar vein to Directors Walton Peteet and K. K. Legett, urging a Board investigation.[49] Later Powell wrote to Governor Thomas Mitchell Campbell and then met with him in regard to conditions at A&M.[50] No action followed these communications from Powell, but the broth was obviously being stirred.

Around October 1907 a conflict developed between the President and three professors in agriculture, Frederick S. Marshall (animal husbandry), Edwin J. Kyle (horticulture), and Adoniram J. Smith (animal husbandry). In reply to a request from Smith, approved by Marshall, to take a class to the circus in Bryan to study draft animals, Harrington tossed the paper into the wastebasket and said, "I will consider it under no circumstances."[51] Earlier, Alva Mitchell, instructor in architectural engineering and drawing, had been rebuked by Harrington for allegedly exceeding his authority in making preparations for a Farmers' Congress meeting on campus, which had soured their personal relationships.[52] Other misunderstandings arose between Harrington

---

[47]*Ibid.,* 152-154.

[48]Minutes of the Board of Directors, November 9, 1907, II, 60.

[49]*Ibid.,* February 12, 1908, II, 71.

[50]Casey, *The History of the A. and M. Trouble,* 152-155; *Farm and Ranch,* March 14, 1908, clipping in Louis L. McInnis Scrapbook, Texas A&M University Archives.

[51]Minutes of the Board of Directors, February 12, 1908, II, 72-73.

[52]Casey, *The History of the A. and M. Trouble,* 156-157.

and Asa J. Neff, in charge of the campus laundry, and between Harrington and Walter W. Evans, superintendent of the Farm, who objected to Harrington's firing of Curtis Carson, a Farm employee. One account suggests that the real cause of the "Harrington strike" involved the refusal of Mrs. Curtis Carson and, later, Mrs. Edwin J. Kyle to agree to prolonged breast feeding of the Harrington infant, which was quite sickly. Both ladies had infants of their own and Dr. Joe Gilbert, the campus physician, recommended against any continuing effort to feed two babies by either. The Harringtons were completely distraught and frantic in their efforts to save their child, which led to a number of unfortunate episodes on campus.[53] Each of these faculty animosities compounded the hostility of the students toward Harrington.

In this highly charged emotional climate Harrington became involved in a direct confrontation with the students over a planned Corps trip to a football game in Dallas between Texas A&M and The University of Texas on October 12. The students received a special order from the President two days before the trip to the effect that the Corps could not go to the game in a body as had been expected, and that each individual who made the trip must obtain written permission from home. For most of the boys it was impossible to write and receive a reply from their parents by mail. Many telegraphed and by extraordinary efforts succeeded in obtaining enough permissions and money to charter the special train needed for the trip to Dallas. Even then, after the students had chartered the train for a return from Dallas at 11:00 P.M. on October 12, President Harrington reportedly telegraphed the railroad directing that the train leave Dallas at 8:00 P.M. rather than at 11:00 P.M., which directive the railroad ignored.[54] But the whole affair thoroughly convinced the students of the arbitrary and uncompromising nature of President Harrington.

Later, on a planned Thanksgiving Day excursion to Austin, the students again felt victimized when President Harrington routed the trip over the Houston and Texas Central line, rather than the International and Great Northern road, which they customarily used, and preferred. On another occasion, when the cadets prepared to leave for the Christmas holidays, they received an order that no student could leave campus until 4:30 P.M. — the close of the school day — which would prevent those going north from catching that day's train. At the last minute, 1:30 P.M., the President relented,

---

[53]Minutes of the Board of Directors, February 12, 1908, II, 72-73; Casey, *The History of the A. and M. Trouble,* 45-47; Samuel E. Asbury, "Statement on the Real Cause of the Harrington Strike," November 21, 1950, in Samuel E. Asbury Papers, Texas A&M University Archives.
[54]Casey, *The History of the A. and M. Trouble,* 19.

but the northbound train had already pulled out of the station, which compounded the irritation of the cadets.[55]

Upon the approach of the Christmas holidays another episode created a severe breach between Charles W. Hutson, the professor of history, Dr. Joe Gilbert, the College physician, and the President. The Hutsons were visited during the holidays by their son from New York and his wife and infant child. The child had developed whooping cough upon their arrival in College Station, and Mrs. C. W. Hutson telephoned Dr. Gilbert, and the mothers of all small children on campus, including Mrs. Harrington, informing them of the case of whooping cough. Dr. Gilbert prepared to impose the "usual quarantine," preventing visitors from going to the Hutson house, but President Harrington directed that a smallpox quarantine be established confining every member of the family to the house, and he further tried to have Arthur Carey Hutson's family removed from the campus. "Old Man" Hutson reacted with outraged indignation and flatly refused to allow his son's removal. Harrington countered by preventing the cook and cook's family from going upon the Hutson premises. Another of the Hutson sons, Miles, was then in school and was similarly confined to the Hutson house.[56] Dr. Gilbert also felt aggrieved because he believed that his authority and professional competence had been in effect questioned by President Harrington. A later account of events at the A&M College in the San Antonio *Daily Express* attributes the A&M troubles largely to the disagreement between Dr. Gilbert and President Harrington. Gilbert had something of a "hero image" among cadets and the public because during the Galveston storm of 1900 he had carried a young "damsel in distress" from the wreckage of the storm, and married her immediately afterwards.[57] The entire Corps of Cadets felt similarly outraged because the Hutson family had also been extremely popular, and because Miles Hutson was one of them. In the spirit of the "one big fraternity" which the Corps of Cadets was on the way to becoming, a wrong to one member wronged all. The cadets went home for the Christmas holidays in a churlish mood, and many of the faculty were in similar bad temper.

By the time school reopened in January the experiences of December had created a unanimity of opinion among the cadets to the effect that President Harrington "must go." Communications to the governor and to Board members from Powell and others led the governor to request a Board meet-

[55] *Ibid.*, 19-20.

[56] Hatton W. Sumners [Dallas, Texas] to Mr. James Cravens, Chairman, Houston, Texas, undated letter in W. D. Roseborough Papers, Texas A&M University Archives.

[57] *Ibid.*; San Antonio *Daily Express*, February 11, 1908.

ing at A&M to investigate the situation.[58] When the cadets heard that the Directors would convene on campus on February 6, the senior class met and agreed to petition the Board for the removal of President Harrington. A petition was prepared, signed by most of the seniors, and submitted to the Board.[59] The Board decided that the petition lacked any substantiating facts and adopted two resolutions. One provided that any complaints against the management or administration of the College in the future should be submitted in writing with a statement of facts to the president of the Board.[60] The second resolution completely exonerated President Harrington of any incompetency and pledged the Board's full support to him:

> Be it resolved by the Board of Directors of the A&M College that we express in heartiest terms our unqualified faith and confidence in the integrity, ability and absolute fairness of President H. H. Harrington in the administration of the affairs of the College; and we further declare, that in his efforts toward keeping the College at its present high degree of usefulness and building it up to even a higher degree of excellence we will give him our unanimous endorsement and support.[61]

The Directors then took the unusual action of signing the resolution as placed in the official minutes. The next day, Friday, February 7, the Board members adjourned and left for home.[62]

Friday night the cadets were unanimous in their feelings of dismay and dissatisfaction upon learning that the Board had destroyed their petition, made no effort to call up a single person whose name was attached, and then wholly backed the President without even making a direct reply to the petition. "It seemed," said Paul Casey, "that the very atmosphere was pervaded by melancholy and silence. Nothing was heard save murmurs until the band struck up the old tune of Home Sweet Home."[63] It was the answer to their dilemma. They would go home.

Commandant Andrew Moses got word of what was brewing and called for a meeting of the senior class to discuss things. Moses strongly advised the boys against any hasty or ill-considered action such as a walk-out. Coach L. L. Larson followed Moses and pointed out that any confrontation with the Administration would sorely injure the athletic program and the school. Later that night a conclave of senior students produced yet another call for a senior-

---

[58]San Antonio *Daily Express*, February 11, 1908.

[59]Bryan *Morning Eagle*, February 16, 1908.

[60]Minutes of the Board of Directors, February 6, 1908, II, 64.

[61]*Ibid.*

[62]*Ibid.*, February 12, 1908, II, 68.

[63]Casey, *The History of the A. and M. Trouble*, 21.

class meeting to be held in the agricultural building. By twelve midnight the seniors had agreed to a "strike," by which they would abstain from all academic duties, but would carry out all military functions and observe all other College regulations.[64]

The seniors sent delegations to awaken every student on campus to inform each student of the action taken and to ask for their support. When classes were called at 8:05 Saturday morning, February 8, not one cadet went to class.[65] Perfect order, discipline, and unusual quiet prevailed on campus. The strike was on.

The action certainly caught the Directors, most of the faculty, and the public in general by surprise. Prior to the meeting of the Board of Directors on February 6 there had been no published reports of trouble or discontent at the College. The Bryan *Morning Eagle,* on February 7, reported simply that the "Board met yesterday" but made no mention of any special problems whatsoever. Not until February 11 did anything appear in state or local papers regarding a problem or strike on the A&M campus.[66] On Saturday, February 8, President Harrington sent telegrams to the Directors, asking them to reconvene. On their return to the campus they found a "well organized strike existing in the student body."[67]

The organization had been so perfected and so skillfully managed by some controlling influence that the Faculty were powerless, and the members of the Board in their individual capacity were unable to break the firm determined stand of the students in their conspiracy against discipline and the continuance of College duties. The demand was made that either the President must resign or the boys would go home, and the sharp, clear cut issue was drawn as to whether we as the governing body of the Institution should control it or the students. There ought to be and could be but one answer to this question.[68]

Monday the tenth of February was a dismal and cloudy day, "such as no student of the college had ever witnessed before and never desires to again."[69] Monday was consumed by meetings between faculty, Directors, and students in formal and informal gatherings which lasted from early morning well into

[64]*Ibid.,* 22.

[65]*Ibid.,* 23.

[66]This writer has found nothing in the local newspapers, the Bryan *Morning Eagle* and Bryan *Daily Eagle,* or in the Galveston *News,* the Austin *Statesman* or the San Antonio *Daily Express;* but see Bryan *Morning Eagle,* February 7, 1908; San Antonio *Daily Express,* February 11, 1908; Austin *Statesman,* February 11, 1908.

[67]Minutes of the Board of Directors, February 12, 1908, II, 68.

[68]*Ibid.*

[69]Casey, *The History of the A. and M. Trouble,* 25.

the night. That morning the entire faculty was convened by the Board of Directors and presented a resolution noting that the "Corps of Cadets is in a state of insurrection," and that the situation was intolerable. The Board directed the faculty to enforce the rules and regulations and "dismiss summarily all students who do not promptly return to their classes and submit to constituted authority." All the faculty, but one, whose name has never appeared in the records, voted approval of the Board resolution.[70] It became obvious to the students that they would receive no support or testimonials from the faculty.

On Tuesday the senior-class representatives requested a "fair hearing" before the Board of Directors, the hearing to be based upon the following seven conditions:

1) That we be allowed a committee of students to sit with the Board.
2) That we be represented by an attorney before the Board.
3) That we be allowed to submit evidence before the Board, both verbal and written.
4) That we be allowed to bring the Board any witness that we may desire.
5) That our attorney be allowed to question all witnesses.
6) That every man who appears before the Board be fully protected.
7) That every member of the Board of Directors be present at the investigation.[71]

The Directors replied to the seniors' communication by noting that it was willing to consider any specific grievance, and that complaints must be properly signed and presented. All complainants and witnesses would be fully protected, but the Board requested all students to resume their proper relations while investigations were proceeding.[72] The Directors did not agree to a formal hearing on the terms desired by the seniors. Nonetheless, the seniors voted to attend classes and most of them did so beginning Tuesday after a senior committee had met with the Board and received assurances of a fair and speedy hearing.[73] The Bryan morning newspaper carried the first report of the whole affair on Tuesday, February 12, when it reported simply, "Seniors agree to return to classes. . . . The students have not been in attendance

[70]*Ibid.*, 26; Bryan *Morning Eagle*, February 16, 1908; Minutes of the Board of Directors, February 12, 1908, II, 68-69.

[71]Casey, *The History of the A. and M. Trouble*, 27; Bryan *Morning Eagle*, February 16, 1908; Minutes of the Board of Directors, February 12, 1908, II, 69-70.

[72]Casey, *The History of the A. and M. Trouble*, 27; Bryan *Morning Eagle*, February 16, 1908; Minutes of the Board of Directors, February 12, 1908, II, 69-70.

[73]Minutes of the Board of Directors, February 12, 1897, II, 70.

upon classes since Saturday, owing to disagreement with College authorities."[74]

Monday night, after all underclass cadets had reached an agreement to resume classes along with the seniors, junior-class representatives called for yet another junior-class meeting, which lasted until 2:00 A.M., and produced a unanimous resolution, supported by a personal pledge from each junior "never to attend another class at the A. and M. as long as Dr. Harrington was president."[75] When classes did convene Tuesday, most of the seniors, but none of the juniors and few sophomores and freshmen, were in attendance. The junior class had assumed leadership in the strike.

Wednesday morning President Harrington convened the faculty, which passed a resolution suspending any student who failed to report for regular class duty by 1:00 P.M.[76] That same morning the seniors presented their formal charges against Harrington to the Board of Directors. There were six charges: (1) that Nathan Powell had been unfairly dismissed, and supporting documents were signed by Powell; (2) that C. W. Hutson had been harassed by the President; (3) that President Harrington had his laundry done without charge — signed by A. J. Neff; (4) that Harrington unjustly prevented the animal-husbandry class under the direction of A. J. Smith from attending the circus in Bryan for educational purposes; (5) that Curtis Carson was unfairly discharged by President Harrington, with a supporting statement of W. W. Evans; and (6) that President Harrington was responsible for a lack of harmony between the cadets and the President, and that he had failed to return their "maintenance fees" due them because of the early dismissal of school during the last session.[77] A committee of five seniors was allowed to call witnesses and conduct the examination.

While the Board proceeded in its investigation, Commandant Andrew Moses posted the faculty's suspension notices and earnestly appealed to students to return to classes. He announced that the regular drill call would be at 3:30 and that any student who had failed to return to class should then turn in his equipment. The boys spent the day polishing their guns, belts, and buckles, and at 3:30, in perfect order, marched to the armory and deposited their gear.[78] That evening most of the cadets, except the seniors, began evacuating the campus.

[74]Bryan *Morning Eagle*, February 12, 1908.
[75]Casey, *The History of the A. and M. Trouble*, 27.
[76]Minutes of the Board of Directors, February 12, 1908, II, 70-71.
[77]*Ibid.*, 71-73.
[78]Casey, *The History of the A. and M. Trouble*, 28.

The hearings ended at 5:30 P.M. and the Board continued its deliberation into the night. On Thursday, February 13, at twelve noon, the seniors and those other cadets who remained on the campus met in the chapel on orders from Captain Moses. Moses read them the decision of the Board. The Directors concluded that the "evidence wholly fails to show that the conduct of President Harrington is subject to any proper criticism," but that on the contrary it shows "a commendable solicitude for the interest and welfare of the student body." Incidentally, this resolution too was entered into the official record of the Board and signed by each Board member. The cadets were stunned. Finally they gave the traditional cheer for the commandant:

> Rah, Rah, Rah;
> Rah, Rah, Rah;
> Rah, Rah, Rah;
> Commandant! Commandant! Commandant!

and by evening most of the cadets were gone.[79]

The Directors concluded their findings with the observation that the "College is in excellent condition."[80] "Students remain emphatic," reported the San Antonio *Daily Express* on the thirteenth, as the news hit the state papers. Former students and the public began to choose sides in the affair. A delegation of the Houston Alumni Association arrived in College Station that afternoon on the same train being boarded by many departing students, and together with Francis Marion Law of Bryan, president of the Alumni Association, and Edwin J. Kyle and Dr. Joe Gilbert among others, they begged the students singly and collectively to remain on campus.[81] They achieved some success. About 100 of the 625 students stayed.[82]

Friday, February 14, the Directors sent a telegram to all parents of departed students notifying them that all students who appeared for classes on Monday, February 17, and who promised to conform to regulations would be reinstated.[83] Seniors, and sophomores and freshmen who remained on cam-

---

[79]Minutes of the Board of Directors, February 12, 1908, II, 74; Casey, *The History of the A. and M. Trouble*, 28.

[80]Minutes of the Board of Directors, February 12, 1908, II, 74.

[81]"To the Members of the Alumni and Ex-Students of the A. and M. College of Texas," undated printed letter signed by James Cravens, Harry L. Wright, Erwin Jesse Smith, Charles C. Todd, Frank August Reichardt, W. D. Roseborough Papers, Texas A&M University Archives; Casey, *The History of the A. and M. Trouble*, 31-32.

[82]Bryan *Morning Eagle*, February 16, 1908.

[83]Minutes of the Board of Directors, February 14, 1908, 75; Bryan *Morning Eagle*, February 16, 1908.

pus, issued their own appeals for a return to class work in line with the Directors' appeal.[84] On the same day the Directors issued a public statement which reviewed in detail the entire situation from February 6 through February 14, and which is for the most part a direct quotation of the official record of the Board.[85] Other than for the points of view taken in the different sources, and for disagreements on the *cause* of the strike, all major sources of information are in complete accord, insofar as the events and facts of the strike are concerned.

The businessmen of Bryan held a public meeting on Saturday the 15th and announced: "We are firmly of the opinion that there exists no reason for the present conditions and that the administration of Dr. H. H. Harrington has been just and that the situation is one that is possible to arise in any school where the regulations are strictly enforced."[86] Francis M. Law reiterated the call for the return of students to the campus, and at the same time commended the "splendid discipline" of the Corps, noting that the students had never been rowdy, but very deliberative,[87] a restraint which makes the Texas A&M protest of 1908 a very different thing from many staged on college campuses in the 1960s. By Friday, February 21, Captain Moses could report only 233 students on campus.[88]

The Houston alumni gathered, with delegates of Alumni Associations around the state, in Houston on Saturday, February 22. The result of an all-day meeting was approval of a resolution asking for a new investigation of affairs at the college:

> We believe that the unsettled state of affairs proves conclusively that something is radically wrong. And that if it had been otherwise, this trouble would have been averted before it reached its present stage. Wherefore be it resolved, that we ask friends of the College throughout the State of Texas to join us in a petition to the Board of Directors of the College to re-open the investigation, and have a public investigation of the condition of affairs of the present trouble in order that the existing evils may be eradicated from the institution.[89]

The alumni engaged the services of Hatton W. Sumners, of Dallas,

---

[84]Casey, *The History of the A. and M. Trouble*, 33-34.

[85]Bryan *Morning Eagle*, February 16, 1908.

[86]*Ibid.*

[87]*Ibid.*, February 22, 1908.

[88]*Ibid.*

[89]Houston *Post*, February 23, 1908; Bryan *Morning Eagle*, February 25, 1908; "To the Members of the Alumni and Ex-Students of the A. and M. College of Texas," undated printed letter signed by James Cravens, Harry L. Wright, E. J. Smith, Charles C. Todd, F. A. Reichardt, W. D. Roseborough Papers, Texas A&M University Archives.

Texas, to represent them. Sumners had served several terms as Dallas County attorney, and had earned a reputation as an honest, aggressive reformer. He earned statewide recognition for breaking up organized gambling in the county between 1900 and 1906.[90] Later he was to appear again on the A&M scene during another crisis, and to go on to become a United States congressman.

The Board of Directors met at College Station in a special meeting on February 24, to consider the petition of the alumni and former students urging that a public investigation be held. In a lengthy reply to the Houston alumni, the Directors said that they had given much time and effort to the matter at hand. The charges made by students and others had been fairly and thoroughly investigated, and among the investigators, added the Directors, were three lawyers. The issue at hand, continued the reply, was a matter of principle: "If the corps of cadets can force the retirement of a President over the judgment of the Board of Directors, they could with equal propriety force the selection of his successor."[91] The Directors were determined to maintain constituted authority, the issues notwithstanding.

At the same meeting the Directors received a letter from a group of parents in Waco, advising the Board that they were returning their sons to A&M, on the condition that Henry Hill Harrington be removed from the president's office in June following commencement. The Directors made an evasive reply, welcoming the return of the students and noting that the Board would do what was best for the College.[92]

For a short while it appeared that things might be returning to normal at the College. The Directors met on the campus in March, and created the office of superintendent of buildings and took care of miscellaneous administrative matters.[93] They met again at Prairie View a few weeks later and received reports on plans for the new engineering building and discussed the construction of a new administration building. Frederick E. Giesecke was appointed College architect in addition to his duties as professor of architectural engineering and drawing.[94] Then in May a new eruption opened the old wounds and indicated that the relative calm on campus was at best a truce.

In a called meeting at Waco, on May 20, 1908, the Directors took note of the continuing discontent on campus evidenced by the inflammatory arti-

[90]Casey, *The History of the A. and M. Trouble,* xxi.
[91]Minutes of the Board of Directors, February 24, 1908, II, 77-79.
[92]*Ibid.,* 79-80.
[93]*Ibid.,* March 27, 1908, II, 82-83.
[94]*Ibid.,* May 11, 1908, II, 84-85.

cles appearing in the student newspaper, the *Battalion*.[95] The Board issued a directive to the President and to the faculty to maintain order on the campus: "In the Opinion of the Board recent issues of the *Battalion* have contained articles highly prejudicial to good order and discipline and the Board directs that the responsible parties be ascertained and adequately punished."[96]

The article particularly offensive to President Harrington and to the Board was one which appeared in a junior-class issue of the *Battalion* on April 22, and which refuted a published statement made earlier by President Harrington that the recent turmoil had been forgotten and that things were now normal at the College. Unfortunately, the issues of the *Battalion* for this period of time are no longer extant. But concern over the articles was sufficiently great that after an investigation failed to turn up specific names responsible for authoring the article, the faculty voted to suspend the seven junior *Battalion* editors from the College. The students again protested, the junior class arguing that they should be held responsible for the articles as a class. Sophomores and freshmen similarly issued resolutions deploring the situation at the College, but no active protests were staged as the students were in the midst of final examinations.[97]

Concurrently with this new crisis on campus a circular letter from the Houston Alumni came to the attention of the cadets and made their cause look more hopeless. This circular letter was a response from the Houston group to a so-called Rogan circular, sponsored by Charles Rogan and others who opposed reopening the College investigations. The Rogan letter accused the Houston group of "going too far." The reply from Houston, signed by James Cravens, H. L. Wright, E. J. Smith, C. C. Todd, and F. A. Reichardt, included the observation:

> In shame and in humiliation and with a deep concern which only an ex-student can understand, we have witnessed the deplorable condition there. And this we want to say by way of parenthesis, the relation between the President and the student body is now as antagonistic as it has ever been, if any difference, perhaps more fixed.[98]

The communication concluded with the observation that there seemed to be nothing the interested alumni could do to change the Board's position on reopening the investigation.[99]

[95] *Ibid.*, May 20, 1908, II, 87.

[96] *Ibid.*

[97] Casey, *The History of the A. and M. Trouble*, 76-88.

[98] "To the members of the Alumni and Ex-Students of the A. and M. College of Texas," undated letter in W. D. Roseborough Papers, Texas A&M University Archives.

[99] *Ibid.*

So the cadets completed their examinations and on June 9 forty-eight seniors received their diplomas. (By June over four hundred cadets had returned to classes.) The next day the Board announced that, upon the request of the alumni, it would begin a public investigation of charges preferred by them against the President.[100] The alumni, represented by Hatton Sumners, presented thirteen charges. Each was thoroughly investigated through witnesses, documents, and cross-examinations in lengthy hearings held between June 10 and June 22, 1908. Attorney Sumners summarized the results of those hearings in reports to the alumni after the investigation closed. The record is voluminous, reported Sumners, "covering nearly 850 typewritten pages." "The case has been so diluted with words," he said, "that it is next to impossible for one not engaged in the investigation to have any idea of what was proven or what led up to the present condition at A&M College." Sumners then attempted, in two lengthy communications to the alumni, to reconstruct the story, event by event and charge by charge.[101] Sumners' reconstruction, considerably amplified, with full consideration of the official records of the University, is the story that has just been told. Its retelling will likely fail to sort out those tangled webs which led to one of the greatest crises in the history of the College. Neither will the legalistic review of the specified charges and the evidence in support or refutation of those charges clarify or place the burden of guilt positively on one or the other participants — on the students, the Board, the President, or the alumni, individually or collectively. It is a thing that happened.

Sumners and others felt that Charge Number 13 had in effect been admitted:

that President Harrington is the executive head of the college, and as such his duties are to command the respect and confidence of the student body, to the end that he may preserve order, maintain discipline and inspire the students to the proper intellectual achievements and moral development; . . . and generally to so direct college affairs as to promote harmony and peace, and create such an atmosphere that uninterrupted and undisturbed work may be done by all connected with the institution.

The rules of the college make him responsible for the discipline of the College.

[100]Minutes of the Board of Directors, June 10, 1908, II, 88-90; June 22, 1908, II, 92-93.

[101]In Hatton W. Sumners to James Cravens, Chairman, Houston, Texas, undated letter, and in Sumners to James Cravens, Chairman, undated letter in W. D. Roseborough Papers, Texas A&M University Archives, Sumners reviews some of the testimony from the proceedings, bearing specifically on the charges. Paul D. Casey's published work, used extensively in this study, reprints a considerable portion of the testimony from the hearings. Casey had access as well to all of the Houston alumni material and reproduced the letters cited above.

That in all these things he has failed utterly, and that A. and M. College, while under him, was brought to the verge of destruction.[102]

The Board concluded otherwise; they found then "*and now* that there was no just cause for complaint against the President." The charges had not been proved, said the Directors, but rather had been affirmatively disproved. Despite the unpopularity of President Henry Hill Harrington with the students, the school "has made genuine progress" under his administration. The Directors attributed the students' dislike of Harrington to his "dignified reserve which is often misunderstood." The Board noted that some 200 to 600 parents had appeared in person or by letter requesting the removal of President Harrington. Even conceding the personal unpopularity of the President as grounds for removal, the Directors reported, they could not have done so until law and order had been established at the College, and until the student body had been taught a lesson that they could not make and unmake college presidents at will. We would "close the school," said the Directors, "before we allow a student body to rise in open and bold defiance of constituted authority."[103]

In February the Board concluded that there was no just cause of complaint against the President and no real grounds for grievance, "such is its conclusion now."[104]

On that day, June 22, 1908, Charles W. Hutson, professor of history and economics, resigned, as did Walter W. Evans, superintendent of the Farm; Asa Judson Neff, superintendent of the power plant; L. L. Larson, the physical director;[105] and instructors Felix S. Puckett and D. E. Mackey. O. F. Chastain replaced Hutson in history and Jake V. Brogdon was named superintendent of the Farm.[106]

On August 7, 1908, the A&M College Board of Directors met in the Elks Hall in Corpus Christi. Henry Hill Harrington presented the Directors his resignation as president of the Agricultural and Mechanical College of Texas: ". . . my continuation as President of your College [he said] may serve in some degree as an embarrassment to you; I therefore tender to you my resignation; to take effect the 1st of September, or at such date as may suit your convenience." "Accepted," answered the Board.[107]

[102]Hatton W. Sumners to M. James Cravens, Chairman, Houston, Texas, undated letter in W. D. Roseborough Papers, Texas A&M University Archives.

[103]Minutes of the Board of Directors, June 22, 1908, II, 91-94.

[104]*Ibid.*, II, 94.

[105]*Ibid.*, II, 94-95.

[106]*Ibid.*, II, 94, 98.

[107]*Ibid.*, August 7, 1908, II, 99.

CHAPTER 11

The Farmers

THE "Aggie" epithet applied to Texas A&M College students is of relatively recent vintage. Little evidence exists that before 1900 any popular nickname was applied to the "students at A. & M. C." Sometime after 1900 the term "Farmers" became popular, but not until the 1930s did "Aggie" come into widespread use. Only in 1949 was the College student annual, the *Longhorn*, changed to *Aggieland*. The term "Farmers" or "Aggie," identifying the major effort or occupation of Texas A&M College students as being related to agriculture or to farming, is a misnomer in almost any day and time, before or since 1900. A far more appropriate descriptive term for A&M students throughout most of the school's history would have been the "Engineers."

In the early Gathright years the College gave little more than lip service to agriculture. The "agrarian reaction" of 1879-1880 produced a sharp revision of the curricula and required students to enroll in either agriculture or engineering. Agricultural training, in conformity to popular and to Grange ideas, was made "practical" to the point that agricultural students were required to do manual field work. The relative distribution of students between the agricultural and the engineering curricula in the academic year 1880-1881 was 18 percent and 82 percent, respectively, denoting the general aversion of Texas A&M students to agricultural studies.[1] A great many of them were from the farm, rural communities, or small towns, and they found nothing exciting about agriculture during the decade immediately following the establishment of the College. Their ambition was to get away from the farm.

Before 1900 the proportion of students enrolled in the agricultural course never exceeded 37.7 percent of the student body, and averaged around 25 percent.[2] In 1888-1889, however, a clear upsurge in enrollment in the agri-

[1]Sub-Committee on Historical Perspective, Land Grant College Centennial Celebrations, "The Agricultural and Mechanical College of Texas, A Land-Grant College in Perspective," Mimeographed [1962], p. 5, Texas A&M University Archives.

[2]Sub-Committee on Historical Perspective, Land-Grant College Centennial Celebrations, "Enrollment at Texas A&M" [typed manuscript], 1-3, in Texas A&M University Archives.

cultural studies occurred, and in 1890 the College for the first time graduated as many agricultural students as engineers. In 1893 eight students received Bachelor of Science degrees in Agriculture while seven students received the Bachelor of Science in Mechanical Engineering, thus for the first and the only time in its history did the College graduate more students in agriculture than in engineering.[3] In 1913-1914 the enrollment in the agricultural studies again increased considerably, with 49.9 percent of the students enrolled in agricultural courses, and from 1914-1917, for the only period of time in the history of the College, the number of students enrolled in agricultural studies exceeded the number of students enrolled in the engineering curricula.[4] The enrollment surge appeared to be a result of congressional passage of the Smith-Lever Act (1914) and the Smith-Hughes Act (1917), providing new job opportunities in extension and vocational agricultural teaching. Since 1954 enrollment in the College of Agriculture has averaged 16 percent of the total enrollment.[5] Throughout most of its history the College has largely been something other than an agricultural school. This fact does not diminish the importance of the agricultural studies, but simply puts the functions of the A&M College into a more nearly accurate perspective than that conveyed by the phrase "Aggie."

The enrollment statistics cited above reflect some important aspects of the agricultural studies at the A&M College. Specifically, the sudden increase in popularity of agricultural studies in 1888-1889, and again in 1913-1914, can be attributed to two very important events in the history of the College, events equally important to the broad development of American agriculture. The first of these milestones was the passage of the Hatch Act and its approval by President Grover Cleveland on March 2, 1887.[6] The second milestone was the passage by Congress of the Smith-Lever Act of May 8, 1914.[7] An analysis of developments under the aegis of these two pieces of federal legislation and the original Morrill Act provide a substantial view of the history of American agriculture as well as an understanding of the development of the agricultural and mechanical colleges. Since events at Texas A&M pertaining to the Smith-Lever Act, which provided for the inception of agricul-

[3]*Ibid.*, College Station *Longhorn, 1908*, p. 148.

[4]"Enrollment at Texas A&M," 1-3; "The Agricultural and Mechanical College of Texas: A Land-Grant College in Perspective," 5.

[5]"Enrollment at Texas A&M," 1-3.

[6]U.S. Department of Agriculture, *Federal Legislation, Regulations, and Rulings Affecting Land-Grant Colleges and Experiment Stations,* 17-18.

[7]Texas A&M, *Biennial Report, 1913-1914,* p. 25; USDA, *Federal Legislation, Regulations, and Rulings Affecting Land-Grant Colleges and Experiment Stations,* 37-40.

tural extension, are dealt with in a later chapter, this chapter of A&M's history reveals the impact which the Agricultural Experiment Station, created by the Hatch Act, had upon the development of the College during its "middle years."

Generally speaking, the advent of the Agricultural Experiment Station program at Texas A&M had much to do with the survival and progress of the College as a whole. Experiment Station work at Texas A&M helped convince the public, not only of the efficacy of "scientific" agriculture and agricultural education, but of the value and prestige of the entire College. The general pattern of national agricultural-experiment-station history is closely paralleled at College Station.

Throughout the United States and in Texas, experimental farming operations began at the agricultural and mechanical colleges many years before the passage of the Hatch Act. The University of Wisconsin had an experimental farm as early as 1866, and the state of Connecticut established an independent agricultural experiment station in 1875, which provided a model for the stations created by the Hatch Act.[8] When Texas A&M opened in 1876 it conducted experimental farming operations of a very marginal nature, under the direction of Professor of Agriculture Carlisle P. B. Martin. Experimental farm operations were expanded by Charles C. Gorgeson between 1881 and 1883, and further by George W. Curtis during his tenure as professor of agriculture between 1883 and 1893.[9] Yet both Gorgeson and Curtis found a strong prejudice against agricultural education among both the students and the public.[10] President Hardaway Hunt Dinwiddie and Curtis experienced some success in their efforts to cultivate the support of Texas farmers for the A&M College between 1883 and 1887.[11]

Not until the spring of 1887 did the Texas State Grange begin to support vigorously the A&M College. In the fall of 1888 the College appeared to be stirring from its doldrums and breathing with new life. The advent of the seemingly sudden popular support from Texas farmers, and the bustle of activity on the campus in 1888, both of which events, happily for Louis L. McInnis, coincided with his election to the chairmanship of the institution,

[8]Charles E. Rosenberg, "Science, Technology and Economic Growth: The Case of the Agricultural Experiment Station Scientist, 1875-1914," *Agricultural History*, XLV (January 1971), pp. 1-3.

[9]Texas A&M, *Annual Report, 1883*, pp. 30-34.

[10]*Ibid.*, and *Annual Report, 1884*, p. 84.

[11]Texas A&M, *Annual Report, 1884*, pp. 1-4; Texas A&M, *Biennial Report, 1883-1885*, pp. 12-13; S. W. Geiser, "George Washington Curtis and Frank Arthur Gulley: Two Agricultural Teachers in Texas," *Field and Laboratory*, XIV (January 1946), pp. 1-13.

can in part be easily explained. The passage of the Hatch Act provided new money for the College, which in years past had been virtually impoverished. The fact that the College now had money which had not come from Texas pockets undoubtedly relieved many Texans of the fear that this A&M College would prove too costly a venture in terms of taxes.

The truth is that the Hatch Act did more than create agricultural experiment stations; it helped establish and secure many tottering public institutions of higher learning. Texas A&M was one of these. There was a very definite tendency at Texas A&M, as there was elsewhere in the country, to exploit the budget of the Experiment Station for the good of the whole institution.[12] Thus for many years Texas A&M salaries for regular teaching faculty were supplemented by Experiment Station funds. The professor of agriculture, for example, doubled as director of the Agricultural Experiment Station, but drew his entire salary from Experiment Station funds, although his primary duty was to teach regular college courses in agriculture. The professor of physics served as Station meteorologist; the professor of veterinary science doubled as Station veterinarian; the professor of chemistry served as chief chemist of the Station; and instructors and lesser individuals worked as assistants to the Station personnel, all drawing a portion, or sometimes all, of their salaries from Hatch Act funds. Even students benefited directly by being able to receive ten cents an hour (as in 1888) for labor, whereas previously the College had no funds with which to pay student labor.[13] One of the most important features of the Hatch Act is its provision of new money to the A&M College.

The agricultural experiment station also made it easier for the agricultural and mechanical college to sell farmers on the idea of scientific farming, and on the value and services of the institution itself. The experiment station, quite often, did help a farmer solve his problems. In fact, in many respects extensive public services by the experiment station generated the need for the Agricultural Extension Service created in 1914. Before 1914 the experiment stations became so involved in extension that they had little time for research or real experimentation. Indeed, sponsorship of an agricultural experiment station, while it was a positive good for the agricultural and mechanical college, also brought problems.

The public, for example, expected the Texas A&M Experiment Station,

[12]See Rosenberg, "The Case of the Agricultural Experiment Station Scientist, 1875-1914," *Agricultural History*, XLV (January 1971), p. 5.

[13]Minutes of the Board of Directors, January 24, 1888, I, 44-46; Texas A&M, *Catalogue, 1887-1888*, p. 77.

and the College generally, to cater to immediate public concerns. Thus the Experiment Station became heavily involved in testing soils, feeds, fertilizers, and seeds for area farmers rather than in genuine scientific investigation.[14] When there were scientific investigations, those investigations were most often dictated by local economic concerns — such as control of Texas fever for Texas cattlemen, and control of the boll weevil for Texas farmers.[15] Because of their work in public relations, Experiment Station personnel were often judged and valued on the basis of personality rather than technical ability.[16] Furthermore, because of the conscious policy of promoting improved relations with farmer organizations, and the sponsoring of Farmer Institutes, and later the Farmers' Congress, Texas Experiment Station and A&M College personnel sometimes found their policies and programs to be dictated by their constituent groups rather than by scientific or academic considerations. The state Legislature also often responded to organized farm lobbies by instituting various research programs and farm services at the A&M College.[17] Legislative enactments included the creation of a Texas Grass Experiment Station in 1891, authorization of a program to devise means of destroying the "Mexican boll weevil" in 1899, a fertilizer-inspection law in 1899, the conception of tobacco-farming experiments in 1909 and in 1911, the establishment of teacher institutes in agriculture in 1909, a pure-feed inspection law in 1905, and the addition of a "department of instruction to determine the spinable value of cotton" in 1909.[18] While these programs, of course, cannot be disparaged, the method of implementing the programs indicates the somewhat subservient nature of the Experiment Station and of the College.

In 1912 the Board of Directors of the A&M College, in accord with the spirit of the Experiment Station and the Extension Service programs, recog-

[14]See Rosenberg, "The Case of the Agricultural Experiment Station Scientist, 1875-1914," *Agricultural History,* XLV (January 1971), pp. 4-6.

[15]Investigations initially planned for the newly established Agricultural Experiment Station included winter feeding to cattle, testing variety of grasses and forage plants, improvement of soil by fertilization and crop rotation, improvement of soil by drainage, and study of the disease of the cotton plant (Minutes of the Board of Directors, June 1, 1888, I, 60).

[16]See Rosenberg, "The Case of the Agricultural Experiment Station Scientist," *Agricultural History,* XLV (January 1971), pp. 4-6.

[17]*Ibid.,* 4-7; Minutes of Board of Directors, June 4, 1889, I, 76; Bryan *Eagle* (w), August 18, 1898, July 21, 1898.

[18]Minutes of the Board of Directors, November 5, 1891, I, 123; *General Laws of Texas, 1897-1902,* p. 9; Minutes of the Board of Directors, June 7-9, 1909, II, 165; *General Laws of Texas, 1909,* 221-223, 278-279, 401; *General Laws of Texas, 1911,* 168-169. See also Clarence Ousley, *History of the Agricultural and Mechanical College of Texas,* 107-135.

nized the primary objective of the College as being to "achieve distinction for civil service to the people of Texas."[19] This objective recognizes the assumption of obligations and responsibilities somewhat uncommon to many institutions of higher learning, and helped create for Texas A&M a unique place in the affairs of the state of Texas.

The Texas Agricultural Experiment Station, as organized by the Board of Directors of the A&M College on January 24, 1888, functioned under the direction of an Agricultural Experiment Station Council. The Council included the chairman of the faculty, the business agent, and the director of the Station. The director was to be elected by the Board and would be given faculty status as well as teaching duties. Professor of Chemistry Henry Hill Harrington served as chief chemist; Professor of Physics John H. Kinealy was meteorologist; and Professor of Veterinary Science Mark Francis was veterinarian. The Directors elected Frank Arthur Gulley, of the A&M College of Mississippi, as first director of the Experiment Station.[20]

The practice of publishing experimental bulletins begun by the College in 1888 was carried on and expanded by the Experiment Station.[21] By 1893 the Station had issued a total of twenty-five *Experiment Station Bulletins* on such topics as the chemical composition of grasses and forage plants, the effects of cotton seed and cotton-seed meal as food for hogs, the causes of alfalfa root rot, and a chemical study of the soils of the state. Bulletins were issued in runs of 6,500 copies.[22] By 1898 the Station reported a mailing list of 12,000 names, with publications (and mailing lists) being divided into three categories: (1) general farm crops, (2) fruits and vegetables, (3) stock husbandry.[23]

The Board of Directors proposed in 1890 to establish an experimental substation in each section of the state "representing a distinct soil and climate at the earliest moment practicable." Operating funds would come out of federal appropriations, but the initial cost had to be borne by the state or come from other sources. Under this policy the Directors announced that experiment stations had been established at Harlem, in Fort Bend County, on the State Farm for sugar-cane studies; at Gatesville, in Coryell County, at the State Reformatory for grass study; at McGregor, in McLennan County (provided by the State Grange), for wheat studies; and at a private orchard near Rusk, in Cherokee County, and at Prairie View Normal, in Waller County,

[19]Minutes of the Board of Directors, August 6, 1912, III, 34-35.

[20]Minutes of the Board of Directors, January 24, 25, 1888, I, 44-45.

[21]Texas A&M, *Annual Report, 1883-1884*, p. 6.

[22]"Fifth Annual Report of the Texas Agricultural Experiment Station, January 1, 1893," in Texas A&M, *Biennial Report, 1891-1893*, pp. 25-26.

[23]Texas A&M, *Biennial Report, 1896-1898*, pp. 10-20.

for fruit experiments.[24] These projects, however, were never funded by special appropriations and soon expired.

The first true experimental substation was established at Beeville, under provisions of an act of the state Legislature in 1892 which provided $5,000 for the location of three substations.[25] Land for the Beeville Station was contributed by the citizens of Bee County in 1895. James H. Connell, who succeeded Frank A. Gulley (1888-1890) and George W. Curtis (1890-1893) as director of the Experiment Station, announced that the projects of the Beeville Substation would include the cultivation of apple, peach, and grape orchards and experiments with olives, oranges, lemons, pineapples, dates, and forty varieties of cotton.[26] The Beeville Station apparently consumed most of the state appropriations, for by 1898 only one other substation had been established and that was at Alvin, without the use of state funds.[27] This "station" soon ceased operations. The Legislature authorized in 1901 the establishment of a second station, which was established northeast of Troup, in Smith County, in 1902. In 1931 it was relocated northwest of Tyler.[28] By 1930 the Texas Agricultural Experiment Station operated sixteen substations in widespread parts of the state. Others had been operated but discontinued.

Substation No. 1	(1895)	Beeville, Bee County, Texas
Substation No. 2	(1902)	Troup (later Tyler), Smith County, Texas
Substation No. 12	(1905)	Chillicothe, Hardeman County, Texas
Substation No. 3	(1909)	Angleton, Brazoria County, Texas
Substation No. 4	(1909)	Beaumont, Jefferson County, Texas
Substation No. 5	(1909)	Temple, Bell County, Texas
Substation No. 6	(1909)	Denton, Denton County, Texas
Substation No. 7	(1909)	Spur, Dickens County, Texas
Substation No. 8	(1909)	Lubbock, Lubbock County, Texas
Substation No. 9	(1909)	Pecos (now near Balmorhea), Reeves County, Texas
Substation No. 10	(1909)	College Station, Brazos County, Texas
Substation No. 11	(1909)	Nacogdoches, Nacogdoches County, Texas
Substation No. 14	(1916)	Sonora, Sutton County, Texas
Substation No. 15	(1923)	Weslaco, Hidalgo County, Texas
Substation No. 16	(1924)	Iowa Park, Wichita County, Texas
Substation No. 19	(1929)	Winter Haven, Dimmit County, Texas

[24]Texas A&M, *Annual Report, December 1, 1890*, pp. 6-7.

[25]Minutes of the Board of Directors, July 4, 1893, p. 151.

[26]Bryan *Eagle* (w), January 17, 1895.

[27]Texas A&M, *Biennial Report, 1896-1898*, pp. 10-20.

[28]Minutes of the Board of Directors, October 16, 1901, p. 243; Ousley, *History of the Agricultural and Mechanical College*, 133.

The greatest accomplishments of the Texas Agricultural Experiment Station research programs included the elimination of Texas fever, through the efforts of Dr. Mark Francis; the improvement of grain sorghum varieties, under the direction of Arthur B. Conner, later director of the Agricultural Experiment Station; the development of Sudan grass, by Charles Vancouver Piper, of the United States Department of Agriculture, Arthur B. Conner, and others; the control of loin disease in cattle, by Dr. Hubert Schmidt and others; the control of soremouth in sheep by Drs. W. Tyree Hardy and I. B. Boughton; and the control of root rot in cotton, by Dr. Jacob Joseph Taubenhaus.[29] The massive amounts of technical information and personal services provided Texas and U.S. farmers by the Texas Agricultural Experiment Station have an inestimable dollar value.

The original Experiment Station Council, established by Louis McInnis in 1888, was dissolved when Governor Lawrence Sullivan Ross became president of the College. Between 1890 and 1901 the Experiment Station functioned under the control of the Board of Directors. In October 1901 the Board created a new Council comprising the president of the College, the director of the Experiment Station, the chemist, the veterinarian, and the horticulturist of the Station. This Council could approve all Station expenditures, determine the character of all experiments, and approve all bulletins published. It was soon abolished upon the arrival of a new director of the Station, William D. Gibbs, in August 1902, and control passed back to the Board of Directors.[30]

In 1909, upon the creation of eight new substations, the state Legislature created a substation board comprising the governor, the commissioner of agriculture, and the lieutenant governor, and placed Substations Nos. 3-11 under the control of this special board. In 1913 a new act, amended by a special called session of the same year, created a control board for the Texas Agricultural Experiment Station, composed of the lieutenant governor and three additional voters appointed by the governor, providing that only the Main Station at College Station should remain under the Board of Directors of the College. In 1921 full control was returned to the A&M Board of Directors.[31]

In 1903 John A. Craig, former professor of agriculture at Iowa A&M and later at the University of Wisconsin, replaced William D. Gibbs as direc-

[29]Ousley, *History of the Agricultural and Mechanical College*, 107-128.

[30]Minutes of the Board of Directors, October 16, 1901, I, 244; *ibid.*, August 4, 1902, I, 268.

[31]Ousley, *History of the Agricultural and Mechanical College*, 130-132.

tor of the Agricultural Experiment Station. Craig left in June 1906, and a year later the Board named A&M President Henry Hill Harrington acting director of the Station. Upon resigning as president of the College in August 1908, Harrington was named director of the Experiment Station, with the implied proviso that he not reside at College Station.[32]

Bonney Youngblood replaced Henry Hill Harrington as director of the Texas Agricultural Experiment Station in 1911. Born on a stock farm in Milam County, Texas, on July 31, 1881, Youngblood entered Texas A&M in 1898 and received a B.S. in Agriculture in 1902. He taught public schools in Henderson and Mineola, Texas, and Paul's Valley, Oklahoma, for a time and in each case introduced elementary courses in agriculture. He returned to Texas A&M and received the M.S. degree in 1907, and then worked with the United States Department of Agriculture for four years before joining the A&M faculty. Youngblood presided over the Texas Experiment Station from 1911 to 1926, during which time the Station earned an outstanding reputation for research and service. In 1926 he went to Washington, D.C., to work in the United States Department of Agriculture, Bureau of Agricultural Economics, and in 1929 became the principal agricultural economist for the United States experiment stations. He retired on September 15, 1950.[33]

Robert Teague Milner, commissioner of agriculture and ex officio member of the Board of Directors of Texas A&M, replaced Harrington as president of the College on August 7, 1908. In background, temperment, and training Milner compared favorably to Lafayette Lumpkin Foster. Both men came to Texas in their youth, Milner having been born in Cherokee County, Alabama, June 21, 1851. Both went into politics, Milner serving in the state Legislature between 1887 and 1892, and Foster from 1882 to 1886. Foster became commissioner of agriculture in 1886, and Milner entered that office in 1906, when it had been reorganized to exclude insurance, history, and statistics. Both Foster and Milner worked for a time as newspaper publishers. Both had relatively little formal education.[34] Both were self-made men. Milner followed a strong line of A&M presidents and was fully as effective as such prestigious predecessors as Lawrence Sullivan Ross and David Franklin Houston.

Milner began to function in his capacity as president of the College on

[32]Bryan *Eagle* (w), September 24, 1903, p. 4; Minutes of the Board of Directors, June 12, 1906, II, 8-9; *ibid.,* June 27, 1907, II, 31; *ibid.,* August 7-8, 1908, II, 103; *ibid.,* September 3-5, 1908, II, 105.

[33]Bryan *Daily Eagle,* September 6, 1950; College Station *Battalion,* September 18, 1950.

[34]Webb and Carroll (eds.), *The Handbook of Texas,* II, 202; College Station *Longhorn,* 1909, pp. 5-6.

the day of his election, August 7, 1908, although he did not officially resign as commissioner of agriculture until August 31, and did not arrive on campus until September 1. According to the student annual of 1909, the *Longhorn,* Milner was sent to A&M to "sit on the lid," and reportedly was doing a good job of it, for the student *Longhorn* editor commented in 1909 that "his presence is breeding an era of good feeling."[35] This seems to have been true, but for an unfortunate episode in 1913. Generally, Milner presided over a growing faculty, and an expanding and somewhat truculent student body. Texas A&M was leaving its childhood behind and entering its adolescence.

Characteristic of the growing pains of this period is the fact that each year from 1906 until the outbreak of World War I many students were forced to live in tents, despite the addition of several new dormitories. In getting Milner's first academic year underway, following the stormy and chaotic preceding year, the Directors hired a number of new faculty, including a librarian, James H. Quarles, and an athletic director, N. A. Merriam. Glenn W. Herrick came as professor of entomology, and Hiram L. McKnight as assistant professor of agriculture.[36] Total salaries for the seventy-five employees of the College (plus several unfilled positions), equalled $114,942.50 for the 1908-1909 academic year.[37] More than half of the salaries were paid from federal grants such as the original endowment, the Hatch Act of 1888 (Agricultural Experiment Station), the Adams Act of 1906 (increased support for Experiment Station), and the Nelson Act of 1907 (supplementing the original Morrill endowment).[38]

One of the most annoying tasks of the College Directors for many years was the assignment of housing to the faculty. Just as there was a scarcity of housing for students, there was a lack of adequate housing for faculty, until such time as the College finally divested itself of responsibility for faculty housing altogether in 1940. In 1906 some members of the faculty made private efforts to resolve the critical housing shortage by organizing the A&M College Club and building a hotel, The Shirley, named for the daughter of Professor John A. Lomax, whose name was selected in a drawing. The Shirley was a large, two-story frame building with four white pillars on the front porch. It had a large lobby, dining room, and kitchen downstairs, with guest rooms upstairs. The Shirley provided temporary quarters for new faculty while residences were being constructed, and some bachelor professors

[35]College Station *Longhorn, 1905,* pp. 5-6; Austin *Daily Statesman,* September 1, 1908.
[36]Minutes of the Board of Directors, September 3-5, 1908, II, 105-109.
[37]*Ibid.,* 115.
[38]*Ibid.,* 115-120.

resided permanently in The Shirley and others ate regularly in the dining room operated by Mrs. Asa J. Neff and her mother, Mrs. Charles B. Stillwell. Cadets waited on tables. Robert Franklin Smith presided regularly at one table, at which sat Charles Puryear, Chaplain Isaac Alexander, David Brooks Cofer, and John David Bond. Smith, Oscar Melville Ball, John W. Kidd, and Frederick E. Giesecke were the original promoters and major stockholders of the hotel, which was built for about $20,000.[39]

In 1910 the stockholders built the Shirley Annex, designed for some fifty bachelor members of the staff. This was a three-story rooming house which saw service through the end of World War I. The original Bachelor Hall, built by the College in 1900, remained in service until 1917, when it was converted into an apartment house. The old natatorium also entered service as a bachelors' quarters in 1908 and housed about nineteen men.[40] The electrification of the gasoline interurban and the advent of the automobile helped solve the critical housing situation for faculty and staff, but only in relatively recent years have the surrounding communities of Bryan-College Station been able to offer fully adequate housing facilities for College students and personnel.

David Brooks Cofer, writing in 1953, gives a very vivid description of the campus in 1910:

> In 1910, the third year of the Milner administration, Texas A. and M. College presented an appearance far different from that of 1953. The College buildings were quite different, the trees now so plentiful and beautiful, were at that time few in number, except cedar trees in clumps and on each side of the road leading to the railroad station, and surely the so-called streets were but dusty or muddy roads, and sidewalks, except cinder and gravel, were non-existent. At this time the front of the campus was toward the railroads, not the present beautiful entrance in front of the present System Administration Building. The front of the 1910 A. and M. looked to the West: the front of the 1953 A. and M. looks to the East.
>
> In President Milner's day the main campus streets, or ways, were the Circle, the Walk to the Old Mess Hall from the front of Old Main Building, Military Walk, running along in front of Gathright, Ross, Foster, and Old Chapel, Quality Row (Throckmorton), the Road from the Flag Pole to the Railroad Station, the Street in front of Old Chemistry Building, Agricultural and Horticultural Building, State Chemistry Laboratory, the street along by the Textile Building, Natatorium, Old Hospital and to the barns. At that time cedar trees lined many of these ways, not live-oak trees as now, and the cedar trees, lining the way on both sides from Old Main to the Railroad Station, were very uniform and really pretty. These cedar trees,

[39]David Brooks Cofer (ed.), *Fragments of Early History of Texas A. and M. College*, 17-18.
[40]*Ibid.*, 18-20.

too, followed the Circle from the President's Home to the Francis house on the opposite side of the common and the drill field.[41]

Cofer goes on to describe the faculty and staff residences, the crowded office and classroom conditions, and the still inadequate utilities and sanitation facilities.

In September 1908 Goodwin Hall was opened for students, and in early October 1908 the Agricultural Building was almost destroyed by fire but for the "heroic efforts of the student body."[42] In December the Directors requested authorization for a summer "normal" school to be conducted on campus between June 15 and July 30, 1909, and extended a five-year lease to William Carson Boyett to continue operation of a "first class grocery store" on campus.[43] In March 1909 the Directors made a new step forward in the world of academics by investigating the possibility of establishing College-sponsored correspondence courses.[44]

Faculty rank and salary were also "modernized" in June 1909. Assistants were to be hired at $800 for twelve months, with annual increases of $50 for four years. Instructors began at $1,000 per year with annual increases of $75 for four years, and assistant professors started at $1,300 with $75 increases each year for four years. Associate professors started at $1,600 with a $100 annual increase. Full-professor salaries, while not specified, ranged from $1,800 to $2,700.[45]

The session 1909-1910 opened with burgeoning student enrollments. As of September 24, 1909, enrollment stood at 757 students, "107 more than there are accomodations [*sic*] for," with "more arriving on every train,"[46] we find recorded in the Minutes of the Board of Directors. The Directors resolved, however, not to turn anyone away, as had been the practice in the past, but requested emergency appropriations from the state, and meanwhile allocated funds from other accounts for purchase of new tents and mess-hall equipment.[47] During the academic year efforts to relieve the crowded conditions took various forms. W. H. Stillwell was given permission to erect and operate a private rooming house on campus. A committee also met with citi-

[41]*Ibid.*, 30-36.

[42]Minutes of the Board of Directors, September 3-5, 1908, I, 106, 129; and October 17, 1908, II, 126.

[43]*Ibid.*, December 5, 1908, 133.

[44]*Ibid.*, March 9, 1909, II, 152.

[45]*Ibid.*, June 7-9, 1909, II, 158-159.

[46]*Ibid.*, September 24, 1909, II, 176-177.

[47]*Ibid.*

zens of Bryan to encourage local people to provide rooms and accommodations for College employees. William C. Boyett, who owned property adjoining the northern portion of the campus, was requested to place some of his property on the market "so that there may be built adjacent to the College a community which would relieve the congested condition on the campus," but by 1912, there having been no such community development, the Directors set aside a portion of the campus for business along the northeastern corners of what are now Ross and Ireland Streets (see fig. 2), although the extension of Ireland past Ross no longer exists.[48]

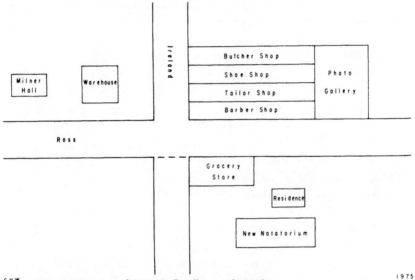

GHW   Figure 2. Diagram of "North Gate" stores in 1912.   1975

In June 1910 the Directors also authorized the A&M College Club to build its "Shirley Annex" adjacent to the hotel, which stood west of the present site of Sbisa Hall.[49] On August 8 the Board directed Frederick E. Giesecke, the College architect, to prepare plans for two new dormitories, each containing 100 rooms. Bids were taken on the two dormitories (Milner and Leggett Halls) and construction began within a month.[50] In 1911 yet another dormitory, named Harvey Mitchell Hall, in honor of Mitchell's role in locating the College, was authorized.[51] An engineering building was completed in

[48]*Ibid.; ibid.*, April 1, 1910, II, 201; June 13-15, 1910, II, 207; October 15-16, 1912, III, 32, 45.

[49]*Ibid.,* June 13-15, 1910, 208-211.

[50]*Ibid.,* August 8, 1910, II, 214; August 22, 1910, II, 215; September 5, 1910, II, 217.

[51]*Ibid.,* November 11, 1911, II, 289.

1919, and the Agricultural Experiment Station building in 1910,[52] but two dis-astrous fires prevented the College from ever achieving any real relief from the pressure on its facilities.

On Saturday morning, November 11, 1911, a fire destroyed the Mess Hall. Only the cold-storage plant, the storeroom, and the dining-room furniture were saved. That day was the only occasion of his long career as supervisor of the mess when Bernard Sbisa served a late breakfast — but he did serve breakfast. That same day a temporary tin-roofed dining hall and kitchen were erected and meals continued without interruption. The Directors met in Houston on November 13-14 and resolved to begin on the site of the old mess hall immediate construction of a new mess hall capable of accommodating 2,500 students. They asked Governor Colquitt for a deficiency appropriation of $100,000. Construction on the new mess hall (Sbisa Hall) began in May 1912.[53]

Disaster struck again on May 27, 1912, when Old Main, with most of the records of the College, was totally destroyed by fire. Frederick Giesecke, who served as architect for the mess hall, was commissioned by the Directors to be architect for a fireproof main building to be built for $200,000. On August 6, 1912, a contract for construction of the building, the Academic Building, was awarded to Texas Building Company of Fort Worth for $190,845 with the copper dome to be constructed at cost plus ten percent, but not to exceed $2,500.[54]

Giesecke was one of the busiest men on campus during the Milner years. In addition to designing and supervising the construction of three dormitories, Milner, Leggett, and Mitchell Halls, and the design and construction supervision of Sbisa and the Academic Building, Giesecke designed the projected Alumni Memorial YMCA (Young Men's Christian Association) building, completed in 1913. Edward B. Cushing played a major role in managing the Alumni campaign for funds to build the YMCA facility. Construction on it began in June 1912, at which time the Board of Directors gave the ground to be "set apart and dedicated for all time for the location of a building to be used for purposes of a Young Men's Christian Association."[55] Giesecke also supervised construction of a Mechanical Engineering Laboratory and designed a new, and for that time very advanced, central heating plant and plan for the campus.[56] He was likely a very overworked and underpaid

[52]*Ibid.*, September 24, 1909, II, 179; February 15, 1910, II, 196.
[53]*Ibid.*, November 13-14, 1911, II, 283-286; March 8, 1912, III, 4; May 20, 1912, III, 13.
[54]*Ibid.*, June 11-12, 1912, III, 14-15; August 6, 1912, III, 31.
[55]*Ibid.*, September 5, 1910, II, 218, 220; March 8, 1912, III, 9; June 11-12, 1912, III, 16.
[56]*Ibid.*, March 8, 1912, III, 9; June 11-12, 1912, III, 16.

man. Giesecke resigned on September 1, 1912, to accept a teaching position at The University of Texas, leaving town, according to his daughter, in the first faculty-owned automobile on campus, a Pratt.[57] He returned to the A&M faculty in 1927.

Obviously, not only Giesecke, but Milner and the entire faculty and staff were thoroughly inundated with work and activity during these years of rapid growth and development. Administration changes, a fresh round of negotiations with the Regents of The University of Texas, and finally a new "student strike" reminiscent of the "great trouble" of 1908, compounded the confusion and the work. Yet, to the credit of Colonel Robert Teague Milner, none of these factors acted adversely upon the growth of the College.

Negotiations continued with The University of Texas over the allocation of University funds. In June 1909 the A&M Directors called for a joint meeting with the Regents to discuss the welfare of the respective institutions, and "if possible to reach an amicable agreement as to the disposition of the revenue arising from the permanent endowment of The University."[58]

A joint meeting of the two executive boards produced a general agreement that the institutions should be formally separated, administratively and financially.[59] In 1910 the Democratic State Convention, which nominated Oscar Branch Colquitt for governor, recommended separation of Texas A&M from The University of Texas. In his message to the Thirty-second Legislature, Governor Colquitt recommended approval of a constitutional amendment separating the two institutions.[60] With the impetus provided by Colquitt, the Regents and Directors worked together to offer an acceptable plan of separation. The A&M Directors agreed that A&M should seek one-half of the Permanent Endowment Fund, and also recommended that both institutions seek a constitutional amendment allowing the Legislature to levy taxes for the support of each institution.[61]

Clarence Ousley presided at the joint meeting of the Regents and the Directors on January 27, 1911, in Austin. Persons present included Regents Alex Sanger, Fred W. Cook, George W. Littlefield, and William L. Stark, and President Sidney Edward Mezes, representing The University; and President Milner, and Directors W. A. Trenckmann, Charles Davis, Laurence J.

[57]*Ibid.*, August 6, 1912, III, 33; interview with Mrs. L. Giesecke Geren, College Station, Texas, May 14, 1971.

[58]*Ibid.*, June 7-9, 1909, II, 161.

[59]*Ibid.*, November 25, 1909, II, 192.

[60]*Ibid.*, January 27, 1911, II, 236; H. Y. Benedict (ed.), *A Source Book Relating to the History of the University of Texas*, 462-463.

[61]Minutes of the Board of Directors, January 27, 1911, II, 236-237.

Hart, John I. Guion, Walton Peteet, and Dr. J. Allen Kyle, and Commissioner of Agriculture Edward R. Kone, representing Texas A&M, with their attorney, Hatton W. Sumners, and Board Secretary James Hay Quarles. Lengthy discussions during the morning session in rooms at the Driskill Hotel produced a consensus, on the basis of which Attorney Sumners prepared a draft of a constitutional amendment presented at the 2:00 P.M. session for approval by the Boards.[62]

The proposed amendment to Section 10, Article 7 reads as follows:

The Agricultural and Mechanical College of Texas located in the county of Brazos, is hereby separated from The University of Texas, and is constituted an independent College, whose leading object shall be, without excluding other scientific and classical studies, and including military tactics, to teach such branches of learning as are related to agriculture and the mechanic arts, in such manner as the legislature may prescribe, in order to promote the liberal and practical education of the industrial classes in the several pursuits and professions of life.[63]

Article 7 would be amended by addition of Section 16:

One half of the million acres of land heretofore set apart and appropriated by section 15 of article 7 of the Constitution, for the endowment, maintenance and support of The University of Texas, and its branches, and one half of other lands so appropriated, or appropriated for the endowment and support of said University is hereby set apart and appropriated for the endowment, maintenance and support of The University of Texas, and the remaining one half of said land is hereby set apart and appropriated for the endowment, maintenance and support of the Agricultural and Mechanical College of Texas and the legislature shall provide for the equal and equitable division of said land as between The University of Texas and the Agricultural and Mechanical College of Texas.[64]

The representatives of the two institutions accepted the proposed amendments, and each board appointed four members of a special legislative committee to press for approval of the amendments, and to work for a statutory act providing a special taxation for each institution. Members of this special committee included Trenckmann, Kone, Davis, and Milner for A&M, and Ousley, Littlefield, Cook, and Mezes for The University.[65] The constitutional amendments and the special tax bill both failed to pass the House, although the Senate did approve a resolution calling for the proposed consti-

[62]*Ibid.*, 240-245.
[63]*Ibid.*, 240-241.
[64]*Ibid.*, 241.
[65]*Ibid.*, 241-246.

tutional amendments.[66] As a result, the A&M-University of Texas problem remained in 1911 as unresolved as ever.

The convening of the legislative session of 1913 again found A&M College and University officials working together. On December 12, 1912, A&M Directors invited University officials to meet with them during the Christmas holidays. At the same time the A&M Directors enlisted the aid of the Farmers' Congress to lobby for legislative appropriations for the College, exemplifying again the proposition that agricultural extension work was "paying off" for the College.[67] On January 6, 1913, University and College Board members met in the parlor of the Westbrook Hotel in Fort Worth. Prior to the joint session A&M Directors adopted a set of guidelines to be presented to the Regents. Those guidelines reflect A&M policy on the question of separating the institutions and dividing the endowment fund:

1) There should be no antagonism between The University of Texas and the Agricultural and Mechanical College of Texas.

2) It is highly desirable that the governing boards reach an agreement upon questions affecting the two institutions.

3) The Agricultural and Mechanical College should be separated from The University and constituted an independent college.

4) The College has an equity in the permanent University fund.

5) By statute, or by constitutional amendment, provision should be made for an ad valorem tax for the benefit of the higher institutions.

6) The shares of The University and the College in the proceeds of such tax should be in the ratio of 40 to 30.

7) The question of enrollment should not be considered in connection with the division of such proceeds.

8) If the Prairie View State Normal and Industrial College is to share in such proceeds, its share should appear as a separate item.

9) Prairie View State Normal and Industrial College should remain under the management of A&M.

10) If no agreement can be reached with the authorities of The University, A&M should present its case independently.

11) Texas A&M should receive 40 percent of the permanent University Fund.[68]

Perhaps the most significant aspect of these policies is that A&M had retreated somewhat from its demand of 1911 for 50 percent of the Endowment Fund.

[66]*Texas House Journal, 1911*, pp. 1622-1638; *Texas Senate Journal, 1911*, p. 1522; Benedict (ed.), *A Source Book of the University of Texas*, 464-466. Unless otherwise denoted Legislative *Journals* are always for the regular session.

[67]Minutes of the Board of Directors, December 12, 1912, III, 48-49.

[68]*Ibid.*, January 6, 1913, III, 51-52.

The "A&M plan" is in sharp contrast to the "One University plan" advocated by many University supporters. Edgar P. Haney, one of the chief authors of House Joint Resolutions No. 28 and No. 39, each calling for consolidation of the A&M College with The University, in cooperation with other "unification legislators," published a brochure summarizing the features of the "one University" bill, and offering testimonials in its favor:[69]

> Briefly stated, the bill provides for the consolidation of the College with The University and its removal, as soon as practicable to Austin. The members of the College Faculty are made members of the Faculty of The University; the students are to be regarded as students of The University; and are to be credited with all work completed at the College; and the alumni of the College are to be given all the rights and privileges of alumni of The University.
>
> The bill further provides that A&M College property shall be converted into a State hospital for the insane. When the buildings have been rearranged to fit them for hospital purpose, they will furnish accommodations for twelve or fifteen hundred patients and will relieve the pressure on the other asylums and on the county jails for years to come.[70]

Consolidation supporters pointed to duplication of efforts by the College and The University — the rival engineering schools, and the duplication of libraries, laboratories, and teaching staff. The purported object of the bill was to "provide a thoroughly efficient, up-to-date and well-managed agricultural college for Texas."[71] The brochure outlined the history of troubles at the College and cited testimonials from a wide variety of persons such as Peter Radford, president of the Farmers' Union; Governor Oran M. Roberts; Dr. Samuel P. Brooks, president of Baylor University; Marion Sansom, former president of the A&M Board of Directors; Frederick S. Johnston, former professor of agriculture at A&M; William Clifford Hogg, of Houston, and others.[72] Supporting newspaper opinion was cited from the Dallas *News,* San Antonio *Express,* Houston *Chronicle,* Austin *Daily Statesman,* and from *Farm and Ranch.*[73] Perhaps the most damning testimony was that of David Franklin Houston, recently appointed Secretary of Agriculture by Woodrow Wilson, and former president of both The University of Texas and the A&M College.

[69]*Texas House Journal, 1913,* pp. 496, 586, 1241, 1622, 1701-1705, 1769-1770; *Statement by Members of House of Representatives Concerning a Bill to Consolidate the Agricultural and Mechanical College and the State University,* 1-25 (hereinafter cited *Statement Concerning Bill to Consolidate).*

[70]*Statement Concerning Bill to Consolidate,* 3-4.

[71]*Ibid.,* 2.

[72]*Ibid.,* 2, 11-20.

[73]*Ibid.,* 20-23.

Houston's letter of March 12, 1913, addressed to Edgar Haney, is worth quoting in full:

> Nothing less than your official request could induce me to express opinion on A. and M. and The University. The present location of A. and M. is exceedingly unfortunate, agriculturally and educationally. An institution needs the support of a highly developed community. The Faculty and students both suffer. Otherwise, it is difficult to prevent stagnation resulting from isolation. I found the best men restive and discontented under conditions at College Station. I could get and keep stronger men in Austin economically. The transfer of the College to Austin would be highly desirable. Consolidation would result in great strength for both institutions, and the A. and M. College interests would be chief gainers. The problems of administration and discipline would be immensely simplified. The College Station plant could be used for indefinite time for the Prairie View Normal or other institutions. On my judgment, the friends of the A. and M. should be the strongest advocates of the proposal.
>
> D. F. Houston[74]

For even the most ardent separatist Houston's evaluation provided a sobering moment of reflection. In a word, the consolidation movement in 1913 is not to be lightly dismissed.

Governor Colquitt provided some incentive to consolidation, despite his official position in support of separation of the two institutions. Colquitt's special message of February 5, 1913, to the Legislature characterized his "Ideal University" as being a campus of "ample acreage" on which he would erect "buildings more magnificent and commodious" than we now have, and "I would call these buildings the 'Agricultural and Mechanical College'." On the same campus he would erect the "State Normal Colleges," the "College of Arts and Industry," the "Law College," and the "Medical College." "In the center of the campus I would build a magnificent main building of Texas granite large enough to afford accommodations not only for the present, but for future generations, and I would call the whole the 'University of Texas'."[75] A view of the modern University of Texas campus in Austin would lend credit to the belief that Governor Colquitt may have had at least part of his dream come true.

Colquitt's message also presented a comparative statement on enrollment and per capita cost:

[74]Benedict (ed.), *A Source Book of the University of Texas*, 479; *Texas House Journal, 1913*, pp. 431-436.

[75]*Texas House Journal, 1913*, pp. 431-436.

The enrollment of The University for the past three years and per capita cost was as follows:

	1910	1911	1912
Enrollment*	1,939	2,038	2,332
Per capita cost*	$248.86	$214.35	$300.56

*Includes Medical School at Galveston.

The enrollment at the Agricultural and Mechanical College for the same three years and per capita cost is as follows:

	1910	1911	1912
Enrollment	1,080	1,129	1,001
Per capita cost	$410.75	$620.84	$704.10[76]

The figures cited by the Governor suggested exorbitant costs of operating the A&M College as compared to similar costs for The University. Several qualifying factors, however, should be considered in conjunction with the above statistics: (1) the per capita costs of 1911 and 1912 were swollen by the emergency appropriations caused by the loss of the Mess Hall and Main Building by fire; (2) while it does not justify waste, part of the cost of operating the A&M College was borne by the federal government, while almost the entire cost of operating The University was borne by the state; and (3) the cost of operating a scientific and technical program *is* greater per capita than the operation of liberal-arts programs.

Colquitt, however, did not ask the Legislature for consolidation, but for separation. In his message of February 5 he submitted his own proposed amendment to the Constitution, which would create the Agricultural and Mechanical College as an independent college under its own Board of Regents, and which would transfer to the A&M College 400,000 acres of The University endowment, as a separate endowment for the College.[77] This plan was similar to the one agreed to by the Regents of The University of Texas, and by the Directors of the Agricultural and Mechanical College in their meetings on January 6, 1913, in Fort Worth.[78]

Numerous amendments to the legislation creating a "more efficient system of public instruction" were proposed in the Legislature in 1913. One would give A&M independence and 600,000 acres of land, and would levy a property tax to be shared in by all Texas colleges.[79] Memorials flooded the House and the Senate in support of and in opposition to consolidation of The University and the A&M College. Notably, memorials from A&M support-

[76]Benedict (ed.), *A Source Book of the University of Texas*, 482-483; *Texas House Journal, 1913*, pp. 431-436.

[77]Benedict (ed.), *A Source Book of the University of Texas*, 485-487; *Texas House Journal, 1913*, pp. 438-440.

[78]Minutes of the Board of Directors, January 6, 1913, III, 51-58.

[79]*Texas House Journal, 1913*, pp. 1701-1703.

ers were overwhelmingly, if not entirely, in favor of separation. The Corps of Cadets presented a petition, as did the Farmers' Congress, and various alumni groups.[80] It appeared that the "Battle of the Universities" was about to be resumed. But the battle, if it was that, ended in another stalemate and another postponement of any decision affecting the relationship of the College and The University.[81] By the opening of the next legislative session the whole scene would be replayed.

An event which added greater intensity to the legislative fight in 1913, and which added incentive to the consolidation movement as well, was the outbreak of fresh "trouble" at Texas A&M. The student strike of 1908 was still fresh in the minds of most Texans, when in December 1912 and January 1913 a series of events created a new crisis and unfavorable public reactions to affairs of the College — just at the moment when the critical legislative session of 1913 was opening. The crisis was related to hazing.

The problem of hazing in the state colleges first became public on March 3, 1911, when a University of Texas student being "hazed" by upperclassmen shot and killed another University student. A resolution deploring hazing passed the Legislature on the same day.[82] The fires at the A&M College in 1911 and 1912 were publicly attributed to "incendiary origins" by Governor Colquitt, which, while having nothing to do with hazing, suggested a lack of student discipline.[83] In April 1912, during the annual Corps march to the Brazos River, a "subfreshman," Norman Samuel Hunter, drowned while attempting to swim the Brazos. Again, there was no hazing, but the event did attract unfavorable attention.[84]

Professor Ernest Langford vividly recalls the San Jacinto Day outing at "Camp Moses" in April 1912. He recollects that upon reaching the river the cadets *en masse* shucked their clothing and rushed in for a swim. In the melee Hunter's disappearance went unnoticed for several hours. Search began, then dragging the river, and finally dynamite was used but to no avail. Hunter's best friend, Sam Perrin, vowed to stay on the river until the boy was found. Perrin stayed on, and spent seven days walking the banks of the Brazos until he found Hunter's body over five miles from the swimming hole. Memorial services presided over by President Milner were held on campus for the cadet. The cadets contributed ten cents each to buy a watch with which to honor Perrin for his loyalty and friendship to his lost comrade.[85]

[80]*Ibid.*, 1682-1683; Benedict (ed.) *A Source Book of the University of Texas*, 488.
[81]*Texas House Journal, 1913*, pp. 1704-1705, 1770.
[82]Benedict (ed.), *A Source Book of the University of Texas*, 466-468.
[83]*Texas House Journal, 1913*, p. 21.
[84]Texas A&M, *Biennial Report, 1911-1912*, p. 21.
[85]Interview with Ernest Langford, College Station, Texas, June 3, 1971.

While there was a tremendous sense of loyalty and comradeship among the cadets, there was also hazing. Extracts from the Faculty Minutes reporting disciplinary cases between 1910 and January 1913 reflect hazing and a not good general student morale, and indicate that things were boiling to a head in December 1912 and January 1913:[86]

October 20, 1910.	Hazing by placing burning sulphur near a sleeping cadet resulting in seriously burning the latter. One [involved]. Cadet dismissed.
November 29, 1910.	Going to Bryan without permit. Confined to campus until February 1.
December 6, 1910.	Desertion. Dropped from rolls and not allowed to return without permission from the Faculty.
January 31, 1911.	Improper language to sentinel on duty. Placed on probation.
February 3, 1911.	Violating probation and drunkenness. Required to withdraw from College. Improper conduct in Bryan. Three cadets. Confined to campus.
February 24, 1911.	Hazing. Five cadets. Two suspended. One expelled and two reduced to private and confined to campus.
March 28, 1911.	Forging a telegram to deceive Commandant. One cadet. Dismissed. Going to Bryan at night without permit. One cadet. Suspended.
April 13, 1911.	Going to Bryan at night without permit. Placed on probation and confined to campus.
May 16, 1911.	Hitting sentinel in head with a stone. Dismissed.
March 5, 1912.	Interfering with electric light system. Confined to campus and put on probation till June 8.
May 7, 1912.	Drinking. Twenty-six cadets. Two reduced to ranks. One confined to campus. Twenty-three given 15 demerits each.
October 24, 1912.	Hazing. Five. Probation.
October 31, 1912.	Hazing. One. Probation.
November 4, 1912.	Hazing. One. Probation.

[86]"Memorandum of Faculty Minutes," vol. 4, in Milner Administration Papers, Texas A&M University Archives, and reprinted in *Proceedings of a Hearing by the Board of Directors of*

January 15, 1913.   Faculty Committee to report on hazing.
January 28, 1913.   Twenty-two cadets. Dismissed.
January 31, 1913.   Hazing. Five cadets. Dismissed.

The above catalogue of events indicates that the problems of hazing appeared to be coming to a head. Ernest Langford, a senior at the time, confirms that a rash of hazing "broke out" about this time.[87] A complaint to College officials about hazing came from Governor Colquitt on October 9, 1912, addressed to Director Walton Peteet. Colquitt warned Peteet of complaints coming to him from irate parents and cited as an example from parents:

We do not object to the boys having small pranks played on them, but when it comes to the boys being stripped of their clothing and thrown down across a bed and whipped on their bare rump and thighs with a leather strap, we think it is time to call a halt.[88]

Student opposition was manifested in December 1912, when a student, Preston Taylor, left the College on account of hazing.[89] Hazing, and faculty efforts to control it and to maintain discipline, touched off the second great student strike on February 1, 1913. The cause of the strike goes back to some rather nebulous events, including hazing and pranks on the campus between December 1 and December 15, 1912. The faculty investigated the problem, and upon resumption of classes after the Christmas holidays, issued stern warnings to the cadets to refrain from some of their more offensive activities. In addition, as the holiday season neared, conflicts between freshman and sophomore cadets had kindled to a hot pitch, and involved the refusal of the "fish" to provide the sophomores with a Christmas tree, and their refusal to clean a "1916" painted on a water standpipe. The hostilities continued when classes resumed in January 1913. The faculty was determined to maintain control. New incidents of hazing, apparently involving strapping, caused the faculty to dismiss twenty-two cadets January 28 and five more January 31.[90]

Members of the freshman and sophomore classes responded on January 31 by presenting a signed petition to the faculty protesting the dismissals, and asking reinstatement of the students.[91] On February 1, 1913, a second petition was presented by members of the junior, sophomore, and freshman classes.

the *A&M College of Texas, Held at Fort Worth, Texas, February 24, and 25, 1913,* pp. 40-43 (hereinafter cited *Hearing by the Board, February 24 and 25, 1913*).

[87]Interview with Ernest Langford, College Station, Texas, June 3, 1971.

[88]*Hearing by the Board, February 24 and 25, 1913,* p. 26.

[89]Minutes of the Board of Directors, December 12, 1912, III, 149.

[90]*Hearing by the Board, February 24 and 25, 1913,* pp. 33-34, 39-43.

[91]"Petition asking Reinstatement, January 31, 1913," Milner Administration Papers, Texas A&M University Archives.

This second petition was considerably more belligerent than the first and concluded with "we make the following demands unconditionally."[92]

1) That all twenty-seven men mentioned in General Order No. 77 be reinstated in good standing and given their daily average as their term grade.

2) That every man whose grade was reduced, due to absence from the College on account of the meningitis situation [a scare, but no cases were reported], have his grade raised to the former standard.

3) That no action be taken in the case of the painting of the 1916 on the stand pipe.

We herewith declare that if these demands are not acceded to, none of the undersigned men will attend any academic duties and from now until such time as our demands are acceded to.

We demand that action be taken on this proclamation and that the result of said action be communicated to us by retreat today, February 1, 1913.

The Junior Class

The Sophomore Class

The Freshman Class

Four hundred and sixty-six students signed the petition. Notably, no seniors, unlike the case in 1908, participated. Perhaps their recollections of the earlier episode were more firsthand, and more vivid. The faculty made a formal reply to the petition, but failed to retract their position. That night the petitioners voted a strike, beginning February 2. At 7:30 A.M., February 2, the entire A&M faculty convened and voted to dismiss from the College the 466 boys who signed the petition of February 1.[93] The same day the action hit the newspapers, the Legislature, and irate parents. The House, on February 5, endorsed President Milner's action in dismissing the students.[94] Some parents protested the dismissal; the Senate promised an investigation; and newspapers throughout the state began to dig into the "sad" affairs at the College, past and present, harking back even to the days of Edmund J. Davis' administration.[95] The Directors convened in special session and lengthy hearings were held at College Station and at Fort Worth. Correspondence *for* and *against* dismissal filled the mail of many public officials, a goodly part of which now fills a niche in the Texas A&M University Archives.[96] The gover-

[92]"Petition by Juniors, Freshmen and Sophomores, February 1, 1913," Milner Administration Papers, Texas A&M University Archives.

[93]*Hearing by the Board, February 24 and 25, 1913*, pp. 34-35.

[94]*Texas House Journal, 1913*, p. 343.

[95]See as an example, Houston *Daily Post*, February 4, 1913, Dallas *Morning News*, February 20, 1913, and a scrapbook of controversial newspaper clippings regarding the "1913 strike," in Milner Administration Papers, Texas A&M University Archives.

[96]See *Hearings of the Board, February 24 and 25, 1913*, pp, 1-45; Minutes of the Board of

nor, the lieutenant governor, and most members of the Texas Legislature became directly or indirectly involved in the affair.[97] The Legislature passed a strong bill prohibiting the "pernicious practice of hazing," the offense being a misdemeanor punishable by fine ($25 to $250) and/or imprisonment (ten days to three months).[98] The publicity also influenced many Texans to consider the pending "consolidation" bill in a new light.

The "strike" ended when the A&M administration extended amnesty to the students, who in very short order realized that they had gone too far. The faculty, the Board of Directors, and public officials had almost overwhelmingly supported the ousting of the dissident students. Each returning student was required to sign an "iron-clad oath" pledge, by which he promised to abide by the rules at all times and to abstain from all hazing. All 466 dismissed students took the pledge. Two of them were summarily dismissed when they "hazed" after taking the pledge.[99] Relative to hazing and its effect on public relations, the whole situation had been a rather nasty affair for the A&M College, but it was perhaps on the whole timely, because the strike contributed to the public alarm which helped bring the whole business of hazing throughout the state, as well as at A&M, under control.

The story was hardly off the front pages of the newspapers when the "consolidation versus separation" argument was renewed. Fueled by the conflict over hazing, the editorials and accusations again flew hot and heavy. A&M's image in much of the state press suffered severely, but it also had its champions.[100] The Dallas *Morning News,* for example, strongly favored consolidation and the removal of the A&M College to Austin while the Dallas *Times Herald* favored separation and independence for A&M.[101] Texas A&M supporters mustered all of their forces for the legislative battle. The fight ended in yet another stalemate when the Legislature failed to approve a constitutional amendment calling for either separation or consolidation, but there was one by-product. The Legislature did approve a proposed constitutional amendment authorizing The University of Texas to issue bonds for

Directors, February 10, 1913, III, 62-63, February 24, 25, 1913, pp. 64-86; "Correspondence and Telegrams, 1913 Strike," Milner Administration Papers, Texas A&M University Archives.

  [97] See Minutes of the Board of Directors, February 10, 1913, III, 62-63, February 24, 25, 1913, pp. 64-86.

  [98] Benedict (ed.), *A Source Book of the University of Texas,* 489-491; *Texas Senate Journal, 1913,* pp. 239-241.

  [99] Minutes of the Board of Directors, June 9, 10, 1913, III, 87-88.

  [100] See "Scrapbook, 1913 Strike," Milner Administration Papers, Texas A&M University Archives.

  [101] Dallas *Morning News,* March 16, 1913; March 23, 1913; Dallas *Times Herald,* July 16, 1913.

buildings construction, serviced by the revenues from the Endowment Fund.[102] Again the state press divided over the amendment, which was considered to be anti-A&M. The A&M Alumni Association mailed circular letters in opposition to the amendment to be voted on by the people of Texas on July 19, 1913. The amendment was defeated at the polls.[103]

The years since 1908, for President Robert Teague Milner and for the A&M College, had been busy, if not chaotic and hectic. Two major fires, student strikes, hazing, administrative changes, politics, controversy with The University of Texas, expansion of agricultural and engineering programs, public relations, public controversy — all would sap the energy of any mortal. Robert Teague Milner was a tough and steady man, who throughout all storms and controversy had his hand firmly on the tiller, but even Milner had had enough. In the last year of his tenure Milner became involved in a running battle with Governor Oscar Branch Colquitt, whom Milner accused of intervening in the internal affairs of the College. On June 9, 1913, President Milner submitted his resignation to the Board of Directors, to be effective October 1, 1913, but he packed his bags and left in August. The Directors belatedly granted him a leave of absence and turned affairs over temporarily to Charles Puryear.[104]

[102]"Scrapbook, 1913 Strike," Milner Administration Papers, Texas A&M University Archives.

[103]Dallas *Times Herald,* July 16, 1913; "Scrapbook, 1913 Strike," Milner Administration Papers, Texas A&M University Archives; Benedict (ed.), *A Source Book of the University of Texas,* 493-495.

[104]Minutes of the Board of Directors, June 9, 10, 1913, III, 90-91; August 18, 1913, III, 100; Interview with Ernest Langford, June 3, 1971, College Station, Texas; "Milner vs. Colquitt Correspondence," Robert Teague Milner Papers, Texas A&M University Archives.

CHAPTER 12

The Engineers

DESPITE the historic preference of Texas A&M students for engineering studies, the engineering curricula, like the agricultural curricula, were forced to struggle, if less constantly, for a place in the sun. The engineers before 1915 had no direct federal assistance comparable to that provided the agricultural programs by the Hatch Act, Morrill Act, Nelson Act, Smith-Lever, or Smith-Hughes Act, although the endowments established by such legislation helped perpetuate the whole program of the affected colleges and universities, including the engineering studies. The engineering curricula at Texas A&M struggled under imposed poverty, and at times from misdirection. Engineers, however, consistently had one great advantage over their "farmer" colleagues. Engineering as a vocation seemed to be more in harmony with the "spirit of the times"; it characterized the age of the industrial and scientific revolution blossoming in America during the last century. Most important, from the time of the very beginning of Texas A&M far more cash-paying jobs were available for engineers than for farmers.

James C. Nagle, chairman of the Department of Civil Engineering at Texas A&M, indicated in 1906 that, despite the greater job opportunities which A&M graduates in engineering enjoyed over the agricultural students during the first quarter-century of the school's existence, the real demand for trained engineers in America was only just beginning. "Our graduates," he said, "find ready employment in lucrative engineering positions." He said further: "Ten years ago scarcely fifty per cent of our graduates could find good engineering openings, but now it would not be difficult to place two or three times the number which we annually graduate from the course in civil engineering at the college."[1]

By 1906 not only were more jobs open for engineers, but Texas A&M graduates were being given greater recognition in the job markets. Charles W. Crawford, professor of mechanical engineering at A&M from 1919 to

---

[1]Texas A&M, *Biennial Report, 1905-1906*, p. 61.

1965 and a graduate of the class of 1919, recalls that with few exceptions during these years the demand for A&M engineers was tremendous. The exceptions included the depression years 1930-1934. Of the thirty mechanical engineers who graduated in 1932, Crawford recalls, only one had a job by commencement. After World War II, he recalls, the demand for engineers became so great that few graduates ever bothered or could afford to forego the attractive salaries in industry in order to pursue graduate instruction. As a result, while agricultural people, who had fewer job opportunities in the post-war era, were returning to colleges under the GI Bill and securing Ph.D. degrees, engineering graduate instruction and some phases of engineering research declined. Beginning about 1960, he says, the situation again began to change and graduate studies became increasingly important to engineers as the competition for jobs became increasingly keen.[2]

Crawford, born in Benchly, Texas, lived in Bryan as a youth, and entered Texas A&M in 1915. The cadets, he said, took great pride in being a military outfit. The uniform was still the traditional gray with black stripes on the trousers and black braid on the blouse front, and on the blouse cuffs. Cadets wore a black bow tie with a blue chambray shirt, when not wearing the blouse. Cadets saluted all cadet officers, who were identified most prominently by the black-and-gold cord on their academy-style cadet hats. Freshmen wore a blue hat cord, sophomores the yellow, and juniors the red, while most seniors held officer rank. On a few occasions, Crawford recalls, hazing did get out of line, although seniors made strong efforts to control things. A report on hazing from a cadet officer was sufficient to have a cadet dismissed from the College, so that their authority had a genuine significance. He remembers that while he was a fish he was "aired out" on a few occasions, that is, turned out of the dormitory in the middle of the night. There were also midnight track meets, "ramming," or the act of giving out demerits by class officers, some paddling, but over all a great amount of *esprit de corps*. A graduate in mechanical engineering, Crawford got his first job with Southern Motors, an automobile manufacturer in Houston, Texas, which for about one year produced the Ranger automobile and farm tractors before going under.[3]

The development of engineering studies at Texas A&M, and indeed throughout the United States, was more a reflection of the needs of the hour than a product of any comprehensive planning. Engineering education, like agricultural education, is of comparatively recent vintage, having been around

[2]Interview with Charles William Crawford, professor emeritus of the Mechanical Engineering Department, College Station, Texas, March 30, 1971.
[3]*Ibid.*

in a formal state for little more than a hundred years. Mortimer E. Cooley, dean of Engineering at the University of Michigan, traced the development of engineering education in the United States over a half-century for an audience at the Texas A&M Semi-Centennial Celebrations in 1926. Cooley suggested that the works of the ancient world "are the best evidence that engineering was then, as today, the material means to the state we designate as civilized:"[4]

Examples of that evidence were the Seven Wonders of the world, the achievements of the Romans, the Greeks, the Egyptians, the Assyrians, the Babylonians, and on back through dim and dark ages to the very beginning when God created the heavens and the earth as told in the Book of Genesis. And who shall deny it when philologists tell us that the G-E-N of Genesis and the G-I-N of engineers are from one and the same root, meaning to create.[5]

Formal training in engineering in the United States began in the early nineteenth century. Cooley suggests that the Rensselaer Polytechnic Institute at Troy, New York, founded in 1824, might be considered the alma mater of civil engineering. The first state school to offer courses in civil engineering was the University of Michigan, which in 1853 offered an engineering course taught by a professor of physics. Civil engineering derived as a separate field of study out of military engineering, which survived from the ancient world, through the Middle Ages, as a distinct and honorable profession. The "civil" simply designated all engineering vocations distinct from the military, and thus civil engineering became the parent of the modern engineering curricula. Mechanical engineering followed civil engineering as a separate branch, being introduced in the period around 1870. After that, and usually in direct response to new developments, new branches of engineering education appeared in rapid order. Because of the foundation work done in physics, rapid advances in electricity and magnetism occurred in the late seventies and early eighties, and formal training in electrical engineering followed.[6]

Chemical engineering appeared in the nineties; agricultural engineering, textile engineering, highway engineering, industrial engineering, marine engineering, petroleum engineering, and aeronautical engineering usually appeared in the first two decades of the twentieth century.[7] Indicative of the

[4]Mortimer E. Cooley, "The Development of Engineering Education during the Last Fifty Years," *1876 . . . 1926, The Semi-Centennial Celebration of the Agricultural and Mechanical College of Texas*, 81-98.

[5]*Ibid.*, 81.

[6]*Ibid.*, 84-86.

[7]*Ibid.*, 85-86.

continuing responsiveness of the engineering curricula to contemporary needs is the advent of such fields as aerospace engineering, as opposed to aeronautical engineering, and nuclear engineering. Within each curriculum one can further specialize — thus the mechanical engineer can work in steam power, internal combustion, hydromechanics, heating and ventilating, refrigeration, automobile and industrial specialties. The engineer has generally moved from the very broad spectrum of an essentially classical education to the limited span of extreme specialization.[8]

Cooley's outline of the development of engineering studies in the United States is strongly validated and paralleled by the development of the engineering curricula at Texas A&M. In the beginning, during the Gathright years, no formal instruction was given at Texas A&M in engineering as such. The would-be engineer received an essentially classic education, but here he was in a much more advantageous position than was the erstwhile student of agriculture. Formal agricultural training had very little if any identification with classical studies. Only a few savants of the Roman world, such as Marcus Porcius Cato *(De agricultura),* ever "studied" agriculture, and the Greeks gave farming even less time and consideration. But many of the Greek and ancient philosophers were proficient mathematicians and physicists, for example Pythagoras (c. 582-500 B.C., geometry), Heraclitus (c. 540-475 B.C., change and flux in the universe), Democritus (460-370 B.C., the original atomic theorist), Euclid (c. 300 B.C., geometry), and Archimedes (c. 287-212 B.C., mathematics and inventions).

The Texas A&M Department of Applied Mathematics under the direction of Robert Page Morris between 1876 and 1879 provided, for all practical purposes, a course in general engineering. The junior class, for example, received instruction in surveying, descriptive geometry, mechanics, and drawing. The senior class studied shades, shadows, and perspective; descriptive astronomy; railroad surveying; strength of materials; arches; framing; freehand drawing; mapping; sketches of tools; and designs for the component parts of machines, bridges, and other structures.[9] The Department of Pure Mathematics under Alexander Hogg offered courses in arithmetic, algebra, trigonometry, geometry, and calculus.[10] All of these studies are fundamental to any engineering curriculum. Thus Texas A&M engineers, even during the classical period, could obtain a very strong engineering foundation.[11] Unlike

[8]*Ibid.,* 88.

[9]Texas A&M, *Catalogue, 1876-1877,* pp. 15-16.

[10]*Ibid.,* 16-17.

[11]This is confirmed in an interview with Charles W. Crawford, College Station, Texas, March 30, 1971.

the agriculturists, the engineers readily found a home in classical studies. The award of the degree of civil engineering to the first two Texas A&M graduates, Louis John Kopke and William Harrison Brown, in June 1880, would have been fully justified on the merits of the curriculum.[12]

Engineering, as well as agricultural, studies at Texas A&M, however, suffered during the agrarian reaction of the 1880-1883 period. The great emphasis on practical training by the agrarians also tended to force the engineers away from the drawing boards and the theoretical studies into the workshops. Under the direction of Franklin Van Winkle the emphasis in so-called engineering studies came to be placed upon woodworking and blacksmithing.[13] While this helped to produce competent machinists, cabinetmakers, and artisans, it did not build creative and knowledgeable engineers. Nonetheless, the basic core of engineering studies, including trigonometry, geometry, calculus, drawing, and surveying, remained a part of the curricula.

Franklin Van Winkle was the first to come to Texas A&M as professor of engineering. His full title was professor of engineering, mechanics, and drawing, and superintendent of the machine shops.[14] Van Winkle's inclinations and efforts lay heavily in the practical application of vocational skills. His class of 1880-1881, for example, did millwright work and set up the machine shop. The class of 1881-1882 built a front gate for the College with handworked iron lettering. The class of 1882-1883 reconstructed the bathhouses and built bathing facilities, and ran a telephone line into Bryan from the campus.[15] Not only did the emphasis upon craftsmanship tend to retard the development of a real engineering curriculum, but the imposition of a three-year program for the entire College, during the era 1880-1886, made it impossible to broaden engineering studies.[16]

During these years the College awarded no engineering degrees, or degrees of any sort, until in 1883 a fourth year of "graduate" study was added which would lead to a Bachelor of Science degree, or a degree in either civil engineering or mechanical engineering. The fourth-year study program leading to the civil-engineering degree included mathematics, English, mineralogy, geology, and one modern language. Fourth-year mechanical-engineering studies included mechanical engineering, mathematics, physics, one modern language, and English.[17]

[12]Texas A&M, *Longhorn, 1908*, pp. 38-40.
[13]Texas A&M, *Catalogue, 1879-1880*, p. 9; *Catalogue, 1882-1883*, pp. 28-30.
[14]Texas A&M, *Catalogue, 1879-1880*, p. 9.
[15]Texas A&M, *Annual Report, 1882-1883*, pp. 5, 10-12.
[16]Texas A&M, *Catalogue, 1882-1883*, pp. 28-29.
[17]*Ibid.*

Van Winkle left A&M in June 1883, and was replaced by Roger Haddock Whitlock, who graduated from Stevens Institute of Technology in Hoboken, New Jersey, in 1882. Whitlock came to Texas A&M as professor of mechanical engineering. Until 1886 Whitlock and Arnold D. Harbers, the shop superintendent, comprised the entire engineering faculty.[18] Engineering studies were supported by the Department of Chemistry and Physics, under the direction of Chairman of the Faculty Hardaway Hunt Dinwiddie. William L. Bringhurst taught courses in physics from 1882 to 1886. In 1888 Henry Hill Harrington assumed the duties of professor of chemistry and physics, with Duncan Adriance as assistant.[19] Physics was combined with civil engineering in 1889, and John H. Kinealy came as the head of that department. He was replaced the next year by Charles Puryear. Puryear became head of the Department of Mathematics in 1889, when Louis McInnis left the College, and James C. Nagle then became head of the Department of Civil Engineering and Physics.[20]

Nagle, in January 1893, recommended the separation of civil engineering from physics.[21] The opportunity was provided when in March 1893 a legislative committee investigating Texas A&M recommended the addition of a course in electrical engineering. Civil engineering then became independent and electrical engineering came under the tutelage of the Department of Physics.[22] In 1902 President David F. Houston strongly recommended the establishment of a separate department of electrical engineering because the "demand for instruction in the latter subject has increased tremendously in the last few years." At the time, incidentally, of the total student enrollment of 467, 98 were enrolled in civil-engineering studies, 116 in mechanical engineering, 206 in agriculture, and the remaining 47 students in electives, special courses, and graduate courses.[23] The Department of Electrical Engineering was organized in 1903 under the direction of Professor Nathan H. Brown, a trained mechanical engineer who came to A&M from Chattanooga, Tennessee, where he had been superintendent of the city electric railway lines.[24]

The state Legislature had a direct hand in the creation of another engineering department, in addition to the electrical, when in 1903 it directed Texas A&M to establish a "department of instruction in the theory and prac-

[18]David Brooks Cofer (ed.), *Fragments of Early History of Texas A. and M. College*, 68.

[19]*Ibid.*, 68; Texas A&M, *Catalogue, 1887-1888*, pp. 15-16.

[20]Texas A&M, *Annual Report, 1889-1890*, pp. 3-4; Texas A&M, *Longhorn, 1908*, pp. 36-40.

[21]Texas A&M, *Biennial Report, 1891-1893*, p. 16.

[22]*Texas House Journal, 1893*, p. 527; Texas A&M, *Biennial Report, 1900-1903*, p. 13.

[23]Texas A&M, *Biennial Report, 1900-1903*, pp. 6, 13.

[24]Texas A&M, *Longhorn, 1908*, pp. 43-44; Texas A&M, *Biennial Report, 1903-1904*, p. 20.

tical art of textile and kindred branches of industry," and it appropriated a wholesome $50,000 for the necessary machinery and staff.[25] The school was established under the direction of James S. Weir, formerly of Mississippi A&M. It boasted a complete cotton-goods manufacturing facility.[26] For the first two years of study the curriculum for mechanical engineers and for textile engineers was the same.[27] In 1909 the Department of Textile Engineering assumed the duties, also delegated by legislative authority, of teaching classes in the "practical art of grading, classing, and determining the spinable value of cotton."[28] Texas had clear intentions after the turn of the century of becoming a part of the new industrial South. She eventually achieved this aim, but it was largely petroleum production rather than textile manufacturing which brought the transformation. Engineers from Texas A&M provided much of the technical know-how to bring about the industrial development in Texas.

Roger Haddock Whitlock is credited by many as being the father of engineering at Texas A&M. David Brooks Cofer writes, "he came to the institution at a time when there were no engineering courses and developed both mechanical and civil engineering."[29] The A&M "school of engineering" obtained its second professor in 1886, when Frederick Ernst Giesecke was named instructor in mechanical engineering and drawing at a salary of $60 per month for nine months, plus room and board. Giesecke was born in Latium, Texas, on January 28, 1869, and grew up in New Braunfels. He entered A&M at the age of fourteen in the fall of 1883, and obtained his certificate of completion in 1886, having been cadet captain and first in his class. During his senior year Giesecke and senior engineering students E. H. Whitlock, M. D. Tilson, Harry L. Wright, C. L. Burghard, I. A. Cottingham, W. F. Woodward, and C. C. McCulloch constructed a working steam engine which was exhibited at the State Fair in Dallas. For many years it could be seen in the lobby of the Engineering Building on campus.[30]

In June 1892 the Directors created a separate Department of Drawing

[25]*General Laws of Texas, 1903*, p. 74.

[26]Texas A&M, *Biennial Report, 1903-1904*, pp. 4-5.

[27]*Ibid.*

[28]*General Laws of Texas, 1909*, p. 220.

[29]Cofer (ed.), *Second Five Administrators of Texas A&M College*, 91-104.

[30]*Ibid.;* Charles W. Crawford, "F. E. Giesecke, Engineer, Scholar, Gentleman," address delivered before Texas chapter, American Society of Heating and Ventilating Engineers, in F. E. Giesecke Biographical Papers, Texas A&M University Archives; Cofer (ed.), *Fragments of Early History of Texas A. and M. College*, 42-47; Cofer (ed.), *First Five Administrators of Texas A. and M. College*, 34.

and placed Giesecke at its head as full professor.[31] In 1904 he obtained the S.B. (scientific bachelor) degree in Architecture from Massachusetts Institute of Technology. In his capacity as College architect, Giesecke became greatly involved in expanding and constructing College buildings during the Milner years. In 1912 Giesecke left A&M to become professor of architecture at The University of Texas and also to serve as head of its Division of Engineering, Bureau of Economic Geology and Technology. In 1923 he went for further graduate work to the University of Illinois, where he received his Ph.D. in mechanical engineering in 1924. In 1927 Giesecke returned to his alma mater to assume the chairmanship of the Department of Architecture. In 1928 he again became College architect and also director of the Texas Engineering Experiment Station. Giesecke turned over his duties as head of architecture to Ernest Langford in 1930. He retired from A&M in 1939, but continued his professional work, receiving a C.E. degree from the University of Illinois on June 7, 1943, at the age of 73. During his lifetime he published many texts and papers on mechanical drawing and hot-water heating systems, in both areas of which he was a pioneer. He died June 27, 1953,[32] a most illustrious representative of the Texas A&M Engineering School.

The history of A&M engineering can be written in the lives of such men as Whitlock and Giesecke, who came on the scene early, and stayed late. Whitlock, who came to A&M in 1883 and who served as acting president on several occasions, left the College in 1906.[33] The third of the great "triumvirate" of engineers at Texas A&M included James C. ("Jimmy") Nagle.

Nagle, born in Richmond, Virginia, October 9, 1865, moved to Texas as a child. He entered The University of Texas in 1887 and received the B.S. degree in Civil Engineering in 1889 and came to Texas A&M as associate professor of civil engineering and drawing, being brought in by Whitlock. While still on the faculty, Nagle earned the M.S. degree from The University of Texas in 1892, the C.E. degree from the University of Pennsylvania, and the Master of Civil Engineering from Cornell, both in 1893 and in absentia. Nagle, with brown hair, blue eyes, and a ruddy complexion, was loved and respected by his students and colleagues.[34] The 1910 *Longhorn* was dedicated to him. It described him as being

[31]Minutes of the Board of Directors, June 8, 1892, I, 135.

[32]Cofer (ed.), *Fragments of Early History of Texas A. and M. College*, 42-47; Crawford, "F. E. Giesecke, Engineer, Scholar, Gentleman"; see also F. E. Giesecke, "Autobiography," Giesecke Biographical Papers, Texas A&M University Archives.

[33]Cofer (ed.), *Second Five Administrators of Texas A. and M. College*, 91-104; Houston *Post*, June 13, 1906.

[34]James C. Nagle Biographical Papers, Texas A&M University Archives; Cofer (ed.), *Fragments of Early History of Texas A. and M. College*, 52-58.

patient and skillful in the classroom and in field practice; abounding in the virtues of hospitality and wholesome good-fellowship; the generous, constant friend of all A. and M. men. . . . a sane, honest, plain man — a big-bodied, big-brained, big-souled man — who has won, and will hold forever, our esteem and love.[35]

Again in 1921 the A&M students dedicated their yearbook to Nagle.[36]

James C. Nagle became the first dean of the School of Engineering by action of the Board of Directors on November 11, 1911.[37] He left A&M temporarily in August 1913 to serve as chairman of the State Board of Water Engineers, but returned in 1917, upon the death of Dean David W. Spence, to resume the office of dean of Engineering. Nagle retired in 1922, having served at Texas A&M for thirty years, and died April 6, 1928.[38]

During Nagle's absence between 1913 and 1917, David Wendel Spence served as dean of the School of Engineering. Born September 22, 1868, Spence obtained a B.S. from The University of Texas in 1889, and the C.E. from the University of Michigan in 1891. He came to A&M in 1892 as assistant professor of civil engineering and drawing at a salary of $1,200 for twelve months.[39] When civil engineering and physics were separated in 1899 Spence became head of physics. He returned to the Department of Civil Engineering in 1903, when physics joined with electrical engineering under the direction of Nathan H. Brown. From 1907 to 1912 Spence worked as consulting engineer for Prairie View State Normal and Industrial College, and became dean of Engineering in August 1912. He died, while dean, on June 28, 1917. Spence was one of that small group of men responsible for the development of the Texas A&M School of Engineering in its early decades. Ernest Langford, who had courses under him while a student at A&M, and who replaced Giesecke as chairman of the Department of Architecture in 1930, recalls Spence as a man of even temper, and a good teacher and engineer, who could be as "hard as nails" when necessary.[40]

After 1920, as Charles Crawford recalls, the complexion of the engi-

[35]Texas A&M, *Longhorn, 1901* (dedication); and Cofer (ed.) *Fragments of Early History of Texas A. and M. College,* 54-55.

[36]Texas A&M, *Longhorn, 1921* (dedication).

[37]Minutes of the Board of Directors, November 11, 1911, II, 288.

[38]Texas A&M, *Biennial Report, 1913-1914,* p. 9; James C. Nagle Biographical Papers, Texas A&M University Archives; Cofer (ed.), *Fragments of Early History of Texas A. and M. College,* 52-58.

[39]Minutes of the Board of Directors, November 2, 1892, I, 141; Texas A&M, *Biennial Report, 1917-1918,* p. 2.

[40]Cofer (ed.), *Fragments of Early History of Texas A. and M. College,* 69; Texas A&M, *Biennial Report, 1917-1918,* p. 2; interview with Ernest Langford, College Station, Texas, March 8, 1971.

neering faculty changed markedly. The "old-timers" began to disappear from the scene and many new faces, and new leadership, appeared.[41] One of those, however, who helped bridge the times, and who held the great respect of his colleagues, was Emil Jerome Fermier, who joined the A&M College faculty in 1906 as chairman of the Department of Mechanical Engineering. President Henry Hill Harrington's *Biennial Report* for 1905-1906 indicated that mechanical-engineering studies had failed to keep abreast of development in other fields,[42] an evaluation which might explain Whitlock's resignation in 1906. A&M lore has it, however, that Whitlock and Harrington were competing for the A&M presidency and that when Harrington won out Whitlock left. In any event, Fermier, who replaced Whitlock, proved eminently capable, and did modernize and improve the studies in mechanical engineering.

Fermier graduated from Purdue University with a liberal-arts degree and after a few years of public-school teaching returned to that institution to obtain a degree in mechanical engineering. Charles Crawford, who worked under Fermier as a student and then with him as a colleague, believed Fermier to be "one of the most astute and smartest men" he ever worked with, and an excellent teacher. Crawford recalls that Fermier died only a few hours after his wife passed away, in the fall of 1927. Fermier's Essex automobile failed to start when he left to telegraph the sad news to the family; so he walked eight blocks from the old St. Joseph (formerly Bryan) Hospital to the telegraph office along the railroad tracks, climbed the steps to the operator's office, sat down and wrote "Nora died tonight about eleven o'clock, . . ." and dropped over dead. When given the news the next morning, Crawford, and many other former students, felt as if they had "lost my father."[43] And so, one by one, the real developers and pioneers of the engineering curricula at Texas A&M passed from the scene, but, while engineering at A&M began to assume a "new look" in the modern era after World War I, that college had been built upon a firm foundation provided by such men as Roger Haddock Whitlock, Frederick Ernst Giesecke, James C. Nagle, David W. Spence, and Emil J. Fermier.

Although Giesecke, Nagle, and Fermier remained active at A&M for many years after World War I, one man in particular is the transitional figure between the old and the new, insofar as engineering is concerned. He was Francis Cleveland Bolton. A 1905 graduate of Mississippi State College in physics and electrical engineering, he joined the A&M faculty in 1909 as pro-

---

[41]Interview with Charles W. Crawford, College Station, Texas, March 30, 1971.

[42]Texas A&M, *Biennial Report, 1905-1906*, pp. 16, 57-58.

[43]Interview with Charles W. Crawford, College Station, Texas, March 30, 1971.

fessor of electrical engineering. Bolton replaced Nagle as dean of the College of Engineering in 1922 and in 1931 became dean of the A&M College. Bolton, with Charles Puryear, is credited by many as having been most responsible for raising academic standards of the A&M College, to make it no longer a "remote cow college," but one of the top technical schools of the nation. He served as the "cotter key which locks the spinning wheel to the shaft, giving the whole mechanism drive."[44]

Other individuals, to be sure, made a contribution to the development of the engineering program during the middle years. Robert J. Potts moved from civil engineering to establish a division of highway engineering within the Department of Civil Engineering in 1910,[45] a move which also marked the advent of the automobile age in Texas. Potts, who left A&M in August 1914, was succeeded by Robert J. Morrison, a graduate of the University of Illinois and of Columbia University.[46] The agriculturists made their entry into the engineering field in July 1914, when the Board of Directors authorized the establishment of a Department of Agricultural Engineering in conjunction with the Department of Agronomy. In July 1915 agricultural engineering was given independent status under the School of Agriculture, with E. C. Gee as its head.[47] In his report to President David F. Houston in 1904 Phineas S. Tilson first recommended the establishment of a division of chemical engineering in the Chemistry Department.[48] In 1906 James C. Blake, then head of Chemistry, again advised the establishment of a course in chemical engineering, and a regular program in chemical engineering came in under Blake's Department of Chemistry in 1908.[49] Architectural engineering did not attain autonomy until after World War I. Architectural engineering was associated variously with drawing or architecture, but by 1906 the College boasted a curriculum in architectural engineering under the direction of Frederick E. Giesecke.[50] By 1910 Texas A&M offered eight degree programs, only one of which, agriculture, was unrelated to engineering. They included architecture, agricultural engineering, chemical engineering, civil engineering, electrical engineering, mechanical engineering, and textile engineering.[51]

[44]Texas A&M, *Biennial Report, 1909-1910*, p. 26; *A Man and His College: Frank C. Bolton* [1-16]; Minutes of the Board of Directors, September 13-14, 1909, II, 173.

[45]Minutes of the Board of Directors, April 1, 1910, II, 210.

[46]Texas A&M, *Biennial Report, 1913-1914*, p. 9.

[47]*Ibid.*, *1915-1916*, pp. 31-32.

[48]*Ibid.*, *1903-1904*, pp. 140-141.

[49]*Ibid.*, *1905-1906*, p. 56; *ibid.*, *1909-1910*, p. 7.

[50]*Ibid.*, *1905-1906*, pp. 53-54.

[51]*Ibid.*, *1909-1910*, p. 7.

In 1913 Texas A&M engineers voluntarily formed the Texas Engineering Experiment Station. The object of the Engineering Experiment Station was "to supply important information to the general public through printed bulletins, and to make important investigations in the field of engineering."[52] In establishing the Station A&M was not far behind the University of Illinois and Iowa State College, which established the first two such facilities in 1903.[53] The Station was formally authorized by the Board on August 25, 1914, at which time Dean David W. Spence was named director. In 1928 Giesecke became director of the Engineering Experiment Station and in 1932 the Station moved into its own building.[54] Although the Station has made significant research contributions, it has never been as well endowed as the Agricultural Experiment Station.

When Robert Teague Milner left Texas A&M in 1913 the College was very clearly prospering in terms of academic programs, financial status, and numerical growth (see table 1). Indeed, a major part of the problems confronted by the administration had to do with growing pains.

William Bennett Bizzell officially succeeded Milner as president of A&M on August 25, 1914, following the interim administration of Charles Puryear, who returned to his duties as dean of the College. At the meeting of the Board of Directors in Houston on November 24, Bizzell "spoke in an optimistic vein of conditions at the college." Following the chaotic experiences of the past year and a half, the Directors felt a tremendous sense of relief, and according to the genial giant, Ike Ashburn, who then functioned as secretary to the Board and director of publicity, "Every member of the Board expressed his appreciation with the President's remarks and the meeting was turned into a love feast."[55] It was a propitious beginning for an administration that was among the most successful in the history of the College.

When Bizzell assumed the office of president several important situations confronted him. (1) The Texas Legislature had provided for the reorganization of the boards of several state institutions, including the Board of the A&M College; (2) Acting-President Charles Puryear had signed an agreement with the United States Department of Agriculture providing for Texas A&M's entry into the field of Agricultural Extension work under the terms

[52]*Ibid.*, *1913-1914*, pp. 15-16.

[53]*Ibid.*, *1915-1916*, pp. 18-19.

[54]Crawford, "F. E. Giesecke, Engineer, Scholar, Gentleman," Texas A&M University Archives; Clarence Ousley, *History of the Agricultural and Mechanical College of Texas*, 99, 162; Minutes of the Board of Directors, August 25, 1914, III, 152.

[55]Minutes of the Board of Directors, August 25, 1914, III, 149-151, and November 24, 1914, III, 153.

of the Smith-Lever Act; and (3) negotiations were again pending with The University of Texas over separation of A&M from The University, and the disposition of the University Endowment.

Table 1.
Texas A&M Enrollment, 1876-1917

Academic Year	Students Enrolled	Academic Year	Students Enrolled
1876-1877	166	1897-1898	337
1877-1878	331	1898-1899	356
1878-1879	248	1899-1900	396
1879-1880	144	1900-1901	382
1880-1881	127	1901-1902	427
1881-1882	258	1902-1903	396
1882-1883	228	1903-1904	378
1883-1884	108	1904-1905	414
1884-1885	118	1905-1906	411
1885-1886	170	1906-1907	515
1886-1887	176	1907-1908	623
1887-1888	214	1908-1909	639
1888-1889	207	1909-1910	834
1889-1890	279	1910-1911	1,082
1890-1891	318	1911-1912	1,129
1891-1892	331	1912-1913	1,015
1892-1893	293	1913-1914	888
1893-1894	313	1914-1915	915
1894-1895	372	1915-1916	1,068
1895-1896	354	1916-1917	1,242
1896-1897	311		

Source: Texas A&M, *Biennial Report, 1905-1906,* p. 13, and *Biennial Report, 1917-1918,* p. 22.

On April 2, 1913, the Legislature enacted a law which reorganized the boards of The University of Texas, Texas A&M, and other state institutions. The law provided that the A&M Board should be composed of nine persons who should be qualified voters. They should be from different sections of the state and should be nominated by the governor and appointed by and with the consent and advice of the Senate. Appointments were for six-year terms, and incumbent Board members were to accept new tenures of two, four, and six years, so that every two years, or at every regular session of the Legislature, three new Board members having six-year terms would be selected.[56] A ruling by the attorney general in January 1914 established that

[56]*General Laws of Texas, 1913,* pp. 191-192.

the secretary of agriculture was no longer to be considered a member of the A&M Board of Directors.[57] The A&M Board still remains under the organizational structure provided by the law of 1913.

One innovation of the Board of Directors in 1913 was the inauguration of an "open house" meeting with all employees of the College. The first such open house was held September 5, 1913, at which time a "free discussion" concerning faculty problems developed. The major problem at the time appears to have been the control of roaming stock, which was trampling lawns and gardens; another problem involved the disposition of dead animals. The meeting was undoubtedly successful, for another open house followed in November.[58] This Board-Faculty meeting established the precedent for the contemporary annual Faculty-Board banquet.

Another innovation denoting the entry of A&M into the modern era was the Board's decision to bring motion pictures to the campus. In April 1913 the Directors appointed a committee to arrange for a series of motion-picture shows for the entertainment of the students, and upon the committee's recommendation they directed the Department of Mechanical Engineering to purchase a "moving picture machine and to make such other arrangements as may be necessary to insure a picture show for the cadets."[59] Also in 1913 the Directors studied the feasibility of installing an elevator in the new Academic Building, which would have been a first in Brazos County, but they decided against it.[60]

In June 1914 the Directors created the position of athletic director, in response to the growing role of organized athletics, particularly football, on the campus. Some problems had developed previously. The Athletic Council, comprising three faculty and three student members which supervised athletic activities, owed $1,105.28 to A. G. Spaulding Company for athletic equipment. The Board of Directors disclaimed any liability for the claim, arguing that organized athletic events functioned on an unofficial basis. The Athletic Council, however, promised in 1913 to liquidate the claim as soon as possible, and indicated that it was an old claim resulting from "unfortunate results of the operation of the athletic teams."[61] The appointment of the athletic director in 1913 made the College the official sponsor of organized athletic events, and ended for all time the questionable status of intercollegiate athletics at the College.

[57]Minutes of the Board of Directors, January 19-20, 1914, III, 124-125.

[58]*Ibid.*, September 4-5, 1913, III, 101; November 3, 1913, III, 119.

[59]*Ibid.*, September 4-5, 1913, III, 106; and January 19-20, 1914, III, 126.

[60]*Ibid.*, September 4-5, 1913, III, 107.

[61]*Ibid.*, September 4-5, 1913, III, 103-104.

Charles B. Moran, who joined A&M as football coach in 1910, succeeded in making the institution football conscious. The *Longhorn* of 1914 boasted that between 1902 and 1913 the Farmers had won 73 football games, lost 18, and tied 4. Although baseball had been temporarily evicted in 1902 and 1903 by football, the baseball team had won 96 games, lost 54, and tied 4 between 1904 and 1913. In 1910 and 1911 the A&M track team won first place in the state meet.[62] In the 1913 season A&M's "young, inexperienced eleven" lost more games than the team had lost in the past four seasons.[63] The 1913 schedule included the following contests:[64]

Texas A&M		*Opponent*
7	Trinity	0
6	Austin College	0
19	Polytechnic College	6
0	Mississippi A&M	6
0	Kansas A&M	12
0	Oklahoma A&M	3
0	Haskell Institute	28
14	Baylor University	14
7	Louisiana State University	7

In the next season, 1914, Texas A&M lost only one game, to the Haskell Indians. The cadets defeated Texas Christian University 40-0, Louisiana State University 63-9, Rice Institute 32-7, Oklahoma A&M 24-0, and Mississippi State University 14-7.[65] In 1915 Texas A&M lost only to Rice and to Mississippi A&M, and for the first time since 1911 played a football game (on Thanksgiving day) against The University of Texas. A&M won by a score of 13-0.[66] A report on the Texas University-A&M football game in 1915 strongly suggests the future course of that institutional rivalry, and the future of intercollegiate football in general:

> Too much can not be said for the spirit manifested by the corps in the entertainment offered to our friends from The University on the occasion of their first visit to our campus in the first big game at College between the schools. The splendid showing made by the corps and the healthy rivalry between the two institutions has perhaps done more than anything of recent years to stimulate interest in athletics

[62]Texas A&M, *Longhorn, 1914,* pp. 270-271, 289.
[63]*Ibid.*
[64]*Ibid.*
[65]*Ibid., 1915,* p. 228.
[66]*Ibid., 1916,* pp. 247-254.

in the State of Texas. The advertising for the two schools concerned, the growth of State pride, the friendships formed, are the biggest reasons possible for the continuance of athletic relations with The University of Texas.[67]

By 1916 it appeared that big-time football had already come. Andrew Cavitt Love, chairman of the Faculty Athletic Committee, reported that "The largest crowd at an athletic contest south of the Mason-Dixon line witnessed the Thanksgiving game against The University at Austin. The crowd was estimated to be 15,800 and the receipts of the game were approximately $21,000." As a result of the "good season," Love continued, A&M had paid its old obligations, met all current expenses, and made needed improvements in athletic facilities.[68] The College, he inferred, had also "cleaned up" its athletics so that it could never again be said that "A&M teams are composed of men that are not gentlemen and that have been coached to play dirty, underhand games."[69] When "Charlie" Moran left, E. H. W. ("Jigger") Harlan, from Princeton, became head coach, and was assisted by Dorsett V. ("Tubby") Graves. Harlan remained for the 1915 and 1916 seasons, after which he was replaced by Dana X. ("Deac") Bible, who had coached a very successful A&M freshman team in 1916. The new athletic director, appointed in 1915, was William L. ("Billy") Driver.[70]

President Bizzell, according to the 1918 *Longhorn*, was largely responsible for putting A&M intercollegiate athletics upon a well-organized, "business-like" basis. Part of the effort involved in 1914 the organization of the Southwest Athletic Conference, of which Texas A&M was a charter member and which in 1916 included the University of Arkansas, Baylor University, Oklahoma A&M, the University of Oklahoma, Southwestern University, Rice Institute, Texas A&M, and The University of Texas.[71]

The Texas A&M-University of Texas football rivalry, which dates essentially from 1915, was in many respects a manifestation of the political rivalry which had existed between the schools even before The University of Texas had become a reality. Since the time of Lawrence Sullivan Ross the political rivalry had been somewhat muted, or at least had been elevated to a higher level — to the board rooms and executive offices. As the political

---

[67]Texas A&M, *Biennial Report, 1915-1916*, pp. 107-108.

[68]*Ibid.*, *1917-1918*, pp. 105-114. Note: The Thanksgiving Day game was played in 1917 against Rice, in Houston; it had not yet become a tradition with The University of Texas and Texas A&M.

[69]*Ibid.*, 114.

[70]*Ibid.*, 105-114; Texas A&M, *Longhorn, 1916*, pp. 242-244.

[71]Texas A&M, *Longhorn, 1918*, pp. 77-84; Texas A&M, *Biennial Report, 1915-1916*, pp. 107-109.

rivalry cooled, the athletic rivalry between Texas A&M and The University intensified and seems to have been largely a by-product of modern football. But politics remained a part of the A&M-University "game."

In January 1914 the A&M Board of Directors received an invitation from the Regents of The University of Texas to unite with them in presenting to and urging upon the Thirty-fourth Legislature the enactment of a proposed constitutional amendment which would (1) make A&M an independent college, (2) allow legislative appropriations and tax levies for capital construction, and (3) specify the interests of A&M in the Permanent Fund, *"if any."* The Directors replied that they were kindly disposed toward the invitation of the Regents. But in June the A&M Directors submitted to the Regents their own proposals, which included items (1) and (2) above, but which specified that there should be *an equal* division of the Permanent Fund, and that a tax levy should be equitably divided. The Directors also urged that efforts should be made to prevent the duplication of work by the two schools.[72] Eventually, the A&M Board of Directors received an invitation from the Regents to meet with them on November 30, 1914, in Austin, for the purpose of considering a tax levy to support higher education. The Directors replied that they thought it inadvisable at the time to ask for a tax levy "in view of the financial conditions now prevailing among the people of the State."[73] The questionable financial conditions alluded to by the Board had to do with the uncertainties caused by the outbreak of war in Europe in August 1914. At the same time the Directors did ask for a meeting with the Regents on December 15, 1914, to consider separation of the institutions.[74] This exchange seems to have involved more "fencing" for position than the assumption of a new approach by either Texas A&M or The University. Both institutions remained essentially committed to the agreements reached between them in 1913, and the final product of the Thirty-fourth Legislature was the approval of a proposed amendment which reflected the 1913 agreements, with some modifications.

The most important "new" development during the 1915 legislative sessions came as a proposal from Governor James Edward Ferguson, who was inaugurated as Oscar Branch Colquitt's successor on January 20, 1915. Ferguson's plan, in retrospect, was one of the most "progressive" solutions to the perennial institutional conflict. But "Farmer Jim" Ferguson was not kindly disposed toward higher education, either that of The University or the A&M

[72]Minutes of the Board of Directors, January 19-20, 1914, III, 128-130, and June 10, 1914, III, 136-137.

[73]*Ibid.,* November 24, 1914, III, 157.

[74]*Ibid.*

variety. "It is apparent to any fair-minded person that Texas is today suffering more from a want of under education of the many than it is from a want of over education of the few," he told the Legislature and people of Texas. "There is a real danger of somebody going hog wild about higher education." Ferguson proposed to establish a Central Board of Control with full fiscal and management authority over The University, the A&M College, and the Medical School.[75] Ferguson's plan did not meet the approval of the Legislature.

The Legislature, however, did approve submitting to the people in 1915 two constitutional amendments affecting The University and the A&M College. One amendment would change Section 3b of Article 7 of the Constitution and create a tax-supported Student Loan Fund. Another would amend Sections 10-15 of Article 7 to separate the institutions, and give A&M 600,000 acres of the University lands and Prairie View State Normal and Industrial College 150,000 acres as a separate endowment. Both propositions were defeated at the polls. The Loan Fund amendment lost by a vote of 27,529 to 102,627, and the separation provision failed by a vote of 81,658 for, to 50,398 against, or fewer than 6,000 votes, to gain the necessary two-thirds majority.[76] The experiences in the Legislature and at the polls in 1913 and 1915 made it appear conclusive that no constitutional settlement of The University question was imminent.

The Thirty-fourth Texas Legislature on January 29, 1915, did accept the provisions of an act of Congress on May 8, 1914, called the Smith-Lever Act, "to provide cooperative agricultural extension work between the agricultural colleges in the several states receiving the benefits of the Act of Congress approved July 2, 1862, and the acts supplementary thereto, and the United States Department of Agriculture."[77] The inauguration of the Texas Agricultural Extension Service under the auspices of the A&M College had an even more profound effect upon the expansion of the College's services than did the Agricultural Experiment Station System. By 1920 one-half million dollars annually came from state and federal sources for agricultural extension work.[78] During the depression crises of the thirties the Extension Service carried on a substantial part of the relief and recovery programs of the New Deal.

Clarence Ousley, a member of the Board of Regents of The University

[75]Benedict (ed.), *A Source Book of the University of Texas*, 505-507.

[76]*Ibid.*, 508-516.

[77]Minutes of the Board of Directors, April 24, 1915, III, 163.

[78]"Organization of the Agricultural and Mechanical College System in Texas," *Bulletin of the Agricultural and Mechanical College of Texas*, 3rd ser., VI (December 1, 1920), p. 10.

of Texas and former editor of *Texas Farm and Ranch*, was appointed director of Extension activities in Texas by the A&M Board of Directors, effective August 15, 1914. Personnel of the Extension Service, comprising three major divisions — county agents, home demonstration agents, and specialists — were housed in Gathright Hall on the A&M Campus. Almost immediately upon its inception the Extension Service helped organize a cotton-holding program to stem the collapse of cotton prices caused by panic at the outbreak of World War I in Europe. By 1917 the Extension Service was deeply involved in stimulating increased farm production for the war effort. In the twenties and the thirties it had to deal with a severe farm depression.[79] Its activities became of such magnitude that it is fully deserving of a history of its own, and deserves at the least a full chapter in the history of A&M.

Ousley soon left Texas to become Assistant Secretary of Agriculture under David Franklin Houston, former president of Texas A&M. Thomas O. Walton, who was to succeed Bizzell as president of A&M in 1925, replaced Ousley as director of the Texas Extension Service.[80] The Extension Service, in conjunction with the Experiment Station, became so enormous in terms of prestige and federal-state endowments, that for a number of years the activities of these agencies completely overshadowed the regular academic functions of the College.

By 1915 the A&M College had evolved into three fairly distinct coordinate divisions: the Division of Resident Teaching, which included the School of Agriculture and the School of Engineering, to be joined in 1916 by the School of Veterinary Medicine; the Division of Agricultural Research, which comprised the Agricultural Experiment Station; the Division of Agricultural Extension, which included farm- and home-demonstration work.[81] These divisions continue to reflect the basic functions of Texas A&M University: teaching, research, and extension. Other actions of the Thirty-fourth Texas Legislature in 1915 having a profound effect upon the growth and development of the A&M College included the authorization of a School of Veterinary Medicine with an appropriation of $100,000 for buildings, and the establishment of a State Forestry Service, both under the auspices of the Board of Directors of Texas A&M. The advent of the School of Veterinary Medicine may be largely attributed to the work of Dr. Mark Francis. The Board of Directors officially established the School on April 10, 1916, named Mark Francis dean and professor of veterinary medicine and surgery, and authorized

[79]Ousley, *History of the Agricultural and Mechanical College of Texas*, 137-149.

[80]*Ibid.*, 139.

[81]"Organization of the Agricultural and Mechanical College System in Texas," *Bulletin of the Agricultural and Mechanical College of Texas*, 3rd ser., VI (December 1, 1920), p. 14.

the granting of the degree of Doctor of Veterinary Medicine.[82] The school began enrolling students in September 1916.

The advent of the Texas Forest Service has its own unique history. By 1915 the "time was ripe" for Texas to do something about preserving her forest resources. The Progressive Movement, with its emphasis on conservation, and the implementation of federal forestry programs, especially by President Theodore Roosevelt, provided the initiative for state legislation. Federal funds for forest preservation under such statutes as the Weeks Law (March 1, 1911) provided extra incentive for states to develop a forest-protection and preservation system. The Forestry Law of 1915 called for the appointment of a state forester by the A&M College Board of Directors, and for the Board's supervision and control over the state forestry programs.[83] While the State Forest Service has been less conspicuous as an academic arm of Texas A&M, it has done for the Texas forestry industry what the School of Veterinary Medicine has done for the Texas livestock industry. Both branches of the A&M system have had a continuing impact since their inception upon bettering the lives and improving the fortunes of Texans.

Despite the failure at the polls of the constitutional amendment to separate the A&M College from The University in 1915, President William Bennett Bizzell hailed that legislative session as one of the most productive in history. He said it had "passed more bills in the interest of the College than any previous legislature."[84] Bizzell now had the gargantuan task of implementing these new programs. Under his direction the Texas Forest Service, the Extension Service, and the School of Veterinary Medicine began to function. Athletics were organized and expanded. Student enrollment increased considerably, and faculty and staff grew at an even more rapid rate. In 1917 the College acquired, in addition to Prairie View State Normal and Industrial College, two new branches, the John Tarleton Agricultural College and the Grubbs Vocational College, which are the subjects of a later chapter. In the years while Bizzell was president Texas A&M received larger appropriations for building construction than the total received from its founding to the beginning of his administration. Added to the awesome tasks of the Bizzell administration was that of supervising the conversion of the College, upon America's entry into World War I, to a "war training school." For several years the normal academic routine at A&M was almost completely disrupted

[82]Minutes of the Board of Directors, April 10, 1916, III, 191-192; Texas A&M, *Biennial Report, 1915-1916*, pp. 19-20.

[83]Texas A&M, *Biennial Report, 1915-1916*, pp. 92-106.

[84]Minutes of the Board of Directors, April 24, 1915, III, 164.

when A&M "went to war." If it was Lawrence Sullivan Ross who brought A&M out of its "dark ages," it was William Bennett Bizzell who took A&M into the modern era.

It all began quite unpretentiously. "One bright, sunshiny day in the early part of September 1914, an alert, earnest young man, of pleasing appearance" but for the fact that his hair was parted in the middle, recounts the student editor of the 1918 *Longhorn,* stepped off the interurban car and after several hours of consultation with Dean of the College Charles Puryear, announced to the world smilingly that he was ready for "what might come."[85] The cadets met their new President Bizzell with some reservations, derived largely from the fact that he indeed parted his hair in the middle, and that he came to them from a "girl" school, the College of Industrial Arts for Women, in Denton, to which he had been elected president in 1910. "However, after several never-to-be-forgotten interviews, following continued violations of the established rules of good conduct and morality, some of these students went away (literally) saddened but wiser young men," intoned the same 1918 student editor.[86]

Bizzell was born at Independence, Texas, not far from the A&M campus, on October 14, 1876. He attended the Baylor-Crane College, at Independence, before going to Baylor University, in Waco, from which he received a Bachelor of Science degree in 1898, and a Doctor of Philosophy degree in 1900. He was principal of Montgomery High School from 1899 to 1901, principal of Navasota High School from 1901 to 1902, and superintendent of Navasota High School from 1902 to 1910, until he was selected to become president of the College of Industrial Arts (now Texas Woman's University). Bizzell specialized in economics and sociology, and published a number of scholarly works including *Austinean Theory of Sovereignty* (1912), *Judicial Interpretation of Political Theory* (1914), *The Social Teaching of the Jewish Prophets* (1916), *Farm Tenancy in the United States* (1912), *Rural Texas* (1923), and *The Green Rising* (1927).[87]

Upon assuming his office at Texas A&M, Bizzell announced that certain policies would prevail at the College, including (1) higher standards of morality, (2) greater religious activity, (3) higher standards of scholarship, (4) proper conduct of athletics, (5) the abolition of hazing, (6) development and improvement of the material equipment of the College, and (7) a greater

[85]Texas A&M, *Longhorn, 1918,* pp. 77-84.

[86]*Ibid.*

[87]*Ibid.;* Frank W. Johnson, *A History of Texas and Texans,* II, 2466-2467; *Who's Who in American Education, 1937-1938,* p. 526.

field of usefulness for the College through Extension Service, the Experiment Station and the Publicity Department. Higher standards of morality were created by Bizzell's insistence upon faculty participation in Sunday school and religious activities, by instituting a school of religious instruction which offered a four-year course on the Old and the New Testaments, and by broadening the work of the YMCA and the erection of a handsome new YMCA building. Bizzell raised admission requirements in 1914, requiring fourteen units of high school work for enrollment in the freshman class, rather than the old criteria of age and a high-school diploma or "special examination"; and beginning in 1915 A&M admission required graduation from an acceptable secondary school designated as of the "first class" by the State Department of Education.[88]

Even while all of the innovative programs were being introduced, and old programs expanded, Texas A&M, like many other colleges and universities in the United States, began to be touched by the war in Europe. Having declared war on France on August 3, 1914, following the chain reaction set off by the assassination of Archduke Ferdinand of Austria in Sarajevo, Bosnia, on June 28, 1914, Germany, by September 5, 1914, had pushed her forces within thirty miles of Paris and had locked the Allied armies in combat. On the eastern front German-Austrian armies were mauling the Russians.

Americans and President Woodrow Wilson were determined not to become a part of the strife, but the imminence of American involvement loomed ever more threatening. On June 3, 1916, Congress passed the National Defense Act, which authorized the establishment of Reserve Officer Training Corps programs at qualifying educational institutions. Texas A&M fully embraced the military training program which so thoroughly complemented the institution's historic military orientation. For the next several years the military and the war almost overwhelmed the academic aspects of the institution, and the mark of the military, if it had not been so before, now became an indelible part of Texas A&M's history and tradition.

[88]Texas A&M, *Biennial Report, 1915-1916*, p. 33; Texas A&M, *Longhorn, 1918*, pp. 77-84.

CHAPTER 13

The War Years, 1916-1918

W ORLD War I was a watershed in the history of the Texas Agricultural and Mechanical College. The College entered the War essentially a local agricultural and mechanical school, in a world where agricultural and technical training still had to prove itself to the small world around it. It was a military school in a world where military schools were quite common, its only claim to the uncommon being its attempt to blend the gentlemanly occupation of the military into the less gentlemanly avocations of commercial farming and engineering. The Texas A&M College of 1920 stood in marked contrast to the Texas A&M of 1915.

In 1915 Texas A&M had little reputation outside of its local environs for its military, agricultural, or engineering capabilities; however, it emerged from the war years with a proven and proud record in all three capacities. Its affiliations and services to Texas and to the nation spread rapidly within a few short years by virtue of its contributions to the war effort and through its affiliated institutions and services — John Tarleton Agricultural College, Grubbs Vocational College, Prairie View State Normal and Industrial College, the Agricultural Extension Service, the School of Veterinary Medicine, the Agricultural Experiment Station and substations, the short courses, Extension Service agents, and Home Demonstration agents. The accompanying map (fig. 3), taken from a 1920 organizational manual of Texas A&M,[1] visually demonstrates the high degree of penetration of A&M College into the everyday affairs of Texas. Five years earlier such a map would have been virtually blank.

Although enrollment remained relatively stable while World War I was in progress, during the regular session ending in June 1920, student population on the main campus was 1,902, more than double the 915 enrolled for

[1]"Organization of the Agricultural and Mechanical College System in Texas," *Bulletin of the Agricultural and Mechanical College of Texas,* 3rd ser., VI, No. 13 (December 1, 1920), map folio.

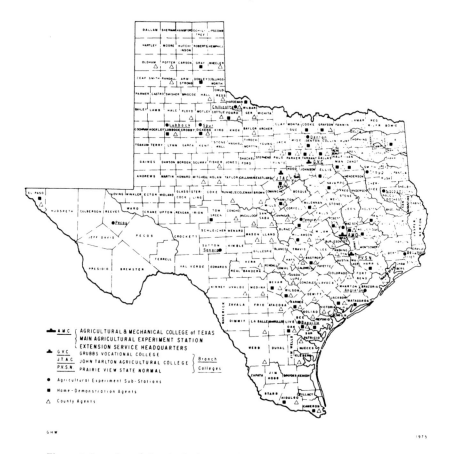

Figure 3. Location of the Agricultural and Mechanical College of Texas, its branches, experiment substations, county agents, and home-demonstration agents, 1920. From *Bulletin of the Agricultural and Mechanical College of Texas,* 3rd ser., VI, No. 13 (December 1, 1920), map folio.

the session ending in June 1915.[2] The Texas A&M "system" in 1920 boasted a total of 980 employees and 6,759 students for the regular and summer sessions and short courses.[3] By comparison, in 1915 the Texas Agricultural Experiment Station listed a total of 51 employees, the Extension Services, 13 employees, the College, including the industrial staff, Feed Control Department, and Office of the State Entomologist, 222 employees, and Prairie View

[2]*Ibid.,* 20-21; Texas A&M, *Biennial Report, 1915-1916,* p. 32.
[3]"Organization of the A&M College System," *Bulletin* (December 1, 1920), pp. 20-21.

State Normal, 62 employees — for a total of 340 employees.[4] The faculty and staff almost tripled between 1915 and 1920.

Despite the fact that several of the years in this period were war years, the physical growth of the main campus between 1915 and 1920 was equally striking. The new YMCA building enjoyed its first full year of service in 1916. A new three-story brick hospital (long needed) was completed in 1916. An animal-husbandry building (the Stock Judging Pavilion, measuring 100 X 200 feet) was built in 1916. A modern fire-proof dairy barn capable of housing 102 cows was erected. Guion Hall, a "magnificent" auditorium with seating for 2,500 people, was completed in 1917 and remained in service until 1970. A three-story brick Experiment Station building was ready for occupancy in 1917. A four-story veterinary-medicine building (Francis Hall), a service laboratory, and a powerhouse were all completed in 1917. Bizzell Hall, a new and modern fire-proof dormitory, was opened in 1918.[5] All of these buildings have continued in service in some capacity for well over a half-century.

Bizzell, a good academician, and a most able administrator and planner, developed a comprehensive ten-year building program for the campus during his first year at A&M. Presented for the consideration of the governor and the Legislature in 1917, the building program was revised intermittently, particularly in 1919 (see table 2). As outlined in 1919 the program specified the type of structures needed and the estimated appropriations required from the Legislature.

"If this program can be realized," said Bizzell, "1926 will see the Agricultural and Mechanical College one of the best equipped and most efficient institutions of its kind in the entire country."[6] The program was largely achieved by 1926.

The Reserve Officer Training Program instituted at Texas A&M by virtue of the National Defense Act of June 3, 1916, had both an immediate and a long-term effect upon the development of the College.[7] It helped regularize and professionalize military training at the College; it provided justification over and above the original Morrill Act of 1862 for the military orientation of the school, which features had in the past been seriously questioned by

[4]Texas A&M, *Biennial Report, 1913-1914*, pp. 33-34, 49-54, shows the budgeted salaries for positions for the 1914-1915 session.

[5]Texas A&M, *Biennial Report, 1915-1916*, pp. 10-12. Ernest Langford recalls assisting in the designing and in the drafting of architectural plans for many of the buildings (interview with Ernest Langford, July 1, 1971, College Station, Texas).

[6]Texas A&M, *Biennial Report, 1915-1916*, p. 30.

[7]*U.S. Stat. at L.* (1917), pp. 116-217.

Table 2.
Ten-Year Building Program, 1917-1927 (by Legislative Session)

Facility Needed	Estimated Appropriation	
Thirty-fifth Legislature	*1917-1918*	*1918-1919*
Agricultural building	$325,000	$25,000
Dormitories	90,000	90,000
Cottages	16,000	16,000
Mechanical-engineering building and shops	20,000	75,000
Physics building, equipment	—	60,000
Remodeling of old chapel for library	6,150	5,000
Extension of sewer system, water mains, and tunnels	10,000	5,000
Central gas plant	15,000	—
Poultry-husbandry buildings	5,000	5,000
Thirty-sixth Legislature	*1919-1920*	*1920-1921*
Gymnasium and armory	$200,000	—
Library	—	$150,000
Completion of dining hall	60,000	—
Agricultural-engineering building	—	75,000
Dormitories	90,000	90,000
Thirty-seventh Legislature	*1921-1922*	*1922-1923*
Extension building	$75,000	—
Chemical building	—	$100,000
Dairy building	75,000	—
Dormitories	90,000	90,000
Machine shops	20,000	—
Wood shops	—	15,000
Foundry	—	15,000
Thirty-eighth Legislature	*1923-1924*	*1924-1925*
Biology building	$75,000	—
Electrical-engineering testing laboratory	—	$50,000
Architectural-engineering building	75,000	—
Dormitories	90,000	90,000
Thirty-ninth Legislature	*1925-1926*	*1926-1927*
Railway mechanical-engineering building	$75,000	—
Ceramics building	—	$50,000
Hydraulic laboratory	45,000	—
Dormitories	90,000	90,000

Source: Texas A&M, *Biennial Report, 1917-1918,* pp. 26-28.

many Texans. The National Defense Act also provided fresh incentive for the continuance and revitalization of the military program. What the National Defense Act failed to accomplish in this regard, the War itself did accomplish. Thus Texas A&M emerged from World War I much more of a professional military institution than when it entered the War.

The National Defense Act was a comprehensive piece of legislation based upon the premise that all able-bodied men between the ages of eighteen and forty-five were subject to military service. One feature of the Act of 1916 was to authorize the President of the United States to establish and maintain in civil educational institutions a Reserve Officers Training Corps. a "senior division" could be established in four-year colleges which agreed to satisfy the specified requirements. The military requirements of the ROTC program were actually less demanding than had been the regular military curriculum of Texas A&M.[8]

On October 3, 1916, Texas A&M officials applied to the War Department for permission to establish a senior ROTC program at the College. The War Department approved the application on October 19, 1916, and the program was funded by Congress and fully instituted at the school beginning in September 1917.[9] Participation in the military training program of the ROTC was mandatory for all freshman and sophomore students. All students at A&M could now receive uniforms from the federal government, and juniors and seniors who voluntarily elected to continue in the ROTC received $8.00 and $9.00 per month, depending upon the allotted "ration," and all expenses for summer training.[10] Upon graduation cadets could be commissioned as reserve officers in the United States Army, and, upon the election of the President, as temporary second lieutenants in the Regular Army.[11]

Irrespective of their decision to elect the advanced ROTC program, all A&M students remained members of the Corps of Cadets and wore the same Army uniform. In September 1917 the cadets put away the old gray-and-black uniforms that had been in use for over forty years, and donned the Army khaki with campaign hats. While the benefits of the program — a uniform, a few dollars a month, and an eventual commission — may sound negligible today, in 1917 the program provided a direct stimulus to enrollment in the nation's colleges and universities. It was with this idea of increasing attendance partly in mind that Bizzell so strongly supported the program for A&M.[12]

[8]Texas A&M, *Biennial Report, 1915-1916*, pp. 15-18.
[9]*Ibid.*, 16, 18.
[10]*Ibid.*, 18.
[11]*Ibid.*, 16.
[12]*Ibid.*, 17-18.

The ROTC program, of course, complemented in every way the military regimen and traditions of the College. Except for a few years in the eighties when fourth-year "graduate" students were exempt, A&M students had always been subject to military discipline. The demerit system, the uniform, and to a considerable extent the daily military activities of the College in 1916 added up to a situation much like that of 1876.[13] After the resumption of a full four-year curriculum, the Directors once again required all students to enroll in the military program, unless specifically exempted by the chairman of the faculty.[14] President Lawrence Sullivan Ross regarded military training and the Corps of Cadets as one of the paramount features of the College. He gave the military program permanence and respectability.[15]

In 1910, under the auspices of Captain Andrew Moses, and despite the earlier difficulties of 1908, Texas A&M earned the Distinguished Institution Award from the United States War Department, marking it one of the top ten military institutions in the United States. The award entitled the president of the College to name a graduating senior, and an alternate, for a direct appointment as a second lieutenant in the United States Army, who would hold the same grade as a graduate of West Point. The award also enabled the College to obtain from the Army two breech-loading rifled cannons with carriages and equipment, which became prized equipment of the Corps of Cadets. The cannons were manned by seniors who had not received appointments as cadet officers. The Corps of Cadets in 1915 comprised three battalions of infantry, a battery of field artillery, a band, and a bugle corps. Texas A&M had the "largest student body under complete military discipline in the United States."[16]

By 1912 the Board of Directors of the A&M College had become more enthusiastic over the military program than they had evidenced in the past. Noting that the military feature was now overwhelmingly approved by the parents and that the program "benefits the physical man, encourages obedience and discipline, promotes courtesy between fellows, teaches sanitation and creates a spirit that is ever present in true manhood," Director J. Allen

[13]Texas A&M, *Catalogue, 1876-1877*, pp. 25-26; Texas A&M, *Biennial Report, 1915-1916*, pp. 85-86.

[14]Minutes of the Board of Directors, June 4, 1889, I, 75.

[15]"Joint Committee Report," *Texas House Journal, 1893*, pp. 527-528. Minutes of the Board of Directors, August 20, 1890, I, 94-95.

[16]Texas A&M, *Biennial Report, 1909-1910*, pp. 9, 19. The cannon were prominently featured in the movie filmed on the Texas A&M campus in 1943, *"We've Never Been Licked."*

Kyle introduced in 1912 several resolutions which were unanimously adopted by the Board:[17]

1) Resolved, that the policy of this Board is to encourage the military in every way that it can.

2) Resolved, that the officers, professors and employees of the College are advised that they should foster the military system, and that if there is among them those who cannot conscientiously support the military feature they are advised that they will seriously hamper the institution by continued opposition.

From 1912 until the final abandonment of the compulsory military training program for all A&M students in 1965,[18] the endorsement of military training and of the Corps of Cadets became a part of the unwritten code of ethics of all Texas A&M faculty and administrators. There was considerable "moral" persuasion to conform or get out.[19] The curious kind of paternalistic atmosphere in which the A&M student was reared created the "one big fraternity" or "family" association which has been so strikingly unique about A&M students and alumni, particularly during its past half-century of existence. This same paternalism perhaps also contributed to a certain academic permissiveness. The decline of the Corps of Cadets in contemporary times marks the end of an era for the A&M College, an era which flourished most vigorously for a full half-century roughly between 1915 and 1965.

President Woodrow Wilson ran for a second term in office in 1916, pointing with justifiable pride to his progressive reform record and to his achievement in keeping America out of the European war. Even then war clouds were drawing very close to American shores. England and France were near exhaustion. American financial commitments to the Allied Powers had become enormous. The Central Powers were readying for their last great offensive. Finally, on January 31, 1917, Germany announced renewal of an unrestricted submarine campaign in the war zone around the British Isles. In March the release of the sensational Zimmerman notes, pledging German aid to Mexico in a war against the United States, in the event the United States entered the war against Germany, shocked the American people. Soon afterwards German submarines sank unarmed American merchantmen in the

[17]Minutes of the Board of Directors, June 11-12, III, 21.

[18]Texas A&M, *Fifth Year Report to the Southern Association of Colleges and Schools* (October 1968), p. 5.

[19]Minutes of the Board of Directors, June 11-12, III, 21.

North Atlantic. On April 6, 1917, Congress approved President Wilson's recommendation for a declaration of War.[20]

In College Station, Texas, on March 21, 1917, the faculty of the A&M College, anticipating the declaration of war, offered the entire facilities of the College to the federal government for war training purposes. The action was ratified by the Board of Directors on March 23:

> Whereas, the President and the Congress of the United States are confronted with a serious international crisis that may at any time result in a declaration of war; and
>
> Whereas, the Agricultural and Mechanical College of Texas is a land-grant institution established by an act of Congress in 1862 presumably for the purpose of preparing men for military service and technical pursuits; and
>
> Whereas, the conditions of modern warfare demand technically trained men for military service; therefore, be it:
>
> Resolved, that we, the Faculty of the Agricultural and Mechanical College of Texas, earnestly request the immediate approval of the Board of Directors, sanctioned if necessary by the Legislature of the State, for the tender to the Federal government of all research and instructional facilities of this College, the same to be subject to the direction of the Secretaries of War and Navy, and that we hereby, individually and collectively, pledge our support to the international policies of the Federal government and earnestly request the Governor and the Legislature of this State to assume undiminished the continuance of appropriations during the continuance of such Federal use irrespective of the suspension of the instructional functions of any or all of the College departments. We urge the favorable consideration of this resolution by the Board of Directors of the College and if necessary by the Legislature also.[21]

A&M was the first college in the United States to offer its facilities and equipment to the government for military purposes.[22] By the end of the month President Bizzell was in Washington, D.C., seeking tents, equipment for the establishment of a cadet cavalry unit, and the assignment of additional Army officers to the College in order to expand the military program. The War Department declined an immediate commitment to Texas A&M, pending the development of adequate storage facilities on campus for war equipment.[23] By April 6, the day President Woodrow Wilson announced the declaration of war against Germany, Bizzell was back in College Station to direct mobilization.

From April 6, 1917, through the end of the academic session in June

[20]Thomas A. Bailey, *A Diplomatic History of the American People*, 632-646.

[21]Texas A&M, *Biennial Report, 1917-1918*, pp. 23, 124; Minutes of the Board of Directors, March 23, 1917, III, 212-213.

[22]Texas A&M, *Biennial Report, 1917-1918*, p. 23; Bryan *Daily Eagle*, March 26, 1917.

[23]Bryan *Daily Eagle*, April 6, 1917.

1919, Texas A&M literally mobilized for war and remained on a war footing throughout the period. "It was a time," recall representatives of the graduating Class of 1921, Elbert L. Robinson, Charles W. Sherrell, and Fred R. Brison, "of considerable confusion."[24] But with all of the confusion there was an intense purposefulness and dedication on the part of faculty and students.

Immediately after the declaration of war the College administration excused practically the entire senior class of the College from further academic duties in order to give these young men an opportunity to enter the first officer-training school, located at Camp Funston, Leon Springs, Texas.[25] Seventy-three of the 150 seniors were finally admitted to the officer-training course, in addition to twenty others who did not have senior rating. The first course was to begin May 14.[26] Other students were enlisting directly in the various services. President Bizzell, upon the urging of the junior class, obtained special permission from the War Department for juniors to attend the Officer Training School in Leon Springs. Some twenty-four juniors signed up for the training course by May 18.[27] The student body of the College was being gradually depleted. Those who remained were on a "war footing," for, while class work was being continued, the stress was on drilling and military exercises.[28] "On April 7, 1917, the day after war was declared," reads President Bizzell's report, "the amount of time devoted to military instruction was increased to ten hours per week, besides a material increase in the time devoted to target practice."[29]

The College had planned an impressive commencement exercise for June, the baccalaureate sermon to be given by Reverend Charles M. Sheldon, author of the popular "social gospel" reform book, *In His Steps*. Governor Charles H. Brough of Arkansas was to have delivered the address. But by June virtually no seniors were left on campus. Texas A&M officials then decided to hold commencement at Leon Springs, and did so in one of the most unusual commencements on record.[30] Seniors in good standing, irrespective of their failure to complete classwork for the session, were awarded diplomas.[31] Faculty, as well as students, rapidly mobilized for war.

[24]Interview with Elbert L. Robinson, Charles W. Sherrell, and Fred R. Brison, College Station, Texas, May 14, 1971.

[25]Texas A&M, *Biennial Report, 1917-1918*, p. 23; Bryan *Daily Eagle and Pilot*. June 2, 1917.

[26]Bryan *Daily Eagle*, May 4, 1917.

[27]Bryan *Daily Eagle and Pilot*, May 18, 1917.

[28]*Ibid.*

[29]Texas A&M, *Biennial Report, 1917-1918*, p. 124.

[30]*Ibid.*, p. 23; Bryan *Daily Eagle and Pilot*, May 18, 1917, and June 2, 1917; San Antonio *Express*, June 4, 1917.

[31]Texas A&M, *Biennial Report, 1917-1918*, p. 125.

In May, Bizzell appointed a faculty committee on organization for national defense, of which Bizzell served as chairman. Members included Charles Puryear, Oscar M. Ball, Clarence Ousley, H. M. Eliot, Bonney Youngblood, Eugene Peter Humbert, and Frank C. Bolton. Clarence Ousley, director of the Texas Agricultural Extension Service, left in July for Washington, D.C., to serve with the National Food Conservation Campaign, as Assistant Secretary of Agriculture under David Franklin Houston.[32] Thomas O. Walton replaced Ousley as director of the Agricultural Extension Service and as a member of the committee.[33] The local defense committee conducted victory-garden campaigns and a War Savings Stamps drive, and acted as liaison with the authorities in Washington.[34] Numerous members of the faculty resigned to enter the Army, or to go into YMCA work, or to accept civilian government jobs. Many others left the College to accept higher positions in other colleges and universities, opening because of the wartime demand for manpower.[35] One professor, A. B. Ray, a chemist, offered his services without pay to conduct research on chemical warfare.[36] Students and faculty of the A&M College made a total commitment to winning the War.

In September 1917 the College received word from the War Department that it had been selected to give Signal Corps training. An initial detachment of 112 men of Depot Company "K" Signal Corps arrived on campus for training on December 9. The detachment, commanded by Lieutenant M. C. Funston, received its technical training from the staff of the Department of Electrical Engineering. Regular military officers conducted the military training. The Department of Electrical Engineering offered also, under its own auspices, a course in "buzzer practice," or telegraphy, to civilians who wished to volunteer for duty with the Signal Corps. In 1918 the Electrical Engineering Department offered a special course in radio communication for civilian junior and senior engineering students, who could take it as a special option. Most junior and senior engineers took the course, a number going on to the Signal Corps officers-training camp, and accepting commissions. The radio course was further modified in April 1918 to handle 300 Army inductees training for service as radio mechanics with the Air Service. In August 1918 the electrical engineers began training new contingents of radio electricians for the Signal Corps. Frank C. Bolton, with the assistance of

[32]*Ibid.;* Minutes of the Board of Directors, June 29, 1917, III, 216.

[33]Texas A&M, *Biennial Report, 1917-1918,* p. 125.

[34]*Ibid.;* Eugene P. Humbert, "Report of the Committee on Organization for National Defense," Texas A&M, *The Alumni Quarterly,* III (February 1918), pp. 18-19.

[35]*Alumni Quarterly,* III (February 1918), 11-12.

[36]Texas A&M, *Biennial Report, 1917-1918,* p. 125.

O. B. Wooten, directed the radio training schools. Bolton also served as director of War Educational Activities for the College.[37] Many of these trainees
went directly from the A&M campus to overseas assignments, and to posts
along the Texas border where American forces had been engaged against
units of Pancho Villa's army, and where the threat of war appeared to be
imminent.[38]

Bolton attended a conference of college administrators in Washington
on January 11 and 12, 1918, to discuss plans for training mechanics and technicians for the Armed Forces. General John J. ("Black Jack") Pershing had
requested 60,000 trained mechanics and technicians for duty in France — far
in excess of the available supply. Texas A&M anticipated training some 2,500
of these men for duty by October 1, 1918. Following the conference, the
Board of Directors reconfirmed the offer of all College facilities to the government for training men in technical fields.[39]

A more intensified training program began in April 1918, with the
arrival on campus of 320 Army trainees to enroll in a pilot course in practical
auto and motor-truck mechanics conducted by the Department of Agricultural Engineering. Fifteen new instructors were employed, and the Army sent
twenty-five automobiles and ten trucks with parts and equipment to be used
for training purposes. Instruction was offered in five divisions: (1) the motor
division, which taught the "dismantling and assembling of the power plant
of autos, trucks and tractors"; (2) the chassis division, which dealt with the
steering gear, transmission, differential, and wheels; (3) the electrical department, which handled instruction in wiring and firing; (4) the lubrication
division, which worked with vehicle maintenance; and (5) the driving department, which gave operating instructions, including a five-mile "obstacle
course."[40]

By September 1918 the Auto Mechanics Course produced 1,731 mechanics for the Army. In August 1918, 800 students were enrolled in the intense,
sixteen-hour-per-day, eight-week course, taught by thirty-three civilian and

[37]Bryan *Daily Eagle and Pilot*, September 10, 1917, November 14, 1917; Frank C. Bolton,
"With the School of Radio Mechanics," *Alumni Quarterly*, III (May 1918), p. 10; Texas A&M,
Biennial Report, 1917-1918, pp. 126-127.

[38]Frank C. Bolton, "With the School of Radio Mechanics," *Alumni Quarterly*, III (May
1918), p. 10.

[39]Texas A&M, *Biennial Report, 1917-1918*, p. 126; Bryan *Daily Eagle and Pilot*, January 17,
1918; Minutes of the Board of Directors, January 28, 1918, III, 229.

[40]R. A. Andree, "With the School of Auto and Motor Truck Mechanics," *Alumni Quarterly*, III (May 1918), pp. 4-5; Bryan *Daily Eagle and Pilot*, April 30, 1918; Texas A&M, *Biennial Report, 1917-1918*, pp. 38, 127.

thirty-eight military instructors. The pilot course proved so successful at Texas A&M that the Army made plans to establish similar courses in 100 additional schools and colleges.[41]

The establishment by the Signal Corps of a course in meteorology on the Texas A&M campus in May 1918 inaugurated a training program that was unique among all American colleges and universities. The program, designed to train weather observers for the Armed Forces, admitted only college graduates. Dr. Oliver L. Fassig, of the United States Weather Bureau, directed the program. The two-month weather-observers program, in common with the other war courses, required two hours of military drill each day in addition to instruction and lab work.[42]

Military training courses operating on campus in 1918 ranged from auto and radio mechanics to horseshoeing. By September 1918 A&M had trained 3,648 soldiers, considerably in excess of the January projections, which called for training 2,500 men: 1,731 men had completed the course in auto mechanics, 1,305 in signal corps and radio, 338 in meteorology, 82 in machining, 30 in horseshoeing, 56 in blacksmithing, 82 in carpentry, 6 in general mechanics, 12 in surveying, and 6 in topographical drafting.[43]

All of the war training was in addition to the regular academic instruction of the College, which admittedly suffered. The fall term of 1918 in particular differed from previous terms. The students who returned to school "had their minds and heart in the war; the quest for knowledge was forgotten."[44]

It was perhaps just as well that the quest for knowledge was forgotten, for the faculty and program of the College were geared for war, rather than academics. Fred R. Brison, Class of 1921, recalls that "the course of study in 1918 was not what we came to study, but a course of study prescribed by the army people."[45] Charles W. Crawford, with the Class of 1919, who attended summer camp at Fort Sheridan, Illinois, in 1918, returned to the campus for the fall session, and after six weeks of "study" the entire class was called to Camp McArthur, at Waco, Texas, to attend the Central Infantry Officers Training School, preparatory to being sent overseas.[46] They never made it

---

[41]Texas A&M, *Biennial Report, 1917-1918*, pp. 38-39, 128; Bryan *Daily Eagle and Pilot*, June 11, 1918.

[42]Bryan *Daily Eagle and Pilot*, May 25, 1918; Dallas *News*, July 21, 1918.

[43]Texas A&M, *Biennial Report, 1917-1918*, p. 128.

[44]Texas A&M, *Longhorn, 1919*, p. 113.

[45]Interview with Fred R. Brison, College Station, Texas, May 14, 1971.

[46]Interview with Charles W. Crawford, College Station, Texas, March 30, 1971.

overseas, for the Armistice was signed in November. By 1918 regular academic studies had become a secondary consideration.

The Student Army Training Corps (SATC) supplanted the regular Army Reserve Officers Training Program in the fall of 1918. The Student Army Training Corps was open to all men over the age of eighteen who planned to attend college. They were allowed to register with the local draft boards and then were immediately inducted into the Army as privates in the SATC. At school they received Army pay and were subject to military discipline. Qualified students were then selected from the SATC to attend officers' training schools. Had the SATC not been established the academic functions on many college campuses would have virtually ceased, for in September the draft age was lowered to eighteen. After that only boys between the ages of sixteen and eighteen would have been found at Texas A&M. Dean of the College Charles Puryear, Bizzell, and others correctly regarded the SATC as a "boost" to the College during the "dark days" of World War I.[47]

The student body, and the military attachments on campus, fluctuated constantly during the academic year in terms of numbers and personnel. The SATC student received instruction in courses prescribed by a national Committee on Education and Special Training, and local college authorities had little latitude in altering or amending the curricula. The SATC curricula at Texas A&M sought to produce Army officers, chemists, and engineers. Instruction in such subjects as English, history, economics, and government was virtually nonexistent. Intensive training in chemistry and engineering was established in twelve-week courses set up for eight consecutive terms.[48] Under the SATC curricula the student could complete his college training in less than two years.

In October a special naval detachment of the SATC arrived at Texas A&M for studies in certain aspects of electrical and mechanical engineering, preparatory to a more intensive training session at the Naval Steam Engineering school, in Hoboken, New Jersey.[49] When the War ended, all of these programs were abruptly scrapped, and the academic confusion became greater rather than less while the school "demobilized."

Academic studies under the SATC programs were accompanied by

[47]Charles Puryear, "The War and the College," *Alumni Quarterly,* IV (November 1918), pp. 3-4; Bryan *Daily Eagle and Pilot,* August 31, 1918; Texas A&M, *Biennial Report, 1917-1918,* p. 32.

[48]Puryear, "The War and the College," *Alumni Quarterly,* IV (November 1918), pp. 3-4.

[49]Bryan *Daily Eagle and Pilot,* September 19, 1918; *Alumni Quarterly,* IV (November 1918), p. 11.

equally intensive military drills under the supervision of Major Fred W. Zeller, in charge of the SATC program at Texas A&M for the Army. SATC students received eleven hours of military instruction during the first two terms, and six hours a week thereafter.[50] The A&M *Longhorn* reminisced in 1919 that "those were the dark days. Military duties from reveille until taps along with academic studies. . . . It was indeed a problem for mere human beings who require sleep to find sixteen hours a day to devote to military activities and duties."[51] In addition to prescribed duties, the College offered its own required war-aims "course of indoctrination to all students and soldiers in training."[52] One other aspect of wartime "indoctrination" at the College should be mentioned. The Board of Directors required all employees of the College to sign a loyalty oath, and to make a financial pledge to a war campaign fund.[53] There is no indication of any objections being raised from any quarter. Texas A&M was at war, and everyone knew it.

By the summer of 1918 the College found itself in a serious housing crisis precipitated by the steadily increasing number of soldiers on hand, and by virtue of the attraction of the SATC program to young men of draft age. In May 1918 the local Bryan *Daily Eagle and Brazos Pilot* reported that 1,000 soldiers and 700 students were on the A&M campus.[54] As against this total of 1,700, only 1,152 students had been enrolled during the regular session of the previous year, and housing facilities had even then been full.[55] By June it was anticipated that if all students expected for the opening of the 1918-1919 session received accommodations, no room would be left for the military personnel.[56] College officials planned to construct temporary frame barracks for the soldiers. Some relief appeared at the end of June, when part of the Signal Corps training program, that portion relating exclusively to aircraft, was transferred to The University in Austin.[57] But then in August the War Department raised the quota of military trainees for other A&M technical courses to 2,000 men.[58]

[50]*Alumni Quarterly*, IV (November 1918), p. 4; Bryan *Daily Eagle and Pilot*, August 17, 1918.

[51]Texas A&M, *Longhorn*, 1919, p. 114.

[52]Bryan *Daily Eagle*, September 19, 1918.

[53]Bryan *Daily Eagle and Pilot*, June 1, 1918; Minutes of the Board of Directors, May 27, 1918, III, 235.

[54]May 28, 1918.

[55]Texas A&M, *Biennial Report, 1917-1918*, p. 31.

[56]Bryan *Daily Eagle and Pilot*, June 8, 1918.

[57]*Ibid.*, June 22, 1918.

[58]*Ibid.*, August 24, 1918.

The College met the housing crisis by constructing, over a period of several months, nine two-story barracks, 140' × 42'. The buildings were constructed by local labor under the supervision of Walter W. Kraft, superintendent of buildings and grounds for the College. The difference in the cost of the buildings and their depreciated value after the war was to be paid for by the federal government. The College chose temporary construction, by their own craftsmen, in order to avoid contractual delays, delivery problems on materials, and "profiteering" on the government.[59] In addition to the barracks, College Maintenance people, with some aid from military labor, constructed onto the mess hall a frame annex seating 1,300 men. Bernard Sbisa, incidentally, fully met the challenge of feeding twice the number the College ordinarily fed. Two quartermaster buildings, an auto-mechanics building, a forge shop, an instructors' quarters, an officers' quarters, a quarters for mess-hall servants, a canteen for the enlisted men, a storage-battery building, and a carpenter shop were all built within a twelve-month period.[60]

Facilities still remained cramped. The unanticipated arrival of many soldiers at College Station with their wives and families created serious difficulties and personal hardships. One dormitory was set aside on campus for soldiers' wives, while the soldiers lived in the barracks. The wives were allowed to eat in the mess hall with their husbands for sixty cents a day. President Bizzell appealed to the citizens of Bryan to help find accommodations for military families and for new instructors and their families. He appealed especially to the Woman's Club of Bryan for assistance. Bizzell also announced that in the future military wives would be discouraged from coming to College Station with their husbands, but at the time it had been a completely unexpected development. Bizzell also reprimanded local citizens who were raising rents charged College personnel. Bizzell announced that relations between the College and the town would be terminated if the practice continued.[61]

Bryan citizens responded energetically to Bizzell's appeal. The Business Club and the Woman's Club of Bryan canvassed the town and secured quarters for 100 additional people, a result which unquestionably strained the resources of the town. The clubs also set a scale of fair rental rates which they posted with A&M authorities.[62] Bizzell next resorted to more tents for housing. Tents had been in use on the campus now since 1906. A&M procured

[59]*Ibid.*, June 8, 1918; Texas A&M, *Biennial Report, 1917-1918*, p. 130.

[60]Texas A&M, *Biennial Report, 1917-1918*, p. 130.

[61]Bryan *Daily Eagle and Pilot*, September 5, 1918.

[62]*Ibid.*, September 9, 1918.

eighty additional tents from the Army and set them up in front of the YMCA Building. Each tent housed six men.[63] Finally, in October, some respite came as a result of the Signal Corps decision to close down its entire training facility on the campus, and to transfer its training to Regular Army posts.[64] By this time a new crisis was afoot.

The heavy influx of people onto the campus severely tried the limited hospital facilities of the College. In the spring of 1918 President Bizzell began to urge the War Department to provide funds for additional hospital facilities. Endless delays seemed to occur and, finally, in October 1918, Bizzell, after a trip to Washington to press the matter, succeeded in getting approval for a $55,000 frame hospital building.[65] By then it was almost too late. The influenza epidemic which was sweeping the United States and Army posts in Europe, struck College Station.

A brief recollection by Charles Crawford of flu at A&M more than adequately tells the story:

> At that time there were two wooden barracks — two-story — on the site of where the mechanical engineering shop is now. There were students in those, enlisted men both upstairs and down, and at times there were so many of those fellows who had the flu and were deathly ill that there weren't enough up running around to even wait on them. We had as many as five or six of those fellows dying a night. The local undertaking establishment couldn't keep enough caskets to bury them in, and they would come out with these long wicker baskets about six feet long shaped like the old Egyptian mummies. The hospital was full and running over. They say some people had a walking case, and that's what I had. I've never seen such horrible looking nasal discharges as there were from the men who had the flu, and of course, much of it went into pneumonia and that's what caused a great many deaths. I don't know if I've ever seen an epidemic that was any worse than that flu was at that time.[66]

Life as a student, faculty member, or soldier at A&M during the War was no easy thing.

In 1918 chapel attendance became no longer compulsory. Attendance had been required since 1886. The *Battalion* and the *Longhorn,* the student newspaper and yearbook, respectively, suspended publication for a time but both soon resumed publication. Commencement exercises were not held for the class of 1918, more than half of whose members were on active duty by

[63]Bryan *Daily Eagle,* September 19, 1918.

[64]*Ibid.,* September 24, 1918.

[65]Texas A&M, *Biennial Report, 1917-1918,* p. 129; Bryan *Daily Eagle,* October 10, 1918.

[66]Interview with Charles W. Crawford, March 30, 1971, College Station, Texas.

the time the semester ended. Seniors who joined the service prior to graduation were eligible to receive an "honor war certificate." Since athletic coaches
were in short supply, the faculty members volunteered for duty. Football continued, although the regular schedule was altered to include Army posts.[67]

One of the by-products of war at A&M was the assignment of the first
woman faculty member to the traditionally all-male college. Mrs. Wanda M.
Farr replaced H. E. Hayden, Jr., as instructor in biology. "Scarcity of available
men made it necessary to select a woman to take the work," reported the
Bryan newspaper, "but she is said to be fit for her position."[68] Mrs. Farr, a
graduate of Ohio State University in 1915, did graduate study at Columbia
University, and taught at Kansas State College before coming to Texas
A&M.[69] While Farr's appointment set a precedent, she has been followed by
very few women instructors over the years.

The War generated a great sense of patriotism, purpose, and fraternity
among Texas A&M faculty, students, and alumni. From "somewhere in
France," on November 10, 1918, the day before the Armistice was signed, a
group of A&M soldiers wrote the editor of the *Alumni Quarterly:*

Dear Brother Alumnus:

If you could look in on us tonight and forget where we were you might easily imagine it a gathering of some of the old boys in the College Mess, except that
our uniforms are of olive drab instead of cadet blue. The cloth is as white, the silver
as gleaming and the food as good as at some of the special spreads that Bernard Sbisa
used to set for us. In fact, the atmosphere of old A. and M. pervades this high ceiled
dining room in France tonight, and its walls have echoed to a "Chigarro garem" and
to "Rough tough, real tuff" in good old A. and M. style. Possibly the waiters think
we have gone crazy or that perhaps we have heard through some private channel that
the Kaiser has committed suicide. At any rate they do not understand "Zese droll
Americaines" but you would and you'd know how good we feel to be here together.

Most of us are at a big flying field not many kilometers from here, while a
few others are at nearby posts. Some others missed being here by a narrow margin;
for instance "Fanny" Coleman left just a few days ago and though we've not heard,
we hope he has a Hun or so to his credit by now. Lane pulled out last week and took
his tin lid with him, so he must have some important business to attend to. Red
Allen is not many kilometers distant, but were unable to reach him with a notice of
this rather impromptu spread.

We have with us tonight three of our ancient enemies, Lt. Ben Rice, Jr., Lt.

[67]Texas A&M, *Longhorn, 1919,* pp. 118, 152; *Alumni Quarterly,* III (February 1918), pp.
21-22; and IV (November 1918), p. 12; Bryan *Daily Eagle and Pilot,* February 14, 1918; Bryan
Daily Eagle, September 20, 1918.

[68]Bryan *Daily Eagle and Pilot,* February 2, 1918.

[69]*Alumni Quarterly,* III (February 1918), p. 8.

Fred C. Roberts and Lt. Martin of The University of Texas, and they have contributed both to the merriment of the evening and to the zest of the reminiscences, particularly anent football scores and student battles.

Regards to Sergeant Kenny, and to the other Sergeants with him, who we know are keeping up with the 2,000 A. and M. men in the Service, and are turning out new ones all the time.

Now we will pledge A. and M. and you and all our brothers overthere and overhere in the wine of France.

"Hold'em A. and M."

Lieut. C. H. Harrison '12, Lieut. J. M. Kendrick '15, Lieut. W. T. Donoho '13, Captain C. A. Biggers '14, Lieut. Dillon T. Stevens '13, Captain R. B. Pearce '11, Lieut. Martin M. Daugherty '16, Lieut. T. K. Morris '16, Lieut. John Fries '12, Lieut. Quinlan Adams '12, and Lieut. Mark P. Thomas '17.[70]

Texas A&M was justifiably proud of its contributions to the war effort. It had trained thousands of men for the Armed Forces in special fields of service and sent most of its able-bodied men to war. Fully one-half of the men who had graduated from A&M since it was established participated as soldiers in the war. Large numbers of the others entered government service. A report in the New York *Times* of July 14, 1918, indicated that Texas A&M, by March of that year, had a larger percentage of its graduates in service (37.5 percent) than any other college or university in the United States.[71] By September 1, 1918, President Bizzell reported that 49 percent of the all-time graduates of A&M were in military service: "Out of the total of 1472 graduates 702 were enrolled in the army or navy. Six hundred and sixty-eight of this number were commissioned officers; 565 under-graduates were commissioned officers, making a total of 1233 officers who received their military education at this institution."[72] The percentages did not reflect the enlistment of undergraduates and former students, large numbers of whom received direct commissions in the Armed Services.

Of the officers sent by A&M there were 2 brigadier generals, 7 colonels, 12 lieutenant colonels, 52 majors, 173 captains, 456 first lieutenants, and 530 second lieutenants. Five hundred and eighty-four of these men were attached to infantry regiments; 198 were artillery officers; and 195 were with the engineers. The air service

[70]*Ibid.*, IV (February 1919), p. 13. Names of those not signed in full in the letter are: Carter H. Harrison, James M. Kendrick, William Thompson Donoho, Chester Arthur Biggers, Rufus B. Pearce, and Thomas K. Morris.

[71]New York *Times*, July 14, 1918; Bryan *Daily Eagle and Pilot*, July 20, 1918; "Governor William P. Hobby Address to Texas Legislature, January 14, 1919," *Texas House Journal*, 1919, p. 89.

[72]Texas A&M, *Biennial Report, 1917-1918*, pp. 22-24.

drew 116 while the remainder of those listed were with the marine corps, signal corps and staff corps. A number of these men have been decorated for bravery and several have received promotions on the field of battle for heroism and unusual discretion under trying and dangerous conditions.[73]

Forty-nine A&M soldiers died in service.[74] Of these, four received the Croix de Guerre posthumously, six were awarded the Distinguished Service Cross, and two were cited by their commanding officers for personal valor. Major Ike Ashburn, who received severe wounds and later returned to the campus as commandant and secretary to the Board of Directors, also received the Distinguished Service Cross. Lieutenant Andrew Moses, former commandant, emerged from the war a brigadier general.[75]

In the early morning hours of November 11, 1918, College Station residents were aroused by repeated blasts of the power-plant whistle. The Armistice had been signed. The War was over. There was great jubilation, and some regret among those who knew they would never get "over there."[76] In the morning the band gathered and began to play patriotic songs. Soon the entire student body and many soldiers began marching behind the band, pied-piper fashion, the five miles to Bryan. When the thousands arrived in Bryan the city declared a holiday and everyone joined in the celebrations.[77]

Charles W. Crawford recalls that the senior class, most of whom were then in training at Fort McArthur, in Waco, had been working as hard as a bunch of men could work, and had developed one of the most polished military outfits possible. "It took us about a week to realize that the war was over after November 11th, and after we realized that I think that was as sorry a military outfit — just fell apart. We realized that the war was over and we were going to get home. We got checked out of there on the first day of December 1918."[78] It was the same everywhere, even in Europe.

Demobilization was as sudden and chaotic as had been mobilization. Disbanding of the Student Army Training Corps began almost immediately. It was announced on November 27, 1918, that the SATC would be completely demobilized by December 21. Confusion reigned on the A&M cam-

[73]*Ibid.,* 23-24.
[74]See "The Gold Book," *Alumni Quarterly,* IV (August 1919), pp. 1-26; see also Appendix C.
[75]"The Gold Book," *Alumni Quarterly,* IV (August 1919), pp. 1-26; College Station *Reveille,* November 21, 1918, June 14, 1919.
[76]Texas A&M, *Longhorn,* 1919, p. 118.
[77]Interview with Fred R. Brison, May 14, 1971, College Station, Texas.
[78]Interview with Charles W. Crawford, March 30, 1971.

pus. Several students at the time, members of the Class of 1921, recall that from November 11 through December 23, as the SATC dissolved, the students did little. There were hundreds of boys on the A&M campus without any classes.[79] During the War regular academic programs had been almost entirely supplanted by the SATC curricula. The situation now was something like that of a war industry having to convert to peacetime.

After Christmas, President Bizzell announced that classes would be resumed, but that there would be two special terms, the first beginning January 3, and the last ending in late June in order to allow students to get two full terms of work and to complete their annual academic studies.[80] Conditions, in other words, remained somewhat abnormal for the remainder of the academic year.

The fall term of 1919 opened on a more normal basis, but with a distinct difference. Many of the students were veterans; all felt older and more experienced. Texas A&M was changed. It was a war school, with an earned and honorable military reputation. There was greater purpose and dedication, a greater spirit of fraternity, in which the military feature assumed a larger role. On May 4, 1919, the bronze statue of Governor General-President Lawrence Sullivan Ross was unveiled. Ross, in many respects, was the patron saint of the Corps of Cadets. Oak trees were planted on campus to commemorate the war dead. Plans began to be formulated for an Alumni Memorial Stadium to be dedicated to those who had given their lives in World War I. On November 11, 1919, General William S. Scott, formerly commandant of the Corps of Cadets, who left A&M with the ouster of Louis L. McInnis, addressed a general convocation of the faculty and cadets commemorating the first anniversary of Armistice Day. At the convocation, commissions were awarded to all cadet officers for the current year.[81] All of these events were symbolic of the fact that Texas A&M had become in spirit, if not in fact, the "West Point of the Southwest." The tradition of service to the country established by A&M in World War I was more than fulfilled again during World War II.

Still, along with the military, Texas A&M had achieved a higher degree of fulfillment in her technical specialties of agriculture and engineering during the war years. The engineers had proven themselves by their ability to

[79]Interview with Charles W. Sherill, Elbert L. Robinson, and Fred R. Brison, May 14, 1971, College Station, Texas; College Station *Reveille*, November 28, 1918.

[80]Interview with Fred R. Brison, May 14, 1971, College Station, Texas.

[81]Texas A&M, *Annual Report, 1919-1920*, pp. 31, 35-36; *Alumni Quarterly*, III (February 1918), p. 15, and IV (May 1919), pp. 11-12, and V (February 1920), pp. 3-4.

train men. The critical shortage of engineers during the War and in the post-War world provided its own justification for the efforts of the A&M College. The agriculturists also effectively convinced farmers and the general public, perhaps for the first time, of the real necessity for scientific farming information, research, and extension. One of the great marvels of World War I was the enormous increase in production by American farmers.[82]

World War I marked a distinct watershed in the history of the A&M College. New problems and contingencies would arise in the new order in which the College emerged, but overall Texas A&M would maintain a basic continuity with the past, for the new American society which emerged after World War I was a society of producers — of engineers, technicians, scientists, and agriculturists. It was the world for which Texas A&M had been originally designed.

[82]Edwin J. Kyle, "The Agricultural Graduate's Part in the War for Democracy," *Alumni Quarterly*, III (February 1918), pp. 10-12; Texas A&M, *Biennial Report, 1917-1918*, pp. 48-49.

CHAPTER 14

Entering the Modern Age

A CASUAL observer of campus activities at Texas A&M in September 1919 would conclude that academic life was finally returning to the kind of "normalcy" advocated by Republican presidential candidate Warren G. Harding. That conclusion would be wrong. Texas A&M would never again experience the kind of existence it had known before World War I. The changes, however, were subtle — more in the state of mind than in anything physical or tangible. Both the students and the College had assumed a new purposefulness. Many of the old doubts and uncertainties about higher education, and about what the College was doing or trying to do, had been removed.

The veteran, as after every war, "brought back to the college unusual earnestness of purpose and a definite sense of social responsibility."[1] The students of the 1920s had a different outlook on life from that which motivated students of a generation earlier. There had been "a mental shake-up," President William Bennett Bizzell said, which was a product of the War, automobiles, moving pictures, radios, and the marvelous mechanical devices of the modern age:[2]

> Students of this generation are totally unwilling to be nose-led or milk-fed. They demand greater freedom of action and less external direction than the college students of other days. They are less inclined to accept the opinions of their professors as infallible expressions of truths, and more inclined to appraise critically the quality of instruction provided for them.[3]

Under the probing of student dissent the world of academia was beginning to give and stretch a little in the 1920s. New educational theories and approaches were tried, often to the alarm of the traditionalists and laymen. Commenting upon Bizzell's evaluation of the modern college student, the Dallas *News* editorialized that "if a person were of a mind to get alarmed over

---

[1]Texas A&M, *Annual Report, 1919-1920,* p. 3.
[2]Dallas *News,* April 25, 1926.
[3]*Ibid.*

the school situation in colleges and universities of today, he would find more to disturb him in the faculties of these institutions than in their student bodies. For bizarre standards of taste and exoticisms of loyalty," continued the *News*, "the extremes of the extremist faculty men are of more moment for harm than the extravagances of youth among their pupils."[4]

College students, according to Bizzell, faced unusual distractions in these modern times. While a career in college should not be a period of "dig, grind and hard labor," too many diversions "fritter" away the student's time. The greatest diversion of the 1920s appeared to be the automobile, believed by many to be at the root of the new sexual license, changing social values, climbing divorce rates, and otherwise unsettling influences. President Bizzell and the A&M faculty took action against this particular diversion by banning the ownership and use of private automobiles by students. "The faculty is firmly convinced that an automobile consumes a needless amount of the student's time and is otherwise objectionable."[5] The "jellybean" and "flapper" of the 1920s caused college administrators and academic people almost as much agony as did the "hippies" of a later era. For the most part, however, the stereotype "jellybean" was little in evidence at Texas A&M, and the "flapper" was entirely absent. Texas A&M remained an all-male military-oriented school.

Texas A&M, along with the nation in general in the 1920s, was a pool of paradoxes. On the national scene prohibition vied with the speak-easy, isolation contradicted a genuine international involvement, and the Ku Klux Klan, lynchings, and gangsterism confounded a people comfortable in their self-righteousness. The Model A puttered along on roads built for wagons, and airplanes flew in skies previously reserved only for birds. In College Station returning veterans refused to have anything to do with military training and were exempted by President Bizzell from participation in the Corps of Cadets.[6] These same men had given the military program at Texas A&M the reputation of being one of the best in the country, and because of them that program was rapidly expanded in the 1920s.[7]

In the 1920s, too, the public began to make an enormous demand upon the nation's colleges and universities and upon Texas A&M. Student enrollment at A&M in the opening session of 1919 was 50 percent greater than that

[4] *Ibid.*, April 26, 1926.

[5] Dallas *Journal*, September 9, 1922.

[6] William Bennett Bizzell Scrapbook, editorial by Harry T. Warner, "The Agricultural and Mechanical College," clipping with no date and no banner, in William Bennett Bizzell Papers, Texas A&M University Archives.

[7] College Station *Battalion*, May 1, 1919.

of any pre-War year.[8] Enrollment continued to climb at Texas A&M throughout the 1920s and the 1930s.[9] President Bizzell pointed out that for each 250 students added to the main campus, approximately nine additional teachers, one dormitory, one laboratory, and enlarged dining and classroom facilities were required.[10] But these new demands upon higher education were countered by a "widespread sentiment of retrenchment in public spending."[11]

From 1918 through the end of his administration as president of Texas A&M, William Bennett Bizzell repeatedly charged the public and the Texas Legislature with the necessity of enlarging appropriations for higher education. He pointed to the rising cost of living and to the competition of private business and employers for academic people. Without an $80,000 emergency appropriation for salary increases by the called session of the Thirty-sixth Legislature in 1923, Bizzell believed the College would have had to cease operations because of the departure of faculty to higher-paying jobs.[12] "The State," Bizzell informed the Finance and Appropriations Committee of the Legislature in 1923, "must recognize the necessity of increasing appropriations commensurate with increasing attendance."[13] Of the 2,700 college students who had finished high school in 1923, Bizzell announced on another occasion, 900 enrolled in A&M. The College, he said, is growing at the rate of 600 students a year. At the time "there are 300 students sleeping in tents at the College while hundreds of others are crowded into present buildings."[14] Texas A&M, of course, along with all other major colleges and universities, survived the combination of fiscal retrenchment and swelling enrollments following World War I, but survival required great effort. Few college or university presidents of that era made so prolific and impressive a sales pitch for higher education as William Bennett Bizzell. Bizzell outranked all of his predecessors in the office of president of A&M in terms of his ability and his efforts as a public-relations man.

One result of the spiraling costs of higher education was a regeneration of efforts by Texas A&M and The University of Texas to resolve the Endowment Fund problems. Having failed in 1915 to secure approval of a constitutional amendment which would separate Texas A&M and The University of

[8]Texas A&M, *Annual Report, 1919-1920*, p. 5.

[9]See Table 9, p. 583.

[10]Dallas *News*, April 10, 1923.

[11]Austin *Statesman*, January 12, 1925.

[12]Texas A&M, *Biennial Report, 1917-1918*, p. 25; Texas A&M, *Annual Report, 1919-1920*, p. 38.

[13]Austin *Statesman*, April 10, 1923; Dallas *News*, April 10, 1923.

[14]Dallas *News*, April 13, 1923.

Texas and which would provide for a division of the Endowment,[15] both institutions continued to press for a settlement. Texas A&M and The University found their efforts substantially diverted between 1915 and 1917 when a new Battle of the Universities began. This time Texas A&M sat on the sidelines while The University of Texas warred with the executive branch of the state government, specifically with Governor James E. Ferguson. The conflict was somewhat reminiscent of the feud between Governor Oscar Branch Colquitt and A&M President Robert T. Milner in 1913; Milner resigned the presidency in that instance charging that the Governor was trying to run the College.[16] Ferguson's war with The University was much the same, only more bitter and prolonged, and terminated very differently.

In his message to the Thirty-fifth Legislature on January 10, 1917, Ferguson rejected public charges that he was "against higher education." But he added:

. . . when higher education becomes either autocratic or aristocratic in its ways or customs and begins to arrogate to itself an unwarranted superiority over the great masses of the people who make higher education possible, and wants to rule with a college diploma alone, then I am against higher education, and I consider it "book learning" gone to seed.[17]

Ferguson believed that for every dollar spent on higher education by the state three should be spent on the high schools.[18]

Ferguson also clearly believed that the governor should run The State University. He attempted to direct the dismissal of a number of The University of Texas faculty in 1917, and when the Board of Regents refused his directive Ferguson attempted to revamp the Board of Regents. The faculty and president of The University of Texas reacted by petitioning the Legislature for a thorough investigation of all aspects of The University. The Senate obliged and sustained the action of the Board of Regents, and subsequently rejected a number of Ferguson's nominations for membership on the Board of Regents. The legislative, executive, and judicial branches all became involved in the struggle over the control of The University. Meanwhile a joint resolution appeared in the House calling for a constitutional amend-

[15]Harry Yondell Benedict (ed.), *A Source Book of the University of Texas*, 513-516.

[16]"Milner vs. Colquitt Correspondence," Robert Teague Milner Papers, Texas A&M University Archives.

[17]Benedict (ed.), *A Source Book of the University of Texas*, 519; *Texas House Journal, 1917*, pp. 20-21; *Texas Senate Journal, 1917*, pp. 8-9.

[18]*Texas Senate Journal, 1917*, pp. 8-9.

ment to separate Texas A&M and The University.[19] The resolution got lost in the chaos of the four consecutive legislative sessions which followed.

The Thirty-fifth Legislature became almost completely preoccupied with the conflict between Governor Ferguson and The University. On June 2, 1917, Governor Ferguson vetoed the $1,640,000 appropriations bill for The University of Texas and the Medical Branch at Galveston, excepting only a single $3,500 salary for one member of the faculty at Austin.[20] Appropriations to Texas A&M of $860,260 for 1917-1918, and $811,275 for 1918-1919 went unchallenged.[21] Appropriately, perhaps, A&M partisans remained discreetly silent during the ensuing legislative battles. A&M had received good treatment from "Farmer Jim" Ferguson.

Ferguson charged that the per-student cost of The University was exorbitant. He said that the president of The State University was an incompetent and overpaid administrator, and a sectarian preacher, each count disqualifying him from the office he held. He objected to the growth of the fraternity system on The University of Texas campus, which he charged created a "well defined line between wealth and poverty." He accused the faculty of gross irregularities, including such practices as absenting themselves from the state for four to nine months a year while drawing one-half to full salaries. "In addition," he said, "it is well known that there are many professors at the State University drawing around $3,000 a year who are not working fifteen hours a week. A great part of the work is done by instructors of little or no educational attainments, and the dignity of the institution is thereby greatly impaired."[22] Many of Ferguson's accusations have a remarkably contemporary ring.

He charged The University with attempting to do work that could be done better and more efficiently by other institutions. He accused a small clique of the faculty with attempting to control the school irrespective of the authority of the Board of Regents. Ferguson amplified this last remark with a review of events on May 28, 1919, when he was presenting his veto plans to the Board of Regents. As he was reading the paragraph of his communication to the Regents having to do with cliques and clans on the faculty, the student body of The University, led by their band, paraded before his office window; they carried banners, Ferguson said, which proclaimed: "We fight autocracy

[19]Benedict (ed.), *A Source Book of the University of Texas*, 518-529, 554-555; *Texas House Journal, 1917*, pp. 223-224, 329.

[20]Benedict (ed.), *A Source Book of the University of Texas*, 539-546.

[21]William Bennett Bizzell, "College Appropriations," *Alumni Quarterly*, II (May 1917), pp. 2-3.

[22]Benedict (ed.), *A Source Book of the University of Texas*, 539-542.

abroad, can we tolerate it at home?" "We are with the Board of Regents in the opposition to the Governor's unconstitutional demand," and "Kaiserism is a menace abroad and likewise a menace at home." Ferguson charged that the faculty was aware of the slogans and the parade. If they did not actually instruct the students in their march, said Ferguson, then they were still responsible for creating the sentiment and the idea for such a parade as a result of their teaching and influence over the students. If the faculty directed such an activity, Ferguson declared, "then I unhesitatingly declare that the State University should be abolished, and never reopened with faculty who would permit such acts."[23]

Simultaneously, Ferguson revoked the appointment of a member of the Board of Regents who had "openly manifested an utter lack of harmony with the views and purposes of the present administration." A court ruled, however, that Governor Ferguson had no constitutional right of removal.[24]

Texas House Speaker F. O. Fuller, on July 23, 1917, issued a call for the impeachment of Governor Ferguson, alleging that the Governor had violated the Constitution, that he had failed to carry out the mandate of the laws, and that he had misappropriated public funds. "He has charged the faculty [of The University] generally of being grafters, liars and traitors in my judgment without reason." He had substituted his own will for the judgment of the Board of Regents, removed members of the Regents without cause, sought the dismissal of faculty without a hearing and generally sought to impose his own "unbridled will," said the Speaker.[25] Seeing that the Legislature was going to meet anyway, Ferguson, claiming he had nothing to hide, convened the Legislature in special session to consider a new University appropriations bill on August 1, 1917.[26]

The House, during the special session, adopted articles of impeachment against the Governor, and approved an itemized appropriations bill for The University of Texas. The Senate, at the same time, refused two appointments by Governor Ferguson to the Board of Regents. Upon the voting of the impeachment charges Ferguson was suspended from office and Lieutenant Governor William P. Hobby became acting governor. On August 29, Governor Hobby called the Legislature into a third called session. Of the twenty-one charges under which Governor Ferguson was tried, the Senate found him guilty of ten, and on September 25 the Governor was removed from office.[27]

[23]*Ibid.*, 542-544.
[24]*Ibid.*, 546-547.
[25]*Ibid.*, 548-549.
[26]*Ibid.*, 549-550.
[27]*Ibid.*, 552-563.

Hobby continued to function as governor. The Legislature also agreed to conduct an investigation of all institutions of higher education.[28] In February 1918 Hobby convened yet a fourth session of the Thirty-fifth Legislature.[29]

Texas A&M, and indeed The University, were left essentially unscathed but not unaffected by the political chaos. If the proceedings settled anything regarding institutional jurisdiction, they determined that the institutional boards of control should have a greater degree of autonomy. In addition, the Legislature, as opposed to the executive office, confirmed its pre-eminence over the affairs of higher education in Texas.

The lengthy sessions of the Thirty-fifth Legislature had two direct impacts upon Texas A&M, over and above the fiscal appropriations. The Legislature settled, at least for the short term, the problem of having two agricultural and mechanical colleges or systems in Texas, and the Legislature provided for an investigation which produced a very favorable report for the A&M College.

The legislative committee investigating A&M visited the campus in December 1917, and conducted intensive hearings. All of the officers and most of the department heads were called to testify. The report of the committee to the Legislature so pleased A&M administrators that the report was appended to the *Biennial Report* of the College.[30] The Board of Directors officially commended the committee and its findings, and the *Alumni Quarterly* summarized the report for the former students.[31]

"The Agricultural and Mechanical College is in first class condition," reported the committee. Per capita operating costs of the institution were quite reasonable, being $241.12 per year for the entire period 1876-1917. In this period the legislators found that Texas A&M had enrolled 18,501 students, and received total legislative appropriations for improvements and operation of $4,460,943.69. The A&M faculty taught an average of eighteen hours per week, and carried out other assigned duties for a total of a forty-hour work week — exclusive of class preparation and study, which added many additional hours to the work load. The average faculty salary for 1916-1917 was $2,000 for twelve months.[32]

The legislative committee recommendations happily supported most of the announced objectives of A&M administrators: (1) the separation of

[28]*Ibid.*, 557.

[29]*Ibid.*, 563-569.

[30]Texas A&M, *Biennial Report, 1917-1918*, pp. 143-157.

[31]Minutes of the Board of Directors, January 28, 1918, III, 229; *Alumni Quarterly*, III (February 1918), pp. 13-14.

[32]Texas A&M, *Biennial Report, 1917-1918*, pp. 144-145.

Texas A&M from The University; (2) the equitable division of the Permanent University Fund; (3) a special tax for permanent improvements at all the state institutions of higher learning; (4) the concentration of all educational and public-service activities in agriculture at Texas A&M (as opposed to the duplication of such activities by the State Department of Agriculture); and (5) more adequate salaries for officers and teachers of the College. Finally, the committee report made some effort to reject the notion that a rival or coequal agricultural and mechanical college should be established by Texas in conjunction with Texas A&M.[33] The fact was that such an idea was very much in the minds of many West Texans between 1916 and 1923.

Because of the remoteness of College Station and its substantial difference in environment and climate from that of West Texas, which was experiencing something of a population boom during the decade around World War I, West Texans wanted their own college. In 1916 the State Democratic Convention declared for the establishment of a "branch" agricultural and mechanical college west of the ninety-eighth meridian, which would be west of Austin, to serve the needs of West Texas.[34] In 1917 the regular session of the Thirty-fifth Legislature passed an act calling for the location of a West Texas Agricultural and Mechanical College to be located west of the ninety-eighth meridian and north of the twenty-ninth parallel, or approximately to the north of San Antonio and west of Austin. The College was to be a "branch" of Texas A&M and under the direction of the Board of Directors, but unlike John Tarleton Agricultural College, at Stephenville, and Grubbs Vocational College, at Arlington, which were designated as junior colleges, the West Texas Agricultural College would essentially duplicate the curricula at Texas A&M.[35]

A&M supporters opposed the establishment of a "rival" institution, even under the auspices of its own Board. Opposition to the bill, abetted by the controversy over higher education in general, led to the repeal of the act in the first called session of the same Legislature. Bizzell, and the legislative investigating commission of 1917, opposed the creation of a "duplicate" A&M College. "Great as is Texas," read the legislators' report, "we do not feel that this sentiment for increased vocational instruction should ever be interpreted to mean the creation of another State Agricultural and Mechanical College."[36] The committee recommended the establishment of not more than

[33]Minutes of the Board of Directors, January 20, 1918, III, 229; Texas A&M, *Biennial Report, 1917-1918*, pp. 147-153.

[34]Texas A&M, *Biennial Report, 1917-1918*, p. 150.

[35]*Ibid.*, 16.

[36]*Ibid.*, 16, 151.

six branch junior agricultural colleges, to include John Tarleton and Grubbs Vocational College, geographically distributed through the various regions of the state.[37]

The Ferguson controversy and World War I temporarily interrupted the dispute over a West Texas A&M College, but the conflict was soon rekindled. The Democratic Party convention of 1920 again considered calling for a West Texas Agricultural and Mechanical College. The Dalhart *Texan* charged A&M's President Bizzell with being one of the "plotters and schemers" who prevented the convention from making the call for a West Texas college a platform demand. In the Thirty-seventh Legislature, of 1921, the newspaper charged Bizzell with subverting a West Texas College bill by having it amended to require that the College be agricultural, military, and coeducational. Governor Neff was then led to veto the bill, said the journal.[38] Addressing itself to Bizzell, the Dalhart *Texan* reflected the heat being generated over the West Texas College issue:

> Political dictators, educational and otherwise, are not invincible. Texans have a way of making them dismount. When patience ceases to be a virtue they are hurled from power or dismissed from office and this is what will happen to the Bryan dictator some fine day. He, too, is riding for a fall. West Texans are coming into their own some day regardless of the plotting of the Bizzells or his south Texas lieutenants.[39]

In 1922 the State Democratic Party incorporated a plank in its platform calling for a "branch agricultural college in West Texas." West Texans, and some East Texans too, as indicated by the Waco *Times Herald*, believed that "every tub should stand on its own bottom," that is, West Texas or any other area of the state should have its own institution "unhampered." The Waco newspaper pointedly remarked that it would also be well for Texas A&M to be independent of The University of Texas.[40] The editor was in effect saying to the A&M College that it should do unto others as it would have them do unto it. For Texas A&M had only recently failed, once again, to have itself separated from The University of Texas.

The confusion of the Thirty-fifth Legislature's sessions having ended with the impeachment of James Edward Ferguson, Lieutenant Governor William Pettus Hobby continued as acting governor, and then in 1918 was

[37] *Ibid.*, 151.

[38] Dalhart *Texan*, April 15, 1921.

[39] *Ibid.*

[40] Waco *Times Herald*, September 11, 1922; see also the numerous clippings in the Bizzell Scrapbooks, William Bennett Bizzell Papers, Texas A&M University Archives, regarding the West Texas College controversy.

elected governor in his own right. Governor Hobby favored the separation of the two state institutions and sought a settlement of the long-standing "identity crisis." In December 1918 he called a meeting of the two governing boards. He desired help, he told them, in framing legislation to settle the "University" problem. He viewed the disposition of the University lands as "the great question at issue," and he wanted to see these lands made a more "liquid asset" for the benefit of the two schools. President Bizzell of A&M and President Robert E. Vinson of The University followed the Governor in addressing the board members. The College and University officers agreed to more conferences, and each board appointed a committee to work directly with the Governor in framing legislation.[41]

In January 1919 the Regents and Board of Directors met again in joint session in the offices of University of Texas President Vinson. The boards adopted an agreement which would provide for a permanent settlement of their age-old differences:

1) The two institutions should be separated.
2) The endowment lands should be taken over by the state for $10 million to be divided between Texas A&M and The University on the basis of one-third to A&M, and two-thirds to Texas University.
3) The $10 million would be funded by a bond issue, the bonds to be invested in the Permanent Fund of each institution.
4) Each school in turn could issue bonds backed by its Permanent Fund for permanent improvements only.
5) The State would reserve mineral rights on these lands and distribute royalties to each institution.
6) The constitutional prohibition preventing the Legislature from appropriating money for permanent improvements at The University should be removed.
7) The constitutional amendment removing the prohibition should also define the general character and work of each institution.
8) The Texas State School of Mines [established by the Legislature at El Paso in 1917] should be made a branch of The University of Texas.
9) Legislation should be prepared to submit the necessary constitutional changes to the people.
10) The governor's attention should be called to the need for a fixed tax to support higher education.[42]

On March 18, 1919, the state Legislature approved a resolution calling for all of the items agreed to by the boards, except the "fixed tax." Several

[41]Minutes of the Board of Directors, December 27, 1918, III, 243, 244.
[42]*Ibid.*, January 29, 1919, III, 246-250.

other problems were to be "cleaned up" by the proposed constitutional amendment. The amendment, in addition to making Texas A&M, The University, and the College of Industrial Arts for Women separate and independent institutions, would make the School of Mines and the Texas State Medical College branches of The University. Prairie View Normal and Industrial College would be a constitutional branch of Texas A&M. The proposed amendment granted authority to the Legislature to make appropriations for "maintenance and development" to all state institutions.[43] The amendment, to be presented to the electorate in November 1919, was simply a more polished version of what had been presented to voters in 1915.

Bizzell, and representatives from The University of Texas, went on speaking tours of the state to promote the educational amendment. Bizzell spoke in San Antonio and in a number of places in Southwest Texas, then went to North Texas and spoke at McKinney, Sherman, Denison, and Denton, among other stops. Bizzell reported upon his return to College Station that he found "no opposition" to the amendment, but a "very great indifference."[44] Early returns from the election showed a slight statewide majority for the amendment, but late returns from the rural areas ran steadily against the separation proposal. As a general rule the cities favored the constitutional amendment, but the more conservative and less involved rural voters opposed.[45] Once again the amendment lost, and Texas A&M-University relations were back to where they had been from the beginning. Nonetheless, over the preceding decade or so a very clear consensus had emerged among educators, legislators, and the concerned public as to how the two institutions should share in the state endowments for higher education. That, of course, was the crux of the matter, and in little more than a decade, that issue would be settled.

Thus once again A&M seemed to be frustrated in its efforts for separation, just as West Texas was seemingly frustrated in its desires to establish an independent agricultural and mechanical college. West Texas, however, soon obtained its college. The interest of A&M supporters in preventing the creation of a rival A&M College in Texas resulted in diluting the legislative charges for a new college, happily to the advantage of the new institution. Rather than being confined to strict agricultural and mechanical subjects, the new college, to be named Texas Technological College, was given a broad

[43]*General Laws of Texas, 1919*, pp. 350-354. See also *Texas Senate Journal, 1919*, p. 998; *Alumni Quarterly*, IV (February 1919), p. 6; Bryan *Daily Eagle*, March 19, 1919; Austin *Statesman*, November 3, 1919.

[44]Bryan *Daily Eagle*, November 3, 1919.

[45]*Ibid.*, November 5, 6, 1919.

educational mandate. Specifically, the new college for West Texas created by legislation of February 10, 1923, was to give "thorough instruction in technology and textile engineering." But it was also to offer the "usual college courses given in standard senior colleges of the first class." These would include courses in "the arts and sciences, physical, social, political, pure and applied" as would lead to the degrees of "bachelor of science, bachelor of arts, bachelor of literature, bachelor of technology and any and all degress given by colleges of the first class." The creating legislation added, for good measure, that the school should "give instruction in technological manufacturing, and agricultural pursuits and domestic husbandry and home economics." The college would have its own independent board of directors.[46] Texas Tech could then develop into almost anything it liked, including a university.

Texas A&M's President Bizzell had a hand in locating Texas Technological College. A locating board, which included the presidents of Texas A&M, The University of Texas, and the College of Industrial Arts, with two other state officials, were charged by the Legislature to locate the college north of the twenty-ninth parallel and west of the ninety-eighth meridian.[47] Bizzell, therefore, by fostering upon the new college a broad academic base, and by aiding in its location at Lubbock, helped lay the foundations for the development of what is now Texas Tech University. Bizzell had also a more direct, and perhaps a more salutary, hand in the organization and development of two other Texas colleges, Grubbs Vocational School (now University of Texas — Arlington) and John Tarleton Agricultural College (now Tarleton State College). That story is reserved for a later chapter.

Although quite competent as a public-relations man and a lobbyist, William B. Bizzell was even more able in the day-to-day administrative affairs of the College. If A&M were to emerge from the chrysalis and become a full-winged thing it had to establish its academic credentials on a national as well as a local basis. Prior to World War I, Texas A&M's national academic standing was virtually nonexistent, at least judging by the Eighth Annual Report of the Carnegie Foundation for the Advancement of Teaching (1914), which had some hard things to say about the institution in College Station:

It is a display of great leniency to term the Agricultural and Mechanical College of Texas an institution of higher education at all. The announcements of its requirements for admission, with the utmost latitude of interpretation, can be made to cover only one year of a high school course, and even this meagre amount of preliminary education is not demanded in full of agricultural students. It is pathetic that

[46]*General Laws of Texas, 1923*, pp. 32-35.
[47]*Ibid.*

the great state of Texas should lead boys to think that they are really studying civil, mechanical, and electrical engineering, and even architectural engineering, upon such a slender equipment of previous training.[18]

Before the report had been published, however, A&M had already made some efforts to overcome the recognized problem of low admission standards. Effective for the 1914-1915 session admission to A&M required fourteen high-school units; beginning September 1915 graduation from an "acceptable" secondary school was required.[49] Dean Charles Puryear, with President Bizzell, worked vigorously and effectively to raise the academic standards of the College. In 1919 admission requirements were made stronger by requiring fifteen high-school units (a unit would be the completion of a designated course of study recognized as part of the basic high-school curricula by the State Department of Education) for full admission to the College. Graduates from fully accredited schools would be admitted on the basis of their diplomas. Students with thirteen units and those who passed the regular entrance examination could be admitted on a conditional basis.[50]

Bizzell and Puryear also worked to raise teaching standards in the College. In 1918 Dean of the College Charles Puryear was appointed to head up a committee, including Dean of Engineering James C. Nagle, and Dean of Agriculture Edwin J. Kyle, to make a survey of teaching standards in the College. Consideration was given to the ability of teachers in the classroom in several competencies: (a) to conduct classes skillfully in theory and practice; (b) to get the most out of the time consumed in class recitation or laboratory; and (c) to maintain interest and attention. Secondly, attention was given to textbooks, including their suitability, use, and effectiveness in student preparation. Each instructor in the College was observed in unannounced visits by the committee. Although it might correctly be anticipated that a committee with the composition of this one would report favorably on A&M teaching standards and abilities, Bizzell regarded it as a successful device for focusing faculty attention on the necessity of maintaining and raising academic standards at the College.[51]

The push for academic excellence was also being made in other less direct ways. Under the theory that sound bodies help build sound minds (which has made physical education an integral aspect of modern academic

[48]Annual Report of the President Pro Tempore, May 30, 1914, College Station, Texas, unpublished typescript in Texas A&M University Archives, College Station, Texas.

[49]Texas A&M, *Biennial Report, 1915-1916*, p. 33.

[50]College Station *Battalion*, June 5, 1919.

[51]Texas A&M, *Biennial Report, 1917-1918*, pp. 18-19.

life in America) Texas A&M initiated compulsory physical training of three hours per week for all first-year students beginning in September 1919.[52] By 1924 A&M had a regular academic Department of Physical Education under the direction of Dana X. Bible.[53]

A "citizenship" course, offered under the auspices of the Department of History, was added to the catalogue as a result of the wartime indoctrination courses. The course was designed to "impress the student with what is distinctive in our Americanism." J. F. McDonald, chairman of the Department of History, taught the course.[54] Course offerings and fields of study expanded rapidly in the years immediately following World War I. The academic structure also began to reflect the changing times.

The basic fields of study offered by Texas A&M before World War I included agriculture, mechanical engineering, civil engineering, textile engineering, electrical engineering, chemical engineering, architecture, and veterinary medicine. By 1920 fields in industrial education, agricultural administration, and agricultural engineering had been added.[55] In addition to these regular courses of study A&M offered graduate instruction leading to the Master of Science in agriculture, agricultural education, architecture, civil engineering, electrical engineering, and mechanical engineering. Two-year courses of study without a degree were offered in agriculture, textile engineering, agricultural engineering, and engineering. An eight-week short course in "autos and tractors," like the citizenship course, was a product of the College's wartime experiences and remained in the catalogue.[56] Texas A&M emerged from World War I more definitively a technical and vocational school than when it had entered the War. The rapidly broadening curricula, however, began to provide a leavening influence.

In 1920 the College maintained twenty-nine academic departments administered variously by the School of Engineering, the School of Agriculture, the School of Veterinary Medicine, or in the case of the "service departments" such as history, English, and mathematics, by the dean of the College. The academic structure of the College, by schools, departments and departmental heads in 1920, is as follows:[57]

School of Agriculture
Edwin Jackson Kyle, Dean

[52]College Station *Battalion,* June 5, 1919.
[53]Texas A&M, *Catalogue, 1924-1925,* p. 224.
[54]Bryan *Daily Eagle,* September 1, 1919.
[55]Texas A&M, *Catalogue, 1920-1921,* p. 87.
[56]*Ibid.*
[57]*Ibid.,* pp. 139-237.

Agricultural Engineering   Daniels Scoates, Chairman
Agronomy   James Oscar Morgan, Chairman
Animal Husbandry   George S. Templeton, Chairman
Biology   Oscar M. Ball, Chairman
Dairy Husbandry   Robert L. Pou, Chairman
Entomology   Sherman W. Bilsing, Chairman
Farm Management   P. K. Whelpton, Chairman
Forestry   Eric O. Siecke, Chairman
Horticulture   Edwin J. Kyle, Chairman
Rural Social Science   W. E. Garnett, Chairman

School of Engineering
James C. Nagle, Dean

Architecture and Architectural
   Engineering   Edwin Bruce LaRoche, Chairman
Chemistry and Chemical
   Engineering   Charles C. Hedges, Chairman
Civil Engineering   James C. Nagle, Chairman
Drawing   Alva Mitchell, Chairman
Electrical Engineering   Frank C. Bolton, Chairman
Mechanical Engineering   Emil J. Fermier, Chairman
Textile Engineering   John B. Bagley, Chairman
Vocational Teaching   Martin Luther Hayes, Chairman

School of Veterinary Medicine
Mark Francis, Dean

Veterinary Anatomy   Mark Francis, Chairman
Veterinary Medicine and
   Surgery   Ross P. Marsteller, Chairman
Veterinary Pathology   Emmet W. Price, Chairman
Veterinary Physiology and
   Pharmacology   Solon N. Blackberg, Chairman

Dean of the College
Charles Puryear

Economics   Frederick B. Clark
English   Charles P. Fountain
History   J. F. McDonald
Mathematics   Charles Puryear
Military Science   Louis R. Dougherty
Modern Languages   Charles Boyle Campbell, Sr.

New departments of agricultural economics, under Chairman F. A. Buechel, and geology, under E. Oscar Randolph, were added in 1922 and reflected extensive new course additions to the catalogue.[58] Charles Perkins Fountain, chairman of the Department of English, who had taught at A&M since 1890, died Christmas morning, 1921, and was replaced by David Brooks Cofer. In 1923 the Department of Agricultural Education was organized with Charles H. Winkler as head. Eugene Peter Humbert headed the new Department of Genetics. Poultry Husbandry, separated out of Animal Husbandry, was chaired by Duncan H. Reid. The Department of Rural Social Science was changed to Rural Sociology, with W. E. Garnett continuing as chairman. Charles Marten replaced Martin L. Hayes in vocational teaching, and the department was renamed Industrial Education.[59] During the next year, 1924, many structural changes occurred.

The Directors approved the creation of the School of Vocational Teaching, originally recommended by President Bizzell in 1918.[60] This development was in direct response to federal Smith-Hughes legislation, which provided matching federal funds for teacher training in agriculture, and in the trades and industries. The act required that provisions be made for practice teaching and for practical training. Bizzell stressed that this work in no way duplicated or conflicted with regular normal-school training.[61] The new school, under the direction of Dean Charles H. Winkler, offered studies in agricultural education, industrial education, and rural education.[62]

The organization of the School of Vocational Teaching, but more especially the creation of the School of Arts and Sciences in June 1924, marked the beginning of a broadening of the A&M academic orientation away from the pure applied technical training in agriculture and engineering, which had been the dominant feature of the College since the 1890s. The new development, however, was slow and has become significant only since World War II. The new School of Arts and Sciences offered a course of study in liberal arts and one in science. The explanation for the new School in the catalogue was to give "undecided" students an opportunity for a broad education, and to prepare students for advanced work in law and medicine and for teaching careers in selected fields.[63]

[58]*Ibid.,* 1922-1923, pp. 142, 204; Texas A&M, *Annual Report, 1921-1922,* p. 11.

[59]Texas A&M, *Catalogue, 1923-1924,* pp. 149, 197, 209, 229.

[60]*Ibid.,* 1924-1925, p. 91; Texas A&M, *Biennial Report, 1917-1918,* pp. 28-29.

[61]Texas A&M, *Biennial Report, 1917-1918,* pp. 28-29.

[62]Texas A&M, *Catalogue, 1924-1925,* p. 91.

[63]*Ibid.,* 83; Texas A&M, *Annual Report, 1925-1926,* p. 10.

Charles E. Friley, who had been serving as College registrar since 1911 (the position called secretary of the College, 1911-1913, then registrar), became dean of the new School. Born in Ruston, Louisiana, Friley moved to Bryan, Texas, with his family and attended the Bryan public schools. He completed a two-year course at Sam Houston State Teachers' College in 1905, studied at Baylor University for two years, and taught in the public schools from 1907 to 1910. In 1910 he enrolled for courses at Texas A&M and the next year was made secretary or registrar. He continued studies at A&M from time to time and in 1919 received a B.S. in Agricultural Education. He then took advanced studies at Columbia University in the summers and received his M.A. in 1923 from Columbia. Friley, a very meticulous man who assisted and supported Bizzell in numerous ways, remained head of the School of Liberal Arts until 1932, when he accepted a similar position at Iowa State College, in Ames.[64] He subsequently became president of Iowa State and presided over it during a period of tremendous growth and development.

Also indicative of Texas A&M's broadening educational role is the establishment of the Graduate School in 1924. Prior to this time graduate instruction was directed by the general faculty through a special committee on graduate instruction. The new Graduate School offered instruction leading to the degree of Master of Science in agricultural administration, agricultural education, agricultural engineering, agriculture, architecture, chemical engineering, civil engineering, electrical engineering, mechanical engineering, rural education, veterinary medicine, and science. Charles Puryear, who continued to function as dean of the College and chairman of the Department of Mathematics, also served as the first dean of the Graduate School.[65]

Of the 117 faculty members during the session 1919-1920, 15 held a doctor's degree, 45 a master's degree, and 53 a bachelor's degree. Twenty held a terminal bachelor's degree from Texas A&M.[66] Numerous additions to the faculty were made in 1920, when student enrollment began growing rapidly. In 1920 the teaching staff comprised 159 persons, including 43 full professors, 41 associate professors, 31 assistant professors, 37 instructors, and 7 assistant instructors. Excluding 13 military-science personnel, 8 vocational-education instructors who taught no college classes, and 5 special teachers unassigned to any academic department, of the 133 regular faculty 59 had the bachelor's degree, 50 the master's degree or a professional equivalent, and 10

[64]Charles E. Friley Biographical Papers, Texas A&M University Archives, College Station, Texas.

[65]Texas A&M, *Annual Report, 1925-1926*, pp. 15-16.

[66]*Ibid.*, *1919-1920*, pp. 14-17.

the doctor's degree. Fourteen teachers had no academic degree.[67] By 1925 A&M retained 183 teaching-staff members, with 20 holding the doctorate, 77 the master's, 71 the bachelor's, and 11 no academic degree.[68]

The rapid faculty enlargement reflected rising student enrollments between 1919 and 1925 (see table 3).

Table 3.
Texas A&M Enrollment, 1919-1925

Year	Annual Total	Regular Session
1919-1920	2,647	1,960
1920-1921	3,088	1,991
1921-1922	2,876	1,625
1922-1923	3,482	1,829
1923-1924	3,819	1,023
1924-1925	4,761	2,172

Sources: Texas A&M, *Bulletin of Information*, Session 1925-1926, *Bulletin of the Agricultural and Mechanical College* II (March 1925), p. 9; Texas A&M, *Annual Report, 1929-1930*, pp. 9-10.

The total enrollment figures include regular-session and summer-session figures. Regular-session enrollment actually did not increase at such spectacular rates. Much of enrollment increase can be attributed to the large summer attendance at the Farmers' Short Courses, which, for example, comprised 2,008 "students" in 1925.[69]

Generally the physical growth of the A&M College in the postwar era was accompanied by an academic broadening and improvement in standards. Indeed, in the decade following the unfavorable report of the Carnegie Foundation for the Advancement of Teaching (1914), Texas A&M's academic standing rose measurably. In 1924 the Southern Association of Colleges and Schools granted the College full academic accreditation.[70] This academic achievement marks the capstone of William Bennett Bizzell's administration. Academically the Texas A&M College of 1924 was a far different thing from the College of 1914.

The building boom on campus during and immediately following

[67]*Ibid., 1920-1921*, pp. 16-20.

[68]*Ibid., 1925-1926*, p. 14.

[69]Texas A&M, *Bulletin of Information, Session 1925-1926, Bulletin of the Agricultural and Mechanical College*, 3rd ser., II (March 1925), p. 9; *Annual Report*, 1929-1930, pp. 9-10.

[70]Virginia Darnell, assistant executive secretary, Commission on Colleges, Southern Association of Colleges and Schools, Atlanta, Georgia, to H. L. Heaton, dean of Admissions and Records, Texas A&M University, College Station, October 19, 1970, in files of Admissions and Records, Texas A&M University.

World War I was deflated by a slow-down in new construction during the first half of the 1920s. The Legislature remained in a mood of fiscal retrenchment. In 1920 a Military Science Building and the Physics Building were erected. After several frustrated attempts Dean Edwin J. Kyle succeeded in getting an appropriation for his long-cherished agriculture building. The quarter-of-a-million-dollar, gray-brick, stone-trimmed building, completed in the summer of 1922, long remained the pride of the School of Agriculture.[71] A mechanical-engineering laboratory covering forty-five thousand square feet, also completed in 1922, provided long-needed facilities.[72] The old Shirley Hotel and the Annex were purchased by the College from its private owners for use as additional housing.[73] The Assembly Hall, capable of seating 2,000 cadets, was completed in 1923, as was a dairy-judging building. In that same year the College constructed a hundred frame houses approximately 16′ × 16′ capable of accommodating two or three students each. The Extension Service building was opened to use in 1924.[74]

In the spring of 1919 the Alumni Association pushed for the development of a memorial athletic stadium to honor A&M's war dead, on Kyle Field, the area set aside by the Directors for athletic purposes and later named in honor of Dean Edwin Jackson Kyle. Dedication of the new stadium, which had steel bleachers capable of seating 10,000 spectators, was to occur in May 1920,[75] but the building-fund campaign foundered before construction began. The College began construction of the existing Kyle Field Stadium in 1927. In 1924, at a cost of $150,000, the College constructed the Memorial Gymnasium, with a seating capacity for 3,500 and with classrooms, lockers, baths, and all modern conveniences. Kyle Field also contained a baseball field with a grandstand for 4,000 spectators, a quarter-mile circular track, and a 200-yard straight-a-way track, plus several tennis courts and intramural fields.[76] Several other memorials, in addition to the gymnasium, were constructed on campus. Trees were planted in March 1920 to commemorate the war dead.[77] The memorial statue of Lawrence Sullivan Ross, sculpted by

[71]Texas A&M, *Annual Report, 1920-1921*, pp. 29-32; *Annual Report, 1921-1922*, pp. 31-32; E. J. Kyle, "The Need for an Agricultural Building at the Agricultural and Mechanical College of Texas," *Alumni Quarterly*, IV (February 1919), pp. 14-15.

[72]Texas A&M, *Annual Report, 1920-1921*, p. 32; *Annual Report, 1921-1922*, p. 31.

[73]Texas A&M, *Annual Report, 1921-1922*, p. 32.

[74]Texas A&M, *Catalogue, 1924-1925*, pp. 46-48.

[75]"The Alumni Memorial Stadium," *Alumni Quarterly*, V (February 1920), pp. 3-4.

[76]Texas A&M, *Bulletin of Information, Session 1925-1926, Bulletin of the Agricultural and Mechanical College*, 3rd ser., II (March 1925), p. 15.

[77]Texas A&M, *Annual Report, 1919-1920*, p. 36.

Pompeo Coppini under a legislative grant, was dedicated on May 4, 1919.[78]

Important building construction completed in 1925 included the Aggieland Inn, designed as a hotel for the use of guests of the College, a critical need now that the old Shirley Hotel no longer operated. A new exchange store opened, and a graduate dormitory also began service in 1925.[79] By 1925 much of what would be the modern Texas A&M, academically and physically, had come into being. Even the new cadet uniform, as it appeared in 1920, would remain little changed over the next half-century.

Despite its newness, the modern Texas A&M College was firmly rooted in its old academic precepts and purposes. It was first and foremost an agricultural and mechanical college. For at least the next thirty years the story of A&M can best be explained as an expansion and development of the institutional foundations existing in 1925.

Another tradition which survived into the modern era was the practice of hazing, which had caused considerable turmoil over the preceding several decades. In 1921, and again in 1924, a public furor over hazing practices at Texas A&M swept the state. After the first incidence the Senate conducted during February and March 1921 investigations lasting over a period of days. The investigating committee reported that hazing was conducted "in a spirit of mischief or to perpetuate a college tradition." Freshmen and sophomores in particular were responsible, and both classes, the senators found, conspired to withhold from disciplinary authorities any information regarding such practices. Hazing, in other words, had become a part of the "private life" of the Corps of Cadets. The most offensive practice the committee found was that of whipping the freshman, or "fish," a practice, it must be recalled, which was indeed ancient at the A&M College. The investigators called upon the students, parents, and alumni to help suppress the more undesirable forms of hazing.[80] College administrators responded with fresh efforts to discourage hazing, including the submission to the student body of an antihazing pledge.[81]

By 1924, however, new incidents had aroused public ire anew. Governor Pat M. Neff received complaints, and the press picked up the story, greatly exaggerated. The word began circulating that a student at Texas A&M had died from being forced to drink tobacco juice. The charges were totally

[78]"Memorial to Governor Ross," *Alumni Quarterly*, III (February 1918), p. 15; "Lawrence Sullivan Ross Statue Unveiled," *Alumni Quarterly*, IV (May 1919), pp. 11-12.

[79]Texas A&M, *Catalogue, 1925-1926*, pp. 39-40.

[80]Texas A&M, *Annual Report, 1920-1921*, pp. 22-24.

[81]*Ibid.*

untrue, but the practice of hazing continued to bring the College into disrepute.[82]

Some of what was going on at the College was indeed hazing, but many of the "underground activities" can better be explained simply as part of the "private life" of the Corps of Cadets. This life is exemplified in the writings of John O. Pasco's *Fish Sergeant,* which by means of fictitious letters home trace the life of a fish through his initiation into the mysteries of becoming an "Aggie."[83] Rather than encouraging brutality, this kind of life generated a "spirit of love, loyalty and devotion" for the school and for the Corps of Cadets among students,[84] Senate investigators concluded in 1921. To be sure, there were those who did not fit the Aggie stereotype. The loss of many of these students and the very existence of a stereotype hurt the College by curtailing the breadth of its academic and character development.

William Bennett Bizzell worked with great vigor through his numerous public speeches and writings to instill throughout the whole state of Texas a strong dedication to the idea of public education and to higher education. His appeals ranged from lofty Jeffersonian philosophy to "candy and tobacco" practicality. American democracy, Bizzell argued, depended largely upon wholehearted support of American educational institutions. Bizzell pointed out that in 1923 Texans spent as much for candy and chewing gum as they spent to educate Texas children, and twice that amount for tobacco.[85] "Civilization costs something," Bizzell told a Grayson County audience.[86] Society must provide equal educational opportunities, he told other gatherings, but he opposed the implementation of state tuition charges as prone to create an "aristocracy of education."[87] While he constantly worked for larger public spending on educational institutions, Bizzell also counseled efficiency and economy in the operation of schools. He advocated longer school sessions and extended summer programs in order to utilize more effectively the facilities of public-school systems.[88]

Bizzell traced the advent of the land-grant college system back to John Milton and his "Tractate on Education," published in 1644, in which Milton

[82]San Antonio *Light,* September 29, 1924; Dallas *News,* March 26, 1924; *Farm and Ranch,* February 2, 1924; see also William Bennett Bizzell Scrapbooks, Texas A&M University Archives.

[83]John O. Pasco, *Fish Sergeant* (College Station, Texas 1940), pp. 1-144.

[84]Texas A&M, *Annual Report, 1920-1921,* p. 23.

[85]Beaumont *Daily Journal,* November 7, 1923; Houston *Chronicle,* June 11, 1923.

[86]Sherman *Daily News,* August 1, 1924.

[87]*Ibid.;* Beaumont *Enterprise,* August 17, 1922; Dallas *News,* June 11, 1924.

[88]Houston *Chronicle,* June 11, 1924.

wrote: "I call, therefore, a complete and generous education, that which fits a man to perform justly, skillfully and magnanimously all the offices both private and public, of peace and war." Milton's statement, and Senator Justin S. Morrill's amplification of that idea, were stated as the Educational Objectives of the Agricultural and Mechanical College of Texas in 1925:

THE EDUCATIONAL OBJECTIVE OF
THE AGRICULTURAL AND MECHANICAL COLLEGE OF TEXAS

This statement from Milton's famous Tractate on Education was the inspiration which led Senator Justin S. Morrill of Vermont to conceive and carry to a successful conclusion the Land-Grant and placed them "upon a sure and perpetual foundation, accessible to all, but especially to the sons of toil, where all the needful sciences for the practical vocations of life shall be taught; where neither the higher graces of classical studies, nor the military drill our country so greatly appreciates, will be entirely ignored and where agriculture, the foundation of all present and future prosperity, may look for troops of earnest friends, studying its familiar and recondite economies, and at last elevating it to a higher level, where it may fearlessly invoke comparison with the most advanced standard of the world."[89]

Bizzell saw the land-grant colleges as truly national institutions. He publicly criticized efforts at state control over the agricultural and mechanical colleges as injurious to the land-grant-college idea.[90] The idea of "nationalized" higher education was so far-fetched that few took Bizzell's arguments seriously. Bizzell, of course, would have disliked federal controls over the land-grant colleges. He simply used the idea as a lever to reduce burdensome state controls.

Bizzell published numerous substantive works while president of A&M. Two of his more notable works were *An Introduction to the Study of Economics* (1923), written in cooperation with Walter Marshall William Splawn, and *Rural Texas*, published in 1924.[91] He never hesitated to speak his mind forthrightly on any and all subjects. While he incurred some enmity, William Bennett Bizzell left Texas A&M in 1925 one of the most respected educators in Texas history.

In January 1925 Texas A&M celebrated Bizzell's decade of service to the College. Testimonial dinners and congratulations poured in from all over Texas.[92] In May, Bizzell received an attractive offer from the University of

[89]Dallas *Morning News*, December 2, 1922; *Bulletin of Information, Session 1925-1926, Bulletin of the Agricultural and Mechanical College of Texas*, 3rd ser., 11 (March 1925), p. 3.

[90]Houston *Dispatch*, November 16, 1924.

[91]*Introduction to the Study of Economics* (New York: Ginn and Company, 1923), 386 pp.; *Rural Texas* (New York: Macmillan Company, 1924), 477 pp.

[92]Dallas *News*, January 8, 1925; Semiweekly *Farm News*, January 13, 1925; see also clippings in William Bennett Bizzell Scrapbook, Texas A&M University Archives.

Oklahoma to become its new head. On June 1, 1925, Bizzell submitted his resignation to the Board of Directors of Texas A&M College, to be effective not later than September 1, 1925. His letter of resignation pointed to his achievements while president of Texas A&M and expressed his gratitude for the support of so many, and his regrets at leaving. But Bizzell also noted that the "retrenchment in public expenditures" in Texas "presented problems of great difficulty."[93] That, and what he may have regarded as an unfavorable political climate for higher education in Texas under the administration of Miriam A. Ferguson, the wife of James E. Ferguson, plus the "larger opportunity . . . to serve the cause of education in a more significant way" in Oklahoma, underlay Bizzell's decision to leave. His departure was lamented and the man was recognized and honored throughout the Texas press as a respected educator and a great Texan.[94]

The Board of Directors commended him as a man who "caught a vision of a matchless service to the State and Nation through the threefold organization of the College in its Experiment Station System, Extension Service and College of Resident Instruction." He had been, said the Directors, "a scholarly Christian gentleman, educator, builder, administrator, clear thinking statesman, ideal citizen and friend of men."[95] The Association of Former Students lauded him "as having made a greater contribution to the College than any other man ever connected with the institution."[96] William Bennett Bizzell brought Texas A&M into the modern era, and it was he who defined its contemporary role as being that of teaching, research, and extension.

Whatever Bizzell had been to Texas A&M, and to Texans, he became even more to the University of Oklahoma and to Oklahomans. On August 1, 1941, at the age of sixty-five Bizzell retired after sixteen years as head of the University of Oklahoma, one of its most able and productive presidents,[97] a man who by every measurement must be considered a truly great educator.

During Bizzell's years at Texas A&M the College matured into a full-grown, accepted, and accredited institution. Texas A&M had entered the age for which it was designed. The modern era demanded production — produc-

[93]Minutes of the Board of Directors, IV, June 1, 1925; Dallas *News,* June 3, 1925; Mexia *Daily News,* June 3, 1925; Waco *Times Herald,* June 2, 1925; Palestine *Herald,* June 4, 1925; see also clippings in William Bennett Bizzell Scrapbook, Texas A&M University Archives.

[94]*Ibid.*

[95]Minutes of the Board of Directors, IV, June 2, 1925.

[96]"Resolutions of the Association of Former Students," June 1, 1925, in William Bennett Bizzell Papers, Texas A&M University Archives.

[97]Kansas City (Missouri) *Times,* July 7, 1941; Roy Gittinger, *The University of Oklahoma, 1892-1942,* pp. 129-165.

tion of cotton, corn, wheat, hogs, oil, textiles, furniture, houses, buildings, and factories. The College promised to begin to produce the farmers, vocational teachers, engineers, and craftsmen who could turn the wheels of American industry. It fulfilled that promise. The College produced the soldiers who in the next great war would help defend the American way of life. Texas A&M plowed ahead with a new zeal, dedication, and purposefulness, and to some extent with a narrowing vision of what tomorrow might bring, losing itself in the business of producing the cornucopia of today.

CHAPTER 15

Branching Out

T HE Texas A&M College System, as it has been styled since 1948, began
to develop even before the A&M College opened for business. The Texas
Legislature established a branch "for the benefit of colored youths" at Prairie
View, in Waller County, by Act of August 14, 1876.[1] In 1917 two "junior,
agricultural, mechanical, and industrial" colleges were established under the
auspices of the Texas A&M Board of Directors, one at Arlington, and
another at Stephenville.[2] When asked to describe the relationship of the
branches with the main campus, Eugene J. Howell, president of Tarleton
State College from 1945 to 1960, replied that there had been "advantages and
disadvantages" in being a part of the A&M System. Howell and his counterpart at Prairie View A&M College, Edward Bertram Evans (president, 1946-
1965), contended that the advantages outweighed the disadvantages.[3] The
Arlington branch, which separated from Texas A&M in 1965, found the association to be a liability rather than an asset.

Each branch has led its own independent and unique existence. All have
shared to a greater or lesser extent, however, common blessings and common
grievances resulting from their relationship as subordinate divisions of Texas
A&M. Eugene Howell, for example, suggested that a leading disadvantage of
being a "branch" is that the Board of Directors and the president (or chancellor) tend to identify with the main campus. Funds are allocated according to
priority — the greater priority always being the parent campus.[4] An analogy
can be drawn between Texas A&M's own experiences as a "branch" of The
University of Texas. Texas A&M believed that as a branch of The University
it failed to receive equitable treatment at the hands of the Regents, particu-

[1]Gammel (ed.), *Laws of Texas*, VIII, 972.

[2]*General Laws of Texas*, 1917, pp. 58, 260.

[3]Interview with President Eugene J. Howell, Tarleton State College, Stephenville, Texas,
September 18, 1971; interview with President Edward B. Evans, Prairie View A&M College,
Prairie View, Texas, October 11, 1971.

[4]Interview with E. J. Howell, Stephenville, September 18, 1971.

larly in regard to the allocation of Endowment Fund money. In the eighties A&M, notably through George Pfeuffer, rigorously opposed the introspective view of The University Board of Regents. Throughout their association with Texas A&M the branches have felt much the same subservient fiscal relationship to the main campus which Texas A&M felt toward The University. It is questionable, however, whether the branches would fare as well financially were they independent of Texas A&M.

Edward B. Evans, longtime president of Prairie View, A&M's oldest branch, believes that the branch status has been financially beneficial over the long pull. Texas A&M branches have shared to some extent in Morrill Land-Grant funds, Second Morrill Act funds, and in Experiment Station and Extension Service funds and programs. Whatever Texas A&M has had, Prairie View has shared, he said.[5] The fortunes, and indeed the misfortunes, of the parent became those of the child.

Each branch of Texas A&M has had its own identity, its own development, and its own unique characteristics. The history of the branches has generally been that of autonomy rather than subservience. If there has been a "policy" in the Texas A&M College System, that policy has historically been self-determination.[6] Each branch has been allowed to seek its own identity — to exult when the goose hangs high, or to stew in its own broth when times are bad.

The Prairie View A&M University, A&M's oldest branch, until contemporary times was the only public institution of higher learning for Negroes in Texas. Its academic history has thus reflected all of the nuances of Southern politics and society. As George R. Woolfolk, author of *Prairie View: A Study in Public Conscience,* so vividly describes it, the College has not only an academic history and a Texas history, but also a black history. Woolfolk's book is much more than a study of a college; it is the study of the black man in a white man's world.[7] The following résumé of the Prairie View branch of Texas A&M highlights and annotates the story told by Woolfolk.

Under the act establishing the "agricultural and mechanical college for the benefit of colored youths" the Legislature appropriated $20,000 and appointed three commissioners (Ashbel Smith, John D. Giddings, and James H. Raymond) to locate the college. The commissioners selected a tract of

[5]Interview with E. B. Evans, Prairie View A&M College, October 11, 1971.

[6]Interview with E. B. Evans and George R. Woolfolk, Prairie View A&M College, Prairie View, Texas, October 11, 1971.

[7]George R. Woolfolk, *Prairie View, A Study in Public Conscience* (1962), pp. 1-404.

land six miles from Hempstead, in Waller County, known as Alta Vista, on which were located buildings suitable for academic purposes.[8]

Alta Vista was a 1,000-acre plantation given by Dr. Richard J. Swearingen to his daughter, Helen Marr Swearingen, upon her marriage in 1858 to Jared E. Kirby. Before and during the Civil War the Kirbys maintained four large plantations, including Alta Vista, and several farms, and entertained on a lavish scale. Kirby became a colonel in the Confederate Army, attached to the staff of General E. Kirby Smith, who for many months during the late phases of the War maintained his headquarters at Alta Vista. Soon after the War Jared Kirby died owing more "than ten times the value of his estate." Helen Marr Kirby worked to save what she could. In 1867 she opened Alta Vista Institute, a boarding school for young ladies. In 1875 she closed her school and moved to Austin to teach, and in 1876 opened a new Alta Vista Institute in Austin. She sold Alta Vista Plantation to the state for $13,000. From 1884 until her death Helen Marr Kirby was dean of women at The University of Texas.[9]

The lands of Alta Vista, to be utilized by the state for the new Negro college, were exceptionally good for farming and other agricultural purposes, and were, in fact, superior to those chosen for the parent institution at College Station. On January 21, 1878, the commissioners formally transferred the property to the Board of Directors of the Texas A&M College, having made repairs and improvements to the property costing $15,787.67. On January 22, 1878, the Directors elected A&M President Thomas S. Gathright the president of Alta Vista Agricultural College to serve without additional salary, and on the same day chose Frederich W. Minor, of Mississippi, as the principal⁺ and sole instructor of the school.[10]

Although announcements of the opening were made in the press and by circular, the school opened on March 11, 1878, with only eight students enrolled. Like its parent institution, Alta Vista experienced a slow start, but unlike Texas A&M, where the enrollments increased as the weeks of the first school term passed, attendance at Alta Vista declined. In January 1879 a visiting delegation from the Sixteenth Legislature "found Professor Minor, but no colored youths seeking instruction."[11] The legislators concluded, "as stated

---

[8]*Texas Senate Journal, 1879*, pp. 205-210; Anderson James Peeler (ed.), *Laws Relating to the Agricultural and Mechanical College of Texas*, 15-16.

[9]*The Alcalde*, IX (January 17, 1922), pp. 944-950, quoted in Woolfolk, *Prairie View*, 332-337.

[10]*Texas Senate Journal, 1879*, pp. 205-210; Peeler (ed.), *Laws Relating to the Agricultural and Mechanical College of Texas*, 33-38.

[11]*Texas Senate Journal, 1879*, pp. 205-210.

by Professor Gathright, there is no demand for higher education among the blacks," but believed that some practical way could be found for Negroes to share in the benefit of the congressional donation of 1862.[12] As the early experiences at College Station had indicated that white students were not highly motivated by the prospect of leaving the farm to attend a college to study farming in order to return to the farm, so in like manner black students were not interested in college training which would merely return them to the drudgery of farm labor.

President Gathright believed the school at Alta Vista should be converted into a manual training school similar to Hampton Roads Institution. Others advised turning it into a coeducational state normal school, for in the beginning, as at Texas A&M, the school opened as an all-male institution. Governor Oran M. Roberts, also president of the A&M Board of Directors, solved the matter for a time by advising the Legislature on February 5, 1879, that Alta Vista should be "safely rented out for the year until it can be employed by the directors as to serve pupils to be taught in it."[13] The idea of converting Alta Vista into a normal school for training teachers won preference, and, indeed, was not incompatible with Gathright's reference to Hampton Normal and Agricultural Institute, as "Hampton Roads Institute" was properly styled. The state Legislature, stimulated by Barnas Sears, formerly president of Brown University and then agent for the George Peabody Fund to promote Southern education, by an act of April 19, 1879, established a "Normal School at Prairie View for preparation and training of colored teachers."[14] In the same session the Legislature created a State Normal for white students at Huntsville.

A dual conception lay behind the creation of the normal program for Negroes. On the one hand the idea coincided with the purpose of the white normal program, to train selected individuals in the practical skill of teaching illiterates. The second role, peculiar to Negro institutions created under the inspiration of Northern philanthropy, was to train

selected Negro youth who should go out to teach and lead their people, first, by example, by cultivating land and making homes; to give them not a dollar that they could not earn themselves; to teach respect of labor; to replace stupid drudgery with skilled work; and to these ends to build up an industrial system, for the sake not only of self-respect and efficient labor, but also for schooling and character.[15]

[12]*Ibid.*

[13]Woolfolk, *Prairie View*, 35-36; *Governor's Messages, Coke to Ross, 1874-1891*, pp. 249-250; *Texas Senate Journal, 1879*, pp. 205-210.

[14]Gammel (ed.), *Laws of Texas*, VIII, 1482; Woolfolk, *Prairie View*, 35-44.

[15]Woolfolk, *Prairie View*, 43-45.

The law establishing Prairie View State Normal School incorporated a tuition plan similar to that provided for Texas A&M, to assure the "success" of the academic program. It should be recalled that in 1878 both the agricultural and the engineering curricula at College Station had been slighted by students, who preferred the liberal-arts curriculum. This problem had been overcome at College Station by firing the faculty, by eliminating all courses except a curriculum in agriculture and one in engineering, and by assigning state tuition grants equally to each curriculum. Similarly, the state tuition grants were made to Prairie View students with the stipulation that they pursue the normal, or teacher-training, curriculum. Students accepting the grants were required to sign a written obligation to teach in the public schools of Texas for a minimum of one year or for a time proportionate to the time enrolled at Prairie View. The law also specified that the school should admit male and female students of at least sixteen years of age.[16]

The Board of Directors of Texas A&M, under the leadership of Governor Roberts, selected E. H. Anderson as principal, and provided for two teaching assistants and a staff of three. The Normal opened October 6, 1879. Twelve state students and four local students enrolled initially, but the ranks swelled to a total of sixty before the end of the term. The Legislature originally appropriated $6,000 for Prairie View from the Public School Fund, and in a special session in 1879 appropriated an additional $1,600 from the University Fund. In 1881 the Legislature allocated $8,000 from the University Fund for Prairie View. Soon afterwards, the idyllic "first summer" for Prairie View Normal ended.[17]

The legal question arose as to whether Prairie View Normal, as a branch of Texas A&M, should also be considered a branch of The University of Texas, and so share in the University Endowment Fund. Governor Roberts had no doubt that Texas A&M, and Prairie View, when established under mandate of the Constitution of 1876, were intended to be branches of The University of Texas.[18] But Roberts was confronted by the fact that the Constitution did not call for a Prairie View Normal, and by the additional fact that the law clearly intended that the Normal School at Huntsville, which could in no way be considered a branch of The University, be funded from the general revenues. Could Prairie View Normal then be considered a branch? Insofar as the original legislation had never been repealed, it could. But insofar as William M. Brown, the state comptroller, was concerned, it

[16]Gammel (ed.), *Laws of Texas*, VIII, 1482.

[17]*Governor's Messages, Coke to Ross, 1874-1891*, pp. 406-408; Woolfolk, *Prairie View*, 47, 69.

[18]*Governor's Messages, Coke to Ross, 1874-1891*, p. 399.

could not be so considered, and he believed the legislative appropriation out of the University Fund was unconstitutional. Brown, on his own action, refused to audit the Prairie View accounts and to pay vouchers on that account.[19] Prairie View, in fact, had run aground upon the same rocks that threatened Texas A&M over the next few years. Texas wanted to build a state university and any disbursements from the University Fund obstructed the development of that university.

In January 1881 Principal E. H. Anderson wrote Governor Roberts that Prairie View had no money and no credit and that its accounts were three months in arrears.[20] The story of how several Houston merchants were called upon to advance money to the school has been told in an earlier chapter.[21] The financial crisis was resolved by an emergency appropriation in 1882, and by the release of unused Morrill Act funds from Texas A&M to Prairie View.[22] In 1883 the Legislature appropriated $7,500 from the General Fund to Prairie View for the two fiscal years ending February 28, 1885,[23] an act based on the assumption that Prairie View was not a branch of The University. Furthermore, in 1882 Prairie View supporters failed in an effort to have the College converted into "a branch of the State University, for the instruction of colored youth."

An act of the Legislature in that year called for a statewide election to select a site for the state university, and another act called an election for locating a colored branch of The University. The electorate chose Austin as the site for both institutions,[24] but no funds have ever appeared for the organization of a colored branch in Austin. Prairie View A&M would remain a subordinate division of Texas A&M, while remaining the only Negro public college in Texas until about 1940. The latter role gave it a greater degree of independence than an "ordinary" branch might have, and also made the institution more sensitive to the vagaries of state politics.

The passing years brought increasingly less involvement of the Negro in state politics as black disfranchisement, effected by a grandfather clause and white primaries, and accompanied by Jim Crow laws, muted the Negroes' voice in state politics. This process, more than the administrative connections to Texas A&M, put Prairie View in more of a dependency status than it might have had, and helped mold it into the "ghetto world," the phrase by

---

[19]*Ibid.*, 406-410.

[20]*Ibid.*, 409.

[21]See Chapter 4.

[22]Gammel (ed.), *Laws of Texas*, IX, 297-298; Woolfolk, *Prairie View*, 68-72.

[23]Gammel (ed.), *Laws of Texas*, IX, 433-434.

[24]*Ibid.*, 285.

which Woolfolk characterized it.[25] Prairie View A&M, between 1878 and 1946, was a separate but unequal institution. The greatest objective of its principals (or presidents) throughout these years was to upgrade the institution continually, and to accommodate the special needs of black citizens while attempting to avoid a confrontation with the white power structure. They strove, in a word, to make the institution a separate but *equal* institution. Most Prairie View principals were able and astute men. Unlike presidents of the parent institution at College Station, Prairie View administrators have generally had long and rather stable tenure.

Since its founding there have been a total of nine principals or presidents of Prairie View A&M. The efforts of L. W. Minor (1878-1879) to organize the Alta Vista College were abortive.[26] E. H. Anderson (1879-1884) established the Normal School and, in the face of severe financial problems, finally saw the normal programs extended to two full academic sessions per year.[27] Anderson, who died in 1884, was replaced by his brother, L. C. Anderson, a strong individualist, and an able administrator and solicitor of public and private funds.[28]

L. C. Anderson noted in 1886 "a decided improvement in attendance and in the educational qualifications of the students." He believed that more male students needed to be enlisted in the academic program, feeling that the girls after being married were forced to give up their commitment to education. Like the main campus in College Station, Prairie View Normal had no adequate water supply, and needed wagons, implements, and more money.[29] In 1887 a committee from the Board of Directors investigated the "1st Assistant Teacher," who had been publicly charged with advocating racial mixing in the schools, in defiance of state laws and the Constitution of Texas. The committee found that in an article published in the *New England Journal of Education* the teacher had indeed advocated racial mixing in the schools, but the Directors recommended retaining him on the faculty.[30] On occasion, as in this instance, the Texas A&M administration provided a useful shield for Prairie View from political attack.

[25]See Lawrence Rice, *The Negro in Texas, 1877-1900* (1970), the entire book; Woolfolk, *Prairie View*, 330.

[26]*Governor's Messages, Coke to Ross, 1874-1891*, p. 406; *Texas Senate Journal, 1879*, pp. 205-210, 509-511; Woolfolk, *Prairie View*, 66-74.

[27]*Texas Senate Journal, 1883*, p. 145; Woolfolk, *Prairie View*, 66-74.

[28]Minutes of the Board of Directors, June 7, 1886, I, 11-15; Woolfolk, *Prairie View*, 74-109.

[29]Minutes of the Board of Directors, June 7, 1886, I, 11-15.

[30]*Ibid.*, I, 20.

The decade of the nineties brought renewed political turbulence and heightened racial antagonisms. The Democratic Party in Texas was threatened by a revolt of farmers who organized a Populist Party, and by the specter of a rejuvenated state Republican Party which threatened to ally with the Populists. Congress, in 1890, began debate on a new Force Bill which white Southerners believed would reinstitute reconstruction. The Negro became an increasingly important and controversial subject.

In this atmosphere a legislative investigating committee reported in 1891 that Prairie View Normal was "doing excellent work for the colored race." The committee advised the Legislature to give the college as much of an appropriation as possible, although it would not be practicable to give everything the principal requested. The committee report used the occasion to criticize "white adventurers," and the "interference by irritating legislation" of people of the North. The report marked the unselfish and unstinted support the state (Democratic Party) had given the Negro in the form of educational institutions and asylums.[31] Principal Anderson "played" these political and social tensions to the advantage of Prairie View, with a finely tuned ear.

He used the increasing preoccupation of the white world with Booker T. Washington's concepts of industrial training to build and improve the normal as well as vocational features of Prairie View. An industrial education course was introduced in 1887. Typesetting, printing, blacksmithing, carpentry, and elementary agriculture were important features of the vocational course. Anderson never lost sight of the paramount feature of the college as a normal school for the training of teachers, who would in turn go out to educate and improve the life of black Texans.[32] A branch of the new Agricultural Experiment Station was established at Prairie View in 1888, when it was organized under Texas A&M's jurisdiction.[33] In 1890 Prairie View came in for a share of the Second Morrill Act funds, but not the one-third originally allocated to it by Governor Ross. The Legislature, on March 4, 1891, gave Prairie View one-fourth of the funds.[34] Perhaps because of the political uncertainties, and because of Lawrence Sullivan Ross' presence at A&M, Prairie View shared in larger legislative appropriations during the nineties, despite the depression.[35]

[31] *Texas House Journal, 1891*, pp. 38-39.
[32] *Report of the Prairie View Normal School*, 1886-1888, xiii, 11.
[33] *Ibid.*, 11.
[34] Gammel (ed.), *Laws of Texas*, IX, 45-56.
[35] *Ibid.*, I, 573-576, 865-866, 1475-1476.

But by 1896 the political storms had calmed in Texas. Populists, Republicans, and Negroes were out. The solid Democratic Party was safely and securely in. Anderson, in the view of the new Democratic solidarity, had courted too many unsavory agencies and political personages. He was, after all, a Republican. When, in 1896, he took umbrage at remarks by a Board member deprecating Negro rights, the Board of Directors summarily dismissed him. Edward Lavoisier Blackshear, a Democrat, replaced him.[36]

Blackshear followed Anderson's pattern in continuing to press for improvement in the academic standards of Prairie View, but was not averse to incorporating the rising interest in industrial training for the Negro into his program. In 1899 the state Legislature provided a "labor fund," similar to the state student grants, anticipating the promotion of vocational training at Prairie View. At the time the Legislature changed the name of the institution from Prairie View State Normal School to Prairie View State Normal and Industrial College.[37] In 1901 Blackshear received legislative approval to offer a four-year course in "classical and scientific studies," which represented a standard college curriculum open to all normal graduates without examination and to others after satisfactory completion of examinations. The college course at Prairie View was then funded with an appropriation of $4,300 for the first two years. Prairie View held its first commencement in 1904.[38] Also in 1901 the Legislature enlarged the program of student aid at Prairie View to cover most of the expenses of 159 students.[39] Sorely needed physical improvements at the institute included construction of two dormitories for men, Foster Hall (1909) and Luckie Hall (1909); a dormitory for women, Crawford Hall (1912); and a combination auditorium-dining hall in 1911.[40]

Prairie View, like the A&M College, had great difficulty in finding a good underground water supply. Until 1911, when Blackshear secured the old power plant from Texas A&M, Prairie View had no electric lights and power, and even after the acquisition lighting was regarded as inadequate. A legislative investigation in 1911 found the facilities, even the new buildings, to be poor, shameful, and inadequate.[41]

In 1914 Blackshear found himself on the losing side of the political fight against James Edward Ferguson. Robert Teague Milner, president at

[36]Woolfolk, *Prairie View*, 108-109.

[37]*General Laws of Texas, 1897-1902*, p. 325.

[38]*Ibid.*, 35; Woolfolk, *Prairie View*, 127-130.

[39]*General Laws of Texas, 1897-1902*, pp. 246-247.

[40]Prairie View A&M, *General Catalog, 1970-1971*, p. 10.

[41]Woolfolk, *Prairie View*, 149-153.

Texas A&M, having earlier found himself in conflict with Governor Oscar Branch Colquitt, left A&M "under pressure" in 1913. Ferguson's "pressure," as A&M officials were to discover, was much more direct and intensive than had been Colquitt's. In 1915 "Farmer Jim" Ferguson agreed to sign a $29,000 appropriation for Prairie View but stated that "Blackshear . . . has got to go." The Board and friends attempted to screen for Blackshear, but he finally had no choice but to resign.[42]

I. M. Terrell, who had formerly worked under Alexander Hogg (a member of the first faculty of Texas A&M) while Hogg was superintendent of schools in Fort Worth, succeeded Blackshear. Terrell was hardly in office before local and faculty hostilities at Prairie View led to his dismissal by the Board of Directors. A group of "concerned citizens" from Prairie View successfully petitioned the Directors to unseat Terrell. Terrell, who had no background in academic affairs, was an abrupt, ambulatory individual who did not fit with the people.[43] The dismissal undoubtedly fully suited the purposes and intentions of A&M President William Bennett Bizzell, who was deeply gratified to see Terrell replaced with his own old childhood friend, Dr. J. Granville Osborne, born and reared on the farm adjoining the Bizzell's near Washington, Texas. As a youth Osborne had saved Bizzell from drowning in the local swimming hole.[44] Osborne became the Bizzell of Prairie View, working in close harmony and purpose with President Bizzell.

Osborne received his A.B. degree from Bishop College, in Marshall, Texas; completed a course in pedagogy at the University of Chicago; served one year as high-school principal in Victoria, Texas; taught chemistry and biology at Bishop College one year; and then returned to Chicago for more work before entering Leonard Medical School at Shaw University. He interned in Philadelphia and returned to Leonard Medical School to teach. In 1913 he completed a year of advanced study to become an eye, ear, nose and throat specialist. Osborne then returned to Navasota, Texas, to practice medicine. Because of the meager returns from medicine he accepted the job of principal of the Negro public school, continuing to practice medicine on the side. In 1916 President Bizzell invited Osborne to serve as physician and instructor in science at Prairie View.[45]

[42]*Ibid.*, 158-159.

[43]*Ibid.*, 175-177. Interview with Edward B. Evans, Prairie View, Texas, October 11, 1971; Minutes of the Board of Directors, April 27, 1918, III, 234; May 27, 1918, III, 237. The Directors also discharged Professor of Agriculture C. H. Waller, and Professor Charles Atherton, and appointed J. Granville Osborne, acting president.

[44]*Ibid.*, 163-168.

[45]*Ibid.*, 163-173.

The Board of Directors permitted a most unusual procedure upon the ouster of Terrell, by allowing the faculty of Prairie View to choose their own principal. They chose Dr. J. Granville Osborne.[46] Dr. Edward B. Evans, who began his work during the administration of I. M. Terrell, recalls Dr. Osborne as one of the most able of all Prairie View administrators. Osborne, he said, "never got the credit he deserves." It was Osborne who wanted to put Prairie View on a real collegiate basis, and did so. He rehabilitated the four-year-degree-granting program in 1919, scrapping the old normal curriculum. The new Division of Education provided a strong curriculum in education, with science courses in liberal arts under the same umbrella. Osborne's action provoked opposition from the faculty, alumni, and state educators. Evans recalls that it created a "furor all over the state." Enrollment in the college fell by almost one-half, to only 400 students, but Osborne held steadfast, and within a year the opposition subsided and the collegiate course remained.[47]

Osborne instituted a nursing school at Prairie View, established an R.O.T.C. program, helped create the Interscholastic League for Negroes, launched a YMCA program, raised teacher salaries, established a teacher-training program in vocational agriculture (home economics and mechanic arts) leading to a Bachelor of Science degree, instituted a regular B.S. degree in agriculture, and expanded the Cooperative Extension Service, initiated at Prairie View at the same time as at A&M, to the point that Prairie View became the effective leader of Negro extension in Texas.[48] Osborne, as Bizzell at Texas A&M, brought Prairie View into the modern era. But like so many aggressive men, Osborne created enemies and pushed many people too hard.

Bizzell's departure from Texas A&M left Osborne vulnerable to attack. "Fergusonism" once again instigated the removal of a Prairie View administrator. Osborne's dismissal came as a product of formal student protests to the Board of Directors, charging Osborne with a break-down of discipline among the faculty, and with an accumulation of minor charges. There were none, not even the faculty, to defend him, and Osborne was "turned out like a janitor," says George R. Woolfolk.[49]

Osborne's successor, Willette Rutherford Banks, nicknamed "Scrap,"

[46]*Ibid.*, 177.

[47]Interview with Edward B. Evans, Prairie View A&M, October 11, 1971; Woolfolk, *Prairie View,* 191-199.

[48]Interview with Edward B. Evans and George R. Woolfolk, Prairie View A&M, October 11, 1971.

[49]Woolfolk, *Prairie View,* 207-208; interview with Edward B. Evans and George R. Woolfolk, Prairie View A&M, October 11, 1971.

the second of thirteen children, was born August 8, 1881, in a cabin in the hills of northeast Georgia. As Woolfolk tells the story,

about three o'clock in the stillness of the morning, a tall brown man, lean and lank, rushed excitedly, half dressed, through the woods to the cabin of Aunt Nancy. His fist pounded impatiently upon the rickety door, arousing the old soul of some ninety years from slumber. He said distractedly to her, "I came for you. Laura is sick." After kneeling by her bed for a brief prayer, Aunt Nancy dressed with the deliberate preoccupied slowness of the aged, Laura's husband all the while pacing the small yard with restless impatience. Lighting her cob pipe and reaching for her walking stick signaled her readiness, and she left with the man for his cabin. They entered quietly. Laura was in great pain. While she writhed in pain in the shadow of death, Aunt Nancy took from her a handful of human flesh weighing four pounds. Holding it in her hands she whispered to the inquisitive father, "It's a ole boy."[50]

Banks went on to complete his education at Atlanta University, became principal of the Kowaliga Community School in Alabama, then president of Texas College, in Tyler, Texas, in 1915. On June 3, 1926, the Texas A&M Board of Directors, upon the recommendations of the State Department of Education and the General Education Board, elected Banks principal of Prairie View Normal and Industrial College.[51] Banks served as principal from 1926 to 1947. Whatever Prairie View A&M is today is in large measure the product of the work of Banks and his staff, and of Edward B. Evans and his administration. These two men guided the affairs of the College for four decades, from 1926 through 1965.

Evans recalls that Banks, who died at Prairie View in 1970, "had an uncanny knowledge of human nature." He had the ability to inspire people who worked with him. He built a strong educational program and a strong faculty. He did much with little. He believed the school should extend its educational program into the community. He sensed the value of working with different units of the state government and had influence with the General Education Board and with the State Department of Education.[52]

Banks initiated the Prairie View Conference on Education in 1931, established the Division of Graduate Study in 1937, helped develop National Youth Administration (NYA) programs on the campus in the thirties, and in 1943 brought the Army Specialized Training Program (ASTP) to Prairie View. In 1945 Banks saw the title and function of Prairie View State Normal

[50]Woolfolk, *Prairie View*, 213.

[51]*Ibid.*, 214; interview with Edward B. Evans and George R. Woolfolk, Prairie View A&M, October 11, 1971.

[52]Interview with Edward B. Evans and George R. Woolfolk, Prairie View A&M, October 11, 1971.

and Industrial College changed by the state Legislature to Prairie View University, with authorization for Prairie View to offer all courses offered by The University of Texas. For one "bright moment" Prairie View had a law school and prepared to offer full university curricula.[33] The 1945 "revolution" in Prairie View affairs came in response to rising federal and local insistence upon full racial equality in all areas of life, including the political, economic, and educational. The new university status for Prairie View was in part a "sop" from the state to grant to Texas Negroes some of their historic demands, and so deter racial mixing and antagonism.

The designation of Prairie View as a university fulfilled what had previously appeared to be but an empty promise to establish a Negro university in Texas, an obligation first imposed by the Constitution of 1876, restated in an election for the location of such a college in 1882, and reaffirmed by legislation and by Democratic Party conventions in the 1890s.[54] By 1945, however, the Negro in Texas, like the whites, had become an urban dweller. Prairie View A&M still represented to most spectators, black and white, the old order of things. Houston and the urban Negro represented the new order. Pressure from Negro and white interests, especially those centered about Houston, brought an early demise to Prairie View University. In 1947 the Legislature created Texas Southern University, in Houston, with all of the authority and implements of the state university for Negroes including a law school and a medical school, the latter now disestablished. The law created a "university in two parts," with Prairie View receiving the acknowledgment, but not the title, of the agricultural and mechanical "part" of the university. Prairie View became Prairie View Agricultural and Mechanical College of Texas, designated for instruction in "agriculture, the mechanic arts, engineering and the natural sciences connected therewith together with any other courses authorized at Prairie View at the time of the passage of this Act, all of which shall be equivalent to those offered at the Agricultural and Mechanical College of Texas."[55] It would appear that after a seventy-year lapse the charter of Prairie View was back to the original authorization of the Morrill Land-Grant College Act.

But by 1947 Texas A&M was no longer the school it had started out to be in 1876, and there could be no turning back the clock for Prairie View. It now had a strong academic foundation and specific authorization to grow academically in any way in which the parent campus grew. Substantial growth

[33]Prairie View A&M, *General Catalog, 1970-1971,* pp. 10-11.

[54]Gammel (ed.), *Laws of Texas,* IX, 285.

[55] Prairie View A&M, *General Catalog, 1970-1971,* pp. 10-11; interview with Edward B. Evans and George R. Woolfolk, Prairie View A&M, October 11, 1971.

and development continued at Prairie View A&M, under the able direction of Edward Bertram Evans.

Evans, a short, solid, light-complexioned Negro, was born in Kansas City, Missouri, in 1894. His parents took great interest in him as a child, his mother teaching him to be polite and kind, and wanting him to be a gentleman, and his father indulging his interest in things mechanical and in animals and livestock. Evans recalls that as a child his school principal passed his home every evening, and Evans would sit on the fence and greet him and tip his hat. After his "graduation" from elementary school, he relates, he got the prize for being the most polite kid in school, a thing he has never forgotten and an event which has served as a constant inspiration. He has always, he said, had great respect for the feelings of others — always tried to treat people the way he would have them treat him.[56]

As a boy Evans worked in a drugstore in Kansas City, sometimes working eighteen hours a day including Sundays and holidays. He lived one block from the Kansas City Veterinary School, and in the drugstore had frequent occasion to talk with students about their studies. He also became acquainted with a Negro veterinarian, C. V. Lowe, employed by the U.S. Department of Agriculture as a meat inspector. Lowe encouraged him to go into veterinary medicine, but the thing that impressed him most, he said, was that Lowe paid his bills with gold. He had never seen so much gold and "wanted to get his hands on some of that." So with eighty dollars in his pocket he arrived in Ames, Iowa, never previously having been out of the city alone, to study veterinary medicine.[57]

Upon arriving in Ames he stopped the first fellow he saw and asked him, "Can you tell me where the colored people live in this town?" The man looked at him "funny" and told him gruffly, "no, I couldn't." Evans thought to himself, "That's funny, he doesn't know where the colored people live." Later, he found a Negro porter in a barber shop and told him he was looking for a place to stay. The porter answered him, "There ain't but two of us [Negroes] in this town and we don't speak." But he did direct him to the other one, who took him in for his first night in Ames.[58]

The next day he tried the International House on the campus, where he received a warm welcome. After being shown to his room, Evans asked how much it would cost. They told him forty dollars a month. Evans said it was like hitting him between the eyes with a sledge hammer. He backed out and

[56]Interview with Edward B. Evans, Prairie View A&M, October 11, 1971.
[57]*Ibid.*
[58]*Ibid.*

finally found a room with a Negro student from South Carolina, also studying veterinary medicine. Evans worked his way through his first college year
shining shoes in a barber shop. The next year he got a job waiting tables in a
Tri Delta sorority house, where he worked for the next three years.[59]

President Evans remembers how in his second year he was put next to a
white South Carolina student who was "a little stiff." Eventually they began
talking to each other and finally became good friends. Evans and his South
Carolina friend, Henry Dukes, vied with each other for top honors. That
experience taught him, Evans says, that "regardless of the prejudices people
have, if you can establish a good relationship where one man can see the
good in the other, and one can know one another as human beings, that's the
best way I know of to establish good will." Evans and Dukes, who became
professor of physiology at Cornell, won Phi Kappa Phi honors at
graduation.[60] Evans received the Distinguished Alumnus Award from Iowa
State University in 1970.

Upon graduation he was still broke. With some enthusiasm he accepted
a job offer in 1916 from Principal Terrell at Prairie View State Normal and
Industrial College at $75 per month. He planned to stay at Prairie View one
year, Evans recalls, but the years passed and he "never looked back." The
greatest shock he ever had in his life, Evans said, was seeing eight hundred
black youths in a dining hall all at one time, ". . . it just took my breath
away."[61]

Evans entered into a long career of service to the school and to the community. At various times he served as professor of veterinary science, director
of athletics, acting registrar, acting director of the School of Arts and Sciences, state leader for Negro Extension Service, and finally principal. In 1947
his title was changed to dean; on September 1, 1948, with the organization of
the A&M College system and the office of chancellor, Evans became the
president of Prairie View A&M College. In 1950 Evans restructured the academic branches of the College to include the schools of Agriculture, Arts and
Sciences, Home Economics, and Engineering, Industrial Education, and Technology. Numerous physical additions were made to the campus, including a
$1-million Memorial Student Center, a $2-million Science Building, a $1.5-
million Health and Physical Education Building, a substantial addition to the
library, and a number of new dormitories. The College was accredited by the
Southern Association of Colleges and Secondary Schools in 1958.[62] Evans
retired on August 31, 1966.

[59]*Ibid.*
[60]*Ibid.*
[61]*Ibid.*
[62]Prairie View A&M, *General Catalog, 1970-1971,* pp. 10-12.

He was replaced for a brief time by Dr. J. M. Drew, who became ill, and, at his request, was relieved of his duties. He was replaced by Dr. Alvin I. Thomas, who was former dean of the School of Industrial Education and Technology.[63] In the following years Prairie View became embroiled in the black militant movement, a situation which in February 1971 led to the temporary closing of the school and dismissal of a number of students who participated in destructive demonstrations.[64] New tensions and pressures were pulling at Prairie View, as at every college in the United States. In the sixties, perhaps more than at any time in the past, Prairie View, as indeed Texas A&M, was being buffeted by the winds of change.

Dr. Evans and Dr. George Woolfolk both agree that over the years the association between Prairie View and Texas A&M has been cordial and beneficial to the branches. They view A&M as having had a "faithful stewardship," but strong disagreement with this view has existed in the past, and continues within the black community of Texas today. The strongest exception to Texas A&M's "faithful stewardship" was made in 1932 in a special report of the Joint Legislative Committee on Organization and Economy, popularly called the Griffenhagen Report, after the specialists hired to conduct the investigation. This report, it must be emphasized, was in most respects critical of Texas A&M, and in few respects laudatory. It included the following recommendations relative to Prairie View:

1) Its control should be removed from the administrative officers of Texas A&M, "which have grossly mismanaged the institution." It should be under the State Board of Education.

2) The agricultural course should be revised so as to include "practical training" during the first two years' work.

3) Trades courses should be offered on a noncollegiate basis "to fit the needs of students who are not high school graduates."

4) The College should be considered not only a "college in the common meaning of that term, but as a general-purpose school for giving to Negroes such training as cannot be secured in public elementary and high schools."

5) Classes having enrollments of ten or fewer students should be discontinued.

6) More practice-teaching facilities should be obtained in Houston or elsewhere.

7) Extension classes should be offered in outlying centers only when enrollment of fifteen or more students can be obtained.

[63]*Ibid.*, interview with Edward B. Evans, Prairie View A&M, October 11, 1971.

[64]Houston *Post*, February 26, 27, and 28, 1971; Bryan *Daily Eagle*, February 25 and 28, 1971, March 4, 1971; *The Battalion*, March 4, 1971.

8) Summer sessions should be reduced from ten to nine weeks.

9) Graduate courses should be discontinued.[65]

Other recommendations included the suggestion that the operation of the College hospital was overly extravagant, that athletics should be entirely self-supporting, that military training should be discontinued, that dining halls and dormitories should be operated on a self-supporting basis, and that two instead of seven trucks were adequate for the College. There were a total of forty-three recommendations.[66]

A brief summary of Prairie View in the main report on Texas A&M College itself was quite blunt:

> Much of the mismanagement and waste in the operation of this institution [Prairie View Normal and Industrial College] is a result of the inefficient administration emanating from the Agricultural and Mechanical College. It has permitted great waste in expenditures for many non-essentials. It has fixed upon the College its own complicated and inefficient accounting system. It has failed completely to understand some of the elementary principles of Negro education. It has dictated nearly every policy and procedure of the Prairie View State Normal and Industrial College. Many of its dictates have been unjustified both on grounds of economy and under sound principles of education.[67]

Had Texas A&M saddled Prairie View with its own peculiar identity, which the Griffenhagen Report took equally strong exception to, and was it guilty of misguiding and misleading Prairie View and the Negro in Texas? If one takes the recommendation of the Committee toward "practical training" to be the correct path for Prairie View as the only institution of higher learning for Negroes in Texas, then indeed Texas A&M was clearly wrong.

The history of Prairie View, in retrospect, can seemingly be divided into three general periods. The first phase is that characterized by the post-Reconstruction period, by the Peabody Fund and Hampton and Tuskeegee Institutes, when black education was a new thing, and when, under New South doctrine, the Negro was to be "uplifted and civilized." During this period Negro education, Prairie View State Normal and Industrial Institute being a case example, was separate and unequal. After *Plessy vs. Ferguson* (1898) and the advent of the progressive era, black education remained separate, but

---

[65]Joint Legislative Committee on Organization and Economy and Griffenhagen and Associates, *The Government of the State of Texas*, XI, *Education: The Agricultural and Mechanical College of Texas and Its Affiliates* (December 31, 1932), pp. 314-318 (hereinafter cited, *The Government of the State of Texas*, XI, *Education*).

[66]*Ibid.*

[67]*Ibid.*, 6.

there was a conscious stirring for equality. Black schools should teach black students what white schools taught white students, not something less. Blackshear, Osborne, and Banks worked stringently for a measure of equality — within the framework of separation, admittedly without great success, but with that always their goal. But in 1932 the Griffenhagen Report was not advocating academic equality, but something less. In the phraseology of the Report, the Report "failed completely to understand some of the elementary principles of Negro education." The Griffenhagen Report would convert Prairie View into a vocational, trades, general-purpose school for Negroes rather than a full collegiate institution which paralleled the academic standards and purposes of white colleges.

The third period of Negro educational history, and the third period of Prairie View history, conforms to the contemporary, to the post-World War II civil-rights movement and the era of *Brown vs. Board of Education of Topeka* (1954), which held that separate educational facilities are inherently unequal. This marked not only a social revolution in the affairs of white schools and colleges, but perhaps even more an academic revolution in the affairs of black colleges, such as Prairie View, whose whole academic and social philosophy had been geared to separation. Integration forced the black colleges to achieve equality whether they sought it or not. Black colleges have been forced into the mainstream of modern education. They are forced to accept full equality, not only in standards, but in academic responsibility. Thus Edward B. Evans and his successors at Prairie View have presided over one of the most volatile and revolutionary eras of Negro education.

What has been the outstanding role of the parent institution throughout the "three ages" of Prairie View development? Generally Texas A&M, contrary to the Griffenhagen Report, has failed to dictate or prescribe the academic or social standards of the institution. If the A&M System has had a "policy" relative to its branches that policy historically has dictated a laissez-faire stance. The branches have for the most part been left to their own devices, to develop their own strengths, and to possess their own foibles.

George Woolfolk, a nationally recognized scholar, and an able spokesman for Prairie View A&M, sees four prominent features of Texas A&M's stewardship: (1) Within the perspective of the time and period in which Texas A&M operated and of the prevailing attitude in Texas and the nation toward black education, Texas A&M has been reasonably responsible. (2) Texas A&M has responded to the dominant trends in the field of developing knowledge and science and has instigated a similar response at Prairie View, providing Prairie View with such things as a branch Experiment Station, an

Extension Service, short courses, and technical know-how. (3) Texas A&M did try to understand the aspirations of black people to seek their own identity and their own dignity. Prairie View has been allowed to develop on its own initiatives. The role of the Board of Directors of A&M has been more to advise than to direct, and to permit considerable latitude to the local administration of Prairie View. The Board, says Woolfolk, has weathered much criticism in behalf of Prairie View and has sheltered it from many storms. (4) Prairie View has profited over the years, in participating in the general esteem the state has for Texas A&M, which he believes to be broad-based and deep. President Evans supports Woolfolk's conclusions.[68]

There is, nonetheless, considerable sentiment among Negroes in the state at large for the complete separation of Prairie View College from the Texas A&M System. Such a course, Evans and Woolfolk believe, is possible under the prevailing rise of the Negro to political affluence and the contemporary ideas of black separatism. Such an eventuality, they feel, would leave Prairie View College vulnerable to the danger of becoming a political football.

John Tarleton, the founder of Tarleton State College, Stephenville, Texas, and John Tarleton Institute, in Knoxville, Tennessee,[69] is a most unusual and enigmatic benefactor of public education. A biographer, C. Richard King, says that Tarleton's personal characteristics paralleled his paradoxical life:

> Although he always carried two rolls of money and had coins sewed in the patches of his clothing, Tarleton preferred to walk the distance from his Palo Pinto-Erath County ranch to the nearest post office because he considered himself financially unable to afford a horse. He fell in love with the red feather of a lady's hat, married the woman, and then charged her half the expenses of a honeymoon trip to Philadelphia.[70]

John Tarleton was born in Vermont in November 1808, and orphaned at the age of six. He left the aunt who was caring for him as soon as he could and worked his way to Tennessee, where he got a job teaching school for $30 a month. Later, about 1825, he accepted a job with Cowan-Dickerson, merchants, and stayed with the firm forty years, living frugally in the back of the

[68]Interview with George Ruble Woolfolk, Prairie View A&M, October 11, 1971; interview with Edward B. Evans and George R. Woolfolk, Prairie View A&M, October 11, 1971.

[69]J. Thomas Davis (ed.), *John Tarleton: A Memorial to the Founder of Tarleton College* (1933), pp. 47-57.

[70]C. Richard King, "John Tarleton," *Southwestern Historical Quarterly*, LV (October 1951), p. 240.

shop and investing his savings in government certificates issued to soldiers as bounties for locating land. At the end of the Civil War, Tarleton bought warrants for ten thousand acres of land in Palo Pinto, Erath, and Hood counties in Texas, at a price of about 12.5 cents an acre. In 1865 he came to Texas, dressed as a tramp, with his money concealed in his clothing. He settled first in Waco, where he opened a mercantile store which he operated until 1880. He then had his land surveyed, blocked it off into tracts of from 100 to 200 acres, and offered it for sale. As no buyers appeared, Tarleton began operating a ranch and fenced in 10,000 acres, from which he sold 600 to 700 calves a year and occasionally offered for sale lots of four hundred four-year-old steers.[71] He became, even by Texas standards, a big cattleman, who had many idiosyncrasies.

One biographer of Tarleton, Lillian Edwards, records that he "walked everywhere." He and his wife divorced in 1876, but remained friends. He ate two meals a day and had a glass of buttermilk for supper; he was never ill, except in Waco when an employee tried to poison him to get his money. He kept large amounts of cash on hand, and always paid his bills promptly and in full, sometimes paying more than was asked. He loved children, and believed in the value of an education. He died of typhoid fever on November 26, 1895, leaving a will filed at Palo Pinto, Texas.[72]

He left his property in Tennessee to the magistrates of the County Court of Knox County, the proceeds from the sale of which were to be used to found The John Tarleton Institute for the education of children between the ages of six and eighteen and of good moral character who were unable to educate themselves. All of his remaining property, "wheresoever located in the United States," he left to the county judge of Erath County, Texas, and to the governor of Texas, and their successors, to maintain in the city of Stephenville "The John Tarleton College" for the education of the children of Erath County between the ages of six and eighteen and of good moral character who were unable to education themselves.[73]

The trustees opened Stephenville College with an endowment of $85,000 on September 3, 1899, in the facilities of a previous private college operated by Dr. Marshall McIlhaney. The new college had a faculty of four, consisting of Lillie Pearl Chamberlain, Harry McIlhaney, Clara Bartholo-

[71]*Ibid.*, 241-245; Davis (ed.), *John Tarleton*, 47-51. There is a conflict between the two authors in the dates of Tarleton's land purchase. King says the purchase was made in 1860 or 1861, Lillian Edwards in the memorial says 1865, which date would fit the land prices and the occasion of Tarleton's leaving for Texas. The patents to the land were dated 1861.

[72]Davis (ed.), *John Tarleton*, 47-54.

[73]*Ibid.*, 54-57.

mew, and President William Hershel Bruce. E. E. Bramlette replaced Bruce, and Lourania Miller replaced Miss Bartholomew in the second year. The school began to grow with new faculty and new students. New rooms were added and between 1902 and 1907 Lillie Pearl Chamberlain served as "lady principal." Around 1909 the school encountered bad times and began to deplete its endowment. In 1913 James F. Cox became president, and new bequests were made by Mollie J. Crow and Mary Corn-Wilkerson. The College struggled fitfully for existence. In 1917 a movement was started to get the state to take over the College as a branch of Texas A&M.[74] Many felt that as a trustee of Tarleton's estate Texas had certain obligations to the school.

Some opposition to Texas A&M's "branching out" developed in Bryan and among Texas A&M alumni, who felt that it would weaken the academic programs and reduce attendance at Texas A&M. Many local businessmen believed that a branch would absorb money which should be coming to the Bryan-College Station area. Opponents to A&M's annexation of the Stephenville college argued the unconstitutionality of such a move, holding that a statewide referendum was necessary. Attorney General Looney, however, rendered an opinion in response to a legislative inquiry, holding that branch A&M colleges were legal and that the Legislature had the power to levy taxes for their support. Looney argued that a college "branch" was simply a matter of nomenclature. A branch would be a "separate and independent institution" whose only connection to another school was to have the same managing board.[75]

The question of having a branch of A&M at Stephenville, as well as at Arlington, had some bearing on the problem of establishing a West Texas Agricultural and Mechanical College west of the ninety-eighth meridian and north of of the twenty-ninth parallel, West Texas A&M College having been called for in 1916 by the state Democratic convention.

In November 1916 a delegation from Sweetwater, Texas, appeared before the A&M Directors asking the Board's support for a legislative bill to establish a West Texas A&M College, the college to be under the direction of the A&M Board. The Directors not only failed to support the delegation, but went on record in opposition to the proposal. The Directors did say, however, that they would favor the founding of junior agricultural colleges under A&M auspices.[76] A bill establishing a West Texas A&M actually passed the

[74]*Ibid.*, 77-81.
[75]Bryan *Daily Eagle and Pilot*, September 6, 7, 1917.
[76]Texas A&M, *Biennial Report, 1917-1918*, p. 150; Minutes of the Board of Directors, November 29, 1916, III, 206.

Legislature in 1917, but was repealed in a later session of the same Legislature. Texas A&M supporters opposed creating a "duplicate" A&M, even under the auspices of the same Board of Directors. A legislative investigating committee recommended instead that A&M establish six junior agricultural colleges to include John Tarleton at Stephenville and Grubbs Vocational College at Arlington. It can be surmised then, that at least in part, Texas A&M's decision to branch out came as a product of pressure from West Texas to establish a "rival" institution. The junior A&M colleges would undermine support for a full-scale West Texas A&M College while providing useful feeder schools and new regional influence for Texas A&M. President Bizzell sought to assure the alumni that "every effort will be made to so correlate the work of these institutions so as not to result detrimentally to the Agricultural and Mechanical College."[77]

It was in this scheme of things that existing institutions already at Stephenville and at Arlington came seeking admission to the A&M "system." The Thirty-fifth Legislature approved on February 20, 1917, a bill "to establish a branch of the Agricultural and Mechanical College of Texas, at Stephenville, Texas, and to be known as the John Tarleton Agricultural College."[78] On March 24 the A&M Board of Directors visited Stephenville. The citizens of Erath County, as recipients of John Tarleton's will, donated the existing college facilities and campus to the state, plus an additional endowment of 500 acres of land and $75,000 to be used for a student-loan fund. The Directors accepted the land and endowments, and prepared an itemized budget for the school.[79] On June 29 the Directors appointed James F. Cox, who had served as president of Stephenville College since 1913, as dean of the branch college.[80] The College began operation in September 1917, offering the last two years of high school and courses in agriculture, home economics, and the arts and sciences for the first two years of college.[81]

The first faculty of the newly constituted John Tarleton Agricultural College, in addition to President Cox, consisted of these persons:

E. E. Binford — Professor of Agriculture

A. L. Darnell — Professor of Animal Husbandry and Dairying

S. F. Davis — Professor of Chemistry and Physics

George O. Ferguson — Professor of History and Rural Economics

[77]Texas A&M, *Biennial Report, 1917-1918*, pp. 16, 150-151; W. B. Bizzell, "New Agricultural College," *Alumni Quarterly*, II (January 1917), pp. 3-4.

[78]*General Laws of Texas, 1917*, p. 58.

[79]Minutes of the Board of Directors, March 23, 1917, III, 212-213.

[80]*Ibid.*, June 29, 1917, III, 217.

[81]*The Government of the State of Texas*, XI, *Education*, 161.

L. C. Sellers — Registrar and Accountant
J. S. Ward — Assistant Professor of Modern Languages
Mrs. Lillie Pearl Chamberlain — Instructor in Applied Arts
C. A. Hale — Instructor in Mathematics
Miss Leaffa Ranall — Professor of Domestic Science
A. B. Hays — Director of Athletics
E. L. Reid — Professor of Biology
R. A. Smith — Professor of English
J. L. Riley — Professor of Mathematics
Miss Lillian Kiber — Professor of Domestic Arts [82]

Shortly after legislative approval of the Stephenville branch of A&M, a bill was passed and approved March 26, 1917, establishing at "Arlington, Tarrant County, Texas, a junior agricultural, mechanical, and industrial college to be known as Grubbs Vocational College."[83] The citizens of Arlington donated to the state 100 acres of land and the campus and buildings of the Carlisle Military School, which had ceased to operate and was in the custody of Judge V. W. Grubbs of Tarrant County.[84]

Established by James M. Carlisle in the 1890s, the Carlisle Military School had a brief, fitful life and expired in 1913. James M. Carlisle, the founder, was born in Coffee County, Tennessee, in 1851, graduated from Emory College, in Georgia, in 1879, and opened a private school in Whitesboro, Texas, the next year. He became superintendent of schools in Corsicana in 1887, and then in Fort Worth in 1890. He became president of the Texas State Teachers Association in 1891, and in August of that year Governor James S. Hogg named him state superintendent of public education. He began the military school in 1895 after his term of office as superintendent. After 1913 a new proprietor, Henry K. Taylor, operated the school under the name of Arlington Training School, but by 1917 it had closed.[85] As with Stephenville, local interest in maintaining a public school encouraged the citizens of Arlington to seek state support. Arlington's interest in securing a branch of A&M was as timely as was Stephenville's. Texas A&M was being coerced into an expansionist position.

The charter for the College provided a broader academic mandate than that possessed by John Tarleton, Prairie View, or Texas A&M. The College was established for

[82]Minutes of the Board of Directors, October 1, 1917, III, 225.
[83]*General Laws of Texas, 1917*, p. 260.
[84]Minutes of the Board of Directors, June 29, 1917, III, 217-221; and July 31, 1917, III, 222; *The Government of the State of Texas*, XI, *Education*, 214.
[85]Walter Prescott Webb and H. Bailey Carroll (eds.), *The Handbook of Texas*, I, 296-297.

the education of white boys and girls in the state in the arts and sciences in which such boys and girls may acquire a good literary education of academic grade, at least, together with a knowledge of agriculture, horticulture, floriculture, stock raising, and domestic arts and sciences, including the several branches and studies usually taught in the established institutions of like character, with such limitations as may be imposed by the governing board of the Agricultural and Mechanical College of Texas, having in view the training of youth for the more important industrial activities of life, while acquiring faculties for the acquirement of a good practical literary education not below the academic grade.[86]

The first faculty of Grubbs Vocational School, whose name was changed in 1923 to North Texas Junior Agricultural College, included the following:

M. L. Williams — Dean and Professor of Education
J. M. L. Ridgell — Professor of Agriculture
C. H. Alspaugh — Assistant Professor of Horticulture
A. A. Wood — Professor of Chemistry and Physics
Thomas E. Ferguson — Professor of English
J. S. Mendenhall — Professor of Mathematics
Miss Bertie Bolton — Professor of Domestic Science
Miss Cora Reynolds — Instructor in Applied Art
Miss Sallie Body Henry — Professor of Domestic Art
Miss Dora Ella Watson — Instructor in Modern Languages
Miss Adeline Holloway — Instructor in Music
M. A. Scott — Professor of History and Rural Sociology [87]

The College, located between the rising industrial centers of Fort Worth and Dallas, and in a rather densely populated area of the state, offered studies equivalent to the last two years of high school, junior college courses in agriculture, home economics, engineering, and the sciences, and semitechnical or vocational courses for special students below the college level.[88]

The curricula of both John Tarleton Agricultural College and Grubbs Vocational College were modeled and molded on the lines of the Texas A&M curricula and were intended to dovetail into the Texas A&M studies so that students could transfer into the advanced college courses at College Station without loss of credits or time. This tended to discourage academic diversification at the branches. By the 1930s Arlington had become heavily committed to a liberal-arts and technical program stemming from student demands. Tarleton, on the other hand, continued an academic program more

[86]*General Laws of Texas, 1917*, p. 260.
[87]Minutes of the Board of Directors, October 1, 1917, III, 226.
[88]*The Government of the State of Texas*, XI, *Education*, 214-218.

in accord with that of Texas A&M, but, unlike A&M, had strong programs in education and liberal arts. Each branch, particularly the Arlington branch, was to have different experiences, different demands, and a different academic orientation from that of Texas A&M.[89]

Perhaps indicative of the mold which A&M sought to impose upon its branches was the fact that the first major building contracts awarded by the Board of Directors at each of the branches in 1918 were for agricultural buildings — $87,435.30 for an agricultural building at Tarleton; $91,878.00 for an agricultural building at Arlington; and $60,979.00 for an agricultural building at Prairie View.[90] The branches happened to come into the A&M System at a time when agriculture was the order of the day, not only at A&M, but throughout Texas. There was some validity to the Griffenhagen Report of 1932 that Texas A&M was imposing something of an academic strait jacket upon its branches by its rather narrow emphasis upon agriculture and engineering.[91] The good intentions of this emphasis failed to diminish its effect as a source of problems and conflicts within the system. Fortunately the Board's overriding policy of self-determination allowed the branches sufficient leeway to develop independently in other academic areas. Each did so to the point that even by 1932 the aforementioned Griffenhagen Report recognized the unique identity and purpose of each of the A&M branches as something separate and apart from Texas A&M.

James F. Cox, the first dean of John Tarleton Agricultural College, was replaced in 1919 by J. Thomas Davis. Cox became president of Abilene Christian College, in nearby Abilene. Davis was a Bizzell protegé and was groomed for the Tarleton job. When Bizzell left Navasota to go to the College of Industrial Arts for Women (Texas Women's University), in Denton, Bizzell helped select J. Thomas Davis as his successor in the office of superintendent of schools at Navasota. Cox began his job as dean in a strictly caretaker role, for Bizzell called upon Davis to take the dean's job soon after Tarleton became a branch of A&M. In preparation for his new job as dean of an agricultural school, Davis left Navasota and enrolled in agriculture at A&M, securing a B.A. and a B.S. in Agriculture Education in June 1920. He received his appointment as dean at John Tarleton in 1919 before receiving the degrees.[92]

Tarleton's curricula in agriculture and in engineering were closely inte-

[89]*Ibid.*, 214-230.

[90]Minutes of the Board of Directors, January 28, 1918, III, 230-231.

[91]*The Government of the State of Texas*, XI, *Education*, 4-6, 166-168, 220-223.

[92]Interview with Eugene Joseph Howell, Tarleton State College, Stephenville, Texas, September 18, 1971; Texas A&M, *Directory of Former Students, 1876-1957*, p. 85.

grated with those at Texas A&M. Tarleton, under statutory provisions, also offered the last two years of high school. Military training, as at A&M, was compulsory for all male students.[93] The academic growth of Tarleton paralleled that at Texas A&M. While A&M developed along the lines of agriculture, mechanics, sciences, and military science, Tarleton developed along those same lines, with home economics and business administration as distinctive fields.[94]

While Tarleton experienced sustained growth during its early years, it was, and remains, a small college. Enrollment in the regular sessions for 1922-1923 stood at 589, rose to 808 in 1925, 1,013 in 1930-1931, and remained fairly steady throughout the thirties; the postwar years (World War II) brought enormous enrollment increases, as at almost every college in the United States, as veterans returned to college under the GI bill. Since approximately 1950, enrollment at Tarleton has ranged between 2,000 and 3,500.[95] Former President Edward Joseph Howell (1946-1966) believes that one of the unique qualities and attributes of Tarleton State College, as it is known today, is that it is a small college, and retains the personal and comfortable atmosphere of a small college, an atmosphere that has been completely lost on most campuses in contemporary times. Howell does not hope to see Tarleton grow too large, and does not believe that it will. The size of an educational institution, he believes, is necessarily closely correlated to the economic growth of the area it serves.[96] The agricultural, pastoral environment of Stephenville gives little promise of intensive industrial growth, or of unusual population increases.

Tarleton State College is unique too in that it has had only four presidents in its six decades of existence: James F. Cox, J. Thomas Davis, Eugene J. Howell, and William Oren Trogdon. Howell, who became president after World War II, was one of the pioneers at Tarleton, beginning his work there in 1923. He was born in Waco on December 6, 1900, and finished high school there in 1918. He applied for admission to The University of Texas, but could be admitted only on probation because he lacked a foreign language, which in those days was one of the admission requirements to The University. He then applied to A&M, entered in September 1918, studied chemical engineering, and received his B.S. in 1922. Howell then accepted a

[93]Interview with Eugene Joseph Howell, Tarleton State College, Stephenville, Texas, September 18, 1971.

[94]*Ibid.*

[95]*The Government of the State of Texas*, XI, *Education*, 162; interview with E. J. Howell, Tarleton State College, September 18, 1971.

[96]Interview with E. J. Howell, Tarleton State College, September 18, 1971.

job with Gulf Refining Company in Port Arthur. He planned to marry, asked for a teaching job at A&M, which he had previously declined, and soon afterwards received a call from Dean Davis at Tarleton.[97]

Davis offered him a job teaching chemistry at Tarleton. "When do you want me?" Howell inquired. "School has already started, I want you Monday," Davis told him. Davis finally gave him an extra week. During those ten days Howell married, and began the two-day drive to Stephenville in his Model T, with his bride and belongings.[98] Even now, when asked what his first impressions of Tarleton were, Howell says, "Listen, I had no impressions. I was a newlywed."[99]

After teaching only one year Howell was given the jobs of registrar and commandant, a dual assignment in those days, plus a $600 raise, which convinced him he should go into administration. In 1930 Howell went to College Station to assume the duties of assistant registrar under Dean Charles E. Friley. When Friley left A&M, Howell became registrar. A reserve officer, Howell received a call to active duty in June 1941 (prior to Pearl Harbor), and wound up in Washington, D.C. After Pearl Harbor he applied for a combat assignment but received training duty at Fort Hood, Texas, then the Tank Destroyer Training Center. His school record followed him everywhere, says Howell, for throughout World War II his primary duty was that of a registrar (or commanding officer) of officer-training schools. Howell left active duty in 1945, a lieutenant colonel.[100]

He was named dean of John Tarleton Agricultural College in July 1945, was released from active duty in August, and began his long tenure as dean and president on September 1, 1945. One of his most important accomplishments, Howell believes, was guiding Tarleton through its postwar growing pains. Over half the students were veterans, he recalls, and trailers for married students were scattered at various points about the campus. By 1946 the interest of the students clearly leaned toward liberal arts. The faculty was thin in numbers and in Ph.D.'s, there being, he said, only two or three Ph.D's in the entire faculty in 1946.[101]

Howell worked arduously to build the faculty, and in 1949 succeeded in having the name of the College changed to Tarleton State College, which reflected the diminishing role of agriculture in the studies. Howell recalls that the high-school studies were maintained at Tarleton as required by state

[97] *Ibid.*
[98] *Ibid.*
[99] *Ibid.*
[100] *Ibid.*
[101] *Ibid.*

law, although the programs received constantly fewer students, and consistently smaller appropriations from the Legislature. The point was quickly
reached where the academic program was being operated "on the cuff." In
1953 Tarleton received legislative approval to become a four-year-degree-
granting institution, authorized to award the B.A. degree in liberal arts only.
Tarleton awarded its first degrees in 1963, won full accreditation from the
Southern Association of Colleges and Schools in 1966, and has since been
authorized to offer the B.A. in agriculture, business, education, physical education, home economics, industrial arts, mathematics, sciences, and music.[102]

Before his retirement in 1966 Howell presided over considerable physical expansion of the campus. A new student center, a library, an athletic field,
and an agriculture building were constructed. The original agricultural building, incidentally, begun in 1918, has long served as the administration building. Two women's dormitories, two men's dormitories, and expansion of the
science building, shops, and roads occurred.[103] Howell recalls that his administrative relations with the A&M Board of Directors, chancellors, presidents
and deans were always most cordial and effective. He believes that as a
branch of Texas A&M, Tarleton State College profited from the experiences
and prestige of the main campus. In accord with E. B. Evans of Prairie View,
he believes the advantages of being a branch have far outweighed the disadvantages, and anticipates that relationship to continue indefinitely.

Grubbs Vocational School at Arlington, renamed the North Texas Junior Agricultural College in 1923, experienced much the same development as
Tarleton State College, but on a much more intensified scale, especially after
World War II. Because of its proximity to the burgeoning metropolitan Dal-
las-Fort Worth area, Arlington experienced tremendous growth in the forties
and fifties. It early became liberal-arts- and engineering-oriented, with agriculture painfully in arrears.[104] After World War II Arlington was allowed, by
legislative and Board approval, to substantially broaden its curricula, and, like
Tarleton, to grant degrees and establish a full four-year college offering. In
1949, as in the case of John Tarleton Agricultural College, the Legislature
changed the name of North Texas Junior Agricultural College to Arlington
State College, and in 1959 the College was elevated to senior-college rank. In
the late fifties and early sixties Arlington grew at a more rapid rate than
Texas A&M.[105] Marion Thomas Harrington, chancellor of the Texas A&M
University System (1953-1959), which was created by the Board of Directors

[102]*Ibid.;* Tarleton State College, *Catalogue, 1970-1971,* pp. 39-40.
[103]Interview with E. J. Howell, Tarleton State College, September 18, 1971.
[104]*The Government of the State of Texas,* XI, *Education,* 215-219.
[105]The University of Texas at Arlington, *Catalog, 1970-1971,* p. 5.

in 1948, recalls that Arlington's growth placed severe financial strains on Texas A&M, and Arlington, conversely, felt that its subordinate role in the A&M System prevented adequate funding for Arlington State College's tremendous expansion.[106]

Texas, meanwhile, had initiated efforts to correlate more closely and effectively state colleges and universities by the creation of a Texas Commission on Higher Education, which after extensive investigations reported to the Governor on December 1, 1958. The work of the Commission led to the establishment of the Coordinating Board, Texas College and University System, which defined the role and scope of Texas institutions of higher education. Arlington State College, availing itself of the use of politics, seized the opportunity offered by the reorganization to withdraw from the Texas A&M College System and in 1965 became a branch of The University of Texas. In 1967, with legislative approval, the Regents of The University changed the name of the College to The University of Texas at Arlington.[107]

Former Chancellor Harrington recalls that the departure of Arlington, though regretted by the A&M administration, was believed to be in the best interests of both institutions, and occurred with the blessings of Texas A&M. Harrington, and many others, however, regret that Texas A&M failed to retain a System institution in one of the great metropolitan areas of Texas.[108] For better or for worse, much of what Prairie View Agricultural and Mechanical College, Tarleton State College, and The University of Texas at Arlington are today may be attributed to the long stewardship of Texas A&M.

[106]Interview with Marion Thomas Harrington, Texas A&M University, College Station, Texas, September 13, 1971.
[107]The University of Texas at Arlington, *Catalog, 1970-1971*, p. 5.
[108]Interview with Marion Thomas Harrington, Texas A&M University, September 13, 1971

CHAPTER 16

The Veterinarians

VETERINARY medicine had an early but fitful beginning at Texas A&M. Despite initial difficulties, by 1888 veterinary medicine had become a recognized field of study at Texas A&M, supported by its own department — staffed by one man. Happily, that one man was Dr. Mark Francis. Moving steadily ahead from this humble beginning, by the 1930s the School of Veterinary Medicine claimed to have one of the largest and most successful programs in veterinary medicine in the world. Texas A&M's achievement in this field can be attributed largely to the pioneering work of Mark Francis and a handful of other men.

The first official record of instruction in veterinary medicine at A&M occurs in the catalogue for 1879-1880, when D. Port Smythe, the College physician, is listed as "Professor of Biology, Hygiene and Veterinary Science."[1] John Garland James, newly installed as president of the A&M College following the expulsion of Thomas S. Gathright and his faculty in November 1879, created two fields of study, one in agriculture and one in engineering, each with a three-year curriculum. The curriculum in agriculture included a one-semester course in veterinary science. The course description indicated that studies included the anatomy and physiology of domestic animals (with laboratory work in the dissection and study of typical organisms), veterinary pathology (including the nature, causes, symptoms, prevention, and treatment of the general and epizootic diseases of domestic animals), lectures on heredity, and veterinary materia medica (involving the preparation and use of the principal medicines in veterinary practice). Textbooks used in the instruction included Owen's *Comparative Anatomy*, Youatt on the horse, Harris on the pig, Wythe on the microscope, Randall's *Sheep Husbandry*, and Jennings' *Cattle and Their Diseases*.[2] The entire agricultural program, however,

[1]Texas A&M, *Catalogue*, 1879. p. 9.

[2]*Ibid.*, 26; Hubert Schmidt, *Eighty Years of Veterinary Medicine: A Brief History of the School of Veterinary Medicine. 1879-1958*, pp. 1-2; Joseph Harris, *Harris on the Pig, Breeding, Rearing, Management, and Improvement* (1883); Robert Jennings, *Cattle and Their Diseases* (1863); Sir Richard Owen, *On the Anatomy of Vertebrates* (1866-1868); Harry Stephens Randall, *Sheep Hus-*

including the course in veterinary science, virtually ceased to exist when most of the agricultural students changed to the mechanics course during the first fall that the program was offered.[3] The field work required of the agriculture students had less attraction than the shopwork required of the engineering students, and the agricultural studies were almost void of students in the early years. For a number of years enrollment in agricultural studies remained marginal.

Beginning in the fall of 1881 Charles C. Gorgeson, who joined the faculty in 1879 as "Professor of Scientific and Practical Agriculture and Horticulture," assumed the duty of teaching veterinary science. Dr. Smythe continued to serve as College physician until 1884, when John D. Read, M.D., replaced him. Thereafter veterinary science remained in the bailiwick of the agriculturists. Gorgeson prepared himself for his new teaching duties by taking courses in veterinary medicine at Iowa State College, in Ames, during the summer of 1881.[4] Gorgeson faced thin enrollments in the agricultural studies, and lamented the lack of livestock for instructional purposes. "It is about as impossible to teach practical stock-breeding without livestock as to teach carpentry without tools and shop work," he reported prior to his departure from the College in 1883.[5]

George Washington Curtis replaced Gorgeson as professor of agriculture in September 1883. During his first year at A&M Curtis repeated Gorgeson's experience in finding "a prejudice against agriculture among the students."[6] During his second year, however, the agricultural course was substantially reorganized; and students' objections to farm labor were partially overcome by distinguishing between "uninstructive labor," for which the student was compensated at 6 to 10 cents per hour, and "instructive labor," for which he received no monetary compensation.[7] Curtis now offered a course in veterinary anatomy. The first class in veterinary anatomy prepared the skeleton of a horse for instructional purposes.[8] The skeleton remained in use

bandry (1863); Joseph Henry Wythe, *The Microscopist: A Manual of Microscopy and Compendium of the Microscopic Sciences* (1877); William Youatt, *Youatt's History, Treatment and Diseases of the Horse* (1859).

[3]Texas A&M, *Catalogue, 1879,* p. 48.

[4]Charles C. Gorgeson, Ames, Iowa, to Louis L. McInnis, College Station, Texas, August 16, 1881, Louis L. McInnis Papers, Texas A&M University Archives.

[5]Galveston *Daily News,* June 15, 1883.

[6]Texas A&M, *Annual Report, 1883-1884,* p. 13.

[7]Texas A&M, *Catalogue, 1884,* pp. 48-49.

[8]*Ibid.*

on the A&M campus for many years. Over the next few years interest in agriculture and in veterinary studies rose significantly.

A combination of factors paved the way for the advent of a serious program in veterinary studies initiated at the College in June 1888. First, through the efforts of Faculty Chairman Hardaway Hunt Dinwiddie (1883-1887) and George Curtis, farmers and cattlemen around the state became increasingly aware of the merits and the economic value of scientific stockbreeding and care. Texas A&M began to win support for its agricultural programs among the Grange, and, in particular, among Texas farmers and cattlemen.[9] Secondly, the decade of the eighties marked the crossroads for the Texas livestock industry. A practical barbed wire, invented by Joseph G. Glidden, of Illinois, in 1873, began to have a great impact on the Texas open-range cattle industry, which reached its zenith with the "fencing wars" of 1887 and 1888.[10] The Homestead Act, nester farmers, the increased drilling of water wells and the use of windmills, and enclosed pastures brought a rapid end to the day of the open range. The severe winters of 1885 and 1886, followed by protracted droughts, destroyed hundreds of thousands of Texas cattle, and millions more in the northern plains.[11] All of these factors contributed to the end of open-range ranching, and led to more intensive animal-husbandry practices, which in turn created a greater demand for trained veterinarians. Perhaps most influential to the development of veterinary medicine in Texas was the increasing reluctance of northern states to admit Texas cattle, and the reluctance of northern buyers to purchase Texas cattle because of the Texas tick fever. While Texas cattle were generally immune to the fever, contact with northern herds invariably produced fever epidemics which destroyed entire herds. Even before the Civil War, Missouri had enacted laws against the admission of Texas cattle because of the fever (1855), and the Territory of Kansas passed similar restrictions in 1859. By the 1880s the marketing of Texas cattle faced such serious legislative obstacles that the future of the industry was in jeopardy.[12]

The wording of the Hatch Act of March 2, 1887, establishing federally supported agricultural experiment stations, suggests that Texas tick fever, a great concern of the American beef industry, played an important role in the formulation of the legislation. The act calls for "research . . . on the

[9]"Letter from the Master of the Texas State Grange" [A. J. Rose] to the Patrons of Husbandry, Farmers, Mechanics and all interested, February 2, 1887, clipping in Louis L. McInnis Papers, Texas A&M University Archives; see also Chapter 5.

[10]Gammel (ed.), *Laws of Texas,* IX, 600-603.

[11]Lewis Atherton, *The Cattle Kings,* 4-5.

[12]*Ibid.,* 8, 45, 155, 273.

physiology of plants and animals; the diseases to which they are severally subject, with the remedies for the same."[13] According to Mark Francis, the first trained veterinarian at Texas A&M, the work of the Texas Agricultural Experiment Station upon its inception in 1888 "was mainly devoted to the 'Texas Fever' problem."[14] Texas fever and the Hatch Act, which brought about the establishment of an agricultural experiment station at Texas A&M, together with the advent of more intensive stock-raising techniques and a more favorable attitude toward scientific agriculture, combined to bring about the establishment of a comprehensive program in veterinary medicine at Texas A&M in 1888.

Appointed chairman of the faculty on January 24, 1888, Louis Lowry McInnis on that same day presented a plan to the Board of Directors for establishing an agricultural experiment station under College auspices. At the same time he called for the creation of an academic Department of Veterinary Science. The Directors approved both of McInnis' recommendations, and on January 25, 1888, formally recognized the Department of Veterinary Science as one of the eleven academic branches of the College.[15] In April the College received, as a part of its biennial budget, state appropriations of $2,500 for equipment for the Department of Veterinary Medicine.[16] On June 6, 1888, the Board of Directors named Dr. Mark Francis, of Ohio, associate professor of veterinary science and veterinarian of the newly created Experiment Station.[17] This appointment marked the real beginning of A&M's program of veterinary medicine.

Not only was Mark Francis the first veterinarian at Texas A&M, but he became one of the most distinguished men in American veterinary history. He was born at Shandon, Ohio, March 19, 1863, and graduated from Ohio State University in 1887 with the degree of Doctor of Veterinary Medicine.[18] On the occasion of the seventy-fifth anniversary of the founding of Ohio State University, in 1936, Ohio State University President William Oxley Thompson paid Francis the following tribute: "If Ohio State University had trained but one man in the 75 years of its existence, and that man was Dr. Mark Francis of Texas, it had given back to its people more than they had expended upon it in the three-quarters of a century of its existence."[19]

[13]24 *Stat. L.*, 440.

[14]Schmidt, *History of the School of Veterinary Medicine*, 2.

[15]Minutes of the Board of Directors, January 24 and 25, 1888, I, 43, 47.

[16]*Texas Senate Journal, Extra Session, 1888*, pp. 33-34.

[17]Minutes of the Board of Directors, June 6, 1889, I, 59.

[18]"Mark Francis — Biographical," Texas A&M University Archives; Bryan *Eagle,* July 3, 1936; College Station *Battalion,* May 24, 1933; Dallas *Morning News,* June 24, 1936.

[19]*The Norden News,* X (September-October 1936), p. 6; "Mark Francis — Biographical,"

Francis, upon graduation, went to the American Veterinary College in New York, and in the summer of 1888 worked in a veterinary hospital in Cincinnati, Ohio, where he was approached about the job at Texas A&M.[20]

According to an account written by Dr. Mark Francis in 1934, and reproduced by Hubert Schmidt in his very informative *History of the College of Veterinary Medicine* (1958), Francis attributes his move to Texas to Dr. H. J. Detmers, a pathologist with the U.S. Department of Agriculture, and to Judge George Pfeuffer. Francis recalls that Detmers was sent to Texas to investigate the Texas-fever problem and came into contact with Pfeuffer. Detmers, like Pfeuffer, was a native of Germany. Their conferences, says Francis, led to a decision by the A&M Board of Directors to begin instruction in veterinary medicine. Judge Pfeuffer next advised the Board to contact Detmers as a possible head for studies in veterinary medicine. Detmers meanwhile had become head of the Veterinary School at Ohio State University. He declined the invitation but suggested for the job Mark Francis, who had just completed studies at the school.[21]

Francis' recollections are misleading if taken literally. George Pfeuffer died in Austin on September 14, 1886, and could not have personally instigated the hiring of Mark Francis in the summer of 1888. No evidence indicates that the A&M Directors ever "decided" to begin instruction in veterinary medicine (other than for the existing course in anatomy taught by George Curtis) while Pfeuffer was still living and prior to January 1888. A connection between Pfeuffer, Detmers, and Francis, however, could have existed nonetheless. The connecting link would necessarily have been Louis L. McInnis, who served as secretary of the Board of Directors throughout Pfeuffer's association with the College. McInnis was a close confidant of Pfeuffer and would undoubtedly have known of Pfeuffer's association with Detmers, and of any interest Pfeuffer may have had in establishing a program in veterinary medicine. It was McInnis, as the newly appointed chairman of the faculty, who presented the plan for a program in veterinary medicine, who contacted Detmers, and who employed Francis. Thus, while one cannot take Francis' account of his employment literally, the story is one that retains its essential validity. It is quite likely that George Pfeuffer, who died two years before its inception, had something to do with the beginning of a veterinary-medicine program at Texas A&M.

Texas A&M University Archives.

[20] Mark Francis, "History of the School of Veterinary Medicine," in Schmidt, *History of the School of Veterinary Medicine*, 2-3.

[21] *Ibid.*

As Hubert Schmidt remarks, "Mark Francis was prone to hide his light under a bushel." His sketchy remarks recalling the first decade or so of his experiences at Texas A&M grossly understate the magnitude of his achievements with Texas fever, but provide an insight into the character of the man, the physical layout of the veterinary-medicine "plant," and the enormous problems faced by the College. "It was the latter part of July or the first of August when I arrived at College Station," Francis wrote:

The college work at first was merely some classroom lectures to the agricultural students. There were no laboratories or equipment for this work. We had a room about 14 × 16 feet that was on the ground floor of the Main Building (destroyed by fire in May, 1912) that served as office, classroom and laboratory. At the end of the school year — June 1889 — the adjoining room became vacant and was assigned to us as a classroom. In this unsuitable place we toiled for fifteen years. There was no hospital. Along about December 1888 a frame barn was built to serve this purpose. It was about 20 × 36 feet and was near where the Agriculture Building now stands.

Box Stall		Feed Room
	Clinic Room	
Box Stall		Drugs and Instruments

The following year a frame building was provided that served as a dissecting room. This building was moved after some years and is now used as a feed room and horse shed immediately north of our new horse stable.

The Experiment Station work was mainly devoted to the "Texas Fever" problem. The director and I were both strangers in Texas and hardly knew the way to proceed. We decided to go to Austin to consult Gov. L. S. Ross. He was quite conservative but suggested that we go to San Antonio to consult John T. Lytle and other prominent cattlemen there, and to Rockport to consult Col. [George W.] Fulton. We did so. We found these men obliging but got no definite working suggestion from them. Col. Fulton suggested that the sulphur water on his ranch destroyed any virus or infection that may be the cause of this trouble, and he offered a car of cattle to be shipped north to make a practical test of it. This was accepted and I went to Rockport and loaded the animals and went with them to the Missouri Experiment Station at Columbia, Missouri. The Missouri station cooperated with the Texas station fully and is entitled to any credit that came from this work.

While at Columbia, Missouri, I made the acquaintance of Dr. J. W. Connaway who was in active charge there. He has been a competent and reliable associate. The idea at that time was that as the southern cattle show an immunity or a tolerance to this disease there must be in their blood something that is the physiological equivalent of an anti-toxin, and that if we were to secure a quantity of the blood-serum of these apparently immune cattle and inject it into northern cattle, that we could thereby produce a passive immunity or a tolerance that would enable us to import highgrade bulls to Texas without the discouraging losses that usually result when no precautions are taken. I am mentioning these matters in detail so you may understand the background of this work.

We drifted along several years but could not secure funds from the legislature for the necessary buildings or equipment. I think they felt that nothing could be done and it would simply be a waste of public money. They seemed to have little or no confidence in the A&M College. When Gov. L. S. Ross came here as president the attitude of the public changed rapidly. They had confidence in him and became more open minded about affairs here. We were asking for a building for Chemistry and one for Veterinary Medicine but failed to get either.

When Col. L. L. Foster became president of the college after Ross' death, he asked for a building costing $75,000.00 but he returned from Austin and said he could get only thirty-five or forty thousand dollars, and asked what we should do about it. We decided to accept it and build a two-story laboratory. The ground floor to be used for veterinary medicine and the second floor for chemistry. This building stood where Cushing Library now stands and was designed by Dodson and Scott of Waco. It served its purpose fairly well. It was demolished in 1933. The practical work in dissecting large animals was done in it for about ten years. About 1914 the one-story brick building that was used for shower baths for students and stood facing Nagle Street between Francis Hall Annex and the Chemistry building was assigned to us for a dissecting room and was used for that purpose until 1933 when our new dissecting room was completed and the old one demolished.

Our work required someone to help on the laboratory periods and Dr. J. H. Rietz served two years. He resigned and Dr. R[oss] P. Marsteller was appointed to fill the vacancy in 1905. We were having animal husbandry students only at that time. In a few years it was decided to add two more instructors and offer a four year course in veterinary medicine leading to a degree.

About this time the legislature allowed $125,000.00 for a suitable building for a proposed School of Veterinary Medicine but [Governor] O[scar] B. Colquitt, serving his second term, vetoed the item. Gov. J[ames] E. Ferguson became impressed with the favorable results obtained in immunizing bulls against "Texas Fever" on his Bosque County Ranch, February 1, 1916, and told the Board of Directors that he would approve an appropriation for suitable buildings for this purpose. The next session of the legislature provided about $100,000.00 to build this house. The plans were drawn by Endress and Watkins of Houston and it was finally completed and accepted in the summer of 1918.

Our classes were small for several years. Our course of study was submitted to the secretary of agriculture who approved it so that our graduates would be eligible for civil service appointments. In 1932 the directors decided to build a new hospital and clinic building and plans were prepared and the building built at a cost of $225,000.00 which was derived from oil funds.

The A&M College has been in operation about fifty years. We are now starting on the second fifty years, and there is no doubt in my mind that great progress will be made if we only do something that is important and useful.[22]

Francis devoted his life to doing things that were "important and useful."

Joseph F. Nichols, a student in one of Francis' first classes in veterinary medicine, provides an insight into the early (and contemporary) hazards of veterinary medicine:

> At one time we took the temperature of mules by inserting a thermometer under the tail of the mule. I had a great fear of the back end of a mule, but I succeeded in inserting my thermometer and my mule instantly ran gaily away with tail high in the air and from this romping mule I never secured return of the thermometer, so I never learned what its temperature was, and had to pay for the loss of the instrument.

The sequel to Nichols' story is that he transferred to horticulture and graduated with a B.S. degree in Agriculture in 1889.[23]

Mark Francis' research on Texas fever had a more profound impact upon the development of the program in veterinary medicine than did his early teaching experiences. Francis plunged into the Texas-fever problem by interviewing and consulting with cattlemen and public figures, including Governor Lawrence Sullivan Ross. Progress and direction were quite slow until work with ticks began to pay dividends. Through experiments conducted in cooperation with the Kansas Agricultural Experiment Station in 1893 and 1894, transmission of Texas fever was narrowed down to the common Southern tick, the "Boophilus Bovis." Incentive for these experiments had been provided in part by Richard J. Kleberg, of the King Ranch, who also aroused Francis' interest in the use of dipping vats for control of ticks. A "Device for Dipping Cattle to Destroy Ticks" was carefully detailed in the Texas Agricultural Experiment Station bulletin which reported Francis' findings on the tick, but no dipping formula was offered. The discovery that the tick transmitted Texas fever was the key to the problem of how to control the disease.[24]

Efforts to control Texas fever involved eradication of the tick and immunization of livestock. Again, progress was slowed by the meager laboratory facilities and equipment which Francis had at his disposal, but in a cooperative effort between the Texas Agricultural Experiment Station veterinarian, Mark Francis, and the veterinarian of the Missouri Agricultural Experi-

[22]*Ibid.*, 2.

[23]"Reminiscences of Joseph F. Nichols," Texas A&M University Archives.

[24]Mark Francis, "Veterinary Science," *Texas Agricultural Experiment Station Bulletin*, No. 30 (March 1894), pp. 437-458 (hereinafter cited: *TAES Bulletin*).

ment Station, J. W. Connaway, inoculation experiments conducted between 1896 and 1899 produced positive results. Noting that herd losses in cattle infected with Texas fever ordinarily ran from 40 to 70 percent, Francis and Connaway reported the following results from their experiments:[25]

1) The final results of the experiments on inoculation with sterile serum show that such material possesses no protective properties.

2) Immunizing by tick infestation can be employed with success, but on account of maintaining a quarantined pasture, and the necessity of hand-feeding in the case of calves of non-immune cows; this method is not as desirable as that of blood inoculation.

3) In the blood inoculation experiments over 400 pure bred cattle have been used. The losses from inoculation and from subsequent exposure to infected pastures in Texas, have been less than 8 percent.

Continuing experiments, Francis in 1902 issued a second report on Texas fever. This report confirmed the results of earlier experiments, suggested refinements in the pasturing and care of animals during the inoculation reaction, and concluded encouragingly: "a considerable degree of immunity against Texas fever can be brought about by producing an infection with the blood of Southern cattle."[26]

Francis, still not fully satisfied with his experiments on Texas fever, tried yet other inoculation experiments. In 1903 and 1904 he tried subcutaneous and intravenous injections of the soluble salts of quinine to see "if we can really control the disease." He also tried injections of the blood serum from horses. "I regret to say," he reported, "that we made a miserable failure in every instance."[27]

Experiments with eradication of the tick proved more frustrating than work with immunization. Francis built on the Texas A&M campus in 1896 a dipping vat, copied from one constructed by Richard J. Kleberg, Sr., manager of the King Ranch. Kleberg's vat had been constructed for purposes other than the control of the tick, and Francis decided to adapt it to his particular needs. He experimented with strong disinfectants, vegetable oils, mineral oils, and even electricity. The latter experiment proved disastrous. A cow was led into the dipping vat and a charge of electricity applied. The cow dropped dead and the irritated ticks went off to find a new host. Francis conducted some experiments with an arsenic dip, but was restrained from strengthening

---

[25]M. Francis and J. W. Connaway, "Texas Fever," *TAES Bulletin*, No. 53 (1899), pp. 55-106; *31st Annual Report of the State Board of Agriculture of Missouri*, 1899, pp. 309-315, 483-486.

[26]Mark Francis, "Texas Fever," *TAES Bulletin*, No. 63 (1902), pp. 1-60; *33rd Annual Report of the State Board of Agriculture of Missouri*, 1902, pp. 217-237.

[27]Texas A&M, *Biennial Report, 1903-1904*, p. 108.

his dip to the necessary point for fear that it would be too dangerous for public use. While Francis' dip formulas helped control the tick, arsenic dips were later developed which proved entirely successful and effective.[28]

The impact of Francis' work upon the cattle industry of the United States was great; the impact of his work upon the Texas cattle industry was greater still. Texas could now begin to develop quality beef herds by importing new breed stock. Francis' successes marked the beginning of the modern Texas cattle industry. Francis fully deserved the epithet applied to him as "father of the Texas cattle industry."[29]

Despite the perfection of dipping and inoculation practices for the control of Texas fever, Francis reported in 1912 that losses from the disease in the United States still approached $50 million per year in deaths, depreciation in livestock values, and restrictions on trade. He noted that considerable progress in eradicating the disease had been made east of the Mississippi River, where more fencing and small farms made control easier, but in Texas especially the disease remained terribly destructive. "The ticks must go," he said. "We cannot afford this expensive nuisance much longer. . . . It is infinitely wiser and better to do away with the disease than to resort to inoculation, which is but a temporary measure." Achievement of this goal, Francis said, would require trained men for proper management and inoculation of cattle, and in turn, he argued, would necessitate the establishment of a school of veterinary medicine in Texas.[30]

Efforts to control Texas fever provided not only the broad impetus behind the establishment of the School of Veterinary Medicine, but gave a very direct and immediate impulse to Governor James E. Ferguson's support for such a school. To be sure, Francis and the colleagues who joined him in veterinary medicine after the turn of the century were not exclusively preoccupied with Texas fever. In the decades after 1900 the veterinarians at College Station worked extensively and with considerable success in treating or preventing anthrax, black leg, tetanus, rabies, and especially hog cholera.[31] In one year, between September 1917 and September 1918, A&M veterinarians manufactured 116,476 doses of hog cholera serum, bought another 50,000 doses and borrowed 10,000 more, but still failed to meet the demand.[32]

Throughout the "pioneering years" of veterinary medicine at A&M,

[28]Schmidt, *History of the School of Veterinary Medicine*, 4-5.

[29]*Ibid.*, 36-37; *The Norden News*, X (September-October 1936), p. 6; "Mark Francis — Biographical," Texas A&M University Archives.

[30]Texas A&M, *Biennial Report, 1911-1912*, pp. 12-13.

[31]*Ibid.*, 1900-1902, p. 61.

[32]*Ibid.*, 1917-1918, p. 47.

buildings and equipment were invariably wanting. Requests for appropriations usually ranged from $2,000 to $10,000, and legislative handouts invariably provided less than the amount requested, and, on several occasions, special appropriations, even when acted upon favorably by the Legislature, were vetoed by the governor.[33] In 1908 the Veterinary Department received $5,000 for a veterinary hospital. This was used to build a facility containing a central 36 × 36-foot clinic room, eight box stalls, four tie stalls, an office, a feed room, a janitor's room, and a hay loft.[34] In 1913 Texas A&M requested an appropriation of $150,000 for the establishment of a School of Veterinary Medicine. The Legislature appropriated $125,000 and Governor Oscar Branch Colquitt, then "at war" with A&M President Robert Teague Milner, vetoed the appropriation.[35] Finally, in 1915, Texas A&M received approval and financial support for a School of Veterinary Medicine. The success came in part because Governor James E. Ferguson was himself a progressive cattleman who knew the value of the program in veterinary medicine.

The Thirty-fourth Legislature appropriated $100,000 for a veterinary hospital, the money to become available in 1917. At the instigation of the Swine Raisers Association of Texas the Legislature also allocated $15,000 to A&M for a serum laboratory for the manufacture of hog-cholera serum. Ferguson personally supported both bills and was interested to the point that in 1916 he imported for his ranch a number of quality breeding bulls which were immunized against Texas fever by Dr. Hubert Schmidt. Later in the year Schmidt visited Ferguson's ranch to advise him on the management of his herd.[36] It is obvious why "Farmer Jim" Ferguson waged his higher-education war against The University of Texas, not against Texas A&M.

Francis Hall, still standing in 1973, was completed in 1918, two years after the official inauguration of the new School of Veterinary Medicine. On April 10, 1916, the Board of Directors established the School of Veterinary Medicine as a part of the Agricultural and Mechanical College. The School was authorized to award the degree of Doctor of Veterinary Medicine. The Directors named Dr. Mark Francis as dean and professor of veterinary medicine and surgery.[37] By 1918 even the new facilities appeared inadequate. The

[33]*Ibid.,* 1900-1902, pp. 61-62; 1903-1904, p. 86; 1905-1906, p. 53; 1907-1908, p. 14.

[34]*Ibid.,* 1907-1908, p. 14; Schmidt, *History of the School of Veterinary Medicine,* 8. This building was located on what is now the corner of Spence and Roberts Streets at the east end of the existing engineering building.

[35]Texas A&M, *Biennial Report, 1911-1912,* p. 13; Schmidt, *History of the School of Veterinary Medicine,* 3, 8.

[36]Texas A&M, *Biennial Report, 1915-1916,* 11-12; Schmidt, *History of the School of Veterinary Medicine,* 8; Minutes of the Board of Directors, August 25, 1914, III, 151.

[37]Minutes of the Board of Directors, April 10, 1916, III, 191-192.

School converted the old wooden bath house into a dissecting room. In 1933 a veterinary anatomy building with several stables were erected. In 1953 and 1955 the new modern veterinary hospital, office, and laboratory building was erected west of the railroad tracks on Farm Highway 60.[38]

Between 1903 and 1916, when the School of Veterinary Medicine opened, Francis secured the assistance of several able veterinarians, each of whom made significant contributions to the field and to the development of the School. Francis' first assistant in the Department of Veterinary Medicine was Dr. John H. Rietz, who joined Francis in the fall of 1903. Francis, always praising his colleagues, commended Rietz' "intelligent assistance" which contributed to making 1903-1904 for the Veterinary Department "the best year's work in its history."[39] Rietz left after only two years at A&M and was replaced by Dr. Ross Perry Marsteller.

Born in West Lodi, Ohio, on July 27, 1882, Marsteller received his Doctor of Veterinary Medicine degree in 1905, and accepted his first and only teaching position at Texas A&M. Marsteller was a member of the A&M veterinary faculty for forty-five years.[40] When Marsteller joined Francis in 1905 the two men taught various courses in veterinary medicine to thirty-five sophomores and eighteen juniors. Twelve farmers participated in the summer short course. In addition, experiments were continued in Texas fever, and approximately 800 cattle were immunized during an average year against the fever. Other research was conducted on glanders, anthrax, and the more crucial stock diseases. Francis' 1905 annual report ended with the observation, "I can not close this report without saying that whatever success we may have attained, has been due, in considerable degree, to the cheerful and intelligent assistance rendered by Dr. Marsteller."[41] Marsteller and Francis were the prime movers in founding the School of Veterinary Medicine.

In 1910 Francis and Marsteller began advocating the establishment of a regular veterinary-science course by the College, but not until buildings, equipment, and staff were adequate.[42] In 1911 Dr. Ralph Clark Dunn,

[38]Texas A&M, *Biennial Report, 1917-1918*, pp. 46-47; Schmidt, *History of the School of Veterinary Medicine*, 25.

[39]Texas A&M, *Biennial Report, 1903-1904*, p. 86; Schmidt, *History of the School of Veterinary Medicine*, 7.

[40]"Ross Perry Marsteller — Biographical," Texas A&M University Archives. Marsteller retired in 1950 and died January, 1954.

[41]Texas A&M, *Biennial Report, 1905-1906*, pp. 52-54. The 800 immunization count is derived from Francis' observation in the 1903-1904 *Annual Report* that inoculations for the past year had dropped to 424 — one-half the usual level.

[42]Texas A&M, *Biennial Report, 1909-1910*, p. 17.

another Ohioan, born in Tiffin on June 11, 1887, and a graduate of Ohio State University in veterinary medicine, joined the Texas A&M faculty as chief laboratory technician in charge of the production and distribution of anti-hog-cholera serum.[43] Dunn became the third man in the quartet who established the A&M School of Veterinary Medicine and who guided its development through almost half a century.

The 1911-1912 *Biennial Report* now included a strong statement of "Reasons for the Establishment of a School of Veterinary Medicine." This statement noted the number and value of Texas livestock in 1911 (table 4).

Table 4.
Livestock in Texas, 1911

Type	Number	Value
Horses	1,369,000	$100,260,000
Mules	702,000	70,202,000
Dairy cows	1,137,000	33,542,000
Other cattle	7,131,000	109,104,000
Sheep and goats	2,400,000	7,500,000
Hogs	3,205,00	25,000,000
Totals	15,944,000	$345,608,000

Care of this sixteen-million-animal, $350-million-dollar industry, the report continued, rested in the hands of seventy-five licensed veterinarians, several hundred untrained "practitioners," and a third group self-styled as veterinary surgeons whose "barbarous surgery, impossible remedies, and irregular business methods have disgusted the public for years." The report then recommended that "As there exists at present no school or college in this whole section which meets the requirements of the civil service, it seems the legitimate work, if not the duty, of this College to meet the situation."[44] As previously indicated, the budget for the proposed veterinary school was vetoed by Governor Colquitt in 1913, but passed with Governor Ferguson's approval in the 1915 legislative sessions.

Meanwhile, in 1913, the last of the four "founders" of the A&M College of Veterinary Medicine joined the faculty at College Station. Dr. Hubert Schmidt, born near Comfort, Texas, on September 24, 1886. A 1908 graduate of Texas A&M in animal husbandry, he received his D.V.M. from the Royal Veterinary College, in Berlin, Germany, in 1912. He accepted a position with the Texas Agricultural Experiment Station as an assistant to Mark Francis in

[43]"Ralph Clark Dunn — Biographical," Texas A&M University Archives. Dr. Dunn died in May 1972.

[44]Texas A&M, *Biennial Report, 1911-1912*, pp. 11-13.

February 1913. Schmidt first worked with Francis on Texas fever, and later made important studies of diseases of animals caused by mineral deficiencies, such as oiin diseases, loin disease, and creeps.[45] Partly through his work proper mineral supplements have almost eliminated these once prevalent stock diseases from Gulf Coast cattle:

> Probably no other one individual will ever equal Dr. Schmidt in his vast knowledge of the diseases of domestic animals — particularly those of cattle and sheep — in Texas. Parasites, both internal and external, poisonous plants, mineral and vitamin deficiencies, and many acute infectious diseases, were studied and methods developed for their control. He was an acknowledged national authority on anaplasmosis, trichomoniasis and nutritional diseases. At the time of his death, although on full retirement, he was completing investigations on hyperkeratosis.[46]

It was Schmidt who, in 1915 and 1916, treated Governor Ferguson's cattle; and it was Schmidt, who in 1958, sat down to write a "Brief History of the School of Veterinary Medicine." Schmidt died in College Station on January 13, 1958, of injuries suffered from an automobile accident, having almost completed his manuscript, which was published shortly after his death.[47]

Mark Francis was the "father" of veterinary medicine in Texas; Francis and three others — Ross Perry Marsteller, Ralph Clark Dunn, and Hubert Schmidt — were the founders of Texas A&M's College of Veterinary Medicine. These four men achieved a remarkable record of medical discoveries and of service to the profession and to the College. The four men together compiled a record of 173 years of service to A&M, an average of 43 years each: Mark Francis (1888-1936), 48 years of service; Ross Perry Marsteller (1905-1950), 45 years of service; Ralph Clark Dunn (1911-1948), 37 years of service; and Hubert Schmidt (1913-1956), 43 years of service.

The School of Veterinary Medicine opened at the beginning of the forty-first term of the College, September 25, 1916. Only freshman classes were taught the first year, the second, third, and fourth-year classes being added each consecutive year. The School opened before the new veterinary-medicine building was completed and for the first year classes were taught in the chemistry building. Three new men were added to the veterinary faculty in 1916. Dr. Bailey O. Bethel, an A&M graduate who received his D.V.M. from Ohio State, worked in the Hog Serum Laboratory from 1914 to 1916,

[45]"Hubert Schmidt — Biographical," Texas A&M University Archives; Schmidt, *History of the School of Veterinary Medicine,* "Foreword."

[46]"Hubert Schmidt — Biographical," Texas A&M University Archives. Dr. Schmidt retired in 1956, died January 13, 1958.

[47]Schmidt, *History of the School of Veterinary Medicine,* "Foreword" by R. D. Turk; "Hubert Schmidt — Biographical," Texas A&M University Archives.

when he joined the teaching staff. Bethel left A&M in 1918. Lewis H. Wright, a graduate of the Cornell School of Veterinary Medicine, who had taught at Cornell for three years before assuming the duties as head of the Department of Pharmacology at Texas A&M in 1916, also left the College in 1918. Clifford C. Whitney, a graduate of the University of Pennsylvania who taught in the veterinary school there for three years, came to A&M as head of the Department of Pathology. Hubert Schmidt was technically not a member of the first veterinary faculty because he remained in the employment of the Texas Agricultural Experiment Station, but when Whitney left for military service in 1918, Schmidt assumed his duties until a replacement could be found. Schmidt, essentially a research man, continued to "back-up" the teaching faculty throughout his career. The four departments of the new school included Anatomy, headed by Francis; Medicine and Surgery, headed by Marsteller; Pharmacology, headed by Wright; and Pathology, headed by Whitney.[48]

The four-year curriculum in veterinary medicine was, in fact, a regular four-year college course which included fifteen semester hours of biology (including bacteriology and zoology), nine hours of chemistry, twenty-one hours of English, six hours of physics, nine hours of animal husbandry, and three hours each of dairy husbandry and entomology. Students were required to participate in R.O.T.C. and to take twelve hours of military science in the first two years, but were exempt from the R.O.T.C. and Corps of Cadets in the junior and senior years. The remaining courses were in veterinary medicine.[49] The first class in the School of Veterinary Medicine included thirteen students. They were Reddin Raymond Childers, S. L. Courtney, Clarence Boone Franklin, Edwin Mobley Gorman, Richard Henry Harrison, Jr., Joseph Henry Hull, Thomas George Jenkins, Walter Theodore Johnson, Fredrick Alexander Murray, Joseph Jenkinson Reid, Archie Stallings, William Mogford Thaxton, and Hilton Otto Von Rosenberg. World War I interrupted the studies of these students, and of the original thirteen, Harrison, Hull, Murray, and Von Rosenberg graduated in 1920; Childers, Johnson, and Reid finished in 1921; and Stallings completed his work in 1923.[50]

Dr. Richard Henry Harrison, Jr., the first of the four 1920 graduates to receive his diploma, helped organize the A&M Veterinary Medicine Club and was its first president. Harrison played quarterback and halfback on the

---

[48]College Station *Battalion,* July 7, 1916; Schmidt, *History of the School of Veterinary Medicine,* 28-35.

[49]"Announcement of the School of Veterinary Medicine," Texas A&M, *Bulletin,* 3rd ser., VII (July 1, 1921), pp. 11-12.

[50]Schmidt, *History of the School of Veterinary Medicine,* 7-8.

Aggie football team for the four years he was in school, served one year as business manager for the school newspaper, the *Battalion,* and upon graduation was the first A&M student to receive the award of Outstanding Military Student. He became assistant state veterinarian after graduation from A&M, and in 1924 entered Baylor Medical School. Finishing medical school in 1928, Harrison interned in Houston for a year, and after serving several years as surgeon for Humble Oil and Refining Company near Corpus Christi, returned to Bryan, Texas, where he established his medical practice. For many years after 1934 Harrison served as the A&M football-team physician. He served in the Medical Corps during World War II, and retired from the service in 1945 as full colonel. In 1963 Harrison returned his diploma to Texas A&M, a memento of a great moment in the University's history.[51]

Anticipating the first graduating class from the School of Veterinary Medicine, the Thirty-sixth Texas Legislature passed an act "Regulating the Practice of Veterinary Medicine, Surgery, and Dentistry, and Creating a Board of Veterinary Medical Examiners," approved by the governor on February 28, 1919. This act regulated the practice of veterinary medicine in Texas, and established a board of seven qualified examiners to approve state licenses.[52] Within a few years some conflicts arose concerning the practice of veterinary medicine in Texas; most of these, interestingly enough, occurred among the divisions of the Texas A&M System.

County agents of the Texas Agricultural Extension Service and vocational agriculture teachers, many of them trained at Texas A&M, early became accustomed to providing various services to their farmer constituents in the treatment of livestock. On occasion these services exceeded the limits (ill defined even today) between husbandry and veterinary practice. Many of the agents were unquestionably rather well trained in the care of animal ailments, but they were not licensed veterinarians. As more and more licensed veterinarians went out into private practice, more and more conflicts of interest arose.

The problem, common to many states, came to the attention of Clyde William Warburton, director of Extension Work, in Washington, D.C. On April 14, 1931, Warburton issued a memorandum to all state extension services, advising that "County Agents should be discouraged from practicing veterinary medicine, but should call on licensed veterinarians."[53] Complaints continued to appear in Texas. The State Veterinary Medical Association,

[51] Bryan *Daily Eagle,* May 12, 1963.

[52] *General Laws of Texas, 1919,* pp. 143-150.

[53] C. W. Warburton, "Memorandum re Veterinary Extension Work, April 14, 1921," Veterinary Medicine Historical File, Texas A&M University Archives.

organized in large measure through the inspiration of Mark Francis in 1903, in which year Francis became its first president, pressed for a resolution of the problem, particularly in 1933.[54] Thomas O. Scott, president of the Association in 1933, wrote to Marsteller describing incidents of the "illegal practice" of veterinary medicine by vocational agriculture teachers and county agents.[55]

Marsteller and the extension director, Oscar B. Martin, established a joint committee of veterinarians and extension personnel to prepare a report on the situation. The Report of the Committee on Relationship of Extension Workers and Veterinarians, issued May 20, 1933, concluded that improper veterinary practice was engaged in by extension agents, and reiterated that "county agents should refrain from making calls in the treatment of sick animals."[56] Although this did indicate some conflict between the Extension Service and veterinarians, the report also confirmed the fact that the Extension Service had long aided the work of veterinarians in controlling contagious diseases. Renewed emphasis was placed upon the necessity for extension agents to report all contagious diseases to the School of Veterinary Medicine.[57]

O. B. Martin strongly reminded Marsteller of this cooperation by the Extension Service in a letter of May 26, 1933. Agents also reported vaccinations made by them on livestock, he said.[58] A letter from an agent to Marsteller in 1922 indicated that the county agents had indeed long served as a field branch for the veterinarians in the control of diseases.[59] In all fairness to the extension agents, they had served as "practitioners" until the state was adequately staffed with licensed veterinarians. By 1933 the conflict between the services simply indicated that by that time the School of Veterinary Medicine was beginning to fulfill the needs of Texas livestock industry, and that a considerable degree of professionalism had developed. The resolution of 1933 clarified, but did not entirely resolve, the problem of the practice of veterinary medicine by nonprofessionals.

[54]*Texas Veterinary Medical Association,* 1-4, in Veterinary Medicine Historical File, Texas A&M University Archives.

[55]T. O. Scott, President, State Veterinary Medical Association to "Dear Doctor" [Marsteller], April 27, 1933, Veterinary Medicine Historical File, Texas A&M University Archives.

[56]"Report of Committee on Relationship of Extension Workers and Veterinarians, May 20, 1933," Veterinary Medicine Historical File, Texas A&M University Archives.

[57]*Ibid.*

[58]O. B. Martin, College Station, to R. P. Marsteller, College Station, May 26, 1933, Veterinary Medicine Historical File, Texas A&M University Archives.

[59]W. J. Marschall, County Agent, Mason County, to R. P. Marsteller, College Station, Texas, March 22, 1922, Veterinary Medicine Historical File, Texas A&M University Archives.

By 1930 the School of Veterinary Medicine was instructing 161 students, only eighteen of whom, however, were enrolled in the regular veterinary-medicine course. Most of the remaining students were enrolled in animal husbandry and poultry science. While they obtained considerable instruction in veterinary medicine, they received the B.S. degree in the School of Agriculture.[60] Little wonder, then, that a conflict of interest arose between practicing veterinarians and "lay" practitioners such as animal husbandrymen, both of whom were often trained in the same classrooms.

In 1931 R. P. Marsteller was made vice-dean of the School of Veterinary medicine to lend assistance to the aging Mark Francis. Francis died on June 18, 1936; Marsteller served for a time as acting dean, and then on July 5, 1937, the Directors appointed him dean.[61] In 1933 a new hospital, an anatomy building, and barns were completed for the veterinary-medicine complex.[62] Enrollments began to surge during the Depression and burgeoned after World War II. By 1936 the School was facing the situation of being severely overpopulated and understaffed. The American Veterinary Medicine Association became critical of the School's deficiencies and called upon Texas A&M "to increase the staff and the number of departments commensurate with the educational standards and expanding accumulation of knowledge in the field of veterinary medicine."[63]

In November 1936 the Board of Directors was informed that serious problems confronted the School and that improvements in the teaching staff were needed at an early date. Action was taken to limit enrollment and to raise standards by imposing higher entrance requirements for the School of Veterinary Medicine. Previously the normal entrance requirements for admission to the College had also satisfied admission requirements to the School of Veterinary Medicine. Admission to the course in veterinary medicine now required one year, or thirty-five semester hours, of work in an approved college or university. These new requirements were first applied to the class of 1941.[64] The new admission standards made veterinary medicine more than a specialized college curriculum. Later, in 1951, two years of preparatory college work became part of the requirement for admission to the veterinary medi-

[60]Texas A&M, *Annual Report, 1929-1930*, p. 16.

[61]Minutes of the Board of Directors, November 25, 1931, IV, 185; Bryan *Daily Eagle*, July 3, 1936; "Mark Francis — Biographical," Texas A&M University Archives; Minutes of the Board of Directors, July 5, 1937, V, 104.

[62]Schmidt, *History of the School of Veterinary Medicine*, 25.

[63]*Ibid.*, 27.

[64]Minutes of the Board of Directors, November 26, 1936, V, 77; Texas A&M, *Catalogue, 1936*, pp. 17-18.

cine curriculum, further elevating the work into the graduate or professional level.[65]

Furthermore, in response to the criticism of the Veterinary Medicine Association, sixteen new members were added to the veterinary-medicine faculty in 1936 and 1937, which more than doubled the existing staff, a statistic which marks the severity of the situation. The original six faculty members, Francis, Marsteller, Dunn, Bethel, Wright, and Whitney (the latter three being on the staff for only a few years) had been joined in 1919 by August Albert Lenert, a native of Warrenton, Texas, a former student (Class of 1914), and a graduate of Kansas City Veterinary College. W. Tyree Hardy and Ivan B. Boughton joined the Experiment Station at Sonora as veterinarians in 1930 and 1932 respectively. Solon N. Blackberg and Patton W. Burns joined the Department of Pharmacology in 1918 and 1926 respectively. Hubert Schmidt (1918-1956), Emmet W. Price (1919-1926), and Arthur E. Wharton (1926-1937) became members of the Veterinary Pathology Department. Hugh B. Thaxton, after having worked as a graduate assistant under Francis in 1933, became a regular member of the Department of Anatomy in 1934.[66] Between 1919 and 1935 only nine new men had joined the veterinary-medicine faculty, thus to have sixteen new men in two years was a revolutionary occurrence. The sixteen new faculty members who joined in 1936 and 1937 were Charles L. Coleman (1936-1937), T. W. Workman (1936-1938), Richard D. Turk (1936-1967), R. L. Piercy (1936-1939), Harold M. Spangler (1937-1940), Frank B. Wilkerson (1937-1938), Dorris D. Giles (1937-1938), George T. Edds (1936-1950), B. L. Warwick (1936-1948), Frank P. Matthews (1936-1945), John H. Milliff (1936-1971), Ralph C. Dunn (from the Serum Laboratory, 1937-1948), Harold W. Sawyer (1936-1938), Thomas S. Leith (1937-1940), Frederick P. Jaggi, Jr. (1937-1966), and Horatio L. von Volkenberg (1937-1944).[67] Many of these, to be sure, were staff of the Texas Agricultural Experiment Station, attached to the Veterinary Medicine School because of the emergency which arose in 1936.

Two new departments were created in 1937 in response to the crisis. They were the Department of Veterinary Hygiene, with Frederick P. Jaggi, head, and the Department of Veterinary Parasitology, headed by Horatio L. von Volkenberg.[68] Enrollment in the School of Veterinary Medicine continued to climb, and, despite the enlarged staff, enrollment increases maintained continuing pressure on the facilities and capabilities of the School. In 1939

[65]Schmidt, *History of the School of Veterinary Medicine*, 26.
[66]*Ibid.*, 28-35.
[67]*Ibid.*
[68]*Ibid.*, 33-34.

the Board of Directors limited enrollment in the School to one hundred new students each fall. Preference would be given to Texas students, with second priority going to students from states having no veterinary school,[69] such as neighboring Louisiana.

Enrollment declined somewhat during the years of World War II, but the postwar surge created new crises for the School of Veterinary Medicine, and for the entire College. Dean R. P. Marsteller became dean emeritus on September 1, 1946, and Dr. Ralph C. Dunn, the oldest member in point of service, became acting dean. The American Veterinary Medical Association renewed pressure on A&M to upgrade the Veterinary School, and to find a permanent dean.[70] Meanwhile, a substantive reorganization of the College was being effected by President Gibb Gilchrist, Vice-President D. W. Williams, Extension Director Ide P. Trotter, and others. Research and extension services were being integrated into the academic branches.

On September 1, 1948, Dr. Ivan Bertrand Boughton, previously attached to the Agricultural Experiment Station in Sonora, Texas, became dean of the School of Veterinary Medicine. Boughton reorganized the School with veterinary extension and research facilities being incorporated into the academic programs.[71] The reorganization formalized what had in fact long been the School of Veterinary Medicine's practice. Experiment Station and Extension Service people had long been directly involved in veterinary programs. The new organization cut through some of the departmentalization of the College effort which had served only to hamstring effective cooperation. It also made the School of Veterinary Medicine appear to conform more fully to the standards of the American Veterinary Medicine Association.

Boughton, who received his D.V.M. from Ohio State University in 1916, served in the Army Veterinary Corps during World War I, and was professor of animal pathology at the University of Illinois from 1919 to 1925. From 1925 until he joined the Experiment Station staff in January 1932 he was head of the Veterinary Agriculture Department in Haiti. Boughton, who specialized in the parasites of domestic animals and who was a good research veterinarian, developed a vaccine for the immunization of sheep and goats against soremouth. He also conducted informative studies in the poisoning of range animals by bitterweed, mescalbean, and shin oak. Dean Boughton suffered a severe stroke in April 1952, and was relieved for a time by Frederick P.

[69]Minutes of the Board of Directors, August 19, 1939, V, 197.
[70]Schmidt, *History of the School of Veterinary Medicine,* 27.
[71]*Ibid.*

Jaggi, Jr. Boughton resumed his duties briefly in 1953 but found the strain too great.[72]

In August 1953 Dr. Willis W. Armistead became the new dean. Armistead, a 1938 graduate of the Texas A&M School of Veterinary Medicine, engaged in private practice in Dallas for two years before returning to College Station as an instructor in veterinary medicine. He was made assistant professor in 1942, in which year he entered military service with the Veterinary Corps, attaining the rank of major. He returned to his teaching duties in 1946, and was made full professor the following year. In 1947-1948 Armistead served as president of the State Veterinary Association. While dean of the School of Veterinary Medicine, Armistead served as editor of the *North American Veterinarian,* one of the most distinguished journals of the profession. In 1956 he was elected president of the American Veterinary Medical Association. Armistead accepted the position of dean of the Michigan State University Veterinary Medical School in 1957, whereupon Alvin A. Price was selected to replace him.[73]

Alvin A. Price was born in 1917 near Dublin, Texas. He completed two years at John Tarleton State College, then the A&M junior branch in Stephenville, before transferring to Texas A&M, where he completed his B.S. degree in dairy husbandry. Price worked in a creamery in Lockhart, Texas, before entering military service. He saw action in North Africa, Italy, and Trieste with the 362nd Infantry Battalion, and won the Bronze Star during the Po River crossing. He came back to A&M on the G.I. Bill, received his D.V.M. in 1948, joined the faculty, and in 1950 became head of the Department of Veterinary Anatomy. He earned a master's degree in reproductive physiology in 1956 and became dean of the School of Veterinary Medicine in 1957, following the resignation of Dean Armistead. Price is a "firm advocate of the practice of learning by doing. The whole program in veterinary medicine at A&M is oriented toward student participation."[74]

Under Price's leadership admission quotas continued to be enforced in order to maintain the quality of the program. By 1963 only sixty-four new students per year were being admitted to the School. In that year, too, Sonja Oliphant became the first woman admitted to the School of Veterinary Medi-

[72]Veterinary Medicine File, August 3, 1936, Texas A&M University Archives; College Station *Battalion,* February 19, 1952; June 4, 1953; College Station *Texas Aggie,* July 1953.

[73]W. W. Armistead Biographical Papers, Texas A&M University Archives; Houston *Chronicle,* October 24, 1956; College Station *Texas A&M System News,* August 1953, November 1956; College Station *Battalion,* June 30, 1953, July 18, 1957.

[74]College Station *Battalion,* August 22, 1957; Bryan *Brazos Valley Review,* December 5, 1960.

cine, marking another "historic" landmark in A&M history.[75] By the opening of the decade of the 1970s the School of Veterinary Medicine, under the leadership of Price and his successor, George C. Shelton, continued to maintain standards of excellence and of service to the people of Texas. The College offers a preveterinary curriculum, a professional curriculum leading to the D.V.M., and a graduate program for specialization leading to the degree of Master of Science, and Doctor of Philosophy. The faculty are grouped in seven departments: Veterinary Anatomy, Veterinary Medicine and Surgery, Veterinary Microbiology, Veterinary Parasitology, Veterinary Pathology, Veterinary Physiology and Pharmacology, and Veterinary Public Health.[76]

Responding to the ever-changing needs of society, Texas A&M's School of Veterinary Medicine became the first in the nation to offer a program in the medicine of aquatic animals.[77] Much has happened in veterinary medicine since the day when Joseph F. Nichols inserted his thermometer under the tail of his mule and Mark Francis tried electrocuting ticks on the hides of living animals.

[75]Houston *Post*, July 1, 1963.
[76]Texas A&M, *Catalogue, 1971-1972*, pp. 316-325.
[77]Bryan *Daily Eagle*, August 18, 1970.

CHAPTER 17

The Texas Forest Service

THE Texas Forest Service has come a long way since its inception in 1915, was the view expressed by Alfred D. Folweiler in November 1971, while recalling his nineteen years as head of the Texas Forest Service (1949-1967).[1] During the twenties and the thirties agriculture and agricultural extension people had little interest in "tree farming" and an inadequate concept of it. During these years the Forest Service tended to be the step-child of the College's main effort in agriculture and engineering. The Agricultural Extension Service maintained its own forestry specialist, who held no affiliation with the Texas Forest Service.[2] The Forest Service itself was regarded generally as a nonacademic, forest-fire-fighting brigade, which because of political and administrative considerations happened to be associated with the College.

Despite its low-key characterization, a role which it continues to occupy within the broad efforts of Texas A&M University, the Texas Forest Service has worked quietly and efficiently since 1915 for the improvement and protection of Texas forest resources. Its works, like those of the Texas Extension Service, although less publicized, have had a profound impact upon the lives of millions of Texans.

Several uncommon characteristics of the Texas Forest Service tend to distinguish it from other state services. It was the first and, for a time, the only state forestry agency placed under the administrative auspices of the land-grant college. A number of states have since implemented a similar administrative organization. Secondly, the administrative offices of the Texas Forest Service, located at College Station, have been outside of the operational area of the Service, an arrangement which, while not unique, has created certain difficulties. A related geographical situation is that the primary operational activities of the Texas Forest Service are largely confined to

---

[1] Interview with A. D. Folweiler, November 10, 1971, Texas A&M University, College Station, Texas.

[2] Texas Extension Service, "Historical·Notes and Staff Lists by years, 1901-1951," year 1938, Texas Extension Service Papers, Texas A&M University Archives, College Station, Texas.

approximately forty deep East Texas counties, where most Texas timber production exists, a geographical orientation which gives the Forest Service a regional rather than statewide complexion, and which has had its political and fiscal implications. The unforested regions which comprise most of Texas have necessarily had relatively little empathy for the Forest Service, a situation which is being overcome increasingly by the attraction which state parks and recreation areas hold for the entire population of Texas, east or west, north or south.

Texas has approximately 263,513 square miles of land area, of which almost one-fifth is forested. Of the forested portion about one-third, or 12.5 million acres, produces forest products in commercial quantities. The remaining two-thirds of the forested area of Texas is classed as "protection forest," in that its primary use is as protection for the soil, wildlife, and vegetation, and the control of rapid runoff.[3] The tree regions of Texas are further categorized into eight timber classes corresponding to rather well-defined geographical regions, as illustrated on the accompanying map (fig. 4).[4]

The Texas forestry program developed out of the concern of the Progressive Movement (c. 1890-1915) for conservation. National forest reserves were first provided for in the Act of 1891, but, for practical purposes, all American land and "conservation" acts before 1897 intended to provide for the exploitation of natural resources and for the transfer of the public domain to private hands, in numerous instances achieving these ends. The Act of 1897, however, attempted to make forest reservations real timber-preservation areas, but the Act proved ineffectual. Finally, under the leadership of Gifford Pinchot, chief forester, and President Theodore Roosevelt, the National Forest Service was created by an act of February 1, 1905, which transferred federal forest reserves from the Department of the Interior to the Department of Agriculture. Theodore Roosevelt used his executive powers to transfer millions of acres of forest lands and dam sites from the public domain to national forests before being halted by Congress in 1907. The Weeks Law of March 1, 1911, allowed the government to purchase or exchange lands for the creation of new national forests, and, more importantly for Texas and all states, authorized the U.S. Department of Agriculture to enter cooperative arrangements with the states in the protection of "forested watersheds of navigable streams," a term which was given the widest construction.[5]

[3]Texas Planning Board, *A Review of Texas Forestry and its Industries,* 11. Texas Forest Service, *Texas Forest Service: Its History, Objectives and Activities,* 2.

[4]Texas Forest Service, *Tree Regions of Texas,* 3.

[5]*United States Government Organization Manual 1971/72,* pp. 245-246; Roy M. Robbins, *Our Landed Heritage,* 301-343; Texas A&M, *Biennial Report, 1915-1916,* pp. 94-95.

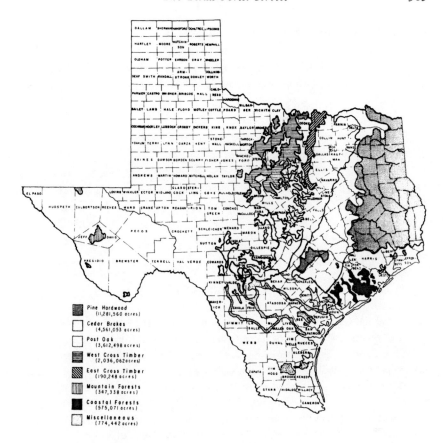

Figure 4. Tree regions of Texas and forested area of each. From Texas Forest Service, *Tree Regions of Texas,* Circular 75 (1970).

As of 1911 Texas had no public program of forest protection or conservation. Considerable interest in such a forestry program and support for it, however, had been developed through the efforts of W. Goodrich Jones, a Temple businessman and banker generally accepted as the "father of Texas forestry." Upon the instigation of Dr. Bernard Eduard Fernow, chief of the newly created Division of Forestry in the U.S. Department of Agriculture, Jones, in 1898, began a crusade for the creation of a state forestry agency. Jones was soon joined by a number of journalists, educators, and lawmakers, such as William L. Bray, of The University of Texas, Moye Wicks, of San Antonio, Clarence Ousley, and others. Support became sufficiently strong for Jones to have a forestry bill introduced into the state Legislature in 1913, a bill which could take advantage of matching funds from the federal government under the terms of the Weeks Law. The bill failed to pass, however, before the close of the 1913 session. In preparation for the session of 1915 Jones called a meeting of some twenty prominent citizens at the Carnegie Library in Temple. These people organized in 1914 the Texas Forestry Association, whose purpose was to give support to the passage of a Texas forestry law. Jones was elected the first president. The association, with the assistance of J. Girvin Peters, of the U.S. Department of Agriculture, succeeded in obtaining passage of the Texas forestry law in 1915.[6]

The original bill drawn up by Jones and Peters had called for a separate Department of Forestry under the auspices of a Forestry Board. Governor Oscar Branch Colquitt and others, however, resisted the proliferation of boards and committees. The bill was redrawn to make the state forestry agency responsible to the Board of Directors of the A&M College as an economy measure. The law is worth quoting:

TEXAS FORESTRY LAW
Chapter 141, Laws of 1915

Section 1. There shall be appointed by the Board of Directors of the Agricultural and Mechanical College of Texas a State Forester, who shall be a technically trained forester of not less than two years experience in professional forestry work; his compensation shall be fixed by the said Board at not to exceed three thousand ($3,000) dollars per annum, and he shall be allowed reasonable traveling and field expenses incurred in the performance of his official duties. He shall, under the general supervision of said board, have direction of all forest interests and all matters pertaining to forestry within the jurisdiction of the State. He shall appoint, subject to the approval and confirmation of said board, such assistants and employees as may be necessary in executing the duties of his office and the purposes of said board, the compensation of such assistants and employees to be fixed by said board. He shall take such action as may be deemed necessary by said board to prevent and extinguish forest fires, shall enforce all laws pertaining to the protection of forests and woodlands, and prosecute for any violation of such laws; collect data relative to forest conditions, and to cooperate with land owners as described in Section 2 of this Act. He shall prepare for said board annually a report of the progress and condition of State forestry work, and recommend therein plans for improving the State system of forest protection, management and replacement.

Section 2. The State Forester shall, upon request, under the sanction of the Board of Directors, and whenever he deems it essential to the best interests of the people of the State, co-operate with counties, towns, corporations or individuals in preparing plans for the protection, management and replacement of trees, wood lots,

[6]Texas Forest Service, *Texas Forest Service: Its History, Objectives and Activities,* 3; Texas A&M, *Biennial Report, 1915-1916,* pp. 94-95; Dallas *Morning News,* August 3, 1950.

and timber tracts, under an agreement that the parties obtaining such assistance pay at least the field expenses of the men employed in preparing said plans.

Section 3. The Governor of the State is authorized upon the recommendation of the Board of Directors to accept gifts of land to the State, same to be held, protected and administered by said board as State forests and to be used so as to demonstrate the practical utility of timber culture and water conservation, and as refuges for game. Such gifts must be absolute, except for the reservation of all mineral and mining rights over and under said lands, and a stipulation that they shall be administered as State forests.

The Board of Directors shall have the power to purchase lands in the name of the State, suitable chiefly for the production of timber, as State forests, using for such purposes any special appropriation or any surplus money not otherwise appropriated, which may be standing to the credit of the State forestry fund.

The Attorney General of the State is directed to see that all deeds to the State of land mentioned in this section are properly executed before the gift is accepted or payment of the purchase money is made.

Section 4. All moneys received from the sale of wood, timber, minerals or other products from the State forests, and penalties for trespassing thereon, shall be paid into the State Treasury and shall constitute a State forestry fund, and the moneys in said fund are hereby appropriated for purposes of forestry in general, under the direction of the Board of Directors.

Section 5. For the maintenance, use and extension of the work under the Board of Directors, and for forest fire protection, there is hereby appropriated the sum of ten thousand ($10,000) dollars annually out of any moneys in the State Treasury not otherwise appropriated, to be placed to the credit of the State forestry fund.

Section 6. Co-operation with Federal Forest Service. The Board of Directors may co-operate with the Federal Forest Service under such terms as may seem desirable.

The law, approved March 31, 1915, provided for the appointment of a state forester by the Board of Directors of Texas A&M at a salary of not more than $3,000 per year plus reasonable expenses. The state forester, in turn, was authorized to appoint assistants and employees as required, their duties and compensation to be prescribed by the Board of Directors. The act allowed the governor to accept donations of land to be set aside as timber, water, and wildlife reserves, and authorized the Board of Directors to purchase land for such purposes out of "surplus money" in the State Forestry Fund. Revenue derived from lands under the jurisdiction of the Forest Service were funded to the exclusive use of the service. The Legislature appropriated $5,000 for each of the two fiscal years ending August 31, 1915, and August 31, 1916.[7] Indifference, as much as opposition, caused largely by the simple

[7]*Texas Forest Service: Its History, Objectives and Activities*, 4.

geographical exclusion of most Texans from involvement in forestry activities, contributed to the narrow margin of favorable votes for the bill. The revised bill passed the House by a six-vote margin, and was approved by a single vote in the Senate.[8]

Upon the encouragement, if not insistence, of President William Bennett Bizzell, the headquarters of the Texas Forest Service was located at Texas A&M, rather than at Austin, though W. Goodrich Jones preferred the capital city.[9] The Directors, "after several months of careful investigation," selected James H. Foster, professor of forestry at New Hampshire College of Agriculture and Mechanics, in Durham, New Hampshire, and a forestry graduate of Yale University, as the first state forester of Texas.[10] Although Foster left in the spring of 1918, reportedly to go into private business, he was a most knowledgeable and energetic first forester, who succeeded in establishing the structure of a working organization and who developed an aura of public approval, despite the severe handicaps of limited funds, a wartime situation, and substantial teaching duties at the College.[11]

As soon as the state forester was named, Texas applied to the federal government for a cooperative agreement under the Weeks Law for a fire-protection system. Texas received $2,500 for the calendar year 1916 for a fire-protection program to encompass about thirty counties and 13 million acres of land in East Texas. On February 1, 1916, Foster appointed George W. Johnson, of Teneha, the agent or forester for East Texas. In September six "federal patrolmen" were hired to work out of Lufkin, Livingston, Jasper, Longview, Teneha, and Linden. Each patrolman was given a district defined by a twenty-five mile radius from his headquarters, the total comprising about one and a quarter million acres of land. Each patrolman was to ride horseback fifteen to twenty-five miles each day, meeting the people in his district, acquainting them with the fire-protection program, posting public fire notices, distributing literature, and, with the help of local citizens, extinguishing small fires. The agent coordinated the work of the patrolmen and was obligated to conduct an intensive survey of the forest resources of the region.[12]

Foster published, in May 1916, *Bulletin 1* of the Department of Forestry, which attempted to create concern over "Grass and Woodland Fires in

[8]*General Laws of Texas, 1915*, pp. 220-221.

[9]*Texas Forest Service: Its History, Objectives and Activities*, 4.

[10]Texas A&M, *Biennial Report, 1915-1916*, p. 14.

[11]*Ibid.*, 92-106; *Biennial Report, 1917-1918*, p. 11; *Texas Forest Service: Its History, Objectives and Activities*, 4.

[12]Texas A&M, *Biennial Report, 1915-1916*, pp. 96-97.

Texas."[13] The lack of concern, or public apathy, appeared to be the most severe and persistent problem in fire-protection work in Texas. It undoubtedly still is. In this brochure Foster indicated that the financial loss caused by fire damage in timber areas to states such as North Carolina exceeded one-half million dollars annually. No systematic efforts to estimate loss caused by fire damage in Texas, however, had ever been carried on before 1916.[14] The simple reporting of fires by the Texas Forest Service subsequently created a strong public concern for "wild" fire, and helped curb losses. One of the most important efforts of the Forest Service during Foster's administration was to compile a "General Survey of Texas Woodlands."[15]

Harry B. Krausz, appointed assistant forester and instructor in forestry in 1916, joined Foster and A. H. Leidigh, soils agronomist with the Texas Agricultural Experiment Station, in preparing the survey. Information for the survey came from the U.S. Bureau of the Forestry, from the U.S. Geological Survey, from The University of Texas, and from reports of the forest patrolmen and county agents of the Texas Agricultural Extension Service.[16] The very composition of the survey indicates that Foster successfully integrated a number of agencies, prominently the Extension Service and the Experiment Station, in the work of the Forest Service.

Although the initial survey was, as the title states, very "general," several interesting tidbits of historical information can be gleaned from the report. The center of the Texas lumbering industry in 1916 was in a relatively small number of counties in the longleaf-pine region — Sabine, San Augustine, Nacogdoches, Polk, Tyler, Jasper, Newton, and parts of Angelina, Trinity, and Hardin Counties. One billion board feet of lumber was produced annually from this region and production was estimated to have reached its maximum. Jasper County alone produced 300 million board feet of timber. The greater part of the longleaf forests had been cut and most of the remaining virgin timber was being harvested. Harvesting methods at the time had "graduated" to the steam skidder, which pulled a heavy chain through a forested area and stripped every living tree. Selective harvesting was unknown,

---

[13]Department of Forestry, "Grass and Woodland Fires in Texas," *Bulletin of the Agricultural and Mechanical College of Texas,* 3rd ser., II (May 1916), pp. 1-16 (hereinafter cited: Texas A&M, *Bulletin).*

[14]*Ibid.,* 9.

[15]Department of Forestry, "General Survey of Texas Woodlands," Texas A&M, *Bulletin,* 3rd ser., III (May 1, 1917), pp. 1-47.

[16]*Ibid.,* 3-4.

although it had actually been practiced under the "earlier methods of logging."[17]

The shortleaf-pine forests which covered the northeastern tier of counties were largely second-growth forests, having been originally cut most heavily in the 1880s, fortunately, by means of the axe rather than the skidder. The bottomland forests, primarily hardwoods, had been heavily cut, but retained significant marketable values. In the post-oak region the timber was considered useful for woodlot purposes. The advent of agriculture and the increased population of the areas of the Edwards Plateau through Central Texas and on the prairies of West Texas had actually increased the timber coverage of those areas. "Within the memory of men now living," reads the report, "this [Edwards Plateau] region was primarily grass covered." The cedar brakes had only recently spread across the land. In the prairies "within the last twenty-five or thirty years the transformation has been so marked as to become a matter of common discussion." Clumps of oak and mesquite, and even extended timber belts, had come to exist where they had never previously been.[18] Why? Because American culture contributed to the control of unleashed fire. Ranchers, farmers, settlers, and towns helped curb the prairie and brush fires which swept uncontrolled through much of Texas during the Indians' day. Many fires were started by the Indians for driving game, and then burned uncontrolled and uncared about until a providential rain or wind quenched them.

Mesquite, according to the survey, spread into Texas from the Matamoros district of old Mexico in the mid-eighteenth century. During the nineteenth century, particularly, livestock hastened the spread of mesquite throughout the prairies, the Edwards Plateau, and even into the post-oak regions, leaving mesquite seeds in their droppings. Harry B. Krausz, the assistant forester, argued that mesquite had commercial possibilities for the Texas lumbering industry in the manufacture of small, turned articles such as gavels, plaques, rings, trays, inlay, and parquet flooring.[19] One wonders, however, whether the essay on mesquite represented a pointed effort by Foster and Krausz to intrigue or excite West Texans to the support of the new forestry program. If so, they are to be commended for their audacity.

Foster, Krausz, and George W. Johnson published a more intensive survey of "Forest Resources of Eastern Texas," in May 1917. This report amplified the general comments of the 1916 survey and provided county-by-county

[17]*Ibid.*, 15-28.
[18]*Ibid.*, 28-34.
[19]*Ibid.*, 39-47.

descriptions of lumbering activities and statistics on them. The report indicated that approximately 14.1 percent of the land area in the forty counties surveyed was still covered by virgin timber, stands of which were rapidly being depleted. Eight and three-tenths percent of the land area was in second-growth timber, 37.4 percent was in culled and cut-over land, and 40.2 percent was agricultural or unforested. The Texas forest industry in those counties ranked third among Texas industries in value of production. Twenty-five thousand people were employed by the industry. Products included lumber, cross ties, posts, piling, staves, poles, fuel, shingles, and limited quantities of charcoal and turpentine. The frequency of forest fires varied widely from county to county with the greater incidence of fires, and the greater lack of concern over their existence, in the cut-over lands.[20]

Foster's sixth forestry bulletin, published in conjunction with Fred H. Miller, who in March 1917 replaced George Johnson as the agent for East Texas, reviewed the causes and concern for forest fires in Texas. The report argued that the long-term losses caused by fire far exceeded the immediate tangible loss. The loss of future forests and game joined soil erosion and depletion as disastrous products of forest fires. It was a common, but mistaken practice, Foster's report indicated, for people to burn grass and timber land in order to improve the range, destroy cattle ticks, and prevent malaria. Burning accomplished none of these things, the report took pains to argue. The first annual compilations of the forest-patrolmen reports indicated that in 1916, 1,132,500 acres of timber lands were burned, with an estimated loss of $656,400. Lightning started two fires; railroads, thirty-three; lumbering activities, forty-seven; brush burning, fifteen; hunters and fishermen, forty; incendiaries, fifty-six; and "other causes," thirty-two.[21] In July 1917 Foster, Miller, and Krausz published a bulletin under the auspices of the Extension Service on "Farm Forestry," and in November 1917 Foster submitted his second and last annual report as state forester. During the second year of its existence the state forestry agency reported 1,207,824 acres burned by fire, with a resulting loss estimated at $777,588.[22]

The primary efforts of the forestry agency in the early days was educational and informational. In terms of actually curbing fire losses, the early years of the Texas Forest Service were failures. The important aspect of Fos-

[20]Department of Forestry, "Forest Resources of Eastern Texas," Texas A&M, *Bulletin,* 3rd ser., III (May 15, 1917), pp. 1-57.

[21]Department of Forestry, "Forest Fire Prevention," Texas A&M, *Bulletin,* 3rd ser., III (July 1, 1917), pp. 2-12.

[22]Department of Forestry, "Second Annual Report of the State Forester," Texas A&M, *Bulletin,* 3rd ser., III (November 15, 1917), pp. 1-7.

ter's work, however, is not the degree of protection provided Texas forests, but the development of the idea that those forests even needed protecting. Foster's primary mission was to overcome public apathy and indifference to timber exploitation, waste, and fire loss. Prior to his work no data existed as to the number of forest fires or the nature or extent of destruction they caused or the economic significance of the forest industry to Texas. With very limited resources Foster made an excellent beginning. The Forest Service surveyed forest resources, published informational tracts, and developed a regular mailing list of almost 2,000 addresses of schools, libraries, and individuals to whom forestry information was channeled. Exhibits were staged at the State Fair and at meetings of the Farmers' Congress. Foster and his patrolmen made numerous public addresses. Blotters and drinking cups bearing forestry slogans were distributed throughout the state. Newspapers and farm journals carried frequent stories and references to forestry matters.[23] Foster helped stimulate a public awakening to forest conservation and forest protection.

By 1917, however, Foster had failed to stimulate effectively the Texas Legislature. Foster reported in November that given the funds available the Texas Forest Service had reached the limits of its capacity. "No less than $20,000 a year should have been made available for the next biennium," but the Legislature provided only $10,000 a year, with a supplemental appropriation of $1,500 to the Extension Service (rather than the Forest Service) for the development of forestry-nursery work. Foster resigned in May 1918, apparently convinced that the future of the Forest Service in Texas was bleak. In addition to his administrative work as state forester, Foster was heavily burdened with teaching duties at A&M. He later became state forester in Vermont and served there for thirty-one years.[24]

On May 27, 1918, the Board of Directors appointed Eric O. Siecke to succeed Foster.[25] Under Siecke's direction the Texas forestry agency made the transition from the role of stressing educational and informational functions to the status of an operations-oriented state department. Indicative of this transition, the state forestry agency, or the Department of Forestry as it was officially known, in 1926 was renamed the Texas Forest Service by the A&M

[23]Department of Forestry, "First Annual Report of the State Forester," Texas A&M, *Bulletin*, 3rd ser., III (February 1, 1917), pp. 7-12; and "Second Annual Report of the State Forester" (November 15, 1917), pp. 1-7.

[24]Department of Forestry, "Second Annual Report of the State Forester," Texas A&M, *Bulletin*, 3rd ser., III (November 15, 1917), p. 7; *Texas Forest Service: Its History, Objectives, and Activities*, 4; Minutes of the Board of Directors, May 27, 1918, III, 235.

[25]Minutes of the Board of Directors, May 27, 1918, III, 235.

Board. A native of Nebraska who had served as professor of forestry at the University of Washington and the University of Oregon, and also as deputy state forester of Oregon, Siecke was an energetic and positive leader of the Texas Forest Service who, during his long tenure as state forester from 1918 to 1942, expanded the operations and effectiveness of the Forest Service. During this period the Forest Service remained heavily "operations-oriented" and dedicated to the control of forest fires. It remained almost independent of the functions and activities of the College, probably becoming in fact increasingly autonomous. There is little evidence that the Board of Directors, or the president of the College, played any positive role in policy formulation, planning, or operations of the Forest Service. This may well have been an advantage. On the other hand, the Board of Directors did serve as a buffer to protect the Forest Service from the vagaries of public pressure and politics.

In 1918, under the "war rules" of the A&M College, Siecke was certified by President Bizzell to be loyal in every respect to the government of the United States and was installed as professor of forestry, forester to the Experiment Station, and state forester.[26] The war and limited appropriations prevented any significant changes in the policies and procedures of the Forest Service during his first year in office. The Forest Service continued to give some attention to public forestry-education work. For fiscal years 1919 and 1920 the Forest Service received a slight increase in state appropriations, from $10,000 to $12,000 annually, but for fiscal 1921 and 1922 appropriations jumped from $12,000 to $20,750 annually. From state and federal sources the fire-protection budget for fiscal 1922 reached $25,239.86 as compared to $7,482.43 for the previous year.[27] Substantive changes and the enlarging of operations began to occur.

The number of fire patrolmen was increased from nine to twenty-two. A Division of Forest Protection, established under the direction of Howard J. Eberly, in 1924 moved its headquarters to Lufkin in order to be within the main operating area. The number of forest patrolmen continued to increase, rising from twenty-eight patrolmen and two inspectors in 1924, to forty-two patrolmen and four inspectors in 1926. Fire-control effectiveness demonstrated a marked improvement over the two decades of the twenties and thirties (see fig. 5), an improvement attributed as much to public education as to practical fire control.[28]

[26]*Ibid.*
[27]Texas A&M, *Annual Report, 1921-1922*, pp. 45-46.
[28]*Ibid.; Annual Report, 1922-1923*, pp. 55-56; *Texas Forest Service: Its History, Objectives, and Activities*, 6.

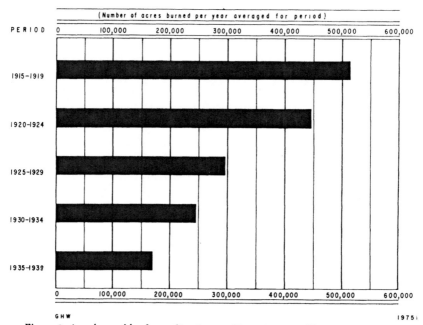

Figure 5. Area burned by forest fires in east Texas (averaged by 5-year periods, 1915-1939). From Texas Forest Service, *Twenty-fourth and Twenty-fifth Annual Reports, 1939-1940,* Bulletin 30 (1940).

The Clarke-McNary Law of June 1924 provided a new supply of federal money for fire protection and for timber management on private lands. Siecke continued to press for increased state appropriations to allow the Texas Forest Service to take full advantage of federal matching-funds programs. The Service increasingly stressed forests as a crop. In 1924 it made the first purchase of cut-over lands for the development of a state forest as authorized under the state Forestry Law of 1915. The first such state forest, of 1,701 acres, was purchased in August 1924 in Newton County, near Kirbyville. In 1944 this forest was named the E. O. Siecke State Forest; it was formally dedicated to Siecke on July 18, 1951. In 1925 a second state forest, of 1,633 acres, was acquired in Montgomery County, near Conroe, later named in honor of W. Goodrich Jones. In 1925 also 1,530 acres, in Cherokee County, known as the I. D. Fairchild State Forest, were transferred to the Forest Service from the State Prison Board. A 600-acre tract, the John Henry Kirby Forest, in Tyler County, was acquired by gift.[29] Profits from the opera-

[29]Texas Forest Service, *Annual Report,* 1926, p. 50; memorandum, D. A. Anderson, College Station, to Henry C. Dethloff, November 23, 1971. The State Forests have been since slightly enlarged.

tion of the forest were designated to provide a student-loan fund operated by the Association of Former Students. A small forest of 118 acres known as the Mission State Forest was operated until 1957, when it was transferred to the Texas State Parks Board. Small additional acreages were later added to these forests which, but for the Cass County hardwood forest leased to the state in 1964, comprise the bulk of state forest lands.[30] The work of the Forest Service, of course, is by no means confined to these rather small acreages, which can be placed more in the category of demonstration forest farms. Beginning in 1934 the federal government began to purchase timber lands for the development of national forests in Texas. Between 1934 and 1937 631,000 acres were acquired by the federal government.[31]

During the Great Depression, Texas public forestry work was expanded tremendously by the Civilian Conservation Corps (CCC) programs operating in conjunction with the Texas Forest Service. In 1934 the Texas Forest Service directed seventeen CCC camps with a total of 3,800 emrollees. The program was gradually reduced until in 1940 only four CCC camps (at Woodville, Alto, Humble, and Newton) remained in Texas, and American entry into World War II ended the program. The CCC "boys" helped modernize the Texas Forest Service and greatly improved fire-protection capabilities. They built fire lanes, roads, bridges, telephone lines, fire towers, and encampments.[32]

By 1938 the Texas Forest Service had developed four major divisions: (1) the Division of Forest Management worked with private timberland owners in providing aid in management, harvesting, and farm products utilization; (2) the Division of Forest Education was primarily concerned with publicity and forestry educational work other than teaching, and was responsible for the publication of *Texas Forest News;* (3) the Division of Forest Research conducted experiments in timber growing on the state forests and research in raising seedlings in the nurseries; (4) the Division of Forest Protection overshadowed all others and, of course, was responsible for the protection of forests and cut-over lands from fire.[33] William E. White, who joined the Forest Service as a patrolman in 1927, headed the Division of Forest Protection in 1938, and in 1942 succeeded E. O. Siecke as director of the Texas Forest Service.[34]

During World War II the Texas Forest Service, which had enjoyed an

[30]*Texas Forest Service: Its History, Objectives, and Activities,* 6.
[31]Texas Planning Board, *A Review of Texas Forestry and Its Industries,* 33.
[32]Texas Forest Service, *A Picture Story of Forestry in Texas,* n.p.
[33]Texas Forest Service, *Handbook for Employees of the Division of Forest Protection,* 7-8.
[34]*Ibid.,* 1; *Texas Forest Service: Its History, Objectives and Activities,* 4.

abundance of manpower during the thirties, found itself facing a critical shortage of men. To compensate, the Forest Service organized the Forest Fire Fighters Service (FFFS), a volunteer organization set up in 1942 under the direction of Governor Coke Stevenson and in cooperation with the Texas Agricultural Extension Service. The Texas Forest Patrol, a unit of the Civil Air Patrol, was organized in 1943 to provide air surveillance of Texas forests during critical fire periods. In 1944 a severe ice storm blanketed East Texas and caused substantial damage to timber, blocked fire roads, broke telephone communications, and placed unusually heavy duties on the limited personnel. Throughout World War II increased timber production was a number-one commitment of the Service. To promote timber production the U.S. Army provided a tour group of veterans called the Forest Fighter Caravan. Educational programs, seedling production from the Indian Mounds Nursery, and research reached a new level of intensity during World War II, despite the limited personnel.[35]

By 1944 the organizational structure of the Texas Forest Service included the director (a state forester) at the head, and a chief clerk and bookkeeper under him. The state forests were administered by the regional forester. The nursery at Alto was under a "chief." A chief also headed the divisions of Forest Products Research, Silvicultural Research, Forest Management, Industrial Forestry, and Information. Two assistants worked under the chief of information. Farm-forestry programs came under the auspices of the farm forester, or two project foresters. The Division of Forest Protection, headquartered in Lufkin, was administered by a chief and an assistant chief. A fiscal clerk, a technical assistant, a radio technician, a law-enforcement agent, a maintenance engineer, three forest engineers, three assistant forest engineers, and two educational assistants were also assigned to the Forest Protection Division. The lesser ranks of the operating arm of the Texas Forest Service in 1944 included 226 men classified variously as patrolmen, lookoutmen, smoke chasers, emergency men, or crewmen. Eighty-eight forest guards were also employed on an annual retainer basis.

Despite the effectiveness of its fire-protection work and progress in forestry research, the Texas Forest Service entered a "postwar slump" from which it was long in recovering. This was unfortunate, for the demands for Texas timber had only begun to be felt. The postwar housing boom placed a new urgency on fire protection, timber management, and production utilization.

Director White resigned his post in early 1948 because of rising discon-

[35]Texas Forest Service, *Texas Forestry Programs, 1943-1944*, pp. 3-4.

tent with the Forest Service from external sources, because of the internal reorganization and upheaval at the College, and because of alleged personal errors in judgment.[36] Sherman L. ("Jack") Frost, chief of the Information Office, replaced White as acting director for a short time, until Frost left to accept the position of executive secretary for the American Forestry Association.[37] David A. ("Andy") Anderson succeeded Frost as acting director in June. Anderson, a native of Aroca, Pennsylvania, received his B.S. degree in Forestry from Pennsylvania State University in 1934 and joined the Texas Forest Service in May 1936. In later years Anderson served as mayor of College Station, thus adding to his other accomplishments.[38]

In January 1949 the Board of Directors named a permanent director of the Texas Forest Service. Alfred D. Folweiler, another transplanted Pennsylvanian born in Northhampton, Pennsylvania, in 1902, served in this office until 1967. Folweiler recalls that one of his forestry professors at Penn State told the 1925 class, "Young men, if you want to get into Forestry, go South." Reminiscent of Horace Greeley's famous invitation of earlier days, "Go west, young man, go west!" the South of the twenties and thirties represented the land of opportunity in forestry and in many other professions. Folweiler, however, went where the jobs were, and his first job was in New Jersey. Asked by an acquaintance, "What in the world is a forester doing in New Jersey?" Folweiler took the comment seriously and moved farther South, first to North Carolina and then to Florida, after having completed graduate studies in forestry at Yale University. Folweiler served as assistant state forester for information and education in Florida from 1931 through 1934, and during the early New Deal became the administrator of CCC camps on private lands in Florida.[39]

Folweiler joined the faculty of Louisiana State University in 1934, took a leave of absence to earn a doctorate in land economics from the University of Wisconsin, published a textbook on forestry, and became involved in a privately endowed research project at LSU. Then the outbreak of war disrupted his program. Finally, in 1943, Folweiler accepted a commission in the United States Army and spent all but two months of the next two years over-

[36]*Texas Forest Service: Its History, Objectives and Activities,* 4-5; interview with Alfred D. Folweiler, November 10, 1971, Texas A&M University, College Station, Texas.

[37]Interview with Alfred D. Folweiler, November 10, 1917, Texas A&M University, College Station, Texas.

[38]"Biographical Sketch," in letter from D. A. Anderson, College Station, to Henry C. Dethloff, College Station, November 23, 1971.

[39]Interview with Alfred D. Folweiler, November 10, 1971, Texas A&M University, College Station, Texas.

seas. In England, Folweiler became acquainted with David W. Williams, who after the War returned to Texas A&M to become vice-president for agriculture. Folweiler returned to Louisiana after the War as manager of International Paper Company lands in the state. In 1948 Folweiler applied for the job of director of the Texas Forest Service, traveled to A&M, where he renewed his acquaintance with Williams, and following a meeting in Lufkin with President Gilchrist and Williams, he received the job, which then paid $8,500 per year, a figure which he noted was 40 percent higher than the salary he had earned while one of the better-paid foresters with International Paper Company.[40]

Folweiler came to A&M during the incubation of substantive changes within the College, and within the Texas Forest Service. At A&M the "System" had just been organized, and the channels of authority between the various branches and agencies were being clarified. The presidents of Texas A&M, Prairie View, Tarleton, and Arlington and the heads of the Experiment Station and the Extension Service technically came to rank equally with the state forester under the direction of the newly created office of chancellor. The previous year, 1948, had been a bad year for the Texas Forest Service. Three changes in leadership, the last two of these leaders being only temporary or acting appointments, contributed to demoralization of the Service. Worse yet, during the year, and during the turnover of directors, Texas encountered its worst series of forest fires in years. The lack of firm leadership and the high incidence of fires helped cause the Texas lumber industry to lose confidence in the Texas Forest Service and helped create rising concern for the diminishing effectiveness of fire-protection operations. All of this at a time when the demand for timber and the prices of lumber were soaring — and the Texas timber industry was itself becoming better organized and more influential. Something, in a word, had to be done, and the impetus came from organized timber interests and principally from the Texas Lumber Manufacturers Association (TLMA).[41]

TLMA decided that something had to be done to improve the quality of fire-protection services in Texas. Two important prerequisites, it believed, would be an interested party on the Board of Directors of Texas A&M, and increased appropriations for the Forest Service from the Legislature. TLMA efforts brought about the appointment of Albert E. Cudlipp, secretary-treasurer of TLMA, to the A&M Board of Directors. He served two six-year terms, from 1948 to 1960. Cudlipp succeeded in bringing Board attention to

[40] *Ibid.*
[41] *Ibid.*

the needs and the importance of the Forest Service. Folweiler attributes much of the progress made during his years as director of the Texas Forest Service to Cudlipp and to Clyde Thompson, who succeeded Cudlipp on the Board, and to the support of Board members Harold Dunn, Rufus Peeples, Henry B. Zachry, and Erwin W. ("Hook") Harrison.[42]

Timber interests believed that the Texas Forest Service was being neglected because of Texas A&M's emphasis upon agriculture and engineering. Forestry, it was believed, played a subordinate role to agriculture, which resulted not so much in intentional injury to forestry programs, as in indifference or benign neglect. The dissidents, however, had no interest in separating the Texas Forest Service from Texas A&M, only a desire to make the Service a more nearly equal partner in the A&M System. Distrust of the agricultural administrators under and with whom the Forest Service operated, particularly of Charles Shepardson, dean of the School of Agriculture, and D. W. Williams, vice-president for agriculture, proved, in part, unfounded. Folweiler soon convinced timber interests that Williams "wore a white hat," insofar as forestry operations were concerned.[43]

One of the most important developments of these years was the establishment of an Advisory Committee to the Texas Forest Service. Chancellor Gibb Gilchrist approved Folweiler's request for a committee of nine men appointed by the Chancellor to represent various components of the Texas timber industry in an advisory capacity. Although Folweiler asked that they be appointed to two-year terms, Gilchrist decided on one-year appointments, although terms have since been extended to two years. This Committee effectively integrated the Forest Service with representatives of the industry it served and helped make it more responsive to owners of forest land and to the forest-products industries.[44]

Folweiler proceeded to reorganize the field-protection services of the agency, dividing the Piney Woods area into six administrative districts, each under a district forester. Heads of the work-area departments, including Forest Management, Information and Education, Forest Products Laboratory, and Fire Control, had both staff and line office responsibilities, each administering his work in the field through the district forester. Standard operating procedures were established for fire-protection work and all other activities, and with the assistance of W. A. Holzmann and William Clyde Freeman in the fiscal office, budgetary controls over the entire Service were implemented for

[42]*Ibid.*
[43]*Ibid.*
[44]*Ibid.*

the first time. Through the cooperation of D. W. Williams, George G. Gibson, and Ide P. Trotter, the Extension Service forestry specialist was eventually integrated into the Forest Service, although the integration consisted essentially of merely housing the specialist in the Forest Service building, a situation Folweiler felt never proved adequate. Silviculture research programs were implemented in cooperation with Robert Donald Lewis, director of the Texas Agricultural Experiment Station. Fire-protection systems were mechanized and the service essentially converted from telephone to radio communication in 1950, although D. A. Anderson and Joseph O. Burnside had introduced some radio equipment as early as 1944. Manpower previously utilized to maintain rights of way and communications was now freed for other services. Reforestation programs were substantially enlarged, in part facilitated by the USDA Soil Bank program, which allowed surplus agricultural lands to be planted in timber. A new seedling nursery was developed at Magnolia Springs, near Kirbyville, to serve the reforestation program.[45]

The expanded operations and upgrading of the Forest Service required substantial increases in state appropriations. Again the Forest Service was fortunate in having concerned men in and out of the Legislature working in behalf of forest programs. Senators Otis Locke, Martin Dies, Jr., and A. M. Aikin, Jr., among others, worked actively in the Legislature in behalf of the Forest Service. Governor Allan Shivers (1949-1957), a native of East Texas, was kindly disposed to the strengthening of the Texas Forest Service. In industry such men as Ernest L. Kurth, Aubrey Carter, Arthur Temple, Jr., and Harry Seaman gave strong support to forestry programs.[46] The result was that funds available to the Texas Forest Service grew from $286,066 in 1948 to a total of $1,936,118 in 1968.[47]

The Gulf States Cooperative Tree Improvement Program, financed in part by private industry, the Texas Forest Service, and the Agricultural Experiment Station, had its origins in the 1950s and was the first genetic tree-improvement program in the South. Dr. Bruce Zobel gave the program a "splendid start."[48] The outbreak of a Southern-pine beetle epidemic in the fifties led to the establishment of the Southern Forest Research Institute, funded originally by private forest owners in Texas and by the Boyce Thompson Foundation. Later other public and private funds became availa-

[45]*Ibid.; Texas Forest Service: Its History, Objectives and Activities,* 3-14.

[46]Interview with Alfred D. Folweiler, November 10, 1971, Texas A&M University, College Station, Texas.

[47]*General Laws of Texas,* 1947, p. 658; *General Laws of Texas,* 1967, p. 2267.

[48]*Texas Forest Service: Its History, Objectives and Activities,* 14; interview with Alfred D. Folweiler, November 10, 1971, Texas A&M University, College Station, Texas.

ble. During two five-year research programs, directed in part by Dr. Jean Pierre Vité, a graduate of Georg August University, of Göttingen, Germany, the Institute pioneered in the use of nonchemical insect-control techniques.[49] One product of the concern over forest-pest epidemics was the passage of the Forest Pest Control Law (1963) by the Texas Legislature. This law allowed the Texas Forest Service to enter upon private lands for the control of forest pests without the owner's authorization, just as the original Forestry Law of 1915 had allowed patrolmen to enter upon private lands for the control of fire.[50]

Folweiler retired as director of the Texas Forest Service in September 1967, and was succeeded by Paul R. Kramer, a native of Columbus, Ohio, who acquired his forestry education at Washington State University and Yale University. After work with the Tennessee Valley Authority and the U.S. Forest Service, Kramer joined the Texas Forest Service as forest-products technologist in 1948, and became head of the Forest Products Laboratory, in Lufkin, in 1955.[51]

Kramer and the Forest Service expanded forestry research and reforestation and management programs. The Service has given increased attention to a program initiated by Folweiler by which small timber tracts are organized into "aggregates" under cooperative management and fire-protection programs. Kramer revitalized the older Cooperative Forestry Improvement Program (now Gulf State Cooperative Tree Improvement Program), and converted the Magnolia Springs Nursery into a seed orchard. Public education, as well as forest protection, continues to constitute a major effort of the Texas Forest Service. Research programs have developed new and improved tree-farming practices; trained foresters have taught timberland owners the best forestry practices, and the Forest Service, in cooperation with other state and federal agencies such as the U.S. Forest Service and the Texas Forestry Association, has worked persistently to create in the public a concern for conservation and forest preservation.[52] Over the years these efforts have been tremendously successful.

Today the Texas Forest Service remains on the basic organizational structure established in 1949. The four major departments include Forest

[49]Interview with Alfred D. Folweiler, November 10, 1971, Texas A&M University, College Station, Texas.

[50]*Ibid.*

[51]"Biographical Sketch of Paul R. Kramer," in letter from D. A. Anderson, College Station, Texas, to Henry C. Dethloff, College Station, Texas, November 23, 1971.

[52]Interview with Alfred D. Folweiler, November 10, 1971, Texas A&M University, College Station, Texas; *Texas Forest Service: Its History, Objectives and Activities,* 6, 8.

Management, Information and Education, the Forest Products Laboratory, and Fire Control. Six administrative districts in the Piney Woods, headquartered variously at Linden, Henderson, Lufkin, Woodville, Kirbyville, and Conroe, supervise field operations. A seventh division headquartered at College Station administers field operations in the post-oak region.[53] The Service, in cooperation with the Texas Forestry Association, sponsors public billboards and a Youth Forestry Shortcourse, and directs the Sears-Roebuck Foundation Forestry Awards Program.[54]

Overcoming, belatedly, one of the most chronic deficiencies in the forestry program of Texas A&M University, the University established an undergraduate degree program in forestry in 1969. Texas A&M's failure to pursue earlier an academic program in forestry caused the creation of a forestry program at Stephen F. Austin State College, in Nacogdoches, in 1946. The lack of an academic program in forestry at A&M contributed in some degree to the alienation of the Forest Service from the academic and research programs of the University and, until recent years, weakened efforts to develop tree-improvement programs in conjunction with the plant sciences.[55]

Texas A&M made some overtures toward beginning forestry training in 1946, when the Department of Range Management, which had been organized the previous year, became the Department of Range Management and Forestry. Robert Raymond Rhodes joined the Department as Texas A&M's first professor of forestry, but the courses in forestry were optional, no degrees were granted in the discipline of forestry, and range management continued to be the emphasis. In 1965 the School of Natural Biosciences was created; it comprised the Departments of Recreation and Wildlife Management (now Wildlife Science) and Range Management and Forestry. The Texas Coordinating Board authorized Texas A&M to grant doctoral degrees in forestry, but incongruously, no master's or undergraduate degrees. The forestry academic program remained a paper tiger. Finally, on September 1, 1969, with the authorization of the Coordinating Board, the Department of Range Management and Forestry divided to become the Department of Range Science and the Department of Forestry Science, the latter headed by Robert Glenn Merrifield. Not until that time was an undergraduate degree program in forestry initiated.[56] Despite the great contemporary emphasis on the eco-

[53]*Texas Forest Service: Its History, Objectives and Activities*, 6, 8.

[54]*Ibid.*, 13.

[55]Interview with Alfred D. Folweiler, November 10, 1971, Texas A&M University, College Station, Texas.

[56]Interview with Robert Glenn Merrifield, December 1, 1971, Texas A&M University, College Station, Texas; Texas A&M, *General Catalogue, 1971-1972*, pp. 50-55, 213-214.

logical studies represented by the curricula of the School of Natural Biosciences, no director of the School has ever been appointed, and the programs remain somewhere in the netherworld of Texas A&M academics.

The forestry programs and the Texas Forest Service throughout their history have carried a low profile within the state and within the Texas A&M academic system, but in dollars and cents and in public service the forestry programs and the Texas Forest Service have had a profound impact upon Texas. The Texas Forest Service has strongly adhered to A&M's recognized obligation of service to the people.

CHAPTER 18

An Extension of the University

"Extension work is hereby defined as all work intended to extend the usefulness of the College to the people of the state." (Texas A&M, Board of Directors, October 15, 1912)

COOPERATIVE agricultural extension work in the United States is usually traced to Dr. Seaman A. Knapp's farm-demonstration work on the Walter C. Porter farm near Terrell, Texas, in 1903.[1] In 1914 the Smith-Lever Act provided federal funding and the basic organizational structure for a nationwide extension program.[2] Knapp and the Smith-Lever Act are the crossroads, but along that roadway are numerous milestones which have combined to shape and build agricultural extension work in America. The development of agricultural extension is a complex and cumulative historical process, in which Knapp and the Smith-Lever Act are vital elements, and which had as its broad purpose to instruct people outside of the academic and scientific community in better farming and living techniques. The story of agricultural extension in Texas is a microhistory of the Agricultural Extension Service of the United States Department of Agriculture.

The passage of the Morrill Land-Grant College Act in 1862 marks the real beginning of organized public agricultural extension work in the United States. Teaching, research, and extension developed as coordinate divisions of the land-grant-college effort. The Agricultural and Mechanical College of Texas, formally dedicated on October 4, 1876, first conceived of its extension obligations in the 1880s, developed extension programs in the 1890s, adopted the format of modern extension (including demonstration farms, county

[1]Texas Extension Service, "Historical Notes and Staff Lists by Years, 1903-1951," Texas Extension Service Papers, Texas A&M University Archives; USDA, Bureau of Plant Industry, *The Work of the Community Demonstration Farm at Terrell, Texas,* by Seaman A. Knapp, Bulletin 51, Part II (February 17, 1904), pp. 3-8; Joseph C. Bailey, *Seaman A. Knapp: Schoolmaster of American Agriculture,* pp. 149-168; Oscar B. Martin, *The Demonstration Work: Dr. Seaman A. Knapp's Contribution to Civilization,* 3-4; Alfred C. True, *A History of Agricultural Extension Work in the United States, 1785-1923,* p. 60.

[2]Bailey, *Seaman A. Knapp,* 276; True, *A History of Agricultural Extension,* 100-129; 38 *Stat. L.* 372.

agents, and club work) in the first decade of the twentieth century, created a Department of Extension in 1910, entered a cooperative agreement with the United States Department of Agriculture and formally organized a statewide extension program under a College Extension Committee in 1912. Texas A&M organized the Texas Agricultural Extension Service under the provisions of the Smith-Lever Act of 1914, which provided for cooperative agricultural extension work between the land-grant colleges and the United States Department of Agriculture. Extension, by that time, had already become an established fact in Texas and in many other states.

The idea of extension is implicit in the Morrill Land-Grant College Act, which seeks to promote the "liberal and practical education of the industrial classes." The benefits of the educational program are intended for a very broad spectrum of society, not just for the student enrolled. The idea of extension and of the dissemination of knowledge for the public welfare also entered into the development of the National Patrons of Husbandry, or Grange, in the late 1860s and 1870s. Oliver Hudson Kelley, the founder of the Grange, sought to create a Masonic-type order concerned with improving the condition of the farmer materially, socially, and intellectually.[3] The Grange, or Patrons of Husbandry, was first organized in Texas at Salado in July 1873 by R. A. Baird, of the national Grange. As a nonpartisan agrarian order the Texas Grange offered to farm families a fourfold plan for cooperation in business, happier home life, more social opportunities, and better educational advantages. When Texas A&M College was opened the Grange was working toward the establishment of a cooperative college and experimental farm at Austin. By 1878 the Texas Grange became concerned that Texas A&M was failing in its obligations to the masses of people (the farmers) by adhering during its early years to the classic, literary curricula. Meeting at Bryan in January 1878, the Texas State Grange demanded that the A&M College establish an experimental farm, on which the farmers could learn new and improved techniques of cultivation.[4] The idea of a "demonstration" farm influenced the passage of the Hatch Act and the establishment of the agricultural experiment stations. The agricultural experiment stations were conceived and operated, at least in part, in the purely practical atmosphere of a demonstration farm. Because so much of their work involved practical demonstration work, and because their experimental work was largely dictated by

[3]Solon Justus Buck, *The Granger Movement*, 39-41.

[4]Frederick Eby (ed.), *Education in Texas, Source Materials*, 705; see also additional Grange criticism in Bryan *The Brazos Pilot*, January 23, 1880, reprinted in College Station *The Texas Collegian*, January, 1880.

local practical farm requirements, the experiment station at the outset was almost as much involved in extension as in experimentation.[5]

In 1879 Governor Oran M. Roberts echoed Granger concern and pointed to the need to demonstrate the practical application of knowledge to agriculture:

> And when it is found that by attending the school it will be learned how to produce two ears of wheat and corn and two bolls of cotton by the same labor and capital that have been heretofore producing but one, then it will be understood that this is a new field of learning the most extensive and the most beneficial to our race that has engaged the educators of any previous age.[6]

The Board of Directors established an experimental farm in October 1879, too late to stem the tide of criticism which led to the discharge of the entire faculty in November.[7]

The agrarian reaction sought to establish the entire program of the College on the basis of practical agriculture and practical mechanics. The man in charge of agricultural studies at Texas A&M during the period was Charles C. Gorgeson. A graduate of Michigan State College (A&M) in 1878, Gorgeson studied at the Agricultural College of Iowa, at Ames, in 1886, while Seaman A. Knapp was there as professor of practical and experimental agriculture. Gorgeson, who achieved a distinguished record as an agriculturist in Tokyo, Kansas State College, and Alaska, began his practical demonstration work at Texas A&M in 1880.[8] Gorgeson likely was influenced as much by his Michigan training as by Knapp's influence on agricultural studies at Iowa, for both Michigan State and Knapp represented the "narrow gauge" school of thought about the Morrill Land-Grant Act, to the effect that the act "intended to create a new education for, and the advancement of, the plain people."[9] Although Gorgeson began the "experimental farm," his successor at Texas A&M, George Washington Curtis, an 1883 graduate of Iowa State

---

[5]Charles E. Rosenberg, "Science, Technology and Economic Growth: The Case Study of the Agricultural Experiment Station Scientist, 1875-1914," *Agricultural History*, XLV (January 1971), pp. 1-20.

[6]Oran M. Roberts, Austin, Texas, to Thomas S. Gathright, College Station, Texas, May 21, 1879, reprinted in Galveston *News*, November 15, 1879.

[7]Anderson James Peeler (ed.), *Laws Relating to the Agricultural and Mechanical College*, 23.

[8]S. W. Geiser, "George Washington Curtis and Frank Arthur Gulley: Two Early Agricultural Teachers in Texas," *Field and Laboratory*, XIV (January 1946), pp. 2-3; C. C. Gorgeson, Ames, Iowa, to Louis L. McInnis, College Station, Texas, August 16, 1881, Louis L. McInnis Papers, Texas A&M University Archives; Texas A&M, *Annual Report, 1883*, pp. 30-34; Bailey, *Seaman A. Knapp*, 79.

[9]Bailey, *Seaman A. Knapp*, 81.

College,[10] made more positive contributions to the development of the extension concept in Texas.

During his first year at College Station, Curtis recommended the establishment of "farmers' institutes" in the "next year or two" so as to allow "free discussion and experimentation." He also began the publication of bulletins making available to the public the results of experimental farm work.[11] Curtis undoubtedly drew directly upon the experiences of Iowa State College with farmers' institutes, they having been initiated in Iowa in 1870.[12] Meanwhile Curtis, Chairman Hardaway Hunt Dinwiddie, and his successor Louis L. McInnis, achieved signal success in proselytizing for the College with the Texas State Grange.[13] In December 1888 Texas A&M College made a formal request to the Legislature for funding of farmers' institutes.[14] Appropriations were sufficient to allow the Directors in June 1889 to authorize a farmers' institute in each congressional district.[15] The first farmers' institute in Texas was held in Henrietta, Texas, on January 10 and 11, 1890, with the cooperation of John G. James, the local banker, and former president of Texas A&M.[16] Farmers' institutes were held at random in various parts of the state for the next eight years.

In July 1898 James H. Connell, who replaced Curtis as professor of agriculture and director of the Agricultural Experiment Station, organized a massive Farmers' Camp Meeting on the A&M College campus. At this meeting Connell and President Lafayette Lumpkin Foster organized the Texas Farmers' Congress, of which Connell became the first president.[17] This Congress met annually on the A&M College campus from 1898 to 1915.[18]

The Congress proved a most effective device in bringing the farmer in to see demonstration farm work, to hear lectures, and to obtain practical sci-

---

[10]Geiser, "George Washington Curtis and Frank Arthur Gulley," *Field and Laboratory*, XIV (January 1946), pp. 3-6.

[11]Texas A&M, *Annual Report, 1883-84*, pp. 4, 6.

[12]True, *A History of Agricultural Extension*, 11; see for a history of farmers' institutes, *ibid.*, 14-42.

[13]H. H. Dinwiddie, College Station, Texas, to Louis L. McInnis, Forest, Mississippi, August 8, 1884, Louis L. McInnis Papers, Texas A&M University Archives; Texas A&M, *Biennial Report, 1883-1885*, pp. 12-13; Minutes of the Board of Directors, June 6-9, 1887, I, 26-27.

[14]Texas A&M, *Annual Report, 1888*, xviii-xix.

[15]Minutes of the Board of Directors, June 4, 1889, I, 76.

[16]*The Farmers' Institute of the Fifth Congressional District*, Henrietta, Texas, January 10 and 11, 1890, pp. 1-4, pamphlet in Louis L. McInnis Papers, Texas A&M University Archives.

[17]Bryan *Eagle*, June 23, 1898; July 21, 1898; August 18, 1898; July 21, 1904; see also Texas Farmers' Congress, *Proceedings*, 1898-1915.

[18]Texas Farmers' Congress, *Proceedings*, 1898-1915.

entific farming information. The Farmers' Congress was Texas A&M's first well-organized extension activity. In addition to the Congress, Farmers' Institutes continued to be held at random times and places about the state. Concurrent with this activity the *Farm and Ranch* journal, published by Clarence Ousley, sponsored a variety of agricultural clubs for boys and girls. In 1903 Connell, who later replaced Ousley as editor of *Farm and Ranch*, succeeded in getting the Farmers' Congress to assume sponsorship of junior agricultural clubs on a statewide basis. The Congress, in a meeting at College Station in July 1903, organized the Farm Boys' and Girls' Progressive League, which became a predecessor of 4-H Club work.[19]

Texas A&M's Farmers' Congress, club work, institute work, and the unofficial extension work of Experiment Station personnel were soon supplemented by federal programs which developed out of efforts to fight the spread of the boll weevil, ravaging Texas at the turn of the century. Here Seaman A. Knapp enters the picture. Seaman A. Knapp left Iowa State College in 1887, and immediately became involved in efforts to develop agricultural enterprises, and especially the rice industry in the prairies of southwest Louisiana. In his first official capacity with the U.S. Department of Agriculture, Knapp was commissioned as a "plant explorer." The success of his mission to Japan in returning with the Kiushu variety of rice, which helped found the modern rice industry, led to his being commissioned in the summer of 1902 as special agent with the Department of Agriculture.[20]

Knapp's work in southwest Louisiana attracted widespread interest and produced a variety of inquiries. One of these came from Edward Howland Robinson Green, manager of the Texas Midland Railroad, whose mother was Hetty Green, a partner of John Pierpont Morgan. According to Francis Kamp McGinnis, a Texas A&M graduate of 1900, he advised F. B. McKay, the general passenger agent of the Texas Midland Railroad, that the best way to increase freight loadings was to increase the production of cotton, corn, and livestock in the territory served by the railroad. McKay contacted Green, who in turn requested special assistance from the Department of Agriculture. The Department put Knapp in touch with Green.[21] At the same time, during

[19]Texas Extension Service, "Historical Notes and Staff Lists, 1903-1951," Texas Extension Service Papers, Texas A&M University Archives.

[20]Bailey, *Seaman A. Knapp*, 133-137; Henry C. Dethloff, "Rice Revolution in the Southwest, 1880-1910," *Arkansas Historical Quarterly*, XXIX (Spring 1970), pp. 66-75.

[21]Reminiscences of Francis Kamp McGinnis (May 1956), Texas A&M University Archives. Green established a large and expensive experimental farm near Terrell in November 1903. Knapp verifies the role of F. B. McKay in "Texas Extension Service Historical Notes and Staff Lists, 1903-1951," date of January 29, 1904, Texas A&M University Archives.

late 1902, Knapp and Beverly T. Galloway, chief of the Bureau of Plant Industry, were establishing government-operated demonstration farms close to Calvert, Texas, and Shreveport, Louisiana.[22] Green's invitation to have Knapp visit and conduct a series of meetings with farmers at Terrell, Texas, was first declined by Knapp, who believed that the effort would be local, rather than regional, in scope. Green met Knapp in New York in the winter of 1902, and again urged Knapp to give assistance and direction to farm problems in Texas.[23] Farmers in Greenville, Texas, and in Terrell, Texas, now acted independently of Green to contact Knapp, this time proposing his assistance in establishing a community demonstration farm, rather than in lecturing. Knapp, who was now tremendously pressed for time, outlined certain conditions under which local farmers would manage the demonstration farm under his direction. The farmers agreed, and Knapp met with farmers at Greenville on February 24, and at Terrell, Texas, at the Odd Fellows Hall, on February 25, 1903. That spring the Greenville Demonstration Farm and the Porter Demonstration Farm, at Terrell, began operations.[24]

The Walter C. Porter Demonstration Farm proved eminently successful.[25] On October 22 Secretary of Agriculture James B. Wilson and his entourage, including Knapp, Jasper Wilson, Beverly T. Galloway, William Jasper Spillman, and Arthur W. Edson, visited the Farm. Wilson later addressed a large crowd in Terrell, remarking on the advances in agriculture, and the problems. "You should pay more attention to your agricultural college," he told them, among other things. In all, he was greatly impressed with results on the Demonstration Farm.[26]

What made the Porter Demonstration Farm so important and so unique was that it was not a "government farm," nor a "corporate farm," but a local, community farm operated at local expense. Perhaps equally important, it was a clear, "demonstrable," success. The Greenville effort was equally successful, but less publicized.[27]

An immediate product of Wilson's tours through the South and the

[22]Bailey, *Seaman A. Knapp*, 150.

[23]*Ibid.*, 151-152.

[24]Texas Extension Service, "Historical Notes and Staff Lists, 1903-1951," Texas A&M University Archives; Bailey, *Seaman A. Knapp*, 152. The Porter Demonstration farm was owned by Walter C. Porter and operated by his son, S. B. Porter.

[25]Bureau of Plant Industry, *The Work of the Community Demonstration Farm at Terrell, Texas, by Seaman A. Knapp*, Bulletin 51, Part II (February 17, 1904), pp. 1-4.

[26]Texas Extension Service, "Historical Notes and Staff Lists, 1903-1951," date of November 4, 1903, Texas A&M University Archives.

[27]Bailey, *Seaman A. Knapp*, 159.

Southwest, which brought him to Terrell, was a congressional emergency appropriation of $250,000 to fight the boll weevil. One-half of this appropriation was given to the Bureau of Entomology and one-half to the Bureau of Plant Industry. Following the inspection of the Porter Demonstration Farm, forty thousand dollars was allocated to Seaman A. Knapp by the Bureau of Plant Industry to develop demonstration farms similar to the Terrell project. In January 1904 Seaman A. Knapp established headquarters in the Old Masonic Temple in Houston, Texas, and extension by demonstration began in earnest.[28]

Knapp's first effort was to mobilize the "industrial agents" of Texas railroads to support efforts in combating the boll weevil and to promote better farming techniques among farmers served by their roads. Then, between February 1 and February 24, 1904, Knapp appointed thirty-three "special agents" for a tenure of two to six months, and at salaries of $60 to $80 per month, with traveling expenses and free passes on the railroads, whose job was to establish demonstration farms and to disseminate information sent out by Knapp. George W. Curtis, former professor of agriculture at Texas A&M, was one of these agents.[29] They served various areas of the state, usually including seven or eight counties, as need arose. In 1906 the businessmen of Tyler, Smith County, Texas, appealed to Knapp for a full-time resident, special agent in the county, and agreed to pay part of the agent's salary if he could be appointed. On November 12, 1906, William C. Stallings was named county agent of Smith County, the first such county agent in the United States.[30]

Texas A&M officially entered the picture in 1905, when the state Legislature failed to make appropriations for the continuance of Farmers' Institute (and Farmers' Congress) work at A&M. Knapp agreed to help fund the College's program, in return for which the director of Farmers' Institutes, James W. Carson, of the A&M faculty, agreed to take charge of a minimum of twenty demonstration farms.[31] Thus was established the very important precedent for A&M College direction of "county" or demonstration-agent work.

The demonstration idea rapidly spread across Texas and into other

[28]True, *A History of Agricultural Extension,* 60; B. T. Galloway, Lakeland, Florida, to O. B. Martin, College Station, Texas, March 18, 1928, copy of letter in Texas Extension Service, "Historical Notes and Staff Lists, 1903-1951," Texas A&M University Archives.

[29]Texas Extension Service, "Historical Notes and Staff Lists, 1903-1951," date of February 24, 1904, Texas A&M University Archives; see also Houston *Post,* January 29, 1904.

[30]Texas Extension Service, "Historical Notes and Staff Lists, 1903-1951," year 1906, Texas A&M University Archives.

[31]*Ibid.;* Texas A&M, *Annual Report, 1906,* pp. 40-41.

states, including Louisiana and Mississippi. Knapp moved his headquarters to Lake Charles, Louisiana, in 1906, and for 1907 placed Texas under the direction of three state agents, William F. Proctor for East Texas, James L. Quicksall for West Texas, and W. D. Bentley for the Panhandle and western Oklahoma. The East Texas region was divided into ten districts, each under a district agent. Six of the district agents in East Texas were in fact county agents who received part or all of their salaries from county sources.[32] Cooperative demonstration work expanded rapidly under this pattern until 1911, with an increasing number of agents becoming county agents. Two important events altered developments in 1911. One was the death of Seaman A. Knapp, on April 1, and the other was approval by the Texas Legislature of a bill authorizing county commissioners courts to appropriate money for ·agents' salaries.[33] Knapp had gone to Washington, D.C., to head up the Division of Farmers' Cooperative Demonstration Work, but had continued to maintain an interest in demonstration work in Texas.

In the interim, between 1907 and 1911, other developments were altering the course of extension work. On September 25, 1907, special agents Tom M. Marks, W. D. Bentley, James L. Quicksall, and Captain F. S. White, of the Rock Island and Frisco Railroad, were confronted by the failure of a "corn show" in Jack County, Texas. The farmers simply had failed or refused to show their corn.

Bentley said to Marks, "You can't teach an old dog new tricks."

"Then," replied Marks, "next year, we will try the young dogs."

Marks went on to organize the first Boys' Corn Club in Texas, and followed it in the spring with a highly successful corn show. Quicksall and the other state and district agents promoted the expansion of Boys' and Girls' Corn Clubs throughout the state. In 1908 Knapp went to Washington, D.C., as head of the Division of Farmers' Cooperative Demonstration Work, in the Bureau of Plant Industry. Knapp's division immediately began to promote the expansion of boys' and girls' clubs, and by 1912 youth-club activity had become a national program of Farm Demonstration work.[34] The 4-H insignia was soon afterwards devised by Oscar Baker Martin, Texas director of boys' and girls' club work, and later director, Texas Agricultural Extension Service.[35]

---

[32]Texas Extension Service, "Historical Notes and Staff Lists, 1903-1951," year 1907, Texas A&M University Archives.

[33]*Ibid.*, 1911.

[34]*Ibid.*, 1907, January 1909.

[35]Texas Extension Service, *I Pledge My Heart: The Story of Boys' 4-H Club Work in Texas* (1938), pp. 1-5. A three-leaf clover insignia was developed in Iowa in 1911, signifying "head, hands, and heart."

Thus, the Corn Clubs, rather than the Boys' and Girls' Progressive League, sponsored by the Farmers' Congress, became the immediate antecedent of 4-H Club work. But in practice, the clubs were often organized and administered by the same people, or persons having common affiliations; and in 1912 Texas A&M assumed direction of the entire demonstration program in Texas, and by 1915 the Farmers' Congress and its work had yielded to the Cooperative Demonstration program. Although local boys' and girls' clubs had developed in Illinois and Ohio in 1900 and 1902 respectively, and under the auspices of the Texas Farmers' Congress in 1903, and had appeared in Mississippi and Kansas in 1907, Texas Corn Clubs provided the immediate impetus which led to Knapp's systematic organization of boys' and girls' club work in 1909.[36]

Between 1906 and 1911 the extension idea was also being promoted by the General Education Board, a John D. Rockefeller-funded organization, which concluded a cooperative agreement with the Department of Agriculture on April 20, 1906.[37] During the same period the Association of American Agricultural Colleges and Experiment Stations became concerned with promoting extension work.[38] Additional signs of the changing times included action by the Texas Legislature to expand the experiment-station program, and approval of a law providing in 1909 for summer "teacher institutes" in agriculture for instructing teachers in elementary agriculture.[39] In 1910 Texas A&M established correspondence courses in agricultural education for teachers, and in soils, crops, dairying, animal husbandry, and horticulture for farmers. The Directors also established a Department of Extension with Claude M. Evans as head, responsible for correspondence courses, fair projects, and institutes.[40]

Shortly before Seaman A. Knapp's death on April 1, 1911, the Texas Legislature approved a bill which gave the county-agent-extension program in Texas a firm base, thus opening new horizons in extension work. The bill provided that county commissioners courts, the fiscal and executive authority in county government, could allocate up to $1,000 per year in county revenues

---

[36]True, *A History of Agricultural Extension Work*, 37-41, 65-68.

[37]*Ibid.*, 61-62; Texas Extension Service, "Historical Notes and Staff Lists, 1903-1951," date of April 20, 1906, Texas A&M University Archives.

[38]True, *A History of Agricultural Extension*, 54-57.

[39]*General Laws of Texas, 1909*, p. 221.

[40]Minutes of the Board of Directors, February 15, 1910, II, 195-196; Texas Extension Service, "Historical Notes and Staff Lists, 1903-1951," year 1910, Texas A&M University Archives.

for farmers' cooperative demonstration work.[41] Whereas county demonstration work, that is, the maintenance of agricultural specialists in each county, had previously depended upon essentially limited federal appropriations to the general account of the Bureau of Plant Industry or upon donations to the General Education Board, and upon private contributions within each county, every county in Texas now had the wherewithal to hire its own county agent without dependence upon private donations or federal funds. By October 1911 thirteen Texas counties had either converted to the new system of funding county agents, or had initiated new programs. Each year in 1911 and 1912 approximately ten new counties obtained county agents. Between 1911 and 1913 many states of the Union passed varying kinds of legislation providing public funds for cooperative extension work. Included in this type of legislation were bills providing state or local funds for the organization of farm bureaus which became the local sponsoring organization for extension agents.[42] The advent of the farm bureau marked yet a new chapter in the extension story, a development well treated in Gladys Baker, *The County Agent;* William J. Block, *The Separation of the Farm Bureau and the Extension Service;* and Grant McConnell, *The Decline of Agrarian Democracy,* among others.[43] The significance of this new state legislation is that it facilitated the expansion of the extension program and "localized" what otherwise might have been a federal or national program.[44]

The Texas Legislature also authorized, in 1911, each county to establish its own demonstration farm under the control of the county commissioners court. By this time, however, the demonstration-farm approach had been superseded by the county-agent system, which enabled each farmer, in effect, to "demonstrate" on his own farm. Furthermore, the demonstration-farm law required a donation of land to the county, and included a number of encumbering stipulations,[45] so that it failed to have any significant impact upon extension activities.

[41]*General Laws of Texas, 1911,* pp. 105-106.

[42]Texas Extension Service, "Historical Notes and Staff Lists, 1903-1951," years 1911 and 1912, Texas A&M University Archives. True, *A History of Agricultural Extension Work,* 76-100.

[43]Baker (Chicago, 1939); Block (Urbana, Ill., 1960); McConnell (Berkeley, California, 1953).

[44]See Henry C. Dethloff, "Missouri Farmers and the New Deal: A Case Study of Farm Policy Formulation on the Local Level," *Agricultural History,* 39 (July 1965), pp. 141-146.

[45]*General Laws of Texas, 1911,* pp. 208-211; *Farmer's Cooperative Demonstration Work, by Bradford Knapp* [1913], in Texas Extension Service, "Historical Notes and Staff Lists, 1903-1951," year 1913, Texas A&M University Archives.

In August 1912, the A&M Directors announced a new extension policy for the College:

> Realizing that the A. & M. College of Texas can be and should be of great service in many ways to the citizens residing throughout the State, and that the most widely distinguished institutions of the A. & M. Colleges of other states are those that are assisting and co-operating in agricultural and engineering lines with the people, the tax-payers of their states, it is hereby made the declared policy of this Board and of Texas A. & M. College to achieve distinction for civil service to the people of Texas.[46]

An Extension Committee, including Dean of Agriculture Edwin J. Kyle, Dean of Engineering David W. Spence, State Chemist George S. Fraps, and Director of the Experiment Station Bonney Youngblood, became active on September 1; in October Dean of the College Charles Puryear, Publicity Agent Ike S. Ashburn, Jr., and President Robert Teague Milner were made members. The new Extension Committee defined the role and function of Texas A&M's extension program, recommended specific actions, including the expansion of correspondence courses and faculty participation in public and professional affairs, and reported to the Board of Directors. The "new idea" at A&M was essentially that there was much more to College work than teaching. "Teaching," one Committee report read, "is one-half or less than one-half of the real function of the Scientific (State) College, under the modern idea of educational work."[47]

On October 1, 1912, the United States Department of Agriculture concluded a Memorandum of Understanding between the Bureau of Plant Industry and the A&M College. The agreement gave Texas A&M supervision over cooperative farm demonstration work, and boys' and girls' club work in Texas, under the direction of the Bureau of Plant Industry.[48] W. F. Proctor was named state agent, with J. L. Quicksall as assistant state agent in charge of all existing district and county agents. Claude M. Evans, superintendent of A&M's Department of Extension, became state agent in charge of boys' and girls' club work, with Howard H. Williamson and J. O. Allen his assistants.[49] College Station quickly became the center of fervent activity.

---

[46]Minutes of the Extension Committee, 1, Texas A&M University Archives.

[47]*Ibid.,* 1, 3, 5-10; Minutes of the Board of Directors, October 15, 16, 1912, III, 39-40.

[48]Minutes of the Extension Committee of the Agricultural and Mechanical College of Texas, 12-15, Texas A&M University Archives.

[49]Texas Extension Service, "Historical Notes and Staff Lists, 1903-1951," year 1912, Texas A&M University Archives; Minutes of the Extension Committee, 12-15, Texas A&M University Archives.

The new Extension Service established "tent headquarters" in two tents next to the agricultural building. Federal funds and Texas county funds allowed numerous additions to the field force, including for the first time women demonstration agents. Mrs. Edna W. Trigg, appointed on January 16, 1912, to work in Milam County, was the first "lady agent" in Texas. By the end of the year sixteen home-demonstration agents were at work in Texas. Under the direction of H. H. Williamson enrollment in boys' and girls' club work rose to over 15,000. Exhibits, fairs, shows, and demonstrations were held in almost every area of Texas during the next two years. By 1913 the county agents and agricultural extension had become well-established institutions in Texas.[50] As the advent of the Experiment Station had rejuvenated and expanded the academic affairs of Texas A&M before the turn of the century, so the development of agricultural extension promoted a great awakening at the College and added impetus to a genuine surge of academic progress so ably directed by President William Bennett Bizzell between 1914 and 1925.

The Smith-Lever Act of 1914 was in many respects an anticlimax, or perhaps more appropriately, the Christmas wrapping on an already well-prepared parcel. The Smith-Lever Act, insofar as Texas and many other states of the Union were concerned, formalized an existing situation, but more important, it provided substantial funding for the operation of the Agricultural Extension Service. The act provided $480,000 for the first fiscal year, with $10,000 to be paid each state accepting the terms of the act, and

there is also appropriated an additional sum of $600,000 for the fiscal year following that in which the foregoing appropriation first becomes available, and for each year thereafter for seven years a sum exceeding by $500,000 the sum appropriated for each preceding year, and for each year thereafter there is permanently appropriated for each year the sum of $4,100,000 in addition to the sum of $480,000 hereinbefore provided.[51]

These funds were to be apportioned to the states, to the colleges or the administrative agents of the program, on the basis of the proportion of rural population within each state to the total rural population of all the states. Federal appropriations were to be matched by state, county, college, or local funds, which in Texas as of 1914, far exceeded federally scheduled appropriations.[52]

[50]Texas Extension Service, "Historical Notes and Staff Lists, 1903-1951," years 1912 and 1913, Texas A&M University Archives; Minutes of the Extension Committee, 16-49, Texas A&M University Archives.

[51]38 *Stat. L.* 372.

[52]*Ibid.*

David Franklin Houston, former president of Texas A&M, and now Secretary of Agriculture under Woodrow Wilson, wrote Charles Puryear, acting president of A&M, on May 12, and again on May 25, 1914, regarding procedures under the terms of the Smith-Lever Act, approved by President Wilson on May 8. Houston indicated that a States Relations Service, within the Department of Agriculture and under the direction of Alfred Charles True, would be established to administer the program. Interim approval by the governor of Texas, pending formal approval by the Legislature which was to convene in 1915, was required. There was some initial confusion and delay when Governor Oscar Branch Colquitt first declined to make any commitment, but the matter was soon cleared up and Colquitt's acceptance was received by the Department of Agriculture.[53] Colquitt may still have been miffed by his late encounters and public exchanges with former A&M President Robert T. Milner.

Charles Puryear signed a Memorandum of Understanding with the United States Department of Agriculture establishing the organizational structure and scope of extension programs under the new act. This memorandum essentially lumped all existing extension programs, committees, personnel, and funds in Texas together, with Smith-Lever funds allocated to Texas, under the administrative control of Texas A&M's Agricultural Extension Service, which now reported to the newly organized States Relations Committee and Director Alfred C. True.[54] Texas A&M's Board of Directors approved the agreement on June 29.[55] On August 10, 1914, the Directors named Clarence Ousley as Texas director of Agricultural Extension, and defined his duties and the new advisory duties of the existing Extension Committee on August 25.[56] The Texas Legislature accepted the terms of the Smith-Lever Act on January 29, 1915, naming Texas A&M the administrative agency and recipient of federal funds.[57] As had occurred when federal Hatch Act funds came to A&M, there was in 1915 a substantial enlargement of fac-

---

[53]David F. Houston, Washington, D.C., to Charles Puryear, College Station, Texas, May 12, 1914; Houston to Puryear, May 25, 1914; Puryear to Houston, June 2, 1914 (copy); A. C. True, Washington, D.C., to George S. Fraps, College Station, Texas, June 20, 1914; Oscar Branch Colquitt, Austin, Texas, to David F. Houston, May 18, 1914 (copy); Colquitt to Houston, June 15, 1914 (copy); Colquitt to Puryear, June 25, 1914; Texas Extension Papers, Texas A&M University Archives.

[54]See "Memorandum of Understanding, 1914," Texas Extension Service, "Historical Notes and Staff Lists, 1903-1951," Texas A&M University Archives.

[55]Minutes of the Board of Directors, June 29, 1914, III, 138-144.

[56]*Ibid.*, August 10, 1914, III, 146; August 25, 1914, II, 151.

[57]*Ibid.*, April 24, 1915, III, 163.

ulty and staff, and attractive salary raises to many personnel. The president's salary, for example, was raised from $5,000 to $6,000 per year.[58]

New agricultural specialists appointed to the Extension staff in 1915 were these: F. H. Blodgett, plant pathology; Walton Peteet, farm reporter; Claude M. Evans, animal husbandry; Robert L. Pou, dairying; William Bradford Lanham, horticulture; Fred W. Kazmeier, poultry; James C. Olsen, farm engineering; G. M. Garren, agronomy; and Fred Clark, seed selection.

For the first time Negro county and district agents were appointed in the Texas extension program. Negro extension work was headquartered at Prairie View under the direction of R. L. Smith.[59]

Clarence Ousley became Assistant Secretary of Agriculture on June 25, 1917, and Thomas O. Walton, who would play a long role as president of Texas A&M between 1925 and 1944, became acting director of Extension. Ousley resigned his position as director effective July 1, 1919, at which time Thomas O. Walton became director.[60] On July 1, 1923, the States Relation Service within the U.S. Department of Agriculture was abolished and the Extension Service, with a director at its head, Clyde William Warburton, replaced it. Organization on the state level in Texas had also been streamlined. T. O. Walton was director; William B. Lanham, assistant director; H. H. Williamson, state agent; Remus W. Persons, assistant state agent in charge of boys' club work; Sterling C. Evans, assistant boys' club agent; M. Helen Higgins, state home-demonstration agent; and Mildred Horton, assistant state home-demonstration agent. There were, in addition, nine district agricultural agents, nine district home-demonstration agents, one district agent at large, and about twenty-eight specialists, all headquartered at College Station.[61]

When Walton became president of the College in 1925 Charles H. Alvord replaced him as director. Alvord resigned on November 30, 1927, on the eve of the silver anniversary of the Extension Service. There were now about 300 county and home-demonstration agents in the field and 48 staff members at College Station.[62] Oscar B. Martin, born in South Carolina, November 8, 1870, and an early associate of Seaman A. Knapp's as national head of boys' club work after 1909, became director of the Texas Agricultural

[58]*Ibid.*, July 6, 1915, III, 170-171.

[59]Texas Extension Service, "Historical Notes and Staff Lists, 1903-1951," year 1915, Texas A&M University Archives.

[60]*Ibid.*, 1916-1919; Minutes of the Board of Directors, July 1, 1919, III, 254-255.

[61]Texas Extension Service, "Historical Notes and Staff Lists, 1903-1951," years 1920-1923, Texas A&M University Archives.

[62]*Ibid.*, 1927; Texas A&M, *Annual Report, 1927-1928*, pp. 22-23.

Extension Service. Martin had been regional director for extension under the U.S. Department of Agriculture in 1924, before accepting the position in Texas. Martin was a tireless worker for "teaching by demonstration" as opposed to what he termed the "dogmatic (or theoretical) school" of teaching. Martin guided the Texas Extension Service through its greatest years of growth and public service. He died at College Station on June 30, 1935, and was eulogized by the Association of Land-Grant Colleges and Universities as one who gave "a life of devotion and dedication to the philosophy of the demonstration and a deep, sincere interest in, and love for, people."[63]

H. H. Williamson succeeded Martin as director on July 8, 1935, at a time when Extension activities had grown to gigantic proportions by virtue of the Capper-Ketcham Act (1928), which provided large new federal appropriations to the states, and more particularly because of the Agricultural Adjustment Act of 1933, the New Deal agricultural recovery program which became the model for modern farm programs. The county agent became the field force for the New Deal farm programs. The home staff and field force of the Texas Extension Service were correspondingly enlarged.[64]

The Bankhead-Jones Act of 1935 provided more money for both the Texas Agricultural Experiment Station and the Extension Service. In May of that year, before becoming director of Texas Extension, Williamson led 4,200 farmers to Washington, D.C., to "thank Congress for all it has done for downtrodden farmers." As a result, he said, "We met with President Roosevelt on the White House lawn, at which time he delivered the first speech of his 1936 campaign." Years later he told a reporter, "In less than two weeks after we'd left Washington, Congress passed another act, the second Agricultural Act. I'm real proud of that."[65] The second act to which Williamson referred was the Soil Conservation and Domestic Allotment Act of 1936, rather than the Second Agricultural Adjustment Act of 1938. Both of these acts became important to Texas Agricultural Extension, but not for the reasons inferred by Williamson. Both acts phased out the county agent as a New Deal farm-program administrator, except in an advisory capacity.

In various states and even on the federal level, the Agricultural Extension Service became increasingly critical of Agricultural Adjustment Administration programs. Two "farm program" administrative agencies, in effect, had developed by 1938, with virtually parallel lines of authority. There were

[63]Martin, *The Demonstration Work*, 191-236.

[64]Texas Extension Service, "Historical Notes and Staff Lists, 1903-1951," years 1928-1935, Texas A&M University Archives; see also Dethloff, "Missouri Farmers and the New Deal," *Agricultural History*, 39 (July 1965), pp. 141-146.

[65]Bryan *Daily Eagle*, August 26, 1970, p. 2.

administrative conflicts and there were conflicts in policy — not the least of which was that the Extension Service was geared to "production," the AAA to "control."

World War II brought tremendous external and internal pressures to bear upon the College and the Texas Extension Service. For one thing, as in World War I, the Texas Extension Service had a job to do — to promote agricultural production. For another thing there was a tremendous turnover in personnel, especially among the younger men going into service and then later returning. In addition, there were tremendous technological breakthroughs and developments in every area of science and technology — and in agriculture. By 1943 these pressures combined to create a crisis in the Texas Extension Service.

The immediate incitement to the crisis was the simple recognition by the Board of Directors that Texas A&M needed to change with the times. The Directors recognized that the kind of substantive change they had in mind required a change in top personnel. In August 1943 the Directors asked Howard H. Williamson to resign as director of the Extension Service. He declined, and in August the Directors "refused to rehire him."[66]

The reasons for Williamson's departure are numerous and complex, but appear to have been largely internal rather than external. Specifically, a "power struggle" developed within Extension between the "Williamson faction" and the "Eudaly faction," the latter involving prominently Ernest R. Eudaly and George P. McCarthy. Moreover, the 700-800 employees of the Texas Extension Service comprised a powerful political organization within the state which was vulnerable to political pressures. Williamson was criticized for being "too kind," and not trimming back on the employee rolls. The Extension Service, furthermore, had no real association or involvement with the teaching and research functions of the College; its alienation from these activities diminished its effectiveness. In addition, Texas A&M itself was in the throes of change. Williamson and President Thomas O. Walton, who also retired under pressure in August 1943, appeared to some too inflexible and rigid.[67] Later, Williamson was named agricultural relations adviser to the Office of Price Administration (OPA) by Chester Bowles.[68]

[66]Houston *Post*, August 12, 13, 1943; Dallas *Morning News*, August 12, 1943; Houston *Press*, August 12, 19, 1943; Bryan *Eagle*, August 19, 1943; Fort Worth *Star-Telegram*, August 20, 1943; H. H. Williamson, College Station, Texas, to "All Extension Employees," August 14, 1943, in Texas Extension Service Papers, Texas A&M University Archives.

[67]*Ibid.;* Houston *Post*, August 20, 1943, February 15, 1944; Dallas *Morning News*, August 20, 1943; interview with Ide Peebles Trotter, November 17, 1971, College Station, Texas.

[68]Dallas *Morning News*, December 1, 1943.

A rapid turnover occurred on all levels of the Texas Extension Service with the departure of Williamson, now partly inspired by conflicts with the Agricultural Adjustment Administration. George E. Adams, vice-director for extension, replaced Williamson until December 1943, when he was relieved. His public reaction was that "he was relieved to be relieved," and he left then for a hunting trip.[69] Ernest R. Eudaly was named director to replace Adams, and James D. Prewit became vice-director in December 1943, but the Directors, who had effectively assumed administrative control over the Extension Service, had failed to consult Washington authorities as required by the Cooperative Agreement with the federal government. Eudaly was a 1910 Texas A&M graduate in animal husbandry, and a "second-generation" extension agent. Between January and July 1944 the Texas Extension Service became a statewide and even national storm center, when Milburn L. Wilson, national director of the Extension Service, after a two-week personal inspection of the Texas situation, refused to accept Eudaly's nomination as Texas director. Controversy and recrimination raged throughout the state Extension Service. There were numerous dismissals and departures from the Service, including that of Miss Mildred Horton, vice-director of extension and home demonstration. Miss Maurine Hearn, who succeeded Miss Horton, came under fire. There were accusations of attempted federal control of A&M. Finally, in October a settlement was reached under the auspices of recently elected Texas A&M President Gibb Gilchrist. Eudaly, never having been confirmed by Washington in his new post, resigned from the Extension Service. Ide Peebles Trotter, former head of A&M's department of agronomy, became the new director in October, with the approval of M. L. Wilson.[70] Trotter accepted the position with the understanding that Texas A&M's Board of Directors had finished its internal administration of Extension affairs. He then worked hard to still the chaos and factional bickering in the Extension Service.

During the next year the storm clouds lightened. Inequities, where they had developed, seemed to be corrected. Trotter sent the district representa-

[69]Dallas *Morning News*, December 14, 1943; George E. Adams, College Station, Texas, to "Dear County Agent," December 20, 1943, Texas Extension Service Papers, Texas A&M University Archives.

[70]Houston *Post*, February 12, 20, May 14, June 22, 25, August 3, 5, October 6, 15, 1944; Dallas *Morning News*, March 19, April 30, May 14, June 22, August 3, 4, 5, October 6, 15, 1944; Fort Worth *Star-Telegram*, April 14, 30, May 15, 20, June 22, 25, July 7, October 6, 15, 1944; Bryan *Daily Eagle*, April 25, May 15, June 2, 21, 22, 23, 24, 29, July 5, 6, August 3, 8, October 5, 16, 1944.

tives away from College Station to headquarters in their home districts. Maurine Hearn was retained as state home-demonstration agent; H. H. Williamson received an assignment as assistant director of extension work in Washington, D.C., working under Director M. L. Wilson.[71] President Gibb Gilchrist and the Directors also reorganized the College administration so as to place the Texas Extension Service under the auspices of the newly created vice-president for agriculture (see fig. 6).[72] David Willard Williams, who in September 1946 became the first vice-president for agriculture, recalls this as a necessary and most productive administrative reorganization, and Ide P. Trotter pointed out that it was the first step in integrating the three basic divisions of the College of Agriculture — Teaching, Research, and Extension.[73]

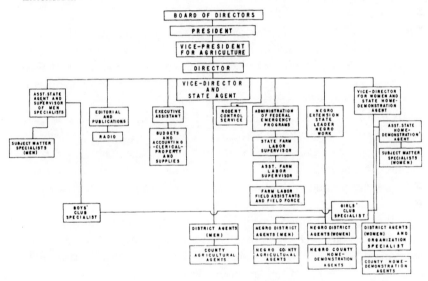

Figure 6. Organizational chart of the Texas Agricultural Extension Service, 1946. From *Bulletin of the Agricultural and Mechanical College of Texas, Catalogue*, part 9 [1946].

[71]College Station *Battalion,* November 7, 1944; Bryan *Daily Eagle,* 1945, September 26, 1945; USDA, "Advance Release," January 4, 1945, in Texas Extension Service Papers, Texas A&M University Archives.

[72]Fort Worth *Star-Telegram,* October 15, 1944.

[73]Interview with David W. Williams, College Station, Texas, September 15, 1971; interview with Ide P. Trotter, College Station, Texas, November 17, 1971.

A fundamental reorganization of the Service occurred in 1946, when the academic divisions of the School of Agriculture were integrated to include personnel from the academic School of Agriculture, the Texas Agricultural Experiment Station, and the Agricultural Extension Service. This reorganization attempted to reflect the announced policy of coordinating Texas A&M's teaching, research, and extension activities.[74] These basic activities of the College had long been recognized, but no effort had been previously made to harmonize or coordinate those functions. David W. Williams and Ide P. Trotter played a major role in modernizing and updating the Texas Extension Service and the College, for the challenges and demands of the postwar world.

Ide Trotter served as an effective "trouble-shooter" in a most troublesome time for the Texas Extension Service. Trotter, born in Brownsville, Tennessee, on December 12, 1895, received his early training at Mississippi College and Mississippi A&M, and did advanced work at the University of Missouri and at the University of Wisconsin, receiving his Ph.D. from Wisconsin in 1933. From 1923 to 1936 Trotter served as Extension agronomist in Missouri, and headed a number of AAA New Deal programs. He came to Texas A&M as head of the Department of Agronomy in 1936, and in 1944 became director of the Texas Extension Service.[75] He helped plan the reorganization of the administrative structure of the Texas Extension Service, clarified lines of authority, assisted in the integration of Extension, academic, and research personnel within the College, upgraded the Extension staff with special advanced training and degree programs sponsored, in part, by the Sears, Roebuck Foundation; instituted a special training program for Negro employees; and in 1949 left to his successor in office, George G. Gibson, a modernized and more effective Extension Service. Trotter recalls that James D. Prewit, his vice-director of Extension, was a most efficient and effective "Operations man" who handled the day-by-day mechanics of the Service. One of the most important accomplishments, Trotter believes, was to establish at Prairie View A&M a national training program for Negro extension personnel. Trotter moved on to his second trouble-shooting role in 1949, becoming dean of the then struggling Graduate School.[76]

[74]Houston *Post,* October 31, 1946; see "Memorandum, December 5, 1946," Texas Extension Service, "Historical Notes and Staff Lists, 1903-1951," Texas A&M University Archives.

[75]Ide Peebles Trotter Papers, Biographical data, Texas A&M University Archives.

[76]John E. Hutchison, College Station, Texas, to Ide Peebles Trotter, College Station, Texas, December 18, 1959, Ide Peebles Trotter Papers; Texas Extension Service, "Historical Notes and Staff Lists, 1903-1951," year 1949; College Station *Battalion,* March 11, May 25, 1949; interview with Ide P. Trotter, November 17, 1971, College Station, Texas.

Director George G. Gibson, who replaced Trotter, continued to build and to improve the quality and efficiency of the Texas Extension Service. Gibson joined the Service in 1935 as a county agent in the field. He later moved to Texas A&M as assistant dairy husbandman. He furthered the racial integration of the Service and expanded the role of extension work on the farm and in rural and urban communities. Gibson did much to professionalize the Texas Extension Service, and to broaden "extension" as a basic facet of modern public education. In 1954 Congress revised the Smith-Lever Act, giving the Service specific authority to promote and lend assistance to industrial projects in rural communities. In 1955 Texas A&M concluded a new memorandum of understanding with the United States Department of Agriculture on cooperative extension work in agriculture and home economics. The memorandum specifically recognized the work of the Texas Agricultural Extension Service as "cooperative extension" rather than agricultural extension. The new terminology was significant in view of the expanding role of the Extension Service. The agreement also provided that all full-time Texas extension personnel receive a joint appointment from the Texas Agricultural Extension Service and the United States Department of Agriculture. This provision was clearly intended to "nationalize" the operation of the Extension Service and to diminish the possibility of state-national conflict within the Service. The memorandum also provided for revised federal appropriation formulas, auditing by state and federal auditors, and funding on a line-item basis.[77]

John E. Hutchison succeeded Gibson as director of the Texas Extension Service in 1958. He has enjoyed the longest tenure of any director of Texas Agricultural Extension. Hutchison joined the Extension Service as a county agent in Matagorda County, completed a master's degree in horticulture at Texas A&M, came to College Station as the Service's horticultural specialist, and during a leave of absence obtained his doctorate from the University of Chicago. During the sixties and seventies the role and scope of public education on every level were changing and being broadened to meet rapidly changing social needs. The Texas Cooperative Extension Service responded vigorously to the challenges of the day. It has provided a unique and important underpinning to the educational processes in Texas. The primary function of the Cooperative Extension Service is *education,* stresses Hutchison.

[77]Memorandum of Understanding between the Texas Agricultural and Mechanical College System and the United States Department of Agriculture on Cooperative Extension Work in Agriculture and Home Economics, approved by Ezra Taft Benson, March 17, 1955, pp. 1-3; interview with John E. Hutchison, December 15, 1971, College Station, Texas.

Education involves more than the dissemination of information, he says, but a process of changing the whole person, including his skills, capacities, insights and attitudes. Thus the Extension Service is committed to affecting the very processes of change. Its programs have embraced a "sophisticated system of informal education" which seeks to apply relevant knowledge to a problem. The contemporary county agents have become a field staff of educational generalists. The county agent is the catalyst, organizer, and innovator of new public-service programs, which under authority of Congress, are no longer exclusively farm- and rural-oriented. The county agent initiates the assembling of a large and diverse staff of specialists from the Extension Service and the University complex as problem solvers.[78]

Facilitated by the early integration of the teaching-research-extension functions of the University complex, Director Hutchison initiated the development of Research and Extension Centers throughout Texas. Jointly staffed by research and extension-area specialists, who by their training and capacities are most informed as to the needs of the counties and extension districts assigned under them, the Research and Extension Center provides a problem-solving team immediately responsive to the local county agents, the program-building committees, and other clientele.[79]

The County Program Building Committee is a vital innovation of the modern Texas Extension Service. Program building is a continuous process, involving county leaders, county Extension agents, and other local agencies and resource persons, by which county problems and county objectives are identified and pursued through a program of education and action. The Program Building Committee defines and helps achieve long-range social, economic, and educational goals of the community. County programs include such goals as increasing agricultural income, lowering levels of pollution, care for the aged, and community improvement.[80]

New programs of the Texas Extension Service which illustrate its contemporary character include the V. G. Young Institute for County Government. This institute provides a continuing educational program for elected

[78]Interviews with John E. Hutchison, December 15, 1971, and June 6, 1973, Texas A&M University, College Station, Texas; John E. Hutchison, "The Basic Model of Agricultural Extension as It Has Evolved in the United States," address to the Seminar on Extension Education, Tunis, Tunisia, February 8-19, 1966.

[79]Texas Agricultural Extension Service, *Extension Advances Progress '72: Annual Report of the Texas Agricultural Extension Service* (College Station: Texas A&M University, 1972), 1-67.

[80]Texas Agricultural Extension Service, *Program Building Handbook* (College Station: Texas A&M University, n.d.), 1-32; Victoria County, "Your County Program" (mimeographed), 1-41; Dallas County, "Long Range County Program" (mimeographed, 1969), 1-58.

and nonelected officials of county government in Texas through short courses, conferences, and other training experiences. The Extension Service also conducts special programs for the aging, sponsored by the Governor's Commission on Aging. State and federally funded programs in mental health and mental retardation are administered by Extension personnel. One of the largest programs administered by the Extension Service is a human-nutrition program. Established in January 1969, the program operates in fifty-four Texas counties, in both urban and rural areas, employs over 900 local aides, operates exclusively on federal funds, and seeks, through on-the-spot instruction from Extension-trained local aides, to improve diets by training consumers in food purchasing and preparation. The Texas Extension Service also operates six area-development programs embracing over 155 counties. These programs strive to raise regional income through improved production, marketing, and money-management practices in the established regional industries. Indicative of the scale of Extension activities is the statewide program called "3.76 in '76," calling for $3.76 billion in gross farm sales for Texas in 1976, a figure surpassed before the deadline.[81] As at the time of its founding, the Texas Cooperative Extension Service continues to fulfill a vital role in Texas and Texas A&M University life.

[81]Interviews with John E. Hutchison, December 15, 1971, and June 6, 1973, Texas A&M University, College Station, Texas; Texas Agricultural Extension Service, *Extension Advances Progress '72*, 1-67.

CHAPTER 19

Semicentennial Years

THE first decade of A&M's second half-century began auspiciously with the "Semi-Centennial Celebration and the Inauguration of Thomas Otto Walton, LL.D., as President of the College." Anniversary Day and the inauguration, by declaration of the Board of Directors, was set for Saturday, October 16, 1926, fifty years and twelve days after the earlier inauguration ceremonies on that barren, almost empty, wind-swept knoll, when Governor Richard Coke and President Thomas S. Gathright hailed the birth of Texas' first public institution of higher learning.

Texas A&M had truly come a long way, but the next fifty years would bring even more profound changes. The first ten of that next fifty years brought substantive developments in the school's history. A new president, who was to enjoy the longest tenure of any, Thomas Otto Walton, entered office. The College's endowment was substantially enriched by the discovery of oil on University lands and by the division of those oil revenues between The University of Texas and Texas A&M. A great building program began, during which process the campus was turned to face east instead of west — to face a new highway and the modern era, bidding farewell to the railroad tracks and the pioneering days through which the College had passed. Finally, in the 1930s, by action of the Board of Directors, through the declaration of the courts, and with the approval of most former students, the modern era at Texas A&M was reserved exclusively for men — for almost another half-century.

It made one proud to be an "Aggie" and a Texan during those three days of Semi-Centennial celebrations, October 15-17, 1926. On Friday morning, October 15, delegates and guests registered at the Y.M.C.A, Building and then proceeded to Guion Hall, where Dean Edwin Jackson Kyle introduced Dean Eugene Davenport, of the University of Illinois, who spoke on "Agricultural Education during the Past Half-Century." Mrs. Durant S. Buchanan, of Bryan, provided an interlude with her song "The Morning Wind." Then

Kyle introduced his colleague, Dean Charles E. Friley, who spoke on "The Agricultural and Mechanical College of Texas, Past, Present and Future." At 1:15 P.M. faculty and guests had lunch at Sbisa Hall, and then returned to Guion to hear Dean Mortimer E. Cooley, of the University of Michigan, speak on "The Development of Engineering Education," and Dr. Daniel A. Penick, of The University of Texas and president of the Southwest Athletic Conference, speak on "Intercollegiate Athletics." Thus far everything reflected perfectly the nuances of the time, for in many respects the mid-1920s also inaugurated the golden days of agriculture, engineering, and athletics at Texas A&M.[1]

Beginning at four-thirty in the afternoon the Corps of Cadets passed in review before the distinguished assemblage. The Corps was already full with history and tradition, but like agriculture, engineering, and athletics, it had its future ahead of it, not in the past. That evening Oscar Melville Ball, head of the Biology Department, presented a concert by the Prairie View Singers, followed by the main address of the evening, "Fifty Years of Science," by Dr. Edwin E. Slosson, director of Science Service, in Washington, D.C. Slosson took his audience from Leonardo da Vinci to the Wright brothers; from Auguste Comte (who said we shall never be able to study the chemical composition of the celestial bodies) to Sir William Ramsay (discoverer of helium); from steam to the internal-combustion engine; and from Roger Bacon to Albert Einstein — in a word, into the brave new world of the twentieth century. Cadet Colonel Robert L. Edgar extended greetings on behalf of the student body; Dean Charles Puryear brought greetings from the faculty; and Judge Marion S. Church ('05) spoke in behalf of the alumni.[2]

Saturday brought the inauguration, which included an address by William Bennett Bizzell. Thomas Otto Walton praised an "Education That Serves the Whole People." He noted the contributions of past presidents, board members, faculty, and the various colleges and divisions, and he pledged his life in the earnest and faithful performance of his duties. The afternoon and evening were filled with a football game (University of New Mexico vs. A&M), open houses, receptions, and the anniversary dinner. On

[1]*1876 . . . 1926, The Semi-Centennial Celebration of the Agricultural and Mechanical College of Texas and the Inauguration of Thomas Otto Walton, LL. D., as President,* 18, 35-116 (hereinafter cited: *1876 . . . 1926, The Semi-Centennial Celebration*). Bryan *Daily Eagle,* October 11, 1926; Dallas *Morning News,* October 13, 1926; Houston *Post-Dispatch,* October 13, 1926; see also Texas A&M College Publicity Department, Press Clippings, Book No. 1, September 1926-November 1926, Texas A&M University Archives.

[2]*1876 . . . 1926, The Semi-Centennial Celebration,* 19, 117-139.

Sunday Dr. Glenn L. Sneed, of the Trinity Presbyterian Church in Dallas, preached the "anniversary" sermon in Guion Hall.[3]

Thomas Otto Walton came to the president's office up through the ranks of the Agricultural Extension Service. He came there, in part, with the blessings of James E. Ferguson, who had occasion on July 14, 1925, to attend the meeting of the A&M Board of Directors in the offices of the First National Bank in Austin. Ferguson's wife, Miriam A., was then governor. At this meeting the Directors considered twenty-five candidates to fill the vacancy left by Bizzell. Fifteen of these were eliminated and the final decision was made in Houston on September 3, 1925, at the Rice Hotel with "Farmer Jim" Ferguson not present. Walton was elected by a 6-3 vote.[4]

Walton had scarcely assumed his new office when it was discovered that the chief clerk of the Agricultural Experiment Station over a period of years had embezzled at least $5,301.73 in federal funds, and possibly other unspecified amounts, estimated as high as $100,000. Then, too, classes had scarcely gotten underway before an outbreak of venereal disease struck the campus. The president and Directors acted expeditiously in both crises. The clerk was discharged, indicted, and arrested, and his assets were impounded by the courts. New financial controls were established. The College surgeon was authorized to charge students $10.00 for the "private" treatment of V.D., with $5.00 going to A&M and $5.00 to the doctor.[5] Yet another serious incident creating statewide concern was the death of an A&M student, Charles M. Sessums, during a Texas A&M-Baylor football riot in Waco on October 6, 1926.[6] Walton's administration was early destined to be one of persisting crises, of which depression and war were the more outstanding.

A composite, and somewhat statistical, review of the College as it passed its half-way mark, when compared with a similar analysis of conditions ten years later, indicates the advent of change, growth, and some turbulence during the interval. On August 31, 1925, the College had 69 permanent buildings valued at $3,552,778.86. Ten years later the number had grown to 109 permanent structures valued at $8,034,115.94. Over 6,000 acres of land were added to A&M holdings in the same time period. Enrollment in the

---

[3]*Ibid.,* 20-21, 141-216.

[4]Minutes of the Board of Directors, IV, 41-46.

[5]*Ibid.,* IV, 50-51, 58, 63-64.

[6]Honey Grove *Citizen,* December 17, 1926; Tyler *Journal,* November 19, 1926; Channing *News,* November 26, 1926; Midland *Reporter,* November 19, 1926; Galveston *News,* November 1, 1926; Houston *Press,* November 1, 1926; Dallas *News,* December 9, 1926; Houston *Post-Dispatch,* December 9, 1926. See also Texas A&M College Publicity Department, Press Clippings, Book No. 2, February 1926-February 1927, Texas A&M University Archives.

main college rose from 2,379 in 1925-1926 to 4,915 for the 1936-1937 academic year. On the advent of A&M's fiftieth year the College had granted a total of 1,836 degrees. By the end of the 1936-1937 year, 5,729 degrees had been awarded. In 1926 the recently established graduate school (1924) awarded 23 M.S. degrees, and in 1936 49 M.S. degrees and two professional degrees in engineering. The faculty in 1926 numbered 193 persons, almost half of whom had no advanced degree. By 1936 81 percent of the faculty had advanced degrees, including 20 percent who held the Ph.D.[7]

The pace of change at Texas A&M increased with World War II, and appeared to increase by geometrical progression thereafter. What had been good and true in 1926 seemed to have less and less applicability as the years passed. Despite the innovations and improvements, too soon time and circumstances began to pass by Thomas Otto Walton and the A&M College. As Will Rogers, who was fast becoming the homespun prophet of the era, said, "The faster I go, the behinder I get"; it seemed to apply too well to Texas A&M.

There was a bustle of activity, indeed, throughout Walton's administration, 1925-1943. In July 1926 the Directors purchased 150 acres of land contiguous to the original tract from William Carson Boyett for $30,000. Boyett, in order to avoid the appearance of a conflict of interest, resigned from the A&M Board of Directors during the meeting at which the purchase was contracted.[8] At the same meeting the Directors agreed to close the College Zoo and sell all the animals but the deer and elk.[9] According to Ernest Langford, the Zoo had been started about 1920 by President Bizzell, "who thought an institution like this needed a zoo." The Zoo, located across the railroad tracks from the west gate of the campus, at one time housed several lions and tigers, numerous snakes, an elephant, a huge ostrich, and an assortment of native American animals. By 1925, however, the animals had become a time-consuming, expensive, and noisy factor, and Bizzell himself had become disenchanted with his project before he left A&M. Walton closed it down in 1926.[10] How much money was derived from the sale of the animals is not recorded. That fact alone suggests that it must have been a meager amount. In any event, College Station and A&M once had a zoo.

In October 1926 the Department of Agricultural Economics was

[7]*Progress Report for Twelve Years of the Agricultural and Mechanical College of Texas, 1924-1937*, pp. 5-7, 11, 78.

[8]Minutes of the Board of Directors, July 27, 1926, IV, 80.

[9]*Ibid.*

[10]Interview with Ernest Langford, College Station, Texas, March 9, 1972.

divided into four new departments, the Department of Agriculture and Land Economics, the Department of Accounting and Statistics, the Department of Farm and Ranch Management, and the Department of Marketing and Finance.[11] Among other things, this division marked what must be considered the inception of A&M's College of Business Administration. The College R.O.T.C. program added a unit of engineers in 1927.[12] Three new dormitories were dedicated that year, Francis Marion Law Hall, Puryear Hall, and Thomas Otto Walton Hall.[13] In the same year the Directors let the contract for the E. B. Cushing Library,[14] usually styled the Cushing Memorial Library. Effective in September 1929, the Department of Petroleum Engineering and a curriculum in that area were established at the request of representatives of the oil industry.[15] The Directors conducted their own investigation into the perennial hazing problem in 1928, and in 1929 prohibited the practice of having freshmen clean the rooms of upperclassmen, and banned "fish calls," which involved the rousing of the entire freshman class at odd and uninviting hours for unusual and usually uninviting tasks.[16] But the traditions persisted and the Directors were again busily investigating hazing.[17]

Despite increased crowding in the dormitories, the Directors agreed in May 1930 not to build any more frame shacks on the campus.[18] These "Hollywood shacks," as they were called, had become the post-World War I version of the earlier tent city. The "Hollywood shack" was a frame building 16 × 16 feet in which at first two, and later three or four, boys lived. A few such structures were still extant in the College Station area in the 1970s.

In April 1930 the citizens of Brenham petitioned the A&M College to assume control of Blinn Memorial College, a private community college then encountering rough days because of the onset of the Great Depression — which is now a thriving junior college with a branch in Bryan. The Directors took no action on the "offer" other than to refer the question to its Committee on Branches.[19]

Also in 1930 Texas A&M inaugurated its first group life-insurance plan for employees. The plan was first set up with Southwestern Life Insurance

[11]Minutes of the Board of Directors, October 15, 1926, IV, 81.

[12]*Ibid.,* IV, 86.

[13]*Ibid.,* April 13, 1927, IV, 88; July 4, 1927, IV, 95.

[14]*Ibid.,* November 23, 1927, IV, 98, 99.

[15]*Ibid.,* December 3, 1928, IV, 113.

[16]*Ibid.,* 113; February 5, 1929, IV, 115.

[17]*Ibid.,* November 26, 1930, IV, 159.

[18]*Ibid.,* May 30, 1930, IV, 146-147.

[19]*Ibid.,* April 21, 1930, IV, 146-147.

Company, of Dallas, which continues to exercise an A&M employees' life and hospitalization plan in the 1970s.[20] Throughout the twenties and thirties the A&M Board of Directors seemed preoccupied with business arrangements — oil leases, building contracts, deposits, interest rates, bonds, and fiscal controls.[21] These were the days, of course, when money was especially important and in short supply.

With the end of World War I some degree of laxity crept into the military regimen of the College. Veterans were exempted from the Corps of Cadets, a number of women attended the College, foreign students and graduate students appeared in increasing numbers, and some regular students displayed an aversion to the military system. In order to leave no doubts on the matter, the Directors issued a statement in May 1930, reaffirming the military character of the school:

> Effective with the opening of the session 1930-31 all non-military students [those not in the R.O.T.C. program] who live in dormitories, except graduate students or foreign students and those physically unable to perform military duties, will be required to wear the regulation uniform with some insignia to indicate they are not members of the R.O.T.C. They will be organized into companies and placed in charge of a [civilian] supervisor who will maintain orderly conduct and who will have general charge of the group.[22]

The military "position" of the College had changed little since 1876. Times, however, had changed. The old question of admitting women to Texas A&M arose with fresh urgency in the 1920s and 1930s.

The College opened its doors as an agricultural and mechanical college in 1876, and, perhaps by default as much as by design, as an all-male military institution. Few women attended college in those days, fewer still pursued instruction in the then "unfeminine" fields of farming and engineering. As for the military orientation of the school, it must be said that few schools in the South were without some form of military program. Thus, in the beginning there was no real conspiracy or plot to exclude women from the institution. Indeed, in 1876, before classes began at A&M, a Texas Senate committee which inspected the new College facilities, recommended that the school be open to both sexes.[23] While the first catalogue of the College announced the admission of only male students fourteen years of age or older,[24] presumably the issue of coeducation never arose during the first two decades because no

[20]*Ibid.*, November 26, 1930, IV, 157; February 23, 1931, IV, 168.

[21]*Ibid.*, February 23, 1931, IV, 168.

[22]*Ibid.*, May 30, 1930, IV, 153.

[23]Ernest Langford, *Getting the College Under Way*, 46.

[24]Anderson James Peeler (ed.), *Laws Relating to A&M*, 21-22.

women applied for admission and it was generally accepted that Texas A&M was an all-male school.

The advent of Lawrence Sullivan Ross on the campus reaffirmed in the public mind the all-male, military, chivalric connotation of the College, while in fact, Ross, perhaps in part yielding to local pressures, had no objection to coeducation. The break in the tradition began in 1893, when Ethel Hutson, daughter of Professor Charles W. Hutson, attended classes for two years as a "lecture student," but received no credits for her work.[25] Sophie and Mary Hutson, Ethel Hutson's twin sisters, enrolled in the civil-engineering course and completed all required studies in 1903. They received certificates of completion at commencement, but no degrees.[26] In the 1890s public interest in coeducation at A&M was aroused when the state began serious consideration of founding a girls' industrial school.

President Ross was reportedly "besieged" by promoters of the girls' industrial school, who desired to incorporate the school under the auspices of the A&M Board of Directors. Ross responded favorably, even to the point of recommending that the school be located on the campus with the A&M College. "Governor Ross," said the Bryan (weekly) *Eagle,* "believes in co-education, and readily conceded the point that the cadets would be improved by the elevating influence of the good girls, whose training would go on under their eye. Both sexes," he said, "are benefited."[27]

Interest in establishing a female institution in conjunction with Texas A&M heightened over the next few years, especially among the businessmen and citizens of Bryan, who recognized the economic opportunities and many of whom desired to secure a college education for their daughters. In 1899 a special committee of Bryan citizens, including William R. Cavitt, William Smith Howell, Henry Bates Stoddard, Louis L. McInnis, John Whitfield Doremus, J. Robert Astin, and Amos W. Buchanan, was designated to head the local effort to locate the proposed girls' industrial school at A&M. The committee prepared a brochure arguing *Reasons for Locating the Girls' Industrial School at the A&M College.* The brochure stressed the economic advantages derived from the use of common facilities and faculty, and the "refining influence" of the young ladies on the boys at A&M.[28] Texas A&M and The University of Texas supporters each petitioned the state Legislature in

[25]College Station, *The Olio,* 3, 49.

[26]Ernest Langford, "It's History — Women at A&M," unpublished manuscript in Texas A&M University Archives, 3.

[27]April 2, 1897.

[28]W. R. Cavitt *et al.,* 1-4, in Coeducation Papers, Texas A&M University Archives.

1899 for a bill establishing a girls' industrial school as an adjunct of their existing institution. By an 11-10 vote the Senate passed a bill favoring the College Station location for the school, but the bill failed to win approval in the House.[29] Finally, in 1901, the Legislature approved a bill creating the "Texas Industrial Institute and College for the Education of White Girls of the State of Texas in the Arts and Sciences" under a separate Board of Regents, to be located by a special commission appointed by the governor.[30] That the school would have its own governing authority prejudiced the commission against locating the woman's college in College Station or Austin.

Perhaps partly in hopes of influencing a decision from the commission locating the woman's college, Texas A&M established its first summer session for the period June 18-July 28, 1901, and opened its doors for that session to women. A "separate dormitory, in charge of a matron" was "set apart for the ladies in attendance." Only a few daughters of the regular faculty and staff attended that session, and no further summer sessions were held until 1909.[31] Presumably, the opening of the girls school, now Texas Woman's University, in Denton in 1901, alleviated the "necessity" for summer sessions which admitted women to Texas A&M.

Between 1900 and 1910 a number of women followed the precedent established by Ethel Hutson and attended classes in the regular session at A&M. Emmie Fountain, daughter of Professor Charles P. Fountain and later wife of Ross P. Marsteller, entered as a special student in 1900; Esther and Frances Davis, step-daughters of James C. Nagle, studied at various periods between 1902 and 1910; and in 1910 Marjorie Goforth, Hertha Thompson, Bernadine McKnight, Virginia Spence, and Alma and Linda Giesecke attended classes.[32] In 1909 the Texas Legislature authorized regular summer sessions for Texas A&M, with the proviso that both sexes be allowed to attend.[33] No record, however, indicates the awarding of any degrees to women as a result of summer work.

In 1915 the Texas A&M Board of Directors made its first official policy statement excluding women from the regular sessions at A&M. The occasion arose when Clara B. Dismukes Vander Las offered to endow a chair of

---

[29]Bryan *Eagle*, (w) May 11, 18, 1899.

[30]*General Laws of Texas, 1897-1902*, pp. 306-309.

[31]Byrnes, *Foster*, 174.

[32]Linda Giesecke Geren, Fort Worth, Texas, to Editor, *The Texas Aggie*, January 6, 1969, Coeducation Papers, Texas A&M University Archives.

[33]*General Laws of Texas, 1909*, pp. 221-223.

domestic science. The Directors "respectfully and appreciatively" declined on the grounds that the endowment would make the college coeducational.[34] Despite this ruling, time and circumstances continued to promote flexibility in the all-male rule.

During World War I teacher shortages resulted in the employment of Texas A&M's first woman instructor, Mrs. Wanda M. Farr, in botany.[35] After the War married veterans brought their wives to the campus, and provision was made for many of them to attend classes as "special unofficial students." Seven women attended in 1922, fourteen in 1923, and a total of thirty were enrolled by 1925, when President William Bennett Bizzell departed.[36] Dr. Bizzell saw "no reason for not admitting a reasonable number of girls to this institution, especially the daughters of the employees of the College . . . and mature young people who [sought] the particular advantages offered by this College."[37] Under Bizzell's leadership Texas A&M appeared to be moving very gradually to a coeducational status.

In August 1925 Mary Evelyn Crawford, the sister of Charles W. Crawford, professor of mechanical engineering, became the first woman to receive a degree (Bachelor of Arts) from the College. Commenting on her experiences at Texas A&M, Mrs. Lon B. Locke (née Mary Evelyn Crawford) wrote years later:

> I attended A&M two summers and one long term. . . . As far as I remember there was no objection to my registration. . . . I registered at A&M because I wanted to finish college and it was much cheaper to stay at home. . . . I completed all of my required work in a satisfactory manner so I suppose they just felt that I had earned my degree.[38]

But the postwar trend to admit women, the "open-door" attitude of President Bizzell, and the Mary Evelyn Crawford precedent failed to convert the school into a coeducational facility.

Sensing the necessity for dealing with coeducation, the A&M Board of

[34]Minutes of the Board of Directors, December 30, 1915, III, 187.

[35]Bryan *Daily Eagle and Pilot*, February 2, 1918; *Alumni Quarterly*, III (February 1918), p. 8.

[36]College Station *Longhorn*, 1922, p. 140. Tommy DeFrank, "Early Coeducation Tries Failed To Materialize," College Station *Battalion*, February 10, 1966; Polly Westbrook, "A History of Coeducation at Texas A&M University," unpublished manuscript in Coeducation Papers, Texas A&M University Archives.

[37]Quoted in Ernest Langford, "It's History — Women at A&M," 4; and Polly Westbrook, "A History of Coeducation at Texas A&M University," unpublished manuscript in Coeducation Papers, Texas A&M University Archives, 8.

[38]Mrs. L. B. Locke, College Station, Texas, to Ernest Langford, College Station, Texas, February 12, 1969, Coeducation Papers, Texas A&M University Archives.

Directors spent agonizing hours, after Bizzell's departure, over the problem. On July 14, 1925, the Directors ruled that "only the relatives of college employees and women who seek special education unavailable elsewhere" should be admitted to A&M.[39] Compared to the policy adopted in 1915 involving the Vander Las endowment, this was a definite move toward coeducation. Critical alumni quickly pointed this out to the Directors, who, on September 3, completely reversed their decision of a few weeks previous, by ruling that "no girls should ever be admitted to the College."[40] Sometime later the Directors apparently realized that this flat statement contradicted the law requiring the admission of women in summer school and they made that exception.[41]

From 1925 until 1933 no women attended A&M classes as special or regular students. By 1933, however, as the Depression deepened and faculty salaries were lowered by 25 percent, the Directors eased the "men only" ruling to the extent of allowing daughters of faculty and staff to enroll in the regular session.[42] This sprang the lid of Pandora's box. If daughters of faculty could attend the school, why not the daughters of other local townsmen or Texans anywhere, who might be inconvenienced if they were not admitted to A&M? A number of Bryan girls who had no relatives on the A&M faculty or staff applied for admission for the fall of 1933. Their admission was categorically denied.

Local parents, irritated by the exclusion of their daughters, in September 1933 filed a writ of mandamus in Bryan's Eighty-fifth District Court against President Thomas O. Walton and the Board of Directors. In the midst of hard times A&M offered the only educational facility available to the daughters of local Bryan families. Leadership in the suit was taken by J. E. Stanford, secretary of the Bryan Chamber of Commerce, whose daughter, Alia, had attended one year at the College of Industrial Arts for Women in Denton, and one summer session at A&M. Other girls involved included Jane Singletary, who had one year at The University of Texas; Francis Locke, who had attended three summers at A&M and one and a half years at Texas; and Lucille Vick. Other complainants included Mrs. William Edgar Neely, Mrs. Orval A. Fox, and Mrs. Louise B. Jones.[43]

[39]Minutes of the Board of Directors, July 14, 1925, IV, 44.

[40]*Ibid.*, September 3, 1925, IV, 6.

[41]*Ibid.*, February 23, 1926, IV, 66.

[42]T. O. Walton *et al.*, "Hearings," 3-56, Coeducation Papers, Texas A&M University Archives.

[43]Bryan *Daily Eagle*, January 5, 1934; College Station *Battalion*, February 15, 1966; J. E. Stanford *et al. vs.* T. O. Walton *et al.*, "Hearings," in Coeducation Papers, Texas A&M Univer-

In their meeting of September 23, 1933, the Directors discussed the mandamus suit, which could open A&M to women on a regular basis. They decided to defend the "men only" policy with "the best legal talent that can be secured and if necessary to take the case through the Supreme Court of Texas."[44] The Directors retained as their attorneys Judge Nelson Phillips and his son, who cooperated with an assistant attorney general of the state of Texas, Homer DeWolfe. The plaintiffs retained Charles Christopher Todd, a former student and prominent jurist and alumnus.

The hearings, beginning on October 3, in Bryan, were reported in 105 pages of testimony. Argument presented by the plaintiffs included appeal to the law creating The University of Texas, and the reasoning that since A&M was a branch of The University the law providing for coeducation in The University was equally applicable to the branch. It maintained also that the legislative intent requiring the admission of women in summer sessions under the 1909 legislative act, and the fact that the branches of A&M were themselves coeducational, argued, in the view of the plaintiffs, that Texas A&M was being discriminatory, unlawful, arbitrary, and capricious in excluding women during the regular sessions. Todd also introduced a letter from the state attorney general of 1931 addressed to Director Byrd E. White which stated that the "Board of Directors . . . is wholly without authority in passing any kind of an order barring from the College female students."[45]

Members of the Board of Directors unanimously went on record in support of the "men only" ruling. Francis Marion Law said that the ruling was justified by the fact that Texas A&M had a strong military orientation. He believed that open admission of women would lead to a deterioration in the quality of the school. Henry C. Schumacher ('92) said simply that he did not believe in coeducation. George R. White thought that the exclusion of women was in the best interests of the school. Guy Anderson, who was not a former A&M student, admitted that he did not believe in coeducation and advised that women would be better off to go elsewhere. Joseph Kopecky also favored the exclusion of women. President Thomas O. Walton cited the separation of the sexes as a long-standing principle of education. Perhaps cap-

sity Archives; Mrs. W. E. Neely, *et al. vs.* Board of Directors of A&M College of Texas *et al.,* "Brief for the Respondents," and "Reply Brief for Respondents," in Coeducation Papers, Texas A&M University Archives.

[44] Minutes of the Board of Directors, September 23, 1933, IV, 248.

[45] Stanford *vs.* Walton, "Hearings," 3-56, in Coeducation Papers, Texas A&M University Archives.

ping the arguments of the defense were petitions and letters signed by the A&M Mothers' Clubs of Fort Worth, Dallas, Waco, San Angelo, and San Antonio — all opposed to admitting girls to Texas A&M.[46] The simple fact seemed to be that Aggies, most parents, and the administrators did not want coeducation at Texas A&M.

The trial itself, beginning October 31, lasted two days, with Board members and plaintiffs testifying before Judge William C. Davis.[47] Judge Davis concluded that

. . . if the legislature had seen fit to declare in specific language the status of all the other institutions of learning . . . with respect to the admission of both sexes, and with reference to A&M it remains silent, the only logical conclusion that can be reached is that the Legislature intended to leave to the discretion of the Board of Directors of the College the admission of girls and women.[48]

Judge Davis refused the writ of mandamus. For two more decades the old issue of coeducation lay dormant, only to erupt again with new vigor in 1953, and finally in 1963 a different resolution began to emerge. One impact of the "men only" policy at Texas A&M during the next several decades may have been, as a faculty-staff-student study reported in 1962, that the exclusion of women impeded the development of academic excellence at Texas A&M,[49] and, as argued by some, slowed the rate of enrollment growth at the institution.[50]

During the same years in which the controversy over coeducation at Texas A&M raged another equally important fight flared over the distribution of funds from the Permanent University Fund. These funds were those derived from the sale and lease of University lands. The total land endowment of The University of Texas equaled 2,100,000 acres in 1930.

The original 50 leagues (221,420 acres) endowment by the Republic of Texas, after settlement of conflicting claims, produced 216,805 acres surveyed for The University endowment. This land was sold, without reservation of mineral rights. The grant of one section of land to The University out of

[46]*Ibid.*, 57-105.

[47]Minutes of the Board of Directors, October 31, November 1, 1933, IV, 251; Mrs. W. E. Neely *et al. vs.* Board of Directors of the A&M College of Texas *et al.*, "Brief for the Respondents," 1-66, and "Reply Brief for the Respondents," in Coeducation Papers, Texas A&M University Archives.

[48]Bryan *Daily Eagle,* January 5, 1934.

[49]Texas A&M University, *Faculty-Staff-Student Study on Aspirations,* 86-90.

[50]"The Agricultural and Mechanical College of Texas: A Land-Grant College in Historical Perspective," unpublished memorandum prepared by Sub-Committee on Historical Perspective, Texas A&M Self-Study 1962, Texas A&M University Archives.

every ten granted to railroads, made by the Texas Legislature in 1858, but never effected, was replaced by an outright grant of one million acres by the Constitution of 1876. The state Legislature in 1883 granted an additional one million acres each to the public schools and to The University. The total 2,289,682 acres finally granted to The University of Texas as a surveyed land endowment, produced, after adjustments for inaccurate surveys, sales, and the settlement of conflicting claims, a modern land endowment of 2,100,000 acres.[51]

Texas A&M and The University of Texas in Austin had battled furiously down the years for the revenues derived from these lands, especially in the 1880s, when Senator George Pfeuffer challenged exclusive control of the land endowment by the Regents. After the turn of the century a settlement was reached whereby the revenues from the lands would be used by The University, Texas A&M to obtain compensation by legislative appropriations. For years, however, Texas A&M received a nominal sum (usually $500) from the Permanent Fund, as evidence that the "branch" retained its rights in the endowment. During the first two decades of the twentieth century the Board of Regents and the A&M Directors pressed repeatedly for a permanent division of the Endowment Fund and for a separation of the two institutions by constitutional amendment. The efforts were unsuccessful. A constitutional settlement appeared to be out of reach. The problem of dividing endowment money, however, failed to be critical until the mid-1920s, largely because the money derived from University lands was nominal and came mostly from surface leases and land sales.

Santa Rita, however, changed all of that. Santa Rita was a discovery oil field located on University lands which came into production in 1923.[52] By 1926 oil royalties flowing into the University Permanent Fund reached $250,000 per month, and the total royalties accumulated up to that time equalled more than $5 million.[53] Texas A&M's "share" in the University lands now became of vital importance to the "branch."

On September 21, 1925, A&M Directors resolved to take two courses of action in regard to the school's claims to the Endowment Fund: (1) Texas A&M would first seek an out-of-court settlement of the matter with the Board of Regents; (2) failing any agreement, Texas A&M would retain an

[51]Thomas Lloyd Miller, *The Public Lands of Texas, 1519-1970*, pp. 120-125.

[52]Martin W. Schwettmann, *The University of Texas Oil Discovery — Santa Rita*, 1-40; Walter E. Long, *For All Time To Come*, 83-84.

[53]Dallas *Morning News*, November 25, 1926.

attorney and take the school's case for a share in the revenues to court.[54] A&M Director Byrd E. White made the preliminary contacts on the question with the Regents and in November reported back to the A&M Board that he had been promised by the Regents that "something would be done about the matter" in their scheduled meeting of December 8.[55] But in February White reported that the Regents had taken no action and that he had "exhausted all means at his command to get an agreement with the Regents."[56] The Directors then decided to retain Judge Nelson Phillips, formerly chief justice of the Texas Supreme Court, at a fee of $1,000, to investigate the situation, to give an opinion on A&M's legal position, and to advise on the best course of action.[57]

Phillips advised negotiation. Negotiations were renewed on Thanksgiving Day, November 25, 1926, when the A&M Directors met with the Regents at the Driskill Hotel prior to the annual gridiron contest between Texas A&M and The University of Texas.[58] Francis Marion Law presided at the joint session, where "the utmost friendliness and a spirit of cooperation existed throughout the entire two-hour meeting."[59] A&M Directors present included Law, Byrd E. White, Walter G. Lacy, Pinckney L. Downs, Jr., Mrs. J. C. George, Henry C. Schumacher, Walter L. Boothe, and William A. Wurzbach. Secretary Stephen G. Bailey recorded the minutes. President Thomas O. Walton attended, as did Andrew P. Rollins, president of the Former Students Association, and Steve A. Lilliard ('10). Regents from The University of Texas included H. J. Lutcher Stark, Chairman of the Board of Regents, Marcellus E. Foster, Edward Howard, Sam Neathery, Mrs. J. H. O'Hair, Mart H. Royston, George W. Tyler, and R. G. Storey. Others included C. D. Simmons, secretary to the Regents, Texas University President Walter Marshall William Splawn, and Judge Thomas Watt Gregory, president of the Ex-Students Association.[60] The boards agreed to appoint each a committee of three to investigate the questions at issue, including separation of the institutions and claims by each to the Permanent Fund. A report was to be returned before the next regular session of the Legislature.[61] These

[54] Minutes of the Board of Directors, September 21, 1925, IV, 52.

[55] *Ibid.*, November 25, 1925, IV, 62.

[56] *Ibid.*, February 23, 1926, IV, 66.

[57] *Ibid.*

[58] *Ibid.*, November 25, 1926, IV, 84.

[59] Dallas *Morning News*, November 27, 1926.

[60] *Ibid.*

[61] Minutes of the Board of Directors, November 25, 1926, IV, 84.

initial negotiations, however, led nowhere.[62] Newspapers around the state reacted only slightly to reports that the royalties from University lands might be shared with A&M. Several papers reported cynically that "A&M Wants in on the Swag," but most approved of a division of funds.[63] The big news continued to be the death of Cadet Sessums at the A&M-Baylor football game. After all, Texas had been through the fund division-institutional separation business many times before without results.

Several more years passed without any agreement being reached by the two institutional boards. By 1929 the A&M Directors determined to take their case to court. In April of that year Texas A&M formally notified the Board of Regents that Texas A&M "claims an interest in the University Land Funds."[64] In August the Directors asked the state attorney general for a legal opinion regarding A&M's claims to a share of the Permanent Fund.[65] The Regents now decided to reopen negotiations.

On January 21, 1930, the A&M Directors and the Regents met together in Austin. Judge Robert Lynn Batts, who presided, indicated that the Regents desired to "work in complete harmony" with the Directors. Francis M. Law replied with similar remarks for the Directors. Director Byrd E. White posed the question of the hour as being whether the Regents admit "that the A&M College is a branch of the University and is entitled to a portion of the Permanent University Endowment Fund and the income from this Endowment." H. J. Lutcher Stark, of the Regents, asked White whether, if A&M was considered a branch, the constitutional prohibition against using legislatively appropriated money for buildings could not apply also to A&M. White replied that the Directors thought not. Lutcher Stark asked whether A&M wanted to be considered a branch for "instructional" purposes only, or a real branch. Judge White evaded the question, saying that the Constitution provided the answer. Dr. Edward Randall (Regent) asked whether, if A&M were considered a branch, such status would not dissolve the A&M Board? White replied that all previous attempts to consolidate the two schools under one board had failed.[66]

Judge Batts then summarized the position of the Regents:

[62]Minutes of the Board of Directors (meeting of Joint Committee), December 15, 1926, IV, 85, and April 22, 1929, IV, 118.

[63]Marshall *News*, December 12, 1926; Vernon *Record*, November 15, 1926; Dallas *Morning News*, November 25, 27, 1926.

[64]Minutes of the Board of Directors, April 22, 1929, IV, 118.

[65]*Ibid.*, August 23, 1929, IV, 127.

[66]*Ibid.*, January 21, 1936, IV, 134-135.

We will have no legal scrap or litigation. We do not intend to let that happen. . . . There has been no question with the University in recognizing the A&M College being a branch of the University, but it has been a question of whether A&M was willing to be recognized as a branch. . . . We agree that you are a branch of the University of Texas from a legal standpoint. We recognize the Legislature has a right to make appropriations from the University funds for A&M for buildings. It is also believed that the Legislature will in all probability appropriate this money for maintenance and other purposes at the University and A&M College. We have no disposition to postpone the matter, but want to dispose of it now.[67]

The two boards then agreed to appoint a joint committee to discuss the division of revenues. "Harmony prevailed during the entire meeting."[68]

On March 8 the A&M Directors received and approved the recommendations of the joint committee on revenue, which provided that A&M would receive $100,000 for four years, and thereafter would receive one-third of the royalties from University lands. On the same day the Regents of The University of Texas rejected the agreement.[69] The two boards then convened in joint session in the Educational Building of The University and agreed to continue negotiations. The special committee was enlarged and a meeting set for the home of Judge R. L. Batts, in Austin, at 9:00 A.M. on March 30.[70]

This time a revised proposal offered Texas A&M $150,000 for the fiscal year ending August 31, 1931, and for the next three fiscal years. Beginning September 1, 1934, Texas A&M would receive one-third of the income from the Permanent University Fund, excluding income from surface leases, which was to be reserved to The University. In addition, the two governing boards would jointly request the Legislature to change the law to allow funds to be used for building construction and equipment, and to borrow on those funds for periods not exceeding fifteen years.[71] The A&M Directors and the Regents approved this proposal on April 21, Judge Batts noting in behalf of the Regents that "there should be no discord between the two institutions. We must necessarily work together keeping in mind the young men and young women of Texas." But of the seven Regents present, Batts indicated that four voted for the agreement and three against.[72] The reluctance of the Regents can be understood. First, the money in the Permanent Fund had been essentially under the exclusive control of the Regents from the beginning.

[67] *Ibid.*, 135.
[68] *Ibid.*, 136.
[69] *Ibid.*, 138.
[70] *Ibid.*, 140-141.
[71] *Ibid.*, 143.
[72] *Ibid.*, 142-145.

Secondly, some of the Regents believed that A&M intended to use royalties and legislative appropriations for building construction, the use of royalty money for that purpose at the time being denied The University. Thirdly, Texas A&M appeared to be offering little, but taking a lot.

By 1930 standards more money was actually flowing into The University of Texas coffers from oil revenues than The University could effectively spend, especially given the prohibition on spending that money for capital improvements. The University needed A&M's help in getting that prohibition removed, and while it is a startling statement by contemporary standards, it simply did not need all of the money accumulating in the Permanent Fund. Both schools then, and higher education in Texas, stood to benefit by an agreement for the division of funds and the removal of restrictions over the use of those funds. Unquestionably, the outstanding factor that has made Texas higher education effective and competent, if not outstanding, has been the, availability of vast and essentially unrestricted sums of money for the exclusive use of Texas colleges and universities. Few states of the Union have so well endowed their higher institutions of learning. A glance at table 5 underscores the enormity of this endowment, and the impact of the oil discoveries in the decade of the twenties.[73]

In perfecting the bill to be submitted to the Legislature in January, the committee made a few adjustments. The bill, as presented, provided that A&M should get $200,000 for three years, rather than $150,000 for four years; that surface leases should be stated "grazing leases"; and that income from the grazing leases, *and* from state bonds in the Permanent Fund derived from the sale of the original fifty leagues dedicated by the Republic of Texas, should be reserved entirely to The University.[74] The Texas Legislature approved the bill on April 8, 1931. This agreement has operated to the present. It has been, said former A&M President and Chancellor Marion Thomas Harrington, "the lifesaver of Texas A&M and The University."[75]

The impact of this new source of money upon Texas A&M was immediate, and in view of the crucial financial conditions ensuing from the darkening Depression, the results were even spectacular. One is led to wonder if Texas A&M and The University could have survived the Depression without the oil revenues. As it was, both did survive — exceedingly well. The oil revenues, supplemented by federal funds derived from such New Deal programs

[73]Thomas Lloyd Miller, *The Public Lands of Texas, 1519-1970*, p. 280.

[74]Minutes of the Board of Directors, January 5, 1931, IV, 160-163.

[75]Interview with Marion Thomas Harrington, College Station, Texas, September 13, 1971.

Table 5.
Total Income Received from University Lands, 1895-1970

Year	Annual Total	Year	Annual Total
(1859-1928)	($16,338,017.74)		
1929	$ 1,809,848.63	1950	$ 9,217,510.48
1930	4,350,962.40	1951	17,909,955.33
1931	1,958,792.90	1952	23,160,000.29
1932	1,383,332.81	1953	34,502,967.17
1933	1,146,754.06	1954	25,992,880.54
1934	1,502,773.11	1955	24,326,801.83
1935	946,190.20	1956	37,851,428.27
1936	1,158,784.97	1957	22,395,771.38
1937	3,096,823.25	1958	18,848,656.42
1938	2,333,443.47	1959	25,334,163.33
1939	1,503,686.65	1960	19,324,013.06
1940	1,135,373.31	1961	17,614,356.61
1941	815,193.28	1962	19,652,195.18
1942	1,325,045.16	1963	18,055,414.00
1943	3,242,083.63	1964	20,441,339.18
1944	22,337,032.25	1965	29,595,184.11
1945	4,288,338.32	1966	28,262,978.33
1946	8,884,763.33	1967	17,770,159.59
1947	6,812,473.76	1968	23,944,331.43
1948	17,308,665.28	1969	41,347,970.79
1949	12,879,703.57	1970	19,827,918.29
	Total	1859-1970	$610,127,077.69

Source: From *The Public Lands of Texas, 1519-1970,* by Thomas Lloyd Miller, p. 280. Copyright 1972 by the University of Oklahoma Press.

as the Federal Emergency Relief Administration (FERA) and the Public Works Administration (PWA), converted what might have been a dismal period of stagnation into a time of progress and achievement for The University and for Texas A&M.

From 1876 through 1929 Texas appropriated a total of $3,389,664.91 for buildings and equipment at Texas A&M.[76] Between 1929 and 1937, the years of most severe depression, Texas A&M spent $3,165,850 on construction, an amount almost equal to the total spent on capital improvements during the school's first fifty years (see table 6).[77] During these same years, 1929-1937, enrollment increased from about three to five thousand students. Had there

[76]Texas A&M, *Annual Report, 1928-1929,* pp. 15-16.
[77]Texas A&M, *Progress Report for Twelve Years, 1925-1937,* pp. 48-49.

Table 6.
The Building Program, 1929-1937

Facility	Location	Cost
1929-1930		
Cushing Library	College Station	$225,000
Hart Hall Dormitory	College Station	215,000
Auditorium	Stephenville	90,000
		$530,000
1930-1931		
Walton Hall Dormitory	College Station	$250,000
Shop Building	Prairie View	80,000
		$330,000
1931-1932		
Conversion from steam to hot water	College Station	$ 9,000
Petroleum Building	College Station	167,500
Tunnel	College Station	26,300
Classroom Building	Prairie View	60,000
		$262,800
1932-1933		
Administration Building	College Station	$ 350,000
Agricultural Engineering Building	College Station	176,600
Animal Industries Building	College Station	209,300
Veterinary Anatomy	College Station	19,000
Veterinary Hospital	College Station	132,900
Veterinary Stables	College Station	35,600
Swimming pool	College Station	92,000
Streets and roads	College Station	71,400
Girls Dormitory	Prairie View	52,000
		$1,138,800
1933-1934		
Horse barn	College Station	$ 24,000
Sewage disposal plant	College Station	28,000
Sewage lake	College Station	5,500
Outfall sewer	College Station	2,600
New sewer system	College Station	28,200
Lateral heat lines	College Station	24,150

Facility	Location	Cost
	1933-1934 (cont.)	($112,450)
Pipe lines in tunnel	College Station	34,100
Water system	College Station	29,000
Power-plant additions	College Station	42,800
Fuel-combustion		
system	College Station	33,900
Incinerator	College Station	7,500
Gymnasium	Arlington	31,000
Science Building		
(1st unit)	Stephenville	<u>75,000</u>
		$365,750
	1934-1935	
Addition to Creamery	College Station	$ 40,000
Power magazine	College Station	500
Science Building		
(2nd unit)	Stephenville	<u>70,000</u>
		$110,500
	1935-1936	
Girls Dormitory	Stephenville	$ 33,000
Hospital additions	College Station	92,000
Temporary Office		
Building	College Station	<u>20,700</u>
		$145,700
	1936-1937	
Addition to Board		
Quarters	College Station	$ 12,000
Mess Hall addition	College Station	20,000
Project houses	College Station	108,000
Remodeling sewage		
plant	College Station	800
Air conditioning of		
President's Home	College Station	4,500
Project houses	Prairie View	17,000
Farm buildings	Arlington	60,000
Gymnasium	Prairie View	<u>60,000</u>
		<u>**$282,300**</u>
	Grand Total	$3,165,850

Source: Texas A&M, *Progress Report for Twelve Years, 1925-1937*, pp. 48-49.

been no endowment funds available this growth could not have occurred.[78] One coincidental observation that may be derived from the table is that the great bulk of money was spent on the main campus at College Station, a condition which the branches continued to lament.

In addition to the physical improvement of A&M facilities, the building program of this era had yet another intangible, symbolic impact upon the College. Texas A&M turned away from the railroad and the west, leaving its pioneering days behind, and faced the new highway, the east, and a new era. On July 4, 1931, Texas A&M deeded the State Highway Department 7.9 acres of land along the eastern boundary line of the campus, to be used for the right-of-way of the new State Highway 6. The following year the A&M Directors let the contract for the new administration building, the Systems Building, for $372,600,[79] which magnificent edifice served as the gateway to the new university for the next four decades, until it too became symbolically overshadowed by the skyscraper, space-age structures of the 1970s.

[78]*Ibid.*, 78.
[79]Minutes of the Board of Directors, August 20, 1932, IV, 218.

CHAPTER 20

Depression Years

COLLEGE Station, Texas, had even less in common with Wall Street in 1929 than it does today; even so, what happened there, and throughout the country, on October 24, 1929, profoundly affected Texas A&M and the community of which it was a part. On that day the stock market crashed, sending waves of financial panic into every nook and cranny of the nation, College Station included. On Thursday, October 29, further market collapses shook the entire country, the fifty leading stocks losing an average of $40 per share; within a period of six weeks stock values declined by 50 percent and continued downward. Banks, overextended, were forced to close; factories and businesses, unable to meet payrolls, went out of business; consumers, without paychecks or credit, quit buying; farmers, caught since 1921 in a depression of their own, found no markets for the abundance of farm commodities produced and forced a new wave of foreclosures and hard times. Unemployment spiraled from 1.5 million in 1929 to over 12 million in 1932. This was the Great Depression.[1]

Compared to the impact of the Depression on other people and other places, the impact at Texas A&M was mild. Indeed, compared to other institutions A&M did marvelously well in the 1930s — largely because of the flow of royalty money which began in 1932. Nonetheless, compared to normal times, the Depression years brought suffering to A&M, too. It took almost two years for the reverberations of the stock-market crash to strike A&M. In 1930 and 1931 an increasing number of bank failures began to create concern among Texas A&M managers over the security of institutional funds. On October 29, 1931, the A&M Board of Directors held an emergency meeting to consider how A&M funds and investments might best be protected. The situation was viewed as critical.[2] Enrollment for the opening session of the 1931-1932 year, 2,584, was down by almost 500 students from the

---

[1]John Kenneth Galbraith, *The Great Crash, 1929,* pp. 1-212; David A. Shannon, *The Great Depression,* 1-171.

[2]Minutes of the Board of Directors, October 19, 1931, IV, 184.

1928-1929 level of over 3,000.[3] Parents simply lacked the cash to send their boys to college. In November 1931 the Directors announced a reduction in room rent for students from $30 to $15 per semester.[4] Throughout the Depression student fees at A&M were quite nominal. The total costs of a semester in college for the student at College Station were less than $145. Student fees for each semester included these items: matriculation fee (tuition), $25.00; room rent, $15.00; medical service fee, $5.00; maintenance (board), $96.00; and room key deposit (first semester only), $1.00.[5] Despite the relatively low costs, the Depression denied many Texans the opportunity to secure a college education, and worked a real hardship on the families and students who did attend. The ways in which students improvised to defray expenses provide classic hard-times stories. One of the most interesting phenomena was the project houses or student cooperatives that began at Texas A&M at this time.

Until 1932 all A&M students were required to live in dormitories, to wear the prescribed uniform, and to eat in the mess hall. The Board, however, began to allow the president to "make exceptions in exceptional cases."[6] Some of these exceptional cases found that they could rent a house, pool their money, bring food from home or the farm, cook their own meals, and live more cheaply than they could on campus. By 1935 cooperative student housing was on the way to becoming official school policy, thanks largely to the efforts of Daniel ("Dan") Russell, professor of rural sociology.

Dan Russell first experimented with a project house in 1932, when the Department of Rural Sociology was allowed to sponsor a house with twelve boys. The boys did their own cooking and cleaning, purchased food supplies in bulk and supplemented their larder with food from home.[7] The project houses began accidentally, Russell said in an address to the Southwest Social Science Association in 1937:

> An old [vacant] two-story home near the College was rented and twelve boys from one community came down to set up their own home. An aunt of one of the boys came along to be house mother and do the cooking. One of the boys brought along two milk cows and all of the boys were required to bring four laying hens each.[8]

---

[3]Texas A&M, *Progress Report for Twelve Years, 1925-1937,* p. 78.

[4]Minutes of the Board of Directors, November 25, 1931, IV, 185-186.

[5]Y.M.C.A., *The Students' Handbook of Texas A&M College,* 1933-1934, p. 19.

[6]Minutes of the Board of Directors, January 19, 1933, IV, 229-330.

[7]"A&M Co-op Student Housing," typed memorandum dated October 10, 1953, in Dan Russell Scrapbook, Texas A&M University Archives.

[8]Dallas *Morning News,* March 30, 1937.

When they found that they could not get enough food from home to keep them going, the group, with Russell's help, got a wholesale firm to sell them groceries. It worked, said Russell; "the boys all passed their courses and made better grades than the average [student] living in the dormitories."[9] In 1933 and 1934 more project houses were begun under the "exceptions in exceptional cases" rule adopted by the Board, allowing more students to live off campus.

In 1935 Russell submitted a comprehensive proposal to the Board of Directors that would establish a large-scale cooperative housing program under official College auspices. The A&M Board of Directors approved the plan on February 4, 1936.[10] That summer College officials arranged with the Association of Former Students to have the Association build project houses on the A&M campus, the houses to be managed by the College. The final arrangements were completed in April 1937. In addition, the College authorized construction contracts for fourteen project buildings from institutional funds, costing a total of almost $100,000.[11] By the end of 1937 over fifty project houses were in operation on and off campus.

The Texas A&M program became the first college-sanctioned cooperative student-housing organization in the United States, and operated the largest cooperative consumers' project in Texas. The cooperatives had social as well as financial significance. Each cooperative had a sponsor, who recommended students to be housed in the cooperative. Sponsors included county agents, vocational-agriculture teachers, parent-teacher associations, civic clubs, denominational groups, or local former-student clubs. Students in the cooperatives had common interests of locality, social ties, or academic pursuit. Project groups, for example, included the Collingsworth County Cooperative, Northeast Texas Cooperative, Washington County Cooperative, Catholic Cooperative, Industrial Education Cooperative, and for a time the American Legion Cooperative. In 1938 the American Legion of Texas provided $20,000 for a self-supporting cooperative project on the A&M campus. The College assumed the financing of the house and in 1940, when the Legion pressed for a fifty-year lease contract, paid the Legion for its investment.[12]

Texas newspapers were full of the A&M-cooperative story between

[9]*Ibid.*

[10]Minutes of the Board of Directors, September 21, 1935, V, 20; February 4, 1936, V, 34.

[11]Minutes of the Board of Directors, July 17, 1936, V, 59; April 10-11, 1937, V, 84, 89.

[12]"A&M Co-op Student Housing," Dan Russell Scrapbook, Texas A&M University Archives; Odessa *Bulletin,* July 20, 1939; Minutes of the Board of Directors, November 23, 1938, V, 170-171; April 15, 1940, VI, 16.

1936 and 1939. "700 Aggie Students Sweeping and Dusting Way Through College," reported the Beaumont *Journal*, Corsicana *Sun*, Longview *News*, Tyler *Times*, Sherman *Democrat*, Waco *Times-Herald*, Denison *Herald*, Amarillo *News*, and others in 1937.[13] The Corsicana *Light* jibed, "With Colleges grinding out thousands of eligible graduate males annually, and June coming on, what chance, we ask, will his [Russell's] charges have against designing young women who can't cook or keep house and like coffee brought to bed each morning?"[14] The Sherman *Democrat*, Nacogdoches *Sentinel*, Wichita Falls *Times*, Fort Worth *Star-Telegram*, Vernon *Record*, and Texarkana *Gazette*, among others, praised the project-house program and commented on the above-average grades "co-op" students earned.[15]

The average group in a cooperative was twenty-two, but the number ranged from ten to fifty boys. Each house had a matron or housemother, who maintained a "home-like" environment and planned the meals. Each house had a student manager and a treasurer. The manager maintained discipline and assigned duties; the treasurer kept an accurate set of accounts and charged each student his pro-rata share of expenses. The Department of Rural Sociology (Daniel Russell) supervised the accounts of each house and prescribed "house rules" over and above the regular College regulations. In addition, Dan Russell served as the purchasing agent for all of the cooperatives, screened applicants for the position of housemother, maintained files and grades on all students in cooperative housing, helped graduates from cooperatives obtain jobs, served as student counselor, and acted as promoter and publicity agent for the co-op project.[16]

Groceries, meat, bread, kitchen equipment, milk, and most other goods and services, including laundry, were purchased in bulk on open bids. Only day-old bread was bought, at 3.5 cents per loaf. The housemother received room and board and $1 per student per month for her services. Russell estimated that the cooperatives purchased $100,000 in supplies during a nine-month period and that total savings to cooperative students, as compared to

[13]Beaumont *Journal*, March 23, 1937; Corsicana *Sun*, March 27, 1937, August 19, 1937; Longview *News*, March 28, 1937; Tyler *Times*, March 28, 1937; Sherman *Democrat*, March 28, 1937; Waco *Times-Herald*, March 27, 1937; Denison *Herald*, March 28, 1937; Amarillo *News*, March 26, 1937.

[14]March 30, 1937.

[15]Sherman *Democrat*, January 25, 1939; Nacogdoches *Sentinel*, June 6, 1937; Wichita Falls *Times*, March 27, 1937; Fort Worth *Star-Telegram*, May 12, 1936; Vernon *Record*, March 27, 1937; Texarkana *Gazette*, March 28, 1937.

[16]"A&M Co-op Student Housing," Dan Russell Scrapbook, Texas A&M University Archives.

regular maintenance, exceeded $150,000 per year. He estimated that the average household expense per cooperative student was $13.34 per month, and that the per-student expenses ranged from $9 to $15 per month depending on the house.[17]

In 1934 nearly 250 students at Texas A&M lived in off-campus cooperative housing. By 1937 over seven hundred students lived in co-ops on and off the A&M campus. The student co-op idea spread from A&M to The University of Texas campus, where, by 1939, over three hundred students lived in cooperative housing.[18] The idea was picked up at schools around the country, such as the University of Washington, where, according to a *Readers Digest* report of 1939, "Six years ago there were boys living in the cheapest rooms, eating at the meanest lunch counters and too often going to classes hungry. One lived for two weeks on bread and apples."[19] The report continued, "At the University of Oregon a few boys who were crowded into shabby rented rooms and living on boiled rice and milk started an organization which now operates four houses."[20] The college cooperatives in 1939 had a membership of over 100,000 students, the *Digest* noted, and provided the social amenities, business training, and "confident ideals of making democracy work."[21] Dan Russell was described in the *Readers Digest* as the "professor of rural sociology . . . who was worrying about living ghosts — flesh and blood boys who were packing their books to go home as their slim allowances melted to the vanishing point . . . believed that there should be some way for these ambitious boys to continue their studies."[22] Russell played a quiet, rather obscure, unheralded, but positive role in this great movement.

The project-house program was something in which Texas A&M could take justifiable pride. It represented institutional response to a critical public need. It demonstrated that "Aggies" were industrious and conscientious students. The cooperative program reflected the deep and genuine commitment of Texas A&M students, faculty, and administrators to higher education.

Despite the impressive building program at Texas A&M during the Depression decade, hard times affected students, faculty, and staff alike. But for the Depression Texas A&M would have moved into a number of "new directions" in the 1930s, including the development of a nautical school. On May 28, 1931, the Texas Legislature authorized the organization and estab-

[17] *Ibid.*
[18] "Cooperating Their Way through College," *Readers Digest* (June 1939), pp. 43-46.
[19] *Ibid.*
[20] *Ibid.*
[21] *Ibid.*
[22] *Ibid.*

lishment "in one of the harbors of the State of Texas [of] a Nautical School for the purpose of instructing boys in the practice of seamanship, ship construction, naval architecture, wireless telegraph, engineering and the science of navigation," to be under the control of Texas A&M.[23] The bill became a curious piece of legislative double-talk when amended with the proviso, "It is hereby declared to be the intention of the Legislature only to allow interested citizens to support such a school and that it is understood that the State shall never be called upon to appropriate any money for the support of this school at this or any future time."[24] Almost three decades later the Legislature repealed the proviso and established the Texas Maritime Academy. Subsequently, in 1972, the Texas Maritime Academy became a part of Texas A&M University's College of Marine Sciences and Maritime Resources, and Texas A&M was designated by the federal government a Sea-Grant College. The Depression, however, postponed A&M's march to the sea.[25]

On the other hand, the Fireman's School, established by the Forty-second State Legislature in 1931, survived and even flourished during the Depression. An experimental fireman's "short course" was held at A&M in the summer of 1930, under the direction of Harold Rinshaw Brayton. After the approval of legislative support for a regular fireman's training school, Frank C. Bolton, Thomas O. Walton, and Charles C. Hedges were appointed to a committee by the A&M Board of Directors to organize the school. Brayton remained director of the school through 1940, when Hedges replaced him. By 1940 attendance at the school had climbed to 607 men, representing over 286 cities and towns in Texas, and a few from outside the state.[26] In the 1970s the school still flourished, having achieved an international reputation for a unique and significant public service.

In 1932, during what President Herbert Hoover called the "Great Fear," or bank panic, created by the uncertainties of the presidential elections, A&M Directors became concerned over the stability of local Bryan banks in which were deposited substantial College funds. Some of these funds were transferred to larger banks in Houston, and in the same instance the Directors

[23]*Laws of Texas, 1931*, pp. 423-434; Texas Maritime Academy Papers, Texas A&M University Archives.

[24]*Ibid.*

[25]See also Minutes of the Board of Directors, November 10, 1932, IV, 223, response to a letter from Corpus Christi Chamber of Commerce urging establishment of a Nautical Training School, and Chapter 26, which discusses the development of the Sea Grant program.

[26]Minutes of the Board of Directors, November 25, 1931, IV, 187; Dallas *Times-Herald*, October 17, 1939; Yoakum *Times*, September 8, 1939; Bryan *Daily Eagle*, March 15, August 3, 1940; *Harris County News*, March 11, 1941; *Laws of Texas, 1931*, pp. 382-383.

took action to aid local banks by reducing interest charges on College funds paid by the banks to 1.5 percent.[27] A few months later the Directors successfully thwarted an attempt by the state comptroller to transfer all A&M funds from Board control to state control.[28] Throughout the Depression fiscal management became a primary concern of College administrators. The experiences of the Depression finally impressed upon the administrators the necessity of having a regular professional business manager. Elmer N. Holmgreen, instated on February 1, 1941, was the first to fill the position since the departure of General William P. Hardeman in the 1880s.[29]

The darkest days of the Depression came in 1933. In February of that year the administrators began a broad program of retrenchment. A number of staff positions were eliminated and other staff workers were given salary cuts of from 10 to 20 percent.[30] In April the Directors cut the cash reserve in Bryan banks to $5,000, and reduced interest charges to the banks to 1 percent.[31] In an economy measure the Board ordered all classes of less than five undergraduate students abolished, but allowed for special situations. The number of such classes, reported President Walton in November, was reduced from sixty-one to eighteen.[32] Interestingly enough, the "small-class" ruling continues at Texas A&M.

In the spring of 1933 the Forty-third Texas Legislature approved a 25-percent across-the-board salary reduction for all state employees, including college teachers, for the 1933-1935 fiscal years as a part of the appropriation bill. Walton reported in July that "salaries have been reduced, positions eliminated wherever possible, consolidations of departments, and other reductions made." The Directors urged yet further economy measures and directed Walton to confer with deans in devising new measures.[33] As a concession to the faculty for the salary cuts, rent on college-owned housing was lowered from 10 to 9 percent of evaluation.[34] Faculty were hired on a nine-months basis, rather than twelve, and if summer courses failed to "make," teachers were simply unemployed for the summer. Each faculty member, though hired for nine months, received twelve monthly paychecks, and the 25-percent cut in 1933 was effected by eliminating the last three paychecks.

[27]Minutes of the Board of Directors, November 10, 1932, IV, 223, and November 23, 1932, IV, 226, 227.

[28]*Ibid.*, January 29, 1933, IV, 228.

[29]*Ibid.*, December 31, 1940, VI, 77.

[30]*Ibid.*, February 12, 1933, IV, 231.

[31]*Ibid.*, April 15-16, 1933, IV, 232.

[32]*Ibid.*, June 2-3, 1933, IV, 236, and November 29, 1933, IV, 253.

[33]*Ibid.*, July 1, 1933, IV, 246.

[34]*Ibid.*, July 1, 1933, IV, 244.

Marion Thomas Harrington, later chancellor and president of Texas A&M University, recalls that as a newly married instructor in chemistry at Texas A&M, his $1,800 (12-month) salary was cut to $1,535 in 1933, and remained there for a long time. His dollars, however, went much farther, and he used his summer "unemployment" to work on advanced degrees. When the state was broke, he recalls, faculty were paid with warrants — a state-issued promise to pay. These warrants were accepted by local banks and businesses at a small discount, or the employee could hold them until the state was able to redeem them.[35] Charles W. Crawford, in mechanical engineering, remembers that a number of the faculty quit when they got the salary cut, but most did not — there was no place to go.[36] Warrants were still being used, and cashed at a discount by local banks, as late as 1942.[37]

Although small injections of federal money began to be received by Texas A&M in 1934 under various New Deal programs, this money invariably went into minor construction projects. For example, in 1934, $39,800 was received under a PWA (Public Works Administration) grant to remodel the creamery; another $10,500 from the FERA (Federal Emergency Relief Administration) was used for a small paving program.[38] State appropriations to higher education continued to be deficient. Walton indicated to the Board of Directors in April 1935 that the legislative appropriations that year were critically insufficient.[39] New economies effected in 1935 included the discontinuance of the School of Vocational Teaching, "because of high costs and low enrollment."[40]

In 1936 Texas A&M instituted a retirement program which had a dual role. One was to provide an additional benefit to faculty, and so promote better faculty retention; the other motive was to purge the payroll by retiring employees over the age of seventy. The retirement program was established on May 15, 1936, and provided for retirement at the age of seventy with a one-year extension permissible. Maximum retirement pay was to be one-half of the last year's salary, or 25 percent of the average salary over the last five years of employment plus 1 percent for each year of service to the College.[41] The Board of Directors has since made retirement mandatory at age sixty-

[35]Interview with Marion Thomas Harrington, September 13, 1971, College Station, Texas.

[36]Interview with Charles William Crawford, March 30, 1971, College Station, Texas.

[37]Interview with Joseph Milton Nance, April 10, 1972, College Station, Texas.

[38]Minutes of the Board of Directors, July 25, 1934, IV, 265; and April 6, 1934, IV, 256.

[39]*Ibid.*, April 24-25, 1935, V, 4.

[40]*Ibid.*, July 6, 1935, V, 12.

[41]*Ibid.*, February 4, 1936, V, 34; May 15, 1936, V. 45-46.

five, although special extensions may be requested. Texas A&M employees now come under the Texas State Teachers Retirement System and optional retirement plans.

Perhaps the most critical phenomenon of the Great Depression at Texas A&M was the fact that large numbers of A&M students had no jobs waiting for them after graduation. The Class of 1932 was the hardest hit, there being, for example, but one engineer in the graduating class with a job at commencement. Thereafter, a gradual improvement in the employment picture developed, as new government jobs became available with the New Deal recovery agencies, and as business gradually recovered.[42] Throughout the thirties, however, any job at all, at almost any salary, was welcomed by the graduate. Professional people, such as engineers and architects, were especially vulnerable to depression. Signs of recovery, however, had become obvious by 1937.

Between 1932 and 1937 Texas A&M confronted not only problems of depression, but an educational-political crisis equally as grave, in part inspired by the Depression. In 1931 the Forty-first Texas Legislature created the office of state auditor and efficiency expert. The Forty-second Texas Legislature, pressed for funds, resolved to study ways of implementing economies in government, and ways of deriving new avenues of taxation. A Joint Legislative Committee on Organization and Economy retained the services of Griffenhagen and Associates of Chicago, specialists in public administration and finance, to investigate and prepare reports, which were submitted to the Forty-third Legislature in 1933. The following extract of House Concurrent Resolution No. 58, authorizing the investigation, illustrates the critical status of state financing during the depression:[43]

Whereas, the 41st Legislature created the office of State Auditor and Efficiency Expert, and the same has been functioning for nearly two years, and during such time has uncovered many irregularities as well as stopped many unwise practices in our government; and

Whereas, It was the intention of the said Legislature that the cost of State government and functions should be placed on an economical and efficient basis as soon as possible, by such Auditor and other State agencies; and

Whereas, On account of the continued financial depression, and the lowering of the values of taxable property, and the lowering of earning power of the tax-

[42]Interview with Marion Thomas Harrington, September 13, 1971, College Station, Texas; interview with Charles William Crawford, March 30, 1971, College Station, Texas; interview with Ernest Langford, March 8, 1971, College Station, Texas.

[43]Joint Legislative Committee on Organization and Economy, *The Government of the State of Texas*, XI, *Education; the Agricultural and Mechanical College of Texas and its Affiliates*, December 31, 1932 [iv.] (hereinafter cited: *The Government of the State of Texas*, XI, *Education*).

payer, the 42d Legislature has been forced to reach out and find new avenues of taxation to properly carry on the different functions of this government in an efficient and economical manner; and

Whereas, It is the desire of the people of this State and this Legislature to economically administer their governmental affairs without unduly or unfairly burdening the citizens with unnecessary or exorbitant tax levies, and without unduly alarming or over-burdening capital now invested in this State, or contemplating such investment; and

Whereas, There is an undoubted duplication of work, employment and expense in many of the departments in institutions of this State, as well as many unnecessary departments thereof, which duplication both of expense and labor could be done away with, if the Legislature knew how, and in what way such could be reduced; now, therefore, be it

Resolved by the House of Representatives of the State of Texas, the Senate concurring, That the Speaker appoint three members of the House, and the President of the Senate appoint two members of the Senate for the purpose of making a thorough investigation of all State Institutions, and State Departments of any and all kind, including the State Judiciary, the State Departmental, the State Eleemosynary and the State Educational Institutions, with a view to ascertaining if such institutions and departments may be, or can be operated at a greater efficiency, and a lesser expense to the taxpayers of this State; and as to whether or not the policies and operation of such institutions can be changed, in such a way that the cost of government might be reduced, and/or a greater service be rendered by such institutions to the people of this State, and whether some of such institutions or departments may be consolidated and made to function more efficiently and at lesser expense to the people; and as to how the affairs of this State may be run in a more economical manner without affecting the efficiency of such affairs.

The resulting report was highly critical of the Texas A&M academic program, and of the administration of the A&M system.

Recommendations of the legislative committee report proposed substantive and, for A&M people, shocking changes. Not the least of these was the recommendation that the functions of the Board of Directors be transferred to a proposed State Board of Education, which may be considered, incidentally, something of a prototype of the present Coordinating Board, Texas College and University System, formerly the Texas Commission on Higher Education, created in 1965, although the Board proposed in the Griffenhagen Report, unlike the contemporary board, would have strong, centralized powers. It was also advised that A&M discontinue offering degrees in arts and sciences, and that A&M and Texas Technological College only should offer degrees in agriculture. Texas A&M and The University of Texas should be the only schools offering degrees in engineering. The report advised integrating the work of the Extension Service, the Agricultural Experiment Station, and the School of Agriculture. It recommended that the Texas Forest Service be transferred to a proposed State Department of Forests, Fish, and Game, and that John Tarleton Agricultural College be transferred to the control of The University of Texas at Austin. It recommended that control of Prairie View State Normal and Industrial College should be removed from the administrative offices of the Agricultural and Mechanical College "which have grossly mismanaged the institution," and that A&M's branch at Arlington, North Texas State Agricultural College, should drop its agricultural program and become a county-supported junior college.[44]

The Griffenhagen Report could be quite specific as well as broad. The graduate courses offered in the catalogue at A&M, it declared, should correspond approximately to the number of courses actually given, meaning that almost one-half of the courses listed should be abandoned. The number of classes (289) with fewer than ten students should be drastically reduced. Only one summer term of six weeks, rather than two, should be offered. Most liberal-arts classes, it said, should be eliminated from the summer curriculum. Pay for summer instruction should be reduced. Graduate instruction should be offered only in certain departments in agriculture and veterinary medicine. The military system should be relaxed. Competitive athletics should be made self-supporting. Twenty-two (specified) instructional positions should be eliminated. Some eighty student-labor positions should be eliminated. Seven stenographic and clerical positions should be abolished. Thirty positions with the Department of Buildings and Grounds should be abolished — plus virtually all part-time labor. Four hospital employees, two assistant librarians, sixteen designers, engineers, and draftsmen, and a dozen or so miscellaneous other employees should be discharged, advised the report.[45]

Had many of the recommendations from the study been effected, one would think there would be little left of the A&M College. Few of the advised changes ever came to be. To be sure, some of the advice was well founded. As the years passed, a number of the recommended changes were made, although not quite in the manner as anticipated in the Report. An example was revision toward meeting a genuine need for some integration in the functions of agricultural extension, agricultural experimentation, and agricultural teaching. Throughout the College there was little coordination among academics, research, and extension at any level or in any field. Recognition of this situation brought about a substantive reorganization of the

[44]*Ibid.*, 24-25, 72, 74, 149, 158, 208-209, 253-255, 314-318.
[45]*Ibid.*, 72-74, 109-110.

entire College after World War II. Great need for coordination of all institutions of higher learning in Texas did exist, a problem which did eventually achieve some resolution by the creation of the Texas Commission on Higher Education in 1958. This agency was later replaced by the Coordinating Board, Texas College and University System, in 1965. The Arlington branch did eventually drop its agricultural role and become more· subservient to the needs of the urban centers near it. But John Tarleton Agricultural College, Prairie View State Normal and Industrial College, and the Texas Forest Service were not separated from A&M control, probably to the good fortune of those institutions. Graduate studies and liberal arts were not curtailed at Texas A&M, to the great good fortune of that institution; and of the hundreds of employees whom the legislative committee report recommended be discharged, only a few actually were released, to the great good fortune of the majority who retained some employment during the Depression.

In a word, the Griffenhagen Report, generated by a real sense of need, prepared in an honest motive of service to the state, and predicated upon economic efficiency, was in the very broadest sense a perceptive report, but in a literal sense it was irrational, impracticable, and injurious to the course of higher education in Texas. Fortunately, it had relatively little positive impact upon the course of events.

In November 1932 a special meeting of the A&M Board of Directors was held to discuss the content of the Griffenhagen Report, the text of which was not made public until the following month. The discussion at that meeting was not recorded in the minutes,[46] but the content of that discussion can be inferred from subsequent activities. Basically, the Board followed a course of passive resistance. In fact, it never even officially acknowledged the existence of the Report. It may be inferred that the economies of 1933-1935, both by the A&M administration and by the state Legislature, came as a result of the Griffenhagen Report, but this is unlikely. Those economies, or some economies, would have had to come with the deepening of the Depression. The Griffenhagen Report, or certainly Volume XI, concerning Texas A&M, ended up in the limbo land of the legislative archives, and life went on at Texas A&M, much as it had in the past. The Report left in its wake, to be sure, some irritated people at Texas A&M. One of these, Dean Frank C. Bolton, who in all of his life had never been known to cuss, "came very close to doing it," after reading the Griffenhagen Report.[47]

Despite, or perhaps because of, the hard times, the student body at

[46]Minutes of the Board of Directors, November 10, 1932, IV, 222.
[47]Interview with Ernest Langford, April 12, 1972, College Station, Texas.

Texas A&M developed a particularly intensive spirit of cooperation and loyalty to one another, and to the school. The Corps of Cadets, with its "spirit of Aggie land," was at no time before or since so keen as it was during the 1930s and the early 1940s. The camaraderie and student unity at A&M, great from the very beginning of the institution, truly reached the pitch of the one great "fraternity" during the Depression decade. The "Farmers" of the first decades of the twentieth century by 1930 had become the "Aggies" of the modern era. The modern Aggie was of the same stuff as the old "farmer" species, perhaps just a little more concentrated. He was loyal, dedicated, and determined, so much so that at times he appeared bull-headed, immature, and irrational, and he inevitably inspired many of the contemporary "Aggie Jokes." The A&M man became an ethnic species of his own, and he was proud of his distinct status:

"Did you hear about the Aggie library?" goes one joke. "They had to close it when someone checked out the book."

"But he returned it," continues the story; "so they reopened the library. Then they had to close down again when they found the student had already colored the book."

And then there is this one: "Did you hear about the Aggie navy? It's no joke." Indeed it isn't.

"And did you hear about what graduating students got all the jobs this year?"

You guessed it, the Aggies did. Aggies take great pleasure in the unique distinction of being Aggies.

According to the 1933-1934 Y.M.C.A.-sponsored *Students' Handbook,* an Aggie:[48]

Speaks to every cadet and every professor at every opportunity.

Learns the college songs and yells as soon as possible.

Thanks the driver of a car who has given him a ride and helps the driver if he has trouble while the cadet is with him.

Attends all athletic contests that are possible for him to attend and backs the team through thick and thin.

Keeps his shoes shined, his hair combed and his uniform pressed.

Never "razzes" a referee or umpire.

Dresses neatly and is a gentleman while on weekend trips or Corps trips.

Is honest in class room regardless of what he may see others, who are careless of their honor, doing.

Realizes that someone is making a sacrifice to give him the opportunity to be at A. and M. and consequently makes use of his time to the best advantage by consci-

[48]Y.M.C.A., *The Students' Handbook of Texas A&M College,* 1933-1934, p. 31.

entious work whether it be his study time or his leisure. He plays hard and studies hard.

To be sure, an Aggie had other traits and activities as well. He ate "spuds" (potatoes), "blood" (ketchup), "rocks" (ice), "cackle" (eggs), "gun wadding" (bread), "scabs" (post toasties), "sawdust" (sugar), "dope" (coffee), "worms" (spaghetti), and "cush" (dessert). Aggies had "fish" (freshmen), "horizontal engineers" (sleeping students), and "bleed meetings" (freshman "orientation" by upperclassmen), and lived with an "old lady" (roommate). They attended midnight yell practice, polished the bronze statue of Lawrence Sullivan Ross endlessly, and honored their dead with the inspiring "Silver Taps" and monuments. Seniors ended their years at A&M with the unglamorous Elephant Walk, and then the impressive Final Review.[49] Any explanation of an Aggie is inadequate. For greater insight one should read Henderson Shuffler's *Son, Remember . . .,* John Pasco's *Fish Sergeant,* George Sessions Perry's *Texas A&M,* and numerous other biographies, war memoirs, and reminiscences, many of which will be found listed in the bibliography of this work. But if you are not an Aggie, especially of the 1930s vintage, you will never truly know what an Aggie is — or was, for the Aggie of the twenties and thirties is now vintage wine.

One of the great moments in the life of the Aggie occurred on May 11, 1937, when President Franklin Delano Roosevelt visited Texas A&M. Roosevelt, returning from an ocean fishing trip out of Galveston, was enroute by train to visit his son Elliott, who was then a resident of Fort Worth and also a member of the Texas A&M Board of Directors. Roosevelt was received at College Station with a twenty-one-gun salute. He reviewed the Corps of Cadets, spoke briefly to some 20,000 people assembled in the football stadium, and received a white-faced Hereford for his Warm Springs, Georgia, farm. His train pulled away from cheering Aggies along the track, their ears still ringing with the kind things President Roosevelt had said about their school.[50]

The Aggie of the Depression years felt a close identification with his instructors and administrators, who were considered a part of the fraternity. In 1933-1934, College officers and department heads included these persons:[51]

[49]John O. Pasco, *Fish Sergeant,* 14, 17-18, 36-37, 45-47, 55-58, 93-94.

[50]College Station *Battalion,* May 11, 1937; Bryan *Eagle,* May 11, 1937.

[51]Y.M.C.A., *The Students' Handbook of Texas A&M College,* 1933-1934, pp. 16-17; Texas A&M, *Catalogue, 1933-1934,* pp. 112-188.

President · · · · · Dr. Thomas Otto Walton
Commandant · · · · · Colonel John Ellis Mitchell
Registrar · · · · · Eugene Jody Howell

Heads of Departments

Accounting and Statistics · · · · · Thomas William Leland
Agricultural Economics · · · · · Virgil Porter Lee
Agricultural Education · · · · · Charles H. Winkler
Agricultural Engineering · · · · · Daniels Scoates
Agronomy and Genetics · · · · · Eugene Peter Humbert
Animal Husbandry · · · · · David Willard Williams
Architecture · · · · · Ernest Langford
Biology · · · · · Oscar Melville Ball
Chemistry and Chemical Engineering · · · · · Charles Cleveland Hedges
Civil Engineering · · · · · John Jefferson Richey
Dairy Husbandry · · · · · Charles Noah Shepardson
Economics · · · · · Floyd Barzilla Clark
Electrical Engineering · · · · · Martin Collins Hughes
Engineering Drawing · · · · · Alva Mitchell
Engineering Research · · · · · Frederick E. Giesecke
English · · · · · George Summey, Jr.
Entomology · · · · · Sherman Weaver Bilsing
Geology · · · · · John Tipton Lonsdale
History · · · · · Samuel Rhea Gammon
Horticulture · · · · · Edwin Jackson Kyle
Industrial Education · · · · · Edward LaFayette Williams
Landscape Art · · · · · Frederick William Hensel, Jr.
Mathematics · · · · · Walter Lee Porter
Mechanical Engineering · · · · · Charles W. Crawford
Military Science and Tactics · · · · · Ambrose Robert Emery
Modern Languages · · · · · Charles B. Campbell
Municipal and Sanitary Engineering · · · · · Ernest William Steel
Petroleum Engineering · · · · · Robert Lockhart Mills
Physical Education · · · · · Madison Bell
Physics · · · · · Oscar William Silvey
Poultry Husbandry · · · · · Duncan Henry Reid
Rural Education · · · · · William Lycurgus Hughes
Rural Sociology · · · · · Daniel Russell
Textile Engineering · · · · · John Brewer Bagley

Veterinary Anatomy	Mark Francis
Veterinary Medicine and Surgery	Ross Perry Marsteller
Veterinary Pathology	Arthur Edwards Wharton
Veterinary Physiology and Pharmacology	Patton Wright Burns

Other Officers

Librarian	Thomas F. Mayo
Supervisor of Subsistence	William Adam Duncan
Manager of Student Publications	J. Elmo Angell

A number of important changes in administrative personnel occurred during the thirties, but generally turnover in the faculty was relatively small. There was no place for college professors to go.

Frank Cleveland Bolton, who joined the A&M faculty in 1909, and served first as head of the Department of Electrical Engineering, and then as dean of Engineering, was named acting dean of the College in July 1931, replacing Charles Puryear, who was ill at the time. In 1932 Puryear was made dean emeritus and Bolton replaced him on a permanent basis, but continued to serve as dean of Engineering until 1937. In 1937 Bolton added to his title and duties those of vice-president of the College, becoming the first to hold the office since 1890, while retaining the position of dean of the College. That same year Bolton served as acting president while Walton was away on a tour of Europe. In 1948 Bolton was inaugurated as president of Texas A&M and retired in 1950.[52]

Bolton served A&M for forty-one years, a popular and respected administrator. Bolton believed that a man should "choose some type of work you enjoy and believe is worthwhile, and learn all you can about it. . . . The man who learns as much as possible about any subject and applies that knowledge with whole-souled enthusiasm over the years, is almost certain to succeed, whether his field of interest be the collection of old coins or the splitting of the atom."[53] Bolton possessed steadfastness of purpose, inner strength, determination, and personal humility. One day Bolton appeared at work with one hand bandaged, but made no explanation to his associates. It took several days before the word got out that he had "trimmed his fingernails" too closely with an electric saw while he was engaged in his favorite hobby, woodworking.[54]

Thomas Dudley Brooks, former dean of the School of Education at

[52]Minutes of the Board of Directors, July 4, 1931, IV, 182; June 3, 1932, IV, 209; July 5, 1937, V, 104; August 10, 1937, V, 109; R. Henderson Shuffler, *A Man and His College* [1-14].
[53]Shuffler, *A Man and His College* [5-6].
[54]*Ibid.,* [7].

Baylor University, joined the Texas A&M faculty in 1932 as dean of Arts and Sciences and dean of the Graduate School. Brooks replaced Charles E. Friley, who left A&M to become dean of Arts and Sciences at Iowa State College, and later president of that institution.[55] Gibb Gilchrist, who had done a remarkable job as head of the Texas State Highway Department, accepted the position of dean of the School of Engineering in 1937, replacing Frank C. Bolton.[56] Gilchrist quickly began to provide strong leadership in many areas. In 1944 he became president of Texas A&M, and presided during a time of considerable stress, when many substantive changes occurred at A&M. In the same year in which Gilchrist came to Texas A&M, 1937, Ross Perry Marsteller became dean of the School of Veterinary Medicine, replacing Mark Francis.[57]

On the departmental level the Directors created the Department of Wild Game in 1937, with Walter Penn Taylor as head. The Department was renamed the Department of Fish and Game Conservation in 1939.[58] In 1939 the Board created the Department of Aeronautical Engineering, with Howard Walter Barlow as its head, and the Department of Industrial Engineering, headed by Judson Neff.[59] John Thomas Lamar McNew succeeded John Jefferson Richey as head of Civil Engineering in 1940, and Horace C. Spencer replaced Alva Mitchell in 1940 upon Mitchell's retirement as head of the Department of Engineering Drawing.[60] In 1941 the State Board of Registration for Professional Engineers allocated $40,000 to Texas A&M for establishment of an engineering library.[61] This development, as well as the revamping of the engineering curriculum and the addition of new departments, was initiated and effected by Gibb Gilchrist, who worked diligently to improve his school. Gilchrist, it must be noted, was not a popular administrator among rank-and-file College professors, in part, perhaps, because he lacked the usual academic credentials and experience, but mainly because he was quite positive, direct, and blunt in his dealings with people. He was, nonetheless, most energetic and quite effective.

Gilchrist, to be sure, had something of a problem on his hands; like the School of Veterinary Medicine, the School of Engineering came under close scrutiny and considerable criticism from professional evaluators. The Depres-

[55]Minutes of the Board of Directors, June 3, 1932, IV, 208-209; July 9, 1932, IV, 214.

[56]Minutes of the Board of Directors, July 5, 1937, V, 102.

[57]*Ibid.,* 104.

[58]*Ibid.,* August 10, 1937, V, 109; April 30, 1939, V, 184.

[59]*Ibid.,* September 2, 1939, V, 202; March 9, 1940, VI, 10.

[60]*Ibid.,* May 11, 1940, VI, 21; May 30, 1940, VI, 37.

[61]*Ibid.,* May 11, 1940, VI, 21; July 12, 1941, VI, 125; May 21, 1943, VI, 218.

sion, and to some extent professional inbreeding and administrative negligence, contributed to A&M's failure to maintain a progressive academic development in several fields. The program in chemical engineering was refused accreditation by the Southern Association of Schools and Colleges in 1937, and other fields in engineering had been negatively evaluated. The lack of suitable engineering library facilities, furthermore, was critical and contributed to Gilchrist's efforts to secure funds for the development of a reputable library.[62] In some respects, despite the physical growth of the College during the Depression, the era may be characterized in part as one of academic stagnation, one cause of which, indeed, was that Texas A&M had placed too much of its money in buildings and too little in people. This condition became increasingly chronic well into the postwar years.

Administrative and academic reorganization in 1937 and afterwards did help improve the situation. State appropriations to A&M increased in 1937, and salary raises were received by key administrators. The president now received $10,000 per year, the vice-president $7,500, and deans $7,000,[63] but raises were not passed down in a significant manner to faculty, and no wholesale increases to cancel the 25 percent salary reduction made in 1933 ever occurred. The College did choose, however, to initiate a program for hiring "outstanding professors." The Board of Directors agreed in July 1937 to set aside between $40,000 and $50,000 to employ a number of distinguished teachers. The College Executive Committee, including deans and higher officials, subsequently recommended that distinguished professorships be established in petroleum engineering, air conditioning (mechanical engineering), electrical engineering, and civil engineering; and that eleven distinguished professorships be established: seven in various fields of agriculture, three in arts and sciences (including geology, biology, and museum), and one in veterinary science. These professorships were to pay up to $7,000 per year, in unhappy contrast to the salary range of department heads of from about $3,800 to $4,500 per year.[64] Perhaps significantly and interestingly, all of these professorships, including the one in "museum," were in the areas of agriculture, engineering, and the sciences, which fact reflected the continuing emphasis of the College in those areas, to the exclusion of the liberal and fine arts. The museum professorship, incidentally, might have owed its creation to the fact that in April 1937 Mark Francis donated his very excellent fossil collection as a nucleus for a museum of natural history at Texas A&M.[65]

[62]*Ibid.*, May 21, 1943, VI, 218.
[63]*Ibid.*, July 20, 1937, V, 107.
[64]*Ibid.*, July 20, 1937, V, 107; September 10, 1937, V, 113.
[65]*Ibid.*, April 24, 1937, V, 89.

The distinguished-professor program was initiated in 1938, when the Board hired Plato L. Gettys as distinguished professor of economics in business law. Efforts were made to hire a man in petroleum engineering, but without success.[66] But in 1940, with the war spreading in Europe, the Board of Directors elected to hire six reserve officers to teach military science, to be paid for out of the fund reserved for distinguished professors.[67] That, and America's entry into World War II, ended for the time being Texas A&M's program for distinguished professors.

Texas A&M conferred its first honorary Doctor of Laws degree on Francis Marion Law in June 1934. Law, a graduate of Texas A&M ('95), and a member of the Board of Directors since 1917, served on the Board until 1945. During his last twenty years he served as president of the Board.[68] Law, a Houston banker, throughout his association with A&M was a strong and diligent supporter of the College.

In 1936 Texas A&M awarded an honorary Doctor of Laws degree to Jesse H. Jones, "for services to the nation and the state of Texas." Jones, born in Robertson County, Tennessee, in 1874, moved to Texas with his family in 1884, but returned with them to Tennessee in 1886. Jones returned to Texas in 1894 to enter the lumber business. He moved from lumbering into building construction and in 1911 built the Rice Hotel, in Houston. He amassed a large personal fortune from lumbering, construction, banking, and publishing the Houston *Chronicle*. Jones served in an appointive post under Woodrow Wilson, was named a member of the Reconstruction Finance Corporation board by Herbert Hoover, and became its chairman under Franklin D. Roosevelt, who in 1940 appointed him Secretary of Commerce. In 1939 Texas A&M honored Jones again by dedicating the Thanksgiving Day football game, on November 30, to Jesse Jones. He died May 31, 1956, in Houston.[69]

In 1936 the Board of Directors authorized the granting of the regular Doctor of Philosophy (Ph.D.) degree and the Doctor of Science, in agriculture and engineering. The first recipient of the Ph.D. from Texas A&M was Dorris David Giles, a student in animal physiology and nutrition, who received his degree in May 1940.[70] In 1940 Charles Edwin Friley, former dean of Arts and Sciences at A&M, and then at Iowa State, received an honorary

[66]*Ibid.*, January 6, 1938, V, 129.

[67]*Ibid.*, September 25, 1940, VI, 54.

[68]*Ibid.*, June 1, 1934, IV, 262; see also Texas A&M, *75th Anniversary* [24-25].

[69]Minutes of the Board of Directors, October 17, 1936, V, 71; Jesse Holman Jones Biographical Papers, Texas A&M University Archives.

[70]Minutes of the Board of Directors, May 15, 1936, V, 46; Texas A&M, *Catalogue, 1940-1941*, p. 310.

law degree from Texas A&M.[71] Subsequently, in 1941, the Board "regularized" the granting of honorary degrees by providing for the degree of Doctor of Laws (LL.D.), Doctor of Agriculture (D.Agr.), Doctor of Engineering (D.Eng.), Doctor of Science (D.Sci.), and Doctor of Journalism (D.Jln.). In that year honorary degrees were conferred on George McCormick, for engineering achievements; William Lockhart Clayton, the cotton broker, who was unable to be present; Richard J. Kleberg of the King Ranch; and Edwin J. Kiest, of the A&M Board of Directors,[72] who was then critically ill.

Beginning in the twenties the College and the Association of Former Students received numerous private gifts, most of which were used to help young people obtain a college education. W. S. Pearson gave the College $2,500 for "deserving students" in 1926, which sum the College turned over to the Association of Former Students to be administered as a student-aid fund. In 1927 the role of the Association of Former Students in student-aid activities became formalized with Board approval of a Permanent Endowed Student's Loan Fund, administered by the Association.[73] The role of the Association in helping students through school greatly expanded through the Depression years. Texas A&M's Former Students Association is second to none in terms of institutional loyalty and support, and in many years is second only to the Harvard Alumni Association in terms of cash gifts to the school.

Mrs. Emily St. P. Nagle, the widow of Dean James C. Nagle, left A&M $5,000 for the James C. Nagle Memorial Fellowship fund in 1937.[74] Dr. and Mrs. Oscar M. Ball left their estates in separate wills to the College to found the Julia Ball Lee Scholarships in Biology.[75] Walter J. Coulter gave $5,000 in bonds to create a fund "to help boys who need help."[76] Dr. Samuel E. Asbury, assistant state chemist with the Agricultural Experiment Station at A&M, willed all of his wordly goods to the College. Asbury, a one-man unofficial fine-arts promoter on the campus, made vigorous efforts to expose faculty and students to fine music and works of art.[77] Thousands of the former students and friends of the College helped with smaller gifts and with services to the school.

[71]Minutes of the Board of Directors, May 30, 1940, VI, 26.

[72]*Ibid.*, March 8, 1941, VI, 82; see also Appendix E.

[73]*Ibid.*, October 15, 1926, IV, 83; February 22, 1927, IV, 86.

[74]*Ibid.*, September 10, 1937, V, 113.

[75]*Ibid.*, November 25, 1942, VI, 201.

[76]*Ibid.*, January 10, 1942, VI, 164.

[77]*Ibid.*, June 5, 1941, VI, 124; interview with Mrs. Robert R. Lancaster and Mrs. Thomas D. Watts, September 9, 1971, Bryan, Texas.

Substantial endowments were received from W. R. McFarland and family, of Tulsa, Oklahoma, who gave land and money to the Association of Former Students valued at $115,000. Will C. Hogg, the son of former Governor James Stephen Hogg, willed Texas A&M $50,000 and $25,000 to each of the three A&M branch colleges for loans to worthy students. Mrs. J. R. Astin, the widow of J. Robert Astin ('84), left the College a gift of land and money valued at $50,000, to be used for the student-loan fund.[78] In few institutions have the former students shared so vigorously in the growth and development of their alma mater as at Texas A&M.

The construction program, facilitated so greatly by the availability of money from the University Endowment Fund after 1932, was further enhanced by construction loans and grants obtained through New Deal recovery agencies. In June 1937 Texas A&M applied to the Reconstruction Finance Corporation, headed by Jesse Jones, for a $2-million loan to finance construction of new dormitories containing 1,250 rooms. The income from the dorms, then set at $10 per room or $5 per student per month, was to service the twenty-year loan with semiannual installment payments of $55,250. The RFC accepted the application, and contracts for the dormitories were let in November 1938.[79] The buildings were designed to provide the maximum number of rooms at the lowest possible cost, and omitted most of the amenities.[80] Perhaps fittingly, the group of dorms are today popularly referred to as the "Corps Dorms," which have housed the Corps of Cadets after military training became noncompulsory, and which reflect the Spartan military tradition of the Texas A&M Corps of Cadets.

The twelve new dormitories and a mess hall were named in recognition of those who had served the College with distinction: (1) David Wendell Spence, former dean of the School of Engineering; (2) Edwin J. Kiest, of Dallas, member of the Board from 1927 to 1941, and editor and publisher of the Dallas *Times-Herald;* (3) Robert W. Briggs, of Pharr ('17), member of the Board from 1937 to 1945; (4) Charles Perkins Fountain, head of the Department of English from 1904 until his death in 1921; (5) Charles S. Gainer, of Bryan, attorney, Texas legislator from 1914 to 1918, state senator from 1928 to 1932, and a strong supporter of the College until his death in 1955; (6) Walter G. Lacy, of Waco ('93), member of the Board from 1924 to 1941 and president of the Citizens National Bank of Waco; (7) Henry C.

[78]Texas A&M, *Progress Report for Twelve Years, 1925-1937,* p. 64.

[79]Minutes of the Board of Directors, June 4, 1937, V, 98-99; November 24, 1937, V, 123-126; June 14, 1938, V, 147-154; November 5, 1938, V, 164.

[80]Ernest Langford, "Here We'll Build the College," unpublished manuscript in Texas A&M University Archives, 166.

Schumacher, of Houston ('92), member of the Board from 1924 to 1940; (8) Louis L. McInnis, of Bryan, former chairman of the faculty, from 1887 to 1890, and member of the Board from 1905 to 1908; (9) George Rollie White ('95), of Brady, member of the Board from 1926 to 1955; (10) Byrd E. White, of Lancaster, member of the Board from 1922 to 1934; (11) Henry Hill Harrington, former president of Texas A&M from 1905 to 1908; and (12) Joe Utay, of Dallas, member of the Board from 1935 to 1941. The new mess hall servicing the dorms was named for William Adam Duncan, supervisor of subsistence from 1920 to 1937.[81] In 1969 the names for Schumacher, McInnis, and G. Rollie White were changed to honor Medal of Honor winners Turney W. Leonard, William George Harrell, and Eli Lamar Whiteley. Two new dormitories in a different area of the campus were then named for Schumacher and McInnis. G. Rollie White, meanwhile, had become the name for the coliseum.[82]

The Directors used the occasion of the naming of the new dormitories to honor James C. Nagle, former dean of Engineering, for whom the civil-engineering building was named, and Vice-President Frank C. Bolton, in whose honor the electrical-engineering building was named.[83] The memorial gymnasium, completed in 1924, was renamed "Charlie Deware Field House" in November 1939, in honor of Charles A. Deware, Sr. ('09), of Brenham, one of A&M's all-time great athletes and an institution on the A&M players bench until the time of his death.[84] The next year the Directors honored Emil Jerome Fermier, former head of mechanical engineering, by naming the mechanical-engineering building after him.[85]

Other major and minor construction projects in the prewar years included a "Triple A" office building, built with an RFC loan by the College and leased to the Agricultural Adjustment Administration of the U.S. Department of Agriculture.[86] The Board of Directors rooms were air-conditioned in 1940, and a new mule barn was built the same year.[87] Guion Hall was outfitted for picture shows; the Aggieland Inn underwent minor repairs; and the

---

[81]*Ibid.*, 163-166; Minutes of the Board of Directors, October 28, 1939, V, 210; see also, Charles Perkins Fountain, Charles S. Gainer, George Rollie White, Henry C. Schumacher, Edwin J. Kiest, Biographical Papers, Texas A&M University Archives.

[82]*Directory of Former Students 1876-1970*, xii-xiii.

[83]Minutes of the Board of Directors, October 28, 1939, V, 210-211.

[84]*Ibid.*, November 29, 1939, V, 217; Charles Deware Biographical Papers, Texas A&M University Archives.

[85]Minutes of the Board of Directors, May 30, 1940, VI, 26.

[86]*Ibid.*, March 9, 1940, VI, 11.

[87]*Ibid.*, April 15, 1940, VI, 15; August 6, 1940, VI, 44.

two small lakes on College property were drained in an effort to eradicate mosquitoes.[88]

Gibb Gilchrist, newly appointed dean of Engineering, established a Department of Aeronautical Engineering during his first year at A&M, and simultaneously began planning for the development of a flight-training program with suitable airport facilities. In 1939 the Civil Aeronautics Authority received congressional authorization "to cooperate with various colleges and universities over the country in connection with student pilot training courses." Gilchrist applied to the CAA for certification for Texas A&M to give primary flight training, and primary and secondary ground-school courses, and certification was approved.[89] The subsequent development of Texas A&M's airport facility, better known as Easterwood Airport, became a lesson in bureaucratic red tape, administrative headaches, and success.

In the spring of 1940 Congress budgeted $25 million for WPA (Works Progress Administration) airport construction projects. A grant under the WPA program, Gilchrist learned, required certification from the War Department that the project would be suitable for purposes of national defense. After some delay and confusion Texas A&M received the necessary War Department approval for its projected airport project. While negotiations were pending with the WPA and the War Department, Congress allocated $40 million dollars to the Civil Aeronautics Authority to develop 250 airports around the country. Texas A&M then applied to the CAA for an airport-construction grant, assuming that the WPA grant would fail to materialize. The CAA awarded a $75,000 grant to A&M, and soon afterwards, the WPA informed the College that it would be the authorizing agency for the project, and that the airport project would be a joint effort by the CAA and the WPA with grants from both sources totaling $229,970, far exceeding College expectations.[90]

By May 1940 the project had been confirmed by the necessary authorities, and upon the recommendation of Dean Gilchrist the Board directed that the airport be named Jesse E. Easterwood Airport, "because it was felt that his life and activities best typify the spirit of the A. and M. College." Jesse Easterwood left A&M in 1917 to enlist in the Naval Air Service, received a commission as ensign and won promotions to the rank of lieutenant. He served with the British Royal Flying Corps in 1918, and completed sixteen successful raids behind German lines. Easterwood was killed in a plane acci-

[88]*Ibid.*, June 1, 1939, V, 196; October 14, 1939, V, 206; July 12, 1941, VI, 128.
[89]Bryan *Daily Eagle* (Supplement), September 4, 1941.
[90]*Ibid.*

dent in the Canal Zone on May 19, 1919, and was awarded posthumously the Navy Cross.[91]

The airport was developed on 500 acres of College property located on the western edge of the campus. To this acreage the College added other portions of land by purchasing tracts from adjacent landowners. Construction of runways was completed in May 1941, lights were added with an additional $75,000 WPA grant, and the facility was formally dedicated on May 22, 1941.[92] Texas A&M became one of the few colleges in the country which owned its own airport facility, which in later days became a not altogether happy circumstance. Time passed almost too fast. War training for pilots was soon shifted to a new Air Force training facility west of Bryan, and within a few decades the "air age" had given way to the "space age."

The most significant campus development program of the prewar era involved the exclusion of faculty housing from the campus. Because of the isolation of the College from commercial and residential development, the College, since the beginning, had been forced to provide housing for its instructors. After World War I more and more of the faculty had chosen to live off campus, some in Bryan, but many in homes of their own construction on private property adjacent to the campus. The advent of the automobile age, combined with the rapid growth of the College and its personnel, and the lean budget of the College for housing construction between 1925 and 1941, further forced the development of an off-campus community during the twenties and thirties. By 1938 a sufficient community had developed that a number of "local citizens" headed by John Thomas Lamar McNew, professor of highway engineering, began planning for the incorporation of the community. McNew appeared before the Board of Directors in March 1938, indicating the desire of local residents to be incorporated into a town. The Directors had no objections, and advised the citizens to incorporate a complete belt of land around the campus,[93] a suggestion which was implemented in October 1938. College Station, Texas, which had originated as a "flag station" on the old Houston and Texas Central Railroad in 1876, and which added a post office in 1877 but little more before 1900, became an incorporated city under the General Laws of the State of Texas in 1938. Elections for

[91]*Ibid.;* Minutes of the Board of Directors, May 11, 1940, VI, 25.

[92]Bryan *Daily Eagle* (Supplement), September 4, 1941; see also "Easterwood Airport," Texas A&M University Archives. The tracts purchased to add to airport properties included John Ettle, 24 acres; Dowling Tract, 127 acres; Martinez Tract, 25 acres; John T. Ettle, 9.1 acres; E. C. Jones. 6.4 acres (Minutes of the Board of Directors, October 4, 1941, VI, 144; May 14, 1942, VI, 188).

[93]Minutes of the Board of Directors, March 12, 1938, V, 134.

city offices, organized under the council-manager form of government, were held on November 18, 1938. John H. Binney was elected mayor, John S. Hopper, city marshall, and George B. Wilcox, Ernest Langford, Luther G. Jones, Letcher P. Gabbard, and Alva Mitchell, aldermen. Frank G. Anderson followed Binney as mayor, and in 1942 Ernest Langford replaced Anderson. Langford served in that post, without remuneration, as did all city officials other than the marshall, until 1966. In 1940 the census recorded 2,200 inhabitants of College Station, Texas, and thirty years later, over 20,000.[94]

The development of an incorporated town relieved the College of one of its greatest burdens, that of housing its own personnel, which throughout the years abetted the charges that the College was "poorly located" and required the duplication of facilities which one might ordinarily find in a more urban setting. The Directors seized upon the opportunity to end permanently College-supported housing. In September 1939 the Directors adopted a resolution requiring that "on or before September 1, 1941, all campus residences be vacated and those that are vacated prior to that time be not re-rented or occupied." This did not include residences occupied by officials required to live on campus.[95] The next year officials conducted a survey, at the Board's direction, to see whether the faculty would like to buy the campus houses, to be moved to locations off campus, and in March 1941 the sale of campus houses was authorized.[96] The Directors then agreed to pay each faculty member for any improvements made in the fifty-three University-owned homes, with adequate depreciation. Fifty-three faculty members subsequently received varying portions of $8,477.25 paid out for improvements.[97] College Station and neighboring Bryan subsequently received a fresh influx of population and many new homes.

By 1941 the Depression was over. It left a number of interesting legacies at Texas A&M; more buildings and lower salaries, more students and fewer courses, an airport, a fireman's school, a nonfunded maritime academy, project houses, government projects, an incorporated town, a legislative committee indictment, and a school spirit unparalleled in the history of the College. Then came World War II.

[94]College Station, Texas, Papers, Texas A&M University Archives.
[95]Minutes of the Board of Directors, September 2, 1939, V, 204.
[96]*Ibid.,* August 6, 1940, VI, 43; March 8, 1941, VI, 86.
[97]*Ibid.,* January 10, 1942, VI, 166.

CHAPTER 21

The Fighting Texas Aggies

MEN from Texas A&M fought and died on every battlefield of World War II. The school, said Douglas MacArthur, commander of American forces in the Pacific in 1942, "is writing its own military history in the blood of its graduates."[1] In 1946 Dwight D. Eisenhower, chief of staff, said:

> No more convincing testimony could be given to the manner in which the men of Texas A&M lived up to the ideals and principles inculcated in their days on the campus than the simple statement that the Congressional Medal of Honor has been awarded to six former students, that 46 took part in the heroic defense of Bataan and Corregidor, and that nearly 700 are on the list of our battle dead.[2]

Almost twenty thousand Texas A&M former students served in the Armed Forces during World War II, some fourteen thousand of them as officers, and twenty-nine of these in the rank of general. Texas A&M furnished more officers than did even the United States Military Academy at West Point.[3] Aggies were at Pearl Harbor, Bataan, Corregidor, Midway, and Guadalcanal, with James Doolittle over Tokyo, at Normandy, North Africa, Italy, and the Battle of the Bulge. "The men of Texas A. & M.," General Omar Bradley told the graduating Class of 1950, "can stand up to any men in the world and compare favorably their education and training for leadership — leadership in the pursuits of peace, and if it comes to war, leadership in battle."[4]

Although largely ignored by the American people, World War II had been brewing in Europe and Asia for years. The seeds of the second world war, indeed, were sown in the Peace of Versailles. Open warfare began in Asia when Japan invaded Manchuria in 1931, and some half-dozen years later,

---

[1]College Station *Texas Aggie*, November 20, 1943.

[2]Houston *Post*, April 22, 1946. Note: Later figures put the list of dead at 950.

[3]*Ibid.*; Texas A&M, *Annual Report, 1944-1945*, p. 5; Texas A&M, *1876 . . . 1951, 75th Anniversary* [10-11].

[4] Texas A&M, *1876 . . . 1951, 75th Anniversary* [11].

marched into China. In 1935 Italian dictator Benito Mussolini invaded Ethiopia, and in the same year Adolph Hitler, of Germany, who had lately abolished constitutional processes and all political parties but the National Socialist German Workers' Party (Nazi), and had made himself "Fuehrer," proceeded to rebuild German armies. Between 1936 and 1939 Hitler fortified the Rhineland, and took Austria and Czechoslovakia piece by piece. Mussolini seized Albania. Then Hitler invaded Poland from the West, and Russia, which had lately entered into an alliance with Hitler, moved in from the East. Great Britain and France declared war on Germany on September 3, 1939. By June 1940 Hitler had conquered Denmark, Norway, Belgium, Holland, and France, and possessed two-thirds of Poland. He then turned his armies against Russia.

The United States, said Franklin D. Roosevelt, "hates war" and "hopes for peace." But while the American Congress debated neutrality legislation, it authorized the rearmament of America for war. In September 1940 Congress, at the urging of Roosevelt, passed the Selective Service Act. While both presidential candidates, Franklin D. Roosevelt and Wendell L. Willkie, promised to keep America out of war, war moved inexorably closer. Its imminence began to be felt at Texas A&M in early 1939, when the Board of Directors authorized President Thomas O. Walton to offer the services of the College to the national government in any needed capacity.[5] Pointing to the necessities of national defense, in late spring Texas A&M launched a campaign urging Texas high-school boys to attend a military college.[6] Charles Monroe ("Tennessee") Johnson, who graduated in June 1939, was probably the first Aggie to go to war. He felt so strongly about Hitler's aggression in Europe that in May of 1940, he temporarily renounced his American citizenship, hitchhiked to Canada and joined the Canadian Seaforths with which he served for the next five and one-half years.[7] While Franklin D. Roosevelt and Winston Churchill in August 1940, at sea "somewhere in the Atlantic," worked over the text of the Atlantic Charter, which provided a statement of Allied war aims, Texas A&M conducted a survey of its facilities useful to national defense.[8]

The following month, September 1940, as National Guard units began to be called to active duty, students began to leave the campus. The College returned all unspent fees to those called to duty. Ross Hall was repaired and converted to the use of the military-science program. The Directors author-

[5]College Station *Battalion*, March 7, 1942.
[6]*Ibid.*
[7]Charles Monroe Johnson, *Action with the Seaforths*, flyleaf.
[8]Minutes of the Board of Directors, August 6, 1940, VI, 39.

ized a short course in chemical warfare, and in June 1941, while Hitler's armies rolled through France, the Directors went on record in support of a bill to provide universal military training.[9] Thus by late 1941 Texas A&M was as well prepared or as ill prepared for war as was the rest of the nation. Suddenly, on Sunday, December 7, 1941, Texas A&M, with the rest of the United States, was swept into the whirlwind of war.

The A&M campus was quiet that Sunday afternoon. Many students were at the campus theater watching "A Yank in the R.A.F." The film snapped and amidst the proverbial catcalls and boos the theater manager, Charlie Tiegner, announced, "If you would care to know, Japanese forces have just bombed Pearl Harbor." There was shock and disbelief, followed by yells, "Beat the hell out of Japan," and "Let's take a Corps trip to Tokyo."[10] Many Aggies were already close to the Japanese Empire — prominently at Corregidor, Bataan, Mindanao, and Midway.

President Franklin D. Roosevelt, on December 8, 1941, asked Congress for a declaration of war against Japan; that afternoon the Academic Council of Texas A&M, representing the faculty and the administration, adopted a resolution extending all facilities of the College to the national government for the war effort.[11] President Walton and Colonel Maurice D. Welty, commandant of the Corps of Cadets, meanwhile urged all students to remain in school. "When your country needs you, it will call," they said.[12] And it did. Some, to be sure, had already been called.

When Colonel George F. Moore, commandant of the Corps of Cadets and a 1908 graduate of Texas A&M, left College Station in 1940, he selected thirty-five graduating Aggies to precede him to his new post in the Philippines. When the Japanese invaded the Philippines in December 1941, American forces retreated into the Bataan Peninsula, across the bay from Manila. In April 1942, after a bitter defense and prolonged siege, Bataan fell. Some survivors managed to cross over to the adjoining American fortress of Corregidor under the command of Lieutenant General Jonathan M. Wainwright, where Major General George Moore commanded units at Fort Mills. On April 21, 1942, twenty-five Aggies, including Moore, celebrated San Jacinto day on Corregidor. They drank toasts of water to the Texas heroes of 1836, sang A&M songs, told stories of their college days, and had their "muster"

---

[9]*Ibid.*, September 25, 1940, VI, 52, 53; March 8, 1941, VI, 85; June 5, 1941, VI, 121; July 12, 1941, VI, 125.

[10]College Station *Battalion*, December 9, 1941.

[11]*Ibid.*

[12]*Ibid.*

interrupted by Japanese shells. Within two weeks they were dead or imprisoned.[13] Corregidor had fallen. Those A&M heroes were these men:[14]

	Class	*Hometown*
Major General George F. Moore	1908	Fort Worth
Major Tom Dooley	1935	McKinney
Major (Marine) Paul A. Brown	1929	Galveston
Major John V. King	1922	College Station
Captain Chester A. Peyton	1935	Corpus Christi
Captain William Mark Curtis	1932	Covington
Captain Roy M. Vick, Jr.	1935	Bryan
Captain Wilbert A. Calvert	1938	Archer City
Captain Henry J. Schutte, Jr.	1939	Houston
Captain Graham M. Hatch	1931	Dallas
Captain Jerome A. McDavitt	1933	San Antonio
Captain Stockton D. Bruns	1935	Louise
Captain Willis A. Scrivener	1937	Taft
Lieutenant John McCluskey	1936	Anderson
Lieutenant David Snell	1937	Dallas
Lieutenant Lewis B. Chevallier	1939	Marshall
Lieutenant Carl Pipkin	1940	Beaumont
Lieutenant Clifton Chamberlain	1940	Wichita Falls
Lieutenant William Hamilton	1940	Dallas
Lieutenant Charlton Wimer	1939	San Antonio
Lieutenant William Boyd	1938	Amarillo
Lieutenant Andy James	1940	Dalhart
Lieutenant Urban C. Hopmann	1940	Beaumont
Lieutenant Stanley Friedline	1940	Grand Saline
Sergeant Hugh Hunt	1938	Carthage

Thus was formed the Corregidor Chapter of the Alumni Association of the Agricultural and Mechanical College of Texas.[15] The Aggies at Corregidor were commemorated by Congress in 1942,[16] and by the initiation of a

[13]*Ibid.*, April 23, 1942; Houston *Post*, November 11, 1942, April 7, 1946, April 21, 1946; *Time*, May 4, 1942, p. 23; College Station *Texas Aggie*, November 6, 1942; College Station *Longhorn*, 1943, p. 66.

[14]"A&M Men Present at Famous Aggie Muster on April 21, 1942, on Island of Corregidor," Corregidor Muster File, Association of Former Students Office, Texas A&M University.

[15]News release by Senator Tom Connally, April 21, 1942, in Corregidor Muster File, Association of Former Students Office, Texas A&M University.

[16]*Congressional Record*, 77th Cong., 2nd sess., vol. 88, pp. A1453-A1454; College Station *Battalion*, April 23, 1943; College Station *Texas Aggie*, May 5, 1942.

unique and now traditional muster ceremony on the College Station campus in 1943. In these ceremonies a poem written by Dr. John Ashton ('06), of the Department of Rural Sociology, not to be published, but for the oral tradition only, was read to the assembled cadets. As the names of the heroes of Corregidor were read, a friend and comrade answered the roll call, "Here!"[17] So the former men of A&M live on in A&M tradition.

After the reconquest of the Philippines by American forces a number of Aggies visited Corregidor. One of these, Lieutenant Colonel Ormond Simpson ('36), reported, "It is a scene of incredible physical devastation. There is not a square foot that has not been fought over, shot up or bombed."[18] Captain Robley David Evans ('40), taken prisoner in the Bataan attack and a survivor of the March of Death who spent almost four years in the Canatuar (POW) Camp, recalled that some 6,000 men were in the camp. Vitamin deficiency and hunger produced blindness, and death, sometimes at the rate of fifty or sixty men a day. A teacup and a half of cooked rice, and a thin soup made with camote, or sweet potato, comprised the daily ration. "Funny thing," said Evans, "the worst part of that blindness were the lice that infested our cells. We could feel them, but we couldn't see to hunt them."[19]

The desperate defense by American forces in the South Pacific also involved A&M men in action at Mindanao, the Coral Sea, and Midway. In early 1942 James Connally ('32), a cousin of then Texas Senator Tom Connally, led a bombing mission of five planes from Java to Mindanao in the Philippines through violent weather, sank a Japanese freighter in the midst of a convoy, and landed on Mindanao to rescue twenty-three stranded American pilots. Connally received the Distinguished Service Cross for the action. He died later in combat over Yokohama, Japan, in 1945. In 1949 the old Waco Army Air Field was renamed James Connally Air Force Base in his honor.[20] Connally's brother, Clem ('38), received the Navy Cross in 1942 for his action as a dive-bomber pilot in the battle of the Coral Sea.[21]

At the battle of Midway in June 1942, which blunted Japanese striking power in the Pacific, Captain Charles Gregory ('38) flew fifty-seven combat

[17]Instructions for 1943 Muster and John Ashton, "Heroes Roll Call," in Corregidor Muster File, Association of Former Students Office, Texas A&M University.

[18]Lieutenant Colonel Ormond Simpson, Philippines, to E. E. (Mac) McQuillen, College Station, Texas, April 21, 1945, in Corregidor Muster File, Association of Former Students Office, Texas A&M University.

[19]College Station *Texas Aggie*, November 1, 1945.

[20]College Station *Battalion*, April 23, 1942; College Station *Texas Aggie*, March 20, 1942; Waco *Tribune Herald*, October 2, 1960; Houston *Post*, October 13, 1967 (Connally AFB deactivated); see also James Connally Biographical Papers, Texas A&M University Archives.

[21]College Station *Texas Aggie*, November 6, 1942.

hours in four days.[22] George H. Gay ('40) flew a Navy torpedo plane in the battle. He was the only survivor of Torpedo Squadron 8; all fifteen of the Squadron's planes were shot down, including Gay's. Described as an average cadet, Gay had failed the Army physical for pilot training, but had been accepted by the Navy. When rescued from the sea after the battle the doctors asked Gay what treatment he had given his burns. Gay answered, "Well, I soaked 'em in salt water for ten hours." During the War he won the Navy Cross, with Air Medal, and several citations for bravery.[23] Although in the earlier phases of the War fewer Americans served in the European and African theaters than in the Pacific, among the Aggies who were in combat across the Atlantic was Captain John I. Hopkins, Jr. ('40), who flew bomber missions against German columns in the Egyptian desert.[24]

By October 1942 about 6,500 Texas Aggies were in service, most of them officers, and twenty-three were known to have been decorated for bravery.[25] Among these twenty-three were Major Hervey H. Whitfield ('34), Distinguished Flying Cross; General George Moore ('08), Distinguished Service Cross; Lieutenant Harry Schreiber ('36), Purple Heart; Major Henry C. Dittman ('39), Distinguished Service Cross; Lieutenant Elbert D. Reynolds ('32), Distinguished Flying Cross; Major Louis E. Hobbs ('28), High Valor Award; Major Paul A. Brown ('28), Silver Star; Lieutenant Thomas C. Day ('41), commendation for bravery; Lieutenant William R. Walker ('45), Distinguished Flying Cross; Lieutenant William H. Baker ('42), Distinguished Flying Cross; Lieutenant James M. Rowland ('41), Silver Star (posthumously); Lieutenant John Jefferson Keeter, Jr. ('40), Silver Star (posthumously); Lieutenant Hiram A. Putnam ('38), Distinguished Flying Cross (posthumously); Colonel Noel Pazdral ('27), Silver Star (Medical Corps); Lieutenant Everett Davis ('39), Soldiers Medal for Heroism; Colonel William D. Old ('24), Silver Star; and Lieutenant Jaime S. Morris ('39), citation for heroism.[26]

A number of Texas Aggies participated in one of the most daring events of the early War years — General James Doolittle's April 1942 raid on Tokyo. At a time when things were particularly bleak for Allied Forces in the

[22]*Ibid.*, July 9, 1942.

[23]*Ibid.*, July 9, 1942, February 1, 1944; Houston *Post*, November 11, 1942, September 13, 1951; Colonel Red Reeder, *The Story of the Second World War: The Axis Strikes, 1939-1942*, p. 234; Ira Marion, "An Aggie Goes to War," episode No. 96 of the Blue Playhouse, 1-19, TQN Program File, Association of Former Students Office, Texas A&M University.

[24]College Station *Texas Aggie*, October 15, 1942.

[25]Houston *Post*, November 11, 1942.

[26]*Ibid.*; College Station *Battalion*, April 23, 1942.

Pacific, the bombing raid on the Japanese mainland was a badly needed morale booster for the Allies. With no American air base within range of Japan, Doolittle and his volunteers took off from carriers in land-based bombers for a one-way trip over Japan, intending to land when they ran out of fuel, "somewhere in China." Major John A. Hilger ('32), known as "Jack" and "Sissy" Hilger at A&M, was second in command under Doolittle. Hilger's brother, Ted Adair Hilger ('34) was killed in combat off the Java coast shortly before the flight. Other former students accompanying Hilger and Doolittle included Lieutenant William N. Fitzhugh, Captain Robert Manning Gray ('41), and Major James M. Parker ('41), all of whom, with Hilger, were awarded the Distinguished Flying Cross.[27] Until the attack on Guadalcanal in November 1942 American forces were everywhere on the defense. There was little "war planning" as such; American forces responded as best they could to enemy attacks.

At "home" there was also considerable confusion and a lack of "war planning" during the first years of conflict. At Texas A&M there was less planning and more "response" to given needs and situations, the most critical need being manpower for the Armed Forces. As an initial response to this need A&M officials placed the institution and its branches on a three-semester basis of sixteen weeks, for a twelve-month school year, allowing students to earn degrees in three, rather than four, calendar years.[28] In January the Directors additionally authorized the establishment of the first military training program on campus, a program to train 2,050 airmen in air navigation and as bombardiers.[29] Texas A&M's great contribution to the war effort included not only sending its students to war, but the training of 23,604 Army personnel in engineering, science, and management war-training courses; the training of 13,364 Navy and Marine personnel in radar and radio operation and maintenance; the schooling of 4,000 Air Corps preflight cadets; and the training of 4,105 students in the Army Specialized Training Program.[30] Just as industry was converting from peace-time to war-time production, so too was Texas A&M converting to war production.

As a part of the war program at A&M, discipline was tightened, physical training was increased, and the "indoctrination" of freshmen was relaxed.

---

[27]Carroll V. Glines, *Doolittle's Raiders*, vii, 42-43, 263-265, 278, 417-418, 429; College Station *Texas Aggie*, July 9, 1942, May 25, 1942; Houston *Post*, September 13, 1942, November 11, 1942; College Station *Longhorn, 1943*, p. 352.

[28]Minutes of the Board of Directors, January 10, 1942, VI, 167; College Station *Battalion*, January 13, 1942.

[29]Minutes of the Board of Directors, January 10, 1942, VI, 169.

[30]Texas A&M, *Annual Report, 1944-1945*, p. 5.

Students were called to reveille formation, followed by morning calisthenics, with expanded "phys-ed" in the afternoon. The commandant, Maurice D. Welty, prohibited "bleed sessions," fish-room orderlies, and the running of "details" by freshmen.[31] In January the minimum age requirement for appointment as Army officers was lowered to eighteen years.[32] In February the regular R.O.T.C. program added a Quartermaster Corps.[33] Throughout the early months of the War students were leaving campus to join the services. Others felt confused by the fact that on the one hand they were advised to stay in school and to continue their studies in those areas recognized by the federal government as vital to national defense, including engineering, medicine, dentistry, veterinary medicine, and the sciences, and on the other hand, if they did remain in school, they often found themselves drafted.[34]

Adding to the confusion, the War Department during 1942 created a number of new training programs which were often revised after being established. In May the War Department organized the Army Enlisted Reserve Corps for college students. Under this plan students could enlist in the services and attend college on an inactive-duty status. In their second year of college they were required to pass a general examination in order to continue in school. Those who failed to pass, or to show promise of leadership capacity, were immediately inducted into active duty.[35] The idea of the program was to give college students a greater degree of "job security" and the opportunity for academic planning. Under this program all contract R.O.T.C. sophomore students were required to enlist in service before taking advanced courses. If any student then failed to complete advanced study or dropped out of school he was immediately inducted into service.[36] In theory those who maintained a good academic record could expect to finish school and be commissioned.

In practice academic studies gave way almost entirely to the necessity of providing manpower for war. The tenuous academic security theoretically provided by the Enlisted Reserve Corps (ERC) soon evaporated. In September 1942 Secretary of War Henry L. Stimson announced that all college-stu-

[31]College Station *Texas Aggie,* January 31, 1942.

[32]College Station *Battalion,* January 31, 1942.

[33]*Ibid.,* February 28, 1942.

[34]College Station *Texas Aggie,* February 20, 1942.

[35]U.S. War Department, Bureau of Public Relations, "News Release, May 14, 1942," in Army, Navy, Marine Programs, WW II, Texas A&M University Archives; Texas A&M, *Annual Report, 1941-1942,* pp. 10-11.

[36]College Station *Battalion,* May 2, 1942.

dent members of the ERC would be called to active duty as soon as they reached the age of eighteen.[37] Some time passed, however, before any blanket calls of eighteen-year-olds came. In the meanwhile rumors were rife on the A&M campus. Students heard that the Army was to take over the school and that no more diplomas would be granted, thus ending for the time all regular academic pursuits. Other rumors held that because of A&M's status as an "essential military" school, the normal academic and military training program would be continued.[38]

The War Department also soon scrapped advanced R.O.T.C. training entirely and substituted the Army Specialized Training Program, which, while conducted on campus, further removed the cadet from civilian study.[39] In December 1942 all juniors and some seniors, a total of 1,306 men, who had been in advanced R.O.T.C. were called to active duty and assigned to Texas A&M for one semester in the Army Specialized Training Program as enlisted men at enlisted men's pay. At the conclusion of the semester they were sent to replacement training centers and then to an officer-candidate school prior to commissioning. Some of the seniors were commissioned directly after training at the replacement centers or at branch schools.[40]

In October 1942 the Former Students Association of Texas A&M addressed a letter to the President of the United States, the Texas delegation in Congress, the Secretary of War, and General Lewis B. Hershey expressing concern over the confusing draft situation and advising the adoption of a coordinated national policy.[41] The letter emphasized that:

> College men want to do their part to win the war. They should be told what their part is to be, where and how they can best serve, and what their Nation wants and expects them to do.

The Present Situation

College and university men face this confused and confusing situation:

1. Their own and national leaders have urged them to stay in school to better prepare themselves for war service.

2. Army, Navy, Marine, and other military divisions shoot high-powered appeals for enlistment in various reserve programs.

3. Local draft boards operate without a definite national rule and are often as confused as are college men.

---

[37]*Ibid.*, September 12, 1942.

[38]*Ibid.*, January 30, 1943.

[39]Texas A&M, *Annual Report, 1942-1943*, pp. 7-8.

[40]College Station *Battalion*, December 31, 1942; College Station *Texas Aggie*, January 5, 1942, March 19, 1943; Texas A&M, *Annual Report, 1942-1943*, p. 7.

[41]*Congressional Record*, 77th Congress, 2nd sess., vol. 88, part 10, pp. A3784-A3785.

4. By implication, at least, promises are made, then broken; for example, the statement of the Secretary of War that Army Enlisted Reserves would be called upon reaching military age.

5. No required or recommended curriculum has been established. No physical education or military training has been provided in many schools. Exceptions are the Reserve Officers' Training Corps land-grant institutions where military training is given. An outstanding exception is the Agricultural and Mechanical College of Texas, where 6,000 students live under military rule and where military training is required and emphasized.

6. Lowering of conscription age to 18 greatly increases the vital need of a definite, established, and followed policy in regard to college students.

The Result

A total lapse in the college training of men is threatened. If that training is of value in the war program, then action now should be taken to protect and control it.

By January 1943, however, most doubts about the draft situation had been removed; everyone available was going to war. Juniors and seniors at A&M had been inducted into service, but many of them remained on campus for a time, and most other eighteen-year-olds, including those in ERC, were being called to active duty. As a result the campus was being rapidly depopulated of all students except those under age, those having physical disabilities, those awaiting induction, a few returning veterans, and those servicemen in training schools. In May 1943, within a period of forty-eight hours, the 1,306 juniors and seniors who had been previously inducted, left the campus.[42] By 1944 the only students having academic deferments of any kind were those in veterinary medicine.[43]

Texas A&M enrollment, which reached a high of 6,679 students in 1941, declined only slightly, to 6,549, by the opening of the fall session in 1942, but then dropped precipitously between 1942 and 1943. By February 1943 enrollment had dropped to fewer than 4,000 students, and by September was down to 2,205. In December 1944, 1,893 students were enrolled, of whom 1,025 were below the age of eighteen. Thirty-one were over the draft age of thirty-eight (later raised to forty-five), 65 were returning veterans, 180 had physical disabilities, 190 were in veterinary medicine, 356 were in the reserves awaiting call, one was on active duty, and 45 were foreign students.[44]

[42]Texas A&M, *Annual Report, 1944-1945*, p. 13.

[43]*Ibid., 1943-1944*, p. 5.

[44]Texas A&M, Committee on Postwar Planning and Policy, "Forecast of Postwar Enrollment," March 21, 1944, p. 17, in Texas A&M University Archives; College Station *Battalion*, January 30, 1943; December 8, 1944.

Enrollment in the graduate program declined even more drastically. From a high of 376 graduate students in 1940, the number in graduate studies dropped to 48 in 1943.[45] Essentially all available manpower at A&M had gone to war.

During the early years of the War the ranks of college professors and employees also declined critically. By October 1942, 322 A&M employees had entered the Armed Services or taken jobs in war industries. Soaring salaries in industry attracted many older professors and employees away from the College. As a result the first real hike in salary levels since the advent of the Great Depression was effected by the Board of Directors in October 1942, in an effort to retain faculty and staff.[46] A year later the teacher shortage continued to be critical, but throughout 1944 and 1945 the "shortage" suddenly turned into a glut, as the civilian student body all but disappeared.[47] By March 1945 some faculty were attempting to return to their teaching positions only to find they were no longer needed. The school had become overstaffed and employees were encouraged to find temporary employment in industry.[48] Generally, although there were periods of imbalance, the supply of teachers was proportionate to the supply of students.

Students and faculty at the College during the War years put in a six-day work week ending at 4:00 P.M. on Saturday. A compulsory study and quiet period began at 7:00 P.M. in the dormitories, and in the hours from 8:00 A.M. to 4:00 P.M. "study conditions" were maintained in the dormitories.[49] Faculty members lectured fifteen to eighteen hours a week, counseled students, graded papers, and worked on various special projects, on research, and in war drives. The Agricultural Extension Service managed the Food for Freedom program designed to increase farm production and to reduce consumer dependence on commercial production by encouraging home "victory gardens." The Agricultural Experiment Station engaged in research work to stimulate production, and experimented with new crops and various substitute products. Experiment Station staff taught courses in Army mess management in the military-science program and special short courses. One important development, perfected by Professor Robert E. Karper, was the produc-

[45]Texas A&M, *President's Report on the Agricultural and Mechanical College of Texas, May 15, 1943*, p. 12.

[46]Texas A&M, *Annual Report, 1941-1942*, p. 7; Minutes of the Board of Directors, October 10, 1942, VI, 193.

[47]Texas A&M, *President's Report, May 14, 1943*, p. 1; Texas A&M, *Annual Report, 1943-1944*, p. 6.

[48]Texas A&M, *Annual Report, 1943-1944*, p. 6.

[49]College Station *Battalion,* January 30, 1943.

tion of starch from grain sorghum. Starch was in short supply during the War because of the loss of sources of supply of cassava roots in the East Indies.[50] Engineers staffed and directed many of the war schools on campus.

The Army Air Force established its preflight training school on campus in February 1943, and assigned 4,092 students for special training.[51] The following month the College contracted to train five hundred engineers for the Army in a specialized training program.[52] In May the Directors requested the establishment of a V-12, naval officer-training program at A&M, for training 400-600 men.[53] Texas A&M contributed even to the war-propaganda effort.

In 1943 a "war movie" entitled "We've Never Been Licked" tied the spirit of Aggieland to national defense. Produced by Walter Wanger, and directed by Jack Rawlins, with script by Norman Reilly Raine (author of the Tug Boat Annie stories, tremendously popular in the *Saturday Evening Post* during the 1940s and 1950s), the movie depicts the story of Brad Craig (Richard Quine), who enrolls at A&M fresh from Japan, where he had been living with his father, Colonel Craig, who was on overseas assignment. In the setting of the marching Corps, Aggie traditions, friendly coeds from Texas State College for Women, and kindly professors, Craig becomes something of an outcast. His notoriety becomes greater when he becomes chummy with two Japanese students and the Japanese gardener. On the eve of the Japanese attack on Pearl Harbor, a plot to stage an attempt by the Japanese to steal an important chemical formula from the campus laboratory is exposed at A&M. Although Craig foils the theft of the vital formula, he has played the part of the "double agent," and is linked by the cadets and officials to the plot.[54]

The "traitor," who by now has only one friend left in the cadet corps, Cyanide Jenkins (Noah Berry, Jr.), is drummed out of the Corps and dismissed from the College in disgrace. Craig turns up in Japan when war begins with the United States and serves the Japanese as a "Tokyo Rose." During a decisive naval engagement Craig is aboard a Japanese fighter plane broadcasting an account of the Japanese attack. He intercepts the broadcast of American fighter pilots, recognizes the voice of Cyanide Jenkins, seizes control of the plane and radios to the Americans the location of the Japanese fleet. Craig, now obviously always loyal to his country but having selflessly

[50]Houston *Post*, November 11, 1942; Texas A&M, *President's Report, May 15, 1943*, p. 19.

[51]College Station *Texas Aggie*, February 18, 1943; Texas A&M, *Annual Report, 1944-1945*, p. 12.

[52]Minutes of the Board of Directors, March 13, 1943, VI, 208.

[53]*Ibid.*, May 21, 1943, VI, 215.

[54]Houston *Post*, April 14, 1946; College Station *Battalion*, July 28, 30, December 3, 5, 12, 1942; January 4, 1943; College Station *Texas Aggie*, August 13, 1943.

played the role of a secret agent, then dives to attack a Japanese carrier and is killed. The sequel to the story, with which the movie actually opens, are ceremonies in Kyle Field honoring Texas A&M's men in service, and the announcement of the posthumous award of the Congressional Medal of Honor to Brad Craig.[55]

The filming of the movie, most of which was done on campus, involved the entire A&M student body and faculty, townsmen, and coeds from TSCW. In October 1942 the producers sponsored a contest, the winner of which was to receive a $50.00 war bond and introduction to one of the stars, Anne Gwynne, for the best essay on what was meant by "the spirit of Aggieland." Cadet Bob Gulley won first prize and John Stout second.[56] Rawlins, the producer, attended yell practices, football games, classes, and social events in order to capture the "spirit."[57] Filming began in November; some 500 students, joined by 204 TSCW coeds, volunteered to remain on campus during the Thanksgiving holidays to film various scenes. Producers provided free meals for all at Aggieland Inn during the shooting.[58]

During the week of December 7-11 classes at A&M were virtually suspended in order to provide time for filming. For the shooting of the memorial scenes at Kyle Field the producers invited everyone for miles around to sit in the stadium during appointed hours on December 12 and 13, and enticed the crowd with free fried-chicken dinners and barbecue. A full-page advertisement in the Bryan *Eagle* extended the invitation. This effort, however, failed to produce the expected crowds, and according to a disgusted Aggie reporter, only about six hundred townspeople showed up and worse yet, some $700.00 worth of food was wasted — this being the worst offense a hungry Aggie could imagine.[59] President Thomas O. Walton refuted rumors that faculty members were being paid to perform, and, while indicating that the school was honored to be selected for the movie, regretted that so much class time was being lost.[60]

All in all the movie was a tremendous success — at least among Aggies, and continues to be that. "We've Never Been Licked" shows at the Grove Theater, outdoors on campus, at least once a year, and is a vital and proud part of the Aggie tradition.[61]

[55]*Ibid.*

[56]College Station *Battalion*, October 8, 1942, November 21, 1942.

[57]*Ibid.*, October 10, 1942.

[58]*Ibid.*, November 17, 1942; December 1, 1942.

[59]*Ibid.*, December 5, 12, 1942, January 4, 1943.

[60]*Ibid.*, December 12, 1942.

[61]Note: The author saw the movie in the Grove in the summer of 1970.

When the first American Occupation forces moved into Tokyo after the Japanese surrender in 1945 the first official entry into the city was made by a tank of the First Cavalry Division, emblazoned with the Aggie slogan "We've never been licked," and flying the Texas flag.[62] Texas A&M men, and the Aggie spirit, not only contributed to the war effort in terms of spirit and sheer numbers, but in terms of unexcelled examples of courage and determination. Seven A&M men received the nation's highest decoration, the Congressional Medal of Honor, for their combat service.

One of these, Second Lieutenant Lloyd D. Hughes, of Corpus Christi, Texas, scheduled for graduation with the Class of 1943, volunteered for the Army Air Force in 1942 and received his wings at Lubbock, Texas, in November 1942. By the spring of 1943 Hughes was with the Ninth Air Force units operating in North Africa. In August 177 B-24 Liberator bombers, one of them commanded by Hughes, left bases in North Africa for a strategic bombing mission against refineries at Ploesti, Rumania, a major source of German fuel supplies. It was one of the earliest attempts to strike the vital Nazi refineries, and involved a grueling and difficult 2,000 mile round trip. Flying through heavy antiaircraft fire, the bombers struck their targets at tree-top level. Hughes' plane received two direct hits, lost most of its fuel, and was in flames, but Hughes persisted in making his attack, and did so successfully. He then attempted a crash landing, but was killed on impact, although most of his crew survived. Of the 177 aircraft engaged in the strike, 73 failed to return. For his heroic action Hughes was posthumously awarded the Medal of Honor. At Texas A&M a dormitory was named in his honor.[63]

Allied bombing raids of Axis fuel refineries in Rumania and Hungary were a part of the offensive against the Axis underbelly, Sicily and Italy, in 1943. On July 10, 1943, under the overall command of Dwight D. Eisenhower, the British Fifteenth Army Group, under Field Marshall Sir Harold R. L. G. Alexander, spearheaded by General Bernard L. Montgomery's Eighth Army, and the newly organized American Seventh Army, under George S. Patton, invaded Sicily. After a thirty-day campaign Sicily was taken and German troops withdrew across the Straits of Messina into Italy. In September the American Fifth Army, under Lieutenant General Mark W. Clark, led the Allied invasion of Italy. For the next two years Allied invasion forces

---

[62]Wick Fowler, Austin, Texas, to Earl Rudder, College Station, Texas, January 27, 1967, World War II Papers, Texas A&M University Archives.

[63]Lloyd H. Hughes Biographical Papers, Texas A&M University Archives; Lieutenant General Ira C. Eaker, "Strategic Air Power Over Europe," *Bombs Away! Your Air Force in Action*, 206; Bryan *Eagle*, April 20, 1946.

encountered stubborn German resistance at all points — notably at Salerno, Cassino, and Anzio.[64]

As American forces clung tenaciously to the Anzio beachhead, Lieutenant Thomas W. Fowler, a tank-platoon leader, won the Congressional Medal of Honor "for conspicuous gallantry and intrepidity, at risk of life, above and beyond the call of duty, on 23 May 1944, in the vicinity of Corano, Italy." German attacks had opened a gap in American lines. Fowler, in charge of a tank platoon, reorganized the remnants of two infantry platoons caught in an enemy mine field. In a tank and on foot, Fowler cleared a path through the twenty-five-yard mine field, even to the point of leaving his tank and pulling up mines with his bare hands, and then led his troops through, all the while under severe enemy fire. Fowler personally administered aid to nine wounded infantry men, and gave aid to a tank crew under attack during the desperate encounter. His action closed the line and averted what might have been terrible consequences to the entire American force. Fowler emerged untouched in the battle. Ten days later he was killed at the head of his tank platoon when the Fifth Army began its drive on Rome.[65]

Fowler, then twenty-two years old, was born in Wichita Falls, Texas, and entered Texas A&M in 1939. He received his B.S. degree in 1943, and was commissioned a second lieutenant in the Cavalry in May of that year. Fowler Hall, a barracks for the Officer Candidate School at Fort Knox, Kentucky, was named in honor of Thomas Fowler, who was the first Medal of Honor winner graduated from the armored-force officers' school at Fort Knox.[66]

After the fall of Rome in June 1944 Fifth Army units pursued German forces up to the rugged Gothic Line in the North Apennine Mountains, where the bitterest fighting of the already bloody Italian campaign ensued. In the attacks on the keystone of the Gothic Line, Mount Altruzzo, Sergeant George Dennis Keathley, A&M Class of 1935, died in action after so inspiring his men that "they fought with incomparable determination and viciousness."[67]

Company B, 338th Infantry Regiment, Eighty-fifth Division, was

[64]See *American Military History, 1607-1958*, pp. 425-434.

[65]College Station *Texas Aggie*, December 4, 1944; New York *Times*, July 7, 1945; Bryan *Eagle*, April 20, 1946; Thomas W. Fowler Biographical Papers, Texas A&M University Archives.

[66]New York *Times*, July 7, 1945; Thomas W. Fowler Biographical Papers, Texas A&M University Archives.

[67]Bryan *Eagle*, April 20, 1946; George Dennis Keathley Biographical Papers, Texas A&M University Archives.

stopped in its attack on the western ridge of Mount Altruzzo by three consecutive Nazi counterattacks. In the midst of the attacks all Company officers were killed and Sergeant Keathley assumed command. He crawled from casualty to casualty, giving first aid to the living and collecting from the dead ammunition, which he distributed to his surviving men. During the final German attack Keathley was mortally wounded in the stomach by a "potato masher" grenade, but he arose and began firing his rifle, giving orders and encouragement to his men for some fifteen minutes until he dropped dead. Inspired, the men "fought with unwonted determination" and repulsed the attack. The Germans soon withdrew, leaving their dead and wounded. Three days later, September 17, 1944, Mount Altruzzo fell to the Eighty-fifth Division. Keathley received posthumously the Congressional Medal of Honor.[68]

As the Italian campaign reached its pinnacle in the spring and summer of 1944, the Allies launched the invasion of Europe on the coasts of Normandy. On D-Day, June 6, 1944, Allied assault forces struck the beaches of the Contentin (Cherbourg) Peninsula. Preceding them was a special Provisional Ranger Force, assigned specific tactical objectives. This special Ranger unit, comprising 225 men commanded by Lieutenant Colonel James Earl Rudder, of Brady, Texas, a graduate of John Tarleton Agricultural College and Texas A&M, Class of 1932, had the job of scaling the cliffs at Pointe du Hoe and destroying an enemy battery of six coastal guns which commanded both American landing beaches, Utah and Omaha,[69] where at least nineteen other Texas A&M officers with the Second Division accompanied the invasion forces.

Rudder, who coached football and taught school in Brady, Texas, after graduation, and who then joined the coaching staff at John Tarleton Junior College, was called to active duty in 1941. In 1943 he was given the job of selecting and organizing the Second Ranger Battalion at Camp Forrest, Tennessee. The Battalion engaged in training exercises in Florida and on the Isle of Wight in England. At 4:05 A.M. on D-Day the Rangers embarked in their amphibious craft in choppy cold seas, and headed for Pointe du Hoe, which commanded the landing beaches of Omaha and Utah. The Rangers, scheduled to be the first unit ashore, were to hit the beach at 6:30 A.M., five minutes after the naval barrage ended, scale cliffs "as high as a nine-story office building," and within thirty minutes destroy the six German guns. For the assault Rudder and his officers had devised a system of grappling hooks fired

---

[68]*Ibid.;* College Station *Texas Aggie,* April 18, 1945; E. J. Kahn, Jr, and Henry McLemore, *Fighting Divisions,* 108-109.

[69]James Earl Rudder Biographical Papers, Texas A&M University Archives; Omar N. Bradley, *A Soldier's Story,* 269-270; College Station *Texas Aggie,* September 1, 1945.

by mortars, and sectional steel ladders. "No soldier in my command has ever been wished a more difficult task than that which befell the 34-year old commander of this Provisional Ranger Force," Omar N. Bradley wrote later.[70]

Rudder, ordered by his immediate superior to follow the assault forces in, insisted on leading his men in. "I'm sorry, sir," he said, "but I'm going to have to disobey you. If I don't take it — it may not go." Rudder was the first man ashore at Pointe du Hoe, and may well have been the first of the Allied assault forces ashore at Normandy. Many of the landing craft, including the supply boat, capsized in the heavy seas; mortars misfired and ropes on the grapnels were so wet and heavy from seawater that the missiles failed to reach the top of the cliffs. As the Rangers clambered up the steep cliffs German soldiers at the top rolled grenades down on them and cut the lines, but finally a foothold was gained at the top and the guns were seized and demobilized before they were ever fired at the invading forces on the beach.[71]

Once on top, the troops were cut off from relief forces and supplies, and the Rangers held on for two days until Allied forces from the beaches joined them in the position. Rudder was wounded twice, once in the leg by a bullet and once on the arm by debris from an exploding shell, but remained in command. For that action and later service Earl Rudder, one day to become president of Texas A&M, won the Distinguished Service Cross, the Legion of Merit, the Silver Star, the Bronze Star with Oak Cluster, the Purple Heart with Oak Leaf Clusters, the French Legion of Honor with Croix de Guerre and Palm, and the Belgian Order of Leopold with Croix de Guerre and Palm.[72] As commander of the 109th Infantry Regiment, Rudder played a vital role in repulsing the German attack in the Battle of the Bulge.

Ten years after the war Rudder and his son revisited Pointe du Hoe. He found a grapnel at the base of the cliff, and a rope still in place hanging from the top. A rusty gun and a shattered concrete bunker were the only evidence that there had ever been a war. "It would make a good place for raising sheep," Rudder remarked.[73] The invasion in June 1944, however, had marked only the beginning of the battle for Europe.

Allied forces were hamstrung for months by a determined German defense, particularly at vitally needed port facilities. Finally, as the supply sit-

---

[70]*Ibid.;* W. C. Heinz, "I Took My Son to Omaha Beach," *Colliers* (June 11, 1954), pp. 21-27; Lieutenant G. K. Hodenfield, "I Climbed the Cliffs with the Rangers," *Saturday Evening Post* (August 19, 1944), pp. 18-19, 98.

[71]*Ibid.*

[72]*Ibid.*

[73]W. C. Heinz, "I Took My Son to Omaha Beach," *Colliers* (June 11, 1954), pp. 21-27. General Rudder again revisited the site on the twenty-fifth anniversary of the landing.

uation eased, the invading armies began to move inland. Paris and most of France fell, but German resistance stiffened to peak with the Battle of the Bulge in December 1944 and January 1945. Shortly before the German counterattack in December, while advancing into Kommersheidt, Germany, with the invading armies, Lieutenant Turney W. Leonard, a 1942 Texas A&M graduate, aided his tank-destroyer company, a tank company, and 1,100 infantrymen in repelling an attack by two enemy divisions.[74]

Leonard, second in command to Captain Marion C. Pugh, who graduated from Texas A&M in 1941, fought with his tank-destroyer company of twelve guns and one hundred men into Kommerscheidt only to find American units trapped by two superior German divisions. After establishing a foothold in the town, Pugh returned to division headquarters for reinforcements and ammunition; he got no reinforcements but received orders to hold. On his return his ammunition trucks were destroyed and Pugh reached Kommerscheidt in the morning. Leonard and his men had fought all that night, repulsing a German attack. On the second day, November 5, the Americans were attacked from three sides. Casualties were high, and every infantry officer was killed. Leonard left his guns to reorganize the infantry, whom he led in the first attack.[75] Scouting out the enemy alone, "Turney found enemy tanks in a haystack that was boarded at the bottom and our destroyers knocked them out. When ᵤ.e leaders of several infantry units were killed, he took over these groups and reorganized them to keep them in the fight."[76] He was wounded many times but returned to his station.

During the second and third German attacks, spearheaded by a newly entered German Panzer division, Leonard stood on a "bare blazing hilltop and fought with his guns." Using a submachine gun and grenades he knocked out a fifty-caliber machine gun, killed several enemy snipers, directed fire into a German half-track, and remained in the thick of the fighting until a direct shell hit took off the lower part of his arm.[77] "By his superb courage, inspired leadership and indomitable fighting spirit, Lieutenant Leonard enabled our forces to hold the enemy attack and was personally responsible for the direction of fire which destroyed six German tanks."[78] Leonard tied a tourniquet around the stump of his arm and headed for a first-aid station. It was the last

[74]College Station *Texas Aggie,* December 1, 1945; Dallas *Morning News,* April 18, 1946; Bryan *Eagle,* April 20, 1946.

[75]*Ibid.*

[76]College Station *Texas Aggie,* December 1, 1945.

[77]*Ibid.*

[78]*Ibid.*

time he was ever seen. Captain Pugh later wrote a recommendation for Turney Leonard, "the bravest man he ever saw."[79]

As a student at Texas A&M, Leonard was cadet captain of I Company, a Distinguished Student, and an honor graduate in military science. Leonard landed at Omaha beach with the invasion forces and had been in the thick of fighting until reported missing in action. He was posthumously awarded the Congressional Medal of Honor.[80]

American and Allied forces pushed slowly ahead into Germany but in mid-December were rolled back by massive German counterattacks. Company L, Fifteenth Regiment, Third Division, had been promised a rest at the rear on Christmas Day after having fought uninterruptedly for 169 days. When the German offensive struck, Company L was rushed forward to replace a whole battalion of the battered Thirty-sixth Division. The day after Christmas the Company failed in an attack on Sigolsheim, Germany, which was heavily fortified. In the attack forty of the ninety-six men died, and the company commander was severely wounded. Lieutenant Eli Whiteley, who finished A&M one year ahead of Turney Leonard, was made acting company commander. Headquarters ordered another attack immediately. Whiteley told the commanding colonel he would be court-martialed before leading his men to a senseless slaughter. The colonel told Whiteley he would relieve him of his command and replace him with a man who would fight. Whiteley told the colonel he would kill the man who tried to relieve him. No relief came.[81]

That night Whiteley moved his fifty-five men into town and in the early morning began fighting house to house. Whiteley was wounded in the arm and shoulder while leading a charge on a house, but entered and killed its two defenders. "Hurling grenades before him, he stormed the next house alone and killed two and captured eleven defenders." At another house, where his men were held down by heavy fire, Whiteley blasted a hole in the side with a bazooka, rushed in alone with a submachine gun under his good right arm, killing five SS troops and capturing twelve more. Whiteley's company captured the village, but not before Whiteley received another wound in his eye. Whiteley was decorated with the Congressional Medal of Honor.[82] Whiteley returned to his College to become a professor of agronomy. He

[79]Dallas *Morning News,* April 18, 1946.

[80]College Station *Texas Aggie,* December 1, 1945.

[81]New York *Times,* August 19, 1945; Dallas *Morning News,* September 9, 1962; Houston *Chronicle,* September 29, 1968; College Station *Battalion,* November 10, 1971; E. J. Kahn, Jr., and Henry McLemore, *Fighting Divisions,* 5-6.

[82]New York *Times,* August 19, 1945; Houston *Chronicle,* September 29, 1968; College Station *Texas Aggie,* September 10, 1945; Bryan *Eagle,* April 20, 1946.

received his Ph.D. in 1959 from Texas A&M, and lives and works on into the centennial years. He told a reporter years later that he had been angry that day back in 1944, and, besides, he said, "I was better trained than anyone else in the unit" to do the job.[83]

During the battle for Europe, Texas A&M aviators fought the Germans in the sky. Lieutenant Colonel Dexter Hodge ('39), a B-24 pilot, earned the Flying Cross, the Silver Cross, the Distinguished Service Cross, and three oak-leaf clusters.[84] Major Julian R. Thornton, Jr. ('40) won the Distinguished Flying Cross and the Air Medal with three oak-leaf clusters. Thornton, also a B-24 pilot, returned from one mission with his oxygen system, electrical system, part of his instruments, and two engines knocked out, his plane in flames, most of his men wounded, and a full load of live bombs which could not be released.[85]

During 1944 and 1945 fighting was as intense in the Pacific as in Europe. American invasion forces hit the Philippines in 1944 and were still fighting as the War ended. Attacks on key island positions such as Iwo Jima and Okinawa were bitter, costly affairs. On Iwo Jima alone twenty thousand men of the invading force of 100,000 died in action. American marines struck Iwo Jima on February 19, 1945, and by March could measure their progress in yards. Japanese forces were heavily entrenched and gave fanatical resistance. In the battle for Nishi Ridge on this three-by-five-mile island atoll, on one day alone, Saturday, March 3, the Fifth Marine Division lost 8 officers, 127 men killed, and 518 casualties. On that day, too, five men of the Fifth Division won Medals of Honor. One of these was Sergeant William Harrell, a former Texas A&M student who attended between 1939 and 1941.[86]

In 1941, when war erupted, Harrell tried to enlist in the Air Force and Navy, but was rejected, by the Air Force at least, for color blindness. He got work in a Port Arthur refinery, and in 1942 succeeded in enlisting in the Marines. He served in New Zealand and New Caledonia before being sent to NCO School (noncommissioned officers school) and was a sergeant with the Fifth Division in the invasion of Iwo Jima. Before dawn on March 3 Harrell was on watch when the Japanese attacked his position. A grenade broke his thigh and tore off his left hand. With his right hand he killed a Japanese poised over him with a saber, while another shoved a grenade under his head. Harrell pushed the grenade out with his good hand, killing another Japanese soldier with the grenade but losing his other hand. During the attack he

[83]Texas A&M, *Catalogue, 1972-1973*, p. 361; Houston *Chronicle*, September 29, 1968.

[84]College Station *Texas Aggie*, April 17, 1941.

[85]*Ibid.*, February 1, 1944.

[86]Richard F. Newcomb, *Iwo Jima*, 222-223; College Station *Texas Aggie*, February 1963.

killed at least five of the enemy, and was found at dawn still alive with a dozen Japanese dead around him. President Harry S. Truman personally decorated Marine Sergeant Harrell for bravery.[87]

After the war William G. Harrell continued to serve his country in a conspicuous manner as chief of the Prosthetic and Sensory Aids Service of the Veterans Administration regional office in San Antonio. In addition to the Medal of Honor for his wartime service, he received the Purple Heart and the Good Conduct Medal. "The good conduct medal," he said, "was the hardest to get."[88]

One other Texas A&M former student won the nation's highest award for heroism during the War. Horace S. Carswell, Jr., attended the College in 1934-1935, before transferring to Texas Christian University, in Fort Worth, where he completed his education in 1939. During the last year of the war in the Pacific, Carswell served as deputy commander of the 308th Bombardment Group. In a mission to bomb Japanese shipping off the coasts of Japan, Carswell's plane was shot to pieces: "With consummate gallantry and intrepidity, Major Carswell gave his life in a supreme effort to save all members of his crew. His sacrifice, far beyond that required of him, was in keeping with the traditional bravery of American war heroes."[89] Subsequently, in 1949, Tarrant Field, near Fort Worth, was renamed for Major Horace S. Carswell, Jr.[90]

Bergstrom Air Force Base, located five miles from Austin on the south side of the Colorado River, was named for another Aggie, J. A. Earl Bergstrom ('29), killed by the Japanese in a bombing raid on Luzon, in the Philippines, on December 8, 1941, the second day of the War. Originally known as the Del Valle Army Air Field when constructed in 1942, it was later named for Bergstrom, the first war casualty from Austin, Texas.[91]

In the air war in the Pacific, Captain J. Thorpe Robbins ('40) was one of America's leading air aces. A squadron leader of the Head Hunters, attached to the Fifth Air Force Fighter Unit on New Guinea, Robbins, by 1944, accounted for eighteen enemy planes. His squadron had downed a total of 203. Edward H. Wims, in *American Aces in Great Fighter Battles of World War II,* acknowledged Robbins as being "one of the great fighter pilots in the

[87]Richard F. Newcomb, *Iwo Jima,* 222-223; Bryan *Eagle,* April 20, 1946.

[88]William G. Harrell Biographical Papers, Texas A&M University Archives.

[89]Dallas *Morning News,* February 11, 1946.

[90]"World War II Casualties File," Association of Former Students Office, Texas A&M University.

[91]Walter Prescott Webb and H. Bailey Carroll (eds.), *The Handbook of Texas,* I, 149-302; World War II Casualties File, Association of Former Students Office, Texas A&M University.

war."[92] Colonel Carl Storrie ('28), commander of the 318th Bombardment Wing stationed on Guam after its recapture, played an important part in developing low-bombing techniques over Japan.[93]

For every example of unusual heroism by A&M men in the War, there were a thousand examples of men doggedly and determinedly doing their job. The record of the fighting Texas Aggies is a proud and extensive part of the record of American fighting men in World War II. That record would not be complete without mentioning the twenty-nine A&M men who reached the rank of general during the War — a record achieved by few colleges or military institutions in the country:

Major Generals

Roderick R. Allen, 1915	George F. Moore, 1908
Andrew D. Bruce, 1916	Bennett Puryear, Jr. 1906
Percy W. Clarkson, 1915	Otto P. Weyland, 1923
Howard C. Davidson, 1911	Robert B. Williams, 1923
Harry H. Johnson, 1917	Ralph H. Wooten, 1916
Edmond H. Leavey, 1915	

Brigadier Generals

Oscar B. Abbott, 1914	Aubrey L. Moore, 1923
George H. Beverly, 1919	Douglas B. Netherwood, 1908
William C. Crane, Jr., 1910	Robert R. Neyland, Jr., 1914
John F. Davis, 1912	William D. Old, 1924
Claudius M. Easley, 1916	Nat S. Perrine, 1917
William E. Farthing, 1914	John L. Pierce, 1919
Arthur B. Knickerbocker, 1921	John T. Walker, 1917
William L. Lee, 1927	John A. Warden, 1908
Alvin R. Luedecke, 1932	Jerome J. Waters, 1913

Major General Roderick R. Allen commanded the Twelfth Armored Division, which between November 1944 and May 1945 demolished the Colmar Pocket, broke through the Siegfried Line, and drove German forces across the Rhine and into Germany.[94] General Andrew D. Bruce selected the site of Fort Hood and began there a tank-destroyer training program designed to counter Hitler's Panzer division, for which he received the Distinguished Service Cross. In 1943 he commanded the Seventy-seventh Army Division,

[92]College Station *Texas Aggie*, May 12, 1944; Sims, *American Aces*, 82-101.
[93]College Station *Texas Aggie*, November 1, 1945.
[94]Eleanor M. Allen, Washington, D.C., to Ernest Langford, College Station, Texas, September 18, 1970, Roderick R. Allen Papers, Texas A&M University Archives.

which fought on Guam and Okinawa.[95] Ernie Pyle, the noted war correspondent, was killed while covering action of the Seventy-seventh Division on Ieshima. Bruce wrote the epitaph for Pyle's grave, "On this spot the 77th Infantry Division lost a buddy, 18 April 1945."[96]

General Percy Williams Clarkson commanded the Eighty-seventh Infantry Division and the Thirty-third Infantry Division, the latter of which headed the attack on Baguio, in the Philippines.[97] Brigadier General William C. Crane left A&M in 1910 and completed his education at West Point. An artillery officer, he served in Africa and Italy during the war.[98] General Howard C. Davidson commanded the Tenth Air Force in Burma against the Japanese.[99] John F. Davis completed his junior year at A&M before entering West Point, where he graduated in 1915. The foster son of Dean James C. Nagle, Davis served one tour at Texas A&M in the mid-twenties as instructor in military science and tactics and attained the rank of brigadier general during World War II.[100] Major General Harry H. Johnson served as military governor of occupied Rome, and later transferred to the war front in the Pacific.[101] Arthur B. Knickerbocker ('21), an outstanding quarterback during his days at A&M, was the Texas adjutant general under Governor Coke Stevenson during most of the War years.[102] General Edmond H. Leavey attended Texas A&M for two years before obtaining an appointment at West Point. During the War he served in Ireland and North Africa, and as chief of staff for the Armed Services in the Western Pacific.[103]

Major General George F. Moore, commander of forces at Corregidor, a 1908 graduate of A&M and former commandant, was awarded the Distinguished Service Cross by General Douglas MacArthur for his defense at Corregidor.[104] Major General Bennett Puryear, Jr., the brother of Dean Charles Puryear and a 1906 graduate of A&M, commanded marine training detachments at Quantico, Virginia.[105] General Otto Paul Weyland ('23) commanded the Nineteenth Tactical Air Command and supported Patton's Third

[95]Second Division Association, *The Indian Head*, September 1954; Dallas *Morning News*, September 1, 1954.

[96]Dallas *Morning News*, September 1, 1954.

[97]Houston *Post*, April 15, 1946; Honorary Degree File, Texas A&M University Archives.

[98]College Station *Texas Aggie*, September 22, 1944.

[99]*Ibid.*, May 7, 1945.

[100]John F. Davis Biographical Papers, Texas A&M University Archives.

[101]New York *Times*, May 27, 1956.

[102]College Station *Texas Aggie*, March 8, 1943; Dallas *Morning News*, October 8, 1951.

[103]New York *Times*, May 27, 1956.

[104]College Station *Longhorn*, 1943, p. 66; Houston *Post*, November 11, 1942.

[105]Houston *Press*, April 15, 1946.

Army drive through France. "Without the close cooperation of Gen. O. P. Weyland's 19th Tactical Air Command we wouldn't have dared to leave our flanks hanging in the air, deep in Nazi territory," said Patton.[106] Weyland later became the first Aggie to attain the rank of a four-star general, as commander of Far East Air Forces, in 1952.[107]

Major General Robert Boyd Williams was commander of the First Bomber Command at El Paso, and of the First Bombardment Division of the Eighth Air Force in Great Britain in 1943, and commanding general of the Second Air Force in Colorado Springs, Colorado, in 1944.[108] Major General Ralph H. Wooten headed the Army Air Force Technical Training School at Boca Raton, Florida.[109] Oscar L. Abbott, known as "Ock" to his 1913 classmates, held the wartime rank of brigadier general.[110] Brigadier General George H. Beverly attended A&M for two years, leaving in 1917. During World War II he was with the Fifteenth Air Force in the North African, Sicilian, and Italian campaigns.[111]

Brigadier General Claudius M. Easley fought on Leyte and was assistant commander of the Ninety-sixth Infantry Division on Okinawa, where he was killed in action.[112] General William E. Farthing commanded the Seventh Air Force Base Command in Hawaii in 1942.[113] Brigadier General William L. Lee served on the staff of Douglas MacArthur with Dwight D. Eisenhower in the Philippines between 1935 and 1938, where he was chief of the Philippine Air Force. In World War II, when he won his promotion to general, he was commander of the Forty-ninth Bomber Wing of the Fifteenth Air Force. He flew twenty-three combat missions and was referred to as the "Toughest Guy in the Air Force."[114] Alvin Roubal Luedecke, who finished at Texas A&M in 1932, advanced through the ranks to become brigadier general in 1944. He served as air attaché at numerous South American legations through 1942, was chief of Air Section, American Intelligence Service, Miami Beach, Florida, 1942-1943, and deputy chief of air staff to the commanding general of the Army Air Forces in the China-Burma-India Theater from 1943 to 1946.[115]

[106]College Station *Texas Aggie,* June 19, 1951.

[107]*Ibid.,* July 18, 1952.

[108]Honorary Degree File, Texas A&M University Archives.

[109]College Station *Texas Aggie,* July 15, 1943.

[110]Honorary Degree File, Texas A&M University Archives.

[111]College Station *Texas Aggie,* December 4, 1944.

[112]Article in Austin Mother's Club Scrapbook, Texas A&M University Archives.

[113]College Station *Texas Aggie,* October 15, 1942.

[114]*Ibid.,* August 20, 1942, December 15, 1944; Robert Sherrod, "Toughest Guy in the Air Force," *Saturday Evening Post* (March 26, 1955), pp. 144, 147.

[115]*Who's Who in America* (1966-1967 ed.), p. 1305.

After civilian service elsewhere, he returned to Texas A&M in 1968 as associate dean of the College of Engineering and coordinator of research for the Texas Engineering Experiment Station. In 1970 he was made executive vice-president, and upon the death of James Earl Rudder, in March 1970, he became acting president of A&M, until the Office of President was filled on a regular basis by the appointment of Dr. Jack K. Williams, effective November 1, 1970, whereupon General Luedecke became executive vice-president of the University.

Brigadier General Aubry L. Moore served as chief of staff of the Tenth Air Force during the last years of World War II.[116] Douglas B. (Spike) Netherwood was a pre-World War I aviation pioneer who rose to the rank of brigadier general and died in a plane crash in the States during the War.[117] Robert (Bob) Neyland left A&M to complete his education at West Point. As a coach at the University of Tennessee he created one of college football's outstanding dynasties, completing twenty-one years of coaching with 171 wins, 27 losses and 12 ties. He became a brigadier general during the War.[118] W. Donald Old, a brigadier general, was decorated for gallantry in evacuating by air nearly 5,000 sick and wounded during the siege of Burma in 1942.[119] General Nat S. Perrine commanded Camp O'Reilly in the Philippines during part of the War.[120] Brigadier General John L. Pierce ('19) was chief of staff, Armored Command, Fort Knox, Kentucky.[121] John T. Walker graduated in 1917 and served with the Marines through World Wars I and II. He commanded the Twenty-second Marine Regiment during the assault and capture of Eniwetok Atoll in the Marshall Islands, where he received the Navy Cross for "extra-ordinary heroism and meritorious devotion to duty." He was chief of staff of the First Provisional Marine Brigade during the invasion of Guam.[122]

Brigadier General John A. Warden, a 1908 graduate of Texas A&M, served in the Quartermaster Corps at Fort Francis E. Warren, in Wyoming, during the War years.[123] Jerome J. Waters ('13) was artillery commander of the Seventy-sixth Infantry Division at Fort Meade, Maryland, in 1941, and in November 1942 went to China, where he organized a field-artillery school for

[116]College Station *Texas Aggie*, May 7, 1945.

[117]Houston *Post*, November 11, 1942; Houston *Press*, April 16, 1946.

[118]Dallas *Morning News*, February 19, 1953; Houston *Post*, March 19, 1962.

[119]College Station *Texas Aggie*, May 5, 1943.

[120]Houston *Press*, April 15, 1946.

[121]College Station *Texas Aggie*, September 17, 1943.

[122]*Ibid.*, August 15, 1950.

[123]Houston *Post*, November 11, 1942.

the Chinese.[124] Texas A&M's claim to a Navy admiral was in the person of Rear Admiral Albert MacQueen Bledsoe, who attended A&M in the fall of 1913 before going to Annapolis. From 1942 to 1944 he was director of enlisted personnel in the Bureau of Navy Personnel in Washington, D.C. In 1944 he commanded the U.S.S. *Denver,* winning commendations in the battle for the recapture of Corregidor, and the Navy Cross in the Battle of Leyte Gulf.[125]

The chronicle of the fighting Texas Aggies will never be fully written; but the sense of achievement and of accomplishment has undergirded the Aggie tradition with a quiet, proud sense of duty and purposefulness. One or two final anecdotes to the story should be related. Major Archer B. Swank ('36) served as an aide at the Teheran Conference. He recalls that Joseph Stalin looked like an East Texas dirt farmer. He witnessed what may have been the first stubborn impasse between Russia and the West when he noticed Stalin pounding on the bathroom door. "In a moment, with an irate and inquiring expression on his face, out strode Churchill."[126]

Finally, Colonel Tom Dooley, adjutant to Lieutenant General Jonathan Wainwright and one of the Aggies taken prisoner on Corregidor, was selected to witness the Japanese surrender aboard the U.S.S. *Missouri* in 1945,[127] a tribute to those who gave so much in the defense of their country. By War's end over 950 A&M men had lost their lives in service.

These men, whom words are inadequate to describe, will never be forgotten at Texas A&M. In 1951 the Memorial Student Center was dedicated

In humble reverence . . . to those men of A. & M. who gave their lives in defense of our country. Here is enshrined in spirit and in bronze enduring tribute to their valor and to their deep devotion. Here their memory shall remain forever fresh — their sacrifices shall not be forgotten.[128]

[124]College Station *Texas Aggie,* May 30, 1951.

[125]Bryce O. Templeton, Mountain Lake, New Jersey, to F. C. Bolton, College Station, Texas, March 14, 1948, Honorary Degree File, Texas A&M University Archives.

[126]College Station *Texas Aggie,* February 1, 1944; Dallas *Morning News,* March 5, 1961.

[127]College Station *Texas Aggie,* September 10, 1945.

[128]*Dedication of Memorial Student Center, Agricultural and Mechanical College of Texas, April 21, 1951,* p. 3; Appendix C.

CHAPTER 22

Reconstruction of the College

T EXAS A&M College experienced a profound postwar reconstruction, realignment, and near rebellion. The painful experiences of the postwar era were the products of essentially three things: (1) the War had brought profound changes in American technology and educational horizons; (2) Texas A&M, along with most of the nation's higher institutions of learning, especially the land-grant colleges, was still living on the fruits of the vintage academic years of the 1920s and 1930s and was not highly susceptible to change; and (3) Texas A&M had been tremendously successful in war and it was inconceivable to many that changes were needed or that she could be faced with failure in peace. Pride, tradition, an outstanding war record, and a false sense of security created a greater resistance to change at Texas A&M than at most institutions of higher learning. Indeed, the postwar reconstruction of the College lasted nearly twenty years, rather than the more common adjustment period of merely the four or five years immediately following World War II.

After World War II the Corps of Cadets and veteran students on campus demonstrated a curious ambivalence between progressivism and traditionalism. The Corps of Cadets, for example, began to ritualize many of the practices of former days which had been, at best, customs. Thus, yell practice, muster, the bonfire, and observance of memorials were increasingly codified and ritualized, and while the form was retained the earlier meaning was often lost. Hazing became more of a ritualistic practice in the postwar years than the *bon-vivant,* fraternal initiation of earlier years. Because it had become more of a ritual, it was more sacrosanct to the Corps of Cadets. An attack upon hazing by the administration after World War II created a profound reaction among cadets, who believed they were doing what was right, as well as among former students, who were in effect being memorialized by the rituals. The success of the administration in breaking up hazing, one of the sacred rituals, dispirited the Corps of Cadets and created a pervasive background of gloom which enshrouded the entire institution for many years — even while truly substantive reforms and changes were taking place.

The fact that the Corps of Cadets, former students, faculty, and administrators were truly and justifiably proud of A&M's war record also created a hostility to change. Why change a system that had proven itself? Indeed, faculty and students after World War II loudly touted A&M's war record. The students symbolically revered A&M's war record simply by membership in the Corps of Cadets. Simply to be a cadet, and to adhere to the traditions of the Corps, was widely regarded as a form of patriotism and loyalty to school, country, and former students, especially by the postwar generations of young A&M students who had not participated in the War, but who were proud of what had been done, and who desired to share at least by association in the "fraternity" the glory of that accomplishment. But these same young people were confounded by the fact that after the War their campus was flooded by those very veterans whom they so greatly emulated, and who almost without exception rejected the forms, the ritual, the hazing, and even the uniform which the young cadets used as demonstration of their esteem and respect for their predecessors. These were frustrating times for Aggies, young and old.

The frustrations continued for many years. Change in any form became something of a threat. Change in the forms of abolishing compulsory membership in the Corps of Cadets, of civilian students on campus, of racial integration, and, worse yet, of coeducation at Texas A&M became fundamental, heart-rending, emotional issues, rather than questions involving simple administrative mechanics. The broadening of the liberal-arts studies, the surge in the pure sciences, the relative decline of the traditional applied studies in agriculture and engineering in the face of the expanding university complex, and perhaps even the advent of the "computer age" on campus, came to be regarded by many as more than elements of change and progress, but as an upheaval of the entire social order. Change is something that was felt by the entire American society after World War II. Texas A&M, where the changes were more rapid and more keenly felt, in a way, was an intensified microcosm of that society.

The replacement of Thomas O. Walton, president of the College, and of Howard H. Williamson, director of the Texas Extension Service, in 1943, and the appointment of Gibb Gilchrist to the presidency in 1944 marked the advent of Texas A&M's era of reconstruction. Problems had begun to beset the College well before these events occurred. The desperate reconstitution of the veterinary-medicine program after 1937, and the loss of accreditation in the chemical-engineering program in 1937, as well as the keen dissatisfaction with Coach Homer Norton that developed within the Former Students Association at that time, signaled storm warnings. Each difficulty, at least for the moment, was amicably resolved. Later, during the first years of the War, as new problems arose they were generally deferred, overlooked, or temporarily resolved.

When in 1943, the regular academic program reached a virtual standstill because of the lack of students, the Board of Directors began to plan more carefully for the years ahead. In 1942 a survey of the College had been conducted at the instigation of President Walton by a number of prominent academic men from other schools and colleges. The Survey Committee included Andrey Abraham Potter, dean of Engineering at Purdue University; Harlow Leslie Walster, dean of Agriculture at North Dakota State Agricultural College; and John S. Tigert, president of the University of Florida. This committee recommended that Texas A&M needed (1) material improvement in basic research by teachers at the College; (2) additional funds for the College library; (3) additional space for classrooms, laboratories, and offices, and an adequate student center; and (4) the development of a well-rounded four-year liberal-arts curriculum in the School of Arts and Sciences, which School was found to be in need of more teachers, more space, and more books. In the School of Engineering the committee found teachers overloaded and the physical plant inadequate and poorly adapted to the needs of the school. The engineering curriculum needed to be broadened to include studies in the humanities, government, and the social sciences.[1] The report showed the need for substantive changes at Texas A&M.

The Directors, concluding that Texas A&M had become a "Model-T" technological institute, in 1943 laid the blame at the door of Thomas O. Walton. They reported that concern over Walton's administration first became acute in 1940, when the Board by a tie vote barely retained him in office. In 1941 the Directors actually voted him out of office, but then reconsidered the vote and decided to retain him on a one-year probation. In 1942, "entirely because of the war situation, the board unanimously decided to retain Dr. Walton for another year."[2] But in August 1943, by a vote of five to three, Walton failed of re-election. He was then given the opportunity to resign the presidency, which he did "after consultation with my physician and acting upon his advice," his resignation to take effect at the pleasure of the Board. It was the Board's pleasure to accept the resignation immediately. At the time the Directors also re-elected all officers of the College, except Howard H. Williamson, head of the Agricultural Extension Service. The Directors

[1]Houston *Press*, March 11, 1944.
[2]Dallas *Morning News*, March 12, 1944.

assigned to Vice-President Frank Cleveland Bolton the duties of the presidency on an interim basis, and named Thomas Otto Walton president emeritus, Walton to draw full salary for one year, and one-half salary for a second year.[3] At the time it was obvious that the Directors wished to make the succession to the presidency as smooth as possible, and to preclude any upheaval or unfavorable publicity over Walton's departure. The Directors, however, were soon frustrated in their effort. All hell broke loose.

Things were relatively quiet on Monday, August 9, through Thursday, August 12, following the news release regarding President Walton's resignation. The newspapers, and official Texas A&M sources, were laudatory of Walton's long years of service to the College and to the state.[4] But by Friday, August 13, the newspapers, and other obviously interested parties, had begun to raise questions. The official announcement regarding H. H. Williamson's dismissal as director of the Extension Service did not come until Wednesday, following Williamson's statement to a reporter, "I've been told that I've been fired." The public, the press, and some former students promptly linked Williamson's dismissal with Walton's resignation. So apparently did Governor Coke Stevenson and the state legislators.[5]

State Senator Penrose Metcalfe, an alumnus and loyal supporter of Walton, sent pointed telegrams to several A&M Directors asking whether they had forced the resignation of Walton, and if so, why? He threatened an investigation into the matter by his special textbook educational committee if the standing Senate General Investigation Committee headed by Senator Houghton Brownlee did not investigate.[6] On Wednesday, August 18, Brownlee's Senate Committee voted to inquire into administrative changes at the College.[7] Meanwhile the state press mentioned Gibb Gilchrist, former state highway engineer and the dean of Texas A&M's School of Engineering, and

[3]*Ibid.;* Minutes of the Board of Directors, August 7-8, 1943, VI, 228-229. The Minutes of the Board do not show a vote for the re-election of President Walton. They do show the letter of resignation from President Walton and the acceptance of the same. Subsequent reports indicate that the vote was 5-3, and that Francis Marion Law, Major General H. J. Brees, and John Burns supported Walton, while Herbert L. Kokernot, Neth L. Leachman, G. Rollie White, Robert Briggs, and A. H. Demke voted no.

[4]Dallas *Morning News,* August 10, 1943; August 11, 1943; Fort Worth *Star-Telegram,* August 11, 1943; August 12, 1943; Houston *Post,* August 10, 1943; San Antonio *Express,* August 13, 1943.

[5]Dallas *Morning News,* August 13, 1943; August 14, 1943; Fort Worth *Star-Telegram,* August 13, 1943.

[6]Dallas *Morning News,* August 13, 1943.

[7]Houston *Post,* August 19, 1943; Fort Worth *Star-Telegram,* August 19, 1943; Dallas *Morning News,* August 19, 1943.

former Texas Governor Dan Moody as likely successors to the A&M presidency.[8] The press also linked Texas A&M Former Students Association officials and the head of the Texas Farm Bureau and the Texas Agricultural Adjustment Administration to Walton's dismissal.[9] Brownlee's Senate Committee concluded, after preliminary hearings held the following week, that the arrangements entered into by the Board with Dr. Walton were in order.[10] Things were quiet for several months.

Then, at the Thanksgiving meeting of the Board of Directors in 1943, Board President Francis Marion Law read a letter to the Directors from Walton in which Walton indicated that he had recovered from his illness and asked the College to assign him duties as president emeritus. The Directors replied to the effect that the position held no duties. Walton then raised the question as to whether the Board of Directors could legally pay him a salary without assigning duties. The Directors, irritated by Walton's persistence, asked the attorney general for an opinion on the matter. The attorney general ruled that the salary paid under such conditions was in fact beyond the authority of the Board of Directors. The Directors notified Walton accordingly and suspended payment of his salary. In February, Walton again asked for an assignment of duties, which would fulfill the requirements for drawing a salary pursuant to the ruling of the attorney general. On February 19 the Directors again declined to assign duties. Walton then decided to enter suit against the Directors for $18,000, on the contractual obligation.[11] At this point the controversy gave way to accusations, counteraccusations, and new revelations.

The Walton affair, in part, reflected internal A&M policy conflicts of ancient vintage. Should compulsory military and the all-male policies be perpetuated or should "allowances" be made? The division among Aggies over these questions goes far back into A&M history, to the days of Lawrence Sullivan Ross and the efforts to develop a Woman's College in conjunction with A&M, to the 1915 Clara Dismukes Vander Las decision, by which the Board refused an endowment for a chair of home economics on the grounds that A&M was an all-male institution, and to the 1925-1926 coeducation disputes.

[8]Fort Worth *Star-Telegram*, August 19, 1943; Houston *Post*, August 19, 1943; Dallas *Morning News*, August 19, 1943.

[9]Dallas *Morning News*, August 14, 1943.

[10]*Ibid.*, March 9, 1944.

[11]*Ibid.*, March 9, 11, 12, 1944; Houston *Post*, March 8, 9, 12, 1944; Houston *Press*, March 9, 1944; Fort Worth *Star-Telegram*, March 8, 9, 10, 12, 1944; Bryan *Daily Eagle*, March 7, 8, 11, 1944.

In 1941 Joe Utay's reappointment to the Board of Directors was allegedly blocked by State Senator George Moffett, an Aggie, reportedly at the request of the Association of Former Students. Utay apparently was one of those who might favor changes being made at the expense of Aggie traditions. In 1943 Neth Leachman, appointed to the Board by Governor Coke Stevenson, led the fight against Walton and represented the "same interests" as had Utay.[12] Those "interests" were never spelled out by the newspapers, and perhaps really could not be spelled out, for they involved rather intangible attitudes, rather than literal programs. The attitude had to do mainly with the Corps of Cadets, and coeducation at Texas A&M. The Board of Directors in 1943-1944 wanted to perpetuate the all-male military tradition of the College, while at the same time renovating and modernizing the academic program. The Corps of Cadets and many former students wanted to preserve the tradition, if necessary at the expense of academic modernization. Some former students, faculty, and administrators wanted to modernize, and, if necessary, at the expense of the traditions. No interest group had genuinely clear-cut concepts about what it would or could not do. The question became whether substantive academic changes could be effected without altering long-established procedures and traditions.

Walton appears to have gotten caught on the horns of this Aggie dilemma. He announced in March 1944 that his retirement from A&M had not been for reasons of ill health, but that he and the Board had been in disagreement over matters of policy for the past three to five years, and that he had known that for the past three years his work as president had not been pleasing to the Directors.[13] Walton said that he believed the Board placed too much emphasis on military training, and that it failed to re-elect faculty without a hearing or showing cause, and that the Board had directed that the 1942 survey committee not include complimentary material in its report. Walton said that complimentary findings were later excluded from the report by the Directors.[14] The Board of Directors followed Walton's announcements with a special meeting at Fort Worth in March 1944, preceded by a press conference, at which Board members agreed to answer "all questions that may be asked."[15]

An official statement issued at the meeting by the Directors reviewed

[12]Houston *Post*, March 9, 1944.

[13]Dallas *Morning News*, March 16, 1944; Fort Worth *Star-Telegram*, March 16, 1944.

[14]Houston *Post*, April 1, 1944; Dallas *Morning News*, March 16, 1944.

[15]Bryan *Daily Eagle*, March 8, 1944; Fort Worth *Star-Telegram*, March 12, 1944; Dallas *Morning News*, March 12, 1944.

events regarding the Walton case. Basically, Walton and the Directors agreed on the facts. The Directors held, however, that Walton's leadership had failed to keep pace with the College's growth, that he had not supported the Board's policies with "wholehearted compliance," and that the Directors had been "greatly concerned over Dr. Walton's failure to exercise better control over the hazing situation." The College, said Francis Marion Law, "had gone off and left" Walton.[16]

Law at the same time indicated that the A&M Board of Directors had offered the presidency to former A&M dean of Liberal Arts, Charles E. Friley, who had become president of Iowa State College. Friley declined the offer. Later conversations with Friley revealed a number of reservations he had about the situation at A&M, and especially the fact that A&M placed too much emphasis on military affairs. He also disliked the item-by-item appropriation method used in the Texas Legislature, and he believed that there was overspecialization in the College and that it should have a broader program of instruction in some of the cultural subjects.[17] Walton concurred with Friley's evaluation that too much emphasis was placed on the military at Texas A&M, but Walton did not indicate any desire to broaden the curriculum away from its preoccupation with agricultural and engineering programs. The Directors realized the need for fundamental academic changes, but did not desire changes in A&M's military orientation. Inevitably, changes in academic policies became impaled on the resistance to change in student life.

More than broad policy issues, to be sure, was involved in the change in top officials at Texas A&M in 1943. Hazing was a problem, and Walton, like many of his predecessors, had great difficulty in controlling it. Secondly, Gibb Gilchrist unquestionably desired the A&M presidency and had many powerful friends in his support, including Board member Robert W. Briggs, of San Antonio,[18] one of those who led the fight against Walton. But most important, although there is no question that Texas A&M had made great progress under Walton's administration, the College appeared to be falling behind academically, and seemed to be floundering without any clear objectives.

Walton replied to the Board's statements, arguing that the Directors exceeded their executive functions by trying to administer the school directly

[16]Bryan *Daily Eagle*, March 11, 1944; Dallas *Morning News*, March 12, 1944; Fort Worth *Star-Telegram*, March 12, 1944.

[17]Dallas *Morning News*, March 12, 1944.

[18]Interview with Henry B. McElroy, June 26, 1972, College Station, Texas.

to the detriment of good faculty-administrator-public relations. "The College," he said, "is facing the worst crisis in its history." He offered to drop any civil action against the College if the Directors would resign from the Board.[19] The Board declared that it would not resign.[20] Subsequently, the Senate General Investigating Committee decided to reopen inquiries into the A&M situation. The dirty A&M linen was fully aired in hearings in Austin lasting well into April. All sides publicly counseled "doing what was best for A&M."[21] The most important thing that needed to be done was to elect a permanent president for A&M.

Finally, on May 25, 1944, the Texas A&M Board of Directors named Gibb Gilchrist to the presidency by a five-to-three vote. Frank Bolton, then acting president, was the runner-up.[22] Gilchrist, former head of the Texas Highway Department, and dean of the School of Engineering at Texas A&M, was a proven and successful administrator. Born at Wills Point, in Van Zandt County, Gilchrist attended Southwestern University at Georgetown 1905-1906, and graduated from The University of Texas in 1909 with a B.S. in Civil Engineering. From 1910 to 1917 he was construction engineer with the Santa Fe Railroad, and after military service in World War I he became a resident and division engineer with the state Highway Department in San Antonio and San Angelo. From 1925 to 1927 he engaged in private business — during the Miriam A. ("Ma") Ferguson years — and in 1927 was appointed state highway engineer.[23] Gilchrist was largely responsible for modernizing Texas' highway system. He was credited with administering $300 million of Texas highway construction during his ten years as head of the Texas highway system. He retired from that position with the reputation of being scrupulously honest, competent, tough, and strong. It was a reputation he retained as president of Texas A&M.

Gilchrist launched into his new job with his usual vigor and determination. He reorganized the academic and administrative structure of the College. He upgraded many of the departments, created the Texas A&M Research Foundation, organized a freshman division, and abolished the more

[19]Dallas *Morning News*, March 16, 1944; Houston *Post*, March 16, 1944.

[20]Dallas *Morning News*, March 17, 1944.

[21]Fort Worth *Star-Telegram*, March 29, 31, April 1, 3, 23, 28, May 1, 1944; Houston *Post*, March 29, 31, April 1, 3, 28, 30, 1944; Dallas *Morning News*, March 31, April 1, 3, 28, 30, May 9, 1944; San Antonio *Express*, March 31, 1944.

[22]Minutes of the Board of Directors, March 25, 1944, VII, 36-37.

[23]Gibb Gilchrist Biographical Sketch, Texas A&M University Archives; Houston *Post*, May 26. 1944; Dallas *Morning News*, May 26, 1944; Fort Worth *Star-Telegram*, May 26, 1944.

serious forms of hazing. He became on the one hand one of the most admired and successful Texas A&M presidents, and on the other one of the most disliked and controversial figures ever to be on campus. He provoked a near revolution at Texas A&M, without, however, changing the basic character of Texas A&M as an agricultural and mechanical college for males only, with compulsory military training.

Gilchrist announced in September 1944, after months of study, that his plan for A&M was twofold: (1) to focus engineering and agricultural research and instruction, in conjunction with the basic sciences, on the development and utilization of Texas resources, and (2) to establish community technical-training centers throughout Texas, where the agricultural and engineering arts could be taught in job-training, short-term programs. Gilchrist sought to establish research centers at Texas A&M to deal with specific farm, forestry, ranch, and industrial problems; and to provide an effective post-high school educational program to allow students to learn in two years some vocational activity.[24] While Gilchrist offered a "New Vision at A&M,"[25] the vision was distinctively framed by the old agricultural and engineering precepts. There would be no revolution, but there would be greater efficiency.

Gilchrist's first year in office was a relatively quiet and constructive one. War still raged overseas. The campus remained underpopulated. A number of administrative changes occurred. Frank C. Bolton resumed full-time duties as vice-president and dean of the College. Charles Noah Shepardson replaced Edwin Jackson Kyle as dean of Agriculture, Kyle accepting an appointment as ambassador to Guatemala. Howard W. Barlow, head of the Department of Aeronautical Engineering, succeeded Gilchrist in the office of dean of Engineering.[26] Over the next few years there was to be an almost complete turnover in administrative personnel, including department heads.

Between 1944 and 1947 over one-third of the academic departments acquired new heads. Numerous changes were made in the academic structure by the combination or division of older departments, and by the creation of new ones. For example, agricultural economics, under Justus W. Barger, and agricultural sociology, under Dan Russell, were combined to form the Department of Agricultural Economics and Sociology, under Letcher P. Gabbard. The Department of Fish and Game, under Walter Penn Taylor, became the Department of Wildlife Management, under William B. Davis. The new Department of Range and Forestry was organized under Vernon G. Young.

[24]Dallas *Morning News*, September 10, 1944.
[25]*Ibid.*, September 12, 1944.
[26]Texas A&M, *Catalogue, 1947-1948*, pp. 6-9.

The Department of Accounting and Statistics was moved from the School of Agriculture to the School of Arts and Sciences. The Department of Education, under William L. Hughes, joined the Department of Psychology, under Charles H. Winkler, to become the Department of Education and Psychology under George B. Wilcox. The Department of Geography was organized under George W. Schlesselman. Geology, under Frederick A. Burt, was transferred from the School of Arts and Sciences to the School of Engineering, under a new head, Shirley A. Lynch. The Department of Military Science became the School of Military Science and Tactics. The process resulted in demotions, promotions, faculty competition and jealousy, the addition of many new faculty — and change — which is particularly disconcerting in an academic atmosphere.[27]

Changes in personnel occurred also at the top administrative levels. The confused succession to H. H. Williamson in Agricultural Extension has already been noted. George E. Adams, Ernest R. Eudaly, James D. Prewit, and Ide P. Trotter were successively named to head that organization within a period of three years. As already indicated, Edwin J. Kyle ended his long career as dean of Agriculture to be succeeded by Charles N. Shepardson. Ross Perry Marsteller ended a long tenure as dean of Veterinary Medicine to be replaced by Ivan B. Boughton. Gilchrist's place in the School of Engineering was filled by Howard W. Barlow. Thomas Dudley Brooks retired as dean of Arts and Sciences to be replaced by Marion Thomas Harrington. Paul B. Pearson assumed the position of dean of the Graduate School, but served only one year. Arthur B. Connor, director of the Agricultural Experiment Station, was replaced by Robert Donald Lewis, and Gilchrist's place as director of the Engineering Experiment Station was filled by Thomas Reese Spence. Paul S. Ballance served as acting Librarian when Thomas Mayo was named head of the Department of English.[28] Over the next few years changes in key administrative personnel would be almost as numerous as in the 1943-1947 period.

Substantive changes occurred in the School of Agriculture. The academic divisions of the School were integrated with service personnel from the Agricultural Extension Service and the Agricultural Experiment Station. David W. Williams recalls that upon being made vice-president for agriculture in 1946, he told Gibb Gilchrist, "This is lousy the way we are organized." There was no interrelationship, exchange, or mutual support

---

[27]Texas A&M, *Catalogue, 1943-1944*, pp. 8-9, 84-201; *Catalogue, 1947-1948*, pp. 71-280.
[28]Texas A&M, *Catalogue, 1943-1944*, pp. 8-9; *Catalogue, 1947-1948*, p. 6.

among the teaching, extension, or research branches of Texas A&M's agricultural program. Gilchrist replied, "Well, what can we do about it?" Subsequently, Ide P. Trotter, director of the Extension Service; R. D. Lewis, director of the Experiment Station; Ivan Boughton, dean of veterinary medicine; Alfred D. Folweiler, director of the Texas Forest Service; and Williams implemented a plan based upon an organizational scheme formulated by Williams during his early years (1920s) at Texas A&M. This plan placed extension, research, and academic personnel under the same departmental roof, with one departmental head in charge. This, said Williams, involved a very big shake-up, but resulted in making the agricultural effort far more efficient and effective.[29]

In addition to the academic changes, College authorities formulated and announced the objectives of the A&M College as follows:

OBJECTIVES OF THE A&M COLLEGE OF TEXAS

In conformity with the Constitution and the laws of the State of Texas, the purposes and principal objectives of the A&M College of Texas are declared as follows:

I.

A state-wide system in accord with the recognized needs of the people of Texas and dedicated primarily to the broad fields of agriculture, engineering, and military science, with principal offices at the main college, for white male students only, located at College Station; with such authorized branch colleges including the branch college for negroes at Prairie View, extension services, experiment stations, and other facilities throughout the State as may be required to meet all objectives.

II.

An environment for student bodies comparable to that which usually prevails in the substantial Texas homes from which these students come, superior instruction including requirements in the study of the national and state governments under which we live, with constant training in leadership, character, tolerance, clean living, and physical drill and development, at a cost alike to all at the lowest possible minimum commensurate with substantial living conditions and superior instruction; a staff of competent and worthy teachers and employees, supporters of our republican form of government and of the Constitutions of the United States and of Texas, eligible and qualified by training and example to teach our students, to work in their interest, and to work toward other declared objectives of the system.

III.

A strong and effective system of military training for male students of the main college or of any of its branches, compulsory for all except those to whom credit may be granted for active military experience or equivalent training.

[29]Interview with David W. Williams, September 15, 1971, College Station, Texas; see also Chapter 18.

IV.

Leadership in agriculture, including veterinary medicine, forestry, and wild game; and in engineering, including the mechanic arts and technical and industrial training; scientific and classical studies; and auxiliary phases connected with the two broad fields, with the highest possible type and quality of coordinated instruction, research, and extension work.

V.

Provision of such graduate instruction and such research facilities and personnel in agriculture and engineering as may be required for the maintenance and advancement thereof or to provide any level of instruction or research needed.

VI.

State-wide extension services and other state-wide work in the broad phases of agriculture and engineering as may come within the range of our objectives, and the appropriate dissemination of information in those fields to the homes, the farms, the branches, and the fields of endeavor of the people of Texas.[30]

The objectives of the College as stated in 1945 reflected little divergence from the historical role of the school. But a reorganization of student-life administration did break with precedent.

Gilchrist inaugurated new plans for student administration and control. The old Discipline Committee was abolished to be replaced by a faculty panel or jury selected for the occasion. A director of student affairs assumed control over student life, completely replacing the commandant from such obligations. John W. Rollins ('17), named director of student affairs, had the job of maintaining the student environment. Texas A&M, like most colleges of that day, acknowledged "responsibility for and claims a decisive influence over not only the curricular work of the student but his total experience and development during the time which he spends on the campus."[31] This responsibility became increasingly difficult to administer as the years passed; but Texas A&M continues to strive for that goal of "environmental control" in the 1970s, at a time when most institutions have essentially disclaimed all responsibility for student extracurricular life and morality. The efforts to exercise that environmental control produced a crisis in 1946-1947.

Gilchrist asked the Board of Directors to secure a tract of land "on some running stream in West Texas" where a summer camp for freshmen could be established. There the orientation and classification tests, medical examinations, and other indoctrination could be completed. The camp would serve as a recruiting and screening device for the College as well as a head-

[30]Texas A&M, "President's Report to the Board of Directors, May 23, 1945," mimeographed report in Texas A&M University Archives.
[31]*Ibid.*

start program for the student.[32] Gilchrist also advised the establishment of a recreation area within a reasonable distance of the campus, "where fishing, swimming, boating, outdoor games, and relaxation facilities of all kinds may be available."[33] He also proposed to strengthen the military training program by offering a curriculum leading to a degree in military science, and to continue efforts to establish a Naval R.O.T.C. program on campus. He also proposed to establish at Beaumont, Texas, a "terminal course in marine engineering and naval architecture" as authorized by the laws of Texas, but never previously funded.[34]

Gilchrist did not attain all of the objectives he established, and those realized were not always as at first evisioned. The "summer camp" project was established on the Texas A&M Adjunct near Junction, Texas, where in 1946 the people of Junction donated 411 acres of land along the South Llano River for educational and research purposes.[35] The College offered an effective program of summer school, recreation, and guidance and counseling at Junction until 1971, when the facility was turned over to Texas Tech University. The envisioned recreational facility near the campus ostensibly became the golf course which opened in 1950. Students could earn a major in military science, but no degree, and the Naval R.O.T.C. program finally appeared on campus some twenty-five years later (1972). The proposed marine-engineering program at Beaumont ultimately became the Texas Maritime Academy in Galveston.

One of the most important accomplishments of President Gilchrist's administration was the establishment of the Texas A&M Research Foundation. It was organized and incorporated as a nonprofit organization of the state of Texas on November 14, 1944. Fifty prominent men, most of them former students, comprised the membership of the Foundation. A fifteen-man Board of Trustees functioned as the governing board, and the first officers of the Foundation included George Chance, president; Everett E. McQuillen, secretary-treasurer; and Dean of Engineering Howard W. Barlow, acting director.[36] The Research Foundation allowed industrial and private grants to be made to Texas A&M for research projects that would otherwise have been beyond the scope and legal authority of the College to pursue.

[32]*Ibid.*, 5.

[33]*Ibid.*, 6.

[34]*Ibid.*, 8.

[35]Minutes of the Board of Directors, July 13, 1946, VIII, 79; Texas A&M, *Catalogue, 1967-1968*, p. 37.

[36]Texas A&M, "President's Report, May 25, 1945."

This was very much in accord with President Gilchrist's research-team, task-force concept of applying institutional resources to agricultural and industrial problems. During the first year of operation the Research Foundation sponsored $157,300 in research contracts dealing with such problems as the desalting of crude petroleum, studies in electric-power transmission and distribution, the development and use of a mass spectrometer, and the location of hurricanes with radio direction finders.[37] Under the supervision of Arne Arthur Jakkula, appointed the first full-time executive director of the Foundation in September 1946, the Foundation grew to become a vital program of the institution which brought in millions of dollars annually in gifts and equipment, and which attracted top scholars, scientists, and graduate students to the institution. It was Jakkula, said David W. Williams years later, "who made the Research Foundation go."[38]

In 1946 the Foundation coordinated $470,000 of research projects and by the 1960s programs were being maintained to the value of millions of dollars a year. One of the more outstanding of the early research programs was an investigation into the causes of oyster mortality. When the oil companies began intensive offshore production, Texas fishing industries immediately attributed the epidemics in the oyster beds to oil pollution and began suing the companies for millions of dollars in damages. The companies responded by investigating the situation through a research project headed by the Texas A&M Biology Department. The result of that work was to prove that a bacteria was destroying the oyster beds, which relieved the oil companies of costly damages, and which provided the fishing industry the technology for controlling the disease, virtually saving the oyster industry.[39]

Through programs sponsored by the Research Foundation, Texas A&M was able to provide unique and invaluable services to man. The research programs in turn provided the impetus to expansion into new fields of inquiry, such as oceanography, meteorology, space, nuclear power, and medicine. The oyster-research project marked A&M's first venture into oceanography. This field of inquiry ultimately grew to the point that Texas A&M became designated a Sea Grant College in 1971. In many respects the establishment of the Texas A&M Research Foundation marked the advent of the new Texas A&M University complex which began to be realized in the 1960s and 1970s.

[37]*Ibid.*

[38]Texas A&M, "President's Report, June 25, 1947," p. 21; interview with David W. Williams, September 15, 1971, College Station, Texas.

[39]Interview with Marion Thomas Harrington, September 13, 1971, College Station, Texas; Texas A&M, "President's Report, May 10, 1948."

The development of the Texas A&M College Development Fund parallelled the growth of the Research Foundation. Although organized in June 1942, the Development Fund really began operation on December 1, 1945, when R. Henderson Shuffler ('29) was named executive director. The purpose of the Fund was to solicit financial support for the College from friends and alumni, and to sponsor special projects beyond the ordinary scope of College finances. Shuffler organized an impressive program publicizing the goals of the Fund and achieved early successes. The Fund first adopted projects to provide one hundred scholarships annually, to build a College chapel, a golf course, and an "institute of Agriculture, Industry and Natural Resources." Initial successes included receipt of the Krueger Award Fund, the Edgar W. Brown gift of American Saddle Horses, a gift of a registered Hereford bull from J. N. Edens, and a Texas Frozen Food Locker Association Scholarship. Between 1945 and 1946 the Development Fund obtained gifts valued at $491,116.57, and total gifts from the inception of the program by 1948 were valued at $1.3 million. The Association of Former Students accepted a project aimed at establishing fifty scholarships known as Opportunity Awards, and a number of agricultural scholarships were given by Mr. and Mrs. Jesse H. Jones. In September 1947 Henderson Shuffler became director of Information for the College, and Everett E. McQuillen ('20), who helped organize the Development Fund program in 1945, became Fund director.[40] The Texas A&M Development Fund, like the Research Foundation, greatly enhanced the educational and service programs of the College over the years.

The most immediate and pressing problem facing Texas A&M and other schools and colleges throughout the nation after World War II was the "matter of instruction, feeding, housing and otherwise providing for" the returning veterans flocking back to the campus under the G.I. Bill.[41] Wartime enrollment "bottomed" at somewhat over 2,000 students in the 1943-1945 academic years, and rose slightly, to 2,718 students, by January 1946. The onslaught of students struck in September 1946, when over 8,200 students registered for classes. Enrollment climbed to 8,651 for the 1946-1947 academic year, and remained in that vicinity for the next three years.[42] Many of the students were married. Married students were something of a novelty on American college campuses at the time, and were even more unusual on

[40]Texas A&M, "President's Report to the Board of Directors, May 25, 1945," pp. 2-3; "President's Report to the Board of Directors, May 30, 1946," p. 13; *Report of the President, 1946-1947*, p. 40; "President's Report to the Board of Directors, May 10, 1948."

[41]Texas A&M, "President's Report, May 25, 1945," pp. 13-14.

[42]See Table 9.

the Texas A&M College campus. A housing crisis quickly developed at A&M.

Two dormitories, Hart and Walton Halls, and the cooperative housing units on campus were converted into married-students' apartments in 1945.[43] The next year the College began to build temporary family dwelling units under Federal Public Housing Authority contracts. These temporary units became a part of the permanent scene at A&M, as on most college campuses.[44] Additional temporary structures were obtained from the Federal Works Agency for instructional purposes.[45] Trailers, owned by married students, were also accommodated on the campus, the College providing the utilities.[46] In 1946 faculty and staff began a work day which lasted from 7:00 A.M. to 6:00 P.M. five and one-half days a week, with many graduate classes scheduled in the evenings.[47]

In the late spring of 1946 Texas A&M obtained the use of Bryan Air Force Base, which was then being deactivated. Through a combination of College and student effort, the facilities were converted within a three-month period into dormitory and classroom spaces. Many veterans, denied rooms on the campus, took squatters' initiative and went out to the "Annex" and made rooms available and ready for their occupancy. In the first year of operation some seven hundred students occupied the Bryan Air Base facility. Marion Thomas Harrington, professor of chemistry, was named to supervise the facility with the title of assistant to the dean of the College.[48]

The next year, 1947, all entering freshmen were automatically assigned to the Annex until it was filled with about 1,500 boys. The annex became essentially a freshman division of the College. In 1948 Harrington returned to the main campus to replace Thomas D. Brooks, dean of Arts and Sciences, who retired from administration. John Paul Abbott, professor of English, became the director of the Annex. The Annex continued in use as a freshmen division until June 1950, when declining enrollments and the building program on the main campus allowed the College to accommodate the entire student body on the campus.[49]

Because of the heavy enrollment of veterans after the war, the Directors

[43]Minutes of the Board of Directors, September 7, 1945, p. 2; November 28, 1945, p. 19.

[44]*Ibid.*, June 12, 1946, VIII, 29.

[45]Texas A&M, *Report of the President, 1946-1947*, p. 3.

[46]Texas A&M, "President's Report, June 25, 1947," p. 5.

[47]Texas A&M, *Report of the President, 1946-1947*, p. 7.

[48]Interview with Marion Thomas Harrington, September 13, 1971, College Station, Texas.

[49]*Ibid.*

discontinued the policy of requiring nonmilitary students to wear the uniform. Most of these men were declining to wear it anyway.[50] The heavy enrollment and the heterogeneous composition of the student body caused the Board and staff concern over disciplinary control. It was obvious that the military department of the College, which regulated the Corps of Cadets, could not be responsible for the control of civilian students. The veterans simply would not hear of a young kid in uniform telling them what to do. The veterans, in fact, formed their own Veterans Student Association, but the Association was not governed by official College regulations. The Directors decided to adopt new comprehensive policies regarding student life, which would reflect the new student-body composition and which would reassert official College control over all student affairs. In November 1946 the Directors created the position of dean of men to supervise student life, with the professor of military science and tactics to exercise control and discipline over only the Corps of Cadets. This meant, in effect, that for the first time in its history Texas A&M had a recognized civilian student body, and that the civilian rather than the military regimen was being given priority. The Directors, to be sure, retained the essential military features of the College by requiring all students under twenty-one years of age entering as freshmen to take two years of military science. All students who had served in the Armed Forces for twelve months were exempt from the military-science requirement and from the necessity of wearing the uniform.[51]

The Directors were aware also that some of the old customs of the Corps could no longer apply to the postwar student body. The Board prohibited an upperclassman from requiring any student to perform room services or personal services for him, nor could upperclassmen require any student to run errands. There could be no use of the board or any instrument of physical hazing on or by any student. There could be no called extra drills at any time unless authorized by the College authorities.[52] The new regulations, in the opinion of the Corps of Cadets and many former students, struck at the heart of the Aggie traditions and the military regimen of the College.

Colonel Guy F. Meloy officially presented the new Articles to the Corps on January 21, and directed the cadets to become familiar with the regulations. At that time several students publicly tore up the regulations, and oth-

---

[50]Minutes of the Board of Directors, September 27, 1946, VIII, 98.

[51]*Ibid.*, November 17, 1946, VIII, 118.

[52]*Ibid.*; College Station *Battalion*, January 21, 1947; Houston *Press*, January 29, 1947; Waco *Times-Herald*, January 29, 1947; Bryan *Eagle*, January 29, 1947.

ers left them in their seats.[53] The next night, a Wednesday, the entire Cadet Corps of 2,100 students staged a protest march on President Gilchrist's home. Unofficial sources reported that over 200 commissioned and noncommissioned cadet officers submitted their resignations to Gilchrist, and told him that they would not serve as cadet officers unless the new regulations were repealed. Spokesmen for the group told Gilchrist that "the new rules for the discipline of the Corps had taken from the Cadet officers their major responsibilities." Gilchrist said very little, but what he said left the cadets speechless: "I accept [your resignations] with regret."[54] The protest march suddenly collapsed.

Senior officers gathered together in a postmarch meeting, where they voted to return to their units and requested the restoration of their commissions. The seniors also presented a list of recommendations, which was released to the newspapers. The recommendations were these: (1) that cadet officers be granted more voice in issuing orders; (2) that seniors retain privileges over freshmen; (3) that two weeks' notice be given for impending changes in regulations; (4) that the system of selecting faculty to the panels to "try" students charged with infractions of the rules be changed; (5) that the Senior Court be allowed to try minor cases; (6) that no regular military officers be housed in the dormitories; (7) that the present uniform be retained if desired by a majority vote; (8) that seniors have the right to ratify cadet officers nominated by College authorities; (9) that threats to deprive officers of advanced R.O.T.C. contracts be removed; (10) that extra drill be permitted when company commanders desired; and (11) that freshmen be removed from the Annex to the main campus. The cadet seniors praised Colonel Meloy and cast a vote of "no confidence" for Gilchrist, who they said had "no respect for their dignity and did not give their requests proper consideration."[55] Cadet Colonel Edward D. Brandt, who had not participated in the protest march, told reporters that there was no student rebellion, although the cadets had ignored Colonel Meloy's orders not to march on the President's home. He added that the cadets did not want to see the "throwing away of customs and traditions."[56]

A few days later the College administrators received a new list of "demands," including the removal of Lieutenant Colonel Bennie A. Zinn

[53]Dallas *Morning News*, January 30, 1947.
[54]*Ibid.;* Waco *Times-Herald*, January 29, 1947.
[55]Dallas *Morning News*, January 30, 1947.
[56]*Ibid.*

from all disciplinary control over the Corps of Cadets, the removal of President Gibb Gilchrist, and the restoration of all cadet-officer ranks.[57] College authorities refused a mass reinstatement of cadet officers, and announced that each case would be considered individually. Furthermore, each officer had to agree in writing to observe the rules, and each was given demerits and extra-duty hours for disobeying orders and neglect of duty.[58] After three days of almost continuous meetings, and Colonel Meloy's absolute refusal to bargain with them in any way ("I will not bargain with you," he told them. "You have forfeited any such right."), 143 of the cadet officers accepted the school's ultimatum. The cadet-officer applications for reinstatement were forwarded for action to the dean of men, J. W. Rollins, with final action by President Gilchrist.[59] The administration and civilian control of the military establishment at Texas A&M was unbowed and unbroken.

Public support for Gilchrist's stand against hazing poured in by mail, telegraph, and telephone. G. Rollie White, president of the Board of Directors, publicly endorsed "wholeheartedly and unanimously," Gilchrist's efforts to abolish all forms of hazing.[60] Some of the comments comprised a sore indictment of the cadet officers. Said a Dallas *Morning News* editorial, "Schoolboy soldiers who cannot grasp the first principle of soldiering have no right to run anything military — least of all the right to run A&M College."[61] Gilchrist blamed hazing for the high proportion of freshman drop-outs at A&M, noting that 48 percent of the freshmen living in Corps dormitories left school the first semester. Representatives from the Corps of Cadets, however, began a planned program of visitations to ex-student clubs to explain the Corps "position."[62]

Inevitably, the *Daily Texan,* published at the rival University of Texas, summed it all up:

> The spirit of Aggieland is all but broken. Or at least, if the howls of outrage rising from the Brazos bottoms can be accepted at face value, that weird complex of tradition, custom, and precedent which your true Aggie would defend to the end in days gone by has been so abrogated that it is no longer recognizable. It may not be broken, but it's sadly bent . . .

[57]Waco *Times-Herald,* February 1, 1947; Bryan *Eagle,* February 1, 1947.

[58]Dallas *Morning News,* January 31, 1947.

[59]Houston *Chronicle,* February 1, 1947; Dallas *Morning News,* February 1, 1947; Waco *Times-Herald,* February 1, 1947.

[60]Dallas *Morning News,* January 31, 1947; San Antonio *Light,* January 30, 1947; Houston *Post,* January 31, 1947.

[61]Dallas *Morning News,* January 31, 1947.

[62]Dallas *Morning News,* February 2, 1947; Houston *Chronicle,* February 2, 1947.

Student officers, facing the ultimate in loss of glamor, rushed virtually in a body to request reinstatement. They kept their sabres, but not much else.[63]

By early February fifty-seven of the cadet officers were reinstated, Edward D. Brandt was secure as Cadet colonel, and eighty-seven others were returned to the ranks as privates.[64]

One father of two A&M graduates pointed to one aspect of the situation which likely contributed to the cadets' frustrations at Texas A&M. Said William C. Goins, of Gladewater, Texas, "There is not much glamour left in wearing a cadet uniform and playing soldier when you are constantly observed and criticized by a lot of disillusioned, battle weary veterans, with rows of ribbons on their chests, who are fed up with the Army."[65] The young postwar cadets were confounded in their well-meant attempts to emulate their predecessors.

But the cadets, just as inevitably, did not, and could not, give up. On the A&M campus seniors resorted to entering into written, notarized contracts with freshmen to perform personal services, at an established fee.[66] Colonel Meloy then banned contracts.[67] Just as inevitably, the cadets began to stir favorable sentiment and support for their position.[68] Cadet representatives appeared before the Directors and criticized Gilchrist for his aloofness and for the suppression of free speech. But the Directors reaffirmed their support for the President and the new policies, and the faculty's Academic Council supported the Directors.[69]

In March the cadet officers cast a vote of "no confidence" in two Corps officers, Cadet Colonel Ed Brandt and Lieutenant Colonel Jack Nelson, who in turn tendered their resignations to Meloy. Meloy refused to accept them.[70] Gloom and dissatisfaction spread to all parts of the campus. Numerous meetings were held by students, including one of seniors and another of veterans, where each assembly approved resolutions asking for the dismissal of President Gibb Gilchrist. The veterans, who had taken no part in the Corps *vs.*

[63]Austin *Daily Texan*, February 2, 1947.

[64]Fort Worth *Star-Telegram*, February 4, 1947; Houston *Post*, February 4, 1947; Austin *Daily Texan*, February 5, 1947.

[65]Dallas *Morning News*, February 6, 1947.

[66]Bryan *Eagle*, February 8, 1947; Houston *Post*, February 10, 1947; Houston *Chronicle*, February 11, 1947; San Antonio *Light*, February 11, 1947; Waco *Times-Herald*, February 11, 1947.

[67]Bryan *Eagle*, February 9, 1947.

[68]Fort Worth *Star-Telegram*, February 9, 11, 1947.

[69]Dallas *Morning News*, February 27, 1947; Fort Worth *Star-Telegram*, February 22, 1947; Bryan *Eagle*, February 22, 27, 1947.

[70]Houston *Chronicle*, March 25, 1947; Dallas *Morning News*, March 25, 1947.

administration conflict, announced that they were looking after their own interests, and that their interests and those of the school would best be served by the resignation of the President. The press, some legislators, and public citizens attended the veterans' meeting. The veterans almost unanimously expressed dissatisfaction with the Gilchrist Administration and its policies, criticized the intimidation of faculty and students, and charged that appropriations to the College were inadequate. The veterans challenged President Gilchrist to answer six questions, dealing with a $200,000 appropriation for a classroom and laboratory building which had never been built, the "too high price" paid by the College for land along the Brazos River, profits of the Exchange Store, the construction of a $100,000 (unused) wind tunnel, the refusal to accept Bryan Army Air Field as an outright gift, and the lack of a tenure system for A&M faculty.[71] While the protest of the regular College students created little favorable response from Texans, a protest from veterans was something else.

The veterans' announcements produced an immediate statewide response. On Thursday, March 27, the House of Representatives voted to investigate the A&M situation. Accusations against Gilchrist began to mount. The Board of Directors released a statement defending the administration, saying that it had ordered the President to eradicate hazing and that he was doing his job. The Directors said they were "determined to develop a College second to none in educational opportunities and useful services."[72] President Gilchrist presented a letter to the Board of Directors answering each question raised by the veterans and concluded with the observation that

> The whole program is being modernized and made more efficient. We are making some real progress in getting outstanding men here. The people of Texas deserve real service from their institution. We are on the move aggressively to achieve the objectives for which the institution was created. The opportunities in the fields mandated to us by the constitution are limitless. Objectively, we propose to make this institution second to none. Nothing should be permitted to stand in the way of this movement.[73]

Gibb Gilchrist was clearly a man with a vision, and with determination.

Gilchrist's answers to the questions raised by the veterans were unequivocal and thwarted all charges of indiscretion or misuse of funds. The

[71]Dallas *Morning News*, March 27, 1947; Bryan *Eagle*, March 26, 28, 1947.

[72]Fort Worth *Star-Telegram*, March 28, 1947; Waco *Times-Herald*, March 29, 1947; San Antonio *Light*, March 29, 1947; Houston *Chronicle*, March 29, 1947; Minutes of the Board of Directors, March 28, 1947, VIII, 140-141.

[73]Minutes of the Board of Directors, March 28-29, 1947, ff. p. 142.

Board of Directors, in supporting the President, said that "the presidency of this institution is not an issue for controversy between this board and the student body of the College."[74] But the public and the Legislature began to feel that "where there is so much smoke, there must be fire."[75] The state Senate called for a joint legislative investigation.[76] The Board of Directors began a series of military trials of students charged with "disobedience of orders, insubordination and flagrant disregard of constituted authority." Of 139 cases tried, 83 cadets were penalized by demotions, demerits, or confinement to the campus, 35 were dismissed from the Corps, and 21 were found innocent.[77]

The legislative investigation began on Tuesday, April 8, lasted through the month, was resumed in mid-May for several weeks, and involved hundreds of witnesses and over 2,000 pages of testimony.[78] Politics, personalities, grudges, school loyalty, personal ambition, conservatism, liberalism, reactionism, and a host of motivations were revealed. President Gibb Gilchrist recalled it as one of the most excruciating experiences he ever encountered.[79]

Highlights of the hearings included appearances by William S. Andrews, president of the Veterans' Student Association, who argued that Gilchrist was ill-equipped to be an educational leader.[80] Texas A&M Board members, faculty, and administrators who appeared, on the other hand, with few exceptions strongly supported the President and school policies. One of the exceptions was Floyd B. Clark, head of the Department of Economics at A&M, who had earlier had personal differences with President Gilchrist. Clark, even before the hearings began, announced at the Southwest Social Science Association meeting where he was giving a professional paper, that the election of Gilchrist to the presidency "was the most unfortunate thing in the history of A&M." He continued to attack Gilchrist before the legislative committee. Subsequently, Clark was fired by Gilchrist.[81]

---

[74]Bryan *Eagle,* March 29, 1947; Fort Worth *Star-Telegram,* March 30, 1947; Waco *Sunday Tribune-Herald,* March 30, 1947; Denton *Record-Chronicle,* March 30, 1947.

[75]Galveston *News,* March 30, 1947.

[76]Houston *Post,* April 1, 1947.

[77]Waco *Times-Herald,* March 31, 1947; Bryan *Eagle,* March 31, April 1, 1947; Houston *Chronicle,* April 1, 1947.

[78]Houston *Press,* April 2, 1947; Waco *News Tribune,* April 8, 1947; Bryan *Eagle,* April 8, 10, 22, March 15, 1947; Houston *Post,* April 9, 11, 1947; Houston *Chronicle,* April 10, 11, 15, May 14, 1947.

[79]Interview with Gibb Gilchrist, August 27, 1971, College Station, Texas.

[80]Houston *Post,* April 9, 1947.

[81]Bryan *Eagle,* April 5, 22, 1947; Houston *Post,* April 5, 9, 1947; Austin *Daily Texan,* April 23, 1947; Dallas *Morning News,* April 22, 1947; Waco *Times,* June 27, 1947.

Thomas O. Walton also criticized Gilchrist and the Directors before the legislative committee. The legislative committee subpoenaed the "secret files" of former President Thomas O. Walton, and Walton himself appeared on the stand. Walton said that he lost his job by refusing to be a rubber stamp for the Board of Directors, and that Gilchrist had misled the Board in formulating rules for the Corps of Cadets. He said hazing was a smokescreen, and that Gilchrist erred in trying to use force rather than to guide. He believed that a number of faculty and Extension Service people had been wronged by Gilchrist, who had fired or demoted them.[82]

President Gilchrist and Dean of the College Frank C. Bolton both testified regarding hazing, which they termed the heart of the matter. "Hazing," Bolton said, "had become worse than it had been in the past ten years."[83] One of the student witnesses linked local business interests to attempts to oust Gibb Gilchrist from the presidency.[84] A House member said that Gilchrist was "one of those men who can't get along with anybody. Gibb does what he thinks is right but fails in human relationships."[85] Other witnesses linked Aggie antipathy to The University of Texas to Gilchrist's troubles. Gilchrist's being a University graduate prompted Aggie hostility to Gilchrist.[86] Soon the mothers became rightfully angry over the whole business and demanded, in a meeting of the State Federation of Mothers Clubs of Texas A. and M. College, the resignation of President Gilchrist.[87] The greater public response to the A&M situation, however, was favorable to the Administration and its policies, but the affair did arouse grave misgivings and doubts.

The investigating committee submitted a majority report on June 6, 1949, which concluded that there was no ineptness in the A&M Administration, and that there had been no misapplication or misappropriation of funds. The report concluded that the effort of the Administration to comply with the laws prohibiting hazing was the principal factor in the dispute, and that outside influences and designing and disgruntled persons had seized upon the occasion to discredit the Administration. The investigators did advise the College to divorce the office of president from the directorship of the branch colleges and other activities of the College in the interest of greater effi-

[82]Houston *Chronicle*, April 10, 15, 1947; Austin *Daily Texan*, April 15, 1947; Bryan *Eagle*, March 15, 1947.

[83]Houston *Chronicle*, April 15, 1947; Lufkin *News Daily*, April 15, 1947; Wichita *Record News*, April 15, 1947; Bryan *Eagle*, April 22, 1947.

[84]Waco *News Tribune*, April 24, 1947; Fort Worth *Star-Telegram*, April 23, 1947.

[85]Waco *Times-Herald*, April 23, 1947.

[86]Austin *Daily Texan*, April 29, 1947.

[87]Dallas *Morning News*, May 12, 1947; Houston *Chronicle*, May 12, 1947.

ciency. A minority report by three legislators reached essentially the same conclusions, but reprimanded President Gibb Gilchrist and his Administration for failure to command the full respect to which they should be entitled, but added that this in no way reflects upon the "successful administrative abilities of the president in other fields of endeavor."[88] The cessation of the hearings brought a return of "domestic tranquility."

The Board of Directors then distributed a copy of the disputed, but now validated, "basic policy" to every student.[89] The veterans asserted that political expediency had dictated the findings of the investigating committee, and, while noting that unhealthy conditions remained in existence, they desired to restore harmonious relations.[90] Charles Murray, student editor of the *Battalion,* wrote an editorial proposing that A&M cease being a military school and become a "civilian ROTC College." Murray was given the "drown-out" treatment, that is, inundated with buckets of water while in his room, by irate cadets.[91] But there, for the public and for the students, the entire episode met an inglorious end.

In the late spring the Directors initiated planning for a student-union building, and created the position of director of the Student Union. William R. Carmichael was named director of athletics, replacing Homer Norton; Marion Thomas Harrington became dean of Arts and Sciences, replacing Thomas Dudley Brooks; Walter L. Penberthy was named dean of men, replacing John W. Rollins; and Paul B. Pearson became dean of the Graduate School, also previously held by Brooks.[92] The College adopted an official seal in September 1947, elevating to this status the "unofficial" seal which had long been in use. It, in the official language,

shall consist of a star of five points, imposed upon a "T" and encircled, on one side by a live oak branch, and on the other by a laurel branch. At the base of the "T" shall be the date 1876, the official opening of the College, and circling the outer rim of the seal shall be the words, "The Agricultural and Mechanical College of Texas."[93]

Texas A&M acquired from the United States in November the Bluebonnet Ordnance Plant at McGregor, Texas, for experimental work related to agriculture, and renamed it the "A&M College Bluebonnet Farm."[94]

[88]Dallas *Morning News,* June 7, 1947; Austin *Daily Texan,* June 7, 1947.

[89]Waco *News Tribune,* May 29, 1947.

[90]Houston *Press,* July 1, 1947; Texas City *Sun,* June 30, 1947.

[91]Houston *Chronicle,* June 19, 1947.

[92]Minutes of the Board of Directors, March 28-29, 1947, VII, 150; June 25-26, 1947, VIII, 175.

[93]*Ibid.,* September 25-26, 1947, IX, 5.

[94]*Ibid.,* November 25-26, 1947, IX, 28-29.

The Board's real response to the investigating committee's findings came in May 1948. The Directors created the Texas A&M College System, to be administered by a chancellor. Each component of the System would be administered by an executive officer designated the president. The executive officer in charge of each agency and service would be a director. The chancellor was to be appointed at the pleasure of the Board. The System officers would be nominated by the chancellor and approved by the Board. Lesser officials, teachers, and employees would be appointed by the director or president, with the advice and approval of the chancellor, and subject to confirmation by the Board of Directors.[95]

Gibb Gilchrist was named chancellor; David W. Williams, vice-chancellor for agriculture; Frank C. Bolton, president of the A&M College; Eugene J. Howell, president of John Tarleton; Ernest H. Hereford, president of North Texas Agricultural College; Edward B. Evans, president of Prairie View Agricultural and Mechanical College; and Marion Thomas Harrington, acting dean of the College and dean of the School of Arts and Sciences — effective September 1, 1948.[96]

During the four years of Gibb Gilchrist's administration as president of Texas A&M great changes had come to the College, and yet beneath the surface things were strangely unchanged. It was still an agricultural and mechanical college with a predominant military and exclusively all-male orientation, but an agricultural and mechanical college which possessed new capabilities. Trials and tribulations and even more profound changes lay ahead.

[95]*Ibid.*, May 9-10, 1948, IX, 63-64.
[96]*Ibid.*, 65.

CHAPTER 23

Gig'em Aggies

MODERN, organized sports, particularly football and baseball, began at Texas A&M in the 1890s. The "dark ages" of athletics at A&M lasted until about 1915, when the organization of the Southwest Conference invigorated the entire athletic program at Texas A&M, and throughout the state and region. Even before this, by 1910, Texas A&M Aggies had already gone "hog-wild" over football. At the end of World War I "big-time" intercollegiate athletics were here to stay. Thirty-five thousand people, for example, jammed the new football stadium at Austin on Thanksgiving Day in 1924 to witness what had already become a regional if not a national classic, the annual football game between Texas A&M and The University of Texas.[1]

Commented one unenthusiastic reporter of the event, which sentiment was presumably echoed by A&M's President William Bennett Bizzell, "The country is simply going hog-wild over football. America is essentially a nation of sports, and we would not deny them a reasonable pastime in this regard, but Americans are extremists, just the same. Therefore," he continued with irrefutable logic, "we are going to extreme on football. A school these days is graded more on their foot ball attainments than on their literary achievements."[2] Half a century later, the game and its critics have changed little.

Football began on the Texas A&M campus in the fall of 1892. By February 1893 the cadets claimed that "A&MC now boasts a crack football team," but there were no recorded football contests until November 29, 1894, when A&M defeated Ball High School, in Galveston, by a score of 14-6.[3] In the same month the "Farmers," as they were then called, played their first

---

[1]Unidentified newspaper clipping, dated December 6, 1924, in William Bennett Bizzell Papers, Texas A&M University Archives.

[2]*Ibid.*

[3]Bryan *Eagle*, December 6, 1894; Texas A&M University, *1971 Football Press Guide*, 78.

football game with The University of Texas, in Austin, and lost by a disastrous 38-0. It was to rank as the second-worst defeat in terms of point spread at the hands of the Texas Longhorns. Frank D. Perkins coached the Aggies in their first official football season, in 1894, and Arthur P. Watts was team captain.[4] In 1898 The University beat the Aggies 48-0; not until 1970 did Texas again achieve a 38-point advantage over the Aggies.[5]

No competitive football games were played in 1895, but the following year Professors Andrew McNarin Soule and Horace W. South volunteered as coaches. Three games were played, the first with Ball High School, in Galveston, which ended scoreless, the second with Austin College, which the Aggies took by 22-0, and the third with Houston High School, which the Aggies won 28-0. Perkins, who coached in 1894, played and was team captain in 1896.[6] The Aggies also adopted their first official College Yell in 1896:

> Rah! Rah! Rah!
> Hi! Ho! Ha!
> AMC
> Boom! Cis! Bah!
> College![7]

The Aggies were a rough-tough, hell-raising bunch, according to Josh B. Sterns, one of the pioneers of Texas A&M football. Sterns, born January 15, 1878, in Harris County, entered A&M in September 1894, when he was sixteen years old. As he recalled many years later, he was "Probably the first Aggie to receive seven letters, three in football, one in baseball, one in track, one in hell raising and one from the faculty telling me they didn't need me anymore."[8] In an interview of May 1971 Sterns reflected briefly on his football career at A&M, recalling a time when Governor [Lawrence Sullivan] Ross called him into his office. When he entered the office in Old Main, he said, Ross said nothing, but busily peered at a number of papers on his desk through a reading glass. Finally Ross said to him,

"Do you know what I'm looking at?"

"No Sir, I have no idea," replied Sterns.

"I'm trying to see your last month's grades," Ross said. "Do your folks know you are up here?"

[4]Texas A&M University, *1971 Football Press Guide*, 78, 81.
[5]*Ibid.*, 77-78.
[6]*Ibid.*
[7]College Station *Battalion*, October 1896, p. 26.
[8]Josh B. Sterns Reminiscences, "Sentinel Duty," Texas A&M University Archives.

"Yes, I suppose they do," Sterns answered.

"Well, what did they tell you to do?" Ross demanded.

Sterns says he thought for a minute and decided there was no need to prevaricate; he answered truthfully, "I want to play football, baseball, box, wrestle, run and jump and have a good time!"

"By God!" said Ross, "I believe it. Unless your grades improve I'll send you home."

They didn't send him home then, "but later they did!" Sterns recalls.[9]

In 1897 Sterns became team captain, played tackle, broke his ankle, and left school. He came back, though, to graduate in civil engineering in 1903. In his 1897 season the boys hired their own coach, C. W. Taylor, for whom the hat was passed at the football games. The Aggies lost to Houston High School (0-10), and to Texas Christian University (6-30), but defeated Austin College (4-0).[10] In 1898 the Aggies, coached by H. W. Williams, played six games, winning four and losing two, including the previously mentioned drubbing at the hands of Texas.[11] In 1899 the "Cadets" lost to Texas 6-0. The referees ruled an A&M touchdown illegal, and the *Battalion* opined that the Aggies were robbed:

> Our players proved that they have grit,
> And played an honest game;
> The referee robbed them 6 to 0;
> They held Varsity just the same.[12]

A&M played The University in football every year from 1898 through 1911, and often twice each year. Of the twenty games played between the institutions during these years, the Aggies won four — in 1902, 1909 (two), and 1910.[13] The Dallas *News* reported the 1902 upset victory of College over Texas:

> For the first time in the history of the game in Texas the State University team went down in defeat before the State Agricultural and Mechanical College eleven and it was the first time that team has ever scored against the varsity. The

---

[9]Interview with Josh B. Sterns, College Station, Texas, May 14, 1971.

[10]*Ibid.;* Texas A&M University, *1971 Football Press Guide,* 77-78; George Sessions Perry, *The Story of A&M,* 74, 128, 241, 246-248.

[11]Texas A&M University, *1971 Football Press Guide,* 78.

[12]College Station *Battalion,* December 1899, p. 14.

[13]Texas A&M University, *1971 Football Press Guide,* 84.

College boys and their friends are painting the town red tonight, while everything is silent and dark on the local campus.

The explanation of the unexpected is that College simply had the best team.[14]

The A&M faculty, however, did not share the cadets' enthusiasm for football and organized athletics. The College had hired George S. Whitney in 1901 as the first regular full-time "physical director," who was to direct the "athletic sports of every character among the students," at a salary of $1,000 for nine months. Whitney, apparently, was overly conscientious. Whitney and others secured the services of James E. Platt for football coach in 1902, and A&M converted a 1-4-0 record of 1901 into a 7-0-2 record in 1902. But prior to the 1902 season the faculty, alarmed at the increasing student preoccupation with sports, passed a ruling prohibiting the A&M football team from meeting other Texas education institutions in competitive events. A vigorous student protest in the form of petitions to the president and the Board of Directors caused the faculty to rescind their action. Whitney, after one year, left A&M, having been caught in the middle of the academics *vs.* athletics squabble, the first, but not the last of its kind.[15]

While the faculty had been overruled in the conflict, it had not been entirely ignored. The Directors called for the creation of a permanent student-faculty committee to supervise athletic activities. Texas A&M's General Athletic Association, which in 1906 was renamed the Athletic Council, has since 1902 been responsible for recommending men for coaching positions to the Directors, scheduling games, awarding letters to players, allocating funds to the various sports, and directing ticket sales, concessions, and athletic business policy.[16] In 1935 the Board of Directors established its own Athletic Committee, which first comprised Joe Utay, Walter G. Lacy, and Guy Anderson, the latter soon being replaced by Roy B. Davis.[17] This committee, on occasion, met with the Athletic Council and was the Council's liaison with the Board of Directors.

Soon after the 1902 furor over athletics at A&M, college athletics was

[14]Dallas *Morning News*, November 28, 1902.

[15]Minutes of the Board of Directors, July 23, 1901, I, 242; June 10, 1902, I, 261; March 26, 1902, I, 257.

[16]College Station *Longhorn*, 1903, p. 110; *The Contributions of Edwin Jackson Kyle to the Development of the Athletic Program at the Agricultural and Mechanical College of Texas*, 3 (hereinafter cited: *The Contributions of E. J. Kyle*).

[17]Minutes of the Board of Directors, April 24-25, 1935, V, 2.

regularized by the organization in Waco, Texas, of the Southwestern Inter-Collegiate Athletics Association on March 12, 1904. This Association, the forerunner of the Southwest Conference, included at first Baylor University, Southwestern University, Trinity University, The University of Texas, and Texas A&M, who were soon joined by Austin College, Fort Worth University, Missouri School of Mines, the University of Oklahoma, and Washington University.[18] Replaced by the Texas Intercollegiate Association in 1910, the Southwestern Athletics Association and its successor established some very broad policies as to player eligibility and game rules, but both organizations had little power of enforcement.

In 1905, the year following the organization of the first regional athletic association, Texas A&M's award to lettermen was changed from a "C" for College, to a "T" for Texas. The "T" Association, with membership open to all students and former students who had represented A&M in intercollegiate athletic contests, was formally organized on November 14, 1907. The "T" was awarded until 1915, when the "T" was overlayed with the "AMC" (A**M**C) to distinguish the A&M "T" from The University of Texas "T."[19]

Most of the early football games were played on the drill field at Texas A&M, where spectators simply stood, or sat in carriages around the playing field. Some games were played in Bryan at the fairgrounds, which boasted a grandstand. On November 10, 1904, the Board of Directors set aside an area of the campus as a permanent athletic field.[20] At that time Edwin Jackson Kyle, an 1899 graduate of Texas A&M, who received degrees at Cornell in 1901 (B.S.A.) and 1902 (M.S.A.) and who joined the A&M faculty as professor of horticulture and horticulturist to the Experiment Station, was chairman of the Athletic Council. Kyle first had the area fenced off with a barbed-wire fence, soon replaced with a wooden fence. According to Kyle, who later became dean of the College of Agriculture and, upon his retirement from A&M in 1944, ambassador to Guatemala, on October 4, 1905, lumber was purchased for wooden bleachers to be built on the football field. In addition, the covered grandstand at the Bryan fairgrounds was purchased, Kyle giving

---

[18]College Station *Longhorn, 1906,* p. 127.

[19]Bryan *Daily Eagle,* November 29, 1951; College Station *Longhorn, 1910,* pp. 184-186; *Longhorn, 1915,* p. 294.

[20]Minutes of the Board of Directors, November 10, 1904, I, 288.

his personal note for the transactions, since the Athletic Council had no money. The stadium provided seating for about 500 people.[21]

Work on the stadium was completed during the 1906 football season. The *Longhorn* for that year depicts the last game played on the drill field, and the first played on the new field. Boasted the College annual, "An athletic field has been completed this year, which is beyond doubt the best athletic field in the State. The fence encloses 250,000 square feet, and bleachers with seating capacity of five hundred has been erected."[22]

The athletic field soon became known as Kyle Field, but, as time passed, considerable confusion existed over the origins of the name. Was it in honor of Edwin Jackson Kyle, who served as dean of Agriculture between 1911 and 1944 and who was chairman of the Athletic Council 1904-1911, 1932-1934, and 1937-1944? Or was it named for Dr. J. Allen Kyle, a member of the Board of Directors from 1911 to 1915? While still unresolved in the minds of many old-timers who unhesitatingly recollect that the field was named "Kyle" in honor of the Director, the Board of Directors has decreed that Kyle Field was indeed named for Edwin Jackson Kyle, who was without question a great inspiration and tireless worker in the development of Texas A&M's athletic program. So be it.[23]

In 1908 enthusiasm for sports, especially football, reached a high point at College Station, but in that year the Aggies, or Farmers, as they were known, completed their first losing season in six years with a 3-5-0 record. The two losses to "Varsity" were particularly onerous. The first loss occurred in Dallas on October 12. Cadet preparations for this game, it may be recalled, led to confrontations with President Henry Hill Harrington, which in turn contributed to the student strike in 1908. The second of these two matches with The University of Texas was played in Houston, on Monday, November 9, where at one point Texas led 14-0. Enthusiastic Longhorn supporters conducted an impromptu victory ceremony by rushing with brooms in hand onto the field, where they figuratively swept the Aggies from the playing field. The demonstration infuriated the cadets, who swept onto the field to stop the Varsity celebrations. A general riot reigned on the girdiron. "In the

[21]*The Contributions of E. J. Kyle*, 2-7; College Station *Texas Aggie* (May 1967), p. 11; Edwin Jackson Kyle Biographical Papers, Texas A&M University Archives.

[22]College Station *Longhorn, 1906*, p. 138.

[23]*The Contributions of E. J. Kyle*, 1-15; interview with Mrs. L. Giesecke Geren, College Station, Texas, May 14, 1971; interview with Ernest Langford, College Station, Texas, April 21, 1971.

melee," said a Waco reporter, a University student "was seriously stabbed. Numbers were bruised, clothing was torn, hats were smashed and the fracas was one of serious description. The police were powerless to quell the disturbance for a time." Interestingly enough, no arrests were made, but relations between Texas A&M and The University of Texas student bodies, already strained, were considerably soured by the event.[24]

Coach Ned A. Merriam was replaced in 1909 by Charles B. Moran, who told the public "he came here to win." Indeed he did, compiling 38 wins, 8 losses, and 4 ties in six football seasons. Moran acquired the reputation of being a tough, mean fighter, who, it was thought on occasion, used professional ballplayers in his line-up, and who certainly imported some fine talent, as from the Haskell (Indian) Institute in Oklahoma. He was withal the "Great Coach of the Texas Aggies" from 1909 to 1914.[25] His 1912 team still holds the season scoring record for the Aggies with 366 points to 26 against nine opponents. Moran's teams included the "immortals" Caesar ("Dutch") Hohn and Tyree Bell, among others.[26]

Basketball made its first appearance on the A&M campus in 1913, largely as a result of the efforts of Frank Decatur Steger, the general secretary of the YMCA, who, without additional compensation, coached A&M basketball through its first three years. During the 1913 season the Aggies played Marlin High School, defeating Marlin 78-8; Galveston YMCA, winning by 72-14, and in a second encounter losing by 25-27; Sam Houston Normal Institute, downing them 72-9 in the first match and 40-12 in the second; and closing the season with a 24-26 loss to Houston High School. Eddie Dreiss was team captain and assistant coach.[27] Enthusiasm for basketball was slow to build, the A&M *Longhorn* noting in 1914 that basketball "fits into the dull times of the winter months and greatly helps us to tide over from the football season to baseball and track."[28] But the 1915 *Longhorn,* dedicated to

[24]Waco *Daily Times Herald,* November 10, 1908; Texas A&M University, *1971 Football Press Guide,* 78, 84; College Station *Longhorn, 1910,* pp. 184-186.

[25]*The Contributions of E. J. Kyle,* 8-10; Ernest Langford, "Here We'll Build the College," unpublished manuscript in Texas A&M University Archives, 135-137; Texas A&M University, *1971 Football Press Guide,* 77, 97.

[26]Caesar Hohn Biographical Papers, Texas A&M University Archives; Texas A&M University, *1971 Football Press Guide,* 77.

[27]College Station *Longhorn, 1913,* p. 230.

[28]Clovis McCallister, "Beginning of Basketball at A&M, 3/5/64," unpublished memorandum in Athletics — Basketball File, Texas A&M University Archives.

Coach Steger, was more appreciative of the sport, "at last basketball has made a good start in gaining an equal footing with our other college sports."[29]

Although track and baseball were replaced in importance after 1900 by the enthusiasm for football, in point of time they were the first organized sports on the A&M campus. Texas A&M played its first baseball game on April 1, 1891, against Navasota. The game erupted into a "rhubarb" and the game was finally awarded to A&M by a score of 9-0. The next year the teams met again, A&M defeating Navasota by a score of 21-12. In 1893, the year in which football first appeared on campus, baseball was reported to be "on the decline." No competitive games were held other than one between the seniors and the faculty, for which no score was ever reported.[30] Baseball experienced a brief rejuvenation in 1894. The Aggies played 4 games, winning 3 and losing 1, but no games were recorded thereafter until 1904, when the Aggies resumed an uninterrupted baseball schedule. Wirt Spencer, the first regular baseball coach, coached the baseball team from 1904 until 1908, compiling 49 wins, 28 losses, and 3 ties. Moran coached the team through 1914, his teams making a much poorer showing on the diamond than on the gridiron, with 50 wins, 46 losses, and 5 ties.[31]

Texas A&M held its first invitational track meet in 1899, and continued the field day annually thereafter. In 1910 the Aggies produced their first great track team. The team won the first annual track meet of the Texas Intercollegiate Athletic Association, held at Sherman, Texas. William A. McDonald broke the Texas Intercollegiate record in the 120-yard hurdles and Roger Hooker tied the record in the 16-pound shotput. Outstanding performances were turned in by Jimmie Johnson and Meredith James in the pole-vault event. In the spring of 1911 Texas A&M initiated the first invitational track meet for high schools on a Texas college campus, the annual Interscholastic Track Meet.[32] Track, baseball, and basketball, however, generally remained subservient to football.

About 1910 the Company Athletic League was organized on campus and provided College-wide participation in organized sports. Players were required to have passing grades, and to be eligible for the College team. The winning teams in the events (baseball, football, basketball, and track) won

[29]*Ibid.*

[30]*The Collegian,* II (April 1891), pp. 14-15; *The College Journal,* IV (April 1892), pp. 15-16; III [*sic*] (March 1893), p. 23; College Station *Battalion,* October 1, 1893.

[31]Texas A&M University, *1972 Spring Sports Press Book,* 15.

[32]Bryan *Eagle,* April 5, 1900, April 28, 1904; *The Contributions of E. J. Kyle,* 11-12; Minutes of the Athletic Council, May 10, 1945, I, 16.

team sweaters, and, beginning in 1914, an all-company team was selected from competitors.[33] The competitive events not only provide recreation for the cadets, but serve as a training school for the regular teams.

Organized athletics at Texas A&M and elsewhere in the Southwest came of age with the organization of the Southwest Conference in December 1914. In May of that year representatives of eight colleges in Texas, Louisiana, Arkansas, and Oklahoma met in Dallas to discuss the organization of an athletic conference. The Texas Intercollegiate Athletic Association had disintegrated when The University of Texas withdrew following football disputes with Texas A&M in 1908-1910. The University suspended all football games with A&M after 1911, but, in the years following, sentiment was strong at both institutions for renewing association ties. Finally, at a December 1914 meeting, Texas A&M, Baylor University, Oklahoma A&M, Rice Institute, Southwestern University (Georgetown), and the Universities of Arkansas, Texas, and Oklahoma agreed to a compact creating the Southwest Conference. Louisiana State University, one of those originally interested in the conference organization, failed to join. Southwestern University, at Georgetown, withdrew in 1916; Southern Methodist University entered in 1918; Phillips University was a member between 1919 and 1921; Oklahoma withdrew in 1920; Texas Christian University joined in 1922; Oklahoma A&M dropped out in 1925; and Texas Tech entered in 1960, leaving, with the entry of the University of Houston in more recent years, the Southwest Conference with its current composition.[34]

Charles B. Moran, who had become a source of irritation to The University of Texas and other would-be conference members, resigned his coaching position at Texas A&M in December 1914. A&M students threatened to strike if Moran was not retained by the College, but President William Bennett Bizzell flatly said that he would not tolerate a strike, and Moran went.[35] Texas A&M then reorganized its athletic program under the headship of an athletic director. William L. Driver, formerly the coach at the University of Mississippi, when interviewed for the job of head coach at Texas A&M, agreed to come only as athletic director, and with the understanding that the College would implement his plan for a reorganization of the athletic pro-

[33]College Station *Longhorn, 1914,* pp. 289-290.

[34]Dallas *Morning News,* December 1, 1929, June 2, 1955; Texas A&M University, *1971 Football Press Guide,* 85-87.

[35]Minutes of the Athletic Council, December 4, 1914, I, 3; *ibid.,* January 17, 1915, I, 3-4.

gram. Driver conceived of college athletics as being physical education as much as competitive sports. Athletics, he said, should be taught in the classroom, as well as in the field.[36]

Driver was hired as athletic director and as head coach in basketball. E. H. W. ("Jigger") Harlan, of Princeton University, became head coach in football, and Dorsett V. ("Tubby") Graves, of Missouri, joined the staff as baseball coach and assistant in football.[37] Dana X. Bible, from Mississippi College, came to A&M in 1915 as freshman coach. Freshman teams were organized and games played with preparatory schools and with normal schools. Bible's freshmen won four out of their five games in the fall of 1915. In 1916 Bible went to Louisiana State University as assistant coach, but returned to Texas A&M in time to become head football coach for the 1917 season, replacing Harlan. Bible's coaching career was quickly interrupted by war. He joined the Aviation Corps in January 1918, but was back on the Texas A&M campus the following year. Beginning with the 1917 season, when the Aggies went undefeated and unscored on, Bible began to compile one of the most remarkable coaching records of all time.[38]

In both 1918 and 1919 his Aggie teams were undefeated and unscored on. The Thanksgiving Day game between Texas A&M and The University in 1919 marked two "firsts" in football history. Believed to be a "first" was a play-by-play radio broadcast of the A&M-Texas football game, by the ham radio station, 5 YA, located in the Electrical Engineering Building on campus, which station soon became, in 1922, the pioneer radio station WTAW. The station was sold by the College in 1959. In 1919 through the efforts of Dean Frank C. Bolton and a group of ham fans, including operator William A. Tolson, and two assistants, Harry M. Saunders and B. Lewis Wilson, Texas A&M broadcast a play-by-play account of the game. The announcer used abbreviations rather than descriptive phrases. "TB A 45 Y; T FP 8Y L," the announcer carefully tapped on a telegraph key, which broadcast meant "Texas's ball at the 45-yard line; Texas attempts a forward pass but is thrown for an 8-yard loss." A ham receiver in Waco reported that a near riot occurred as Texas and Aggie football fans crowded close to his receiver.[39]

[36]*Ibid.,* March 28, 1915, I, 9-10.

[37]*Ibid.,* June 4, 1915, I, 20.

[38]Texas A&M, *Annual Report, 1915-1916,* pp. 107-108; Dana X. Bible Biographical Papers, Texas A&M University Archives.

[39]College Station *Battalion,* November 26, 1953.

The 1919 game also marked the first annual Thanksgiving Day game played between The University of Texas and Texas A&M. The University first played A&M in football in 1894, and beginning in 1898 met the Aggies each year except for 1912-1914, when football relations between A&M and Texas were severed over player disputes in which Moran figured prominently. Between 1900 and 1909 the teams often met twice each year. With the organization of the Texas Intercollegiate Association in 1910, games were to be an annual affair but could be played on varying dates and at different cities. After the organization of the Southwest Conference, Texas A&M succeeded, in 1916, in getting The University to agree to play on Thanksgiving Day each year at alternate schools, the first engagement under the agreement occurring in 1919.[40]

The winning football season in 1919 produced enthusiastic support among the former students and football fans for the College's athletic program. The College Athletic Council, which has responsibility for the financial and administrative affairs of the intercollegiate athletic program, began to search for ways of enlarging the football "stadium," and decided to begin with a fund drive among former students. By October 1919 some $2,200 had been raised in contributions by the Athletic Council. In January the stadium campaign was turned over to William L. Driver and Dean Charles E. Friley. By March 4, 1920, little additional headway was made, the fund equalling only $2,467.50. The fund drive floundered at that point, and the funds and stadium program were turned over to the Former Students Association. The Former Students initially made plans to make the proposed stadium an alumni memorial to the men who had given their lives in World War I, and to lay a dedicatory cornerstone at the May 1920 commencement. As the fund drive continued to peter out, the plans were scrapped. The money accumulated over the next few years was loaned back and forth from the Association of Former Students to the Athletic Council for operating expenses.[41] Finally, in 1927, the College decided to build a new stadium with funds derived from the sale of revenue bonds.

Meanwhile Bible's A&M football team continued to compile an out-

---

[40]Minutes of the Athletic Council, October 23, 1916, I, 41; Bryan *Daily Eagle,* November 29, 1951.

[41]Minutes of the Athletic Council, June 30, 1919, I, 77; October 15, 1919, I, 79; January 27, 1920, I, 88; March 4, 1920, I, 92; March 1, 1922, I, 134; "The Alumni Memorial Stadium," *Alumni Quarterly,* V (February 1920), pp. 3-4.

standing record. In 1920 the Aggies won 6, tied 1 (LSU 0-0), and lost to Texas by a score of 3-7. The next year the record was 6-1-2, with the Aggies playing in one of the first postseason bowl games of record, the Dixie Classic, played at Fair Park Stadium, in Dallas, on Monday, January 2, 1922, against the "Praying Colonels" of Centre College of Kentucky. Centre College was undefeated and unscored on in their regular 1921 season, having played some of the nation's best teams such as Clemson, Harvard, Kentucky, and Auburn.[42]

A report of that game said,

> The Texas Aggies outprayed the Prayin' Colonels. It was the most spectacular, nerve tingling, and enthusiastic football game ever staged in the Southwest; one in which Coach D. X. Bible's fighting mystery team with their dazzling methods of attack and their dogged defense was far too great to be overcome by the hitherto undefeated "Miracle" eleven from the famous blue grass region. The Aggie squad, though only a bunch of youngsters, displayed unexcelled judgment, accompanied by undaunted fight and refused to be turned back.[43]

The score ended A&M 22-Centre College 14.

The Texas Aggies, dubbed the "Southern Champions," were "delirious with joy." Another small college was put on the football map; it was the "biggest surprise . . . since the United States adopted the alleged Eighteenth Amendment [prohibition]." Centre College had reportedly been a four-to-one favorite.[44] The game was unquestionably a hallmark in A&M football history.

The 1921 Centre game became legendary for yet another reason. During the game E. King Gill, a 165-pound reserve sophomore fullback, was in the press box serving as a spotter for Waco sports writer Jinx Tucker. As the rough game wore on, and injuries took their toll, the Aggies were down to only one backfield substitute. Bible called Gill down to the playing field and asked him to suit up; Gill donned injured Aggie captain Heinie Weir's uniform, who put on Gill's civilian clothes. Gill did not play in the game, but the legend says that his readiness spurred the Aggies to the upset 22-14 victory. Since that experience Aggie coaches have called upon the fabled "Twelfth Man" on several occasions, and the Corps of Cadets soon adopted

[42]Texas A&M University, *1971 Football Press Guide*, 79; *Texas A&M College vs. Centre College* (Football Program), in "Athletics — Football — Centre College," Texas A&M University Archives, College Station, Texas.

[43]*The Collegiate World*, IV (January-February 1922), pp. 2, 31.

[44]E. J. Howell and Karl Opryshek, *Southern Champions: A Football Treasure*, 1-32.

the custom, now a hallowed tradition, to stand at all football games, signifying their readiness to be the "Twelfth Man."[45] Gill graduated from Texas A&M in 1924 with a degree in engineering. He coached for a year before entering the Baylor School of Medicine. Earning his M.D. degree and entering private practice, in 1929, he retired at his Rockport, Texas, home in 1972.[46]

Bible continued to coach at Texas A&M until September 1, 1929. During Bible's eleven football seasons as coach at College Station, including the year 1918, when D. V. Graves substituted for him, the Aggies compiled a record of 72 wins, 19 losses, and 9 ties. Texas A&M won five Southwest Conference championships during those years; two of Bible's teams were unbeaten, untied, and unscored on. Bible left A&M to become head coach at the University of Nebraska, from 1929 to 1936, and in 1937 returned to Texas to become head coach at The University of Texas from 1937 to 1946. He retired as athletic director in 1956, after fifty years in football, one of the all-time truly great coaches.[47]

Football and competitive school spirit reached an intense degree during the 1920s, which in turn produced two notable events — one of them unsavory, and the other a unique feature of Aggie school spirit. At the Baylor-A&M football game in Waco in 1926 Baylor students put on a half-time show interrupted by a cadet who mistakenly assumed that the automobile being driven around the field was to be used in a derogatory demonstration against A&M, as had been done with a "bucking ford" the previous year. The Aggie attacked the car containing Baylor co-eds and proceeded to "rock" it. Baylor students rushed to drive away the offending cadet, and the Aggies rushed out to protect him. A riot followed, during which Cadet Charles M. Sessums was killed.[48] After their return to College Station, angry cadets decided to march on Baylor University, with their cannon in tow, and level it to the ground. Anxious moments were experienced by A&M administrators

[45]Bryan *Daily Eagle*, February 4, 1972.

[46]*Ibid.*

[47]Dallas *Morning News*, August 23, 1956; Houston *Post*, November 9, 1957; Bryan *Daily Eagle*, January 22, 1961; Minutes of the Athletic Council, December 26, 1928, I, 214.

[48]See Texas A&M College Publicity Department, Press Clippings, Book No. 2, February 1926-February 1927, Texas A&M University Archives, citing for example, Honey Grove *Citizen*, December 17, 1926; Tyler *Journal*, November 19, 1926; Channing *News*, November 26, 1926; Midland *Reporter*, November 19, 1926; Galveston *News*, November 1, 1926; Houston *Press*, November 11, 1926.

and by railroad officials, who feared that the cadets would make good on their resolve to commandeer a train and "attack" Baylor, before the cadets were finally dissuaded from their plot.[49] While the postgame events at College Station never became widely known or publicized, the riot at the Baylor game attracted statewide attention. Athletic relations between Texas A&M and Baylor were suspended until 1931.[50]

Another consequence of the 1920s football spirit was the institution of a new Aggie tradition, the bonfire, burned in preparation for the game against The University of Texas. Somewhere back in the earlier days bonfires were built on campus to rouse enthusiasm for sporting events. Ernest Langford recalls that back in his school days, between 1908 and 1912, fires were burned by excited students in anticipation of games — usually the "Varsity" game where rivalry was most keen.[51] In the snapping fall months of November or December, when the games were usually played, students, letting off steam at night before the coming event, welcomed a warm fire to crowd around. Gradually the pre-Texas University-game bonfire became a custom, then a "tradition." Frank G. Anderson, a former commandant, and a coach at Texas A&M in the fall of 1920, remembers seeing in that year his first bonfire, a "well aged tradition at that time."[52]

The bonfire, he said, was made of community trash, limbs, boxes, lumber scraps, and debris. Among the cadets' favorite materials for use in the bonfire were untended, unwatched, and, hopefully, unoccupied outhouses. The fire was lighted to the accompaniment of speeches and yells, and was usually burned out by the time the speechmaking had ended. The occasion, however, was not regarded as sufficiently memorable to be mentioned in the student annual, the *Longhorn*, until 1928, when a pile of junk destined to be the Aggie bonfire was first pictured. By this time the bonfire could be presumed to have become a "tradition." There were no other bonfire pictures featured before 1940 other than in the 1930, 1936, and 1938 *Longhorns;* but fires were being built each year in preparation for the game with The Univer-

[49]Tyler *Journal*, November 19, 1926; Galveston *News*, November 1, 1926; Houston *Press*, November 11, 1926.

[50]Dallas *Morning News*, December 9, 1926; Houston *Post-Dispatch*, December 9, 1926; Texas A&M University, *1971 Football Press Guide*, 79.

[51]Interview with Ernest Langford, April 21, 1971, College Station, Texas.

[52]Frank G. Anderson, "The bonfire as it was," College Station *Battalion*, January 18, 1972.

sity of Texas. By 1935 enthusiastic cadets were outdoing themselves in their resourcefulness in acquiring "junk" for the bonfire. "On the morning following the 1935 bonfire," Frank G. Anderson, then the newly appointed commandant, reported, "a very irate farmer came to my office to say that the boys had carried off his log barn, lock, stock and barrel." He demanded payment for his barn and the commandant assessed each company to raise the money.[53]

Because of the 1935 experience bonfire building was placed under the control of the commandant, who carefully regulated the collection of bonfire material and the actual construction of the fire. In 1936 the commandant directed the cadets to a grove of dead cottonwood trees near what is now Easterwood Airport. The College provided saws, axes, and trucks, and in 1936 the Aggies had their first log and their first "legal" bonfire. The first log bonfire, said Anderson, was not large, but it got the job done. Anderson in later years could not condone the building of taller and bigger bonfires with fresh-cut logs. Some junk, as well as logs, continued to be used for the bonfires during the thirties; the 1936 *Longhorn* features a bonfire composed largely of junk; the 1938 *Longhorn* features one with a combination of junk and logs; and in 1942 the fire was mostly junk.[54] The bonfire tradition emerged bigger and better after World War II. The first center pole for a bonfire made exclusively of logs was raised for the 1946 bonfire, and in 1947 two logs were strapped together in vertical extension to create the first high center pole.[55]

The 1947-1948 handbook for freshmen, the *Cadence*, described the traditional bonfire proceedings as follows:

Thanksgiving Bonfire

On the night before the annual football game with the University of Texas, the corps stands at attention to the strains of the Spirit of Aggieland, while a gigantic bonfire burns. During the two weeks before the Thanksgiving Day football game, all cadets spend their free periods gathering fallen trees, timber, and other inflammable materials that are authorized by owners. All of these are stacked in one enormous pile which often towers as high as fifty or sixty feet.

A nightly guard is mounted around the drill field to protect the materials from being set aflame by students from the rival school. All passers-by are questioned to see that no person other than loyal members of the Aggie cadet corps is allowed to go near the huge pile of inflammable materials.

[53]*Ibid.*
[54]"Athletics — Bonfire," Texas A&M University Archives.
[55]*Ibid.*

The bonfire symbolizes two things; a burning desire to beat the team from the University of Texas, and an undying flame of love that every loyal Aggie carries in his heart for the school.[56]

Since that time the bonfires, and opposition to the bonfires, have been growing taller and larger.

A companion tradition to the bonfire was Aggie yell practice. Its origins are hazy, but a little imagination easily suggests how such activities might develop on any college campus. In the post-World War II years the Aggie customs of earlier years became ritualized to become the traditions of today. Yell practice was one such custom to become ritualized, and incoming freshmen had to meticulously follow the ritual. The following description of yell practice in the 1947-1948 *Cadence* is presented for more than informational purposes; it is for the *instruction* of "fish:"

Yell Practice

Yell practice represents more than just another campus event. It is that time and place where enthusiasm, especially for athletic teams, is generated. The new student often gets his first feeling of real school spirit on these occasions.

During the football season, yell practice is held immediately after supper on the designated days. The meeting place is in front of the steps of Goodwin Hall. The primary purpose of these practices is to enliven the corps for the football game on Saturday.

At the practice the band takes it place on the platforms on each side of the steps in front of Goodwin Hall. The yell leaders take their places on the steps. In fan-like shape and on the area in front of the steps are the other members of the corps: the freshmen nearest, the sophomores next, behind them the juniors, and in the outskirts, the seniors.

The band plays. Yells are practiced. Talks concerning the coming game and the great Aggie spirit are made. These are fine, enthusiastic occasions, long remembered in the hearts of the Aggies. Often former students attend these meetings and speak to the corps, urging the students to keep up the same spirit and loyalty which has been a part of the school through the years. It is just such meetings that have provided the scenes for nationwide radio broadcasts.

Whenever the team plays a game away from the college the whole corps turns out to see them off and assure them of the students' support. The team is escorted to the train by the band and the cadet corps and a yell practice is held around the train. When the team returns, the cadet corps gives them a riotous welcome regardless of the score of the game and escorts them back to the campus.

At midnight of the day before every home conference game, the band mem-

[56]Texas A&M, *The Cadence*, 1947-1948, pp. 71-72.

bers stream out of their dormitory with glowing torches playing the Aggie War Hymn. Immediately from every dormitory on the campus come students who fall in line behind the band as it marches to Goodwin Hall and climbs on the steps for a yell practice.

After a victorious game on Kyle Field, the entire corps falls in line behind the band as it marches to the fish pond in Prexy's Triangle. Here the cadets celebrate the victory by throwing yell leaders into the pond. After this the band and corps proceed to the steps of Goodwin Hall where, for a few minutes, the yell leaders lead the group in rejoicing over the events of the afternoon.[57]

Madison Bell, or Matty, as he was called, inherited Bible's job of athletic director and football coach in 1929. As athletics became increasingly competitive in the Southwest Conference, the job of recruiting at Texas A&M became more than proportionately tougher. Bible, according to David W. Williams, went to Nebraska in part because there he could recruit from the entire state without serious competition from any rival institutions. In addition, the military regimen of the A&M College was often unattractive to many prospective athletes. Recruiters from other Texas institutions such as The University of Texas, SMU, Rice, Baylor, and TCU all gave the prospect the same story about Texas A&M, "You don't want to go down there. They blow a horn to put you to bed and blow a horn to get you up. No girls, no social life, no nothing. Now the kid hears this six or eight times, he believes it."[58] Thus, what might be called the "Aggie Syndrome" began to have a debilitating effect on Bible, Bell, Homer Norton, and coaches of more recent vintage.

Bell encountered rough sledding in 1929, winning 5 and losing 4 football games. It got rougher in 1930, when the Aggies won only 2 of 9 games. But 1931 brought new hopes with the Aggie eleven taking 7 of 10 games to place third in the Southwest Conference. After that it was mostly downhill again, and although a good 6-3-1 record was earned on the gridiron in 1933, Madison Bell's days were numbered. Homer Norton, whose Centenary College team in Shreveport, Louisiana, had trounced A&M in the 1933 season, was hired to replace Bell before the season was even over. Bell went as assistant coach to SMU and later became head coach there. He carried his team to the Rose Bowl in 1935, in which year Bell's SMU Mustangs defeated Texas A&M 24-0, with the Aggies failing to make a single first down.[59]

[57]*Ibid.*, 67-69.

[58]Interview with David W. Williams, September 15, 1971, College Station, Texas.

[59]Texas A&M University, *1971 Football Press Guide*, 79; *The Contributions of E. J. Kyle*, 12-14; interview with David W. Williams, September 15, 1971, College Station, Texas.

Homer Norton had a few bad years as head coach of the Texas Aggie football eleven. In 1934 the Aggies won 2, lost 7, and tied 1. In 1935 the record was 3 wins, 7 losses. Nineteen thirty-six was better, with 8 wins, 3 losses, and 1 tie. Norton produced three outstanding players on his 1936 team: Joe Routt, A&M's first All-American football player, who made All-American and All-Southwest Conference at guard; Charles DeWare, All-Southwest Conference center and the son of an earlier football great by the same name; and Roy Young, All-Southwest Conference tackle. In 1937 Routt repeated his honors, as did Young at tackle. Dick Todd, a brilliant halfback, and Virgil Jones, a great guard, both made All-Southwest Conference, but the Aggies ended the 1937 season with a 5-2-2 record at fifth place in the Conference.[60] A&M students and former students desperately wanted to go back to the winning ways of former years. Norton was in trouble. "The student body was in revolt against the coaching staff; the former students were worse. The faculty members were greatly disturbed. The Board of Directors were so concerned they told the President of the College it was up to him to straighten out the situation."[61]

According to Edwin J. Kyle, who resumed the duties of chairman of the Athletic Council in 1937, by 1938 "Everyone wanted a new coach. Some wanted a clean sweep of the entire coaching staff. Students and former students were demanding a showdown."[62] The 1938 season ended with the Aggies winning 4, losing 4, and tying 1, again placing them fifth in Conference standings. It was decided, however, to "stand pat" with Norton, who had two more years to run on his contract. It turned out that the impatient Aggie football fans were well advised in this course. The Texas Aggies won 11 regular-season games in 1939, A&M's only national championship, the Southwest Conference, and the Sugar Bowl in the first annual Sugar Bowl contest, where A&M defeated Tulane University 14-13. Five men made the All-Southwest Conference team: Joe Boyd, tackle; "Jarring" John Kimbrough, fullback; Marshall Robnett, guard; Herb Smith, end; and Jim Thomason, halfback. Boyd and Kimbrough were also named All-Americans.[63] The Aggies defeated Texas 20-0 during that season, in Kyle Field on Thanksgiving Day before a capacity crowd who witnessed ceremonies dedicating the

[60]Texas A&M University, *1971 Football Press Guide*, 79, 88, 95.

[61]*The Contributions of E. J. Kyle*, 14.

[62]*Ibid.*, 15.

[63]Beaumont *Enterprise*, January 1, 1956; Texas A&M University, *1971 Football Press Guide*, 80, 86, 88.

game to Jesse Holman Jones, head of the Reconstruction Finance Corporation, which had financed A&M's new dormitory-construction program.[64]

Norton's maroon and white did it again the next year, 1940, taking 9 of 10 contests on the gridiron, and the Cotton Bowl, first played in 1937, in which they defeated Fordham 13-12. John Kimbrough, guard Charles Henke, and tackle Joe Routt were outstanding players in that game, with Marion Pugh's conversion in the third quarter paving the way for the Aggie win. Kimbrough and Marshall Robnett at guard secured All-American honors in 1940.[65] Homer Norton won a new $10,000-a-year contract with Texas A&M.[66] In 1941 Texas A&M won the Conference again, with a 9-2 record.[67] In each of the War years, 1942-1945, the Aggies maintained a full schedule of games, but coaches, players, and contestants were constantly changing. As the War ended, player recruitment at the all-military, all-male Texas A&M College became more difficult. Norton's 1946 team ended the season with 4 wins and 6 losses; the 1947 eleven won 3, lost 6, and tied one.[68] The Aggies' great days in football now, for the most part, lay in the past. After 1941 Texas A&M won the Southwest Conference Championship on only two occasions, in 1956, under the tutelage of Paul ("Bear") Bryant, and in 1967, under Gene Stallings.[69]

The football fever, however, never diminished. Two large factors contributed to continuing Aggie frustration and a rather rapid turnover in the Texas A&M coaching staff: (1) continuing insistence upon a winning team; and (2) the handicap of intense recruiting competition from state and regional institutions which became national "football powers" in the postwar years, including all of the Southwest Conference members — The University of Texas, the University of Arkansas, Rice University, Baylor University, Southern Methodist University, Texas Christian University, and Texas Tech University — plus such regional powers as the University of Oklahoma and Louisiana State University, plus a myriad of smaller colleges which attract many fine athletes.

[64]*Texas A&M* vs. *University of Texas* (Football Program) November 30, 1939, in Athletics — Football, Texas A&M University Archives; Minutes of the Board of Directors, March 11, 1939, V, 182.

[65]Beaumont *Enterprise,* January 1, 1956; Texas A&M University, *1971 Football Press Guide,* 80, 86, 88, 95.

[66]Minutes of the Board of Directors, January 13, 1940, VI, 4.

[67]Texas A&M University, *1971 Football Press Guide,* 80, 86.

[68]*Ibid.*

[69]*Ibid.*

Homer Norton completed his coaching career at Texas A&M after the 1947 season, when illness and the poor athletic record forced his retirement. Robert H. ("Harry") Stiteler, Sr., an A&M graduate ('31) who had achieved an outstanding record in state high-school football coaching, replaced Norton. Under Stiteler the Aggies won no football games in 1948 and one in 1949, but came through with seven wins and four losses in 1950. Stiteler left under a cloud caused by the poor record and by personal difficulties which involved him in some unfavorable publicity. Raymond George took over for three years but achieved little better results on the gridiron. In 1954 the Aggies obtained the services of Paul ("Bear") Bryant, a proven coach of national reputation whose Aggie teams won the Southwest Conference in 1956, defeating The University of Texas in the process by a score of 34-21, a feat which Texas A&M has accomplished on only three occasions since 1939, the other occasions occurring in 1951 and 1967. The victory by the Aggies over the Longhorns in 1956 marked A&M's first win over Texas on Kyle Field. Jim Meyers, 1958-1961, and Henry C. ("Hank") Foldberg ('45), 1962-1964, both coached consecutive losing seasons. Gene Stallings ('57), another former student and a protégé of "Bear" Bryant, took over in 1965 and led the Aggies to a 1967 Southwest Conference championship, and to the Cotton Bowl, where Texas A&M defeated "Bear" Bryant's Alabama eleven by a score of 20-16. But Stallings ended his coaching career at A&M with a final record of 22 wins, 39 losses and 1 tie. Still seeking the winning combination, the Aggies obtained Emory Bellard from The University of Texas football staff in 1972, to try the new wishbone formation. By 1974 Bellard could present forty-four returning lettermen, ten of whom received postseason honors in 1973. Aggie gridiron expectations and hopes appeared fulfilled for the centennial season.[70]

One conclusion might be readily drawn: football infected the Texas Aggies in the 1890s; they were "hog-wild" over football by the 1920s; they still are! Football, of course, was not the whole show, but it was the big show, which is why the résumé of Texas A&M's athletic history is dominated by football.

Basketball, track, and baseball continued to thrive, but only as minor attractions, until in recent years the minor sports have experienced a rejuvenation which has converted them to major sports. Contributing to this change in emphasis is the fact that as college football has become more professionalized, with increasingly less student-body involvement and participation, stu-

[70]*Ibid.*, 80, 84, 86-87.

dents and fans have turned to the sports where the opportunities for participation and involvement appear to be greater. Since the organization of the
Southwest Conference in 1915 Texas A&M has won the basketball crown on
seven occasions, 1920-1923, 1964, and 1969, when the Aggies went on to the
NCAA playoffs. Aggies tied for the Southwest championship in 1951. After
Dana X. Bible left A&M in 1927 the football and basketball head-coaching
jobs were handled by separate people. Basketball coaches since 1927 have
been Charles Francis Bassett, 1928-1929; John Bond Reid, 1930-1935; Herbert
("Hub") Raymond McQuillen, 1936-1941; Marty Karow, 1942, 1946-1950;
Manning Smith, 1943-1945; John Floyd, 1951-1955; Ken Loeffler, 1955-1958;
Bob Rogers, 1958-1963; and Shelby Metcalf, 1964-.[71]

The Aggie baseball team has captured the Southwest Conference championship on seven occasions since 1915, and tied for the crown three times.
Championship teams were produced by Roswell Gunby ("Little Hig") Higginbotham in 1931 and 1934, Jules Verne ("Siki") Sikes in 1937, Lilburn
("Lil") John Dimmitt in 1942, Homer Norton in 1943 (tying with Texas),
and in 1955. Tom Chandler, who became head baseball coach in 1959, has
produced championship teams in 1959 and 1964; in 1966 the contest ended in
a four-way tie for the honors, with Texas A&M being one of the four.[72] Baseball coaches since 1915 have been Con Lucid, 1916; Dorsett V. ("Tubby")
Graves, 1917-1920; Dana X. Bible, 1921; Paul Santell, 1922; H. H. House,
1923-1925; Claude J. Rothgeb, 1926-1928; Bob Countryman, 1929-1930; Roswell G. Higginbotham, 1931-1935; Jules Verne Sikes, 1936-1938; Marty
Karow, 1939-1942, 1948-1950; Lilburn J. Dimmitt, 1943, 1946-1947; Homer
Norton, 1944-1945; Roy C. ("Beau") Bell, 1951-1958; and Tom Chandler,
1959-.

Since the organization of competitive intercollegiate track teams by
Texas A&M in 1902, the Aggies have produced some outstanding teams and
individual competitors. Texas A&M won the Southwest Conference championship eleven times between 1915 and 1970, and finished second on numerous occasions. All-time great track men include the following:[73]

Texas Aggie Olympians, Track All-Americas

Jack Mahan — 1920 Olympic Team (5th in javelin)

Roy Bucek — 1942 All-America (hurdles)

Pete Watkins — 1942 All-America (high jump)

---

[71]Texas A&M University, *1971-1972 Basketball Press Book*, 1-44.
[72]Texas A&M University, *1972 Spring Sports Press Book*, 3-24.
[73]*Ibid.*, 25-50.

Jitterbug Henderson — 1943 All-America (javelin)

Art Harnden — 1946 All-America (440 dash), 1948 All-America (440 dash), 1948 Olympic Team (1st in 1600-meter relay)

George Kadera — 1948 All-America (discus)

Walt Davis — 1951 All-America (high jump), 1952 All-America (high jump), 1952 Olympic Team (1st in high jump), 1952 World Record (6-11½ in high jump)

Darrow Hooper — 1951 All-America (shot put), 1952 All-America (shot put), 1952 Olympic Team (2nd in shot put), 1953 All-America (shot put)

Bobby Ragsdale — 1953 All-America (broad jump)

Randy Matson — 1964 All-America (shot put), 1964 Olympic Team (2nd in shot put), 1965 All-America (shot put), 1965 World Record (70-7¼ in shot put), 1966 All-America (shot put and discus), 1967 World Record (71-5½ in shot put), 1968 Olympic Team (1st in shot put)

Curtis Mills — 1969 All-America (440 yard dash). Won NCAA meet with world record 44.7. Also ran on All-America 440-yard relay team which finished third in NCAA in 39.5.

Jack Abbott — 1969 All-America (440-yard relay, 39.5)

Scott Hendricks — 1969 All-America (440-yard relay, 39.5)

Rockie Woods — 1969 All-America (440-yard relay, 39.5)

The minor sports on campus began to blossom somewhat after the organization of a regular physical-training program in 1915. Tennis appeared at the turn of the century, but the coaches were usually faculty volunteers. Tennis was made a competitive intercollegiate sport under the rules of the Southwest Athletic Conference in 1915. During World War I the tennis team was coached by James Sullivan, in the Feed Control division, and by William Henry Thomas, professor of English, but no matches were held. The first tennis tournament on campus appears to have been held on May 14, 1920.[74] The first College letter in tennis was awarded to Francis K. McGinnis, of the Class of 1900, but relatively few other letters were awarded between that time and 1925. Early tennis lettermen in this era included Daniel N. Murphy, 1910; Earle H. Varnell, 1921; John R. Wilson, 1921; Adolph E. Hinman, 1924; and Walter E. Anderson, Billy Cobb Barse, James Edmundson, and Carl M. Underwood, all in 1925.[75]

[74]Texas A&M, *Annual Report, 1917-1918,* p. 113; Minutes of the Athletic Council, May 14, 1920, I, 102-103.

[75]Texas A&M University, *1972 Spring Sports Press Book,* 56-57.

Boxing was introduced on the campus in 1917 by the Military Science Department, as were rifle and pistol shooting, all of which became recognized minor sports in later years. Boxing and wrestling matches were held under Athletic Council auspices in 1920. Soccer first came on campus in the spring of 1918, when a match was held against a Baylor University team, with the Aggies losing 3-0. A polo team was officially organized on campus in 1923, but received no financial support from the Athletic Council. In 1937 the Athletic Council recognized football, basketball, baseball, and track as major sports, and cross country, swimming, rifle shooting, golf, and tennis as minor sports; boxing was specifically excluded as a minor sport. In 1938 polo, fencing, and pistol shooting were given recognition as minor sports. William Merl Dowell was named head coach in tennis and Harry Stiteler head coach in golf in 1947.[76]

Swimming came of age at Texas A&M largely through the efforts of Arthur D. Adamson, who joined the Texas A&M faculty in 1934, the same year that the P. L. Downs Natatorium opened. Adamson, a native of London, England, grew up in New Zealand, where he acquired fame as a swimmer and twice won the national championship in the 100-yard freestyle event. While a swimming instructor at Texas A&M, Adamson completed his college education ('39). He retired in 1970 as professor emeritus, having coached thirty-two years of swimming at A&M, during which time he and his teams acquired national distinction. Five of his "boys" became All-America Swimmers. His swim teams won the Southwest Conference championship in 1945 and 1956, and shared the title in 1944. The Aggies were Conference water-polo champs in 1939 and 1965. In 1963 Adamson was elected to the Helms Hall of Fame, in Los Angeles. He died in College Station in 1972.[77]

The minor sports, and to some extent even football, suffered severely in the early years from the lack of adequate facilities, such as an indoor gymnasium, competitive-sized swimming pools, and modern stadium facilities. The first nominal athletic facility on campus was the Natatorium, constructed in 1894, but its major function was for bathing rather than swimming. In 1908 a larger swimming-bathing facility was built at a cost of $9,000 but again its prime purpose was bathing. Its secondary role appears to have been the initia-

[76]Texas A&M *Annual Report, 1917-1918,* p. 113; Minutes of the Athletic Council, November 8, 1923, I, 151; May 14, 1920, I, 102-103; June 4, 1937, II, 3-4; April 12, 1938, II, 9; July 2, 1947, II, 78.

[77]College Station *Battalion,* May 11, 1956; June 20, 1963; March 24, 1971.

tion of "fish," rather than swimming.[78] A recreational pool constructed in the basement of the YMCA in 1917 remained in use until 1934.[79]

Wooden bleachers on Kyle Field remained in use until 1927, when the first phase of a stadium-building program was completed, comprising the first five sections of what is still a part of the Kyle Field Stadium. It was designed by architects Henry Norton June, Ernest Langford, and engineer Carl Edward Sandstedt, and built at a cost of $76,718.84.[80] The construction of 1927 and 1929 was financed by stadium-revenue bonds, which with the advent of the Depression fell into near default. The College and its Athletic Council struggled to maintain interest payments on the bonds, and in 1936 the bonds were refinanced by authority of the state Legislature. A&M's experience with these bonds was harrowing but they were finally redeemed and paid off in full.[81] A second building program of sixteen units was completed in 1929 at a cost of $259,693.68. A third, upper-deck unit was added in 1954 at a cost of $346,000. Seating capacity at this point reached 35,000; in 1969 a further enlargement raised the seating to its present 49,000, at a cost of $1,840,000, one-half million dollars being used to carpet the field with "astro-turf," an artificial playing surface, surrounded by a tartan track.

Texas A&M had no indoor gymnasium until 1924 and the construction of DeWare Field House, named in honor of Charles A. DeWare, Sr. ('08), who lettered in football in each year 1905-1908, and who was regarded as one of the all-time greats of A&M football history. DeWare, a resident of Brenham, Texas, was paralyzed in his lower limbs a few years after graduation. He continued to lead a vigorous, active life and remained a strong supporter of his College and of A&M's football teams. He was elected president of the Association of Former Students in 1921.[82] The P. L. Downs Natatorium was erected in 1934 and named in honor of Board Director Pinckney L. Downs, Jr. ('06), who was largely responsible for the planning, promotion, and procurement of appropriations.[83] "Pinky" Downs continued to serve A&M in a variety of ways, for many years being the "Official Greeter" of the Univer-

---

[78]Texas A&M University, *Directory of Former Students, 1876-1970*, p. xi; Minutes of the Board of Directors, November 9, 1907, II, 52-60; College Station *Longhorn, 1908*, p. 27.

[79]Texas A&M *Annual Report, 1915-1916*, p. 117.

[80]Ernest Langford, "Here We'll Build the College," 135-137, unpublished manuscript in Texas A&M University Archives; *The Contributions of E. J. Kyle*, 12.

[81]Minutes of the Board of Directors, April 15-16, 1933, IV, 234; June 2-3, 1933, IV, 238-239; May 31, 1933, IV, 260; May 15, 1936, V, 51; May 30, 1936, V, 53; July 17, 1936, V, 57-58.

[82]Texas A&M University, *Directory of Former Students, 1876-1970*, xii.

[83]Minutes of the Board of Directors, June 1, 1934, IV, 263.

sity. In 1946 Texas A&M constructed its first concrete tennis courts, twelve in number, at a cost of $35,000. The eighteen-hole golf course, which is now a prominent feature surrounding the eastern part of the campus, was opened in 1950. The G. Rollie White Coliseum, erected in 1954, was named for Director White. The Wofford Cain Olympic Swimming Pool, named for Director Cain, was opened in 1962.[84] A bowling alley was built in the YMCA in 1934, and replaced by the new facilities in the Memorial Student Center in 1950, and again in 1973.[85]

Henderson Hall, a dormitory for freshmen and varsity athletes completed in 1958, was named for Robert William ("Jitterbug") Henderson ('42), a great all-around Aggie athlete who earned eleven letters in five major sports in addition to three freshman numerals and letters in two minor sports while at Texas A&M. Elected to the Texas Legislature in 1952, Henderson died of multiple sclerosis in 1954, at the age of thirty-six. Henderson Hall, like the $3-million athletic dormitory completed in 1973 which supersedes it, provided Aggie athletes all of the amenities of life, including a swimming pool, academic counselors, and dieticians. The newest athletic dormitory has beds for 208 boys on full-time athletic scholarships. In 1972-1973 Texas A&M had some 215 men on full-time athletic scholarships apportioned approximately as follows: football 152, basketball 16, baseball 14, track 20, swimming 6, golf 4, and tennis 3. Approximately 60 additional part-time scholarships are apportioned among the various sports. The total number of athletic sholarships is now prescribed by Southwest Conference rules.[86]

The Aggie mascot, Reveille, dates from 1931, when a group of cadets were returning from Navasota in their Model-T. Along the road they discovered a stray puppy, which they brought back to the campus. The next morning at reveille the puppy howled vigorously in tune with the bugle call, and he was promptly dubbed "Reveille." When, a few days later, Reveille romped onto the football field with the Aggie band at a half-time show, Aggie fans had their mascot. Each year the head yell leader provided a dog-blanket for the mascot, and Reveille and his successors became part of the Aggie "tradition."[87]

The Fightin' Texas Aggie Band, described as "thunder and blazes under

[84]Texas A&M University, *Directory of Former Students, 1876-1970*, xii-xiii.

[85]*Ibid.*, xii; Minutes of the Board of Directors, November 29, 1934, IV, 269.

[86]Ernest Langford, "Here We'll Build the College," 196; interview with Marvin Tate, associate athletic director, Texas A&M University, August 29, 1972, College Station, Texas.

[87]John Pasco, *Fish Sergeant*, 95-96.

tasteful restraint," began in 1894, when Joseph F. Holick and Arthur N. Jenkins organized a thirteen-piece cadet band. By the 1930s the band had grown to a 100-man marching military band, and in the post-World War II years, grew even more rapidly to become by 1968 a 267-member band. For three decades it was under the direction of Colonel Edward V. Adams ('29) until he was succeeded in 1973 by Major Joe T. Haney. Its outstanding attributes have been not merely size, but precision instrumentation and precision drill performances. The Aggie Band has appeared on nationwide television, and has record sales in the millions. It is an outstanding and nationally recognized organization, a fact even more remarkable since its members are entirely volunteer, and since Texas A&M, unfortunately, has never had a music or fine-arts program which might ordinarily generate a band of the caliber of the Fightin' Texas Aggie Band.[88]

Although music has not been a part of the Texas A&M curriculum, the band, the traditions, and the deep sense of school loyalty have produced what are regarded, by Aggies at least, as an outstanding choral group and several famous school songs. The "Singing Cadets," under the direction of Robert Boone, have in recent years made national tours and nationally televised show appearances. Among the songs have been *The Twelfth Man,* with words and music by Mrs. Ford ("Lil") Munnerlyn, and *I'd Rather Be a Texas Aggie,* with words and music by Jack Littlejohn ('39). *The Texas Aggie War Hymn* was composed by James V. ("Pinky") Wilson, of Florence, Texas, while on duty with the American Expeditionary Forces in France in 1918. Some former students recall that Wilson had been working on the song while a student at Texas A&M, for a College quartet had sung something similar just prior to the War. The music was set on paper about 1921 by George Fairleigh, then director of the Aggie Band, and the words and music were copyrighted that year. The song reflects the competitive spirit and traditional rivalry between The University and Texas A&M.[89]

The official school song, *The Spirit of Aggieland,* reflects the history, traditions, and deep affection of students and former students for their alma mater. It was written in the summer of 1925 by Marvin H. Mimms, a junior at Texas A&M. The music was composed by Bandmaster Richard J. Dunn and the song was introduced to the student body in the fall of 1925. It has

---

[88]"Corps of Cadets — Aggie Band," Texas A&M University Archives; see also *Texas Aggie* (November 1966), pp. 3-7.

[89]"Songs — Texas A&M University," Texas A&M University Archives.

since remained a great favorite and a great song.[90] Just as that song continues to denote high points in A&M sporting events, so it denotes the climax and the conclusion of this brief résumé of Aggie athletics:

THE SPIRIT OF AGGIELAND
1925

Some may boast of prowess bold,
Of the school they think so grand,
But there's a spirit can ne'er be told,
It's the spirit of Aggieland.

Chorus

We are the Aggies — the Aggies are we,
True to each other as Aggies can be,
We've got to Fight, boys,
We've got to Fight!
We've got to fight for maroon and white.
After they've boosted all the rest,
They will come and join the best,
For we are the Aggies — the Aggies are we,
We're from Texas A. M. C.

Second Chorus

T-E-X-A-S, A-G-G-I-E,
Fight! Fight! Fight-Fight-Fight!
Fight! Maroon! White-White-White!
A-G-G-I-E, Texas! Texas! A-M-C!
Gig'em, Aggies! 1! 2! 3!
Farmers Fight! Farmers Fight!
Fight-Fight-Fight
Fight-Fight-Fight
Farmers, Farmers, Fight!

[90]*Ibid.*

CHAPTER 24

An Age of Anxiety, 1948-1958

DURING the decade 1948-1958 Texas A&M confronted, and even courted, change without really changing. Compared to the Depression decade, the War years, and the years of postwar reconstruction, the decade marked a time of relative tranquility, but a time too, of considerable anxiety. There was concern for the things that were clearly coming, but were not yet quite here, things such as coeducation, elective military training and a resulting regular civilian student body at Texas A&M, racial integration, a burgeoning program of research and graduate study, and the development of a broader university complex. There was concern too for the things that were already here, not just in College Station, but "afoot" in all the land. In this ten-year period the face of America was being remade.

Thirty-nine million babies were born in that decade. Total population of the United States during this decade increased by thirty million. In ten years American life changed from what would now be considered the primitive to the modern. Narrow roads gave way to highways and superhighways; television came into almost every home; automobiles with power steering, power brakes, automatic transmissions, and tubeless tires appeared before new suburban houses, sometimes in pairs. There was a chicken, packaged and frozen, for every pot; there was air conditioning and the modern kitchen, with freezers, dishwashers, and electric gadgets defying description. There were power tools, fiberglass boats, instant foods, hi-fidelity, FM radio, filtered cigarettes, supermarkets, drive-ins, jet planes, power mowers, new jobs, new ideas, and a chilling cold war.[1] Underway was a technological revolution to which Texas A&M's engineers and agriculturists had undoubtedly contributed greatly, but which now seemed to be leaving the old College behind. Somehow, the faster she went the behinder she got; but in that, Texas A&M, of course, was not alone. It was endemic to the times.

The creation of the Texas A&M College System in 1948 brought Gibb Gilchrist to the chancellor's chair, and Frank Cleveland ("Bear Tracks") Bol-

[1]See Joseph Saten (ed.), *The 1950's: America's Placid Decade,* especially pp. 16-22.

ton to the presidency of the College. Bolton, inaugurated on November 18, 1948, had at that time completed almost forty years of service at Texas A&M, having joined the A&M faculty in 1909 as the first head of the new Department of Electrical Engineering. Bolton became dean of Engineering in 1922, dean of the College in 1931, and served as acting president in the interim between Thomas O. Walton's administration and the election of Gibb Gilchrist to the presidency in 1944.[2] He was a man for whom faculty, former students, and other associates held deep respect and admiration. An associate described him as a very steady, fine, dependable, sincere man, a good engineer, but pretty much restrained by tradition, who rarely strayed far from the middle.[3] Bolton in many ways characterized the more outstanding traits of the A&M College — steady, dependable, competent, clothed in tradition, rarely departing far from the middle.

Bolton's administration as president of A&M College could be considered routine, but effective. Many of the political chores and the political storms were lifted from the President's shoulders by the presence of the chancellor, Gibb Gilchrist. Gilchrist, too, handled the chores of administering the branches, the services, and the agencies, which previously consumed a great amount of the president's time, and which chores became greater as time passed. Bolton and his successors until 1965 could focus more attention on the academic and administrative affairs of the main College.

The organization of the System offered distinctive administrative advantages to the president of Texas A&M, as well as to the presidents of the branch colleges and the directors of the services. The chancellor was in theory a Systems man and not a Texas A&M College man. In practice Texas A&M College continued to be the parent institution, and not a peer. In theory the chancellor held the reins on the powers of the president of Texas A&M. But an organizational fallacy crept into the System as a result of the fact that although Texas A&M College was bigger, more important, and more expensive than all of the other branches and services combined, it was administered by an official technically subservient to the chancellor. With both offices located on the same campus the problem was even more delicate and ticklish. It was a case of the tail trying to wag the dog. Chancellors Gibb Gilchrist (1948-1953) and Marion Thomas Harrington (1953-1965) managed to coordinate the System from the chancellor's post with considerable success, but by 1965 the dog would have no more of it, and the control over the System was returned to the Office of the President.

[2]R. Henderson Shuffler, *A Man and His College* [1-8].
[3]Interview with David W. Williams, September 15, 1971, College Station, Texas.

Generally, between 1948 and 1965, Gilchrist and Harrington were successful chancellors because they left the real administrative control over the branches and services in the hands of the presidents and directors. Between 1948 and 1958 Presidents Frank Cleveland Bolton (1949-1950), Marion Thomas Harrington (1950-1953 and 1957-1959), David H. Morgan (1953-1956), and David W. Williams (acting, 1956-1957) were the real heads of Texas A&M, not merely figureheads. With the exception of D. H. Morgan, the leaders and administrators of Texas A&M and of the System between 1948 and 1958 were the same men who guided the College through the era of postwar reconstruction. Although the titles and positions often changed, and some retirements occurred, a fairly distinct administrative team managed Texas A&M from 1944 to 1956. This team included Gibb Gilchrist as president and chancellor, 1944-1953; Tom Harrington, dean of Arts and Sciences, dean of the College, president and chancellor, 1948-1965; David W. Williams, vice-president for agriculture, vice-chancellor for agriculture and acting president, 1946-1956; Homer Lloyd Heaton, registrar, dean of Admissions, 1944-1972; William Clyde Freeman, comptroller and vice-president, 1952-; John C. Calhoun, Jr., dean of Engineering, vice-president and vice-chancellor for engineering, vice-chancellor for development, 1955-1963, vice president for programs, 1965-1971, and vice-president of academic affairs, 1971-; Ide Peebles Trotter, director of the Texas Agricultural Extension Service and dean of the Graduate School, 1944-1960; Alfred D. Folweiler, director of the Texas Forest Service, 1949-1967; and Robert Donald Lewis, director of the Texas Agricultural Experiment Station, 1946-1967.[4]

After 1948 continuity and longevity in departmental officers was also common. Letcher P. Gabbard headed Agricultural Economics and Sociology from 1947 to 1953. He was succeeded by Tyrus R. Timm, who chaired the Department from 1953 through 1970, when Sociology was made a separate department in the College of Liberal Arts under Robert Leonard Skrabanek. Fred Rufus Jones served as chairman of the Department of Agricultural Engineering from 1940 to 1959. Ernest Langford chaired the Department of Architecture from 1929 to 1957. Jack C. Miller headed Animal Husbandry from 1947 to 1956, when he became dean of the School of Agriculture. Ogburne D. Butler replaced Miller in Animal Husbandry and remained head of that department into the seventies. Thomas William Leland, between 1926 and 1958, developed the Department of Business and Accounting into a Division of Business Administration in the School of Arts and Sciences. Clifton

[4]Texas A&M, *Catalogue, 1948-1949*, pp. 5-6; *Catalogue, 1958-1959*, pp. 4-5; *Catalogue, 1968-1969*, pp. 348-349.

Childress Doak headed Biology from 1937 until his retirement in 1960. James D. Lindsay chaired the Department of Chemical Engineering from 1944 to 1965.[5]

Other men who directed departments continuously through most or all of the decade 1948-1958 included Frederick William Jensen, Chemistry; Isaac W. Rupel, Dairy Science; Walter W. Delaplane, Economics; George B. Wilcox, Education and Psychology; Martin C. Hughes, Electrical Engineering; William E. Street, Engineering Drawing; Adolphe Ferdinand DeWerth, Landscape Architecture; Chauncey B. Godbey, Genetics; George Wilhelm Schlesselman, Geography; Shirley A. Lynch, Geology; Carl E. Tishler, Physical Education; Samuel R. Gammon, History; Guy W. Adriance, Horticulture; Chris H. Groneman, Industrial Education; Donald B. Burchard, Journalism; Charles W. Crawford, Mechanical Engineering; Joseph J. Woolket, Modern Languages; Dale F. Leipper, Oceanography and Meteorology; James G. Potter, Physics; Gustav McKee Watkins, Plant Physiology and Pathology; John H. Quisenberry, Poultry Science; Vernon G. Young, Range and Forestry; John Milliff, Veterinary Anatomy; August A. Lenert, Veterinary Medicine and Surgery; Richard D. Turk, Veterinary Parasitology; Patton W. Burns, Veterinary Physiology and Pharmacology; and William B. Davis, Wildlife Management.[6] Insofar as administration is concerned the decade 1948-1958 is characterized by continuity rather than by change.

Stability, rather than change, was characteristic also of student enrollment at Texas A&M during the decade. After an initial decline from the high fall enrollment of 8,536 students in 1948-1949, a decline explained by the reduced number of veterans returning to the campus, enrollments at Texas A&M averaged something less than 7,000 students per year. Table 7 denotes enrollment by schools and by years. Characteristic of these years is a relative decline in enrollment in agricultural studies, general stability in engineering, and growth in arts and sciences. Enrollment for the 1948-1958 decade at Texas A&M should also be viewed in the light of the surge in enrollment generally characteristic of Texas institutions of higher learning during the same general period. For example, the overall growth for the nineteen fully state-supported institutions of higher learning in Texas, including Texas A&M, between 1951 and 1961 was slightly over 92 percent, or five and one-third times the rate of growth of Texas A&M. Many of the colleges more than doubled enrollment in that period. Arlington State College, an A&M

---

[5]Texas A&M, *Catalogue, 1948-1949*, pp. 9-31; *Catalogue, 1958-1959*, pp. 9-40; *Catalogue, 1968-1969*, pp. 302-349.
[6]*Ibid.*

branch, and Lamar State College of Technology, created a senior college in 1951, grew by more than 600 percent.[7]

Table 7.
Texas A&M Enrollment, 1948-1958

Year	Agriculture	Arts and Sciences	Engineering	Veterinary Medicine	Total
1948-1949	2,382 (27.9%)	1,637 (19.2%)	4,281 (50.1%)	236 (2.8%)	8,536
1949-1950	2,210 (28.4%)	1,657 (21.3%)	3,654 (47.1%)	251 (3.2%)	7,772
1950-1951	1,898 (28.4%)	1,547 (23.2%)	2,928 (43.9%)	302 (4.5%)	6,675
1951-1952	1,710 (26.0%)	1,583 (24.0%)	2,727 (41.0%)	399 (6.0%)	6,583
1952-1953	1,545 (24.6%)	1,416 (22.6%)	2,814 (44.8%)	393 (6.3%)	6,277
1953-1954	1,452 (23.0%)	1,291 (21.0%)	2,893 (47.0%)	410 (7.0%)	6,198
1954-1955	1,300 (21.0%)	1,283 (21.0%)	3,074 (49.0%)	455 (7.0%)	6,257
1955-1956	1,318 (19.0%)	1,479 (22.0%)	3,448 (50.4%)	480 (7.0%)	6,837
1956-1957	1,288 (18.0%)	1,617 (22.0%)	3,728 (52.0%)	420 (6.0%)	7,200
1957-1958	1,165 (16.0%)	1,882 (25.0%)	3,897 (52.0%)	400 (5.0%)	7,474

Source: Texas A&M Century Study, 1962, Report of the Sub-Committee on Historical Perspective.

A subcommittee on historical perspective, working under the auspices of the Texas A&M Century Council, which comprised one hundred outstanding citizens of Texas selected to evaluate the A&M College programs and policies, concluded that Texas A&M, over two decades, 1941-1961, was fast losing its recognition as the second school in the state, coordinate with The University of Texas. The subcommittee attributed this situation to a number of factors, including the facts (1) that Texas A&M no longer had a monopoly on its course offerings and had lost any uniqueness it may formerly have had, vocational training and agricultural and engineering studies having been pre-empted by most other institutions; (2) that the College did not offer a university orientation in name or in course offerings as did many other institutions; (3) that the College was segregated as to gender, unlike every other institution of higher learning in Texas other than Texas Woman's University, which had also experienced a relative decline in enrollment and prestige; (4) that the College's unique insistence upon compulsory military training and military organization of the student body was detrimental to its academic programs and growth; and (5) that the curricula in all fields needed to be broadened with the development of high-quality programs in all areas. These observations failed to be reflected in the final *Report of the Century Council.*[8]

[7]Texas A&M Century Study, 1962 (mimeographed), Report of the Sub-Committee on Historical Perspective, 1-11.

[8]*Ibid.,* 10; Texas A&M, *Report of the Century Council* (1962), pp. 7-11.

The observations and the enrollment figures do reflect, however, the reasons for continuing anxiety throughout the decade 1948-1958, and focus upon the primary concerns of faculty, staff, and administrators for several decades after World War II. To be sure, some progress was made in broadening the curricula and in improving the quality of programs, and some experiments as well as trials (literally) were conducted with noncompulsory military training and coeducation during the decade.

During the presidency of Frank C. Bolton the A&M Board of Directors initiated a new building program, facilitated by the adoption of a constitutional amendment allowing Texas A&M and The University of Texas to fund revenues from the University Permanent Fund, that is, to issue bonds for construction with the revenue from the Permanent Fund pledged for the bonds. The Directors credited Dudley K. Woodward, Jr., for his "able and unselfish leadership and efficient guidance of all phases of activities relative to the submission, adoption and defense of the College Building Amendment."[9] In 1956 another constitutional amendment allowed for a broader base of investment of the University Permanent Fund to generate higher yields, and provided that bonds could be issued for future construction, and for the use of interest to supplement salaries at Texas A&M and at The University of Texas. Construction on campus completed between 1948 and 1958 included the facilities shown in table 8.[10]

Bolton's tenure as president of Texas A&M was in some respects a caretaker regime, since, only nine months after he took office, on September 22, 1949, the Board of Directors named Marion Thomas Harrington to succeed him at the "end of the present school year." Harrington, who had been acting dean of the College and dean of the School of Arts and Sciences since May 1948, was named dean of the College, which position he used for "training" until he assumed the president's office on June 3, 1950.[11] Harrington held a strong executive role at Texas A&M from 1948 until his retirement as chancellor in 1965.

Tom Harrington was born in Plano, Texas, on September 8, 1901. He

[9]Minutes of the Board of Directors, November 24, 1948, IX, 124; Fort Worth *Star-Telegram,* March 11, 1949; interview with Marion Thomas Harrington, September 13, 1971, College Station, Texas.

[10]Texas A&M, *Directory of Former Students, 1876-1970,* xii-xvi; Minutes of the Board of Directors, January 8, 1949, IX, 140; June 14, 1949 ($5 mil. Permanent University Fund Bonds sold at 1.64635 percent interest), IX, 166-167 and Exhibits A-F; May 13-14, 1949 (MSC construction), IX, 171; June 24, 1950, X, 72.

[11]Minutes of the Board of Directors, September 22, 1949, X, 1; interview with Marion· Thomas Harrington, September 13, 1971, College Station, Texas.

Table 8.

Construction on Campus, 1948-1958

Year	Facility	Cost
1948	Easterwood Airport Hangar	$ 10,000
1949	Entomology Field Laboratory and Greenhouse	40,000
1949-1950	Grove Theater and Recreation Area	27,000
1950	Beef Cattle Center	110,000
1950	Memorial Student Center	2,000,000
1950	Biological Sciences Building	600,000
1950	Francis Hall (Business Annex)	134,000
1951	Dairy Center	110,000
1951	Poultry Buildings and Laboratories	168,000
1951	Poultry Classroom Building	96,000
1951	Swine Classroom Building and Laboratory.	96,000
1951	Horse Barns	73,000
1951	Dairy Feeding Barn	70,000
1951	Horticulture Greenhouse	20,000
1951	Coke Building	460,000
1951	Physics Building Addition	216,000
1951	College Water System	700,500
1951	Agricultural Farm Facilities	1,750,000
1952	Engineering Building	570,000
1952	Texas Engineers Library	200,000
1953	Veterinary Hospital	600,000
1954	Laboratories and Greenhouses	330,000
1954	Street and Sidewalk Improvements	200,000
1954	G. Rollie White Coliseum	670,000
1954	Highway Research Center	173,000
1954	Dairy Breeding Center	85,000
1954	Upper Deck to Kyle Field	346,000
1954	Veterinary Sciences Building	881,000
1955	A&M Press Building	347,000
1955	Addition to College Power Plant	670,000
1956	Easterwood Airport Terminal	106,000
1957	All Faiths Chapel (by Former Students)	257,000
1957	Judging Arena for Dairy Center	37,000
1957	Biochemistry Building	1,057,000
1958	Completion of Wind Tunnel	438,000
1958	Addition to Chemistry Building	1,193,000
1958	Henderson Hall (athletic dormitory)	476,000
	Total Construction, 1948-1958	$15,310,500

Source: Texas A&M, *Directory of Former Students 1876-1970.*

enrolled in chemical engineering at Texas A&M in 1918, and, upon graduation in 1922, worked as a chemist for the Texas Company at their refinery in Port Arthur. In 1924 he accepted an offer from the Lone Star Gas Company at their new helium plant in Petrolia, Texas, northeast of Wichita Falls. That summer Charles Cleveland Hedges offered him a teaching job in the Department of Chemistry at A&M. Harrington accepted and remained with the College until his full retirement in 1971. He earned his master's degree in chemical engineering from Texas A&M in 1927, and later earned his doctorate in inorganic chemistry from Iowa State College. He taught chemistry from 1924 until 1946, when he became supervisor of the freshman "Annex" at Bryan Airfield.[12]

Harrington, a good academician and capable administrator, sponsored a number of important innovations and developments while dean of the College and president. He promoted the organization of a Department of Oceanography and Meteorology, which the Board approved in November 1948, and which developed out of the Research Foundation Program which Harrington had also helped frame.[13] In January 1949 Ide P. Trotter, who had performed so well as a troubleshooter in the Agricultural Extension Service, was named dean of the Graduate School, with the assignment to expand and improve the graduate program. Trotter replaced Paul B. Pearson, who left A&M to serve with the Atomic Energy Commission.[14] In July 1949 the Directors named Barlow Irwin athletic director. Irwin provided needed direction and continuity in the College's athletic programs until his retirement in 1968.[15] John Paul Abbott, professor of English, succeeded Tom Harrington as dean of the School of Arts and Sciences in 1949.[16] The College accepted in 1949 the Carl Metzger Collection of rare military and civilian firearms, which is today prominently displayed in the Memorial Student Center.[17] In 1949 a survey of the College library by professional librarians from other institutions provided the impetus for a much needed program of acquisitions and library expansion. The survey reported that the library collection of 163,000 volumes was seriously inadequate for both an undergraduate and a graduate library. Subse-

[12]Interview with Marion Thomas Harrington, September 13, 1971, College Station, Texas.

[13]*Ibid.;* Minutes of the Board of Directors, November 24, 1948, IX, 22.

[14]Minutes of the Board of Directors, January 8, 1949, IX, 141; Houston *Chronicle,* March 11, 1949.

[15]Minutes of the Board of Directors, July 7, 1949, IX, 175.

[16]*Ibid.,* November 23, 1949, X, 31.

[17]*Ibid.,* November 23, 1949, X, 31.

quently additional funds channeled into book acquisitions increased the size of the collection to 183,000 volumes by 1955, still inadequate by most standards, but by 1962 the library reported 434,000 volumes and a marked improvement in the quality of the holdings.[18] By 1972 it had over 716,000 volumes, comprising the fifth largest collection among Texas colleges and universities. In 1950 the Directors established the Division of Business Administration, authorized to grant a bachelor and a master's degree in business administration.[19] Also in 1950, Texas A&M began preparations to celebrate its Seventy-fifth Anniversary.[20] Harrington assumed the president's office on June 3, 1950, the first graduate of Texas A&M to serve as president. Charles Clement French, formerly vice-president of Virginia Polytechnic Institute, replaced Harrington as dean of the College.[21]

Texas A&M celebrated its Seventy-fifth Anniversary on October 4, 1950, with ceremonies in Kyle Field, featuring Governor Allan Shivers of Texas, among other notables.[22] When the speeches ended, the entire student body and guests were hosted at a barbecue beneath the grandstand. A small eighteen-page publication commemorated the event:

> From fighting forest fires in the piney woods of East Texas to poisoning prairie dogs on the High Plains, from developing a new profitable crop for Texas farmers to training the supervisors on her railroads, the activities connected with A. and M. run the gamut of research, extension and teaching needed to meet the problems of a growing state and pave the way for even greater growth tomorrow. Texas has left behind forever the era of the raw frontier, the free range and the simple machine. In a complex society, geared to scientific agriculture and industry, A. and M. has developed to meet the demands of the state to which it belongs.[23]

The brochure stressed the services of Texas A&M to the state in the areas of agriculture and engineering.

Among the outstanding contributions of the College cited by the commemorative brochure were the development of Sudan grass for forage; feterita, a combine-type grain sorghum; the hybridization of cotton, corn, small

---

[18]*Ibid.*, March 11, 1949, IX, 155; Texas A&M, *Institutional Self-Study*, 1963, pp. 99-105; Texas State Library, *Texas Public Library Statistics for 1971*, p. 135.

[19]Minutes of the Board of Directors, January 14, 1950, X, 45.

[20]*Ibid.*, March 24, 1950, X, 51, 55.

[21]Interview with Marion Thomas Harrington, September 13, 1971, College Station, Texas; Houston *Post*, May 11, 1950.

[22]*Ibid.*

[23]Texas A&M, *75th Anniversary, 1876 . . . 1951* [p. 14].

grains and grasses; and the work of Ray E. Dickson of the Spur Experiment Station in developing improved water conservation and terracing techniques. The Agricultural Extension Service, operating as an arm of the College, touched the lives of more than 500,000 Texans in 1949 alone, exclusive of the great works done in the past. The Texas Forest Service undergirded a Texas lumber industry which grossed $125 million annually. The School of Engineering, the Engineering Extension Service, and the Engineering Experiment Station provided technical knowledge, testing, and research for the development of Texas highways and industry, and offered technical training to thousands of Texans annually in fields ranging from plumbing to plant management. Texas A&M paid special tribute to Directors Francis Marion Law and G. Rollie White, and to past educational leaders such as Governor Richard Coke, Senator George Pfeuffer, Lawrence Sullivan Ross, David F. Houston, Thomas O. Walton, Dr. Mark Francis, "the Louis Pasteur of Texas tick fever," and William Bennett Bizzell. Oscar M. Ball was cited for outstanding work in biology, and Helge Ness for his work in the hybridization of plants and the development of the Ness Oak and the Nessberry. Robert E. Karper and J. Roy Quinby pioneered the development of improved grain sorghums. Edgar S. McFadden developed rust-proof varieties of wheat and small grain. James O. Beasley, killed in Italy during World War II, pioneered in work on cotton genetics. Frank C. Bolton, James Nagle, and Gibb Gilchrist made oustanding contributions as engineers and administrators. Under M. T. Harrington, the commemorative brochure continued, "the stage is set for one of the most successful periods in the history of the college."[24]

Harrington's formal inauguration took place on November 9, 1950. John Hanna, president of Michigan State University, addressed the College representatives at a noon luncheon, and in the afternoon Dwight D. Eisenhower, then president of Columbia University, was the inaugural speaker in ceremonies at Kyle Field. Harrington recalls meeting Eisenhower at the railroad station in Caldwell, where the local school children were lined up to see the General. Harrington joined Eisenhower at his breakfast table in his private car. When Eisenhower opened the curtain and saw the children he said to his aide, "What are they doing out there?" "They are waiting to speak to you," was the answer. "Well why didn't you let me know," Eisenhower exclaimed and "jumped up and went out and just went down the line and shook hands with every school kid."[25]

[24]*Ibid.*

[25]Interview with Marion Thomas Harrington, September 13, 1971, College Station, Texas.

A cold norther had blown into College Station the night before. Harrington recalls another memorable gesture made by Eisenhower during the Corps review on the morning of the inauguration:

> We got in the car [at the railroad station in Caldwell], and of course we had the heater on in the car, and he wore a gabardine topcoat like the style at that time was. We drove up to the MSC, and had the R.V. escort, and the Cadet Corps was lined up to go out. He saw that the cadets did not have overcoats. Of course, they may have had lots of clothes on underneath, facing that north wind. He took off his topcoat, after having ridden in the car with the heater on, and handed it to his aide. I kept mine on, and I said, "General Eisenhower, wouldn't you like to have your topcoat?" He said, "No, as long as the students do not have one on, I'll not wear mine."[26]

Harrington recalls the outstanding achievements of his administration as the establishment of the Basic Division, the development of the Research Foundation and the research programs, the construction of the Richard Coke Building and the Memorial Student Center, and the entry of A&M into the Foreign Technical Assistance programs.[27]

Texas A&M's experiences with the freshman division housed at the Bryan Air Force Annex between 1946 and 1950 had proved academically sound. There existed a clear need to provide a basic orientation program for entering freshmen which could help them develop good study habits and channel each student into a field of endeavor where he displayed the greatest aptitude, ability, and interest. Many entering freshmen had ill-conceived ideas of college life and of their professed field of endeavor. As President Gilchrist indicated in 1945, the attrition rate among entering freshmen equalled almost one-half of the entering freshman class during the first year. This represented a costly loss of effort and money, not only for the student and his parents, but for society. The freshman division comprised an earnest effort to make the student's entry into college studies more effective. When A&M closed down its academic program at the Annex in June 1950, the desirability of continuing a basic or freshman division on the main campus was particularly obvious to President Harrington, Chancellor Gilchrist, and Dean of Arts and Sciences John Paul Abbott, who had each had firsthand experiences in the administration of the Annex. The faculty, too, favored the implementation of a formal "basic division" program. The Academic Council, representing the

[26]*Ibid.*
[27]*Ibid.*

faculty, presented a proposal to the Directors in the spring of 1950, and the Board approved the implementation of a Basic Division on September 1, 1950, "for the purpose of providing more adequately for the special needs of the entering students by making possible closer supervision and better guidance during their initial college careers."[28]

John Raney Bertrand, formerly an associate professor of rural sociology, and assistant to the dean of Agriculture, was named dean of the Basic Division. The Basic Division dormitories were separated from the upperclass Corps area, but all entering freshmen continued to be enrolled in R.O.T.C.[29] The Basic Division offered a New Student Week program providing individual and group counseling, achievement and aptitude testing, and general orientation. Entering freshmen could elect to enroll in a general curriculum, or a degree curriculum within the school of their choice. Basic courses included an orientation course, aimed at the selection of attainable life goals; a remedial reading course; college study involving the principles of learning; individual adjustment "designed to help the student understand himself and the nature of the society of which he is a member;" the world of work, directed to the achievement of occupational goals; a survey of man's knowledge, providing a broad humanities background; and the engineering profession, designed to provide intensive information about the specific branches of engineering.[30]

The Basic Division offered "pre-college" work in summer sessions at the Junction Adjunct, where high school graduates could obtain remedial work preparatory to enrolling at A&M, guidance and counseling, and college credit for basic courses such as English, history, and mathematics. Clifford Howell Ransdell, from the Department of Engineering Drawing, who had served as assistant dean, became acting dean of the Basic Division in 1954, when Bertrand resigned to accept the position of dean of Agriculture at the University of Nevada. Robert B. Kamm replaced Ransdell as dean in 1956.[31] Kamm departed in 1958 and his position was never filled. The Basic Division was allowed gradually to fade away. Ransdell remained in charge of the program as associate dean in 1959-1960. In 1960-1961 the position was down-

---

[28]Minutes of the Board of Directors, January 14, 1950, X, 44.

[29]*Ibid.*, May 11, 1950, X, 67-68; Dallas *Morning News*, March 25, May 12, 1950.

[30]Texas A&M, *Catalogue, 1958-1959*, pp. 29-82, 236-237; College Station *Battalion*, January 16, 1950; April 24, 1953.

[31]*Ibid.*, 23, 32; Texas A&M, "Report to the Texas Commission on Higher Education: Role and Scope of the College in Higher Education Systems of Texas," June 24, 1954, p. 4; College Station *Battalion*, August 3, 1954; November 24, 1954.

graded to associate director, and for the 1961-1962 year the position disappeared. Ransdell returned to the School of Engineering as assistant to the dean. The Basic Division was absorbed by the Counseling and Guidance Service, the course offerings gradually disappearing. All that remained by the end of the sixties was a summer program at the Adjunct, near Junction, a freshman orientation week, and an anomalous collection of books, gathered some years after the demise of the Basic Division, shelved separately in the library, and labeled the "Basic Collection" — a bleak reminder of a noble effort gone astray.[32]

What happened to the Basic Division? Two things are likely responsible for the demise of the program — apathy and antipathy. When Harrington left the president's office in 1959 the Basic Division lost its champion; and antipathy to that program had already developed among the schools, which regarded the year of freshman orientation as a year of nonachievement and misdirection. Some deans and many segments of the faculty feared that orientation might orient the freshmen away from their first preference — usually engineering or agriculture; far better that the engineers or agriculturists take upon themselves the responsibility for freshman orientation, counseling, and guidance.[33] And so it has been ever since.

Expansion of the Research Foundation and related programs continued rapidly through the decade of the 50's. In June 1950 the Board of Directors created the Texas Transportation Institute, which was designated by the State Highway Department "to do highway research for and in behalf of the State of Texas and the State Highway Department."[34] The Oceanography Department, organized in 1949, obtained its first seagoing vessel in 1950, a three-masted, 120-foot schooner, the *Atlantic,* contributed to the Texas A&M Research Foundation by Edwin C. and Robert A. Uihlein, of the Joseph Schlitz Brewing Company, of Milwaukee. The vessel could cruise at 9 knots under power or 11 knots under sail, and carried a crew of six or seven and ten scientists.[35] One enthusiastic, but errant, nautical-minded Aggie reportedly sought to enroll in the oceanographic studies for a course in water polo, reported Departmental Chairman Dale F. Leipper soon after the receipt of the vessel.[36]

---

[32]Texas A&M, *Catalogue, 1959-1960,* p. 5; *Catalogue, 1960-1961,* p. 7; *Catalogue, 1961-1962,* pp. 35, 105-107.

[33]Interview with Homer Lloyd Heaton, July 10, 1972, College Station, Texas.

[34]Minutes of the Board of Directors, June 24, 1950, X, 78.

[35]College Station *Battalion,* February 1, 1950.

[36]Dallas Morning News, February 5, 1950.

W. Armstrong Price, an authority on marine geography, joined the Oceanography Department in 1950.[37] In the summer of 1952 the Research Foundation established a storm laboratory, under the Oceanography Department, on Galveston Island, for the study of waves, winds, and hurricanes.[38] In 1953-1954 K. E. Harwell, under a contract from the U.S. Navy Bureau of Ships with the A&M Research Foundation, developed a salinimeter for measuring the salt content and the temperature of ocean water.[39] Arne Arthur Jakkula died in 1953, having firmly established the Research Foundation as one of the most vital centers for academic and scientific development at A&M.[40]

The Memorial Student Center, completed in 1950, was formally dedicated on April 21, 1951, to the men of A&M who gave their lives in defense of the country.[41] The Richard Coke Building, nicknamed "Uncle Tom's Cabin" by the students when President Harrington moved the College's administrative offices into it in 1951, was formally dedicated on May 11, 1957, and named for Governor Richard Coke, a man whom Walter Prescott Webb called "a truly great but little known man of Texas."[42] G. Rollie White Coliseum was completed in 1954.

During the two years 1952-1953 a number of administrative changes occurred in key positions, and some fresh troubles developed. Charles Clement French resigned as dean of the College in 1952 to become president of Washington State College. David Hitchens Morgan, then dean of the Graduate School at Colorado A. and M. (now University), accepted Harrington's invitation to fill the post of dean of the College at Texas A&M. Morgan, a native of Portsmouth, Virginia, was raised and educated in California, where he had considerable experience as a teacher, principal, and administrator in the public schools before moving into college teaching and finally college administration in Colorado.[43] He was dean of the College at Texas A&M for only one year, when Gibb Gilchrist retired as chancellor on August 31, 1953.[44] As the *Battalion* reported, what happened was that Gilchrist turned over the chancellorship to Harrington; Harrington turned over the presi-

[37]Houston *Post*, February 5, 1950.

[38]Houston *Chronicle*, January 27, 1954.

[39]Bryan *Eagle*, January 4, 1954.

[40]College Station *Battalion*, June 2, 1953.

[41]*Dedication: Memorial Student Center*, April 21, 1951 [pp. 1-16].

[42]*Dedication: Richard Coke Building*, May 11, 1957, pp. 1-23.

[43]Bryan *News*, June 29, 1952; David Hitchens Morgan Biographical Papers, Texas A&M University Archives; Minutes of the Board of Directors, June 28, 1952, XII, 11.

[44]Minutes of the Board of Directors, September 27, 1952, XII, 45.

dency to Morgan; and Abbott, who had been dean of Arts and Sciences since 1949, became dean of the College.[45]

The Houston *Chronicle,* in a light, but provocative vein, reflected upon the "awesome" responsibilities of the chancellor's job into which Harrington was moving.

> There isn't a phase of your life in Texas that is not affected by his direction — the life of the prairie dogs and their habits, life on the floor of the Gulf of Mexico, the planning of your cities and towns, whether your firemen are efficient in getting out fires.
>
> The milk you drink, the meat you eat, the mesquite trees on vast ranches, better traffic controls that will get you to the office quicker and safer, the ventilation in your homes and the prickly pear, they are just some of the everyday things that come under his direction.[46]

The *Chronicle* was right in pointing out the diverse and manifold services of the A&M College System which affected the quality of life in Texas.

Harrington lauded retiring Chancellor Gilchrist as "an outstanding administrator of the vast A&M System covering the entire state. He has provided the leadership responsible for establishing the efficient operation of the System. I regret," said Harrington, "that he has reached that number of years in life, according to the rules of the System, that necessitates his going on modified service."[47] Gibb Gilchrist, like Frank Bolton before him, later retired as chancellor emeritus. He remained a strong supporter of Texas A&M until his death in College Station in 1972.

The new president of Texas A&M, David H. Morgan, was something of an unknown quantity, but a man who offered great promise. During his first year on the campus the student newspaper selected Morgan as one of six outstanding members of the faculty.[48] Homer Lloyd Heaton, the dean of Admissions and Records, who served under seven A&M presidents, recalls President Morgan as one of those individuals whom a man worked with — not for. He was, said Heaton, a driver, and a hard and fast worker, and very able. He worked well with student leaders and the Corps of Cadets. He was also, said Heaton, a man who would have a good idea today, and wanted to see it in operation tomorrow.[49] He was an aggressive man who, perhaps, tried

[45]College Station *Battalion,* September 1, 1953; Bryan *Daily Eagle,* August 2, 1953.
[46]Houston *Chronicle,* May 31, 1953.
[47]College Station *Battalion,* April 28, 1953.
[48]*Ibid.,* June 30, 1953.
[49]Interview with Homer Lloyd Heaton, July 10, 1972, College Station, Texas.

to work too fast within the rather unwieldy A&M framework. Before long, Morgan had succeeded in alienating the Board of Directors, the Chancellor, and the Former Students Association.

In July and August 1953 a group of administration, athletic, and alumni leaders made a grand tour of Aggie Clubs ranging from Shreveport, Louisiana, to El Paso, Texas: President Morgan; J. Harold Dunn ('25), president of the Association of Former Students and a member of the Board of Directors; Chancellor Harrington; Walter Lawren Penberthy, dean of men; Colonel Joe E. Davis, commandant; Barlow Irvin, director of athletics; Ray George, head football coach; Charles L. Babcock ('20), of Beaumont, president of the Aggie Club, an organization of former students created for the purpose of aiding the Athletic Department through athletic scholarships; E. E. McQuillen, director of the A&M Development Fund; and J. B. ("Dick") Hervey ('42), executive secretary of the Association of Former Students. Each man gave a talk on some aspect of the College. The tour was a combined informational, promotional, fund-raising effort which proved tremendously successful. It was a prime example of the method by which contemporary A&M administrators have managed to maintain a close liaison with A&M's former students. The speakers characterized Texas A&M as the school with a "difference."[50]

Colonel Joe E. Davis emphasized that difference:

We feel that we have something unique at Texas A&M — a program which is badly needed in these changing times in an unsettled world. Today's children are not being reared as you and I were reared. Their entire environment is totally different. Television, atomic war stories, third dimensional movies, and comic books help to pattern their lives. Times have changed and we are progressing, and this is no plea for the return to what you and I knew. Gone from many of our homes are the opportunities to assume the responsibility of doing small chores. Gone with those responsibilities are many of the opportunities to teach and instill obedience and honesty, and a feeling of closeness and dependence within the family. It seems we haven't the time to know our children and to teach them the greatness of our nation and our democracy. It's these evident gaps which we are trying to bridge in the training of our cadets; it's these things which must be regained if we are to maintain our strength as the greatest of all nations.[51]

President Morgan reviewed the programs of the College, posed the problem of declining enrollments, and alluded to the possibility of coeduca-

[50]*Texas A. and M. Today,* 1-48.
[51]*Ibid.,* 26-27.

tion. J. Harold Dunn and other speakers emphatically and specifically argued against coeducation, Dunn saying "Low cost education and women just don't go together." Morgan concluded his talk by wondering "how large can A. and M. become without losing that certain something which makes it distinctive?"[52]

Morgan worked hard and conscientiously at his new job. He was vitally concerned, said Heaton, about the quality and quantity of A&M's curricula offerings. Out of this concern he appointed a standing Curriculum Committee, with the registrar, Heaton, as chairman. The Committee, said Heaton, had functioned with considerable effectiveness up to the present time. It had not, however, fully achieved the objectives visualized by President Morgan, because the Committee functioned more as a screening committee, or board of review, than as a policy-making and initiating agency. But withal it was an important and constructive program.[53]

Among the important administrative changes made by Morgan was the appointment of John C. Calhoun, Jr., to the job of dean of Engineering, replacing Howard W. Barlow, who became director of the Institute of Technology at Washington State College. Calhoun, who has served in high administrative posts at Texas A&M since his appointment in 1955, was recognized as "one of the nation's top petroleum and natural gas engineers."[54] In 1956 Ide P. Trotter became associate dean of the Graduate School and J. Boyd Page became dean.[55] Walter H. Delaplane, head of the Department of Economics, replaced John Paul Abbott as dean of Arts and Sciences, Abbott becoming dean of the College until 1956, before going to serve with the Texas Commission on Higher Education, where he helped develop the curricula responsibilities of the various Texas colleges and universities. He later returned to A&M as distinguished professor of English and retired from teaching in 1972. When Abbott left A&M in 1956 Dean Page was assigned the responsibilities of the dean of the College in conjunction with his duties as dean of the Graduate School.[56] James E. Adams replaced Charles Noah Shepardson in the office of dean, School of Agriculture, in 1955, when Shepardson accepted a position on the Board of Governors of the Federal Reserve System. When Shepardson left Texas A&M after twenty-seven years

[52]*Ibid.*, 13-19, 43.

[53]Interview with Homer Lloyd Heaton, July 10, 1972, College Station, Texas.

[54]College Station *Battalion*, July 8, 1954; John C. Calhoun, Jr., Biographical Papers, Texas A&M University Archives.

[55]Interview with Homer Lloyd Heaton, July 10, 1972, College Station, Texas.

[56]*Ibid.;* Texas A&M, *Catalogue, 1954-1955, 1955-1956*, p. 7.

of distinguished service to the College, D. W. Williams said that he was a man who has a "rare combination of the academic and the practical, of the discipline required for first-class performance with the sympathy and knowledge of human shortcomings, of the give and take, of hard work and hard play. He is an obstinate taskmaster and an understanding employer." During his career at A&M Shepardson was regarded as "one of the best known soil chemistry and crop production authorities in the nation."[57] For a number of years the frequent turnover among deans and other administrative officers, created largely by the numerous changes in the top echelons of administration and by the attraction of other jobs, caused some disquietude and lack of direction at Texas A&M.

The years 1948-1958 found the Graduate School and the School of Arts and Sciences in particularly critical stages of development. Historically, Texas A&M placed a narrow construction upon the Morrill Act's charges to the Land Grant Colleges — "to teach such branches of learning as are related to agriculture and the mechanic arts." The "scientific and classical studies" were distinctly regarded as inferior and subservient to the dominant role of the institution to provide training in agriculture and engineering.[58] As late as 1948 Texas A&M was unequivocally a school for the training of agriculturists and engineers and little else.

After World War II, with America's entrance into the atomic age and the rising faith in science, students at Texas A&M, as elsewhere, sought more training in the pure and natural sciences. The marked growth of the science curricula and the graduate programs no doubt was aided by the success of the Research Foundation in obtaining research grants, contracts, and paraphernalia, and by the expanding job opportunities in such fields as physics, mathematics, and chemistry. Between 1948 and 1958 the proportion of students enrolled in the School of Arts and Sciences, and in the Graduate School, rose rapidly in comparison to enrollment in agriculture and engineering. Texas A&M awarded its first doctoral degree, in animal physiology and nutrition, in 1940. By 1948 the College had awarded a total of ten Ph.D. degrees and about 1,000 Master's degrees. By 1958 the College had awarded 254 Ph.D.'s and approximately 3,000 Master's degrees, but compared to what would come in

[57]Texas A&M, *Catalogue, 1956-1957*, p. 6; Bryan *Daily Eagle*, April 24, 1955; College Station *Battalion*, July 7, 1955.

[58]Interview with Homer Lloyd Heaton, July 10, 1972, College Station, Texas; Texas A&M Century Study, 1962 (mimeographed), Report of the Sub-Committee on Historical Perspective, 1-11.

the sixties and seventies A&M's production of graduate degrees between 1948 and 1958 represented a marginal effort.[59] Texas A&M was rather ill-equipped to deal with the expansion in the graduate studies and in the sciences which occurred after World War II.

The College's earlier preoccupation with undergraduate studies in agriculture and engineering proved to be a handicap. In part because of the emphasis on undergraduate studies, by 1946 only 17 percent of the entire Texas A&M faculty held the Ph.D. degree.[60] "It was quite obvious that one of the things we needed was improvement of our staff," D. W. Williams recalls.[61] Texas A&M turned to the Rockefeller Foundation, which agreed to provide financial grants to selected faculty members so that they could earn the Ph.D. Over a ten-year period, Williams indicates, some thirty A&M faculty earned Ph.D.'s at institutions of their choice through Rockefeller grants. Williams recalls that John D. Rockefeller III personally visited the campus to discuss the program. It was, said Williams, a "dandy program" that produced positive results.[62] This kind of effort, however, takes years for development, and by 1948 the need for a quality program had already come.

The development of a graduate program also had its own inherent limitations. The Graduate School, commented Dean of Admissions H. L. Heaton in 1972, operates "without portfolio," that is, the dean of the Graduate School does not fit into the regular administrative structure. He has, for example, no faculty on his payroll. He advises and counsels rather than directs. It is a very difficult position to fill.[63] Ide P. Trotter, dean of the Graduate School between 1948 and 1957, achieved considerable success in improving the quality of the graduate faculty, and in enlarging course offerings.[64] Trotter moved too slowly and meticulously for President Morgan, who wanted more immediate results. J. Boyd Page, replacing Trotter in 1957, was able and energetic but served only three years before leaving the College in 1960. Page, recalls H. L. Heaton, was a man on the move. Page was succeeded by Wayne C. Hall (1960-1969), and he in turn by George William Kunze

[59]Texas A&M, *Institutional Self-Study*, 1963, pp. 211-223; Curtis Eric Schatte, *Doctoral Degree Programs at Texas A&M University*, 13.

[60]Texas A&M, *Report of the President, 1946-1947*, p. 8.

[61]Interview with David W. Williams, September 15, 1971, College Station, Texas.

[62]*Ibid.*

[63]Interview with Homer Lloyd Heaton, July 10, 1972, College Station, Texas.

[64]Interview with Ide Peebles Trotter, November 17, 1971, College Station, Texas.

1969-).[65] Under these men the graduate studies at A&M have assumed a dominant role in the total academic effort, but progress prior to 1960 was slow.

The School of Arts and Sciences, like the Graduate School, experienced a period of slow development between 1948 and 1958, only to "come alive" in the sixties and seventies. The School of Arts and Sciences, organized in 1924 under Dean Charles Edwin Friley, offered two courses of study in its early years, "The Course in Liberal Arts," and "The Course in Science."[66] Few students enrolled in either course. Until 1940 enrollment in the School of Arts and Sciences averaged little better than 10 percent of total enrollment. Thomas Dudley Brooks became dean of Arts and Sciences in 1932, holding concurrently duties as dean of the Graduate School. Between 1932 and 1948 some improvements were made in the quantity and quality of course offerings. In 1948 the School of Arts and Sciences contained the following departments:[67] Biology, Clifton C. Doak, head; Chemistry, Charles C. Hedges, head; Business and Accounting, Thomas W. Leland, head; Economics, Clinton W. Randle, head; Education and Psychology, George B. Wilcox, head; English, Thomas F. Mayo, head; Geography, George W. Schlesselman, head; History, Samuel Rhea Gammon, head; Mathematics, Walter L. Porter, head; Journalism (not organized); Modern Languages, Joseph J. Woolket, head; Physical Education, Carl E. Tishler, head; Physics, James G. Potter, head; and Religious Education (taught at local churches with credit from the College).

Majors in the School of Arts and Sciences could be obtained in economics, English, history, journalism, mathematics, modern languages, accounting, business, education, physical education, biology, entomology, chemistry, and physics. Curricula were also available for prelaw, premedicine and predental students.[68] By 1948 enrollment in the School of Arts and Sciences stood at 1,637 students, or 19 percent of the student body. The School continued throughout the 1950s to function basically as a servicing department for the Schools of Agriculture and Engineering.

Between 1948 and 1958 considerable expansion in the School of Arts and Sciences occurred, with most of the development taking place in business and science. The School, by 1958, had four distinct areas recognized in the catalogue, liberal arts, business administration, preparation for teaching, and

[65]Interview with Homer Lloyd Heaton, July 10, 1972, College Station, Texas.
[66]Texas A&M, *Bulletin of Information, 1925-1926,* p. 31.
[67]Texas A&M, *Catalogue, 1947-1948,* pp. 127-183.
[68]*Ibid.*

science. The business curricula added courses and departments leading to a major in building-products marketing, finance, insurance, marketing, and personnel administration, in addition to the original curricula in business and accounting. In the sciences, majors in botany, entomology, meteorology, microbiology, and zoology rounded out earlier offerings in biology, chemistry, and physics, although a straight major in biology no longer existed. Graduate degrees, but no undergraduate degree, were offered in oceanography. Offerings in liberal arts and education did not change between 1948 and 1958, other than for the addition of courses in government offered under the history curricula.[69] Despite its continuing role in offering service courses to agriculture and engineering in the 1950s, a strong foundation was being laid in the School of Arts and Sciences for significant progress in the next decade.

Tom Harrington, who was dean of Arts and Sciences for only one year (1948-1949) before moving up the ladder to become successively dean of the College, president, and chancellor, did more for the School in his latter capacities. A chemist and a fine classroom teacher, Harrington was instrumental in bringing about strong improvements in the science offerings. Abbott, a professor of English and a good administrator, managed the School of Arts and Sciences during a time when overall College enrollment was declining, and when the outbreak of the Korean War further diverted money and interest from the expansion of the School of Arts and Sciences. Walter Harold Delaplane, who succeeded Abbott as dean of Arts and Sciences, was a 1929 Oberlin College graduate who received his advanced degrees at Oberlin and Duke University. He joined the A&M faculty as head of the Department of Eonomics in 1948. Delaplane guided a strong expansion in business offerings and in many respects laid the foundation for what became the College of Business Administration, established in 1968. Delaplane left Texas A&M for a promotion at Southern Methodist University. Frank William R. Hubert succeeded Delaplane as dean on July 1, 1959, after a brief period of service by George Wilhelm Schlesselman as acting dean of Arts and Sciences. Hubert presided over a period of rapid development in the School of Arts and Sciences until 1970, when education, which he had built into a strong program, separated from Liberal Arts to become the College of Education with Hubert as dean. In 1963 the name of the Agricultural and Mechanical College of Texas was changed to Texas A&M University, and the various "schools" became "colleges." During Hubert's administrative control over Arts and Sciences, the four divisions — liberal arts, business, education, and sciences —

[69]*Ibid., 1958-1959*, pp. 113-148.

saw the development of several new colleges. First the Departments of Oceanography, Meteorology, and Geography were united with the Department of Geology in the College of Engineering to create the new College of Geosciences, effective September 1, 1965. Horace R. Byers, the first dean of Geosciences, was succeeded in 1971 by Earl Ferguson Cook. Also in 1965 the College of Sciences under Dean Clarence Zener was created by severing the Departments of Biology, Chemistry, Mathematics, and Physics from the College of Arts and Sciences. John Mack Prescott replaced Zener as dean in 1969. At this time (1965) the remaining departments of what was once the College of Arts and Sciences became the College of Liberal Arts, but included the School of Business Administration, and the Departments of Economics, Education and Psychology, English, Health and Physical Education, History and Government, Journalism, Modern Languages, and Philosophy and Humanities. In 1968 the School of Business Administration became the College of Business Administration with five departments: Accounting, Business Analysis and Research, Finance, Management, and Marketing. Two years later (1970) the Department of Education and the Department of Health and Physical Education were taken from the College of Liberal Arts and united with portions of the Department of Agricultural Education and of the Department of Industrial Education to constitute the College of Education under the leadership of Frank W. R. Hubert. W. David Maxwell was named dean of the College of Liberal Arts after the division.[70]

While President Morgan generally maintained a good relationship with the student body, several problems developed. In 1953 the faculty Student Life Committee established an editorial board for the *Battalion,* arguing that the student editorial staff needed assistance and guidance. The *Battalion* staff rejoined that the administration was attempting to censor and muzzle the student newspaper because it had been somewhat critical of past administrations. The *Battalion* staff resigned *en masse.*[71] Morgan, then dean of the College, appointed a committee to investigate the situation, and the affair was soon smoothed over to the satisfaction of both students and administration.[72]

[70]*Ibid.,* 1943-1944, p. 8; *Catalogue, 1953-1954,* p. 14; *Catalogue, 1954-1955, 1955-1956,* p. 7; *Catalogue, 1959-1960,* p. 5; Texas A&M, "Report of the Self-Study Committee for Standard I — Purpose," June 16, 1972, p. 12.

[71]Houston *Post,* February 23, 1953.

[72]Bryan *Daily Eagle,* March 2, 1953; "Report of the Special Academic Council Committee in the School of Military Science," June 15, 1954, pp. 1-2. Members of the committee included J. H. Quisenberry, S. R. Wright, J. R. Bertrand, S. S. Morgan, C. W. Crawford, H. L. Heaton, and W. W. Armistead, chairman.

Soon after becoming president, Morgan appointed a special faculty committee to study the R.O.T.C. situation. This committee reported in June 1954 that enrollment at Texas A&M was declining relative to enrollment in other colleges of Texas, and that Texas A&M had an unusually high freshman attrition rate. The committee believed that compulsory military training at the College was limiting enrollment and diminishing the College's effectiveness in developing engineers, agriculturists, veterinarians, business executives, and other educated citizens. The committee recommended instituting noncompulsory military training. This, of course, was during the Korean War era, when hostility to military training and overseas service was growing in America. Morgan, with forthright vigor, decided that noncompulsory Corps was a good idea, and with the approval of the Board of Directors, made it effective for the opening of the fall term in 1954.[73] Morgan also moved Corps freshmen into Corps dormitories and civilian students into civilian dormitories.[74]

At the same time the duties of the dean of the Basic Division were increased by the addition of the duties of the dean of Student Personnel Services, a move intended to broaden counseling and guidance services to all students. He was responsible for the operation of the Basic Division, Student Affairs, Student Activities, and the Corps. Bennie A. Zinn headed the Department of Student Affairs, and was in charge of civilian counseling, veterans advising, civilian dormitories, and campus security and housing. Walter L. Penberthy, dean of men since 1947, headed the Department of Student Activities, which directed intramural athletics, student clubs and organizations, organized student activities, music activities, and student concessions. The Corps of Cadets, comprising, of course, the fourth department, was under the direction of the commandant.[75] The reorganization sought to give greater cohesion to a civilian-corps student body.

The change in student-life structure met general approval and acceptance among faculty and students, but some students, especially former students, were unhappy and irritated. Morgan made every effort to meet and counsel with student leaders, especially the Corps of Cadets, to obtain acceptance and support for his new student-life program. A renewal of hazing and the growth of secret organizations such as the mysterious "TT's," or True

[73]Interview with Homer Lloyd Heaton, July 10, 1972, College Station, Texas.
[74]College Station *Battalion,* August 19, 1954.
[75]Bryan *Daily Eagle,* August 8, 1954; Texas A&M, *Catalogue, 1956-1957,* pp. 5, 31, 39.

Texans, were met in positive fashion. Morgan suspended a number of students in the spring for being members of the "TT's," but then reinstated them after the organization was allegedly dissolved. He warned cadets that hazing was illegal and that violations would bring suspension from school.[76] According to Director of Information R. Henderson Shuffler, it was the first time an A&M administrator had ever made a "no-hazing" statement in a public speech.[77] In view of what had occurred some years earlier, when President Gilchrist attacked hazing, Morgan's more radical reforms were implemented with remarkable success.

Morgan and other A&M administrators did not go so far as to allow women to enter A&M during the regular academic terms. Coeducation was a much more controversial issue than even noncompulsory military training. On March 3, 1953, State Senator William T. Moore, a 1940 Texas A&M graduate and resident of Bryan, introduced a resolution in the state Senate which called for the admission of women to A&M. Moore argued that A&M had stagnated since the War and had experienced a decline in enrollment partially because of its refusal to become coeducational. With little deliberation, the Senate adopted the resolution by voice vote. Aggie reaction, headed by State Senator Searcy Bracewell ('38) of Houston, and characterized by a deluge of telephone calls, telegrams, and letters, caused the surprised Senate to reconsider the vote and to rescind the resolution two days later by a vote of 28 to 1. Moore remained resolute, and predicted that A&M would be coeducational within ten years.[78] He turned out to be right. The overwhelming sentiment of the Former Students, however, throughout the decade of the fifties, was against coeducation.

In this climate of opinion Morgan, who held more liberal views on coeducation, made no effort to change the all-male status of the College. Morgan had already made more changes in the College than most former students could easily swallow. Any tampering with the Corps of Cadets or student life as it had been in the past prompted the disaffection of many former cadets and some members of the Board of Directors. Morgan moved too fast. Moreover, he provoked the displeasure of the Chancellor and of the members

[76]Bryan *Daily Eagle*, August 8, 1954; College Station *Battalion*, August 19, 1954; Dallas *Morning News*, September 23, 1954; interview with Walter L. Penberthy, October 24, 1972, College Station, Texas.

[77]Houston *Chronicle*, September 23, 1954.

[78]Polly Westbrook, "A History of Coeducation at Texas A&M University," 13-16. This is an unpublished manuscript in Texas A&M University Archives written by a daughter of a former student, then enrolled at The University of Texas, in 1970.

of the Board of Directors over entirely minor situations. Morgan insisted, upon arriving on the campus, on entire redecoration of the president's residence, which had been refurbished only two or three years earlier. Frequent encounters with the Board of Directors on this issue, which grudgingly acceded to most of his wishes, produced considerable friction.[79]

Although Morgan had been originally recommended to the position of president by Chancellor Marion Thomas Harrington, the two men eventually became estranged, the causes of dissent often being minor issues. One encounter between the two men, for example, involved blowing the whistle on the power plant at the start of the work day, at noon, and at five o'clock. Morgan ordered the procedure stopped; a few days later, on order of the Chancellor and at the request of College employees, the whistling resumed. One of the real handicaps of being president of Texas A&M during the fifties was the physical presence of the chancellor on the campus. Theoretically the president, and not the chancellor, was in charge of campus affairs, but it was virtually impossible for the chancellor, housed on the same campus, not to have an overriding, if not direct, voice in College affairs. The chancellorship might have worked better had the office been removed to another geographic location.[80] Because Morgan incurred the displeasure of former students, the Board of Directors, and the Chancellor, and perhaps because, although he was tremendously capable, he was an impatient man, a man in a hurry to get things done, in early December 1956 he offered his resignation to be effective at the close of the academic year, but the Board of Directors chose to make the resignation effective that same month. Morgan left A&M at the end of the month to become director of Dow Chemical Company's educational program.[81]

D. W. Williams became acting president, in addition to his duties as vice-chancellor for agriculture, on December 22, 1956, and served until September 1, 1957. Williams, born in Vendocia, Ohio, in 1892, joined the A&M faculty in 1919 and headed the Department of Animal Husbandry from 1922 until World War II, when he served as a food and agriculture administrative officer for the Army in England, France, Italy, Germany and Austria. In Austria, Williams was responsible for the reorganization of the federal gov-

---

[79]Interview with Homer Lloyd Heaton, July 10, 1972, College Station, Texas; interview with Marion Thomas Harrington, September 13, 1971, College Station, Texas; interview with David W. Williams, September 15, 1971, College Station, Texas.

[80]*Ibid.*

[81]*Ibid.*

ernment of that country, working under Generals Mark Clark and Albert Gunther. He returned to Texas A&M in January 1946, when he became vice-president for agriculture and immediately headed up the restructuring and quality-improvement effort in the School of Agriculture.[82] Williams was a likable, forthright, vigorous administrator and a good organization man, who stayed in the middle of things.[83] Williams believed when he became acting president that the "organization chart . . . was never straight." In 1957, nearing retirement age, and uninterested in remaining president on either an acting or regular basis, Williams recommended that the president's job be combined with that of chancellor and turned over to Tom Harrington. "I wanted to get rid of this screwy organization and nobody ever quite had the fortitude to do it until Earl [Rudder] came along," he said.[84] The Board of Directors approved Williams' recommendation, and effective September 1, 1957, named M. T. Harrington president and chancellor.[85]

Williams resumed full-time his position as vice-chancellor for agriculture, in which capacity he had administered A&M's international programs since 1953. Texas A&M's cooperation with the Foreign Agricultural Operations, later the Agency for International Development, operated by the Department of State, began in 1953. In that year D. W. Williams and Frank C. Bolton traveled to East Pakistan, where they surveyed the situation and returned to help frame an agreement with the Department of State to provide technical assistance to help the government of East Pakistan develop programs in agricultural education. The first contract provided a $1.7-million grant to A&M to finance the program for three years, with the contract renewable every three years. Texas A&M maintained that contract with East Pakistan until January 1971, during which time from two to fourteen A&M faculty men worked in East Pakistan, while varying numbers of Pakistanis received training in various fields at Texas A&M. In 1954 the Chancellor's Office initiated a foreign technical assistance program for Prairie View A&M in Liberia. A program for Texas A&M also began with Mexico, but was abruptly terminated by order of the State Department when the Mexican government refused to fire some faculty members of a College in Saltillo, who were suspected by the U.S. Department of State of being Communists. "That

---

[82]Interview with David W. Williams, September 15, 1971, College Station, Texas.
[83]Interview with Homer Lloyd Heaton, July 10, 1972, College Station, Texas.
[84]Interview with David W. Williams, September 15, 1971, College Station, Texas.
[85]See Appendix A.

was a mistake," former Chancellor Harrington commented; "we hated to lose that one." Other programs were developed later in such places as Ceylon, Tunisia, the Dominican Republic, and Argentina.[86]

When Williams retired in 1958 he took a three-year tour of duty in Ceylon, where Texas A&M founded and built an agricultural high school and converted it into a junior college. Many active and retiring A&M faculty members have served in overseas assignments. Hundreds of foreign nationals have received basic and advanced training at Texas A&M under the technical-aid programs. Harrington, who later became coordinator of international programs after retiring as chancellor, and Williams both regard the foreign-aid programs as among the most significant and successful services of the University in today's world.[87]

Tom Harrington held the dual office of president and chancellor for two more years, from July 1, 1957, until July 1, 1959. The "Chancellor" designation was dropped during this period and Harrington's office was officially known as "President of Texas A&M and the System." In 1959, partly at the instigation of President Harrington, the Board of Directors reinstated the separation of the Chancellor's Office and the Office of President of Texas A&M. The Board of Directors made Harrington chancellor, and Earl Rudder ('32) president of the College.[88] Earl Rudder, an Aggie with a B.S. in Industrial Education, a major general in the United States Army Reserve and commander of "Texas' Own" 90th Infantry Reserve Division, and hero of World War II, commissioner of the General Land Office of Texas from January 1955 to February 1958, was widely regarded as one of the most unlikely men for the post of an academic presidency, and one who would be least likely to rock the A&M boat or to effect any changes in the College. Those who held this view could not have been more wrong. Rudder restructured, revitalized, and revolutionized the institution. He built a university where a college had been. He dispelled many of the anxieties built up during the decade between 1948 and 1958.

---

[86]Interview with Marion Thomas Harrington, September 13, 1971, College Station, Texas; interview with David W. Williams, September 15, 1971, College Station, Texas.

[87]*Ibid.*

CHAPTER 25

The Rudder Years
A Time of Decision

J AMES EARL RUDDER faced three great crises during his lifetime —
one was at Omaha Beach during World War II, a second was in the Texas
General Land Office, and the third was at Texas A&M. Rudder, a graduate of
John Tarleton Agricultural College who completed his studies with a B.S. in
Industrial Education at Texas A&M in 1932, came to the presidency of
Texas A&M in the midst of one of its greatest crises. A high-school and jun-
ior-college coach between 1933 and 1941, Rudder served with great distinction in World War II. He was one of the first Americans ashore in the land-
ings at Omaha Beach, commanding a daring attack by Rangers on German
gun emplacements at Pointe du Hoe, overlooking the landing areas on
Omaha and Utah Beaches. After the War Rudder lived the quiet but active
life of a rancher, businessman, and mayor of Brady, Texas. He served as a
member of the Texas Board of Public Welfare, and of the State Democratic
Executive Committee. On New Year's Day, 1955, Bascom Giles, veteran
Texas land commissioner, who had recently been re-elected for another term,
failed to qualify for his elective office and so terminated his position. Giles
confronted investigations of alleged fraud and irregularities in administration
of the $100-million veterans' land program. "Accumulating evidence in the
veterans' land scandal which has rocked and shocked the whole state makes
all previous frauds in the state government look petty in comparison," said
one newspaper account. On Tuesday, January 5, 1955, Governor Allan Shivers appointed Earl Rudder to fill the post of Texas Land Commissioner.[1]

Rudder "took the job in all independence — with no strings attached,"
and "worked hard at it."[2] He had a job to do and he did it well. On the heels

[1]James Earl Rudder Biographical Papers, Texas A&M University Archives; Houston
Chronicle, January 6, February 27, 1955; Austin *Daily Texan*, January 6, 1955; Dallas *Morning
News*, January 7, 1955.
[2]Austin *American*, July 10, 1956.

of grand-jury investigations, suits, and journalistic exposés, Rudder pressed immediately for a thorough investigation of the Texas General Land Office by the Legislature. Investigations and trials resulted in indictments and prison sentences for those convicted, including Bascom Giles. The affair was a very nasty business, which involved even the booby-trap bombing of a key witness who was also a friend of Earl Rudder.[3] Rudder initiated thorough reforms in procedures and policies of the Texas Land Office. He expedited the handling of legitimate claims, collected unpaid loans, recovered state losses from forfeited contracts, and expanded the veterans' loan program.[4] In 1956 he won election for a second term in office, and continued to administer conscientiously an expanding and effective land program for Texas.[5] Rudder, who "never quit any job until he felt it was finished,"[6] left the Texas Land Office to return to his first love, Texas A&M College.

On February 1, 1958, James Earl Rudder, a "47-year-old native Texan with an outstanding record of service to Texas and the nation" assumed the duties of vice-president of Texas A&M, a position which made him in actuality the chief administrator of Texas A&M College.[7] Although Marion Thomas Harrington held the joint title of president of the A&M College and president of the A&M System, Rudder was in fact to be the real "president" and Harrington the "chancellor," although the chancellor's post had disappeared in name. Despite Rudder's impressive accomplishments in public service, during peace and war, most academic people counted him at best an "unlikely" candidate to head a major university. Rudder gave every appearance of being an Aggie of the old school, with old-school ties, loyalties, traditions, and basic conservatism. A university in the throes of change, many anticipated, would not be helped along the way by such a man as Earl Rudder.

When Rudder came to Texas A&M in early 1958 he in some ways entered a situation as explosive as the Texas Land scandals he enountered when he became land commissioner in 1955, and even more delicate. When David H. Morgan left the A&M presidency "under fire" in December 1956, the controversy had remained largely under cover. Administrative and policy

---

[3]Dallas *Morning News,* January 6, 1955, March 16, 1955; Houston *Chronicle,* January 6, 1955; Austin *American,* August 7, 1956; Houston *Post,* February 3, 1961.

[4]Dallas *Morning News,* July 26, September 6, 13, 1956; Austin *American,* May 13, June 20, 24, 1956; Austin *American-Statesman,* March 25, 1956.

[5]Austin *American,* December 19, 1957; Dallas *Morning News,* December 22, 1957.

[6]Austin *American,* July 10, 1956.

[7]College Station *Texas A&M System News,* February 1958.

disputes at A&M, however, soon became public. The problem not only involved conflict between the President and the Chancellor, and between the President and the Board of Directors, but between faculty and administrative attitudes regarding compulsory military training and coeducation. Both issues, noncompulsory Corps and women enrollment, became part and parcel of the same package. Both were highly explosive issues; together they were "atomic."

David W. Williams, acting president until September 1, 1957, directed a questionnaire to the faculty at the request of the Board of Directors, seeking their recommendations on a number of questions of policy. One of the questions was to the effect, "Should military training be optional or compulsory?" The Academic Council, representing the faculty, favored optional military training by a vote of 49-1. In November 1957 the Board of Directors voted 5-4 to *restore* compulsory military training, effective in September 1958.[8] The policy change, coming in the face of the faculty's overwhelming disapproval, was made more disconcerting by the fact that news of the change came through "leaks" rather than through an official Board announcement. In December 1957 one member of the Board of Directors was quoted in state newspapers to the effect that military training would indeed be made compulsory for the first two years of college. When reporters questioned President Harrington, he declined to comment, but said only that "Mr. [Lemuel H.] Ridout slipped up."[9]

The story apparently emanated from *Battalion* editor Joe Tindel, who interviewed Ridout after persistent rumors had been circulating around the campus regarding the reinstatement of compulsory military training. After Ridout confirmed the rumor Tindel contacted President Harrington, who acknowledged that the story was correct, but asked Tindel to hold his story until the announcement had been made through faculty channels. Tindel, instead, published the news, which was picked up around the state. His "case" was subsequently reviewed by the faculty-staffed Student Publications Board, which exonerated Tindel and observed that it had been unfortunate that the Board of Directors delayed its announcement so long after the decision was made.[10] Not only had Tindel released the story, but he had editorial-

[8]Houston *Post,* February 10, 1958 (in an article by Leon Hale, entitled "Aggieland's Ordeal").

[9]Bryan *Eagle,* Houston *Post,* Dallas, *Morning News,* Houston *Chronicle,* December 4, 1957.

[10]Bryan *Daily Eagle,* December 5, 1947; Waco *Times-Herald,* December 5, 1957; Dallas *Morning News,* December 7, 1957.

ized in favor of noncompulsory military training "in the interests of future Aggies." Texas A&M did not want to become another West Point, he argued, and civilian students received a broader education and made better grades than did members of the Corps of Cadets.[11] But the issue was already decided. Reaction to the news was varied.

One correspondent, Leon Hale, writing for the Houston *Post* under the banner "Aggieland's Ordeal" identified the issue as a split between the faculty and the Board of Directors. Hale noted that President Harrington and Vice-President Rudder, and all of the Board members but one [Al E. Cudlipp], were ex-Aggies who sought to retain the "old school" in the face of changing times.[12] The old, and still warm, issue of coeducation immediately cropped up in accompaniment with the compulsory Corps controversy. The Houston *Chronicle* noted that coeducation was at the real heart of the controversy. Ninety percent of the cadets, reported the *Chronicle,* opposed coeducation and favored compulsory membership in the Corps.[13] In January 1958 the Bryan *Eagle* set the pace for renewing the fight over coeducation. "A&M cannot play an effective role when hampered by philosophies of 1876," editorialized the *Eagle.* It called upon the Board of Directors to take the necessary steps and make plans to admit women.[14] The *Eagle's* editorial was picked up by many Texas newspapers, the *Eagle* claiming that almost every daily newspaper in Texas had carried the story as released by the news service.[15]

The student newspaper, the *Battalion,* supported coeducation as well as noncompulsory military training, but it obviously failed to reflect the opinion of most students. The Student Senate favored by 11-5 a resolution calling for the resignation of editor Joe Tindel, and "Corps boys" reportedly waged a "bombing" campaign against freshman William Boyd Metts, who had announced the formation of a group called the Aggie Association for the Advancement of Co-Education. Hostile students allegedly intended to run Metts off the campus.[16]

The long-standing coeducation champions, including State Senator William T. Moore of Bryan, now rushed into the fray. In late January the Bryan

[11]College Station *Battalion,* December 4, 1957.

[12]Houston *Post,* February 10, 15, 1958.

[13]Houston *Chronicle,* January 19, 1958.

[14]Bryan *Daily Eagle,* January 5, 1958.

[15]See, for example, on January 5, 1958, San Antonio *Light,* Fort Worth *Star-Telegram,* and Waco *News-Tribune,* and on January 6, 1958, Bryan *Daily Eagle.*

[16]Houston *Chronicle,* January 17, 1958; College Station *Battalion,* February 18, 1958.

Eagle announced that John M. Barron ('35), attorney, would file suit in behalf of Mrs. Lena Bristol, of Willacy County, and Mrs. Barbara Tittle, of Bryan, for their admission to Texas A&M, arguing that Texas women are citizens and taxpayers with the same legal rights as men and to deny them use of public-supported institutions was illegal discrimination. The *Eagle* announced that it had established a fund to finance the fight to the higher courts. The suit was filed on January 29, 1958, in the Eighty-fifth District Court. The Dallas *Morning News* opined that John M. Barron, "a stubby Texas A&M College Aggie" is "destined to go into his alma mater's academic history as either a George Washington or a Benedict Arnold — depending on how you feel about female Aggies."[17]

In March, after a two-day hearing, Judge William T. McDonald gave Mrs. Tittle and Mrs. Bristol authority to enroll in A&M. He said, "The Board of Directors has abused its right to regulate the operation of the college by excluding these women and has even been arbitrary in exercising power in this decision." The rights of women under the Fourteenth Amendment to the Constitution had been violated.[18] Texas A&M appealed the case to the Circuit Court of Appeals, Waco.[19] The Circuit Court heard the arguments in September 1958; John Barron and his father, Judge W. S. Barron, argued that A&M was discriminating against women, and pointed out that of the sixty-nine land-grant colleges in the United States, only Texas A&M refused to admit women. William T. Moore, who had championed the fight for coeducation in the Legislature some years before, sat in the audience.[20]

The Court reversed the decision rendered by Judge McDonald:

> Since the state supports one all-male and one all-female and sixteen coeducational schools, it exalts neither sex at the expense of the other. But to the contrary recognizes the equal rights of both sexes to the benefit of the best, most varied system of higher education the state can supply.[21]

The plaintiffs appealed to the State Supreme Court, which refused to review the Circuit Court's decision. Said John Barron, "I believe that the Texas court did not rule in favor of A&M but instead it ruled in favor of the school's board of directors."[22]

[17]Dallas *Morning News,* January 19, 1958; College Station *Battalion,* April 17, 1959.

[18]College Station *Battalion,* March 19, 1958; Bryan *Daily Eagle,* March 26, 1958.

[19]Bryan *Daily Eagle,* March 27, 1958.

[20]Waco *News-Tribune,* September 19, 1958; College Station *Battalion,* September 19, 1958.

[21]Bryan *Daily Eagle,* October 2, 1958.

[22]College Station *Battalion,* January 5, 1959; Bryan *Daily Eagle,* January 14, 1959.

Vice-President Earl Rudder commented, "the decision is in keeping with the Board of Directors' desire — it is my job to run A&M as the Board wants it to run." When asked about the future, he laughingly replied, "I don't have a crystal ball."[23] Barron soon reported that he had been approached by other women who sought admission to A&M, "It's possible the whole thing may start all over."[24] It did.

In September 1959 Mary Ann Parker, the wife of a Bryan building contractor; Margaret E. Allred, a student at Texas Tech; Mrs. Sarah Hutto, a student at Allen Academy; and Mrs. Mildred Barron, the wife of John M. Barron, all residents of Bryan, Texas, applied for admission to Texas A&M, but were advised that the school was not coeducational. The application forms were sent to them "as a courtesy only, and not subject to any matter of condition." John M. Barron filed suit.[25]

The furor over coeducation on the campus of Texas A&M was regenerated. One "pro-coeducation" student was injured by an ammonia bomb tossed into his room. The editor of the *Battalion* was "busted" in rank for an editorial supporting the admission of women.[26] Judge McDonald, in the Eighty-fifth District Court, ruled *against* the admission of the women to A&M, pointing to the higher court's reversal of the previous case. The case passed to the United States Supreme Court, which refused to reconsider the decision of each of the lower courts. Texas A&M was still an all-male institution with compulsory military training, but, reported the *Battalion* years later, the suits "brought the problem out into the open."[27]

So the furor and contests over both coeducation and noncompulsory military training abated for the moment. Almost unnoticed by the state press, because of preoccupation with the coeducation-military training dispute at Texas A&M, Earl Rudder was named president of Texas A&M on July 1, 1959, when Harrington was made chancellor. The relationship between the two men and the duties they performed were essentially unchanged. But Rud-

[23]College Station *Battalion*, April 7, 1959.

[24]*Ibid.;* Houston *Post*, September 17, 1959.

[25]Houston *Post*, November 6, 1959; Margaret E. Allred, Bryan, Texas, to H. L. Heaton, Registrar, College Station, Texas, August 15, 1959; R. G. Perryman, Associate Registrar, College Station, Texas, to Margaret E. Allred, Bryan, Texas, August 19, 1959; John M. Barron, Bryan, Texas, to H. L. Heaton, Registrar, College Station, Texas, September 3, 1959, and see H. L. Heaton file "Court Cases," Registrar's Office, Texas A&M University.

[26]Houston *Post*, November 6, 1959.

[27]College Station *Battalion*, February 18, 1966; see also H. L. Heaton file, "Court Cases," Registrar's Office, Texas A&M University.

der's authority, the closeness of his relationship to the Board of Directors, and his general popularity with students, former students, faculty, and staff perceptibly increased. Rudder was formally inaugurated president of A&M on March 26, 1960.[28] He faced the difficult task of binding the wounds and quieting the tumult raised over the past two years, while steering Texas A&M ahead in its academic development. It was a most difficult-appearing task, and Rudder, at first, was presumed by many to be unlikely to accomplish the job. But General James Earl Rudder was a fighter who never quit anything until it was finished. As many have said since, he turned out to be the right man in the right place at the right time.

The year 1961 marked the eighty-fifth anniversary of the founding of Texas A&M. One hundred years earlier the land-grant college legislation had been introduced before Congress. In a few years Texas A&M would be called upon for its decennial report to the Southern Association of Colleges and Schools, its major accrediting agency. The recent past had been disturbing; the more distant past was passing in review; the future was full of promise but also brimming with uncertainties. It was clearly time for Texas A&M to do a little soul-searching and self-evaluation. "Realizing that the experiences of the past, properly evaluated, are the foundation-stones of the future, the Board of Directors of the Texas Agricultural and Mechanical College System authorized on April 20, 1961, a long-range planning study of the A. and M. College of Texas."[29]

The next few years were years of quiet, purposeful planning and introspection. Four independent studies of the College were conducted. One study produced the report entitled *Faculty-Staff-Student Study on Aspirations*. Another study, conducted by the Century Council, comprising one hundred outstanding citizens of Texas, many of them former students, produced the *Report of the Century Council*. Another study project, headed by faculty and administrators, resulted in the institutional self-study *Report to Commission on Colleges, Southern Association of Colleges and Schools*. The various study efforts were capped by the Board of Directors' Report, *Blueprint for Progress*. This massive study program involved almost everyone in any way related to the school. It brought many things "out into the open" in a quiet, effective manner. It was both a purgative and a shot of adrenalin. The study efforts calmed the passions of the moment and paved the way for future progress. Each of

---

[28]*Inauguration of James Earl Rudder as President of the Agricultural and Mechanical College of Texas*, March 26, 1960; College Station *Battalion*, September 2, 1959.

[29]Texas A&M, *Report of the Century Council*, 1962, p. 17.

the study groups made a conscious effort to prepare guidelines "to the end that the year 1976 — the one-hundredth anniversary of the opening of A. and M. College — shall see the College in what this Board sincerely believes to be its destined position of state, national, and international prominence among institutions of higher learning."[30]

President Rudder on April 29, 1961, appointed a twenty-four-man committee, representative of faculty and staff members, as a Committee on Aspirations, under the chairmanship of Wayne C. Hall, dean of Graduate Studies, which was to formulate policies for the overall study effort. The Committee was specifically asked by Rudder to explore four areas: (1) What kind of graduate and citizen should Texas A&M seek to produce? (2) What shall be the mission of the A&M College during the next fifteen years? (3) To what degree of academic excellence in research, instruction, extension, and other services should the faculty and staff aspire? (4) What should be the scope and size of A&M College by 1976?[31]

The Committee established work groups and subcommittees, developed a timetable, and launched the study effort with a Faculty-Staff Conference on Aspirations on July 25, 1961, followed by a Forecast Conference to be held in conjunction with the organizational meeting of the Century Council on September 21 and 22, 1961. Rudder opened the July 25 Conference on Aspirations, asking the participants to forget preconceived notions and traditions. "I hope you will look at A. and M. College with the future in mind, visualizing as best you can how all of us as a team can improve this institution and how we can better serve the people of Texas, especially the youth of this state," he said. Rudder introduced Eric A. Walker, president of Pennsylvania State University, who gave a talk on the "Advantages and Pitfalls of Long-Range Planning." Other speakers included Daniel G. Aldrich, Jr., dean of Agriculture, University of California; Paul A. Miller, provost of Michigan State University; and Chancellor Harrington, who discussed the importance of the Century Study to the College. The Conference gave the self-study effort a strong kick-off.[32]

The two-day Forecast Conference of September set a somewhat different tone. It concerned projections, predictions, and future development. Jenkin Lloyd Jones, editor of the Tulsa *Tribune*, discussed "The World and Its Challenges for the College Graduate"; Abraham Hyatt, director of Plans and

[30]Texas A&M, *Blueprint for Progress*, foreword.
[31]Texas A&M, *Faculty-Staff-Student Study on Aspirations*, 3-4.
[32]*Ibid.*, 5-7.

Program Evaluation for the National Aeronautics and Space Administration, talked about "The Space Exploration Program and Its Impact on Science and Technology"; and Richard B. Johnson, chairman, Department of Economics at Southern Methodist University, projected "The Economic Development of the Southwest by 1976."[33] Never before had Texas A&M faculty, staff, students, Board members, and supporters been so mobilized into one concerted and basically harmonious effort. Irrespective of its final product, the self-study programs accomplished much even before they began.

While the various study groups devoted thousands of man-hours and thousands of pages of written material to the evaluation, the final reports comprised a total of about 600 printed pages. Those reports contained both specific and broad statements as to where Texas A&M had been, and where it planned to go. Perhaps the most remarkable thing about them is that most of the recommendations were literally accepted by President Earl Rudder and the administration as a "blueprint for progress." It helped define Rudder's job. Rudder meant to finish the job.

Briefly, the *Faculty-Staff-Student Study on Aspirations* comprised four component parts: (a) the report of the Resident Instruction and Student Life Study Group; (b) the report of the Research Study Group; (c) the report of the Extension Study Group; and (d) the report of the Services Study Group. The final report comprised a summary and distillation of the component parts. The recommendations of the general report are important in view of what came to be.

Texas A&M had no tenure policy for faculty that conformed to national professional standards as established by the American Association of University Professors. In order to promote and encourage the development of more qualified faculty the *Aspirations* report recommended establishing a tenure policy in conformity with national standards. The report further recommended a "marked increase in salary levels" for the higher professional ranks, annual salary increments, merit raises, and the establishment of endowed faculty chairs. "The name of the institution should be changed to foster and maintain a university image." Various fringe benefits should be added for attracting and holding better faculty: improved retirement, medical and hospital insurance, accident and disability insurance, a faculty club, and faculty-staff credit union. Recognition should be given for outstanding teaching and research. Faculty and staff, it was reported, preferred "an end to compulsory

[33] *Ibid.,* 7.

military training and all-male admissions policy" by more than a six-to-one margin.[34]

The *Aspirations* report indicated that the impact of life in a compulsory Corps of Cadets was most critical. "The Corps determines the students' habits, attitudes and ambitions." Corps life became more important than academic life; compulsory military training resulted in attraction of a relatively small number of transfer students to A&M, and was "a primary factor in the relative stability of undergraduate enrollment for the past 20 years." The report warned that "In housing, feeding, and recreation of students, the military emphasis has limited the true pursuit of scholarship and the development of an environment which will contribute to this scholarship." The faculty, said the report, recommends: "(1) that military training be voluntary for all students; (2) that the Corps of Cadets no longer exist as a residential organization; and (3) that an adult supervisor reside in each residential unit."[35]

This was pretty strong stuff. Rumor had it that President Rudder's first reaction to the *Aspirations* report was a loud exclamation followed by tossing the report into the garbage can. He soon fished it out and reread it.

The *Aspirations* report also recommended higher standards for admission to the College, and a substantial improvement of the library, including a new building. Graduate studies should be organized and Graduate Studies should become a Graduate College with a dean at its head; student-government organization should be modernized; greater emphasis and encouragement should be given to research by the faculty, with more funding and released time. "All educational activities of the Texas A. and M. College not properly a function of resident teaching or research should be brought together under a Division of Continuing Education."[36] It is interesting and even somewhat startling to see how very many of these recommendations were implemented by President Rudder, or by his successors.

The *Report of the Century Council* made recommendations of a much less specific nature, reflecting broad policies or preferences. The Council envisioned for the College the development of *an institution of "university" structure,* supported by solid programs in the humanities, the social sciences, and the natural sciences, but it hedged on changing the name of the College. The Council noted the "divided opinion" among its members regarding the

[34]*Ibid.*, 21-23.
[35]*Ibid.*, 24-27.
[36]*Ibid.*, 28-43.

admission of women to Texas A&M, but believed that the "Board of Directors will . . . make a wise and effective disposition of this matter." In view of past disturbances over the question this statement represented a very tolerant attitude by the Council. The Council, unlike the faculty and staff, did strongly endorse the R.O.T.C. program then in effect; that is, compulsory military training for the first two years. Suggestions were made for improving the quality of program and faculty in the schools and divisions of the College.[37]

The report characterized the Texas A&M student body as "predominately of native Texan[s] . . . of middle-to-upper-class socio-economic backgrounds, of generally superior physical development, and of relatively traditional and conservative political and religious attitudes." Texas A&M students generally scored slightly below the national average on college-entrance tests, and the Council advised a "continuous study of selected admissions policy." The student was characterized as "well-disciplined, courteous, friendly, ambitious, courageous and hardworking," perhaps a little less sophisticated, but with "loyalty to state and nation, belief in the American way of life and our democratic heritage, belief in a Supreme Being, a relatively high degree of capacity in their areas of specialization, and a capacity for initiative and leadership." Overall, Texas Aggies were an outstanding body of men.[38]

The regular self-study report to the *Southern Association of Colleges and Schools,* completed in 1963, reflected many of the same attitudes as the other reports, but did add some specific recommendations for building programs on the campus, reflecting the work of a project group operating within the structure of the *Aspirations* study. The report projected a $55-million dollar building program to be completed by 1976. Major facilities believed needed by the College included an Agricultural Analytical Services building, a biochemistry-building addition, an engineering building, a classroom and office building, an oceanography and meteorology building, a golf-course shop, a three-phase library-construction program, a Memorial Student Center addition with adjoining continuing-education facilities, a cyclotron accelerator, nuclear-science center particle accelerator, Data Processing Center addition, and TV closed-circuit studio.[39] By 1975 most of the building projects recommended had been completed, no mean accomplishment, particularly in view of the enormous expenditures necessary.

[37]Texas A&M, *Report of the Century Council, 1962,* pp. 7-53.
[38]*Ibid.,* 56-67.
[39]Texas A&M, *Report to Commission on Colleges, Southern Association of Colleges and Schools,* 43-44.

Although broad in its context, the meaning, purposes, and importance of the Board of Directors' *Blueprint for Progress,* adopted in 1962, cannot be overestimated in its significance to the developing university over the next fourteen years. A particularly penetrating segment of that report had to do with program development:

This Board establishes the following programming objectives, in the belief that if these goals are reached by 1976, the College will indeed be deservedly recognized and respected as one of the outstanding educational institutions of our nation:

The College shall stress systematic and selective program development, emphasizing the necessity to develop strength of programming in those instructional, research, and extension education areas in which the College has been specifically charged with the development of educational leadership.

The College shall place increasing emphasis upon the development of strong interdisciplinary programs in the areas of engineering and the sciences, including the planetary sciences, molecular science, biomedical engineering, energy and raw material resources, electronic data applications, and the behavioral sciences.

The College shall make continuing studies of the possibility of combining both departmental activities and course offerings to more effectively use available funds, facilities and personnel.

The College shall take all feasible measures to strengthen and give greater depth to studies in the humanities and social sciences in all curricula, particularly those of a technical nature, in order that students gain a full appreciation of their American heritage, and be well prepared to assume the responsibilities of citizenship.

The College shall encourage and facilitate the continuing and increasing use of the most modern teaching devices and techniques in College programs.

The College shall place increasing emphasis upon graduate offerings and activities, through further strengthening of the entrance requirements of the Graduate School, and through the institution of graduate programs of greater scope and more intensive depth of offerings.

The College shall institute periodic evaluation of all College programs by qualified individuals, in the interest of maintaining high quality programs, updated curricula, soundness of course content, and effective instructional organization.[40]

The Directors charged "all members of the faculty and staff of the Agricultural and Mechanical College of Texas, in whatever capacity they may serve, that their watchword and goal shall be *excellence.*"[41]

The various self-study reports not only reflect that the times of post-

[40]Texas A&M, *Blueprint for Progress* [8-9].
[41]*Ibid.,* [15].

war reconstruction and anxieties of the decade 1948-1958 were over, but that Texas A&M had been aroused and awakened to new efforts. A number of other studies supplemented the major self-study programs in the early sixties. Thomas R. Spence, manager of physical plants, headed a group which produced enrollment projections. The projections, incidentally, promulgated an enrollment of slightly over 13,000 by 1976,[42] a figure surpassed in 1969. After 1970 most predictions for 1976 approached the 20,000 enrollment figure. By the fall semester 1972 enrollment already exceeded 16,000. An independent study in 1960 by a private management consulting firm of Ernst and Ernst recommended the establishment of several vice-presidencies: one for academic affairs, another for planning and development, and a third for finance and operations. It was advised that the functions of the dean of instruction be merged with those of the vice-president for academic affairs, and that a director of personnel, and a director of auxiliary services be established under the auspices of the vice-president for finance and operations.[43] Another independent study in 1960 advised a restructuring of the College information and publications program to place coordination and control of all information services under a director of information services. In 1962 James L. Lindsey became director of information and publications for the College, replacing L. A. Duewall, who died in that year. R. Henderson Shuffler held a similar office in the System. Other services and even departments handled their own publicity. Gradually these functions were consolidated under "Jim" Lindsey, and finally, effective September 1, 1965, when the Chancellor's Office closed and authority over the System and the University was vested in President Rudder, the Department of Information and Publications exercised complete coordination and control over all information services.[44]

Texas A&M also had policy guidelines established for it by the Coordinating Board, Texas College and University System, which in 1965 superseded the Texas Commission on Higher Education. The Coordinating Board proposed to restrict doctoral-level programs to Texas A&M and three other designated state universities, and to assign to Texas A&M leadership in all levels for agriculture, engineering, architecture, science, veterinary medicine, business adminstration, education and the traditional areas of the liberal arts

---

[42]T. R. Spence, *Enrollment Record and Forecast: A&M College of Texas, 1962-1976*, pp. 1-6, inserts.

[43]Texas A&M, *Report to Commission on Colleges, Southern Association of Colleges and Schools*, 43-44.

[44]*Ibid.*, 44; interview with James L. Lindsey, October 24, 1972, College Station, Texas.

(humanities and social sciences).[45] These policy guidelines reflected the emerging consensus at Texas A&M that the institution should forego its narrower construction of its educational mandates, and proceed on the basis of the broader interpretation of the Land-Grant College Act as pursued by most land-grant colleges in the United States.

Within a year after the completion of the institutional self-study reports two important changes occurred in Texas A&M's perspective. Texas A&M became coeducational, with some restrictions; and the old Agricultural and Mechanical College had a face-lifting, at least in name. On Saturday, April 27, 1963, the Board of Directors agreed to admit women to the College on a limited basis effective June 1. In addition to the "normal requirements" for admission a woman seeking to enroll in the College must be the wife or daughter of an enrolled student or faculty or staff member; or enroll in a course of study or use facilities not available at other state-supported schools. All women, without exception, could enroll in graduate studies.[46] The action caught most Aggies by surprise.

Board President Sterling C. Evans addressed a letter to the former students explaining the Board's decision. Evans noted that a number of programs offered at Texas A&M could be found in no other state institution. There were, he said, 1,800 married students on campus, and many of the wives would like to complete their education. Texas A&M, he said, had experienced difficulty in the past in hiring outstanding faculty because their wives and daughters were denied the opportunity of attending the College. Evans said that the Board had *no* plans to make A&M an "all-out coed institution," adding that "The admission of women on a limited basis will not bring sudden or drastic change to the school." The Directors said they foresaw no changes for the Corps of Cadets.[47] Earl Rudder called a meeting of the entire Corps of Cadets in the G. Rollie White Coliseum. Rudder was greeted with boos and hisses by the angry cadets, who chanted, "We don't want to integrate." At Texas A&M "integration" concerned females, not blacks. Rudder told the cadets that the Board of Directors had absolute authority on the matter, and that the U.S. Supreme Court backed up that authority. Rudder

[45]Texas A&M, Report of the Self-Study Committee for Standard I — Purpose, June 16, 1972, p. 12.

[46]Sterling C. Evans, President A&M Board of Directors, to Association of Former Students, April 1963, in *Texas Aggie* (April 1963), p. 1; Texas A&M, *Catalogue, 1969-1970*, p. 8.

[47]Sterling C. Evans, President A&M Board of Directors, to Association of Former Students, April 1963, in *Texas Aggie* (April 1963), p. 1.

appealed to the cadets' school spirit by arguing that if Texas A&M did not admit women, many students and desirable academic programs would move to Texas Tech.[48] The Corps accepted Rudder's statement, but they never did like it.

One student lamented, "I really didn't think it could come. I didn't want it. It's a helpless feeling. You wake up one morning and you're enrolled in a co-ed school." Some students, in shocked disbelief, said it was like West Point going co-ed. Other students reflected pleasant surprise.[49] One group of cadets formed the Committee for an All Male Military Texas A&M. "We will carry this issue to the people of Texas. The citizens of this state have a right to know why their sons and future generations of young Texas men are now being denied a choice as to the type of institution they can attend."[50]

Reactions from the public and former students were mixed. One thing for sure, a newspaper reporter observed, no Aggie was indifferent, "An indifferent Aggie is about as rare as a dodo bird. Aggies just aren't made that way." A random questioning of Abilene "exes" by the reporter produced such comment as "Big mistake!" "Next they'll abolish the Corps of Cadets." "I'm 54 years old and I still like girls — but not at A&M." "I'm still in shock," said another. "It's about time they had some coeds there and started having a little fun," said one. "It might help out football recruiting!" The last, in view of the dry years A&M had been having on the gridiron, offered many otherwise bitter Aggies some consolation.[51]

The Bryan *Eagle*, long the champion of coeducation at Texas A&M, and unquestionably representative of local citizen opinion on the issue, applauded the move:

The board's action yesterday proves that the college fathers are willing to act in an objective manner not motivated by tradition for tradition's sake. With the board operating in a flexible manner and attuned to the changing world we live in Texas A&M is well on its way to the excellence sought by school officials and the people of Bryan-College Station.[52]

On May 7, 1963, State Representative Will Smith sought to introduce a bill before the Legislature requiring Texas A&M to remain all-male. He

[48]Houston *Post,* April 30, 1963.
[49]*Ibid.,* April 28, 1963.
[50]College Station *Battalion,* August 8, 1963.
[51]"Gal Aggies? Yup! Old Grads React," Abilene *Reporter News,* April 28, 1963.
[52]Bryan *Daily Eagle,* April 28, 1963.

failed to get the necessary four-fifths vote for the introduction of his bill, but did succeed in getting the House to approve a resolution requiring the state to maintain one major university for men and one for women. Over five hundred Aggies turned out to support the resolution and attend the hearings before the State Affairs Committee. The Committee sent the resolution to the floor, where it passed by a vote of 99-22 with Brazos County Representative David Haines leading the fight against it. After passage of the resolution Senator William T. Moore sought to balance the scale by obtaining Senate approval of a resolution supporting Texas A&M's coeducational decision.[53] There the matter rested until the next session of the Legislature, when yet another spirited fight developed over coeducation at Texas A&M.

Twelve women applied for admission to Texas A&M within two days after the policy change was announced. In May 1963 Mrs. Lewis M. Haupt, Jr., and Mrs. Marilyne C. Dieckert, both Texas A&M faculty wives, were admitted to the College, the first regular women students to be enrolled since 1933, when eleven women attended under the "hardship" ruling of the Depression. By September 1963, 150 women were enrolled at A&M.[54] Women could come, but generally they were not made welcome at Texas A&M. Few buildings on campus had any restroom facilities for women, and no dormitories were opened for women during the regular sessions until the fall of 1972. But change was clearly in the air. In 1965 the Board of Directors authorized President Rudder to use his "discretion" in the admission of women. As a result more applications from women for admission were approved and, in fact, all applicants who could meet the same academic qualifications as men were being admitted by the fall of 1969. Finally, by September 1971, all pretenses were abolished by the Board, and women were to be admitted on an equal basis with men. "Texas A&M University is a coeducational university admitting all qualified men and women to all academic studies on the same basis without regard to race, creed, color or national origin."[55] And it was so. After almost one hundred years, one of the major disputes and vexatious issues had been settled. Had Texas A&M lost that certain something that made it distinctive? Many Aggies thought so.

Many Aggies felt that they were being buffeted severely by the winds

[53]Polly Westbrook, "A History of Coeducation at Texas A&M University," 25-26, unpublished manuscript in Texas A&M University Archives; Houston *Post,* May 4, 8, 11, 14, 17, 1963.

[54]*Ibid.*

[55]Texas A&M, *Catalogue, 1972-1973,* p. 8.

of change. Effective August 23, 1963, the Texas Legislature approved a bill changing the name of the Agricultural and Mechanical College of Texas to Texas A&M University. The change had been recommended initially in the *Century Study* and in the *Aspirations* report. Chancellor Harrington and President Rudder announced that the change in name was needed to enhance the prestige of the school, to aid in securing grants, and to help in recruiting faculty. While some had advocated, in conformity to practices of other land-grant colleges, that Texas A&M be designated a "state university," as for example naming the College, "Texas State University," the Texas A&M University designation was an effort to retain, at least in spirit, the old, familiar name. Under the new designation the "A&M" meant nothing — it did not mean Texas Agricultural and Mechanical University — it simply retained the old, familiar sound.[56] But the old, familiar sound was not enough to suit many Aggies. They wanted the old, familiar name back.

Wrote Jack Gallagher for the Houston *Post*, ". . . when they start tampering with the good name of Texas A&M, well they've overstepped their bounds . . . Those curriculum-broadeners went to work and changed Texas A&M College to Texas A&M University. What comes out now is as flat as the Brazos bottoms." He added, "They've ruined something sacred, our song, the song that belongs not just to the Aggies, but to everyone."[57] And many an Aggie still sings in a very loud voice, "We're the Aggies from AMC."

Actually, as the Bryan *Eagle* reported, Aggies were now getting used to the "vicissitudes of life." The change was made rather quietly. In August the campus and local businesses were busy changing names to conform to the new "university" style. The College Station State Bank became the University National Bank. Shaffers Book Store became the University Book Store. Rumors had it, said the *Eagle*, perhaps with tongue in cheek, that College Station was to become "University Terminal."[58]

In November 1964 the Board of Directors of Texas A&M announced yet another change. Chancellor M. T. Harrington would soon retire after having served at Texas A&M for forty-one years in almost every teaching and administrative position in the organization. Effective September 1, 1965,

[56]College Station *Battalion*, April 4, August 22, 1963; Bryan *Daily Eagle*, May 14, August 23, 1963; interview with Marion Thomas Harrington, September 13, 1971; *General Laws of Texas, 1963*, p. 467.

[57]Houston *Post*, November 23, 1967.

[58]Bryan *Daily Eagle*, August 7, 23, 1963.

James Earl Rudder would become president of Texas A&M University and president of the Texas A&M University System. Said Rudder, "Texas A&M is greatly indebted to Dr. Harrington for his contributions," and he added, "I am pleased to follow in the steps of this great man." Rudder announced that he looked forward "to being around to help do the tremendous job that still needs to be done, and I anticipate this will take some time."[59] He added, "Higher education in Texas, and the role Texas A&M is to play in it, especially in graduate studies and research, must achieve a position that is second to none in the nation. All my efforts will be dedicated to this end."[60] Tom Harrington proudly continued to serve his school as coordinator of the international programs until 1971.[61] His was a great example of the strong dedication and able service which so many Aggies have given their alma mater. This kind of service is one of the distinctive qualities that has made Texas A&M a school with a "difference" and a great institution.

Rudder, a dedicated Aggie with unbounded energy and determination, knew no rest. He persistently "got with it," to use one of his own favorite expressions. The men who worked with him were equally as devoted and hard-working. Texas A&M continued to look upon education as serious business. By 1966 the organizational structure of Texas A&M included under President Rudder, John C. Calhoun, Jr., vice-president for programs; William Clyde Freeman, vice-president and comptroller; Thomas D. Cherry, vice-president for business affairs; Wayne C. Hall, academic vice-president and dean of the Graduate College; and Andrew D. Suttle, vice-president for research. Three new colleges and deans were established. Graduate Studies had become the Graduate College under Dean Wayne C. Hall, as recommended in the study reports. The College of Geosciences was established under the direction of Dean Horace R. Byers. The College of Science was established under Dean Clarence Zener. The heads of the older colleges included Fred J. Benson, dean of Engineering and director of Texas Engineering Experiment Station; Frank W. R. Hubert, dean of Liberal Arts; Raleigh Elwood Patterson, dean of Agriculture and director of the Texas Agricultural Experiment Station, who was succeeded in 1967 by Harriott Orren Kunkel; and Alvin A. Price, dean of the College of Veterinary Medicine. James P. Hannigan was dean of students, and William John Graff, former dean of

[59]Dallas *Morning News,* November 26, 1964; College Station *Battalion,* September 2, 1965.

[60]Dallas *Morning News,* November 26, 1964.

[61]Interview with Marion Thomas Harrington, September 13, 1971, College Station, Texas.

instruction, received the title dean of academic administration, although the duties of the office were being transferred to the academic vice-president. Graff's office was to be phased out in 1967. Harold D. Bearden served as director of Texas Engineering Extension Service, and John E. Hutchison as director of Texas Agricultural Extension Service; H. Lloyd Heaton was director of admissions and registrar and was subsequently given the title of "dean"; and Bennett M. Dodson was superintendent of the Texas Maritime Academy.[62]

By 1968 Texas A&M had attained university status, increased its enrollment to almost double that of 1958, expanded its research program monumentally, broadened the curriculum, upgraded academic and faculty standards, and initiated an $85-million building program. Texas A&M had built its $6-million cyclotron complex, and formally dedicated the Olin E. Teague Research Center (the annex to the Data Processing Center), both of which had been recommended in the 1961-1963 study reports. Other construction completed included the nuclear-science center, and expanded facilities for petroleum engineering, architecture, plant sciences, and biological sciences, and new dormitories and apartment houses for married students. The library was being expanded with a four-story modern addition which enveloped the Texas Engineers Library building, and it was being filled with books, microfilm, and journals from a greatly enlarged operating budget. A new president's home was completed in 1965. The College of Business Administration under Dean John E. Pearson had been authorized and was being established. To top it all, Texas A&M won the Southwest Conference championship in football and the Cotton Bowl in 1967.[63] Without fanfare, notice, or disturbance, in a manner atypical of the pattern throughout the South and the Southwest, Texas A&M had also been racially integrated.

In 1970 the College of Education was created, under Dean Frank W. R. Hubert, from components of the College of Liberal Arts, the College of Agriculture, and the College of Engineering. W. David Maxwell was named dean of the College of Liberal Arts. John Mack Prescott became dean of the College of Science in 1969. The College of Architecture and Environmental Design was organized independently of the College of Engineering under Dean Edward John Romieniec. Anything, seemingly, could happen at Texas A&M. By 1971 the old war school had a dean of women, Mrs. Toby Rives

[62]Texas A&M, *Catalogue, 1966-1967*, pp. 4-5.
[63]College Station *Battalion*, February 1, 1968; Houston *Post*, February 1, 1968.

(later appointed associate director of student affairs).[64] Dean Frank Hubert commented in 1967, "We've got people shaken up on this campus." Texas A&M was a university on the move, and Rudder set a quick pace.[65]

At a time when many college campuses were experiencing the shock of campus turmoil and rioting, notably at San Francisco State, Kent State, and others, Texas A&M felt some of the unrest, but only minimally. Rudder promised a "hell of a fight" to any would-be troublemakers at Aggieland.[66] He insisted on keeping the educational processes in smooth operation, and on an orderly basis, and he succeeded in making that insistence stick. Rudder was quite outspoken against the rising trend to unkempt dress and hair styles sweeping the country. "A prof who wears a beard in the classroom is just trying to substitute a beard for knowledge," he said on one occasion.[67] But even in that respect Texas A&M was in the process of change. Long hair, pork-chop sideburns, beards, "hot pants," and bare feet, although they remained the exception, became quite evident on the campus, as on the campuses of other institutions. The cadets in the Corps maintained their traditional, neat, well-groomed appearance.

The Corps of Cadets and Texas A&M's military regimen were not ignored by the "vicissitudes of change." In September 1965 compulsory enrollment of all new freshmen in the Reserve Officers Training Corps and in the Corps of Cadets was abolished in favor of a freedom-of-choice system.[68] Within a few years the number of students who enrolled in the Corps of Cadets and wore the uniform as part of their daily life had declined to fewer than one-half the student body. By the 1970s the Corps of Cadets represented less than one-fourth of the total students enrolled. The Corps was down, but by no means out. The discipline and exuberance of the Corps, which continued to maintain its own "student life area" on the campus, was undiminished, perhaps stronger. The group had become an even more elite and selective organization by virtue of its volunteer status, and by virtue, too, of the rising pay scales and greater attraction of the professional military life in America, which had become a more specialized, professional, volunteer organization itself.

[64]Texas A&M, Report of the Self-Study Committee for Standard I — Purpose, June 16, 1972, p. 12.

[65]Houston *Post*, February 1, 5, 1967.

[66]*Ibid.*, April 3, 1969.

[67]*Ibid.*

[68]Texas A&M, Report of the Self-Study Committee for Standard I — Purpose, June 16, 1972, pp. 18-19; Texas A&M, *Catalogue, 1965-1966*, p. 63; *Catalogue, 1966-1967*, p. 29.

The Corps of Cadets became the "bearer of the flame" of Aggie traditions. The old school, and the old fraternity, did not die; instead they merely changed their complexion. The traditions, or the better ones at least, live on. The Aggie bonfire survives. "It symbolizes every Aggie's burning desire to beat the hell out of Texas on Thanksgiving Day." Silver Taps and Aggie Muster live on. They are beautiful, inspirational traditions which honor those Aggies who are no longer living.[69] They provide a vibrant part of that spirit of "one great fraternity" that has historically pervaded Texas Aggies, and has helped make the student body one with a "difference." Whenever a

student dies, a Silver Taps ceremony is held for him. At 10:30 p.m., all lights in the area of the Academic Building are turned off. People come and stand by the flagpole in front of the building without saying a word. The Ross Volunteers firing squad just as silently marches up and fires three seven-gun volleys. A group of trumpeteers sounds Taps slowly three times. Then everyone quietly leaves.[70]

So the editor of the *Battalion* informed the incoming "centennial class" freshmen in 1972.

Aggie Muster is still held the same day each year, April 21, San Jacinto Day. It honors students and former students who have died since the last muster. Students trace muster back to 1903, but the spirit of A&M student "togetherness" goes back much earlier into the history of the school. San Jacinto Day even in 1876 was a special day for Texas Aggies; Muster later became a ceremonial form of observing that special occasion. The tradition of the Twelfth Man, dating from January 1, 1922, when Coach Dana X. Bible called upon E. King Gill to suit up, lives on. Aggies, in recognition of that occasion, still stand during football games. To be sure, there are now "date sections" where Aggies sit, but every Aggie, at least in spirit, still stands. Where the form no longer exists or is being abridged, the essential tradition and spirit live on. Aggies still gather for midnight yell practice, and passing A&M students continue to exchange the "Howdy."[71] Texas A&M, although it has become a new space-age institution, has preserved its best traditions, and perhaps its greatest tradition has been that of service. The land-grant colleges adopted as their centennial motto "A Century of Service," a slogan fully applicable to Texas A&M University.

Texas A&M has always been more than just a campus or an institution;

[69]College Station *Battalion,* August 2, 1972.
[70]*Ibid.*
[71]*Ibid.*

it early became a way of life and an attitude toward life. An integral part of this life has been the Association of Former Students, organized in 1879, which in the 1970s numbered more than 55,000 Aggies on its rolls. The Association has undergirded the growth and development of the University in spirit and in physical contributions. Since 1940 the Former Students Association has sponsored Opportunity Award Scholarships, so that deserving young Texans might have an opportunity for higher education. The President's Scholarships, initiated in 1967, provide full four- or five-year scholarships of $1,000 per year to outstanding students. Each of the academic deans is given $2,000 each year by the Association to extend the effectiveness of his office in areas where state funds are not available. The Student Loan Fund, started in 1924, has an endowment of over a half-million dollars derived from former students. The Association publishes the *Texas Aggie,* sponsors Distinguished Alumni Awards, Faculty Achievement Awards, and Distinguished Graduate Student Awards. Texas A&M's Association of Former Students, ably directed by Richard O. ("Buck") Weirus, is a remarkable and nationally outstanding alumni group which has helped make Texas A&M a distinctive university with a vital "difference."[72]

The A&M Mothers' Club, founded in Dallas in 1922 under the inspiration and guidance of Mrs. H. L. Peoples, provides a vital ingredient in the unique formula that comprises Texas A&M. Six months after the organization of the Dallas Club, on October 8, 1922, Fort Worth Aggie Mothers organized a club. Brown County (Brownwood) also organized a club in 1922. San Antonio, San Angelo, and Houston mothers organized during the years 1926 and 1927. The Federation of Texas A&M University Mothers' Clubs organized on a statewide basis in 1928, with Mrs. F. L. Thomas as the first president. Mrs. Lewis Gross, president of the Federation for 1973-1974, stated simply the significance of the Mothers' Clubs: "We Mothers feel we are a vital part of A&M; after all, without us there would be no university. Along with sending our sons and daughters to A&M to be developed into citizens of outstanding capabilities, we have sent love, tears, laughter — and cookies." They have given much more. The purpose of the fifty-three clubs and some 2,500 members in the Federation is "By individual and united effort to contribute in every way to the comfort and welfare of the students, and to cooperate with the faculty of the University in maintaining a high standard of moral conduct and intellectual attainment."[73]

[72]*Ibid.*

[73]Mrs. Ernestine Meadows to Henry C. Dethloff, August 24, 1974; *Fifteenth Anniversary, Fort Worth Texas A&M University Mothers' Club, 1922-1972,* pp. 1-6; Federation of Texas A&M

The University continued to build. Construction began on a new $10-million engineering center, which was completed in 1972 and dedicated as the H. B. Zachry Engineering Building. Work began on a fifteen-floor oceanography-meteorology building, costing $7.6 million, to be completed in 1972. Construction began on an $8.5-million addition to the Memorial Student Center, with completion scheduled for the summer of 1975. A $10-million auditorium-continuing-education-conference-tower complex, tied in with new MSC facilities, began to rise on campus. An educational television building costing $600,000 was completed in 1972. Plans and financial programs were initiated for the renovation of Easterwood Airport; a $4-million chemistry annex, an eight-story office and classroom building, a new $8.5-million dormitory complex which included women's dormitory facilities, and general rehabilitation and improvement of the campus grounds and utilities were initiated.[74] Texas A&M was having a face-lifting from bottom to top. There was no question about it, the old A&M College was a new, dynamic university on the go.

Earl Rudder was constantly in the middle of it. He never spared himself. He was tough, but fair. Usually congenial, he could be abrasive if he thought it would help. He held an open mind, and would act on advice contrary to his own preconceived ideas when it appeared that such advice was better informed. He was a forthright, vigorous man, whose integrity, personal honor, and dedication were unquestioned. "Earl Rudder brought Texas A&M University to new heights of achievement, excellence and prestige."[75]

In late January 1970 President Rudder became ill at his home and was rushed to a local hospital. He was quickly transferred to St. Luke's Episcopal Hospital, in Houston, and from there to Methodist Hospital. What at first appeared to be a heart ailment proved to be a cerebral hemorrhage. He underwent brain surgery to remove a blood clot. By February 20 he was reported to be showing improvement. During his illness the Board of Directors appointed three vice-presidents to share responsibility for the administration of the University and the System during Rudder's absence. W. Clyde Freeman, vice-president and comptroller, was delegated authority to act in Rudder's behalf in matters pertaining to the Texas A&M University System. Horace R. Byers, vice-president for academic affairs, was given direction and responsibilities for academic affairs. Tom D. Cherry, vice-president for business affairs, was delegated full charge and responsibility for that office. By

University Mothers' Clubs, *Year Book 1973-74,* pp. 1-56.

[74]Bryan *Daily Eagle,* March 2, 1972.

[75]Houston *Chronicle,* March 25, 1970, quoting Senator Ralph Yarborough.

late February, Rudder's condition had worsened with intestinal and lung complications, and more operations. He died in Houston on March 23, 1970.[76]

Rudder lay in state on the morning of March 25 in the rotunda of the System Administration Building, and that afternoon services for the deceased were conducted in G. Rollie White Coliseum where he was honored by thousands of friends and admirers, including state and national leaders. Former President Lyndon B. Johnson, himself recuperating from a heart ailment, was present, and so were Texas Governor Preston Smith, and members of Rudder's old Ranger command. Rudder was buried in the College Station Cemetery. The Ross Volunteers fired a twenty-one gun salute at the conclusion of the ceremonies while the buglers played "Silver Taps," honoring the Aggie dead.[77] Rudder was one of the truly great Aggies — in both peace and war. "He was always in service to others, either as a teacher or as a leader or as both," said the San Angelo *Standard Times*.[78]

Few men have lived lives the equal of Earl Rudder's in both honors earned and difficult tasks accomplished. But none of the honors which came his way were by any stretch beyond what he deserved. He served his state and his nation throughout his life; that his life has now ended means we have all suffered the loss of a distinguished and dedicated friend.

Eden, Texas, Rudder's home town, in ceremonies on May 30, dedicated its city park as the General Earl Rudder Memorial Park. Texas A&M established the Brown Foundation-Earl Rudder Memorial Outstanding Student Award, first presented to Van H. Taylor, of Temple, cadet commander of the Corps of Cadets, at commencement exercises in May 1971. The Earl Rudder Scholarship, under the President's Endowed Scholar program and sponsorship of the Association of Former Students, was first presented to Harold Mackey Johnstone, of Lake Jackson, Texas.[79] The annual Rudder Memorial Lecture Series, sponsored by the Association of Former Students and honoring the late James Earl Rudder, was initiated to coincide with Aggie Muster in 1972. At Texas A&M the man continues to be known by his works.

After Earl Rudder's death the Board named Major General Alvin Rou-

---

[76]Houston *Chronicle*, February 5, 1970; Austin *American Statesman*, February 5, 1970; College Station *Battalion*, February 4, 5, 6, 18, 1970; Houston *Post*, February 4, 7, 1970, March 25, 1970; Dallas *Morning News*, February 8, 20, 1970; Dallas *Times-Herald*, March 24, 1970; San Angelo *Standard Times*, March 24, 1970.

[77]Houston *Chronicle*, March 25, 1970; Dallas *Morning News*, March 24, 1970; San Angelo *Standard Times*, March 25, 27, 28, 1970.

[78]San Angelo *Standard Times*, March 25, 1970.

[79]College Station *Battalion*, May 12, 1971; College Station *Texas Aggie*, April 1970, p. 14; San Angelo *Standard Times*, May 27, 1970.

bal Luedecke ('32) acting president of the University and of the System while the search went on for "the most qualified person in the United States" to fill the presidency on a permanent basis. General Luedecke retired from the United States Air Force in 1958. He joined the A&M administration as associate dean of Engineering and coordinator of engineering research in 1968, and in 1969 he assumed the duties of associate director of the Engineering Experiment Station. Luedecke, an outstanding officer, won promotion to brigadier general at the age of thirty-three, and was assistant chief of air staff for the China-Burma-India Theater during World War II. He received the Distinguished Service Medal, Legion of Merit with cluster, Bronze Star with two clusters, and the Exceptional Service Medal from the National Aeronautics and Space Administration, among his other awards and recognition. Upon retirement from the Air Force he served as general manager of the Atomic Energy Commission for six years, and, under the Joint Chiefs of Staff and the AEC, directed a series of nuclear tests on Eniwetok and Johnston Islands. He was deputy director of the Jet Propulsion Laboratory at California Institute of Technology before coming to Texas A&M. Luedecke had most excellent qualifications in both military and civilian administration, and a distinguished scientific and engineering background. In all likelihood he was one of the most knowledgeable men on campus in terms of the application of the new technology.[80]

Luedecke was quietly efficient as the *ad interim* administrator of the University. He cleaned up some of the loose ends remaining after Rudder's death and prepared the way for Rudder's successor. This was in itself no mean job, for Rudder's administration had been largely a one-man operation. When it pleased Rudder to by-pass the usual organizational channels, he did so. One of the accomplishments of General Luedecke and the Board of Directors was to remove the final restrictions regarding the admission of women. Although President Rudder had for the past year or two maintained an open-door policy for women, the "daughter-wife" restrictions remained in the book. Beginning in September 1971, Texas A&M became fully coeducational by profession as it had been in practice for several years.

The Rudder years were years when the reconstruction of the old College was finished, and the construction of a new university began. James Earl Rudder had brought together the many fine programs begun since World War II and had helped form those new elements into a compound with the older institutions and traditions to create a more cohesive, integrated, university complex.

[80]College Station *Texas Aggie,* April 1970, p. 13.

CHAPTER 26

The Developing University

J ACK KENNY WILLIAMS became the seventeenth president of Texas A&M on November 1, 1970. At the formal inaugural ceremonies held in G. Rollie White Coliseum on April 16, 1971, Governor Preston Smith, representing the state of Texas, described the kind of man required as administrator of Texas A&M University, and The Texas A&M University System:

> What is called for today is an administrator who rises to the challenge of a complex and difficult task of space-age education but one who is also capable of preserving the traditions which have proved themselves to be valuable.
>
> Such a man is Dr. Williams, an educator, an administrator and a leader.[1]

Williams was born in Galax, Virginia, on April 5, 1920. He graduated from Emory and Henry College with a Bachelor of Arts degree in 1940. Enlisting in the Marine Corps the day after Pearl Harbor, he soon earned a commission and became a platoon leader. With the rank of major, he was a company commander in the Saipan campaign until two Japanese bullets took him out of the War. After the War Jack Williams went to Emory University, where he earned a Master's degree in 1947, and a Ph.D. in history in 1953. He began his teaching career at Clemson in 1947. He was named dean of the Clemson Graduate School in 1957, dean of faculties in 1960, and vice-president for academic affairs in 1963. Williams came to Texas in 1966 as the first commissioner of the Coordinating Board, Texas College and University System, where he helped lay the groundwork for the development of current and long-range planning for the state's junior and senior colleges and universities. He went to Tennessee in 1968 as vice-president for academic affairs for the six-campus University of Tennessee System and served in that capacity until his appointment as president of Texas A&M University and of the Texas A&M University System.[2]

[1]Bryan *Daily Eagle*, April 16, 1971.
[2]*Ibid.; The Inauguration of Jack Kenny Williams as Seventeenth President of Texas A&M Uni-*

Williams, a man with a folksy touch and a persuasive way, follows the "Teddy" Roosevelt advice "to walk softly, but carry a big stick." He is author of numerous scholarly articles and studies in history and education, and a book, *Vogues in Villainy.* He served as chairman of the Commission on Colleges of the Southern Association of Colleges and Schools, and has served as a member of the Executive Committee of the Council of the Federation of Regional Accrediting Commission of Higher Education and of the Educational Plans and Policies Advisory Committee for the Southern Regional Education Board, in addition to duties on many consultation and study groups relating to higher education.[3]

Looking ahead, Williams said in his inaugural address,

> I believe that during the years ahead we will be witness to a geometric rise in the development and adoption of innovative techniques and programs.
>
> In matters large and small, the atmosphere of education is heavy with the smell of change. For some of us this is a heady perfume; for others, it is the pungent odor of brimstone. Either we sail the strange sea, benefited by whatever navigational experience we have and can command, or we will become passengers on educational vessels whose rudders are manned by others.[4]

While Williams indicated that "momentous change is in the air," he reflected upon the past decade of upheaval on American college campuses, and predicted a return to "stability in on-campus governance."[5]

The years since Jack Williams was inaugurated are characterized by an unending series of quiet "happenings." Education at Texas A&M University has grown in an orderly and stable manner in both quantity and quality. Enrollment climbed from 14,316 students in the fall of 1970 to 16,156 in the fall of 1972. In the fall of 1973 student enrollment jumped by 2,364 students to a total enrollment of 18,520, and increased even more in the fall of 1975 to an enrollment of over 25,000 students[6] (See table 9 for a summary of enrollment from 1876 through 1975.) Of these, over 5,000 were women, and over 4,000 were graduate students. More than one half of the twelve thousand

---

versity and Fourth President of the Texas A&M University System, April 16, 1971; Houston *Chronicle Texas Sunday Magazine,* June 13, 1971.

[3]*Ibid.*

[4]Bryan *Daily Eagle,* April 16, 1971.

[5]*Ibid.*

[6]College Station *Battalion,* January 9, 1974; Office of the Registrar, Texas A&M University.

advanced academic degrees awarded by Texas A&M University have been conferred in the last decade.

Not only are the students enrolled at Texas A&M more numerous; they are also more highly qualified. By 1972 sixty-two percent of Texas A&M's students ranked in the top quarter of their high-school classes, as opposed to 36 percent in 1961. The President of the United States, Gerald Ford, then Vice-President under Richard M. Nixon, characterized the Aggies as "doers" rather than "booers," when he addressed the 1974 graduating class at College Station. On that occasion A&M President Jack Williams pointed proudly to the fact that 27.2 percent of the record 1,961 students receiving degrees were honor graduates, having attained a 3.25 or better grade-point average on a 4.0 grading system.[7] TAMU ranks seventeenth in enrollment of National Merit Scholars, and in 1973 led the nation in number of students initiated into Phi Eta Sigma and Alpha Lambda, freshman honor societies.[8] Texas A&M continues to strive for that goal of "excellence" adopted by its Century Study in 1962.

An intensive self-study effort from 1970 to 1972 resulted in formal notification of reaccreditation by the Southern Association of Colleges and Schools, and in the determination of new guidelines and goals for the University:

> Texas A&M University is a Land Grant and a Sea Grant institution dedicated to the attainment of excellence in teaching, research, extension and other public service functions. The University is committed to assist the student in his search for knowledge, to provide him with an understanding of himself, his culture, his environment, and to develop in him the wisdom to assume responsibility in a democratic society.[9]

New faces and new leaders appear in the organizational structure of the University. Jarvis Ernest Miller was named director of the Texas Agricultural Experiment Station in 1971. The following year Edwin H. Cooper replaced Homer Lloyd Heaton as dean of Admissions and Records and Charles W. Powell became dean of men. James R. Bradley was appointed director of Continuing Education. Raymond D. Reed succeeded Edward J. Romieniec as dean of the College of Architecture and Environmental design in 1973. In the same year Dr. George C. Shelton succeeded Alvin A. Price as the head of the

[7]College Station *Battalion,* May 15, 1974.

[8]Lynn Zimmerman, "Texas A&M University Nears One Hundred Years: Tradition, Spirit, Character," unpublished manuscript.

[9]Texas A&M, Report of the Self-Study Committee for Standard I — Purpose, June 16, 1972, p. 1.

Table 9.
Texas A&M Enrollment (Fall Semester), 1876-1975

1876-1877	106	1910-1911	833	1944-1945	2,152
1877-1878	332	1911-1912	895	1945-1946	2,718
1878-1879	248	1912-1913	868	1946-1947	8,651
1879-1880	144	1913-1914	772	1947-1948	8,418
1880-1881	127	1914-1915	775	1948-1949	8,536
1881-1882	258	1915-1916	732	1949-1950	7,772
1882-1883	223	1916-1917	847	1950-1951	6,675
1883-1884	108	1917-1918	874	1951-1952	6,583
1884-1885	113	1918-1919	1,284	1952-1953	6,277
1885-1886	145	1919-1920	1,383	1953-1954	6,198
1886-1887	134	1920-1921	1,393	1954-1955	6,257
1887-1888	214	1921-1922	1,525	1955-1956	6,837
1888-1889	207	1922-1923	1,879	1956-1957	7,200
1889-1890	279	1923-1924	2,091	1957-1958	7,474
1890-1891	317	1924-1925	2,256	1958-1959	7,077
1891-1892	331	1925-1926	2,170	1959-1960	8,094
1892-1893	293	1926-1927	2,395	1960-1961	7,221
1893-1894	313	1927-1928	2,543	1961-1962	7,734
1894-1895	349	1928-1929	2,770	1962-1963	8,142
1895-1896	320	1929-1930	2,734	1963-1964	8,174
1896-1897	282	1930-1931	2,433	1964-1965	8,339
1897-1898	325	1931-1932	2,194	1965-1966	9,521
1898-1899	344	1932-1933	2,001	1966-1967	10,677
1899-1900	382	1933-1934	2,158	1967-1968	11,841
1900-1901	345	1934-1935	2,998	1968-1969	12,867
1901-1902	432	1935-1936	3,430	1969-1970	14,034
1902-1903	354	1936-1937	4,130	1970-1971	14,316
1903-1904	349	1937-1938	4,926	1971-1972	14,775
1904-1905	393	1938-1939	5,582	1972-1973	16,156
1905-1906	369	1939-1940	6,063	1973-1974	18,520
1906-1907	488	1940-1941	6,534	1974-1975	21,463
1907-1908	579	1941-1942	6,679	1975-1976.	25,247
1908-1909	577	1942-1943	6,544		
1909-1910	711	1943-1944	2,205		

Source: Office of the Registrar, Texas A&M University.

College of Veterinary Medicine. Hebbel E. Hoff, of the Baylor College of Medicine, was named dean of Medicine pro tem in 1973 under a new cooperative program in preclinical medical education between Texas A&M University and the Baylor College of Medicine. In 1974 James A. Knight, formerly associate dean of the Tulane University School of Medicine, became Texas A&M's dean of medicine. Dr. Michael E. De Bakey, Baylor's noted heart surgeon, played a key role in developing the cooperative medical program with Texas A&M. Frank Wardlaw, formerly of the University of Texas Press, assumed direction of the newly created Texas A&M University Press in 1974. On November 1, 1974, Dr. Irene Braden Hoadley became director of libraries, denoting the enlarging role of women in the administrative affairs of the University. Leatha F. Miloy became director of Educational Information Services. Tom W. Adair and Nelda Rowell were named assistants to the President. Haskell Monroe was designated dean of Faculties. Lane B. Stephenson was appointed associate director of the Department of University Information. John J. Koldus, III, named vice-president for Student Services, continually reorganizes the student-services programs to cope with larger enrollments and to provide more personal service for the students. In 1975 the Board of Directors became the Texas A&M University System Board of Regents. [10]

Six major new facilities came into use on the campus between 1973 and 1975, while new construction began on others. Buildings dedicated or entered into service were the A. P. Beutel Health Center, the M. T. Harrington Education Center, the Oceanography and Meteorology Building (distinguished guests included famed oceanographer Jacques Cousteau), the Krueger-Dunn Dormitories, the Wofford Cain athletic dormitory, and the J. Earl Rudder Conference Center (including the twelve-story building and the auditorium complex). Expanded Memorial Student Center facilities entered service on an "as ready" basis between 1973 and 1975.[11] The Forsyth Alumni Center opened in 1973. Meanwhile a new landscape panorama, dormitory complex, agricultural building, library, archives facility, and expansion of G. Rollie White Coliseum entered varying phases of planning or construction prior to the advent of the hundredth year.

The Texas Extension Service offered new and broadened services for all Texans: "The Board of Directors of Texas A&M University took a giant step forward when they authorized establishment of Research and Extension Centers at strategic locations throughout the state." The Hoblitzelle Memorial Auditorium and classroom-office building at the Texas A&M University Agricultural Research and Extension Center, in Weslaco, Texas, was dedicated in January 1973. The Corpus Christi Center, dedicated in May 1974, is

---

[10]College Station *Battalion,* January 9, 1974; College Station *Fortnightly,* June 28, July 26, 1974, June 6, 1975.

[11]College Station *Battalion,* January 9, 1974.

the most recent of the nine TAMU centers across Texas. Research and extension centers provide a new outreach of the total University.[12]

Needless to say, the growth, change, and progress were not easy, painless, or noncontroversial. Texas A&M in the mid-seventies had its problems, but of much lesser proportions than those of the nation generally. Inflation eroded salaries, streakers confounded social conventions and plagued administrators, parking and traffic problems provided constant irritations, building and dormitory spaces remained crowded, the football team lost too many games, the costs of education continued to spiral, and gasoline and power shortages added a new dimension to academic as well as everyday life. Exams . . . classes . . . fish . . . the twelfth man . . . muster. The old A&M provides a sturdy foundation for the new.

Few colleges or universities have changed so much in the past few decades as has Texas A&M University; and fewer colleges still, in the face of momentous change, have so well preserved a basic stability, purposefulness, and association with the past. Much of what Texas A&M University is today derives from its essential obligation of service to society as broadly construed from its organic legislation. Texas A&M University has historically regarded itself as a public resource for the development and dissemination of knowledge. Throughout most of its first hundred years its contribution lay in the areas of agriculture, engineering, and military training. With the advent of the semicentennial years, research and training in the natural and physical sciences had become a recognized fourth component of the College's effort, although it was not until post-World War II years that the sciences achieved coequal partnership and recognition with the older, established fields of endeavor. On the eve of its centennial year Texas A&M had not yet achieved contributions in the "classical studies" — the humanities and the liberal arts — equal in stature to those made in the established areas of agriculture, engineering, science, and military training. Instead of moving in the direction of merely "rounding out" the traditional academic studies that might be expected in a university complex, Texas A&M by the 1970s had developed a "new dimension" to the traditional academic activities.

The reconstruction of the forties, the anxieties of the fifties, and the progress of the sixties left Texas A&M a more healthy, viable social organism than it had ever been before. Texas A&M learned to live with change, without rejecting or sacrificing the past. It learned to retain for the present the best of what its past had to offer, to build a new and better house, with-

---

[12]College Station *Battalion,* May 15, 1974.

out destroying the old foundation. It became a more dynamic, progressive, responsive, service-oriented social organism, by seeking new applications in its traditional areas of competency — agriculture, engineering, the sciences, and military training — while selectively entering new fields of endeavor which closely supplemented and supported the old. Texas A&M University has become more than an academic organization. It is a collective body of interdependent missions seeking to help man solve the problems encountered in his "pursuits and professions of life." Because the problems of contemporary life changed so rapidly, the new dimension of the University increasingly came to be its own flexible and dynamic capacity. Today the dynamic quality of Texas A&M is recognizable in the collective body of social-service missions in which the University is engaged, rather than in any single piece of legislation, grant, or action. At Texas A&M extension has come home to rest.

The more than thirty public-service institutes and centers operating under the auspices of the University perform three basic functions. Some are involved in governmental regulation of certain phases of our economic and industrial system; secondly, some are concerned primarily with the social, cultural, and economic development of society; and, thirdly, some are essentially involved in the practical application of new knowledge. Each of these functions or work divisions interact with the teaching, research, and extension capabilities of the traditional academic structure, thus affording the entire university organism a new viable quality. Many of the services performed by Texas A&M are old and well established. Most are new. The integration of the old with the new has created a new threshold of achievement, and new horizons for educational growth. Higher education in general, and Texas A&M in particular, has access to a whole new frontier of endeavor, a second Copernican revolution.

The services performed by the University range from the mundane to the exotic. One of the oldest and most important, and probably most mundane, regulatory functions of Texas A&M is performed by the Agricultural Analytical Services. While dressed up in modern verbiage, this is the Feed and Fertilizer Control Agency established by state law in 1903. In its early years the "agency" simply began as a function of the Department of Chemistry to analyze fertilizers sold in the state when requested to do so by a "customer."[13] As time passed the Agency became a state laboratory where private citizens and public agencies might obtain certified analyses of agricultural chemicals on a fee basis. In conjunction with the service, the state of

<hr>

[13]Texas A&M, *Biennial Report, 1902-1904*, p. 27.

Texas established the Feed and Fertilizer Control Service, which began operation under the auspices of Texas A&M on July 14, 1905. The law provided for regulating the sale of concentrated commercial feeds, and was in part a belated response to the agrarian uprisings of the 1890s, associated with the Texas Farmers' Alliance and Populist movements. Administered by the Texas Agricultural Experiment Station, the Division of Feed Control, as it was originally known, was first headed by Director John A. Craig. Buel C. Pittuck was appointed state feed inspector. The Department of Chemistry, where George S. Fraps was professor of chemistry and state chemist, performed the laboratory work. Long associated with the work of this agency was that well-known and colorful individual Samuel E. ("Doc") Asbury, who served as assistant state chemist. James W. Carson became the first independent director of the Feed Control Division on August 1, 1906, when he also became vice-director of the Agricultural Experiment Station.[14]

The Feed Control Service was funded by a tax on all feeds marketed in the state, each sack to be tagged and certified as to its contents. The tax, originally set at 20 cents per ton, brought in revenues of $101,628.15 during the first fourteen months the Service was in operation. Fertilizer control duties were first handled almost entirely by the state chemist, who reported only 13,500 tons of fertilizer sold in the 1905-1906 season. Later the duties were assumed by the Feed Control Agency. The Service now functions under the authorization of the Texas Commercial Feed Control Act of 1957 and the Texas Commercial Fertilizer Control Act of 1961.

The value of the Feed and Fertilizer Control Service to Texans is inestimable. One can appreciate the service only by being aware of the fraud and misrepresentation which characterized the agricultural chemical industry at the turn of the century. The seller benefits from the development of uniform standards and the elimination of unfair competition; the buyer benefits from being able to obtain the best value for his money.[15] The Feed and Fertilizer Control Service, as well as the more recently established service operations of the University, has aided the development of the academic branches by enabling the institution to bring in new, better qualified personnel, who often served on the regular faculty. Feed and Fertilizer Control funds were also used to supplement the pay of existing personnel who performed addi-

[14]*Ibid., 1905-1906,* pp. 35-38, 42, and *1917-1918,* pp. 61-62; memorandum, John C. Calhoun, Jr., to President Jack K. Williams, Institutes and Centers at Texas A&M University, October 6, 1971 (hereinafter cited: Institutes and Centers at Texas A&M University, October 6, 1971).

[15]*Ibid.*

tional services or research. Each new program initiated by the University in later years often attracted new faculty and new students, and on occasion generated new research developments, services, and academic departments.

Entomology, for example, was one of those academic departments whose development was greatly facilitated by the necessity of providing a specific public service. Although entomology, as the study of "useful and injurious insects," received mention in the first *Announcement and Circular of the State Agricultural and Mechanical College of Texas, 1876-1877,* a regular course in entomology was not offered until about 1890, and the first professional entomologist did not come to Texas A&M until 1899. He was Frederick W. Mally. Born in 1868 a native of Des Moines, Iowa, he enrolled at Iowa State College when Seaman A. Knapp was its president. Mally came to College Station after an act of the Legislature in 1899 called for an expert entomologist whose duties were "to devise the means, if possible, of destroying the Mexican boll weevil." The College established a Department of Entomology in 1899, and, by authority of an act of the Legislature of 1901, established on the campus an apiary under the control of Wilmon Newell. Although Mally left in 1902, and Newell left in 1903, to return, however, in 1910 for another five years, the work in entomology developed rapidly under a succession of able men, and by virtue of new federal and state laws specifying new functions and providing new funds. Newell, for example, helped write the first foulbrood law in 1903, providing for state poultry inspection under the authority of the state entomologist. A primary function of the state entomologist has long been the control of bee diseases, and the hiring of inspectors and the issuance of permits to control the movement of bees across county and state lines. Among the entomologists who made significant contributions during their service at Texas A&M — as state entomologists, teaching faculty, and Experiment Station or Extension Service personnel[16] — were these outstanding men: E. Dwight Sanderson (1902-1904), Albert F. Conradi (1903-1907), Charles E. Sanborn (1904-1909), Sherman W. Bilsing (1913-1952), Maurice C. Tanquary (1919-1923), Robert K. Fletcher (1919-1949), Lloyd R. Watson (1921-1922), and Roy R. Reppert (1920-1960).

The primary mission of the Texas Transportation Institute, established by the Board of Directors in 1950, is described as being:

> To engage in research in various forms of transportation of persons and property, including the economy of transportation, physical plants and property, the

---

[16]V. A. Little, *A Brief History of Entomology at the Agricultural and Mechanical College of Texas,* 1-45.

moving carriers with regard to their trucks or their medium, air transport, and any other phase or activity concerned with the movement of persons or things.[17]

Authorized by the Fifty-first Texas Legislature, establishing Texas A&M as the research agency of the Texas Highway Department, the Institute obtains indirectly a policy-making role in the regulation and control of Texas transportation, particularly in regard to highway construction specifications and highway design and traffic engineering.[18]

Texas A&M's involvement in transportation research dates back to 1914, when highway experimentation was initiated in the College's engineering laboratories. Thirty years later President Gibb Gilchrist, former director of the Texas Highway Department, headed the effort to establish an organized state research program on public transportation. Gilchrist was largely responsible for the cooperative research program entered into by the College and the State Highway Department in 1948, which research is cosponsored by the Federal Highway Administration.[19] Gilchrist brought to Texas A&M Thomas H. McDonald, retiring chief of the Office of Public Roads of the Department of Agriculture, who had held the position from 1919 to 1953, as the Distinguished Research Engineer for the Texas Transportation Institute. McDonald, who died in College Station on April 7, 1957, provided much of the inspiration for the development of the Institute's unique approach to transportation problems, which emphasizes the interrelationship of modes of transportation and economic life. The Thomas H. McDonald Chair of Transportation was established as a living memorial to him after his death.[20]

Located at the Texas A&M Research Annex, the former Bryan airfield, the Institute operates field offices, including a surveillance and research control center on the Gulf Freeway in Houston and a computerized traffic control center on North Central Expressway in Dallas. Work at the Annex is conducted on paving materials and highway design, structural research, traffic control, and automobile impact and safety measurements. Although founded in 1950, the Texas Transportation Institute was not organized in its present form until 1955, when Fred Jacob Benson became the executive officer. Benson, a 1935 graduate of Kansas State College, earned his master's degree at Texas A&M in 1936, and joined the civil engineering faculty of the

[17]Texas Transportation Institute, *Research in . . . Transportation,* Bulletin No. 20 (1960-1963), [1].

[18]*Ibid.* [1-7].

[19][Memorandum] The Texas Transportation Institute [1-2].

[20]*As a Permanent Living Memorial to Thomas H. McDonald,* n.p., n.d. [15 pp.].

College in 1937. He served with the Corps of Engineers during World War II. A nationally recognized research engineer, Benson was named Engineer of the Year in 1955 by the Texas Society of Professional Engineers. In 1956 he was named vice-director of the Texas Engineering Experiment Station and served as director after 1959. In 1957 Benson was made dean of Engineering, but he continued to administer the Texas Transportation Institute until 1962, when Charles Joseph Keese, a 1941 A&M graduate and member of the Civil Engineering Department since 1948, replaced him as director. Under these men the Institute has become one of the most important public-service operations of Texas A&M. Supplementing its work is the Drivers Training Institute, founded by the College in 1948, the function of which is to prepare teachers of driver education.[21]

The Texas Petroleum Research Committee, founded in 1947, is organized under the auspices of the Texas Railroad Commission and utilizes the faculty and staff of both Texas A&M and The University of Texas to research improvements in oil-recovery methods. The work of this Committee, like the research by the Texas Transportation Institute, is often implemented via the policies and regulations of the Railroad Commission affecting petroleum production.[22] The Texas Forest Service, treated in more depth elsewhere, similarly has service, research, and regulatory functions. The Forest Service operates the Forest Genetics Laboratory, Forest Pest Control Laboratory, and Forest Products Laboratory as research services to the forestry industry.[23]

Texas A&M University sponsors also a number of institutes which are concerned primarily with the social, cultural, and economic developments in our society. The Adriance Laboratory, organized in 1956 and named for Guy Adriance ('15), head of the Department of Horticulture from 1935 to 1960, conducts basic research in cooperation with commercial companies related to the needs of the Texas food industry. The Consumer Research Center, like the Adriance Laboratory, operative under the auspices of the College of Agriculture, approaches the foods problem from the point of view of the consumer. Founded in 1971, the Center conducts research on human nutrition,

---

[21]Texas Transportation Institute, *Research in . . . Transportation [1-4]; Tommy Pinkard,* "TTI: *Research in All Directions,*" reprinted from *Texas Highways* (January 1968), pp. 1-11; Louis J. Horn, "Engineering Research Geared for Immediate Implementation," reprinted from *Texas A&M Engineer* (May 1969) [1-4]; Fred J. Benson Biographical Papers, Texas A&M University Archives; Institutes and Centers at Texas A&M University, October 6, 1971.

[22]Institutes and Centers at Texas A&M University, October 6, 1971.

[23]See Chapter 16.

the marketing of food and fiber and household products, residential housing, and human relationships in the home and the market place.[24]

The College of Agriculture sponsors also the Plant Nematode Detection Laboratory, founded in 1969, the purpose of which is to provide the people of Texas with a means of detecting plant losses caused by plant parasitic nematodes and information on how those losses can be reduced. The Real Estate Research Center, which opened in 1972, is designed to provide research and educational programs in rural and urban economics of particular interest to the real-estate industry in Texas and the Southwest. An old service originally performed by the Agricultural Experiment Stations and other agencies of the College is now performed by the Soil Testing Laboratories, located at College Station, Lubbock, and Seymour. The laboratories provide the public with soil analyses for fertilizer and limestone recommendations.[25]

The Texas Water Resources Institute, organized in 1952, promotes and supports research on the water resources and needs of Texas, and sponsors informational conferences on the subject of water resources and management. Although Texas A&M had nothing to do with the Water Resources Institute, its contributions in the area are underlined by the fact that John C. Calhoun, then vice-chancellor for development at A&M and on leave with the Department of the Interior between 1963 and 1965, where he served as assistant and science advisor to the Secretary of the Interior, functioned as acting director of the Office of Water Resources Research in the Department of the Interior for a short time.[26]

The V. G. Young Institute of County Government, organized by the Texas Extension Service and named for Vernon G. Young, a long-time state agricultural agent and vice-director of the Service at the time of his death in 1969, provides a unique continuing educational program for elected and nonelected officials of county governments in Texas.[27] The Architectural Research Center, organized in 1964, seeks solutions to significant ecological problems of mankind, and is particularly concerned with studies of health-related architecture. The Center in 1971-1972 was engaged in $400,000 of sponsored research contracts, the sponsors including the states of Texas and Kentucky, the U.S. Office of Civil Defense, and the World Health Organization. Research by the Center is being projected into studies of environmental-behavioral relationships, architectural-ecological relationships, leisure time-recrea-

[24]Institutes and Centers at Texas A&M University, October 6, 1971.

[25]*Ibid.*

[26]*Ibid.;* John C. Calhoun, Jr., Biographical Papers, Texas A&M University Archives.

[27]Institutes and Centers at Texas A&M University, October 6, 1971.

tional facilities, developing countries' facilities, and disadvantaged population groups' facilities.[28] The Executive Development Program, established in 1953, offers continuing education programs for business executives through seminars and short courses. The Community Education Center, established in 1971, seeks to assist the community in better utilization of local educational resources.[29]

Other special services provided by the University include the Industrial Economics Research Division (1944), which assists Texas industry, cities, and state agencies in the solution of problems relating to economic development. The Electric Power Institute (1965) is supported by private power companies and sponsors research on electric-power systems. The Institute of Electronic Science (1963) trains technicians for employment in the field of applied electronics. The Food Protein Research and Development Center, organized in 1971, includes the National Fibers and Food Protein Committee (formerly the Cotton Research Committee, founded by state law in 1914), the Oilseed Products Research Laboratory (1941), and the Chemurgic Research Laboratory (1945). The Texas Veterinary Diagnostic Laboratory, organized in 1969, provides testing and consultation services for the control of animal disease. In recent years it has participated heavily in the control of the Venezuelan Equine Encephalitis fever (VEE), which has ravaged South and Central America, and which moved into Texas and across the Southwest.[30]

Many of the institutes operating under Texas A&M University are appropriately oriented toward engineering and the practical application of knowledge. The Psychological Services Laboratory, founded in 1967, provides psychological testing services for public schools on a contract basis. The Counseling and Testing Center, mentioned in a previous chapter, provides the University with counseling, group testing, and reporting services. The Data Processing Center, established in 1959, provides computer support to Texas A&M University, affiliated centers and institutes, and other state agencies. The Center entered the 1970s equipped with a highly sophisticated IBM 360/65 third-generation digital computer system, other IBM computing and auxiliary equipment, and a large analog machine. The Institute of Statistics, organized in 1962, in addition to academic programs leading to advanced degrees in statistics, maintains research programs in theoretical and applied

[28]*Ibid.;* Self-Study Committee, Preliminary Self-Study Report, Architectural Research Center, 1972, "Purpose."

[29]Institutes and Centers at Texas A&M University, October 6, 1971.

[30]*Ibid.*

statistics, and provides consultation in statistical methodology to A&M faculty, students, and research programs.[31]

Important supportive roles are played also by the Nuclear Science Center (1961), which provides a source of nuclear radiation for teaching and research activities and is particularly important to the Texas A&M nuclear engineering program, and by the Remote Sensing Center (1968), which applies remote sensing technology to current problems in agriculture and the natural environment.[32] The Thermodynamics Center traces its origins to the American Petroleum Institute Research Project 44 at the National Bureau of Standards, in Washington, D.C., begun in 1942, and to the Manufacturing Chemists Association Research Project in 1955 at the Carnegie Institute of Technology, in Pittsburgh. The two projects were relocated in the Chemistry Department at Texas A&M in 1961 as the Thermodynamics Research Center under the direction of Bruno J. Zwolinski. The Center provides data on "thermodynamic properties, infrared, ultraviolet, Roman, nuclear magnetic resonance and mass spectra of hydrocarbons," prepares "monographs on thermodynamic properties of limited classes of organic compounds," publishes specialized bibliography and monographs in thermodynamics and thermochemistry, and its research staff engage in studies on such problems as "the calculation of ideal gas thermodynamic function from molecular parameters," and "the thermodynamics and kinetics of gas-phase halogenation and isomerization reactions."[33] Texas A&M has clearly entered the age of science.

The Engineering Test Laboratory, organized in 1939, is an industry-designated performance laboratory for manufactured air-moving equipment. The Institute of Solid-State Electronics, originally organized within the Department of Electrical Engineering in 1969, conducts research in materials and device-fabrication technology of integrated circuits. The Institute provides graduate instruction and a program of continuing education through short courses and conferences. It is one of six of its type in the United States and has been engaged in special projects for the National Aeronautics and Space Administration (NASA), and in Army and Navy research projects.[34] The Institute of Tropical Veterinary Medicine (1966) and Laboratory Animals Resource Center (1967) provide resources and training in special areas of veterinary medicine. The international programs, already described, offer a clas-

---

[31]*Ibid.;* [Memorandum] The Texas Transportation Institute [1-2]; Self-Study Committee, Preliminary Self-Study Report, Institute of Statistics, 1972, "Purpose."

[32]Institutes and Centers at Texas A&M University, October 6, 1971.

[33]Texas A&M *Fortnightly,* November 12, 1971.

[34]*Ibid.,* July 14, 1972.

sic example of the practical application of knowledge in the underdeveloped nations of the world.[35]

The remaining institutes and centers operated by Texas A&M University are science- and pure-research oriented. The Human Learning Laboratory, established in 1970, conducts basic research in human learning problems. The Environmental Engineering Division, begun in 1963, conducts research related to the quality of our environment. The Space Technology Division, also established in 1963, engages in space and aerodynamic research. The Bioengineering Division of the College of Engineering, organized in 1969, applies engineering principles and techniques to medical and other biological problems under sponsorship from NASA, the Veterans Administration, and other agencies. Texas A&M initiated a bachelor of science degree program in bioengineering in 1971, one of few such programs in the United States.[36]

One product of developments in bioengineering, biophysics, biochemistry, and veterinary medicine at Texas A&M has been a Texas A&M University System-Baylor College of Medicine affiliation agreement entered into in 1972, providing for an A&M-Baylor partnership in establishing the Institute of Comparative Medicine under the administration of Texas A&M's College of Veterinary Medicine, and cooperative programs in biomedical engineering, graduate studies, and marine biomedical research, and in allied health fields such as physical therapy, health-career teaching, nurse training, and the training of physicians' and veterinary assistants. Organized in Dallas in 1900, the Baylor College of Medicine relocated in Houston in 1943, and became an independent, nonsectarian institution in 1969, under the leadership of its president, Dr. Michael E. De Bakey, an eminent heart surgeon and a pioneer in heart-transplant operations. The affiliation of the academic, technical, and scientific facilities of Texas A&M University with the traditional medical institution is regarded as opening a "new dimension" in higher education and in medicine.[37]

Texas A&M's Cyclotron Institute conducts research in the nuclear aspects of chemistry, physics, biology, engineering, and medicine. Organized in 1963 as an independent agency, the Cyclotron Institute was placed under the administration of the College of Science in 1971. Its principal roles are (1) to conduct basic research on the properties of the atomic nucleus, (2) to develop cyclotron-related techniques and ideas for application to nonnuclear

[35]Texas A&M, Report of the Self-Study Committee for Standard I — Purpose, June 16, 1972, pp. 16-17.

[36]*Ibid.*, 17.

[37]Texas A&M *Fortnightly,* March 24, 1972.

problems, and (3) to provide education and training programs for graduate students and postdoctoral scientists in nuclear physics and nuclear chemistry. The Institute operates the largest accelerator in Texas and one of the most modern and versatile in operation anywhere.[38]

Closely related to geological engineering, the Center for Tectonophysics organized as a research arm of the College of Geosciences in 1967. According to Center Director John W. Handin, "the center trains graduate students in geomechanics, strength of earth materials, structural geology, and petrofabrics by carrying out an integrated program of theoretical, experimental and field research on rock deformation."[39] Texas A&M is a nationally recognized institution for training in applied meteorology. Instruction and research in meteorology, in conjunction with the academic Department of Meteorology, is carried on by the Center for Applied Meteorology, organized in 1971. Horace Robert Byers, who joined the Texas A&M faculty as distinguished professor of meteorology in 1965, and became dean of Geosciences in 1965, served as first director of the Institute. Byers, a member of the National Academy of Science, became academic vice-president of the University on September 1, 1968, and helped guide and formulate Texas A&M's rapidly developing role in the pure and applied sciences.[40]

Many other research centers and institutes at Texas A&M participate in the overall research and extension services of the University. These agencies comprise the dynamic right arm of the developing University. The Coordinating Board, Texas College and University System, revealed that in fiscal 1971 Texas A&M University led the state in volume of research conducted by Texas institutions of higher education. Fields in which Texas A&M made the largest financial outlays for research were engineering, marine science, agriculture, veterinary medicine, and economics.[41] The most important effort of the University in recent decades has been in the areas of marine science and marine resources, leading to the designation of Texas A&M, under Congressional authorization, as one of the four initial Sea Grant colleges in the nation.

Upon Texas A&M's designation as a Sea Grant College, Senator John Tower of Texas declared, "Sea grant college designation recognizes the increasingly important role that Texas is playing in the field of marine

[38]Preliminary Self-Study Report, Cyclotron Institute, 1972, "Purpose."

[39]Texas A&M *Fortnightly*, February 25, 1972.

[40]Institutes and Centers at Texas A&M University, October 6, 1971; Texas A&M *Fortnightly*, June 11, 1971.

[41]Texas A&M *Fortnightly*, January 14, 1972.

affairs. I believe that in years to come, this designation will be as important to Texas A&M as was the land grant designation in the 19th century." United States Secretary of Commerce Maurice Stans said of the Sea Grant program, "I know of few other programs which offer as much long-term promise for the nation." Jack K. Williams, president of Texas A&M, said that "we expect to develop a total program which will do for marine resources what the land grant colleges did for development of agriculture."[42] Despite its recent designation as a Sea Grant College, Texas A&M's programs in marine science and maritime resources have been developing for several decades. Texas A&M, a Sea Grant College, came as a result of the coalescence of a number of diverse developments, including an early, but stillborn, Texas effort to establish a nautical school, the success of the Texas A&M Research Foundation leading to the establishment of programs in oceanography and meteorology, the founding of the Texas Maritime Academy, in Galveston, and recent federal programs supporting maritime training and marine sciences.

The state Legislature enacted in 1931 a law providing that "There shall be established in one of the harbors of the State of Texas a Nautical School for the purpose of instructing boys in the practice of seamanship, ship construction, naval architecture, wireless telegraph, engineering and the science of navigation." The school, provided the Legislature, shall be under the management and direction of the Board of Directors of the Texas Agricultural and Mechanical College. But the country was in the steep slide of depression in 1931, and the Legislature added the proviso that financial support should be from "interested citizens," and that the "State shall never be called upon to appropriate any money for the support of this school at this or any future time."[43] The body had been given form, but no life. Thirty years later the corpse of the nautical school was infused with that vital life ingredient — money.

That infusion, in large measure, came as a result of the energetic and dedicated efforts of a determined group of Galveston, Texas, citizens between 1958 and 1961. The story of the establishment of the Texas Maritime Academy has been written by the men who know it best, Rear Admiral Sherman B. Wetmore, John A. Parker, and Judge Peter J. La Valle, of Galveston. The following account is extracted from their narrative, released in mimeograph form in Galveston on March 1, 1969.[44]

[42]Dallas *Morning News,* September 12, 1971.

[43]*Laws of Texas,* 1931, pp. 423-434.

[44]Texas A&M, Texas Maritime Academy Board of Visitors, The Establishment of the Texas Maritime Academy, 1958/1962 (hereinafter cited: The Establishment of the Texas

Rear Admiral Walter C. Ford, U.S.N. (Retired), then deputy adminis-trator of the U.S. Maritime Administration, addressed a small gathering in the Galvez Hotel in Galveston on May 21, 1958, at a National Maritime Day banquet. Ford briefly reviewed America's maritime affairs and made brief ref-erence to maritime-academy programs.[45] Congress had before it at the time an act "To provide certain assistance to state and territorial maritime academies or colleges," but the act did not become law until three months later, August 18, 1958.[46] By 1958, the merchant shipping of the United States had declined precipitously from the post-World War II levels, when the country had enjoyed pre-eminence in maritime trade. After the banquet, Robert K. Hutchings, a prominent Galveston banker, asked Admiral Ford if it might be possible to establish a maritime training school in Galveston. Ford replied that "the Maritime Administration would like to see one state academy on the Gulf coast." Edward Shreiber, then president of the Galveston Chamber of Commerce, who became mayor of Galveston in 1971, picked up the ball and the next day wrote to Admiral Ford requesting detailed information that might assist in locating a merchant-marine training academy at the Port of Galveston. Ford sent Schreiber considerable information, including a copy of the maritime act then pending in Congress.[47]

In June 1958 Shreiber appointed a Galveston Chamber of Commerce Merchant Marine Academy Committee to investigate the possibilities of establishing such an academy in Galveston. The charter members of that Committee, which continued to function until the opening of the academy in 1962, included Emmett O. Kirkham, chairman and personnel director of Todd Shipyard Corporation at Galveston; Lester E. Briese, general manager of the Galveston division of Todd Shipyard Corporation; Bedford McKenzie, assistant superintendent of the Galveston Independent School District; W. H. ("Swede") Sandberg, general manager of Galveston wharves; Edward J. Shreiber; and J. J. Tompkins, vice-president of Lykes Brothers Steamship Corporation's West Gulf Division, at Galveston. Kirkham's Committee opened correspondence with Ralph A. Leavitt, president of the Maine Marine Academy Board of Trustees and one of its founders, and coauthor of the Maritime Academy Act before Congress. Leavitt gave the Galveston group every assistance, encouragement, and cooperation.[48]

Maritime Academy).

[45]*Ibid.*

[46]Public Law 85-672, 85th Congress, S. 1728.

[47]The Establishment of the Texas Maritime Academy, 1.

[48]*Ibid.*, 1-3.

Kirkham's Committee then sought assistance from State Senator Jimmy Phillips of Angleton, Texas, who agreed to seek enabling legislation to establish the academy, but who advised the Committee to approach Texas A&M, or The University of Texas, and to create their interest and support as sponsors and prospective administrators of a maritime academy. Sid Holiday, general manager of the Galveston Chamber of Commerce, contacted Albert Collier, A&M's oceanography professor in charge of the Marine Laboratory, which served as the research and experimental facility of the Department of Oceanography. The Department of Oceanography, it will be recalled, was authorized by the A&M Board of Directors in 1949 and established under the direction of Dale F. Leipper in 1950. It developed out of the successful research program on oyster preservation sponsored by the Texas A&M Research Foundation through grants from the Texas petroleum industry. Collier became very much interested in the possibilities of a maritime training program, and believed that the building then used by the Laboratory could adequately house a training school during its early development.[49]

The Chamber of Commerce Academy Committee was reappointed for another year with the addition of one new member, Captain Sherman B. Wetmore, a Galveston-Texas City bar pilot, who retired from the U.S. Naval Reserve in 1959 as a rear admiral, and who replaced Kirkham as Committee chairman. Captain Wetmore became an indefatigable worker in behalf of the marine academy project. Within a week of his becoming chairman of the Committee, Wetmore met Collier and Professor Kenneth McFarlane Rae, a member of A&M's oceanography faculty, who reaffirmed A&M oceanographers' interest in broadening the College's Galveston faculty to include a maritime academy. Dale Leipper soon met with Wetmore. Leipper had a strong interest in developing a deep-water base of operations for his oceanography programs. On March 3, 1959, Wetmore's Committee met with President Marion Thomas Harrington, Leipper, Rae, Vice-Chancellor and Secretary of the Board Edward Angell, and Vice-President and Comptroller William Clyde Freeman to discuss the possibilities. Harrington inquired closely about the political and financial support that Galveston might offer the project, and demonstrated considerable enthusiasm and support.[50]

Until this time the Galveston group had been unaware of the 1931 law providing for the creation of a nautical academy under the direction of Texas A&M. Harrington gave each Galveston representative a copy of the law and challenged them to have Section 4A, which prohibited state financial sup-

[49]*Ibid.*, 3-4.
[50]*Ibid.*, 7-10.

port, deleted by legislative action. Wetmore's Committee now had a clearly defined task and carried it through with remarkable success, aided by Committee Cochairman John A. Parker, Senator Jimmy Phillips, and Representatives Jerome Jones, of Galveston, and Peter J. La Valle, of Texas City. By March 27 the offending prohibition in the 1931 act had been deleted, but academy supporters refrained from asking for state financial support at that time, believing that to do so would have invited an unwelcome legislative and political battle for which they were unprepared. It was decided to wait until the next legislative session, in 1961, to seek funding.[51]

During the remainder of 1959 Wetmore's Committee corresponded with officials of public and private maritime institutes and agencies, and conferred again with Texas A&M officials, with whom they seriously considered the opening of a maritime training school in Galveston. Late in the year Galveston maritime-academy supporters received a temporary setback when some members of the Houston, Galveston, and New Orleans Propeller Clubs began to oppose the establishment of a maritime academy on the Gulf Coast, arguing that the National Maritime Academy at King's Point, New York, could best serve the needs of Southern and Texas boys who wanted maritime training.[52] This opposition was generated, in part, simply by strong school loyalty among merchant-marine personnel.

A more serious crisis arose when, in February 1960, Galveston supporters received a sudden and unexpected "cold shoulder" from Texas A&M officials. What had happened was that Texas college and university officials decided earlier that year not to ask the state Legislature to fund any new projects at the 1961 session. It was believed, with good reason, that state revenues would barely be sufficient to fund the ordinary expenses of higher education, and rather than risk a serious budget fight, University officials agreed to curb requests for new expenditures. The entire maritime-academy project was virtually thrown by Texas A&M back into the lap of Wetmore's Committee. The situation looked bleak if not desperate. Then in March, Earl Rudder, recently appointed to the presidency of Texas A&M, in company with Dale Leipper made a trip to Galveston, where he met with a few members of Wetmore's Committee and other Galveston civic and business leaders, including A. J. Stjepcevich, president of W. L. Moody and Co. Bank, an old friend of President Rudder. Rudder told the men that because of the agreement with other college officials, Texas A&M could not sponsor, or even assist in securing funding for a Galveston maritime academy. But Rudder

[51]*Ibid.*, 10-12.
[52]*Ibid.*, 12-16.

reaffirmed A&M's interest in the project, and advised the Galveston people to by-pass the academic channels, and try on their own through ordinary political channels to get money from the Legislature to found the academy.[53]

The legislative and political obstacles to this kind of independent funding were quite large, but the Galveston supporters proved peculiarly astute. Wetmore's Committee, and particularly Wetmore, began buttonholing every political figure they could find, including Waggoner Carr, candidate for the office of attorney general of Texas, and at that time speaker of the House. Carr, not coincidentally, was vice-chairman of the vital State Legislative Budget Board, which House member Peter J. La Valle had decided upon as the key to the funding request. All other state agencies and boards channeled their spending requests to the Budget Board; the Budget Board then prepared the final spending bill presented to the Legislature for approval. La Valle believed that by going straight to the Budget Board maritime-academy supporters could by-pass much of the competition for state funds, and, if the request were approved by the Board, could probably succeed in securing appropriation of the money by the Legislature.[54] It was unorthodox, but effective.

In July, at the invitation of the Budget Board (Waggoner Carr), Galveston representatives presented their case before the Board, which gave them a cordial but noncommital hearing. Thereafter, Wetmore, Representative La Valle, Maco Stewart, and State Senator A. R. ("Babe") Schwartz, among others, worked diligently to secure legislative passage of an academy appropriation when and if it appeared in the appropriations bill. The overall picture, however, was not bright or even promising. The electorate clearly favored retrenchment in state spending to new taxes. The regular session of the Legislature met and adjourned without being able to agree on state appropriations. Finally, in the last minutes of a special session in mid-summer, when reportedly the legislative clock was turned back to avoid the need for issuing a call for yet another special session, the appropriations bill cleared the Legislature — including an appropriation for a maritime academy in Galveston.[55]

Success had been the result in part of luck, but more the product of hard work and "good politicking." One of the boldest and most successful efforts to nurture passage of the appropriation for the maritime academy occurred in March, when Admiral Wetmore, at the suggestion of Senator Schwartz, suc-

[53]*Ibid.*, 19-23.
[54]*Ibid.*, 23-29.
[55]*Ibid.*, 23-29, 32-36.

ceeded in getting the Massachusetts Maritime Academy training ship *Bay State* to change its itinerary and visit Galveston for a four-day stopover. The Galveston Chamber of Commerce then chartered a plane to bring thirty members of the Texas House and Senate to Galveston for a visit; Texas A&M officials also turned out for the affair. The Kirwin High School Band and the Ball High Tornettes, a precision dance team, gave the visitors a red-carpet welcome at the airport. The visitors were then escorted aboard the *Bay State* "with bugle, boatswain's pipes, side boys, and the ships band." The whole affair was an impressive event, followed by dinner at Gaido's, a well-known Galveston seafood restaurant. Gale winds delayed the adjournment, but no one seemed to mind.[56] That one event probably did more to sell the Legislature on the need for a maritime school than all of the other letters, appearances, and publicity combined. The Legislature approved $195,040 for the Galveston maritime facility, and $90,000 to Texas A&M for the instruction of Texas Maritime Academy cadets on the main campus. An additional grant of $75,000 was secured under the terms of the Maritime Academy Act of 1958, and a stipend of $600 annually for each student enrolled.[57]

President Rudder and his staff immediately began to organize the school. Wetmore, Parker, and their associates recommended Captain Bennett M. Dodson for superintendent of the Maritime Academy, and the Board of Directors secured his services beginning February 1, 1962. Dodson had just completed his final tour of duty with the Navy as chief of staff and commander of the Service Force, U.S. Pacific Fleet. During his career Dodson had lectured at the Naval War College, taught at the California Maritime Academy, served as executive officer of the battleship *Iowa,* coauthored two textbooks on mathematics for navigators, and commanded a number of ships and ship squadrons. Despite limited funds and perhaps more than ordinary difficulties in establishing a new institution, Dodson by 1967, when he retired, had built a good foundation for the developing Maritime Academy.[58]

With the appointment of a fifteen-man Board of Visitors, chaired by Admiral Sherman B. Wetmore, and the procurement of Bennett M. Dodson, superintendent, the Texas A&M Board of Directors formally established the Texas Maritime Academy on February 24, 1962. In September 1962 twenty-seven freshmen enrolled at Texas A&M for basic academic instruction prior

[56]*Ibid.,* 29-32. Admiral Wetmore, who piloted the *Bay State* out to sea, received a serious leg injury when he jumped off the ship's ladder into the pilot boat and was hospitalized for four months.

[57]*Ibid.,* 38, 40-42.

[58]*Ibid.,* 42-46.

to their transfer to the Galveston facility. In the summer of 1963 the maritime cadets boarded the *Empire State IV*, the training ship of the State University of New York Maritime College, for the first annual summer cruise sponsored by the Texas Maritime Academy.[59] By 1965 the midshipmen were sailing aboard A&M's own training vessel, the *Texas Clipper.*

During the early struggle of the Texas Maritime Academy for survival, Mrs. Mary Moody Northen, a Galveston resident and member of Texas A&M's Century Council study group organized in 1962, became interested in the institution. After her first offer of a large expanse of Galveston beachfront property was declined by Texas A&M, because it was unsuited to the Academy's need for a harbor front, Mrs. Northen obtained a grant of one million dollars for the procurement of "facilities for the Texas Maritime Academy at Galveston."[60] The grant was instrumental in the expansion of the Academy.

Within a decade of the founding of the Texas Maritime Academy, Texas A&M University, which for almost a century had been a land-locked, land-grant College, had marched to the sea and had become one of a very small group of elite institutions designated as Sea Grant Colleges. "Have you heard about the Aggie Navy?" headlined the Dallas *Morning News* Sunday magazine, the *Southwest Scene,* on June 6, 1971, "It's no joke!"[61] "Old Army" had a "New-look Navy!" reported the Houston *Chronicle* Sunday magazine.[62]

The *Alaminos*, one of four research vessels assigned to the Department of Oceanography, is a 186-foot converted freighter and the sister ship of the ill-starred U.S.S. *Pueblo,* which when captured by the North Koreans during the cold war nearly provoked the outbreak of a renewed hot war with Korea. The *Alaminos* is outfitted with seven laboratories and a $250,000 electronics lab. Other oceanographic research vessels include the *Orea,* a 100-foot steel-hulled vessel accommodating seven crewmen and nine scientists; the *Leprechaun,* an 82-foot converted Navy PT boat used for shallow offshore research and donated to Texas A&M by Emmet Vaughey, of Jackson, Mississippi; and the *Kasidah II,* a 110-foot converted yacht. Three vessels are assigned to the Civil Engineering Department: the *Excellence,* a 56-foot vessel for monitoring water quality; the *Mariner,* a 50-foot heavy-duty vessel for biological related

[59]*Ibid.;* Texas A&M, *The Texas Maritime Academy,* 1963-1964, pp. 1-13.

[60]The Establishment of the Texas Maritime Academy, 46-48.

[61]Dallas *Morning News,* Sunday magazine *Southwest Scene,* June 6, 1971, cover, 6, 8, 10.

[62]Houston *Chronicle,* Sunday magazine *Texas,* May 9, 1971, cover, 16-23.

studies; and the *Duet,* a 62-foot shallow-draft vessel also for monitoring water quality.[63]

But the pride of the Texas A&M Navy is the *Texas Clipper.* Obtained on a loan basis from the U.S. Maritime Administration under the provisions of the Maritime Academy Act of 1958, the *Texas Clipper* is the converted S.S. *Excambion* of the American Export Line, a 473-foot combination passenger-freight vessel built in 1944. During the summer the *Texas Clipper* serves as the training ship for A&M maritime cadets, who board her for lengthy cruises to northern Europe, the Mediterranean, or South America.[64] The Texas Maritime Academy student yearbook, *Voyager,* each year documents the exciting cruise itinerary of the *Texas Clipper.*[65] During the regular academic semester, until the opening of new facilities at the Mitchell Campus on Pelican Island in 1972, the *Texas Clipper* was the floating dormitory for Maritime Academy midshipmen.[66]

Rear Admiral James D. Craik, U.S.C.G. (Retired), in 1967 replaced Admiral Dodson as superintendent of the Texas Maritime Academy. In the same year Alfred R. Philbrick, Jr., joined the Maritime Academy as executive officer, and commander of the *Texas Clipper.* Increasing enrollments forced the 1965-1970 freshman classes and the 1967-1970 sophomore classes to be housed on the College Station campus. The division of the Maritime Academy student body created numerous academic problems. Finally, by 1971, when enrollment reached about 175 students, the opening of new dormitories made it possible to house all midshipmen in Maritime Academy facilities. Problems with staff and administration also developed, but by 1971 the Maritime Academy had clearly moved out of its precarious period of incubation. What was most impressive about the program was that its products were finding jobs — good jobs at impressive salaries — a sure sign of success. The Texas Maritime Academy and forces outside of the Academy proper were moving A&M's venture into marine sciences and maritime resources along at a rapid clip.

A prime stimulant to Texas A&M's expansion in these areas was Congressional approval of the Sea Grant College and Program Act of 1966. The act provided "for the establishment of a program of sea grant colleges and

[63]*Ibid.,* 16-23; Texas A&M, *The University and the Sea* (January-February 1972), p. 11; Texas A&M University, *Sea Grant* [6-7].

[64][Memorandum] Training Ship *Texas Clipper,* to the author from Rear Admiral James D. Craik, U.S.C.G. (Retired); Texas A&M, *Sea Grant* [7-8].

[65]See, for example, Texas Maritime Academy, *Voyager,* 1969, pp. 50-83.

[66]Texas A&M, *Sea Grant* [7-8].

education, training and research in the fields of marine sciences, engineering and related disciplines."[67] Congress assigned administration of the program to the National Science Foundation, which directed it until 1971, when control was transferred from the National Science Foundation to the National Oceanic and Atmospheric Administration of the United States Department of Commerce.[68] No institutional Sea Grant College designations were made by the National Science Foundation, which instead initiated projects designed "to implement the establishment of education, training and research in marine resources." National Science Foundation projects were generally of two kinds: first, for the support of specific projects and investigations, and secondly, for institutional support to develop broad capabilities in marine education.[69]

The first institutional programs were awarded in September 1968. In that year Texas A&M received the third-largest institutional sea grant in the nation, in the amount of $475,000; in the second year, beginning in September 1970, Texas A&M received the second-largest grant of $750,000; and, beginning in September 1971, Texas A&M received a sea grant of $1.4 million. During these years Texas A&M contributed a total of $2 million in matching funds to the programs, to bring total funding to $5.8 million.[70] A Sea Grant Program Office, under the direction of Vice-President for Programs John C. Calhoun, was organized to administer the sea-grant efforts.[71] Under the auspices and coordination of Calhoun, many things in the way of marine studies began to happen.

"In the first year of the program," reported Calhoun, "72 individual faculty persons and 58 students participated. Eleven theses were completed under the sponsorship of the Sea Grant Program and a total of 13 new academic courses were developed."[72] The inspiration and impetus of the sea-grant projects stimulated independently funded programs related to marine resources, such as the Center for Dredging Studies, organized under the sponsorship of the Department of Civil Engineering and the Texas Engineering Experiment Station in 1968. The Center engages in basic research of interest

---

[67]An address by Dr. John C. Calhoun, Jr., director, Sea Grant Program, Texas A&M University, March 1, 1970, *Sea Grant . . . Goals and Accomplishments*, 1-2 (hereinafter cited: Calhoun, *Sea Grant . . . Goals and Accomplishments*).

[68]Texas A&M, *Sea Grant [2]*.

[69]Calhoun, *Sea Grant . . . Goals and Accomplishments*, 2.

[70]Texas A&M, *Sea Grant [2]*.

[71]Calhoun, *Sea Grant . . . Goals and Accomplishments*, 11.

[72]*Ibid.*, 13.

to the dredging industry with funding from private companies such as Bauer Dredging Company, Inc., of Port Lavaca, Texas; C. F. Bean, Inc., of Plaquemine, Louisiana; Williams-McWilliams Co., of New Orleans, Louisiana; and Grant Contracting Company of Greenville, Ohio. In 1969 the Coastal Engineering Laboratory, featuring prominently a number of unique "wave tanks," was organized to complement work in both oceanography and dredging studies.[73] In a similar manner, other developing resources of the University, such as the Data Processing Center, Institute of Remote Sensing, Nuclear Science Center, and Marine Biomedical Institute, contributed to the development of the marine sciences. Thus the pieces which had been slowly and painfully constructed in earlier years were finally being meshed together, providing a unique environment for academic and scientific instruction and research.

In 1970, under sea-grant support, Texas A&M expanded its marine studies often by cooperating with area agencies, institutions, or companies. Dow Chemical Company, the Brazoria County Mosquito Control District, the Brazoria County Commissioners Court, the Texas Agricultural Extension Service, and Texaco Corporation, for example, became cosponsors with Texas A&M for a project related to the pond-growth of shrimp. An instructional program in underwater welding began in cooperation with the Texas State Institute of Technology, and curricula in ocean-instrument technology and deck and fisheries technology began in conjunction with Galveston College. Other programs were begun or envisioned with Lamar Tech University, at Beaumont, Bates College of Law, at the University of Houston, Texas A&I College, at Kingsville, Brazosport Junior College, at Freeport, and Del Mar College, in Corpus Christi.[74] In the same year Texas A&M provided assistance to a special legislative study committee, headed by Representative Ray Lemmon, for consideration of the oceanographic needs of Texas' marine-related economy.[75] By 1971 Texas A&M's Industrial Economics Research Division was developing a workplan for an offshore "superport" facility in the Gulf of Mexico.[76] By 1972 the superport idea had become a viable political issue in the Gulf states.

While all of these and many more marine programs were being devel-

[73]Texas A&M, Department of Civil Engineering, *Center for Graduate Dredging Studies* (informational brochure); Texas A&M, *Graduate Study in Oceanography, 1971-1972*, p. 6.

[74]Calhoun, *Sea Grant . . . Goals and Accomplishments*, 14, 17.

[75]Texas A&M, *Sea Grant [4]*.

[76]*Ibid.*

oped, Calhoun's Sea Grant Program Office was identifying the broader educational, research, and training needs of the region for the development of
marine resources, and was designing a program of activities and a possible Sea
Grant College administration.[77] Calhoun's work in sea-grant affairs was
meanwhile gaining national recognition. On January 20, 1970, Secretary of
the Interior Walter J. Hickle appointed him chairman of the Department's
Marine Affairs Action Group, to review the programs and policies of the
Department of the Interior relating to marine affairs. Calhoun, who had been
named academic vice-president by A&M President Jack K. Williams on June
4, 1971, succeeding Horace R. Byers, was appointed to the National Council
on Oceans and Atmosphere by President Richard M. Nixon, on October 20
of that year.[78] During its first two years of operation Texas A&M's Sea Grant
Program Office held a number of conferences and workshops designed to
promote regional interest and cooperation, and maintained a flow of public
information through such reports as *Marine Affairs in Texas, Project Activities
Report; 1968-1969, Marine Resources Activities in Texas,* and a bimonthly news-
letter with a national scope entitled *The University and the Sea.*[79] The Program
Office also released a film about Texas A&M's Sea Grant Program in 1971,
called *Seascape,* which was made available to A&M clubs, civic groups, and
other educational institutions.[80]

Texas A&M made a number of changes in its administration of the sea-
grant program in 1971, to coincide with the designation of the University as a
Sea Grant College, formally conferred in the office of former Secretary of
Commerce Maurice H. Stans on September 17, 1971. On the occasion Secretary Stans recognized Texas A&M University for "the strong programs it has
initiated in areas of applied research, education and training, and advisory and
information services in maritime affairs." A&M President Jack K. Williams
announced the University's intention "to expand our work scope in marine
resources to all facets of the University — in research, education and public
service."[81]

Much of the work of the Sea Grant Program Office was transferred to

[77]Calhoun, *Sea Grant . . . Goals and Accomplishments,* 3-12.
[78]College Station *Battalion,* January 25, 1970; June 9, 1971; Bryan *Daily Eagle,* October
20, 1971.
[79]Calhoun, *Sea Grant . . . Goals and Accomplishments,* 15-16.
[80]Texas A&M, *Sea Grant* [5].
[81]*Dedication Ceremonies of Texas A&M University as a Sea Grant College,* April 6, 1972
[program].

the newly organized Center for Marine Resources, which remained under the direction of Vice-President Calhoun, assisted by Willis H. Clark. Within the Center, Leatha Miloy headed the Department of Marine Resources Information, and Roger D. Anderson was named coordinator of education and training. The Center for Marine Resources identified the six areas of Texas A&M's immediate concern as including marine fisheries, marine commerce, marine sciences, marine environmental quality, marine engineering and technology, and marine resources management.[82]

Texas A&M also began development of the Mitchell Campus on Pelican Island, adjacent to Galveston, on a 100-acre tract of land donated by the George P. Mitchell family, with construction grants from the Moody Foundation. The campus was to be the home of the new College of Marine Sciences and Maritime Resources, organized on September 1, 1971, by authority of the Sixty-second Texas Legislature. In August 1972, however, the name was changed by the Texas State Legislature to Moody College of Marine Sciences and Maritime Resources. Components of the new College included the Texas Maritime Academy, which maintained its old identity, but was improved and expanded in respect to curricula, students, faculty, and facilities. The Galveston Marine Laboratory and the Coastal Zone Laboratory were among the chain of Texas coastal laboratories envisioned as elements of the College of Marine Sciences and Maritime Resources.[83] President Williams named William Howard Clayton, professor of oceanography at Texas A&M since 1954, a graduate of Bucknell, and formerly associate dean for research in the College of Geosciences, as dean of the Moody College of Marine Sciences and Maritime Resources.[84]

Formal dedicatory ceremonies marking Texas A&M's status as a Sea Grant College were held in the H. B. Zachry Engineering Center on April 6, 1972. Robert M. White, head of the National Oceanic and Atmospheric Administration, United States Department of Commerce, made the main address. Sea Grant Merit Awards were conferred on those men and women who had made outstanding contributions along the way of Texas A&M's march to the sea. A commemorative plaque marked the milestones in the history of the developing Sea Grant Program:[85]

[82]*Center for Marine Resources and Texas A&M a Sea Grant College* [brochure].

[83]*Galveston: Texas A&M University's Doorway to the Sea* [brochure].

[84]*Dedication Ceremonies of Texas A&M University as a Sea Grant College,* April 6, 1972 [program].

[85]*Ibid.*

TEXAS A&M UNIVERSITY
SEA GRANT COLLEGE

In Recognition of the University's Commitment
to Development and Conservation of Ocean and
Marine Resources.

1949	Department of Oceanography & Meteorology Established
1971	Sea Grant College Designation made to Texas A&M University by U.S. Department of Commerce. College of Marine Sciences and Maritime Resources, Galveston, Established.
1972	Texas A&M University Dedicated as a Sea Grant College.

The Department of Oceanography, under department head Richard A. Geyer, since 1966, remained an integral part of Texas A&M's sea-grant effort. A new Department of Marine Science, under Sammy Ray, was organized in 1972 within the Moody College of Marine Sciences and Maritime Resources to develop a program on the graduate and undergraduate levels. The College of Geosciences, under Dean Earl Cook, comprises, with Oceanography, the Departments of Geography, Geology, Geophysics, and Meteorology, the latter having been separated from Oceanography in 1967. Major areas of specialization for research and graduate study in oceanography include biological oceanography, chemical oceanography, and physical oceanography. From its founding in 1949 until the mid-1960s, Texas A&M's Department of Oceanography produced about 25 percent of the nation's graduate degrees in the field.[86] In 1973 the Departments of Oceanography and Meteorology occupied their new fifteen-story quarters in the Oceanography and Meteorology Building adjacent to and overshadowing the Systems Building, a landmark symbolizing the new look and new dimensions of Texas A&M University.

"The oceans," Sea Grant Program originator Athelstan Spilhaus has said, "will offer us more space itself in which to remain human. The sea . . . beautiful and dangerous, elegant and strong, bountiful and whimsical . . . not only challenges us, but offers 'every man in the street' the exciting participation of being 'man in the sea'."[87]

A result of the rapid changes in the frontiers of knowledge has been the necessity not only to educate, but to re-educate on a continuing basis the products of the American educational system. "Because of the accelerating speed of social and economic change, and the consequent acceleration of tech-

---

[86]*Texas A&M, Graduate Study in Oceanography, 1971-1972*, pp. 8-11, 15-23; Texas A&M, *Catalogue 1972-73*, pp. 90-94.

[87]Texas A&M, *Sea Grant* [5].

nical and professional obsolescence among the working population, there must be much greater institutionalization of continuing education for adults."[88] In 1972, declared a report presented to the *Ad hoc* Committee on Continuing Education, Texas A&M restructured its programs of continuing education in response to this need:

> As the land-grant institution for Texas, TAMU has always maintained a strong commitment to education and training beyond the formalized classroom instruction. For many years, this effort was confined almost entirely to the areas of agriculture and engineering. This activity reached every county in Texas and has always maintained a firm tie to the practical needs of citizens of each geographic section as well as a wide variety of professional and technical specializations ranging from such programs as the Fireman's Training School to the Executive Development Course.
>
> In recent years, the scope of continuing education has broadened, both nationally and at TAMU. The number of individuals participating has increased, and the variety of programs has been diversified. While the extensive work of personnel in the broad areas of agriculture and engineering has continued to grow, many new efforts have begun. Now it seems prudent to give direction to these efforts outside the Colleges of Agriculture and Engineering.[89]

This report, presented before the *Ad hoc* Committee for Continuing Education, chaired by Richard Elliott Wainerdi, assistant vice-president for academic affairs in early 1972, recommended that in order to give direction and guidance to the growing continuing-education program at Texas A&M, the University should establish a College of Continuing Education.[90] Numerous meetings of the planning committee, and conferences with deans and administrators, produced plans for a Division of Continuing Education under the supervision of a director having equal status to the directors of the Texas Forest Service and the Texas Extension Service.[91] Authorized by the Board of Directors, and approved by the Coordinating Board, Texas College and University System, Texas A&M's Division of Continuing Education provides a vital educational service to the people of Texas in the best traditions of the Morrill Land-Grant College Act. It offers an educational system which is

---

[88]J. Paul Leagans, "Continuing Education: A Fourth Dimension," in *A New Look At Progressive Education,* 261.

[89][Memorandum] Continuing Education at Texas A&M University.

[90]*Ibid.*

[91]*Ibid.;* Robert S. Morrisey, Norman, Oklahoma, to John C. Calhoun, College Station, Texas, February 21, 1972; see also Minutes of the *Ad hoc* Committee for College of Continuing Education, March 23, 28, 1972.

defined as one that "is flexible but with a backbone, a system that is open-ended and that has numerous entry and exit points according to ability and need."[92]

Located in the eleven-story Continuing Education Tower of the new auditorium and conference-room complex adjoining the Memorial Student Center, the Division of Continuing Education, with the College of Marine Sciences and Maritime Resources, and the numerous institutes, agencies, and laboratories sponsored by Texas A&M, all of them interrelated with the basic academic structure of the University, provide a fourth and exciting new dimension to higher education, as Texas A&M enters upon its second one hundred years of service to the people of Texas, and, indeed, to mankind.

Old Aggies, and the new, remain proud of their University. Most Aggies echo the sentiments of State Senator William Moore, who, before the 1974 summer graduates, pleaded guilty "to an unsurpassed love for this institution," generated in part, he said, "because of what it did for me." That is really what Texas A&M is all about, doing things for people.

[92]Leagans, "Continuing Education: A Fourth Dimension," in *A New Look at Progressive Education*, 258.

Members of the Texas A&M Board of Directors and Secretaries to the Board 1876-1976

1876-1877
Thomas S. Gathright, President of the College

Richard Coke, Governor — Ex-officio President
Richard Bennett Hubbard, Lieutenant Governor — Ex-officio Member
T. R. Bonner, Speaker of the House — Ex-officio Member

Bennett H. Davis, Bryan
Charles DeMorse, Clarksville

Edward Bradford Pickett, Liberty
Fletcher S. Stockdale, Indianola

Charles Sherman West, Austin

1877-1878
Thomas S. Gathright, President of the College

Richard Bennett Hubbard, Governor — Ex-officio President
Wells Thomas, Lieutenant Governor — Ex-officio Member
T. R. Bonner, Speaker of the House — Ex-officio Member

Bennett H. Davis, Bryan
Charles DeMorse, Clarksville
Anderson James Peeler, Austin

Edward Bradford Pickett, Liberty
Thomas Morton Scott, Melissa
Fletcher S. Stockdale, Indianola

1878-1879
Thomas S. Gathright, President of the College

Oran Milo Roberts, Governor — Ex-officio President
Joseph Draper Sayers, Lieutenant Governor — Ex-officio Member
John Hughes Cochran, Speaker of the House — Ex-officio Member

J. K. Dixon, Hillsboro
J. W. Durant, Centerville
W. H. Lyday, Bonham

Anderson James Peeler, Austin
Edward Bradford Pickett, Liberty
George Pfeuffer, New Braunfels

1879-1880
John G. James, President of the College

Oran Milo Roberts, Governor — Ex-officio President
Joseph Draper Sayers, Lieutenant Governor — Ex-officio Member
John Hughes Cochran, Speaker of the House — Ex-officio Member

J. K. Dixon, Hillsboro

Anderson James Peeler, Austin

J. W. Durant, Centerville

W. H. Lyday, Bonham

Edward Bradford Pickett, Liberty

George Pfeuffer, New Braunfels

1880-1881
John G. James, President of the College

Edward Bradford Pickett, Liberty, Chairman

James G. Garrison, Henderson

George Pfeuffer, New Braunfels

Thomas Morton Scott, Melissa

Charles C. Wiggins, Houston

1881-1882
John G. James, President of the College

John D. Thomas, Bryan, Chairman

James G. Garrison, Henderson

George Pfeuffer, New Braunfels

Thomas Morton Scott, Melissa

Charles C. Wiggins, Houston

1882-1883
John G. James, President of the College

John D. Thomas, Bryan, Chairman

James G. Garrison, Henderson

George Pfeuffer, New Braunfels

Thomas Morton Scott, Melissa

Charles C. Wiggins, Houston

April 1, 1883-July 19, 1883
James Reid Cole, Acting President of the College

1883-1884
Hardaway Hunt Dinwiddie, President (Chairman of the Faculty)

George Pfeuffer, New Braunfels, President

William R. Cavitt, Bryan

James G. Garrison, Henderson

Thomas Morton Scott, Melissa

Charles C. Wiggins, Houston

1884-1885
Hardaway Hunt Dinwiddie, President (Chairman of the Faculty)

George Pfeuffer, New Braunfels, President

William R. Cavitt, Bryan

George M. Dilley, Palestine

James G. Garrison, Henderson

Thomas Morton Scott, Melissa

1885-1886
Hardaway Hunt Dinwiddie, President (Chairman of the Faculty)

George Pfeuffer, New Braunfels, President

William R. Cavitt, Bryan

George M. Dilley, Palestine

James G. Garrison, Henderson

Thomas Morton Scott, Melissa

1886-1887
Hardaway Hunt Dinwiddie, President (Chairman of the Faculty)

Christopher C. Garrett, Brenham, President

William R. Cavitt, Bryan

George M. Dilley, Palestine

James G. Garrison, Henderson

Archibald Johnson Rose, Salado

1887-1888
Louis Lowry McInnis, President (Chairman of the Faculty)

Christopher C. Garrett, Brenham, President	George M. Dilley, Palestine
William R. Cavitt, Bryan	Lafayette Lumpkin Foster, Austin

Archibald Johnson Rose, Salado

1888-1889
Louis Lowry McInnis, President (Chairman of the Faculty)

Archibald Johnson Rose, Salado, President	William R. Cavitt, Bryan
Jno. Adriance, Columbia	J. D. Fields, Manor

Lafayette Lumpkin Foster, Austin

1889-1890
Louis Lowry McInnis, President (Chairman of the Faculty)

Archibald Johnson Rose, Salado, President	William R. Cavitt, Bryan
Jno. Adriance, Columbia	J. D. Fields, Manor

John E. Hollingsworth, Austin

July 1, 1890-January 20, 1891
William Lorraine Bringhurst, Acting President of the College

1890-1891
Lawrence Sullivan Ross, President of the College

Archibald Johnson Rose, Salado, President	William R. Cavitt, Bryan
Jno. Adriance, Columbia	J. D. Fields, Manor

John E. Hollingsworth, Austin

1891-1892
Lawrence Sullivan Ross, President of the College

Archibald Johnson Rose, Salado, President	William R. Cavitt, Bryan
Jno. Adriance, Columbia	J. D. Fields, Manor

John E. Hollingsworth, Austin

1892-1893
Lawrence Sullivan Ross, President of the College

Archibald Johnson Rose, Salado, President	William R. Cavitt, Bryan
Jno. Adriance, Columbia	J. D. Fields, Manor

John E. Hollingsworth, Austin

1893-1894
Lawrence Sullivan Ross, President of the College

Archibald Johnson Rose, Salado, President	William R. Cavitt, Bryan
Jno. Adriance, Columbia	J. D. Fields, Manor

John E. Hollingsworth, Austin

1894-1895
Lawrence Sullivan Ross, President of the College

Archibald Johnson Rose, Austin, President
George W. Bowman, Plano

William R. Cavitt, Bryan
John Benjamin Long, Rusk

David A. Paulus, Halletsville

1895-1896
Lawrence Sullivan Ross, President of the College

Archibald Johnson Rose, Austin, President
George W. Bowman, Plano

William R. Cavitt, Bryan
John Benjamin Long, Rusk

David A. Paulus, Halletsville

1896-1897
Lawrence Sullivan Ross, President of the College

Frank A. Reichardt, Houston, President
Frank P. Holland, Dallas

Jefferson Johnson, Austin
George Cassety Pendleton, Belton

Charles Rogan, Brownwood

1897-1898
Lawrence Sullivan Ross, President of the College

Frank A. Reichardt, Houston, President
Frank P. Holland, Dallas

Jefferson Johnson, Austin
Charles Rogan, Brownwood

Marion Sansom, Alvarado

January 17, 1898-July 1, 1898
Roger Haddock Whitlock, Acting President of the College

1898-1899
Lafayette Lumpkin Foster, President of the College

Frank A. Reichardt, Houston, President
Marion Sansom, Alvarado
Frank P. Holland, Dallas

Jefferson Johnson, Austin
John W. Kokernot, San Antonio
A. P. Smyth, Mart

Patrick Henry Tobin, Denison

1899-1900
Lafayette Lumpkin Foster, President of the College

Marion Sansom, Alvarado, President
Jefferson Johnson, Austin
John W. Kokernot, San Antonio
William Malone, Hunter

A. C. Oliver, Douglasville
Frank A. Reichardt, Houston
A. P. Smyth, Mart
Patrick Henry Tobin, Denison

1900-1901
Lafayette Lumpkin Foster, President of the College

Marion Sansom, Alvarado, President
Jefferson Johnson, Austin
John W. Kokernot, San Antonio
William Malone, Hunter

A. C. Oliver, Douglasville
Frank A. Reichardt, Houston
A. P. Smyth, Mart
Patrick Henry Tobin, Denison

1901-1902

Roger Haddock Whitlock, Acting President of the College

Marion Sansom, Alvarado, President

Louis David Amsler, Hempstead

W. J. Clay, Austin

Augustine Haidusek, La Grange

George Taylor Jester, Corsicana

K. K. Legett, Abilene

Frank A. Reichardt, Houston

Patrick Henry Tobin, Denison

1902-1903

David Franklin Houston, President of the College

Marion Sansom, Fort Worth, President

Louis David Amsler, Hempstead

A. J. Brown, Dallas

W. J. Clay, Austin

Augustine Haidusek, La Grange

K. K. Legett, Abilene

Frank A. Reichardt, Houston

1903-1904

David Franklin Houston, President of the College

Marion Sansom, Fort Worth, President

Louis David Amsler, Hempstead

A. J. Brown, Dallas

W. J. Clay, Austin

Augustine Haidusek, La Grange

K. K. Legett, Abilene

Frank A. Reichardt, Houston

1904-1905

David Franklin Houston, President of the College

Marion Sansom, Fort Worth, President

Louis David Amsler, Hempstead

A. J. Brown, Dallas

W. J. Clay, Austin

Augustine Haidusek, La Grange

K. K. Legett, Abilene

Frank A. Reichardt, Houston

1905-1906

Henry Hill Harrington, President of the College

K. K. Legett, Abilene, President

John M. Green, Yoakum

Augustine Haidusek, La Grange

Robert Teague Milner, Austin

Louis L. McInnis, Bryan

Walton Peteet, Dallas

Thomas David Rowell, Jefferson

W. P. Sebastian, Breckenridge

1906-1907

Henry Hill Harrington, President of the College

K. K. Legett, Abilene, President

John M. Green, Yoakum

Augustine Haidusek, La Grange

Robert Teague Milner, Austin

Louis L. McInnis, Bryan

Walton Peteet, Dallas

Thomas David Rowell, Jefferson

W. P. Sebastian, Breckenridge

1907-1908

Henry Hill Harrington, President of the College

K. K. Legett, Abilene, President

Louis L. McInnis, Bryan

John M. Green, Yoakum

Augustine Haidusek, La Grange

Robert Teague Milner, Austin

Walton Peteet, Dallas

Thomas David Rowell, Jefferson

W. P. Sebastian, Breckenridge

1908-1909
Robert Teague Milner, President of the College

K. K. Legett, Abilene, President

John M. Green, Yoakum

Augustine Haidusek, La Grange

Edward Reeves Kone, Austin

A. R. McCollum, Waco

Walton Peteet, Dallas

Thomas David Rowell, Jefferson

W. P. Sebastian, Breckenridge

1909-1910
Robert Teague Milner, President of the College

K. K. Legett, Abilene, President

Augustine Haidusek, La Grange

Laurence Joseph Hart, San Antonio

Edward Reeves Kone, Austin

A. R. McCollum, Waco

Walton Peteet, Fort Worth

Thomas David Rowell, Jefferson

W. P. Sebastian, Breckenridge

1910-1911
Robert Teague Milner, President of the College

W. A. Trenckmann, Austin, President

R. L. Bennett, Paris

Charles Davis, Steele's Store

John I. Guion, Ballinger

Laurence Joseph Hart, San Antonio

Edward Reeves Kone, Austin

J. Allen Kyle, Houston

Walton Peteet, Fort Worth

1911-1912
Robert Teague Milner, President of the College

Walton Peteet, Fort Worth, President

R. L. Bennett, Paris

Charles Davis, Steele's Store

John I. Guion, Ballinger

Laurence Joseph Hart, San Antonio

Daniel W. Kampner, Galveston

Edward Reeves Kone, Austin

J. Allen Kyle, Houston

1912-1913
Robert Teague Milner, President of the College

Edward Benjamin Cushing, Houston, President

Erwin Hugh Astin, Bryan

R. L. Bennett, Paris

John I. Guion, Ballinger

Laurence Joseph Hart, San Antonio

Edward Reeves Kone, Austin

J. Allen Kyle, Houston

Walton Peteet, Fort Worth

1913-1914
Charles Puryear, Acting President of the College

Edward Benjamin Cushing, Houston, President

Erwin Hugh Astin, Bryan

Thomas E. Battle, Marlin

R. L. Bennett, Paris

John I. Guion, Ballinger

Laurence Joseph Hart, San Antonio

J. Allen Kyle, Houston

Walton Peteet, Waco

J. Sheb Williams, Paris

1914-1915
William Bennett Bizzell, President of the College

John I. Guion, Ballinger, President
Erwin Hugh Astin, Bryan
Thomas E. Battle, Marlin
H. A. Breihan, Bartlett

Asbury Bascom Davidson, Cuero
Laurence Joseph Hart, San Antonio
John R. Kubena, Fayetteville
William A. Miller, Amarillo

J. Sheb Williams, Paris

1915-1916
William Bennett Bizzell, President of the College

John I. Guion, Ballinger, President
Erwin Hugh Astin, Bryan
Thomas E. Battle, Marlin
H. A. Breihan, Bartlett

Asbury Bascom Davidson, Cuero
Laurence Joseph Hart, San Antonio
John R. Kubena, Fayetteville
William A. Miller, Amarillo

J. Sheb Williams, Paris

1916-1917
William Bennett Bizzell, President of the College

John I. Guion, Ballinger, President
Erwin Hugh Astin, Bryan
Thomas E. Battle, Marlin
H. A. Breihan, Bartlett

Asbury Bascom Davidson, Cuero
John T. Dickson, Paris
Laurence Joseph Hart, San Antonio
John R. Kubena, Fayetteville

William A. Miller, Amarillo

1917-1918
William Bennett Bizzell, President of the College

John I. Guion, Ballinger, President
Erwin Hugh Astin, Bryan
H. A. Breihan, Bartlett
Asbury Bascom Davidson, Cuero

John T. Dickson, Paris
Laurence Joseph Hart, San Antonio
John R. Kubena, Fayetteville
F. Marion Law, Houston

William A. Miller, Amarillo

1918-1919
William Bennett Bizzell, President of the College

Laurence Joseph Hart, San Antonio, President
H. A. Breihan, Bartlett
Asbury Bascom Davidson, Cuero
John T. Dickson, Paris

John R. Kubena, Fayetteville
F. Marion Law, Houston
William A. Miller, Amarillo
W. S. Rowland, Temple

Roy Lester Young, Houston

1919-1920
William Bennett Bizzell, President of the College

Laurence Joseph Hart, San Antonio, President
H. A. Breihan, Bartlett
Asbury Bascom Davidson, Cuero
John T. Dickson, Paris

John R. Kubena, Fayetteville
F. Marion Law, Houston
William A. Miller, Amarillo
W. S. Rowland, Temple

Roy Lester Young, Houston

1920-1921
William Bennett Bizzell, President of the College

Laurence Joseph Hart, San Antonio, President
H. A. Breihan, Bartlett
John T. Dickson, Paris
T. N. Jones, Tyler

John R. Kubena, Fayetteville
F. Marion Law, Houston
William A. Miller, Amarillo
W. S. Rowland, Temple

Roy Lester Young, Houston

1921-1922
William Bennett Bizzell, President of the College

Laurence Joseph Hart, San Antonio, President
John T. Dickson, Paris
Mrs. J. C. George, Brownsville
T. N. Jones, Tyler

F. Marion Law, Houston
C. E. Marsh, Austin
W. S. Rowland, Temple
J. M. Wagstaff, Abilene

Roy Lester Young, Houston

1922-1923
William Bennett Bizzell, President of the College

Laurence Joseph Hart, San Antonio, President
Walter L. Boothe, Sweetwater
John T. Dickson, Paris
Mrs. J. C. George, Brownsville

F. Marion Law, Houston
C. E. Marsh, Austin
W. S. Rowland, Temple
Byrd E. White, Lancaster

Roy Lester Young, Houston

1923-1924
William Bennett Bizzell, President of the College

Laurence Joseph Hart, San Antonio, President
Walter L. Boothe, Sweetwater,
Pinckney Lovick Downs, Jr., Temple
Mrs. J. C. George, Brownsville

Walter G. Lacy, Waco
F. Marion Law, Houston
W. S. Rowland, Temple
Byrd E. White, Lancaster

Roy Lester Young, Houston

1924-1925
William Bennett Bizzell, President of the College

F. Marion Law, Houston, President
Walter L. Boothe, Sweetwater
William Carson Boyett, College Station
Pinckney Lovick Downs, Jr., Temple

Mrs. J. C. George, Brownsville
Walter G. Lacy, Waco
Henry C. Schuhmacher, Houston
Byrd E. White, Lancaster

William A. Wurzbach, San Antonio

1925-1926
Thomas Otto Walton, President of the College

F. Marion Law, Houston, President
Walter L. Boothe, Sweetwater
William Carson Boyett, College Station
Pinckney Lovick Downs, Jr., Temple

Mrs. J. C. George, Brownsville
Walter G. Lacy, Waco
Henry C. Schuhmacher, Houston
Byrd E. White, Lancaster

William A. Wurzbach, San Antonio

1926-1927

Thomas Otto Walton, President of the College

F. Marion Law, Houston, President

Pinckney Lovick Downs, Jr., Temple

Edwin J. Kiest, Dallas

Walter G. Lacy, Waco

W. T. Montgomery, San Antonio

Henry C. Schuhmacher, Houston

Byrd E. White, Lancaster

George Rollie White, Brady

William A. Wurzbach, San Antonio

1927-1928

Thomas Otto Walton, President of the College

F. Marion Law, Houston, President

Pinckney Lovick Downs, Jr., Temple

Edwin J. Kiest, Dallas

Walter G. Lacy, Waco

W. T. Montgomery, San Antonio

Henry C. Schuhmacher, Houston

Byrd E. White, Lancaster

George Rollie White, Brady

William A. Wurzbach, San Antonio

1928-1929

Thomas Otto Walton, President of the College

F. Marion Law, Houston, President

Pinckney Lovick Downs, Jr., Temple

Edward J. Kiest, Dallas

Walter G. Lacy, Waco

W. T. Montgomery, San Antonio

Henry C. Schuhmacher, Houston

Byrd E. White, Lancaster

George Rollie White, Brady

William A. Wurzbach, San Antonio

1929-1930

Thomas Otto Walton, President of the College

F. Marion Law, Houston, President

Pinckney Lovick Downs, Jr., Temple

Edward J. Kiest, Dallas

Walter G. Lacy, Waco

W. T. Montgomery, San Antonio

Henry C. Schuhmacher, Houston

Byrd E. White, Lancaster

George Rollie White, Brady

William A. Wurzbach, San Antonio

1930-1931

Thomas Otto Walton, President of the College

F. Marion Law, Houston, President

Pinckney Lovick Downs, Jr., Temple

Edward J. Kiest, Dallas

Joseph Kopecky, Halletsville

Walter G. Lacy, Waco

W. T. Montgomery, San Antonio

Henry C. Schuhmacher, Houston

Byrd E. White, Lancaster

George Rollie White, Brady

1931-1932

Thomas Otto Walton, President of the College

F. Marion Law, Houston, President

Pinckney Lovick Downs, Jr., Temple

Edward J. Kiest, Dallas

Joseph Kopecky, Halletsville

Walter G. Lacy, Waco

W. T. Montgomery, San Antonio

Henry C. Schuhmacher, Houston

Byrd E. White, Lancaster

George Rollie White, Brady

1932-1933

Thomas Otto Walton, President of the College

F. Marion Law, Houston, President

Guy T. Anderson, Calvert

Edward J. Kiest, Dallas

Joseph Kopecky, Halletsville

Walter B. Lacy, Waco

Henry C. Schuhmacher, Houston

Louis J. Wardlaw, Fort Worth

Byrd E. White, Lancaster

George Rollie White, Brady

1933-1934

Thomas Otto Walton, President of the College

F. Marion Law, Houston, President

Guy T. Anderson, Calvert

Edward J. Kiest, Dallas

Joseph Kopecky, Halletsville

Walter B. Lacy, Waco

Henry C. Schuhmacher, Houston

Louis J. Wardlaw, Fort Worth

Byrd E. White, Lancaster

George Rollie White, Brady

1934-1935

Thomas Otto Walton, President of the College

F. Marion Law, Houston, President

Walter G. Lacy, Waco, Vice-President

Guy T. Anderson, Calvert

Edward J. Kiest, Dallas

Joseph Kopecky, Halletsville

Henry C. Schuhmacher, Houston

Louis J. Wardlaw, Fort Worth

Byrd E. White, Dallas

George Rollie White, Brady

1935-1936

Thomas Otto Walton, President of the College

F. Marion Law, Houston, President

Walter G. Lacy, Waco, Vice-President

Guy T. Anderson, Calvert

Edward J. Kiest, Dallas

Joseph Kopecky, Halletsville

Henry C. Schuhmacher, Houston

Joe Utay, Dallas

Louis J. Wardlaw, Brady

George Rollie White, Brady

1936-1937

Thomas Otto Walton, President of the College

F. Marion Law, Houston, President

Walter G. Lacy, Waco, Vice-President

Robert W. Briggs, Pharr

Roy B. Davis, Plainview

Edward J. Kiest, Dallas

Elliott Roosevelt, Fort Worth

Henry C. Schuhmacher, Houston

Joe Utay, Dallas

George Rollie White, Brady

1937-1938

Thomas Otto Walton, President of the College

F. Marion Law, Houston, President

Walter G. Lacy, Waco, Vice-President

Robert W. Briggs, Pharr

Roy B. Davis, Plainview

Edward J. Kiest, Dallas

Elliott Roosevelt, Fort Worth

Henry C. Schuhmacher, Houston

Joe Utay, Dallas

George Rollie White, Brady

1938-1939
Thomas Otto Walton, President of the College

F. Marion Law, Houston, Chairman

Walter G. Lacy, Waco, Vice-President

Robert W. Briggs, Pharr

A. H. Demke, Stephenville

Edward J. Kiest, Dallas

Herbert Lee Kokernot, Jr., Alpine

Henry C. Schuhmacher, Houston

Joe Utay, Dallas

George Rollie White, Brady

1939-1940
Thomas Otto Walton, President of the College

F. Marion Law, Houston, President

Walter G. Lacy, Waco, Vice-President

Robert W. Briggs, Pharr

A. H. Demke, Stephenville

Edward J. Kiest, Dallas

Herbert Lee Kokernot, Jr., Alpine

Henry C. Schuhmacher, Houston

Joe Utay, Dallas

George Rollie White, Brady

1940-1941
Thomas Otto Walton, President of the College

F. Marion Law, President

Walter G. Lacy, Waco, Vice-President

Robert W. Briggs, San Antonio

A. H. Demke, Stephenville

Edward J. Kiest, Dallas

Herbert Lee Kokernot, Jr., Alpine

Joe Utay, Dallas

George Rollie White, Brady

1941-1942
Thomas Otto Walton, President of the College

F. Marion Law, Houston, President

George Rollie White, Brady, Vice-President

H. J. Brees, San Antonio

Robert W. Briggs, San Antonio

D. S. Buchanan, Buda

John C. Burns, Fort Worth

A. H. Demke, Stephenville

Herbert Lee Kokernot, Jr., Alpine

Neth L. Leachman, Dallas

1942-1943
Thomas Otto Walton, President of the College

F. Marion Law, Houston, President

George Rollie White, Brady, Vice-President

H. J. Brees, San Antonio

Robert W. Briggs, San Antonio

D. S. Buchanan, Buda

John C. Burns, Fort Worth

A. H. Demke, Stephenville

Herbert Lee Kokernot, Jr., Alpine

Neth L. Leachman, Dallas

1943-1944
Frank Cleveland Bolton, Acting President of the College

F. Marion Law, President

George Rollie White, Brady, Vice-President

H. J. Brees, San Antonio

Robert W. Briggs, San Antonio

D. S. Buchanan, Buda

John C. Burns, Fort Worth

A. H. Demke, Stephenville

Herbert Lee Kokernot, Jr., Alpine

Neth L. Leachman, Dallas

1944-1945
Gibb Gilchrist, President of the College

F. Marion Law, Houston, President

George Rollie White, Brady, Vice-President

H. J. Brees, San Antonio

Robert W. Briggs, San Antonio

D. S. Buchanan, Buda

John C. Burns, Fort Worth

A. H. Demke, Stephenville

Herbert Lee Kokernot, Jr., Alpine

Neth L. Leachman, Dallas

1945-1946
Gibb Gilchrist, President of the College

George Rollie White, Brady, President

Herbert L. Kokernot, Jr., Alpine,
  Vice-President

H. J. Brees, San Antonio

D. S. Buchanan, Corpus Christi

Erwin W. Harrison, South Bend

John W. Newton, Beaumont

Rufus R. Peeples, Tehuacana

Roy C. Potts, Belton

Henry Reese, III, Gonzales

1946-1947
Gibb Gilchrist, President of the College

George Rollie White, Brady, President

Herbert L. Kokernot, Jr., Alpine,
  Vice-President

H. J. Brees, San Antonio

D. S. Buchanan, Corpus Christi

Erwin W. Harrison, South Bend

John W. Newton, Beaumont

Rufus R. Peeples, Tehuacana

Roy C. Potts, Belton

Henry Reese, III, Gonzales

1947-1948
Gibb Gilchrist, President of the College

George Rollie White, Brady, President

Herbert L. Kokernot, Jr., Alpine,
  Vice-President

Tyree L. Bell, Dallas

Erwin W. Harrison, South Bend

Carl C. Krueger, San Antonio

John W. Newton, Beaumont

Rufus R. Peeples, Tehuacana

Roy C. Potts, Belton

Henry Reese, III, Gonzales

1948-1949
Frank Cleveland Bolton, President of the College

George Rollie White, Brady, President

Herbert L. Kokernot, Jr., Alpine,
  Vice-President

Tyree L. Bell, Dallas

Erwin W. Harrison, South Bend

Carl C. Krueger, San Antonio

John W. Newton, Beaumont

Rufus R. Peeples, Tehuacana

Roy C. Potts, Belton

Henry Reese, III, Gonzales

1949-1950
Frank Cleveland Bolton, President of the College

George Rollie White, President

John W. Newton, Beaumont, Vice-President

Tyree L. Bell, Dallas

Erwin W. Harrison, South Bend

Carl C. Krueger, San Antonio

Rufus R. Peeples, Tehuacana

Al E. Cudlipp, Lufkin   Roy C. Potts, Belton
                              Henry Reese, III, Gonzales

1950-1951
Marion Thomas Harrington, President of the College

George Rollie White, Brady, President   Erwin W. Harrison, South Bend
John W. Newton, Beaumont, Vice-President   Carl C. Krueger, San Antonio
Tyree L. Bell, Dallas   Rufus R. Peeples, Tehuacana
Al E. Cudlipp, Lufkin   Roy C. Potts, Belton
                              Henry Reese, III, Gonzales

1951-1952
Marion Thomas Harrington, President of the College

George Rollie White, Brady, President   Erwin W. Harrison, South Bend
Tyree L. Bell, Dallas, Vice-President   Carl C. Krueger, San Antonio
Robert Allen, Raymondville   Rufus R. Peeples, Tehuacana
Al E. Cudlipp, Lufkin   Henry Logan Winfield, Fort Stockton
                         James Winfred Witherspoon, Hereford

1952-1953
Marion Thomas Harrington, President of the College

George Rollie White, Brady, President   Erwin W. Harrison, South Bend
Tyree L. Bell, Dallas, Vice-President   Carl C. Krueger, San Antonio
Robert Allen, Raymondville   Rufus R. Peeples, Tehuacana
Al E. Cudlipp, Lufkin   Henry L. Winfield, Fort Stockton
                            James W. Witherspoon, Hereford

1953-1954
David Hitchens Morgan, President of the College

George Rollie White, Brady, President   Wilfred T. Doherty, Houston
Henry L. Winfield, Fort Stockton,   J. Harold Dunn, Amarillo
   Vice-President   Reginald H. Finney, Jr. Greenville
Robert Allen, Raymondville   Erwin W. Harrison, South Bend
Al E. Cudlipp, Lufkin   James W. Witherspoon, Hereford

1954-1955
David Hitchens Morgan, President of the College

George Rollie White, Brady, President   Wilfred T. Doherty, Houston
Henry L. Winfield, Fort Stockton,   J. Harold Dunn, Amarillo
   Vice-President   Reginald H. Finney, Jr., Greenville
Robert Allen, Raymondville   Erwin W. Harrison, South Bend
Al. E. Cudlipp, Lufkin   James W. Witherspoon, Hereford

1955-1956
David Hitchens Morgan, President of the College

Wilfred T. Doherty, Houston, President
Al E. Cudlipp, Lufkin, Vice-President
Robert Allen, Raymondville
Price Campbell, Alpine

J. Harold Dunn, Amarillo
Reginald H. Finney, Jr., Greenville
Lemuel H. Ridout, Jr., Dallas
James W. Witherspoon, Hereford

Henry B. Zachry, San Antonio

1956-1957

David Willard Williams, Acting President of the College

Wilfred T. Doherty, Houston, President
Al E. Cudlipp, Lufkin, Vice-President
Robert Allen, Raymondville
Price Campbell, Alpine

J. Harold Dunn, Amarillo
Reginald H. Finney, Jr., Greenville
Lemuel H. Ridout, Jr., Dallas,
James W. Witherspoon, Hereford

Henry B. Zachry, San Antonio

1957-1958

Marion Thomas Harrington, President of the College

Wilfred T. Doherty, Houston, President
J. Harold Dunn, Amarillo, Vice-President
Price Campbell, Abilene
Al E. Cudlipp, Lufkin

Eugene B. Darby, Pharr
Reginald H. Finney, Jr., Greenville
Herman F. Heep, Austin
Lemuel H. Ridout, Jr., Dallas

Henry B. Zachry, San Antonio

1958-1959

Marion Thomas Harrington, President of the College

Wilfred T. Doherty, Houston, President
J. Harold Dunn, Amarillo, Vice-President
Price Campbell, Abilene
Al E. Cudlipp, Lufkin

Eugene B. Darby, Pharr
Reginald H. Finney, Jr., Greenville
Herman F. Heep, Austin
Lemuel H. Ridout, Jr., Dallas

Henry B. Zachry, San Antonio

1959-1960

James Earl Rudder, President of the College

Henry B. Zachry, San Antonio, President
Al E. Cudlipp, Lufkin, Vice-President
Price Campbell, Abilene
Eugene B. Darby, Pharr

Sterling C. Evans, Houston
Herman F. Heep, Austin
John W. Newton, Beaumont
Lemuel H. Ridout, Jr., Dallas

Samuel Benjamin Whittenburg, Amarillo

1960-1961

James Earl Rudder, President of the College

Henry B. Zachry, San Antonio, President
Al E. Cudlipp, Lufkin, Vice-President
Price Campbell, Abilene
Eugene B. Darby, Pharr

Sterling C. Evans, Houston
William J. Lawson, Austin
John W. Newton, Beaumont
Lemuel H. Ridout, Jr., Dallas

Samuel B. Whittenburg, Amarillo

1961-1962
James Earl Rudder, President of the College

Eugene B. Darby, Pharr, President
John W. Newton, Beaumont, Vice-President
Sterling C. Evans, Houston
Hugo C. Heldenfels, Corpus Christi

William J. Lawson, Austin
Lemuel H. Ridout, Jr., Dallas
Clyde Thompson, Diboll
Clyde H. Wells, Granbury

Samuel B. Whittenburg, Amarillo

1962-1963
James Earl Rudder, President of the College

Eugene B. Darby, Pharr, President
John W. Newton, Beaumont, Vice-President
Sterling C. Evans, Houston
Hugo C. Heldenfels, Corpus Christi

William J. Lawson, Austin
Lemuel H. Ridout, Jr., Dallas
Clyde Thompson, Diboll
Clyde H. Wells, Granbury

Samuel B. Whittenburg, Amarillo

1963-1964
James Earl Rudder, President of the University

Sterling C. Evans, Houston, President
John W. Newton, Beaumont, Vice-President
Albert Phillip Beutel, Lake Jackson
Hugo C. Heldenfels, Corpus Christi

Leland F. Peterson, Fort Worth
Gardiner Symonds, Houston
Clyde Thompson, Diboll
Clyde H. Wells, Granbury

Samuel B. Whittenburg, Amarillo

1964-1965
James Earl Rudder, President of the University

Sterling C. Evans, Houston, President
John W. Newton, Beaumont, Vice-President
Albert Phillip Beutel, Lake Jackson
Hugo C. Heldenfels, Corpus Christi

Leland F. Peterson, Fort Worth
Gardiner Symonds, Houston
Clyde Thompson, Diboll
Clyde H. Wells, Granbury

Samuel B. Whittenburg, Amarillo

1965-1966
James Earl Rudder, President of the University

Hugo C. Heldenfels, Corpus Christi,
President
Clyde H. Wells, Granbury, Vice-President
Albert P. Beutel, Lake Jackson
Wofford Cain, Dallas

Sterling C. Evans, Houston
Leland F. Peterson, Fort Worth
Gardiner Symonds, Houston
Clyde Thompson, Diboll
Samuel B. Whittenburg, Amarillo

1966-1967
James Earl Rudder, President of the University

Hugo C. Heldenfels, Corpus Christi,
President
Clyde H. Wells, Granbury, Vice-President

Sterling C. Evans, Houston
Leland F. Peterson, Fort Worth
Gardiner Symonds, Houston

Albert P. Beutel, Lake Jackson   Clyde Thompson, Diboll
Wofford Cain, Dallas   Samuel B. Whittenburg, Amarillo

1967-1968
James Earl Rudder, President of the University

Leland F. Peterson, Fort Worth, President   Sterling C. Evans, Houston
Samuel B. Whittenburg, Amarillo,   Hugo C. Heldenfels, Corpus Christi
  Vice-President   Peyton McKnight, Jr., Tyler
Albert P. Beutel, Lake Jackson   Gardiner Symonds, Houston
Wofford Cain, Dallas   Clyde H. Wells, Granbury

1968-1969
James Earl Rudder, President of the University

Leland F. Peterson, Fort Worth, President   Wofford Cain, Dallas
Samuel B. Whittenburg, Amarillo,   Sterling C. Evans, Houston
  Vice-President   Hugo C. Heldenfels, Corpus Christi
Ford D. Albritton, Jr., Bryan   Peyton McKnight, Jr., Tyler
Albert P. Beutel, Lake Jackson   Clyde H. Wells, Granbury

1969-1970
James Earl Rudder, President of the University

Clyde H. Wells, Granbury, President   Sterling C. Evans, Houston
Albert P. Beutel, Lake Jackson,   Hugo C. Heldenfels, Corpus Christi
  Vice-President   Peyton McKnight, Jr., Tyler
Ford D. Albritton, Jr., Bryan   Leland F. Peterson, Fort Worth
Wofford Cain, Dallas   Samuel B. Whittenburg, Amarillo

March 30, 1970-November 1, 1970
Alvin Rubal Luedecke, Acting President of the University

1970-1971
Jack Kenny Williams, President of the University

Clyde H. Wells, Granbury, President   Sterling C. Evans, Houston
Albert P. Beutel, Lake Jackson,   Hugo C. Heldenfels, Corpus Christi
  Vice-President   Peyton McKnight, Jr., Tyler
Ford D. Albritton, Jr., Bryan   Leland F. Peterson, Fort Worth
Wofford Cain, Dallas   Samuel B. Whittenburg, Amarillo

1971-1972
Jack Kenny Williams, President of the University

Clyde H. Wells, Granbury, President   Sterling C. Evans, Houston
Albert P. Beutel, Lake Jackson,   Hugo C. Heldenfels, Corpus Christi
  Vice-President   Peyton McKnight, Jr., Tyler
Ford D. Albritton, Jr., Bryan   Leland F. Peterson, Fort Worth
Wofford Cain, Dallas   Samuel B. Whittenburg, Amarillo

1972-1973
Jack Kenny Williams, President of the University

Clyde H. Wells, Granbury, President

Albert P. Beutel, Lake Jackson,
  Vice-President

Ford D. Albritton, Jr., Bryan

Harvey C. Bell, Jr., Austin

Hugo C. Heldenfels, Corpus Christi

William H. Lewie, Jr., Waco

Peyton McKnight, Jr., Tyler

Leland F. Peterson, Fort Worth

Samuel B. Whittenburg, Amarillo

1973-1974
Jack Kenny Williams, President of the University

Clyde H. Wells, Granbury, President

Albert P. Beutel, Lake Jackson,
  Vice-President

Ford D. Albritton, Jr., Bryan

Hugo C. Heldenfels, Corpus Christi

William H. Lewie, Jr., Waco

Peyton McKnight, Jr., Tyler

L. F. Peterson, Fort Worth

S. B. Whittenburg, Amarillo

1974-1975
Jack Kenny Williams, President of the University

Clyde H. Wells, Granbury, President

S. B. Whittenburg, Amarillo,
  Vice-President

Ford D. Albritton, Jr., Bryan

H. C. Bell, Jr., Austin

Richard A. Goodson, Dallas

William H. Lewie, Jr., Waco

L. F. Peterson, Fort Worth

Joe H. Reynolds, Houston

Mrs. Wilmer Smith, Wilson

1975-1976
Jack Kenny Williams, President of the University

Clyde H. Wells, Granbury, President

Richard A. Goodson, Dallas
  Vice-President

H. C. Bell, Jr., Austin

Alfred I. Davies, Dallas

William H. Lewie, Jr., Waco

Joe H. Reynolds, Houston

Mrs. Wilmer Smith, Wilson

Ross C. Watkins, Uvalde

S. B. Whittenburg, Amarillo

Secretaries to the Board of Directors[1]

William Falconer	July 15, 1876-January 10, 1877
John T. Hand[2]	January 10, 1877-November 21, 1879
George Pfeuffer (Acting)[3]	November 21, 1879-September 1, 1881
Louis L. McInnis[4]	September 1, 1881-July 1, 1890
William L. Bringhurst[5]	July 1, 1890-February 2, 1891

---

[1]Acting secretaries who served for one meeting or short periods of time have included J. L. Jeffreys (1912), Charles E. Friley (1912), Charles Puryear (1913), Gladys Baker (1943), and Henderson Shuffler (1952).

[2]Member of the Faculty.

[3]Member of the Board of Directors.

[4]Louis L. McInnis was ex-officio secretary to the Board from January 24, 1888-July 1, 1890, while chairman of the faculty.

[5]William L. Bringhurst served ex-officio while acting president of the College.

William R. Cavitt[3]	May 12, 1891-October 16, 1899
J. A. Baker	October 16, 1899-July 19, 1904
S. E. Andrews	January 31, 1905-June 9, 1909
David W. Spence (Acting)[2]	July 12, 1909-September 24, 1909
James Sullivan (Acting)	September 24, 1909-February 15, 1910
James Hay Quarles[2]	February 15, 1910-June 12, 1912
Isaac S. (Ike) Ashburn	January 19, 1913-March 23, 1917
Stephen G. Bailey	June 29, 1917-August 23, 1937
Melle N. Williamson	August 10, 1937-April 1, 1943
T. W. Dunlap	April 1, 1943-November 1, 1944
Mary McMinn (Acting)	November 1, 1944-September 7, 1945
Edward L. Angell	September 7, 1945-September 23, 1961
Edith S. Menefee	September 23, 1961-August 1, 1965
Robert G. Cherry	August 1, 1965-

Presidents of Texas A&M University and Chancellors of the Texas A&M University System 1876-1976

(An extract from the compilation of Ernest Langford, March 19, 1971)

Thomas Sanford Gathright

President   July 15, 1876-November 21, 1879

Born in Monroe County, Georgia, January 5, 1829; died at Henderson, Texas, May 24, 1880; buried at Henderson. Elected president of the Agricultural and Mechanical College of Texas July 15, 1876; relieved of the presidency November 21, 1879, in the reorganization of the College.

John Garland James

President   November 22, 1879-April 1, 1883

Born in Fluvanna County, Virginia, December 1, 1844; died in Dallas, Texas, February 11, 1930; buried in Austin. Elected president of the Agricultural and Mechanical College of Texas November 22, 1879; resigned April 1, 1883.

James Reid Cole

Acting President   April 1, 1883-July 19, 1883

Born in Stokes County, North Carolina, November 17, 1839; died at Dallas, Texas, October 28, 1917; buried at Dallas. Mr. Cole was appointed professor of English language, history, and literature on November 22, 1879, following the dismissal of the Gathright faculty.

Hardaway Hunt Dinwiddie

Chairman of the Faculty   July 23, 1883-December 11, 1887

Born at Lynchburg, Virginia, October 25, 1844; died at College Station, December 11, 1887; buried in Austin. Mr. Dinwiddie came to the College in November of 1879 as professor of physics and chemistry. Following the authorization of the office of chairman of the faculty on July 19, 1883, the faculty elected him as its chairman of the faculty on July 23, 1883, a position which he filled with honor and dignity from that date until his death on December 11, 1887.

Louis Lowry McInnis, A.M.

Chairman of the Faculty   January 24, 1888-July 1, 1890

Born at Jackson, Mississippi, March 24, 1855; died at Bryan, Texas, January 14, 1933;

buried at Bryan. Appointed adjunct professor November 9, 1877; professor of mathematics 1879-1890. Appointed chairman of the faculty by the Board of Directors on January 24, 1888; served until July 1, 1890.

William Lorraine Bringhurst, Ph.D.

Acting President   July 1, 1890-January 20, 1891

Born at Alexandria, Louisiana, August 22, 1844. Professor of physics 1882-1885; of English and history 1885-1893; acting president July 1, 1890, to January 20, 1891.

Lawrence Sullivan Ross

President   January 20, 1891-January 3, 1898

Born at Bentonsport, Iowa, September 27, 1838; died at College Station January 3, 1898; buried at Waco. Served as governor of Texas January 18, 1887, to January 20, 1891. Elected president of the Agricultural and Mechanical College of Texas on July 1, 1890, "to take effect at the end of his present term of office as governor," which was January 20, 1891.

Roger Haddock Whitlock, M.E.

Acting President   January 17, 1898-July 1, 1898
                                                                     December 10, 1901-July 1, 1902

Born in Brooklyn, New York, July 15, 1860. Appointed professor of mechanical engineering in 1883; resigned in 1906. Served twice as acting president: first, January 17, 1898, to July 1, 1898, following the death of President Ross; second, December 10, 1901, to July 1, 1902, following the death of President Foster.

Lafayette Lumpkin Foster

President   July 1, 1898-December 2, 1901

Born near Cummings, Georgia, November 17, 1851; died at Dallas, Texas, December 2, 1901; buried at College Station. Member of state Legislature, state commissioner of agriculture. Elected president of the Agricultural and Mechanical College of Texas on June 7, 1898, and by agreement with the Board of Directors set the effective date as July 1, 1898. Served until his death on December 2, 1901. President Foster was buried in the College Cemetery, a small burial plot which was originally on the site where Duncan Hall is now located. His remains and those of several others were moved in late 1938 or early 1939 to their present location on University property west of the Southern Pacific tracks.

David Franklin Houston, M.A., LL.D.

President   July 1, 1902-September 1, 1905

Born in Monroe County, South Carolina, February 2, 1866; died in New York City, September 2, 1940; buried in Cold Spring Harbor, Long Island, Memorial Cemetery. Dean of the faculty, The University of Texas, 1899-1902; elected president of the Agricultural and Mechanical College of Texas April 7, 1902, but by agreement effective July 1, 1902; resigned August 24, 1905, effective September 1, 1905, to accept the presidency of The University of Texas.

Henry Hill Harrington

President   September 8, 1905-August 7, 1908

Born at Buena Vista, Mississippi, December 15, 1859; died at Kilgore, Texas, August

16, 1939; buried at Bay City, Texas. Professor of chemistry and mineralogy, Texas A&M, at the time of his election to the presidency of the College on September 8, 1905. Resigned August 7, 1908, effective September 1, 1908, or at the pleasure of the board. His resignation was accepted as of August 7, 1908.

Robert Teague Milner

President   September 1, 1908-October 1, 1913

Born in Cherokee County, Alabama, June 21, 1851; died at Henderson. Member of the state Legislature 1887-1892; first commissioner of the Texas Department of Agriculture and as such was an ex-officio member of the Board of Directors, who elected him to the presidency of the Agricultural and Mechanical College of Texas on August 7, 1908. Resigned June 9, 1913, effective October 1, 1913.

Charles Puryear, M.A., LL.D.

Acting President   September 1, 1913-August 24, 1914

Born at Boydton, Virginia, October 21, 1860; died at Bryan, Texas, July 11, 1940; buried at Bryan. Appointed associate professor of civil engineering and physics at Texas A&M in 1889; professor of mathematics 1890-1932; dean of the College 1907-1932. Appointed president pro tem on August 18, 1913; but in view of the leave of absence granted to Colonel Milner (see above), it is a safe assumption that his duties as acting president began on September 1, 1913, and lasted until August 25, 1914. Dean Puryear also served as acting president for another month or six weeks during the interim between the resignation of Dr. Bizzell on June 2, 1925, and the election of Dr. T. O. Walton on September 3, 1925.

William Bennett Bizzell, Ph.D.

President   August 25, 1914-September 1, 1925

Born at Independence, Texas, October 14, 1876; died at Norman, Oklahoma, May 13, 1944; buried at Norman. President of the old College of Industrial Arts, at Denton, Texas, at the time of his election to the presidency of the Agricultural and Mechanical College of Texas on August 25, 1914; resigned June 1, 1925, effective September 1, 1925, to accept the presidency of the University of Oklahoma.

Thomas Otto Walton, LL.D.

President   September 3, 1925-August 7, 1943

Born near Gray, Texas, March 8, 1884; died at Bryan, Texas, February 18, 1961; buried at Bryan. Director of Extension Service at time of his election to the presidency of the Agricultural and Mechanical College of Texas on September 3, 1925; resigned August 7, 1943.

Frank Cleveland Bolton, M.S., LL.D.

Acting President   August 9, 1943-May 27, 1944
President   September 1, 1948-June 3, 1950

Born at Pontotoc, Mississippi, March 24, 1883; died at Houston, Texas, January 31, 1961; buried at College Station. Appointed professor of electrical engineering at Texas A&M in 1909; was vice-president and dean of the College when appointed acting president on August 9, 1943; served until May 27, 1944. Elected president on July 9, 1948, effective September 1, 1948; served until June 3, 1950.

Gibb Gilchrist, C.E.

President   May 27, 1944-September 1, 1948
Chancellor of the Texas A&M System   September 1, 1948-August 31, 1953

Born at Wills Point, Texas, December 23, 1887. Appointed dean of the School of Engineering in 1937; elected president of the Agricultural and Mechanical College of Texas May 27, 1944; served until September 1, 1948, when the Texas A&M College System was created and he became the first chancellor of the System, serving until his retirement on August 31, 1953. Gilchrist died in College Station in 1972, and was buried in College Station.

Marion Thomas Harrington, Ph.D.

President   June 3, 1950-September 1, 1953
                                                                    September 1, 1957-July 1, 1959
Chancellor   September 1, 1953-August 31, 1965

Born at Plano, Texas, September 8, 1901. Dean of the College when elected president of the Agricultural and Mechanical College of Texas on September 22, 1949, effective "at the end of the present school year." This was interpreted to be June 3, 1950, and on that date he officially took over the reins of the presidency. He served until September 1, 1953, when he became the second chancellor of the System, succeeding Mr. Gilchrist. Dr. Harrington was elected president a second time on August 23, 1957, and in addition to his duties as chancellor served as president from September 1, 1957, until July 1, 1959. He retired as chancellor on August 31, 1965. He was the first graduate of Texas A&M University to serve as president and also as chancellor.

David Hitchens Morgan, Ph.D.

President   September 1, 1953-December 21, 1956

Born at Portsmouth, Virginia, January 2, 1909. Dean of the College when elected president of the Agricultural and Mechanical College of Texas on June 17, 1953, effective September 1, 1953; resigned December 21, 1956.

David Willard Williams, M.S.

Acting President   December 22, 1956-September 1, 1957

Born at Venedocia, Ohio, August 20, 1892. Vice-president for agriculture when appointed acting president on December 22, 1956; served until September 1, 1957.

James Earl Rudder, LL.D.

President of Texas A&M University   July 1, 1959-March 23, 1970
President of the Texas A&M University System   September 1, 1965-March 23, 1970

Born at Eden, Texas, May 6, 1910; died at Houston, Texas, March 23, 1970; buried at College Station. Vice-president when elected president of the Agricultural and Mechanical College of Texas June 27, 1959, effective July 1, 1959. On September 1, 1965, when Dr. Harrington retired as chancellor of the Texas A&M University System, the title was changed to president, and Mr. Rudder, in addition to his duties as president of Texas A&M University, became president of the Texas A&M University System, which dual position he held until his death on March 23, 1970.

Alvin Roubal Luedecke, LL.D.

Acting President   March 30, 1970-November 1, 1970

Born at Eldorado, Texas, October 1, 1910. Associate dean of the College of Engineering when appointed acting president on March 30, 1970; served until November 1, 1970.

Jack Kenny Williams, Ph.D.

President of Texas A&M University   November 1, 1970-
President of the Texas A&M University System   November 1, 1970-

Born at Galax, Virginia, April 5, 1920. Vice-President for academic affairs, University of Tennessee System, when elected president of Texas A&M University and president of the Texas A&M University System on September 11, 1970, effective November 1, 1970.

Texas A&M Students Who Died in the Military Service of Their Country

WORLD WAR I AND WORLD WAR II

CLASS OF 1900
*Joseph Daniel Carter

CLASS OF 1906
John H. Pirie

CLASS OF 1907
*Coney Uncas Woodman

CLASS OF 1908
*Vories P. Brown, Jr.
*George Little Harrison
Douglas B. Netherwood

CLASS OF 1909
*Jesse L. Easterwood

CLASS OF 1910
James G. Ellis, Jr.

CLASS OF 1911
John William Butts
*John Lamar Matthews
Clinton Warden Russell
Benjamin Fiske Wright

CLASS OF 1912
*Graham Daniel Luhn
*Frank William Slaton

CLASS OF 1913
*William Fowler Bourland
*Romeo Willis Cox
*James Ronald Findlater
*John Bolanz Murphy
*Robert Walker Nolte
*Herbert N. Peters

CLASS OF 1914
J. H. Burford
*Benjamin H. Gardner, Jr.
*Hamlet Park Jones
*Hadyn Potter Mayers
Hugh Andrew Wear

CLASS OF 1915
Crawford H. Booth, Jr.
*Charles Hausser
James Herbert Hinds
*John Hartwell Moore
*George Francis Wellage
*Richard P. Woolley

CLASS OF 1916
Claudius Miller Easley
*Cyrus Earle Graham
*Harry Lamar Peyton
*Ferdinand Regenbrecht
*Edmund Laretz Riesner
Walter Gustave Schultz
George Watson Splawn

CLASS OF 1917
*Thomas Reed Brailsford
Myron J. Conway
*Samuel Reid Craig
*Norman G. Crocker
*James Francis Greer
*Willford MacFadden
John August Otto, Jr.
Stanley Ezra Perrin
*Charles Edward Rust
George A. Woody

CLASS OF 1918
*Elmer Curtis Allison
*Farris Shelton Anderson
*Edwin Mobley Gorman
*Luke Witt Loftus
*John Clyde McKimmey
*Wendell Francis Prime
*Charles Leroy Teague
J. M. Woodson
Horace Conrad Yates

CLASS OF 1919
C. Barfield
*Richard Platt Bull, Jr.
Manson Franklin Curtis
*Eric Albert Goldbeck
*William George Thomas
*John Percy Thompson

CLASS OF 1920
*Walter Sherman Keeling

CLASS OF 1921
*Walter Gustavos Bevill
*Edward Bishop Crook
Roswell G. Higginbotham
John Allen Pierce
Maynard Goldman Snell

CLASS OF 1923
Welborn B. Griffith, Jr.

CLASS OF 1926
Elbert Beard Anding
Adolph Hartung Giesecke
Rufus Hayden Rogers

*World War I
casualties

CLASS OF 1927
Clarence Reid Davis
Earl Emerson Jackson
Ralph T. Smith

CLASS OF 1928
Lacy Noel Bourland
Paul Armstrong Brown
George Edward Miller
James McKinzie
  Thompson

CLASS OF 1929
John August E. Bergstrom
William Edwin Davis
John Hopkins Dodge
John Robertson Jefferson
Jack William Kelly
John Looney Lester

CLASS OF 1930
William L. Hughes, Jr.
Joe Burke Michael
Oscar Stanley Tom

CLASS OF 1931
Gideon Henry Bigham
Graham McFee Hatch, Jr.
William Cruse McMurrey
Wesley John Neumann
J. Wesley Ray
John Finis Rettiger
James Donald Richter

CLASS OF 1932
James Otis Beasley
Joseph Hunt Bourland
James Thomas Connally
William Mark Curtis
Jeth Wesley Dodson
Courtney W. Fichtner
Felix Berkeley Lester
Edward Albert Obergfell
James Howard Perkins
William Clinton Vincent

CLASS OF 1933
Joseph J. Backloupe
Madison D. Beaty
Harold Furman Blodgett
George Cooke Brundrett
George Perry Cook, Jr.
Harney Estes, Jr.
Oliver Edwin Ford

Claude Lewis Madeley
Chester Alan Peyton
William P. Ragsdale, Jr.
Jackson McLane Tarver

CLASS OF 1934
Cary McClure Abney, Jr.
Harold B. Chamberlain
William J. Collier, Jr.
Lewis Griffin Compton, Jr.
Earl Oxford Hall
Ted Adair Hilger
William Lester Jameson
Stephen Anson Jones
Travis Edward Perrenot
Rosson Nat Reid
Thomas Knox Smithwick
Warren D. Stubblefield, Jr.
Bill Jeff Williams
Harold Edward Wright

CLASS OF 1935
John Franklin Barnett, Jr.
Henry Vincent Baushausen
Aubrey Roy Biggs
Robert Wayne Blodgett
John William Crow
Charles Martin Dempwolf
Gustave Herman Froebel
Sydney Robert Greer
Aubrey Peter Meador, Jr.
James Randolph
  Oppenheim
Perkins Gardner Post
Joe Aluis Rosprim
Robert Wilson Russi
Roy McMahan Vick, Jr.

CLASS OF 1936
James Carlton Barham
John Letcher Chapin
Raymond Scott Evans
Bose Gorman
Marvin Earl Hiner
James Russell Holmes
Marshall Arlon Langley
Paul Ostis Mayberry
John Brown McCluskey, Jr.
Louis Oliver Moss
Hollis Ulrich Mustain
Paul Edison Payne

CLASS OF 1937
Olen Williford Abbott
Newton Bryan Birkes
James Madison Blanks
Wilbert Adair Calvert
Bailey Gordon Carnahan
Maxey Cleburne Chenault
Ray Esther Dickson, Jr.
Clifford Hardwick
Otto Heye
George Dennis Keathley
Norman Jarvis McKendry
John Henry Morehead
James Edwin Rountree
Joseph Eugene Routt
Willis Arthur Scrivener
Lee Marion Sommers
Chester Isaac Tims
John Thomas Whitfield
S. Theodore Willis, Jr.

CLASS OF 1938
Woodrow Radford Allen
Edwin Park Arneson, Jr.
Edgar Beaumont Burgess
Horace Seaver Carswell, Jr.
Weldon Davis Cauthan
Dale P. Cleveland
Frank Monroe Colburn
John Charles Conly
George Stevens Gay, Jr.
Henry Troy Gillespie
Rudyard Kipling Grimes
Joe Benjamin Guerra
James Albert Harris
Addie Joss Hogan
Noah Horn
James Frank House
Truman DeWitt Peale
Orville Kennard Puryear
Hiram Aldine Putnam
August Max Schmidt
Lee Joseph Shudde
Robert Neal Smith
William J. Stringer, Jr.
William Marion Taylor, Jr.
Carol Hightower Thomas
Joe Gordon Turner
Warner Rox Underwood
Jack McGee Vinson
James Barclay Whitley

Lillard Graham Wilmeth

CLASS OF 1939

Augustus Jared Allen
Johnson Butler Allen
Robert Balch
Robert Clinton Beck
Freeman Harold Bokenkamp
Gaines Maness Boyle
Joe Wayne Bradford
John Pierre Bradley
Floyd Edwin Breedlove
Jesse Lee Brown
John Frank Burns
William Arthur Burton, Jr.
Daniel Lynell Cajka
Charles W. Carpenter
Jack Whalon Clark
Jack Grady Wilson Cooper
David Elworth DeLong
Hugh Alan Derrick
Gerald Parker Elder
Allen Tatum Fowler
Harry Franklin Goodloe
Robert Edward Greenwell
Raymond Louie Gregg
James Richard Griffin
Howard Preston Hardegree
Frank Petty Haynes
Charles Daniel Heller
Philip S. Isis
James Herman Kaden
Lloyd Wyatt Kelly
Boyd Calfee Knetsar
Kenneth Edwin Krug, Jr.
Leonard Gage Larsen
Henry Archer Lowrance, Jr.
David B. McCorquodale
Birdwell J. McKnight
Ernest Benge Miller
Ross Ivon Miller
Herbert Moss Mills
Maurice Allen Morgan
John B. Naughton
James William Parker
Herbert Hoover Perritte
Francis Morgan Potts
Warren Putman Rece
William Robert Ross
Henry John Schutte, Jr.
Harold Thomas Scott
William Harvey Shuler

David Louis Silverman
Clarence E. Simpson, Jr.
Marvin Judson Smith
Claud Paul Strother
Willis Albert Teller
Milton David Wallace
John Chapin Watkins
Marl Avant Westerman
Robert Joseph Williams
Paul Oscar Wofford

CLASS OF 1940

Charles Benton Adams
William Andrew Adams
T. P. Aycock
Robert Miller Baird
Alfo Leroy Baker
Samuel Johnson Baldwin
Percy Berten Bennett
William Mayo Bills
Howard Louis Bowman
Rolland John Bowman
James Hugh Brantley
Foster Cochran Burch
Wilson B. Buster, Jr.
Walter Mark Cabaniss, Jr.
John Erwin Carpenter, Jr.
Foster Lawson Cash
Walter Junior Clemans
Walter Pershing Crump
Jessie Cleveland Draper
John Henry Duncan
Ioland Edmund Dutton
John Evans Edge
Allen William Erck
Orman Lester Fitzhugh
Thomas Rex Francis
Stanley Friedline
Clifford Patrick Garney
Arthur Edward Gary
Paul Raymond Gregory
Charles Hugh Hamner
John L. Hanby
Duke W. Harrison, Jr.
William Lee Hastings, Jr.
Douglas Henderson
John Jefferson Keeter, Jr.
Marshall H. Kennady, Jr.
Paul Allard Kirk
John Clifford Knight
John Poiterent Lackey, Jr.
Ollie Jack Laird

Sam Winston Lane, Jr.
Louis Jules Lippman
Samuel Webb Lipscomb
Tommie Grantham Martin
Ashbell Green McClung
Charles Robert McIntire
Melvin Royce Millard
Joe Clifton Moseley
Chester Ellis Moudy
Wayne Livingston Mueller
John Willis Muse
Conrad John Netting, III
Roy Adolphus Nichols
Hansford George Olney
Ferdinand B. Paris, Jr.
Brady Oscar Parker
Ralph Isaiah Parlette
Hugh Buster Parris
Marvin Mather Pearson, Jr.
Philip Edgar Pearson
Boyce Penrod, Jr.
Carl Harold Pipkin
William Harrison Reeder
William Conner Richards
Charles L. Ricks, Jr.
William Riley Roberts
Fred Sullivan Rodway
Glen C. Roloson
John Jacob Sanders
Radcliffe S. Simpson
Herbert Everett Smith
Gordon S. Stephens
John Darrell Stukenburg
Rollins C. Syfan, Jr.
George Elias Turner
Henry William Waters
George Walton Wells, Jr.
Richard Djalma Williams
Dennis H. Woodruff
Albert Boyce Yearwood, Jr.

CLASS OF 1941

Thomas Hubert Arkarman
James Marvin Atkins, Jr.
Jack Bruner Bailer
Dwight Watkins Barry
Clyde Webb Beatty, Jr.
Alexander Henry Beville
August John Bischoff
Rex Harvey Blankenship
Howard Leo Blessington
Edmund Francis Boyle

Claude Francis Brewster
Billy Dean Brundidge
Ben Davis Cannan, Jr.
Gus Calhoun Cardwell, Jr.
Daniel R. Chamberlain
Austin Wilkins Clark
Roger Bently Clements
Albert Dale Cotton
Alvin Cowling, Jr.
Herbert Winfield Cumming
Jerral Walter Derryberry
Vincent DeSalvo
James Thomas Drake
James Musick Drummond
Ballard Powell Durham
John Lindsey Eddins
John Green Ellzey
Meinrad Joseph Endres
Walter Lafayette Evans
Ed A. Felder
Barry Church Francks, Jr.
William Faris Gammon
Charles Earl Gaskell
Warren George, Jr.
Tommy Glass
Robert Manning Gray

Lawrence Smith Gready, Jr.
Robert Bruce Gregory, Jr.
Burt Olney Griffin
Paul Grabow Haines, Jr.
Miller Hammons, Jr.
Curtis Olen Hancock
John Robert Harshey
Ralph Beaver Hartgraves
Henry William Heitmann, III
Richard Gordon Hill
Travis Vestal Hodges
Edward D. Hughey
Kenneth McFarland Irby
Andy Marmaduke James, Jr.
Abraham Simon Kahn
Sidney Caldwell Kimball
Edward Carr King
Robert Trimble Kissinger
Clarence Leroy Korth
Jim Lewis Kuykendall
George Lawrence Leger
Arthur Cornelius LePage
Henry Arthur Lewis
Joseph Paul Lindsey, Jr.

Hugh Bland Lockhart
Joe Wallace McCrary
John Easton McCrary
John Preston McKinney
Herbert Welton McMinn
Lynn Howard Mead, Jr.
Kenneth Taylor Merritt
Wendell Deering Neely
Patrick Cluney Noel
Samuel Jackson Parks
William Henry Paschal
Harvey Claude Pollay
Edward Herman Prove
John Daniel Ragland
Robert Smith Roddy
James McDonald Rowland
John Doyle Scoggin, Jr.
Leo Theodore Sharum, Jr.
Charles Thomas Sherman
Keith Willard Short
Charles Savage Simmons
Frank Pierce Smart
Paul Jones Stach

Joel Bryan Stratton
Herbert Carl Stucke
Robert Jackson Sudbury
Charles Vernon Thornton
Aubry Lawless Tobias, Jr.
Leo Tomaso
Richard Herley Torrence
Vester Lamar Turner
Richard Lee Vickrey
Charles Oldham Watts
Percy Alton Weaver
M. J. White
Clarence Emil Phillip Wisrodt, Jr.

CLASS OF 1942
John Harold Allen
Barney R. Anderson, Jr.
Michael Joseph Arisco
William Henry Baker
Jack Michael Balagia
William Spencer Barstow
Frank Parrish Blassingame
H. O. Borgfeld, Jr.
Byron Leo Bostick
David Lee Braunig
Howard Horace Brians
Aaron Lewis Brinkoeter

William Lee Bryce
Raymond Salter Carter
William Brame Cartwright
Newton Vincent Craig
Paul Howard Damrel
Frank Percy Daugherty, Jr.
Brice Coulter Diedrick
Clayton Norwood Duvall
Robert Cromwell Elliott
Robert Smith English
Worthington A. Franks
Virgil Dewey Fugler
Porter Frederick Fuqua
Charles William Gerhardt
Thomas Henry Gilliland
John Pershing Gilreath
Bobby Mack Godwin
Jack Emitt Golden
William Richard Grady
Earl Vetten Green
James Haywood Gulley
Henry Buford Hales, Jr.
Gambrell W. Haltom
Rex Woodrow Hamilton
John Emmett Harris
Walter Manning Hart
Weldon Henderson Holland
J. D. Holzheauser
Joe Berl Huddleston
George Arthur Huser
Charles Largent Hynds
James Edward Inglehart
Henry Douglas Jackson
Gaines H. Jenkins, Jr.
William Charles Jenn
Robert Guy Johnson
Ransom Dudley Kenny, Jr.
Thomas Sylvester King, Jr.
Ivy D. Kuykendall
Foster Lee Lemly
Turney White Leonard
Edwin Robert Lewis
Otis Forest Lowry

George Leslie Mauldin, Jr.
James Walter McCaslin
Willis Douglas Michie
Roger Morwood
Robert Derace Moser
Kirby Clarence Musick
William Lynn Oler
John Paul Olsen

Robert Brownwell Parker
Edwin Forrest Patterson
Robert Lawrence Plagens
George W. Proctor
William Marion Rascoe
Robert Lee Ravey
Charles Glynn Ray, Jr.
Arthur Mills Rider
Addison C. Rumbaugh, Jr.
James Roan Sanders
Otto Eugene Schroeter
Raymond Carl Schuette
Edward Miles Schuyler
Felix Ernest Scott
Sam Fred Semo, Jr.
Henry R. Smith
Reuben Alonzo Smith, Jr.
Herman Henry Spoede, Jr.
Theodore R. Stellmacher
George Lawson Stidham
William Conwell Swain
Anthony Tirk, Jr.
Victor Pat Tumlinson
Lisle Reed Van Burgh, Jr.
John Charles Walden
Raymond Frank Watson
Frank Gordon Weisiger
Goode Shockley Wier, Jr.
James Maurice Williams
Theophulus A. Williams
Eugene Dickens Wilmeth
Tom Fred Wilson
Jack Preston Wolfe
John Shelton Zimmer

CLASS OF 1943
Charles L. Babcock, Jr.
Newell Moore Ballard
Clarence Vance Berdine
James Edgar Bragg
Charles Earl Butler
William B. Caraway, Jr.
Paul D. Chaney
Joe Robert Clark, Jr.
Thomas Ray Coffey
Wiley Harold Craft
Joe Brooks Dalton
Robert Earnest Daw
Garland Edwin Dennis
Louden Charles Doney, III
Kyle Nichols Drake

Carl Bill Ehman
Alfred Anthony Esposite
Joseph Edward Fisher, Jr.
Thomas Weldon Fowler
William Gerard Fraser, Jr.
Edward Fry
Ben Prentice Gafford
William Byron Gibbs
Sam Tom Gillespie
Louis Vinc Girard
William Gammon Goodman
Henry G. Goodwin, Jr.
William Soul Gordon
Dulane P. Gunn
Ferris Sam Harris
Ralph Edwin Hill
Richard Lloyd Hoefle
William Murray Holland
Lloyd Herbert Hughes
Clifford Clark Hutchison
James Hull Japhet
Stephen Charles Kaffer
Charles Edwin Kingery
Jimmie Stewart Knight
James Wafer Mabry, Jr.
William P. Malone, Jr.
Joe Townley Mann
Horace Lowell Markland
Randolph Magruder Martin
Harold M. Massey
Albert Lee Matteson
J. C. McCrary
Donald W. McIntyre
George Perry McMillan, Jr.
William Walter Miller, Jr.
Marvin Claude Mitchell
William Brooks Morehouse
Durward Duvon Morrison
Robert Frederick Mumm
James Tom Myers
Jack Cameron Nagel
Otto Austin Nance, Jr.
John Negri, Jr.
Joseph Terry Newman
William Pinner Noa, Jr.
Sam Oliver
Philip Hackley Parker
William Waldo Partlow
James Perry Passons

Thomas Albert Patton
Herbert Gamble Perkins
Zug Chesley Phelps
Thomas Sharp Porter, Jr.
Patrick Benjamin Quinn
Amos Clyde Railey
William D. Richardson
George Eugene Roberts
Walter Eugene Rogers
Julian Warner Saunders
Harry Oscar Schellhase
George Thomas Schleier
James Henry Scholl
James Adam Scott, Jr.
Carlton A. Sheram, Jr.
Elwyn Marvin Shinn
Charles Willard Smith, Jr.
Lucian E. Taliaferro
Quincy W. Thompson, Jr.
Raymond Leon Tucker
George William Turrill
William Stone Tyler
Archibald S. Ware, Jr.
Harold Douglas Weedon
Warren Henry Welch, Jr.
William B. Wetzel
Howell Roy Young

CLASS OF 1944
Bob John Aderhold
Earnest R. Alexander
Richard Eugene Alston
Lee Ernest Barton
Charles M. Brazelton, Jr.
Thomas Cleo Brown
Joseph Henry Bunch
Jack Coogan Cameron
Robert H. Canterbury
Roy James Cantlon, Jr.
James Durham Cantrell
Elbert Sheridan Clark
Harold Tyrus Cobb
James Wilson Coke
Harrell Leonard Cole
John Daniel Connell
Granville William Cowan
Paul Clifford Crouch
Harry Pearston Curl
John Grandison Delamater
Weldon Warren Dyess
Herbert Dave Erp, Jr.

Cloy Donald Farley, Jr.
Harold Fink
Ralph Leroy Fisher
William Gonzalez
Leslie Talbert Gordy
Edward Allen Gripp, Jr.
Croswell Hall, Jr.
Charles E. Harrington, Jr.
Melvin G. Hass
Richard L. Haxthausen
Roy David Hughes
Luther Gordon Kent
Joe Don Kunkel
Willard Leo Kunze
Robert Morris Livingston
Joseph Courand Maroney
Bobby Lee Massey
Joe John Maucini, Jr.
John Lomax May, Jr.
Forrest Warren McCargo
Edward Albert McKelvey
Charles Carroll McKivett
Raymond Lee Merritt
Frank Allen Milliken
Ben Frank Mills
William Mason Moran
John Marshall Mullins

Irving Murland
James Elias Naham, Jr.
James Earl Newberry
Roy Herbert Nunn, Jr.
Harland Brady Parks
Garrett Columbus Parnell

Robert Alton Pegues
Frank Edward Phenicie
Aubry Durward Poindexter
Robert King Porter, Jr.
Anson Farrand Rideout
Claude Archer Riggs
Howell Clay Robinson
Howell Raymond Rollings
Isaac Samarel
Wilbur Reginald Sanders
John Henry Seay
Forrest David Sharpe
Gerald E. Spofford
Louis Thomas Statton
James Harold Steward
Frederick D. Storey, Jr.
Richard Andrew Stromberg

Fred William Sutherland
Lonnie Collins Tucker, Jr.
Oscar Glenn Turner
Carl R. Van Hook
Kenneth Glenn Varvel
Burton Leon Wade
George Amos Williams
Otto Thomas Willrich

CLASS OF 1945

Frank G. Albritton
Billy Lavern Allman
Theodore E. Armstrong
Addison A. Bachman
William P. Ballard, Jr.
Max Hoyt Barrett
David Irving Binder
James Carlock Black
Jeff George Blair
William B. Blocker, Jr.
Carl Andrew Brannen, Jr.
Edwin Earnest Brashear
Robert Reese Braswell
Doyle Lee Brown
Jarvis Orr Butler
Henry Joseph Canavespe
Victor Clesi, Jr.
James Rufus Collins, Jr.
James Edward Connolly
Donald Hugh Cooper
George Lafayette Davis
Harry Lewis Davis
John Joseph Dee, Jr.
Roy Young Deveny, Jr.
Charles Leroy Dickens
Marshall Clyde Dunn
Weldon Eugene Duty
Alfred Robert Ehlers, Jr.
Raymond Arthur Emery, Jr.
Leslie Andrew Evans, Jr.
Wilbur Randal Flenner, Jr.
Marion Flynt, Jr.
Henry Lee Forrest
Paul Froberg
Warren Kay Garrett
Bryce Charles Gibson, Jr.
Jack Harold Glenn
Norbert Joseph Gorski
Taswell Fielden Hackler
George Allen Halsell, Jr.
Charles E. Harrell, Jr.

Mark Willard Hertz
Cecil Martin Holekamp
Robert Martin Hyde
Ben Barton Isbell, Jr.
William Perkins Johnson
Rufus Jefferson Lackland, III
Daniel Richard Lamberson
Joseph Dan Longley
William F. Lovett, Jr.
Paul Manning, Jr.
Edmundo Martinez

Joe Thornton Mason, Jr.
Cyrus Marion McCaskill
Jim Ragsdale McCutcheon
Maxey Ward McGuire
Lee Earl Meyer
James Philip Miller
Melvin Wesley Miller
James Richard Mitchell
Roger Taylor Newton
James Bertrand Noland
Robert Francis Olsen

David Harrison Payne
John A. Pennington
Harold Stacy Pettit
Fred Philip Pipkin, Jr.
Ira Elbert Pritchett
Walter Sidney Radley, Jr.
Winifred Thomas Rapp
William Walter Redus

Henry King Roark
Pat Neff Roberts, Jr.
Harry Connor Robison
Edward William Roeder
Henry Andrew Rougagnac
Theophilus M. Schnell
William Bradbury Sieber
Billy E. Smith
Herbert Gibson Smith, Jr.
Leonard Roy Steidel, Jr.
Lewis Albert Stein
Homer Jordan Stengel
Charles Henry Taylor
Leonard Tracy Tew
Odis Bert Torbett
Hal Wayne Townsend
Bill Trodlier
Arthur Milton Tubb, Jr.
J. T. Turbeville, Jr.

Alfred W. Walker, Jr.
Benton Joseph Walker, Jr.
George Wilbur Wallace, Jr.
John Earl Watkins, Jr.
Frank Felix Weaver, Jr.
Herbert John Weeren, Jr.
Grady A. Whitehead, Jr.
Burl Tankersley Wiley, Jr.
Robert Willis Willeford
Rual H. Williams
James Murphy Willis, III
James Hamilton Wilson
Tommy Hereford Winn
Lawrence Miller Wolf
Guy Booth Wyrick
John Marvin Young

CLASS OF 1946
Mercer Greene Abernathy
Johnnie Mack Allman
Calvin Floyd Ballard
Max E. Ernst Bergfeld, Jr.
Lynwood Weldon Beyer
Maurice Block, Jr.
William Gary Boatright
Dwight Kendall Booth
Earl Taylor Brown, Jr.
Ormiston Dalton Brown
William Emmett Bruton
Fred Gordon Buckner
Albert Basil Capt
Arthur Aymar Cater
Donald Marion Cortimilia
Philip Albert Davidson
Ben Luker Dean
John Allstin DeBell
Eduardo Diego DeLachica

Albert C. Deutsch, Jr.
Kenneth Horace Doke
Roger Eugene Edwards
Ernest William Genthner
Ward Crockett Gillespie
Connie Claude Hagemeier
Samuel David Hanks
Elwood Henry Herrmann
Jack Copeland Herron
Gano Ladon Hobgood
Gus Thomas Hodge, Jr.
Donald Edgar Hudson
David Reynolds Hughes
Robert Winston Hull

George Norwood Jackson
Jay Neal Jones
William David Jones
Monte William Kaufman
George Henry King
David Vance Lamun
Sam David Lasser
John Galen Lawrence
Thomas Ross Leary
Monteith T. Lincecum
Miles Joseph Luster
Billy Maurice Magee
Warner Harrison Marsh, Jr.
William Gould McCarter
Theodore R. McCrocklin
Lawrence Howell McGinnes
William G. Medaris, Jr.
John Franklin Mingos
Cyril Dwight Moreland
Thomas Jackson Paul
Thomas Ray Perkins
James Francis Perry

James Byron Price, Jr.
Charles Appelt Ragsdale
Hubert T. Roussel, Jr.
John Clovis Sanford
Charles Douglas Saur
Robert Henry Shimer
Ray Parks Shipley
Stanley Dean Smith
Hugh Albert Stanberry, Jr.
Leander C. Stedman, Jr.
William James Summy
Luther Marney Tillery
John Wiley Waldrop
Fred Shelfer Wilcox, Jr.
Robert Vardy Wynne
Horace Edwin Yeary, Jr.
Bobby Joe Younger

CLASS OF 1947
Bland Massie Barnes, Jr.
John Vernon Cox, Jr.
David Allen Harris
Herbert Allan Heinemeier
James Harold Henry
Herbert Otto Koehler, Jr.
Jack Storey Lipscomb
Sam William Noto, Jr.
William Levert Pietzsch
Thomas Lee Sirman
Douglas E. Stillwagon
Arthur G. Stricklin
Harrell Gene Tilley

CLASS OF 1948
Rodman Laferne Boggs
John Batiste Roemer

THE WAR IN KOREA

CLASS OF 1925
Charles S. Ware

CLASS OF 1938
Jess E. Evans

CLASS OF 1939
John Melvin Cook
Harvey H. Storms

CLASS OF 1940
Sidney Clyde Hill

CLASS OF 1941
James G. Willis, Jr.

CLASS OF 1942
Rupert J. Costlow
Edwin James Hernan

CLASS OF 1943
Peter Haynes Bowden
William S. McCarson
John A. Mercer, Jr.

CLASS OF 1944
William C. Knapp
Earl Martin Seay
Maurice H. Smith

CLASS OF 1945
Gerald M. Camp
James L. Garrison, Jr.
Will H. Gordon, Jr.
George G. Greenwell
Robert S. Roberts

Stanley E. Tabor

CLASS OF 1946
Joe R. Allison
David R. Blakelock
William Perry Brown
James Callan III
Cecil E. Newman, Jr.

CLASS OF 1947
Edgar Byron Gray
Leon Waddell Pollard, Jr.

CLASS OF 1948
Cornelius D. Duyf
Frederick Peter Forste
John F. Helm
Walter Norton Higgins
Jack Laughlin

CLASS OF 1949
Milton L. Cagle
George E. Hill, Jr.
Lynn B. Whitsett
Beau R. Wilson
Robert H. Wood

CLASS OF 1950
Mabry E. Cain
Frank T. Davidson
Jerry K. Deason
James R. Holland, Jr.
Gordon Dean Leesch
Gene R. Mauldin
William C. Rodenberry
Kenneth G. Rogers

CLASS OF 1951
Paul C. Coffin, Jr.
Autry W. Frederick
Weldon D. Gardner
Jerry Jackson, Jr.
Jimmie D. Lester
Robert Leach Pierson
Aubrey W. Pollard
David Ames Rives

CLASS OF 1952
Lewis Earl Jobe
Sterling R. Peterson

CLASS OF 1953
Mondal R. Ammons
Albert W. Beerwinkle

THE WAR IN VIETNAM

CLASS OF 1935
Bruno A. Hockmuth

CLASS OF 1936
Morris B. Montgomery

CLASS OF 1942
Roy H. Thompson
Leonard D. Holder

CLASS OF 1944
William M. Andrews
John S. Bonner

CLASS OF 1948
Walter S. Van Cleave

CLASS OF 1949
Edward L. Williams

CLASS OF 1950
Elden Golden

CLASS OF 1951
Roger J. Coslett
Frank F. Trochak

CLASS OF 1952
Royal Clifton Fisher
Teddy J. Tomchesson

CLASS OF 1953
Charles R. Rawlings

CLASS OF 1954
Heriberto A. Garcia

CLASS OF 1955
Russell W. Condon
Hadley Foster
Julius J. Jahns
Richard E. Steel

CLASS OF 1956
Dolton M. Estein
John M. Kessinger
Ernest McFeron
Condon H. Terry, Jr.

CLASS OF 1957
Charles C. Jones
Tedd M. Lewis
Foy Manion Mathis
Edward W. Wyatt

CLASS OF 1958
James C. Caston
Don Thomas Elledge
Robert D. Johnson
George P. McKnight
Milton R. Roberts

CLASS OF 1959
Donald D. Blair
Allen G. Goehring

Donald Rey Hawley
John F. Martin
Allan L. Smith
Ronald D. Stewart

CLASS OF 1960
Billy J. Coley
William F. Cordell, Jr.
Floyd Wayne Kaase
Byron C. Stone
James M. Vrba, Jr.

CLASS OF 1961
James Claud Thigpin
Gerald J. Walla
Gregory Kent Whitehouse

CLASS OF 1962
Thomas H. Ralph, Jr.
James L. Reed
Ralph B. Walker II

CLASS OF 1963
Charles F. Allen II
Donnie Ray Dehart
Johnny L. Garner
George Gutierrez, Jr.

CLASS OF 1964
James R. Hottenroth
George L. Hubler

Edward J. Korenek
Colin E. Lamb
Thomas A. McAdams
John B. Price

CLASS OF 1965
Wesley W. Carroll
John C. Dougherty
John Hernandez
Charles David Jageler
Aubrey G. Martin
Richard A. Oman
Jose C. Santos
Albert J. Tijerina, Jr.
Victor H. Thompson III
R. Bryson Vann
Jerry Don Vick

CLASS OF 1966
Jack Patrick Blake
Joseph Bush, Jr.
Michael R. Callaway

Clyde W. Campbell
James A. Dimock
Larry K. Kaiser
Carl E. Long
Donald J. Matocha
James E. Neely
Eugene C. Oates III
James R. Stevens
Stephen R. Tubre
John Terrell Whitson

CLASS OF 1967
Layne H. Conevey
Converse Rising Lewis III
John E. Russell
Arthur D. (Dave) Smith
John R. Tesch
David E. Yates

CLASS OF 1968
Marvin S. Arthington
Tom M. Boyd III

James M. Butler
Terrel V. Garrett
Richard E. Harlan
Michael D. Noonan
Jack E. Ogdee
Kevin A. Rinard
George T. Taff
James Ned Woolley

CLASS OF 1969
James H. Cartwright
Robert Henry (Bob)
    Johnson
Sanderfierd Jones
William J. Kildare
Henry J. Rockstroh, Jr.

CLASS OF 1972
Phillip R. (Randy) Pannell

MILITARY DEAD OTHER THAN IN COMBAT

CLASS OF 1921
John E. Bloodworth, Jr.

CLASS OF 1923
John H. Claybrook

CLASS OF 1924
George A. Whatley

CLASS OF 1925
Hansel Turner Beckworth
DeWitt Creveling

CLASS OF 1927
Wilburn E. Langlotz

CLASS OF 1929
E. O. Rigsbee, Jr.

CLASS OF 1930
Alvis B. Duke

CLASS OF 1931
Marvin Hays

CLASS OF 1932
George W. Davis

CLASS OF 1934
Wilkie A. Rambo
Louis Shone
Cy Wilson

CLASS OF 1936
Harlan C. Buttrill
Jack K. Wehrmann

CLASS OF 1937
Joe W. Compton

CLASS OF 1938
Charles B. Calvin
Keith Maxwell
Herbert L. Peavy
William M. Roberts
K. Darwin Smith

CLASS OF 1939
Alfred J. Knippa
Charles D. Trail

CLASS OF 1940
Earle Warren Aldrich
Randolph W. Barker
Sidney C. Hill
James I. Hopkins
Kyle H. Morris
Samuel W. Smith
Hugh Ryland Williams
Gail Young

CLASS OF 1941
H. D. Bratcher

John K. Field
Jack S. Griffin
Dale Hatcher
Rogers Hornsby, Jr.
Robert A. Pegues
Ernest E. Schott

CLASS OF 1942
Dexter L. Ator
Harold Ballard
George Kelly
Patrick L. Kelly
Bernard J. Kulhanek
Richard W. Menger
William P. Moore
Roy Mundell
Graham Raht
Deed C. Thurman
Jones F. Webb

CLASS OF 1943
William C. Collins
John T. Cox
John M. Davis
R. G. Dumphy
Robert H. Reeves

CLASS OF 1944
Richard Bartlett
Alvin Caudle
Clarence T. Konecny
William D. Lewis
Eugene Moore Shadle
Dayton L. Warren

CLASS OF 1945
Herbert J. Aldridge
Francis J. Brock
John H. Fowler, Jr.
Frank Reilly, Jr.
Jack Woods
William N. Walterman

CLASS OF 1946
Julian Berry, Jr.
Bobby R. McClure
Ben Sevier
Emmett Clyde Teague

CLASS OF 1947
Jack E. Farquhar
John R. Gaddis
George Alan Hall
Jere Lewis

CLASS OF 1948
H. E. McDowell
Herbert Richardson
John H. Stotts
James Benson Walker

CLASS OF 1949
James W. Guiles
Cecil McCord, Jr.
Charles W. Mitchell
Lovick P. Moore, Jr.
James F. Morris
Alexander Ortiz
Alex F. Sears
Willis L. Sutton
Jimmie R. Tatum
Henry D. Wolz

CLASS OF 1950
Billy R. Bennett
Joe T. Rabb
Carlos Reyes, Jr.
John W. Schmidt

Fred Walters

CLASS OF 1951
Robert T. Asher
Joseph A. Bodine
Edgar T. Butler, Jr.
Alfred V. Chapin, Jr.
Noble N. Clark
Paul C. Coffin, Jr.
John Conner
William S. Henry
Thomas W. McAshan
Billy M. Seargeant
Alan Tom Spencer
Malcolm J. Stokes

CLASS OF 1952
Jack L. Benton
Bart R. Brooks
Ernest Truman Cavitt
Bob Glenn Debenport
Richard Green
Bobby O. Greer
William G. Hartsfield
Donald O. Hughes
Carl E. Martin
Wilson C. Parker
Warren Mason Pierce
James G. Royalty
Alford F. Summy
Ronald D. Wade

CLASS OF 1953
Edward R. Bane, Jr.
Vic H. Bird, Jr.
Leonard R. Bruce, Jr.
Gordon W. Carr
Leonard V. Cleghorn, Jr.
Ira Weldon McCarty
Billy M. McMahan
William H. Moler, Jr.
Alva P. Shepard III
Wallace Travelstead
Carlton Ray Virden

CLASS OF 1954
Hal G. Hegi
William R. Hendrickson
Larry L. McCelvey
Emory F. McWhorter

Jerry L. Maxwell
James Arthur Pankhurst
Donald L. Scott
James R. Sears
Gerald Stull

CLASS OF 1955
Earnest J. Bickley
Harvey M. Hudson
Neely E. Keeper
Robert A. Verduzco
Martin D. Wolfe, Jr.

CLASS OF 1956
Ernest F. Biehunko
R. Buford Miller
Jerald D. Morgan
George W. Parr
Frank Ewing Patterson
Richard M. Tachibana

CLASS OF 1957
Dan C. Rhodenbaugh
Allison Fleming Smith
Rodney H. Smith
Ralph Larry Stout

CLASS OF 1958
Arvin D. Eady, Jr.
James P. Jenrette
Robert R. Wunderlick

CLASS OF 1959
James Addison Hataway
Ronald D. Stewart

CLASS OF 1960
Luther Lee Threadgill

CLASS OF 1961
Norman D. Ayers
Darryl Glenn Bush
James R. Munnerlyn
Jerry Wayne Thornton

CLASS OF 1963
James R. Griffin
William Arthur Holt, Jr.

CLASS OF 1965
John D. Hernandez

All-Time Football and Basketball Records Texas A&M University

FOOTBALL

Aggies		Opp.

1894
Coach: F. D. Perkins

14	Galveston HS (Ball)	6
0	Texas	38
14		**44**

(1-1)

1895
(No Team)

1896
Coach: A. M. Soule
and H. W. South

0	Galveston HS (Ball)	0
22	Austin College	4
28	Houston HS	0
50		**4**

(2-0-1)

1897
Coach: C. W. Taylor

0	Houston HS	10
6	TCU	30
4	Austin College	0
10		**40**

(1-2)

1898
Coach: H. W. Williams

51	Houston HS	0
0	Texas	48
0	Houston HS	6
16	TCU	0
22	Austin College	6
28	Fort Worth U.	0
117		**60**

(4-2)

1899
Coach: W. A. Murray

43	Houston HS	0
0	Sewanee	10
22	Tulane	0
52	LSU	0
33	Baylor	0
0	Texas	6
150		**16**

(4-2)

1900
Coach: W. A. Murray

6	Kan. City Medics	6
0	Texas	5
0	Texas	11
11	Waxahachie Ath. Club	0
44	Henry College	0
61		**22**

(2-2-1)

1901
Coach: W. A. Murray

6	Baylor	0
6	Baylor	17
0	Texas	17
0	Texas	82
0	Baylor	46
12		**112**

(1-4)

1902
Coach: J. E. Platt

11	St. Edwards	.0
0	Trinity	0
11	Baylor	6
22	Baylor	0
0	Texas	0
17	Tulane	5
22	TCU	0
34	Trinity	0
11	Texas	0
128		**11**

(7-0-2)

1903
Coach: J. E. Platt

16	Trinity	0
11	TCU	0
6	Arkansas	0
0	Oklahoma	6
0	Baylor	0
18	Baylor	0
16	TCU	0
0	Trinity	18
5	Baylor	0
6	Texas	29
14	TCU	6
92		**59**

(7-3-1)

1904
Coach: J. E. Platt

49	Deaf & Dumb Inst.	0
5	Baylor	0
29	TCU	0
5	Sewanee	17
6	Texas	34
10	Baylor	0
104		**51**

(4-2)

1905
Coach: W. E. Bachman

29	Houston YMCA	0
20	TCU	0
42	Baylor	0
24	Trinity	0
18	Austin College	11
24	TCU	11
6	Transylvania, Ky.	29
17	Baylor	5
0	Texas	27
180		**83**

(7-2)

1906
Coach: W. E. Bachman

42	TCU	0
34	Daniel Baker	0
22	TCU	0
18	Tulane	0
32	Haskell Institute	6
22	LSU	12
0	Texas	24
170		**42**

(6-1)

1907
Coach: L. L. Larson

34	Fort Worth Univ.	0
0	Texas	0
11	LSU	5
5	Haskell Institute	0
32	TCU	5
18	Tulane	6
19	Oklahoma	0
6	Texas	12
125		**27**

(6-1-1)

1908
Coach: H. A. Merriam

6	Trinity	0
5	Baylor	6
0	LSU	26
13	TCU	10
8	Texas	24
0	Haskell Institute	23
32	Southwestern	0
12	Texas	28
76		**117**

(3-5)

1909
Coach: Chas. B. Moran

17	Austin College	0
0	TCU	0
15	Haskell Institute	0
9	Baylor	6
23	Texas	0
47	Trinity	0
14	Oklahoma	8
5	Texas	0
130		**14**

(7-0-1)

1910
Coach: Chas. B. Moran

| 48 | Marshall School | 0 |
| 27 | Austin College | 5 |

35	TCU	0
33	Transylvania, Ky.	0
0	Arkansas	5
23	TCU	6
14	Texas	8
6	Southwestern	0
17	Tulane	0
203		**24**

(8-1)

1911
Coach: Chas. B. Moran

22	Southwestern	0
33	Austin College	0
16	Auburn	0
17	Mississippi	0
0	Texas	6
22	Baylor	11
24	Dallas U.	0
134		**17**

(6-1)

1912
Coach: Chas. B. Moran

50	Daniel Baker	0
59	Trinity	0
27	Arkansas	0
57	Austin College	0
28	Oklahoma	6
41	Miss. State	7
41	Tulane	0
10	Kansas State	13
53	Baylor	0
366		**26**

(8-1)

1913
Coach: Chas. B. Moran

7	Trinity	0
6	Austin College	0
19	Polytechnic College	6
0	Miss. State	6
0	Kansas State	12
0	Oklahoma A&M	3
0	Haskell Institute	28
14	Baylor	14
7	LSU	7
53		**76**

(3-4-2)

1914
Coach: Chas. B. Moran

32	Austin College	0
0	Trinity	0
40	TCU	0
0	Haskell Institute	10
63	LSU	9
32	Rice	7
24	Oklahoma A&M	0
14	Miss. U.	7
205		**33**

(6-1-1)

1915
Coach: E. H. Harlan

40	Austin College	0
62	Trinity	0
13	TCU	10
33	Missouri School of Mines	3
21	Haskell Institute	7
0	Rice	7
13	Texas	0
0	Miss. State	7
182		**34**

(6-2)

1916
Coach: E. H. Harlan

6	Southwestern	0
20	Dallas U.	6

0	LSU	13
62	SMU	0
13	Haskell Institute	6
0	Rice	20
3	Baylor	0
77	Missouri School of Mines	0
7	Texas	21
188		**66**

(6-3)

1917
Coach: D. X. Bible

66	Austin College	0
98	Dallas U.	0
20	Southwestern	0
27	LSU	0
35	Tulane	0
7	Baylor	0
7	Texas	0
10	Rice	0
270		**0**

(8-0)

1918
Coach: D. V. Graves

6	Ream Field	0
12	Camp Travis	6
19	Baylor	0
7	Southwestern	0
19	Camp Mabry	6
0	Texas	7
60	Camp Travis Remount Sta.	0
123		**19**

(6-1)

1919
Coach: D. X. Bible

77	Sam Houston STC	0
28	San Marcos STC	0
16	SMU	0
12	Howard Payne	0
42	Trinity	0
28	Oklahoma A&M	0
10	Baylor	0
48	TCU	0
7	Southwestern	0
7	Texas	0
275		**0**

(10-0)

1920
Coach: D. X. Bible

110	Daniel Baker	0
3	SMU	0
0	LSU	0
47	Phillips U.	0
35	Oklahoma A&M	0
24	Baylor	0
7	Rice	0
3	Texas	7
229		**7**

(6-1-1)

1921
Coach: D. X. Bible

14	Howard Payne	7
13	SMU	0
0	LSU	6
17	Arizona	13
23	Oklahoma A&M	7
14	Baylor	3
7	Rice	7
0	Texas	0
22	Centre College (Dixie Classic)	14
110		**57**

(6-1-2)

1922
Coach: D. X. Bible

7	Howard Payne	13
10	Tulsa U.	13
33	Southwestern	0
46	LSU	0
19	Ouichita College	6
7	Baylor	13
6	SMU	17
24	Rice	0
14	Texas	7
166		**69**

(5-4)

1923
Coach: D. X. Bible

53	Sam Houston STC	0
21	Howard Payne	0
13	Southwestern	0
14	Sewanee	0
28	LSU	0
0	SMU	10
0	Baylor	0
6	Rice	7
0	Texas	6
135		**23**

(5-3-1)

1924
Coach: D. X. Bible

40	John Tarleton SC	0
33	Trinity	0
54	Southwestern	0
7	Sewanee	0
40	Arkansas A&M	0
7	SMU	7
7	Baylor	15
28	TCU	0
13	Rice	6
0	Texas	7
229		**35**

(7-2-1)

1925
Coach: D. X. Bible

20	Trinity	10
23	Southwestern	6
6	Sewanee	6
7	SMU	0
77	Sam Houston STC	0
13	Baylor	0
0	TCU	3
17	Rice	0
28	Texas	0
191		**25**

(7-1-1)

1926
Coach: D. X. Bible

26	Trinity	0
35	Southwestern	0
6	Sewanee	3
63	New Mexico	0
7	SMU	9
9	Baylor	20
13	TCU	13
20	Rice	0
5	Texas	14
184		**59**

(5-3-1)

1927
Coach: D. X. Bible

45	Trinity	0
31	Southwestern	0
18	Sewanee	0
40	Arkansas	6
0	TCU	0
47	Texas Tech	6
39	SMU	13

14   Rice 0
28   Texas 7

262   32
(8-0-1)

1928
Coach: D. X. Bible
21   Trinity 0
21   Southwestern 0
69   Sewanee 0
0   Centenary 6
0   TCU 6
12   Arkansas 27
44   North Texas STC 0
19   SMU 19
19   Rice 0
0   Texas 19

205   77
(5-4-1)

1929
Coach: Madison Bell
54   Southwestern 7
10   Tulane 13
19   Kansas State 0
7   TCU 13
13   Arkansas 14
54   SF Austin STC 0
7   SMU 12
26   Rice 6
13   Texas 0

203   65
(5-4)

1930
Coach: Madison Bell
43   Southwestern 0
0   Nebraska 13
9   Tulane 19
0   Arkansas 13
0   TCU 3
7   Centenary 6
7   SMU 13
0   Rice 7
0   Texas 26

66   100
(2-7)

1931
Coach: Madison Bell
33   Southwestern 0
21   John Tarleton SC 0
0   Tulane 7
29   Iowa U. 0
0   TCU 6
33   Baylor 7
7   Centenary 0
0   SMU 8
7   Rice 0
7   Texas 6

137   34
(7-3)

1932
Coach: Madison Bell
7   Texas Tech 0
14   Tulane 26
26   Sam Houston STC 0
14   Texas A&I 0
0   TCU 17
0   Baylor 0
0   Centenary 7
0   SMU 0
14   Rice 7
0   Texas 21

75   78
(4-4-2)

1933
Coach: Madison Bell
38   Trinity 0
13   Tulane 6

---

34   Sam Houston STC 14
17   Texas A&I 0
7   TCU 13
14   Baylor 7
0   Centenary 20
0   SMU 19
27   Rice 0
10   Texas 10

160   89
(6-3-1)

1934
Coach: Homer H. Norton
28   Sam Houston STC 0
14   Texas A&I 14
6   Temple 40
0   Centenary 13
0   TCU 13
10   Baylor 7
7   Arkansas 7
0   SMU 28
6   Rice 25
0   Texas 13
13   Michigan State 26

84   186
(2-7-2)

1935
Coach: Homer H. Norton
37   SF Austin STC 6
25   Sam Houston STC 0
0   Temple 14
6   Centenary 7
14   TCU 19
6   Baylor 14
7   Arkansas 14
10   Rice 17
20   Texas 6
0   SMU 24

125   121
(3-7)

1936
Coach: Homer H. Norton
39   Sam Houston STC 6
3   Hardin-Simmons 0
3   Rice 0
18   TCU 7
0   Baylor 0
0   Arkansas 18
22   SMU 6
38   U. of San Francisco .. 14
20   Utah 7
0   Centenary 3
0   Texas 7
13   Manhattan College 6

156   74
(8-3-1)

1937
Coach: Homer H. Norton
14   Manhattan College 7
14   Miss. State 0
7   TCU 7
0   Baylor 13
13   Arkansas 26
14   SMU 0
6   Rice 6
7   Texas 0
42   U. of San Francisco .. 0

117   59
(5-2-2)

1938
Coach: Homer H. Norton
52   Texas A&I 0
20   Tulsa 0
0   Santa Clara 7
6   TCU 34
6   Baylor 6
13   Arkansas 7

---

7   SMU 10
6   Texas 7
27   Rice 0

137   71
(4-4-1)

1939
Coach: Homer H. Norton
32   Oklahoma A&M 0
14   Centenary 0
7   Santa Clara 3
33   Villanova 7
20   TCU 6
20   Baylor 0
27   Arkansas 0
6   SMU 2
19   Rice 0
20   Texas 0
14   Tulane (Sugar B.) 13

212   31
(11-0)

1940
Coach: Homer H. Norton
26   Texas A&I 0
41   Tulsa 6
7   UCLA 0
21   TCU 7
14   Baylor 7
17   Arkansas 0
19   SMU 7
25   Rice 0
0   Texas 7
13   Fordham (Cot. B.) 12

183   46
(9-1)

1941
Coach: Homer H. Norton
54   Sam Houston STC 0
41   Texas A&I 0
49   New York U. 7
14   TCU 0
48   Baylor 0
7   Arkansas 0
21   SMU 10
19   Rice 6
0   Texas 23
7   Wash. State 0
21   Alabama (Cot. B.) 29

281   75
(9-2)

1942
Coach: Homer H. Norton
7   LSU 16
19   Texas Tech 0
7   Corpus Christi NAS ... 18
2   TCU 7
0   Baylor 6
41   Arkansas 0
27   SMU 20
0   Rice 0
6   Texas 12
21   Wash. State 0

130   79
(4-5-1)

1943
Coach: Homer H. Norton
48   Bryan AFB 6
13   Texas Tech 0
28   LSU 13
13   TCU 0
0   North Texas AC
     (Arlington) 0
13   Arkansas 0
22   SMU 0
20   Rice 0

13	Texas	27
14	LSU (Orange B.)	19
184		**65**

(7-2-1)

1944
Coach: Homer H. Norton

39	Bryan AFB	0
27	Texas Tech	14
14	Oklahoma	21
7	TCU	13
7	LSU	0
61	North Texas AC (Arlington)	0
6	Arkansas	7
39	SMU	6
19	Rice	6
0	Texas	6
70	Miami U.	14
289		**87**

(7-4)

1945
Coach: Homer H. Norton

54	Ellington Field	0
16	Texas Tech	6
19	Oklahoma	14
12	LSU	31
12	TCU	13
19	Baylor	13
34	Arkansas	0
3	SMU	0
0	Rice	6
10	Texas	20
179		**103**

(6-4)

1946
Coach: Homer H. Norton

47	North Texas State	0
0	Texas Tech	0
7	Oklahoma	10
9	LSU	33
14	TCU	0
17	Baylor	0
0	Arkansas	7
14	SMU	0
10	Rice	27
7	Texas	24
125		**107**

(4-6)

1947
Coach: Homer H. Norton

48	Southwestern	0
29	Texas Tech	7
14	Oklahoma	26
13	LSU	19
0	TCU	26
24	Baylor	0
21	Arkansas	21
0	SMU	13
7	Rice	41
13	Texas	32
169		**185**

(3-6-1)

1948
Coach: Harry Stiteler

14	Villanova	34
14	Texas Tech	20
14	Oklahoma U.	42
13	LSU	14
14	TCU	27
14	Baylor	20
6	Arkansas	28
14	SMU	20
6	Rice	28
14	Texas	14
123		**247**

(0-9-1)

1949
Coach: Harry Stiteler

0	Villanova	35
26	Texas Tech	7
13	Oklahoma	33
0	LSU	34
6	TCU	28
0	Baylor	21
6	Arkansas	27
27	SMU	27
0	Rice	13
14	Texas	42
92		**267**

(1-8-1)

1950
Coach: Harry Stiteler

48	Nevada	18
34	Texas Tech	13
28	Oklahoma U.	34
52	Virginia Mil. Ins.	0
42	TCU	23
20	Baylor	27
42	Arkansas	13
25	SMU	20
13	Rice	21
0	Texas	17
40	U. of Ga. (Pres. C.)	20
344		**206**

(7-4)

1951
Coach: Raymond George

21	UCLA	14
20	Texas Tech	7
14	Oklahoma U.	7
53	Trinity	14
14	TCU	20
21	Baylor	21
21	Arkansas	33
14	SMU	14
13	Rice	28
22	Texas	21
213		**179**

(5-3-2)

1952
Coach: Raymond George

21	Houston	13
14	Oklahoma A&M	7
7	Kentucky	10
6	Mich. State	48
7	TCU	7
20	Baylor	21
31	Arkansas	12
13	SMU	21
6	Rice	16
12	Texas	32
137		**187**

(3-6-1)

1953
Coach: Raymond George

7	Kentucky	6
14	Houston	14
14	Georgia	12
27	Texas Tech	14
20	TCU	7
13	Baylor	14
14	Arkansas	41
0	SMU	23
7	Rice	34
12	Texas	21
128		**186**

(4-5-1)

1954
Coach: Paul Bryant

9	Texas Tech	41

6	Oklahoma A&M	14
6	Georgia	0
7	Houston	10
20	TCU	21
7	Baylor	20
7	Arkansas	14
3	SMU	6
19	Rice	29
13	Texas	22
97		**177**

(1-9)

1955
Coach: Paul Bryant

0	UCLA	21
28	LSU	0
21	Houston	8
27	Nebraska	0
19	TCU	16
19	Baylor	7
7	Arkansas	7
13	SMU	2
20	Rice	12
6	Texas	21
160		**89**

(7-2-1)

1956
Coach: Paul Bryant

19	Villanova	0
9	LSU	6
40	Texas Tech	7
14	Houston	14
7	TCU	6
19	Baylor	13
27	Arkansas	0
33	SMU	7
21	Rice	7
34	Texas	21
223		**81**

(9-0-1)

1957
Coach: Paul Bryant

21	Maryland	13
21	Texas Tech	0
28	Missouri	0
28	Houston	6
7	TCU	6
14	Baylor	0
7	Arkansas	6
19	SMU	6
6	Rice	7
7	Texas	9
0	Tennessee (Gator Bowl)	3
158		**50**

(8-3)

1958
Coach: Jim Myers

14	Texas Tech	15
7	Houston	39
12	Missouri	0
14	Maryland	10
8	TCU	24
33	Baylor	27
8	Arkansas	21
0	SMU	33
28	Rice	21
0	Texas	27
124		**217**

(4-6)

1959
Coach: Jim Myers

14	Texas Tech	20
9	Michigan State	7
7	Miss. Southern	8

28	Houston	6
6	TCU	39
0	Baylor	13
7	Arkansas	12
11	SMU	14
2	Rice	7
17	Texas	20
101		**141**

(3-7)

1960
Coach: Jim Myers

0	LSU	9
14	Texas Tech	14
14	Trinity	0
0	Houston	17
14	TCU	14
0	Baylor	14
3	Arkansas	7
0	SMU	0
14	Rice	21
14	Texas	21
73		**117**

(1-6-3)

1961
Coach: Jim Myers

7	Houston	7
7	LSU	16
38	Texas Tech	7
55	Trinity	0
14	TCU	15
23	Baylor	0
8	Arkansas	15
25	SMU	12
7	Rice	21
0	Texas	25
184		**118**

(4-5-1)

1962
Coach: Hank Foldberg

0	LSU	21
3	Houston	6
7	Texas Tech	3
6	Florida	42
14	TCU	20
6	Baylor	3
7	Arkansas	17
12	SMU	7
3	Rice	23
3	Texas	13
61		**155**

(3-7)

1963
Coach: Hank Foldberg

6	LSU	14
0	Ohio State	17
0	Texas Tech	10
23	Houston	13
14	TCU	14
7	Baylor	34
7	Arkansas	21
7	SMU	9
13	Rice	6
13	Texas	15
90		**153**

(2-7-1)

1964
Coach: Hank Foldberg

6	LSU	9
0	Houston	10
12	Texas Tech	16
7	Southern Cal	31
9	TCU	14
16	Baylor	20
0	Arkansas	17
23	SMU	0
8	Rice	19
7	Texas	26
88		**162**

(1-9)

1965
Coach: Gene Stallings

0	LSU	10
14	Georgia Tech	10
16	Texas Tech	20
10	Houston	7
9	TCU	17
0	Baylor	31
0	Arkansas	31
0	SMU	10
14	Rice	13
17	Texas	21
80		**170**

(3-7)

1966
Coach: Gene Stallings

3	Georgia Tech	38
13	Tulane	21
35	Texas Tech	14
7	LSU	7
35	TCU	7
17	Baylor	13
0	Arkansas	34
14	SMU	21
7	Rice	6
14	Texas	22
145		**183**

(4-5-1)

1967
Coach: Gene Stallings

17	SMU	20
20	Purdue	24
6	LSU	17
18	Florida State	19
28	Texas Tech	24
20	TCU	0
21	Baylor	3
33	Arkansas	21
18	Rice	3
10	Texas	7
20	Alabama (Cotton Bowl)	16
211		**154**

(7-4)

1968
Coach: Gene Stallings

12	LSU	13
35	Tulane	3
14	Florida State	20
16	Texas Tech	21
27	TCU	7
9	Baylor	10
22	Arkansas	25
23	SMU	36
24	Rice	14
14	Texas	35
196		**184**

(3-7)

1969
Coach: Gene Stallings

6	LSU	35
0	Nebraska	14
20	Army	13
9	Texas Tech	13
6	TCU	16
24	Baylor	0
13	Arkansas	35
20	SMU	10
6	Rice	7
12	Texas	49
116		**192**

(3-7)

1970
Coach: Gene Stallings

41	Wichita State	14
20	LSU	18
13	Ohio State	56
10	Michigan	14
7	Texas Tech	21
15	TCU	31
24	Baylor	29
6	Arkansas	45
3	SMU	6
17	Rice	18
14	Texas	52
170		**304**

(2-9)

1971
Coach: Gene Stallings

41	Wichita State	7
0	LSU	37
7	Nebraska	34
0	Cincinnati	17
7	Texas Tech	28
3	TCU	14
10	Baylor	9
17	Arkansas	9
27	SMU	10
18	Rice	13
14	Texas	34
144		**212**

(5-6)

1972
Coach: Emory Bellard

36	Wichita State	13
7	Nebraska	37
17	LSU	42
14	Army	24
14	Texas Tech	17
10	TCU	13
13	Baylor	15
10	Arkansas	7
27	SMU	17
14	Rice	20
3	Texas	38
165		**243**

(3-8)

1973
Coach: Emory Bellard

48	Wichita State	0
23	LSU	28
24	Boston College	32
30	Clemson	15
16	Texas Tech	28
35	TCU	16
28	Baylor	22
10	Arkansas	14
45	SMU	10
20	Rice	24
13	Texas	42
292		**231**

(5-6)

1974
Coach: Emory Bellard

24	Clemson	0
21	LSU	14
28	Washington	15
10	Kansas	28
28	Texas Tech	7
17	TCU	0
20	Baylor	0
20	Arkansas	10
14	SMU	18
37	Rice	7
3	Texas	32
222		**131**

8-3

BASKETBALL

Aggie		Opp.
	1913	
	Coach: F. D. Steger	
78	Marlin HS	8
72	Galveston Y.M.C.A.	14
72	Sam Houston NC	9
25	Galveston Y.M.C.A.	27
40	Sam Houston NC	12
24	Houston HS	26
311		**96**
	(4-2)	
	1914	
	Coach: F. D. Steger	
W	Galveston Y.M.C.A.	L
W	Sam Houston NC	L
W	Howard Payne	L
L	Galveston Y.M.C.A.	W
L	Houston HS	W
W	Sam Houston NC	L
W	Howard Payne	L
	(No scores available)	
	(5-2)	
	1915	
	Coach: F. D. Steger	
36	Sam Houston NC	5
30	Dallas U.	7
30	Baylor	11
16	Rice	27
35	Baylor	23
20	TCU	28
40	Dallas U.	10
34	Decatur BC	30
41	Decatur BC	26
36	Decatur HS	21
36	Decatur Gym Club	22
39	Sam Houston NC	28
30	Sam Houston NC	13
17	Southwestern	10
30	Southwestern	11
470		**272**
	(13-2)	
	1916	
	Coach: Tubby Graves	
62	East Texas NC	5
45	Southwestern	5
57	Decatur BC	17
39	Baylor	8
41	Baylor	6
34	Tulane	10
30	Tulane	13
25	Rice	20
28	Baylor	24
24	Baylor	22
24	Dallas U.	14
9	Rice	16
22	Rice	24
440		**184**
	(11-2)	
	1917	
	Coach: Lt. W. H. H. Morris	
47	Southwestern	16
39	Southwestern	11
16	Rice	19
21	Rice	13
15	LSU	24
14	LSU	30
26	Tulane	42
37	Daniel Baker C.	5
36	Daniel Baker C.	0
31	Baylor	8
20	Baylor	13
29	TCU	18
42	TCU	18
24	Rice	25
27	Rice	20
16	Texas	38
19	Texas	24
29	Texas	15
16	Texas	24
504		**363**
	(11-8)	
	1918	
	Coach: Bill Driver	
21	Camp Arthur	19
26	Southwestern	13
14	Rice	18
25	Rice	21
17	Simmons	19
0	Simmons	2
	(Game forfeited)	
14	Baylor	23
19	Baylor	9
15	Okla. A&M	8
21	Okla. A&M	19
31	Baylor	25
22	Baylor	15
15	Texas	27
21	Texas	12
9	Texas	8
	(Game forfeited to Texas Acct. Dwyer being ineligible)	
12	Texas	17
26	Rice	27
21	Rice	29
329		**311**
	(9-9)	
	1919	
	Coach: Bill Driver	
31	TCU	12
40	Southwestern	12
35	Southwestern	15
24	U.S. Marines (Galveston)	8
36	U.S. Marines (Galveston)	11
41	Baylor	8
29	Baylor	5
24	TCU	25
25	SMU	18
56	Baylor	18
24	Baylor	26
19	Texas	28
22	Texas	15
43	SMU	12
30	Texas	20
15	Texas	22
24	Kelley Field	22
17	San Antonio YMCA	29
535		**304**
	(14-4)	
	1920	
	Coach: Bill Driver	
36	Baylor Medics	25
32	Baylor Medics	14
36	Baylor	10
52	Baylor	10
45	Simmons	12
21	SMU	15
18	SMU	16
39	Rice	16
28	Rice	10
16	Texas	15
15	Texas	8
20	SMU	15
22	SMU	14
28	Baylor	8
37	Baylor	11
43	Rice	13
28	Rice	13
27	Texas	9
17	Texas	13
560		**247**
	(19-0)	
	1921	
	Coach: D. X. Bible	
28	Baylor Medics	17
21	Baylor Medics	13
32	Simmons	20
17	Simmons	12
20	Rice	19
35	Rice	17
30	LSU	31
28	LSU	28
41	Tulane	28
27	Tulane	30
23	Texas	5
15	Texas	16
15	SMU	5
14	SMU	13
26	Rice	16
28	Rice	18
16	LSU	24
49	LSU	19
13	Texas	16.
18	Texas	13
25	SMU	14
16	SMU	11
546		**387**
	(16-6)	
	1922	
	Coach: D. X. Bible	
37	Sam Houston NC	17
25	Sam Houston NC	9
38	Houston Triangles	16
28	SMU	16
26	SMU	21
15	Baylor	17
17	Baylor	15
22	Rice	7
19	Rice	12
31	Phillips U.	25
30	Phillips U.	18
20	Texas	17
25	Texas	16
34	SMU	14
41	SMU	13
15	Rice	6
13	Rice	9
18	Baylor	19
32	Baylor	19
11	Texas	19
20	Texas	8
517		**313**
	(18-3)	
	1923	
	Coach: D. X. Bible	
48	Sam Houston NC	13
16	Sam Houston NC	17
35	Oklahoma A&M	17
25	Baylor	15
32	Baylor	19
26	SMU	23
21	SMU	23
24	Oklahoma A&M	17
32	Rice	24
15	Rice	26
27	Texas	21
42	Texas	25
36	SMU	21
27	SMU	24
29	Rice	24
25	Rice	23
34	Baylor	30

34	Baylor	14
16	Texas	13
12	Texas	18
556		**407**

(16-4)

1924
Coach: D. X. Bible

27	TCU	26
14	TCU	15
21	Baylor	4
15	Baylor	9
9	SMU	13
9	SMU	16
23	Rice	13
22	Rice	14
22	Texas	33
16	Texas	27
29	SMU	18
18	SMU	31
31	Rice	26
26	Rice	28
32	Arkansas	17
35	Arkansas	27
37	Baylor	13
26	Baylor	14
48	Oklahoma A&M	32
24	Oklahoma A&M	37
22	TCU	16
14	Texas	24
11	Texas	17
531		**470**

(13-10)

1925
Coach: D. X. Bible

25	Sam Houston NC	15
21	Sam Houston NC	14
15	Baylor	13
13	TCU	22
35	Rice	17
26	Austin College	5
15	Oklahoma A&M	24
17	Oklahoma A&M	19
29	Rice	21
24	SMU	35
18	Arkansas	54
17	Arkansas	38
38	SMU	26
21	Texas	14
17	TCU	20
26	Baylor	10
13	Texas	17
370		**364**

(9-8)

1926
Coach: D. X. Bible

13	Sam Houston STC	31
21	Sam Houston STC	18
31	Dallas Ath. Club	29
21	Centenary	17
31	Centenary	26
19	Baylor	22
34	TCU	38
32	Rice	30
32	Rice	28
13	SMU	20
11	TCU	38
32	SMU	30
27	Texas	35
27	Arkansas	37
21	Arkansas	35
27	Baylor	25
19	Texas	32
411		**491**

(8-9)

1927
Coach: D. X. Bible

23	Sam Houston STC	17
22	Sam Houston STC	23

37	Houston YMCA	20
50	Sul Ross	31
40	Sul Ross	25
31	SMU	28
29	Rice	28
27	Arkansas	34
16	Arkansas	25
32	SMU	33
36	Texas	35
20	TCU	36
39	Centenary	20
46	Centenary	26
31	TCU	32
44	Rice	20
28	Texas	39
551		**472**

(10-7)

1928
Coach: C. F. Bassett

32	Sam Houston STC	29
33	Sam Houston STC	31
28	Houston YMCA	31
37	Houston YMCA	41
27	Rice	23
29	Sam Houston STC	34
37	Sam Houston STC	15
25	SMU	39
27	TCU	31
28	SMU	40
30	Rice	33
30	Texas	51
24	TCU	30
19	Arkansas	42
31	Arkansas	46
20	Texas	30
457		**546**

(4-12)

1929
Coach: C. F. Bassett

34	Sam Houston STC	9
28	Sam Houston STC	25
39	Sam Houston STC	24
29	Sam Houston STC	23
39	Southwestern	24
33	Southwestern	15
33	Rice	29
30	Rice	38
27	TCU	22
40	TCU	31
15	SMU	23
29	Southwestern	24
44	Southwestern	16
18	SMU	16
29	Texas	32
23	Arkansas	49
29	Arkansas	38
29	Texas	42
548		**480**

(12-6)

1930
Coach: J. B. Reid

32	Sam Houston STC	20
40	Sam Houston STC	29
32	Houston Triangles	28
24	Houston Triangles	28
26	Centenary	24
17	Centenary	30
19	Sam Houston STC	25
15	Sam Houston STC	21
23	SMU	20
25	TCU	28
17	Rice	23
24	SMU	19
28	TCU	17
25	Texas	33
24	Arkansas	28
23	Arkansas	25
42	Texas	20
17	Rice	26

453		**444**

(8-10)

1931
Coach: J. B. Reid

38	Houston YMCA	33
26	Sam Houston STC	16
43	Sam Houston STC	29
47	San Antonio YMCA	35
23	Southwest Texas STC	20
38	Southwest Texas STC	25
30	Southwestern	34
28	Southwestern	22
31	Centenary	17
35	Centenary	26
19	Arkansas	30
37	Arkansas	34
24	Rice	27
31	Baylor	12
34	Texas	10
18	Baylor	27
32	TCU	34
22	SMU	37
26	Rice	23
25	SMU	23
26	TCU	30
28	Texas	29
661		**573**

(14-8)

1932
Coach: J. B. Reid

45	Humble Oil Co.	9
30	Sam Houston STC	27
40	Texas Oil Co.	35
32	Sproles Transfer Co.	15
29	Rice	40
28	Sam Houston STC	23
38	Centenary	26
26	Centenary	43
23	Baylor	29
33	Baylor	40
23	SMU	30
28	TCU	38
31	Texas	32
27	Rice	6
21	SMU	10
24	TCU	26
28	Arkansas	23
27	Arkansas	33
14	Texas	8
547		**493**

(10-9)

1933
Coach: J. B. Reid

45	Texaco of Houston	46
38	Sam Houston STC	43
38	SFA Teachers College	54
52	Beaumont YMCA	36
74	Baker's Clothiers of Port Arthur	23
30	Brown Paper Co.	41
31	Brown Paper Co.	42
35	Rice	18
24	SMU	28
26	TCU	27
31	Texas	38
20	Baylor	19
33	Baylor	29
26	Rice	18
25	Arkansas	21
25	Arkansas	23
34	TCU	29
32	SMU	22
20	Texas	51
639		**608**

(9-10)

1934
Coach: J. B. Reid

29	Texaco Scotties	20

38	Sam Houston STC	20
21	Texas A&I	24
39	SFA Teachers College	30
44	Centenary	26
41	Centenary	29
30	Hunt Oilers	17
45	Sam Houston STC	27
28	Rice	31
40	SMU	34
34	Texas	29
30	Baylor	14
38	TCU	44
49	SMU	26
32	TCU	40
22	Arkansas	23
35	Arkansas	23
34	Baylor	31
40	Rice	36
25	Texas	27
694		**551**

(14-6)

1935
Coach: J. B. Reid

39	SFA Teachers College	23
35	Sam Houston STC	33
19	Hunt Oilers	43
28	Humble Oilers	30
50	Texas A&I	15
35	Texas A&I	25
32	Rice	46
28	San Marcos TC	23
28	Sam Houston STC	18
41	Texas	40
46	Baylor	23
29	Baylor	33
40	TCU	30
21	SMU	44
29	SMU	35
23	Rice	33
28	Texas	25
41	Arkansas	45
31	Arkansas	51
24	Texas	35
647		**650**

(10-10)

1936
Coach: H. R. McQuillan

20	Houston Regal Brew	15
34	Sam Houston STC	29
40	Beaumont KP	27
24	Jacksonville	23
29	Brown Paper Co., Monroe, La.	33
30	Sam Houston STC	12
18	Arkansas	22
27	Arkansas	34
27	SMU	31
26	TCU	19
27	Baylor	13
28	Baylor	42
32	Rice	38
29	Texas	43
29	Texas	44
28	TCU	27
31	SMU	23
27	Texas	32
506		**507**

(9-9)

1937
Coach: H. R. McQuillan

32	Sam Houston STC	34
26	Sam Houston STC	24
41	Sec Presb of Houston	29
16	Magnolia Oilers	27
18	USC	26
30	Magnolia Mobiloilers	33
33	Louisiana Sulp. Co.	22
21	NTTC	19
27	NTTC	13

27	NTTC	25
25	Rice	32
24	Sam Houston STC	30
37	Baylor	33
14	Texas	23
28	Rice	24
21	Baylor	19
45	TCU	42
32	Arkansas	36
25	SMU	28
19	Arkansas	45
32	Arkansas	36
42	Houston All-Stars	22
30	TCU	21
29	Texas	37
22	SMU	28
696		**708**

(12-13)

1938
Coach: H. R. McQuillan

31	Sam Houston STC	30
29	Sam Houston STC	43
36	Beaumont Mobiloilers	30
39	Magnolia Dealers	49
32	Arkansas	45
22	Arkansas	33
44	Magnolia Dealers	31
45	Rice	39
33	TCU	20
20	SMU	41
28	Baylor	36
48	Baylor	46
43	TCU	27
28	SMU	47
27	Texas	35
27	Sam Houston STC	26
31	Texas	26
52	Rice	45
615		**649**

(10-8)

1939
Coach: H. R. McQuillan

30	Sam Houston STC	25
23	Houston Sec Presb	29
23	Sam Houston STC	26
29	Texas A&I	33
35	Texas A&I	18
35	St. Mary's U.	27
38	St. Mary's U.	52
21	Drury College (Mo.)	47
30	Okla. Baptist College	14
37	Panhandle A&M North Texas	11
39	Rice	51
34	Baylor	38
29	Rice	37
24	TCU	18
29	SMU	40
37	Texas	41
44	TCU	36
28	SMU	48
42	Arkansas	61
38	Arkansas	66
32	Texas	62
23	Baylor	47
700		**827**

(7-16)

1940
Coach: H. R. McQuillan

43	Sam Houston STC	41
44	Sam Houston STC	40
47	St. Mary's U.	48
29	St. Mary's U.	32
31	NTSC	29
31	ECTTC	37
44	Ka. Wesleyan College	46
	Southeast Okla. TC	
46	Ada Oklahoma TC	43
44	TCU	31

40	Sec Presb of Houston	39
49	Baylor	46
44	Rice	62
51	SMU	49
54	Rice	67
36	Baylor	68
25	Arkansas	37
41	Arkansas	38
31	Texas	42
55	TCU	64
39	SMU	46
53	Texas	52
877		**957**

(11-11)

1941
Coach: H. R. McQuillan

21	Sam Houston STC	32
31	Carr-Sweeney of Houston	32
45	Sam Houston STC	33
34	St. Mary's U.	32
42	St. Mary's U.	43
21	Okla. City U.	19
30	Oklahoma A&M	38
34	Rice	68
33	Arkansas	69
36	Arkansas	58
33	Baylor	31
48	Carr-Sweeney of Houston	44
52	TCU	50
37	SMU	43
48	TCU	45
40	SMU	45
46	Rice	50
22	Texas	42
17	Baylor	28
36	Texas	53
979		**855**

(7-13)

1942
Coach: Marty Karow

33	Sam Houston STC	50
56	NTTC	42
43	Phillips 66	74
36	Texas Tech	48
56	LSU	43
52	Centenary	27
29	Kentucky	49
31	Purdue	55
41	Bradley Tech	53
30	Oregon	36
29	Washington U. (St. Louis)	39
32	Texas	46
36	Rice	34
46	Baylor	48
42	Rice	44
54	Sam Houston	42
35	Baylor	38
41	Arkansas	47
31	Arkansas	40
47	SMU	29
33	TCU	27
27	TCU	34
33	SMU	35
46	Texas	42
939		**1022**

(8-16)

1943
Coach: Manning Smith

60	Duncan Field	21
45	95th Division Ft. Sam Houston	39
31	Corpus Christi Naval Air Station	62
39	Duncan Field	33
45	Texas	54
33	Rice	42

54	Randolph Field	41
29	San Antonio Aviation Cadet Center	31
43	Randolph Field	31
53	TCU	26
58	Baylor	66
68	Sam Houston STC	38
43	Sam Houston STC	44
47	Waco Army AF	25
59	Baylor	45
39	TCU	45
39	SMU	51
54	SMU	47
49	Arkansas	74
67	Arkansas	52
30	Rice	40
55	Texas	57

1040		964

(11-11)

1944
Coach: Manning Smith

35	SMU	65
43	Baylor	48
33	Rice	63
39	Baylor	42
30	San Antonio Aviation Cadet Center	53
49	Corsicana Army Air Field	46
41	Texas	77
36	TCU	40
37	SMU	81
33	Rice	67
22	TCU	55
59	Brooks Field	48
30	Randolph Field	62
38	Bergstrom Field	45
36	Texas	81
35	Arkansas	70
38	Arkansas	68

634		1011

(2-15)

1945
Coach: Manning Smith

34	Bergstrom Field	30
26	Normoyle 4051 Base Unit, San Antonio	43
42	Ward Island Navy School	47
20	Corpus Christi Naval Air Station	63
43	Camp Normoyle	57
39	San Antonio Aviation Cadet Center	72
27	Ward Island Navy School	76
27	TCU	30
31	Corpus Christi Naval Air Station	68
22	Rice	53
28	SMU	50
59	Texas	87
42	Baylor	30
29	Baylor	28
25	Rice	68
33	McCloskey General Hospital	46
43	SMU	73
40	TCU	52
35	Texas	70
36	Arkansas	87
21	Arkansas	80

702		1213

(3-18)

1946
Coach: Marty Karow

51	Camp Bowie	17
40	Southwest La. Inst.	32
50	La. State University	51
41	Bergstrom Fld. Flyers	42
50	SHSTC	27
43	Army Pilots Personnel Training School	40
36	AAF Pilot Personnel Dist. Cent.	37
32	Kelley Field	33
44	Corpus Christi NAS	59
45	SMU	38
41	TCU	51
42	Texas University	46
34	Rice Inst.	36
56	Corpus Christi NAS	59
47	TCU	55
53	SMU	49
44	SHSTC	34
50	Texas University	44
59	Rice Inst.	64
48	Baylor Univ.	54
41	Baylor Univ.	44
56	Arkansas Univ.	55
45	Arkansas Univ.	53

1048		1020

(9-14)

1947
Coach: Marty Karow

49	NTSC	59
52	Siena College	47
59	Morehead Teachers College (Over time)	55
46	Murray Teachers Col.	49
63	Bradley Tech	91
42	St. Louis University	57
18	Univ. of Kentucky	84
58	Stephen F. Austin Col.	52
36	George Pepperdine Col.	53
51	Texas Tech	46
41	Univ. of Houston	60
50	Brooke Army Medical Center (Over time)	46
48	TCU	41
35	SMU	68
51	Baylor Univ.	59
52	Rice Inst.	39
39	Baylor Univ.	44
41	Texas Univ.	61
57	Houston YMCA	67
48	Rice Institute	53
40	Texas Univ.	69
56	Univ. of Arkansas	62
58	Univ. of Arkansas	71
48	TCU	38
59	SMU (Over time)	58

1197		1429

(8-17)

1948
Coach: Marty Karow

63	Abilene Christian	54
40	S. E. Okla State	37
37	S. E. Okla. State	40
43	East Texas State	52
65	Sam Houston State	55
57	Sam Houston State	47
64	Baldwin Wallace	81
40	Ohio State	54
44	Seton Hall	46
45	Louisiana State	44
30	SMU	47
55	Denton (NTSC)	59
43	Arkansas U.	58
46	Arkansas U.	57
41	Baylor U.	57
48	Texas U.	69
47	Rice Inst.	49
52	Baylor U.	70
51	SMU	46
48	TCU	22
48	Rice	52
26	SMU	62
41	TCU	46

1116		1258

(7-17)

1949
Coach: Marty Karow

49	Trinity Univ.	56
43	SHSTC	47
58	Abilene Christian C.	40
50	SHSTC	53
55	Louisiana St. U.	58
28	Tulane Univ.	51
50	SW Okla Teachers	30
49	SW Okla Teachers	35
36	Siena College	43
55	Seton Hall College	69
52	Baldwin-Wallace Col.	69
67	Akron Univ.	75
58	TCU	42
37	SMU	55
53	Rice Institute	54
47	Baylor Univ.	53
41	Texas Univ.	50
35	SMU	49
39	TCU	37
57	Arkansas Univ.	62
43	Texas Univ.	56
26	Baylor Univ.	38
46	Arkansas Univ.	61
39	Rice Inst.	53

1111		1236

(5-19)

1950
Coach: Marty Karow

52	Long Island Univ.	66
50	Niagara Univ.	53
51	St. Louis Univ.	55
34	Oklahoma A&M	55
66	Abilene Christian C.	45
73	Abilene Christian C.	38
67	Trinity	49
50	Univ. of Arizona	56
74	N. Texas St. College	33
46	Univ. of Arizona	59
48	Univ. of California	59
49	Stanford Univ.	55
48	SMU	53
49	TCU	55
43	Univ. of Arkansas	35
45	Univ. of Texas	48
56	Rice Institute	37
56	Baylor University	45
50	SMU	56
56	Baylor Univ.	54
46	Univ. of Arkansas	52
52	Rice Institute	62
60	TCU	58
52	Univ. of Texas	53

1274		1221

(10-14)

1951
Coach: John Floyd

40	North Texas State	35
39	Oklahoma City U.	44
42	Siena	56
45	Canisius	44
36	Duquesne	73
50	Southwest Texas	55
52	Southwest Texas	64
40	Sam Houston State	36
45	Univ. of Houston	52
50	Sam Houston State	45
60	Trinity University	40
51	Rice	39
55	Baylor	53
39	TCU	36
44	SMU	51
32	Texas	29
34	Arkansas	33
27	TCU	30
48	Baylor	36
38	Arkansas	46

49	SMU	43
45	Rice	42
40	Texas	42
55	Univ. of Houston	46
50	TCU	44
45	Texas U.	33
34	Texas U.	35
33	Texas U.	32
40	Washington	62

1203   1276

(17-12)

1952
Coach: John Floyd

43	No. Texas State	46
29	Houston U.	38
40	Marshall	46
42	Manhattan	44
52	Tennessee	60
63	Trinity (Tex.)	44
49	Arkansas U.	46
52	Texas Univ.	51
35	TCU	65
47	Arkansas U.	42
55	Oklahoma City U.	62
55	Rice	44
34	SMU	40
47	Baylor	36
44	Houston U.	52
40	Texas	51
41	TCU	52
45	Baylor	52
40	Arkansas	49
61	SMU	47
44	TCU	58
34	Texas	38
46	Oklahoma City U.	42
56	Rice	54

1094   1159

(9-15)

1953
Coach: John Floyd

65	Houston	59
53	NW Louisiana	58
68	E. N. Mex. U.	48
52	Colorado A&M	65
60	Trinity	55
52	SMU	65
49	Arizona	66
54	Texas	58
44	Baylor	60
56	Ark. (2 overtime)	48
36	TCU	67
51	Texas	42
43	Rice	52
51	SMU	43
46	Baylor	47
49	Texas	68
56	Rice	69
46	Arkansas	66
44	Houston	48
59	SMU	73
48	TCU	52

1056   1201

(6-15)

1954
Coach: John Floyd

68	Lamar Tech	88
56	Trinity	46
56	Houston	62
38	OCU	60
56	LSU	77
55	Texas Tech	58
43	Rice	55
50	Baylor	64
41	TCU	69
45	Baylor	47
53	Rice	78
46	Texas	49
52	TCU	69

55	Arkansas	80
48	SMU	92
47	Rice	61
73	SMU	71
49	Texas	66
57	TCU	76
54	Arkansas	67
51	Houston	52
65	Baylor	79

1158   1466

(2-20)

1955
Coach: John Floyd

53	Houston	85
45	Tulsa	57
53	Tulane	82
61	LSU	73
57	West Texas	82
86	Pepperdine	84
66	Texas	61
57	TCU	72
70	Arkansas	74
41	Rice	61
62	Arkansas	59
69	SMU	93
66	Houston	107
77	Baylor	89
58	LSU	47
58	TCU	71
62	TCU	92
34	OCU	55
76	Texas	80
56	SMU	81
68	Baylor	86
64	Texas	74
63	Arkansas	73
52	Rice	67

1464   1805

(4-20)

1956
Coach: Ken Loeffler

43	Tulsa	48
69	Vanderbilt	79
71	Memphis State	84
73	LSU	59
85	Tulane	66
44	U. of Houston	78
81	Rice Inst.	110
59	TCU	67
49	Arkansas	80
90	Baylor	70
77	Rice	89
68	SMU	97
75	U. of Texas	74
66	U. of Arkansas	98
75	Sam Houston State	46
84	TCU	74
56	Oklahoma City U.	76
74	U. of Houston	105
66	Baylor	85
52	U. of Arkansas	61
80	SMU	92
67	TCU	91
61	Rice	85
70	U. of Texas	98

1635   1912

(6-18)

1957
Coach: Ken Loeffler

59	Centenary	67
69	St. Mary's	60
58	Sam Houston	59
81	Trinity	55
68	Loyola	71
63	Miss. Southern	75
83	Florida State	74
69	Georgia Tech	76
80	Miami	86
76	Navy	75

46	SMU	68
44	Rice	66
39	Rice	53
65	Arkansas	73
53	SMU	62
58	Baylor	67
58	TCU	77
69	Texas	67
46	Arkansas	63
59	TCU	62
64	Baylor	61
55	SMU	71
61	Texas	56
55	Rice	57

1478   1601

(7-17)

1958
Coach: Bob Rogers

56	St. Mary's	69
71	Memphis State	68
46	Wake Forest	68
50	Richmond	70
72	Ohio State	69
44	Temple	60
54	TCU	65
49	SMU	59
80	Baylor	63
48	TCU	71
71	Texas	50
59	Rice (OT)	62
57	Baylor	47
44	SMU	36
51	Arkansas	67
55	Texas Tech	57
92	Houston	74
60	Baylor	51
57	Rice	67
68	Texas	74
66	Arkansas	57
79	Texas Tech	63
43	SMU	42
42	TCU	62

1414   1471

(11-13)

1959
Coach: Bob Rogers

61	Trinity	51
57	Houston	45
81	Sam Houston	54
68	Centenary	57
62	Alabama	66
74	Wyoming	64
66	Texas Tech	58
60	Rice	59
61	TCU	45
65	SMU	63
65	Rice	70
49	Baylor	56
63	Arkansas	62
73	Texas	29
71	Houston	64
46	Texas Tech	57
64	TCU	76
65	Baylor	52
61	TCU	80
53	Texas Tech	52
71	Arkansas	72
71	Texas	61
67	Rice	74
66	SMU	70

1540   1437

(15-9)

1960
Coach: Bob Rogers

95	Centenary	38
86	Trinity	47
67	Houston	49
70	Midwestern	43
64	Houston	62

72	TCU	61
84	Texas	74
58	SMU	55
68	Baylor	51
65	TCU	52
64	SMU	66
72	Texas	61
61	Rice	43
69	San Francisco	65
55	Santa Clara	66
89	Texas Tech	59
77	Arkansas	68
94	Rice	53
62	Texas	79
82	Arkansas	61
53	SMU	81
61	Texas Tech	68
64	TCU	56
77	Baylor	63

1708   1421
(19-5)

1961
Coach: Bob Rogers

66	Trinity	48
64	Kansas State	69
66	Houston	61
77	Centenary	54
58	Oklahoma State	60
56	Oklahoma	69
76	Eastern Kentucky	57
62	Air Force Academy	51
82	TCU	69
75	Baylor	61
81	Arkansas	62
68	Texas Tech	74
76	Texas	81
85	Houston	89
86	U. of Pacific	39
80	SMU	66
79	Rice	59
66	TCU	68
74	Texas Tech	71
65	Rice	58
61	SMU	65
86	Texas	69
90	Baylor	69
70	Arkansas	68

1749   1537
(16-8)

1962
Coach: Bob Rogers

58	Centenary	56
64	Houston	49
50	Memphis State	62
55	Lamar Tech	51
62	Auburn	50
71	UCLA	81
69	Wichita	71
71	Seattle	54
71	Okla. City U.	69
59	Arkansas	64
70	Texas Tech	61
54	Baylor	52
75	SMU	55
57	Texas	64
69	Houston	73
79	TCU	72
88	Rice	73
54	SMU	59
54	Texas	48
87	TCU	65
62	Rice	63
89	Arkansas	79
49	Texas Tech	69
84	Baylor	61

1611   1501
(15-9)

1963
Coach: Bob Rogers

91	Centenary	74
74	Lamar Tech	81
78	Memphis State	67
87	Miss. Southern	61
69	Houston	67
67	LSU	61
79	Michigan	82
67	Tulane	53
60	Virginia	59
80	Baylor	54
60	Texas Tech	53
71	Rice	61
68	SMU	71
57	Houston	58
55	Arkansas	66
59	Texas	70
85	TCU	69
76	SMU	70
80	Arkansas	78
73	Texas	83
87	TCU	54
68	Baylor	54
96	Texas Tech	83
70	Rice	73

1757   1602
(16-8)

1964
Coach: Shelby Metcalf

61	Houston	58
71	Utah State	94
71	Utah University	98
96	Sam Houston	63
70	Okla City U.	80
58	Mississippi State	54
61	Washington	53
56	Wichita	70
99	Wyoming	87
75	SMU	61
92	TCU	64
65	Texas	60
65	Houston	73
74	Rice	70
83	Baylor	58
72	Arkansas	64
82	Texas Tech	84
79	Rice	67
77	Baylor	71
60	Arkansas	57
82	Texas Tech	70
75	SMU	70
70	TCU	66
65	Texas	63
62	Texas Western	68

1821   1723
(18-7)

1965
Coach: Shelby Metcalf

73	Memphis State	83
83	Southern Miss.	70
97	Arlington State	80
75	Sam Houston	58
81	Memphis State	71
74	Houston	67
69	Rice	60
49	Houston	59
98	Trinity	72
77	Baylor	80
77	SMU	89
72	TCU	71
93	Rice	55
74	Houston	79
82	Arkansas	79
63	Texas	65
76	Texas Tech	82
77	Baylor	84
104	Rice	93
91	Arkansas	77
102	TCU	95
71	Texas	86
94	SMU	81
73	Texas Tech	98

1925   1834
(14-10)

1966
Coach: Shelby Metcalf

79	Trinity	70
76	SW Texas	66
93	Houston	88
93	Memphis St.	84
89	Rice	81
85	Houston	90
74	Va. Tech	101
86	Xavier	98
72	Bowling Green	85
85	SMU	78
92	Rice	85
75	Arkansas	72
81	Baylor	60
64	Texas	57
85	Houston	97
81	TCU	72
77	Texas Tech	71
82	Texas	110
85	Texas Tech	98
96	TCU	91
65	SMU	82
93	Rice	65
95	Baylor	78
71	Arkansas	94

1974   1973
(15-9)

1967
Coach: Shelby Metcalf

50	Louisiana Tech	53
56	Memphis St.	66
49	Miss. St.	62
68	Alabama	89
78	SF Austin	76
69	N. Tex. St.	72
71	W. Tex. St.	89
54	New Mexico U.	85
67	New York U.	79
69	Rice	66
67	SMU	80
64	TCU	67
46	Arkansas	47
68	Texas	59
74	Trinity	100
65	Baylor	93
70	Texas Tech	67
79	Rice	101
60	Arkansas	53
36	Texas Tech	41
71	Baylor	69
58	Texas	72
71	SMU	85
71	TCU	96

1531   1767
(6-18)

1968
Coach: Shelby Metcalf

84	Louisiana Tech	77
106	Trinity	95
89	West Texas State	83
78	S. W. Texas State	74
65	N. Texas State	71
77	Kansas State	82
52	Kansas	78
80	Seattle	72
77	San Francisco	75
70	Arkansas	75
77	TCU	81

94	Texas Tech	81
77	SMU	78
88	Texas	87
93	Centenary	99
75	Rice	66
67	Baylor	77
117	Tulsa	105
78	Rice	58
67	Baylor	63
71	Arkansas	67
78	TCU	85
81	Texas Tech	83
85	SMU	80

1936   **1892**
(14-10)

1969
Coach: Shelby Metcalf

95	So. Mississippi	82
72	Centenary	65
87	Lamar Tech	98
102	Louisiana Tech	83
74	S. F. Austin	75
60	Wichita State	79
71	Duquesne	93
77	U of Pacific	75
83	Wyoming	81
85	Texas Tech	84
73	Arkansas	68
76	SMU	75
72	TCU	71
71	Houston	85
65	Texas	57
65	Baylor	66
90	Rice	82
70	Texas	69
84	Rice	83
86	Baylor	74
71	Texas Tech	70
79	Arkansas	66
119	SMU	98
71	TCU	94
81	Trinity (NCAA)	66
63	Drake (NCAA)	81
82	Colorado (NCAA)	97

2124   **2107**
(18-9)

1970
Coach: Shelby Metcalf

71	Northwest La.	73
109	Midwestern	80
66	Kent State	68
69	Nebraska	78
63	Colo. St.	54
79	Missouri	81
78	Clemson	63
68	Furman	66
93	Northwestern (ot)	91
64	Arkansas	59
71	Baylor	79
87	Texas	81
84	La. Tech	100
58	Rice	68
84	SMU	74
66	Texas Tech	84
72	TCU	84
79	Texas	70
77	TCU	73
82	Texas Tech	74
84	SMU	81
72	Arkansas	60
68	Baylor	70
91	Rice	86

1835   **1797**
(14-10)

1971
Coach: Shelby Metcalf

82	SFA	89
67	ETSU	61
75	UTA	77
70	Oregon	94
69	Tulane	89
91	ACC	74
71	Tulsa	103
75	Arizona	90
83	Furman	103
61	Citadel	62
66	UNC — Charlotte	62
87	Lamar Tech	82
83	Baylor	108
59	TCU	64
74	Rice	73
65	Texas Tech	76
83	SMU (OT)	89
87	Arkansas	83
69	Texas	78
71	Rice	73
78	SMU	85
66	Tex. Tech (OT)	64
65	Texas	64
71	Baylor (OT)	78
63	TCU	76
92	Arkansas	89

1924   **2086**
(9-17)

1972
Coach: Shelby Metcalf

96	Texas Wesleyan	72
91	Northwestern La.	75
79	Tulsa	90
53	UCLA	117
86	Southwest Texas	68
73	New Mexico	95
77	Creighton	100
65	Michigan State	67
73	LSU	68
72	George Washington	64
66	Virginia Tech (OT)	62
98	Trinity	58
79	SMU	71
89	Arkansas	100
81	TCU	74
85	Baylor	75
80	Rice	70
68	Texas Tech	63
71	Texas	80
71	SMU	75
86	Arkansas	85
75	TCU	67
101	Baylor (OT)	95
69	Rice	73
73	Texas	80
71	Texas Tech	61

2028   **2005**
(16-10)

1973
Coach: Shelby Metcalf

100	Wayland Baptist	60
88	UT Arlington	84
90	Angelo State	81
67	Oklahoma State (OT)	64
72	George Washington	79
99	Oral Roberts	117
81	Brigham Young	83
62	Penn State	55
100	Mississippi	83
102	Wichita State	86
85	Houston	114
73	Arkansas	84
96	Texas Lutheran	77
91	Baylor	80
69	Texas	64
75	Rice	81
67	Texas Tech	68
92	TCU	73

62	SMU (OT)	64
108	Arkansas	82
76	Baylor	63
68	Texas	71
90	Rice	80
76	Texas Tech	75
78	SMU	75
95	TCU	82

2162   **2025**
(17-9)

1974
Coach: Shelby Metcalf

85	Houston Baptist	72
74	Southwest Texas	65
85	Tarleton State	74
87	Stephen F. Austin	62
71	Va. Commonwealth	72
65	George Washington	91
86	Northwestern	84
89	Oklahoma Christian	68
67	Tulsa	88
79	Florida State	99
99	Denver	84
100	Southwestern	87
90	SMU	75
72	TCU	88
61	Texas Tech	63
80	Rice	79
90	Texas	98
62	Baylor	71
86	Arkansas	80
90	TCU	64
68	SMU	70
98	Texas Tech	95
96	Rice	82
81	Texas	88
94	Baylor	72
86	Arkansas	97

2141   **2068**
(15-11)

1975
Coach: Shelby Metcalf

84	Texas Lutheran	74
84	Houston Baptist	77
83	Oral Roberts	84
98	Va. Commonwealth	84
55	Indiana	90
67	Northwestern	55
69	UT El Paso	71
62	Fairfield	57
84	Va. Commonwealth	70
80	UN Las Vegas	78
72	Houston	92
101	Sam Houston St.	71
64	Rice	61
81	TCU	69
62	Texas Tech	55
80	Texas	74
102	SMU	77
89	Arkansas	95
96	Baylor	66
62	Arkansas	60
62	Baylor	55
99	Rice	66
63	Texas Tech	73
94	TCU	81
100	SMU	77
74	Texas	63
79	Cincinnati (NCAA regional playoff)	87

2146   **1962**
(20-7)

Honorary Degrees Conferred by the Texas A&M College

LISTED CHRONOLOGICALLY

Name	Degree Conferred	Date Conferred
Law, Francis Marion	LL.D.	June 1, 1934
Jones, Jesse Holman	LL.D.	November 5, 1936
Friley, Charles E.	LL.D.	May 31, 1940
Kiest, Edwin John	D.Jour.	June 6, 1941
Kleberg, Robert Justus Jr.	D.Agr.	June 6, 1941
McCormick, George	D.Eng.	June 6, 1941
Bennett, Edwin O.	D.Eng.	May 21, 1943
Hoblitzelle, Karl	LL.D.	May 21, 1943
Wallace, Lawrence Wilkerson	D.Eng.	May 21, 1943
Kokernot, Herbert Lee	D.Agr.	May 26, 1944
Dickerson, Adolph F.	D.Eng.	May 26, 1944
Moore, George F.	LL.D.	October 15, 1945
Clarkson, Percy W.	LL.D.	March 22, 1946
Eisenhower, Dwight David	LL.D.	April 20, 1946
Bruce, Andrew D.	LL.D.	April 20, 1946
Davidson, Howard C.	LL.D.	April 20, 1946
Johnson, Harry H.	LL.D.	April 20, 1946
Weyland, Otto P.	LL.D.	April 20, 1946
Williams, Robert B.	LL.D.	April 20, 1946
Wooten, Ralph H.	LL.D.	April 20, 1946
Abbott, Oscar B.	LL.D.	April 20, 1946
Beverly, George H.	LL.D.	April 20, 1946
Easley, Claudius M.*	LL.D.	April 20, 1946
Farthing, William E.	LL.D.	April 20, 1946
Knickerbocker, Arthur B.	LL.D.	April 20, 1946
Luedecke, Alvin R.	LL.D.	April 20, 1946
Netherwood, Douglas B.	LL.D.	April 20, 1946
Perrine, Nat S.	LL.D.	April 20, 1946
Warden, John A.	LL.D.	April 20, 1946
Waters, Jerome J.	LL.D.	April 20, 1946
Leavey, Edmond H.	LL.D.	May 31, 1946

*Posthumously awarded.

Lee, William L.	LL.D.	June 7, 1946
Moore, Aubrey L.	LL.D.	June 4, 1948
Old, William D.	LL.D.	June 4, 1948
Conner, Arthur B.	D.Agr.	June 4, 1948
Boehne, Eugene W.	D.Eng.	June 4, 1948
Walker, John T.	LL.D.	November 13, 1948
Allen, Roderick Random	LL.D.	June 3, 1949
Bradley, Omar Nelson	LL.D.	June 2, 1950
Davis, John F.	LL.D.	June 2, 1950
Hull, Burton Elias	D.Eng.	June 2, 1950
Smith, Marvin Wadsworth	D.Eng.	June 2, 1950
Bolton, Frank Cleveland	LL.D.	June 1, 1951
Charske, Fannin Woody	LL.D.	June 1, 1951
Jones, Marvin	LL.D.	June 1, 1951
Barton, Thomas Harry	LL.D.	May 21, 1954
Harris, David Bullock	LL.D.	May 21, 1954
Tinus, William Cornelius	D.Eng.	May 21, 1954
McLeod, John Hayne	LL.D.	May 27, 1955
Hobbs, Leonard Sinclair	LL.D.	May 27, 1955
Morgan, William Edgeworth	LL.D.	May 25, 1956
Stangel, Wenzel Louis	LL.D.	May 25, 1956
Teague, Olin E.	LL.D.	May 25, 1956
Haydari, Mohamed Darwish	LL.D.	**May 25, 1956

**The Board of Directors has chosen not to award any honorary degrees since 1956.

Emeriti Faculty Members
Texas A&M University

Abbott, John Paul — Professor Emeritus of English (1926, 1972)*

Adamson, Arthur Douglas — Professor Emeritus of Health and Physical Education (1939, 1971)**

Adriance, Guy Webb — Professor Emeritus of Horticulture (1921, 1960)

Atkins, Irvin Milburn — Professor Emeritus of Agronomy (1939, 1969)

Bass, James Horace — Professor Emeritus of History (1940, 1961)**

Blank, Horace R. — Professor Emeritus of Geology (1949, 1967)

Bossler, Robert Burns — Professor Emeritus of Petroleum Engineering (1956, 1966)

Brewer, Alexander Van, P.E. — Professor Emeritus of Mechanical Engineering (1922, 1957)

Brison, Fred Robert — Professor Emeritus of Horticulture (1926, 1964)

Brown, Meta S. — Professor Emeritus of Agronomy (1940, 1974)

Brown, Sidney Overton — Professor Emeritus of Accounting (1959, 1971)

Buchanan, Spencer Jennings, P.E. — Professor Emeritus of Civil Engineering (1946, 1970)

Burgess, Archie Roston — Professor Emeritus of Industrial Engineering (1948, 1975)

Burns, Patton Wright — Professor Emeritus of Veterinary Physiology and Pharmacology (1926, 1967)

Byers, Horace — Professor Emeritus of Meteorology (1965, 1974)

Calaway, Paul K. — Professor Emeritus of Chemistry (1957, 1975)

Chilen, Paul R. — Professor Emeritus of Agricultural Engineering (1967, 1975)

Cleland, Samuel M. — Professor Emeritus of Design Graphics (1941, 1975)

Cofer, David Brooks — Professor of English and Archivist Emeritus (1910, 1957)

Couch, James Russell — Professor Emeritus of Biochemistry and Biophysics (1948, 1974)

CoVan, Jack Philip, P.E. — Professor Emeritus of Industrial Engineering (1946, 1974)

Crawford, Charles William, P.E. — Professor Emeritus of Mechanical Engineering (1919, 1965)

Davis, William B. — Professor Emeritus of Wildlife Science (1937, 1967)

Dillon, Laurence Samuel — Professor Emeritus of Biology (1948, 1975)

Doak, Clifton Childress — Professor Emeritus of Biology (1926, 1967)

Dunn, Ralph Clark — Professor Emeritus of Veterinary Bacteriology and Hygiene (1911, 1950)**

Dyksterhuis, Edsko Jerry — Professor Emeritus of Range Science (1964, 1970)

Eckles, William Elam — Associate Professor Emeritus of Management (1960, 1970)

---

*The two dates in parentheses indicate respectively the date of first appointment to the University staff and the date of appointment to current position.

**Deceased.

Fleming, David Winston — Associate Professor Emeritus of Mechanical Engineering (1927, 1968)

Fletcher, Robert Holton, P.E., — Professor Emeritus of Engineering Technology (1947, 1974)

Folweiler, Alfred D. — Director Emeritus, Texas Forest Service (1949, 1968)

Gaines, J. C. — Professor Emeritus of Entomology (1947, 1971)

Gammon, Samuel Rhea — Professor Emeritus of History (1925, 1957)

Gilchrist, Gibb — Chancellor Emeritus (1937, 1954)**

Hale, Fred — Professor Emeritus of Animal Science (1922, 1965)

Hancock, Charles Kinney — Professor Emeritus of Chemistry (1946, 1973)

Harrington, Marion Thomas — President Emeritus (1924, 1971)

Harris, William Donald — Professor Emeritus of Chemical Engineering (1935, 1974)

Harter, Edward Lin — Associate Professor Emeritus of Chemistry (1921, 1959)

Hillman, John Rolfe — Assistant Professor Emeritus of Mathematics (1938, 1965)

Hobgood, Price, P.E. — Professor Emeritus of Agricultural Engineering (1939, 1974)

Hopkins, Sewell Hepburn — Professor Emeritus of Biology (1935, 1972)

Hoyle, Samuel Cooke, Jr. — Professor Emeritus of Management (1947, 1967)

Hughes, Martin Collins — Professor Emeritus of Electrical Engineering (1923, 1962)

Hurt, John Tom — Professor Emeritus of Mathematics (1936, 1974)

Irvin, Barlow — Athletic Director Emeritus (1948, 1968)**

Jones, Fred Rufus — Professor Emeritus of Agricultural Engineering (1921, 1971)

Jones, Luther G. — Professor Emeritus of Agronomy (1917, 1971)

Jones, William P. — Professor Emeritus of Aerospace Engineering (1967, 1975)

Klipple, Edmund Chester — Professor Emeritus of Mathematics (1935, 1971)

LaMotte, Charles — Professor Emeritus of Biology (1930, 1964)

Langford, Ernest — Professor Emeritus of Architecture (1915, 1957)

Laverty, Carrol D. — Professor Emeritus of English (1939, 1973)

Lewis, Robert Donald — Director Emeritus, Texas Agricultural Experiment Station (1946, 1962)

Liebhafsky, Herman Alfred — Professor Emeritus of Chemistry (1967, 1972)

Lindsay, James Donald, P.E. — Professor Emeritus of Chemical Engineering (1938, 1965)

Linger, Irving Oscar — Professor Emeritus of Economics (1961, 1974)

Little, Van Allen — Professor Emeritus of Entomology (1923, 1964)

Luther, Herbert Adesta — Professor Emeritus of Mathematics (1937, 1975)

McGuire, John Gilbert — Professor Emeritus of Petroleum Engineering (1933, 1975)

Mackin, John Gilman — Professor Emeritus of Biology (1950, 1970)

Middleton, Errol Bathurst — Professor Emeritus of Chemistry (1922, 1962)

Miller, Thomas Lloyd — Professor Emeritus of History (1946, 1974)

Milliff, John Henry — Professor Emeritus of Veterinary Anatomy (1936, 1971)

Mogford, Joseph Sayers — Professor Emeritus of Agronomy (1925, 1971)

Nelson, Al B. — Professor Emeritus of History (1937, 1967)

O'Bannon, Lester Severance, P.E. — Professor Emeritus of Mechanical Engineering (1948, 1967)

Oliver, John E. — Professor Emeritus of Accounting (1959, 1971)

Packenham, Edward S. — Professor Emeritus of Accounting (1947, 1971)

Parker, Grady P. — Professor Emeritus of Education (1940, 1968)**

Pedigo, John Randolph, Sr. — Professor Emeritus of Petroleum Engineering (1953, 1975)

Perry, Bruce A. — Professor Emeritus of Horticulture (1946, 1974)

Porter, Walter Lee — Professor Emeritus of Mathematics (1918, 1959)**
Potts, William McDaniel — Professor Emeritus of Chemistry (1926, 1959)**
Quisenberry, John Henry — Professor Emeritus of Poultry Science (1936, 1972)
Randolph, Neal M. — Professor Emeritus of Entomology (1954, 1975)
Reinhard, Henry J. — Professor Emeritus of Entomology (1947, 1960)
Ross, Henry — Professor Emeritus of Agricultural Education (1935, 1965)
Rotsch, Melvin Medford — Professor Emeritus of Architecture (1950, 1974)
Russell, William Low — Professor Emeritus of Geology (1946, 1963)
Sandstedt, Carl Edward, P.E. — Professor Emeritus of Civil Engineering (1923, 1959)
Smith, Fred E. — Professor Emeritus of Geology (1948, 1971)
Smith, Harris P. — Professor Emeritus of Agricultural Engineering (1974)
Sperry, Omer Edison — Professor Emeritus of Range and Forestry (1946, 1972)**
Stinnett, Tim M. — Professor Emeritus of Educational Administration (1966, 1974)
Thornton, Marmaduke K. — Professor Emeritus of Chemistry (1909, 1954)
Timm, Tyrus R. — Professor Emeritus of Agricultural Economics (1947, 1975)
Tishler, Carl Edward — Professor Emeritus of Health and Physical Education (1941, 1967)
Trotter, Ide Peebles — Dean Emeritus, Graduate School, and Professor Emeritus of Agronomy (1936, 1960)**
Truettner, Willard Irving, P.E. — Professor Emeritus of Mechanical Engineering (1930, 1969)
Vezey, Edward Earl — Professor Emeritus of Physics (1920, 1961)
Ward, Robert Page — Professor Emeritus of Electrical Engineering (1925, 1962)
Watkins, Gustav McKee — Professor Emeritus of Plant Pathology (1949, 1974)
Weekes, Donald Fessenden — Professor Emeritus of Physics (1937, 1971)
Whealy, Roger Dale — Professor Emeritus of Chemistry (1958, 1973)
White, Robert F. — Professor Emeritus of Landscape Architecture (1947, 1975)
Wilcox, George Barton — Professor Emeritus of Education and Psychology (1920, 1959)
Williams, David Willard — Professor Emeritus of Animal Science (1919, 1971)
Woolket, Joseph John — Professor Emeritus of Modern Languages (1925, 1966)
Wright, Samuel Robert, P.E. — Professor Emeritus of Civil Engineering (1923, 1970)

Recipients of Distinguished-Alumni Awards Texas A&M University

Name	Date Awarded
Aston, James W. ('33)	1967
Baker, R. W. "Bob" ('44)	1975
Bell, Tyree L. ('13)*	1964
Benz, M. "Buddy" ('32)	1973
Brockett, Ernest D. "Del", Jr. ('34)	1967
Bruce, Andrew D. ('16)*	1968
Cain, R. Wofford ('13)	1964
Carr, Hal N. ('43)	1972
Colglazier, Robert W., Jr. ('25)	1971
Davis, Roy B. ('27)*	1968
Doherty, W. T. "Doc" ('22)*	1966
Dunn, J. Harold ('25)	1964
Evans, Sterling C. ('21)	1973
Forsyth, James M. "Cop" ('12)	1973
Fouraker, Lawrence E. "Larry" ('44)	1975
Galloway, James H., Jr. ('29)	1970
Goodson, Richard A. ('27)	1966
Greer, Dewitt C. ('23)	1966
Grey, Rex B. ('41)	1971
Halbouty, Michel T. ('30)	1968
Harrington, M. T. "Tom" ('22)	1971
Haynes, Harold J. "Bill" ('46)	1972
Herring, Robert R. ('41)	1974
Johnson, Bernard G. ('37)	1974
Knipling, Edward F. ('30)	1962
Knox, John M. "Jack" ('46)	1971
Krueger, C. C. "Polly" ('12)*	1968
Luedecke, Alvin R. ('32)	1967
Lynch, William W. ('22)	1962
Malina, Frank J. ('34)	1972

*Deceased

McGee, W. C. "mAggie", Jr. ('31)	1969
Morgan, William E. ('30)	1969
Moser, Norman N. ('37)	1971
Mosher, E. J. ('28)	1969
Neeley, M. J. ('22)	1970
Newton, John W. ('12)*	1962
Rudder, James Earl ('32)*	1970
Sanders, Sam H., Jr. ('22)	1970
Sawyer, Horace A. "Tom" ('16)	1967
Schiwetz, Edward M. "Buck" ('21)	1972
Schriever, Bernard A. ('31)	1962
Sherrill, Owen W. ('10)	1974
Teague, Olin E. "Tiger" ('32)	1966
Thomas, J. B. ('11)	1974
Tinus, William C. ('28)	1970
Turner, Francis C. "Frank" ('29)	1969
Varner, Durward B. "Woody" ('40)	1972
Wisenbaker, Royce E. ('39)	1974
Zachry, H. B. "Pat" ('22)	1964

Bibliography

I. PRIMARY SOURCES

A. Official Reports and Documents (excluding the State of Texas and Texas A&M)
B. Official Reports and Documents of the State of Texas and Its Professional Agencies (excluding Texas A&M)
C. Official Reports and Documents of Texas A&M University
D. Newspapers
E. Magazines
F. Manuscripts*
   1. Manuscript Collections
   2. Biographical Papers
G. Interviews

II. SECONDARY SOURCES

A. Books and Monographs
B. Articles
C. Theses, Dissertations, and Unpublished Manuscripts

*Located in Texas A&M University Archives and Manuscripts Collection, unless otherwise indicated.

I. PRIMARY SOURCES

A. *Official Reports and Documents (excluding the State of Texas and Texas A&M)*

Missouri, State Board of Agriculture. *31st Annual Report, 1899.* Jefferson City, Missouri. 496 pp.

_____. *33rd Annual Report, 1901.* Jefferson City, Missouri. 420 pp.

United States, Congress. *Congressional Record.* 77 Cong., 2nd sess., vol. 88, part 10, pp. A1453-A1454, A3784-A3785.

United States, Department of Agriculture. *Federal Legislation, Regulations, and Rulings Affecting Land-Grant Colleges and Experiment Stations.* Department Circular 251. Washington, Government Printing Office, February, 1930. 60 pp.

_____. Bureau of Plant Industry. Knapp, Seaman A. *The Work of the Community Demonstration Farm at Terrell, Texas.* Bulletin 51, part II (February 17, 1904). 8 pp.

United States. *United States Statutes at Large.* 1917.

United States Government Organization Manual, 1971/1972. Washington, Government Printing Office, 1971. 809 pp.

B. *Official Reports and Documents of the Republic and the State of Texas and Professional Agencies (excluding Texas A&M)*

Brazos County. *Brazos County Index to Commissioners Courts Minutes.* Vol. I.

_____. *Deed Records of Brazos County,* vol. M, 142ff.

The Constitution as Amended, and Ordinances of the Convention of 1866. In H. P. N. Gammel (ed.), *The Laws of Texas, 1822-1897.* Vol. V. Austin: Gammel Book Company, 1898.

The Constitution of the State of Texas [1876]. Annotated by D. B. Axtell. Austin: Gammel Book Co., 1901.

Governor. Commission on Higher Education. *Annual Report to the Governor and the Legislature of the State of Texas.* Austin: 1954-1964.

_____. Commission on Higher Education. *Public Higher Education in Texas, 1961-1971.* Austin: 1963. 99 pp.

_____. *Governor's Messages, Coke to Ross, 1874-1891,* ed. by Archive and History Department, Texas State Library. Austin: 1916. 820 pp.

Legislature. *The General Laws of the State of Texas, 1846-1970.* Austin: 1846-1970.

_____. House of Representatives. *Journals of the House of Representatives of the State of Texas.* Austin: 1846-1972.

_____. House of Representatives. *Statement by Members of the House of Representatives Concerning a Bill to Consolidate the Agricultural and Mechanical College and the State University.* n.p., n.d. [1913]. 25 pp.

_____. Joint Legislative Committee on Organization and Economy and Griffen and Associates. *The Government of Texas,* XI, *Education: the Agricultural and Mechanical College of Texas and Its Affiliates.* Austin: 1933. 318 pp.

_____. H.P.N. Gammel (ed.), *The Laws of Texas, 1822-1897.* 10 vols. Austin: Gammel Book Company, 1898.

_____. *Texas Legislative Record,* 17th Legislature. Austin: 1881.

_____. Senate. *Senate Journal of the State of Texas.* Austin: 1845-1972.

_____. Texas Educational Survey Commission. *Texas Educational Survey Report,* VI, *Higher Education.* Austin: 1925. 389 pp.

Professional Organizations. *The Philosophical Society of Texas Proceedings,* 1952. Dallas: The Philosophical Society of Texas, 1953. 40 pp.

_____. Texas State Agricultural Society. *Transactions of the Texas State Agricultural Society; Embracing the Proceedings Connected with Its Organization, the Constitution, and with an Address by the President.* Austin: 1853. 24 pp.

_____. Texas State Horticultural Society. *Initial Report of the Texas State Horticultural Society for 1886-1889.* College Station: December 1889. 106 pp.

Republic of Texas. Congress. *Journals of the Fourth Congress of the Republic of Texas.* 3 vols. Austin: Von Boeckmann-Jones Company, Printers, 1929.

Texas Planning Board. *A Review of Texas Forestry and Its Industries.* Austin: November 1937. 39 pp.

University of Texas. Benedict, Harry Yondell (ed.), *A Source Book Relating to the History of The University of Texas: Legislative, Legal, Bibliographical, and Statistical.* University of Texas Bulletin No. 1757. Austin: October 10, 1917. 854 pp.

_____. *Report of the Board of Regents of the University of Texas, December 1886.* Austin: 1886. 70 pp. Supplement, i-iii.

University of Texas at Arlington, *1970-71 Catalog.*

C. *Official Reports and Documents of Texas A&M University*

Ad Hoc Committee on Continuing Education. "Continuing Education at Texas A&M University" Mimeographed. n.p., [1972].

Association of Former Students. *Directory of Former Students. Bulletin of the Agricultural and Mechanical College of Texas.* 3rd ser., vol. 10 (December 1, 1924). 206 pp.

_____. *Directory of Former Students. Bulletin of the Agricultural and Mechanical College of Texas.* 3rd ser., vol. 15 (May 1, 1929). 202 pp.

_____. *Directory of Former Students, 1876-1938.* [College Station: 1938]. 239 pp.

_____. *Directory of Former Students, 1876-1957.* College Station: 1957. 483 pp.

_____. *Directory of Former Students, 1876-1962.* College Station: 1962. 512 pp.

_____. *Directory of Former Students, 1876-1967.* College Station: 1967. 404 pp.

_____. *Directory of Former Students, 1876-1970.* College Station: 1970. 502 pp.

_____. McGinnis, N. M. (ed.). *Gold Book: Agricultural and Mechanical College of Texas. A Tribute to Her Loyal Sons Who Paid the Supreme Sacrifice in the World War. Alumni Quarterly,* IV (August 1919). 26 pp.

_____. *Texas A&M Today.* College Station: Texas A&M Press, 1953. 48 pp.

Athletic Council. *The Contributions of Edwin Jackson Kyle to the Development of the Athletic Program at the Agricultural and Mechanical College of Texas.* Houston: 1952. 21 pp.

_____. Athletic Council Minutes. 1914-1968. Handscript and typescript.

_____. *Texas A&M 1971 Football Press Guide.* College Station: Texas A&M Press, 1971. 100 pp.

_____. *Texas A&M 1971-1972 Basketball Press Book.* College Station: Texas A&M Press, 1971. 44 pp.

_____. *Texas A&M 1972 Spring Sports Press Book.* College Station: Texas A&M Press, 1972. 64 pp.

Board of Directors. *An Appeal to the Twenty-Second Legislature by the Board of Regents of the University of Texas and the Board of Directors of the Agricultural and Mechanical College, for Appropriations Necessary to Meet the Rapidly Increasing Demands of the People of Texas for Better Facilities for Literary and Technical Education in Those Institutions.* n.p., n.d. 8 pp.

_____. *Announcement and Circular of the State Agricultural and Mechanical College, 1876.* Bryan: Appeal and Post Book and Job Printing Establishment, 1876. 32 pp.

_____. *Annual Report of the Agricultural and Mechanical College* (Title varies). College Station and Austin: 1876-1884; 1919-1946. (See Board of Directors, *Biennial Report,* 1885-1919; see President, *Annual Report of the President,* 1946-1951, 1956-; and see Chancellor, *Annual Report of the Chancellor,* 1951-1955.)

_____. *Biennial Report of the Agricultural and Mechanical College.* College Station and Austin: 1885-1919.

_____. *The Blue Book.* Bryan, College Station: 1910-1919. See Board of Directors, *Laws of the Agricultural and Mechanical College of Texas . . .*

_____. *Blueprint for Progress.* College Station: Texas A&M Press, 1962. [14 pp.].

_____. Century Study. *A Report on Faculty-Staff-Student Aspirations.* College Station: 1962. 213 pp.

_____. Century Study. *Report of the Century Council to the Board of Directors.* College Station: 1962. 70 pp.

_____. Century Study. Spence, Thomas R. *Enrollment Record and Forecast: A&M College of Texas, 1962-1976.* College Station: 1962. 6 pp., inserts.

_____. *College Regulations.* College Station: 1919-1963. See Board of Directors, *Laws of the Agricultural and Mechanical College of Texas . . .*

_____. *Fifth Year Report to the Southern Association of Colleges and Schools* (October 1968). Mimeographed. 53 pp.

_____. *Laws of the Agricultural and Mechanical College of Texas, Established by the Board of Directors with the Rules and Regulations Established by the Faculty.* Title and dates vary. Bryan, College Station: 1883-1918. See Board of Directors, Peeler, Anderson James (ed.), *Laws Relating to the A&M College, 1876-1878; Orders Governing Cadets, 1903-1910;* Board of Directors, *The Blue Book, 1910-1919;* Board of Directors, *College Regulations, 1918-1963; University Regulations, 1963-.*

_____. *Message Accompanying the Report of the Board of the Agricultural and Mechanical College of the State of Texas.* Galveston: 1881. 48 pp.

_____. Minutes of the Board of Directors, 1875-1972. Vols. 1-37. Handscript and Typescript.

_____. *Objectives, Rules, Regulations for the Texas A&M University System, Adopted Sept. 24, 1963.* College Station: 1963. 24 pp.

_____. *Orders Governing Cadets.* College Station: 1903-1910. See Board of Directors, *Laws of the Agricultural and Mechanical College of Texas . . .*

_____. *Organization of the Agricultural and Mechanical College System in Texas, Bulletin of the Agricultural and Mechanical College of Texas,* 3rd ser., VI, No. 13 (December 1, 1920). 21 pp.

_____. Peeler, Anderson James (ed.). *Laws Relating to the Agricultural and Mechanical College of Texas and the Proceedings of the Board of Directors of Said College from June 1, 1875, to January 23, 1878.* Austin: 1878. 39 pp.

_____. President. *Reply to Paper Read by Dr. Thos. D. Wooten before the State Medical Association by the President of the Board of Directors, A&M College.* Galveston: 1887. 10 pp.

_____. *Proceedings of a Hearing by the Board of Directors of the A. and M. College of Texas. Held at Fort Worth, Texas, February 24 and 25, 1913. To Inquire Into and Receive Complaints Concerning Recent Breaches of Discipline at the A. and M. College of Texas.* n.p., n.d. 57 pp.

_____. *Regulations for the Guidance of the Faculty and Staff of the Agricultural and Mechanical College of Texas.* Varying dates. College Station: 1944-. See Board of Directors, *Laws of the Agricultural and Mechanical College of Texas . . .*

_____. *Sanitary Code of the Agricultural and Mechanical College of Texas, August 30, 1918.* College Station: 1918. 11 pp.

_____. *Statutes Enacted by the Board of Directors for the Government of the Agricultural and Mechanical College of Texas.* 2nd ed. College Station: July 1925. 23 pp. See Board of Directors, *Laws of the Agricultural and Mechanical College of Texas . . .*

_____. Self Study. *Institutional Self-Study: Report to Commission on Colleges, Southern Association of Colleges and Schools.* College Station: January 1963. i-xiii, 238 pp.

Bulletin of the Agricultural and Mechanical College of Texas. College Station: November 1, 1883-.

Contains official reports, catalogues, directories, and topical monographs. See individual entries.

Catalogue of the State Agricultural and Mechanical College of Texas. College Station: 1876-1963. See *Catalogue of the University,* 1963-.

Catalogue of Texas A&M University. College Station: 1963-1975. Since 1972 the University has styled the general catalogue as the Undergraduate Catalog.

Center for Dredging Studies, Department of Civil Engineering. *Graduate Study Research and Industrial Testing at the Center for Dredging Studies.* Informational brochure. n.p., n.d. [5 pp.].

Cent r for Marine Resources. *Galveston: Texas A&M University's Doorway to the Sea.* Brochure. n.p., n.d. [8 pp.].

_____. *Center for Marine Resources and Texas A&M, A Sea Grant College* [brochure]. n.p., n.d. [8 pp.].

Chancellor. *Annual Report of the Chancellor, Texas Agricultural and Mechanical College System.* College Station: 1951-1955. See Board of Directors, *Annual* and *Biennial Reports of the Board of Directors,* 1876-1945; President, *Annual Report of the President,* 1946-1951, 1956-.

Committee on Postwar Planning and Policy. "Forecast of Postwar Enrollment," March 21, 1944, Texas A&M University Archives. 14 pp., appendices.

Comptroller. *Financial Report of the Agricultural and Mechanical College of Texas.* College Station: 1934-. Previously published in *Annual* and *Biennial Reports.*

Corps of Cadets. *The Articles of the Cadet Corps.* 2nd ed. College Station: 1949. 32 pp.

_____. *Meeting of the Corps of Cadets with the President of A&M, March 8, 1956.* College Station: Association of Former Students, 1956. 23 pp.

Dean of the Graduate College. *Graduate Study in Oceanography, 1971-1972.* 23 pp.

_____. Post Graduation Studies. *Texas A. and M. Graduates Only Please.* College Station: [1949]. 30 pp.

_____. Schatte, Curtis Eric. *Doctoral Degree Programs at Texas A&M University.* College Station: 1970. 42 pp.

Dean of Men. *The Cadence: A Handbook for Freshmen.* College Station: 1942-. See also YMCA, *Students' Handbook.*

Dedication of the Memorial Student Center of the Agricultural and Mechanical College of Texas. College Station: A&M Press (April 21, 1951). 16 pp.

Jones, Jesse H. *Address by Mr. Jesse H. Jones, Chairman, Reconstruction Finance Corporation, November 5, 1936.* College Station: 1936. 10 pp.

Land-Grant College Centennial. Sub-Committee on Historical Perspective, "The Agricultural and Mechanical College of Texas: A Land-Grant College in Perspective." Mimeographed [1962]. 11 pp.

_____. Sub-Committee on Historical Perspective, "Enrollment at Texas A&M." Typed Manuscript. [3 pp.]. Texas A&M University Archives.

Leachman, Neth L. *Address by Mr. Neth L. Leachman, Dallas, Texas, Member of the Board of Directors, to the Graduating Class, January Twenty-Second, Nineteen Hundred and Forty-Three, The Agricultural and Mechanical College of Texas.* College Station: 1943. [12 pp.].

Morris, Page (Judge). *Baccalaureate Address. Bulletin of the A&M College of Texas.* 3rd ser., vol. 10 (July 1, 1924), 11-28; see also pp. 1-10, 29-48.

Munson, Thomas V. *What Shall My Profession Be? Address Delivered June 5th, 1888, to the Graduating Class of the Agricultural and Mechanical College of Texas.* Denison: 1888. 16 pp.

President. *Addresses at the Inauguration of the State Agricultural and Mechanical College of Texas, 1876.* College Station: 1876. 14 pp.

_____. *Annual Report of the President, Texas Agricultural and Mechanical College.* College Station: 1945-1951, 1951-. See Board of Directors, *Annual* and *Biennial Reports,* 1876-1945; Chancellor, *Annual Report of the Chancellor,* 1951-1955.

_____. *Bulletin of Information, 1925-1926. Bulletin of the Agricultural and Mechanical College,* 11 (March 1925). 44 pp.

_____. Faculty Advisory Committee. *Report of the Faculty Advisory Committee, Texas A&M University, September, 1964.* College Station: [1964]. 50 pp., appendices.

_____. *President's Report on the Agricultural and Mechanical College of Texas, May 15, 1943.* College Station: May 15, 1943. 12 pp.

_____. "President's Report to the Board of Directors, May 25, 1945." Mimeographed. 14 pp., appendices.

_____. "President's Report to the Board of Directors, May 30, 1946." Mimeographed. 20 pp., appendices.

_____. "President's Report, June 25, 1947." Mimeographed. 22 pp., appendices.

_____. *Report of the President, 1946-1947. Bulletin of the Agricultural and Mechanical College of Texas,* 5th ser., IV (March 1, 1948). 90 pp.

_____. "President's Report, May 10, 1948." Mimeographed. 19 pp., appendices.

_____. *1876 . . . 1926: The Semi-Centennial Celebration of the Agricultural and Mechanical College of Texas and the Inauguration of Thomas Otto Walton, LL.D., as President.* College Station: 1926. 246 pp.

_____. *Inauguration of David Hitchens Morgan as Thirteenth President.* Thursday, May 20, 1954. College Station: 1954. 44 pp.

_____. *The Inauguration of Jack Kenny Williams as Seventeenth President of Texas A&M University and Fourth President of the Texas A&M University System, April 16, 1971.* College Station: 1971. [28 pp.].

_____. *Inauguration of James Earl Rudder as President of the Agricultural and Mechanical College of Texas, March 26, 1960.* College Station: [1960]. [14 pp.]. See also *Proceedings of the Inauguration of James Earl Rudder as President of the Agricultural and Mechanical College of Texas.*

_____. *Inauguration of Marion Thomas Harrington as Twelfth President of the Agricultural and Mechanical College of Texas, Thursday, November 9, 1950.* College Station: 1950. 56 pp.

_____. *Proceedings of the Inauguration of James Earl Rudder as President of the Agricultural and Mechanical College of Texas.* College Station: [1960]. 68 pp.

_____. *Progress Report for Twelve Years of the Agricultural and Mechanical College of Texas, 1924-1937.* College Station: A&M Press, 1938. 78 pp.

_____. "Report to the Texas Commission on Higher Education: Role and Scope of the College in Higher Education Systems of Texas," June 24, 1954. Mimeographed. 11 pp., (1)-(9).

_____. *Sixty Facts About the Agricultural and Mechanical College of Texas.* College Station: [1918]. 16 pp.

Prairie View A&M, *General Catalog,* 1970-1971.

Proceedings of the Dedication of the Richard Coke Building. College Station: Texas A&M Press (May 11, 1957). 23 pp.

Registrar. *Annual Register.* College Station: 1956-1964.

_____. *Directory of Faculty, Staff and Students.* College Station: 1915-1975.

Sea Grant. Calhoun, Dr. John C. Jr., Director, Sea Grant Program, Texas A&M University, An Address, March 1, 1970, *Sea Grant . . . Goals and Accomplishments.* Sea Grant Publication No. 301 (March 1970). 19 pp.

_____. *Dedication Ceremonies of Texas A&M University as a Sea Grant College.* April 6, 1972. College Station: 1972. 8 pp.

_____. *Sea Grant Center for Marine Resources.* Reprinted from *The Texas Aggie,* October, 1971, by the Center for Marine Resources, Texas A&M University Sea Grant Program. [11 pp.].

_____. *The University and the Sea,* V (January-February 1972), 11 pp.

School of Veterinary Medicine. *Announcement of the School of Veterinary Medicine. Bulletin of the Agricultural and Mechanical College of Texas.* 3rd ser., VII (July 1, 1921). 20 pp.

Self-Study Committee, Standard I — Purpose. "Report of the Self-Study Committee for Standard I — Purpose," June 16, 1972. Mimeographed. 48 pp.

_____. "Preliminary Self-Study Report, Institute of Statistics, 1972 — Purpose." Mimeographed. [2 pp.].

_____. "Preliminary Self-Study Report, Architectural Research Center, 1972 — Purpose." Mimeographed. [2 pp.].

Seventy-fifth Anniversary Committee. *The Agricultural and Mechanical College of Texas, 1876-1951, 75th Anniversary.* College Station: A&M Press (October 4, 1950). 33 pp.

Special Academic Council Committee. "Report of the Special Academic Council Committee in the School of Military Science," June 15, 1954. [2 pp.].

Student Body Organization. *Aggieland.* College Station: 1950-. Student Annual. See also *The Olio,* 1895; *The Longhorn,* 1903-1949.

_____. *Longhorn, The.* College Station: 1903-1949. See Student Body Organization, *Aggieland.*

_____. *Olio, The.* College Station: 1895. See Student Body Organization, *Aggieland.*

_____. *Yell Book.* College Station: [c. 1921-1938].

Texas Agricultural Experiment Station. *Annual Reports of the Agricultural Experiment Station,* 1888-.

_____. *Bulletins.* 1888-.

_____. Francis, Mark. "Veterinary Science," *Texas Agricultural Experiment Station Bulletin,* No. 30 (March 1894), pp. 437-458.

_____. Francis, Mark, and J. W. Connaway. "Texas Fever," *Texas Agricultural Experiment Station Bulletin,* No. 53 (1899), pp. 55-106.

_____. Francis, Mark. "Texas Fever," *Texas Agricultural Experiment Station Bulletin,* No. 63 (1902), 58 pp.

_____. *Veterinary Science,* Bulletin 30 (March 1894), pp. 438-458.

Texas Agricultural Extension Service. *Bulletins.* 1914-.

_____. *The Agricultural Extension Service. Bulletin of the Agricultural and Mechanical College of Texas,* Catalogue Number: Part IX. College Station: 1946. 45 pp.

_____. *Extension Service Farm News,* 1924-1933.

_____. *I Pledge My Heart: The Story of Boys' 4-H Club Work in Texas.* College Station: 1938. [22 pp.].

_____. Memorandum of Understanding between the Texas Agricultural and Mechanical College System and the United States Department of Agriculture on Cooperative Extension Work in Agriculture and Home Economics, March 17, 1955. 3 pp.

Texas Farmers' Congress. *Proceedings,* 1898-1915. 18 vols.

The Farmers' Institute of the Fifth Congressional District, Henrietta, Texas, January 10 and 11, 1890. 4 pp.

Texas Forest Service. *A Picture Story of Forestry in Texas.* Bulletin No. 29, n.p., n.d. 24 pp.

_____. *Eleventh Annual Report.* College Station: 1926. 64 pp.

_____. *First Annual Report of the State Forester. Bulletin of the Agricultural and Mechanical College of Texas,* 3rd ser., III (February 1, 1917). 16 pp.

_____. *Forest Fire Prevention in Cooperation with the Federal Government. Bulletin of the Agricultural and Mechanical College of Texas,* 3rd ser., III (July 1, 1917). 17 pp.

_____. *Forest Resources of Eastern Texas. Bulletin of the Agricultural and Mechanical College of Texas,* 3rd ser., III (May 15, 1917). 57 pp.

_____. *General Survey of Texas Woodlands. Bulletin of the Agricultural and Mechanical College of Texas,* 3rd ser., III (May 1, 1917). 47 pp.

_____. *Grass and Woodland Fires in Texas. Bulletin of the Agricultural and Mechanical College of Texas,* 3rd ser., II (May 1916). 16 pp.

_____. *Second Annual Report of the State Forester. Bulletin of the Agricultural and Mechanical College of Texas,* 3rd ser., III (November 15, 1917). 7 pp.

_____. *Texas Forest Service: Its History, Objectives and Activities.* Circular 100. College Station: May 1965. 15 pp.

_____. *Texas Forestry Laws.* Circular 7. Revised, 1950, 1955, 1963, 1967. 25 pp.

_____. *Texas Forestry Programs, 1943-1944.* Bulletin 32. 1944. 76 pp.

_____. *Tree Regions of Texas.* Circular 75. Revised 1964, 1970. 11 pp.

Texas Maritime Academy. Wetmore, Sherman B., John A. Parker, and Peter J. La Valle, "The Establishment of the Texas Maritime Academy, 1958/1962." Texas Maritime Academy Board of Visitors, 1969. Mimeographed. 55 pp.

_____. *The Texas Maritime Academy, 1963-1964.* 36 pp.

_____. *Voyager,* 1969. 160 pp.

Texas Transportation Institute. *Research in . . . Transportation.* Bulletin No. 20 (1960-1963). [14 pp.].

_____. *As a Permanent Living Memorial to Thomas H. McDonald,* n.p., n.d. [15 pp.].

Young Men's Christian Association (YMCA). *Students' Handbook of A&M College of Texas.* College Station: 1912-. See also Dean of Men, *The Cadence: A Handbook for Freshmen.*

D. *Newspapers*

Abilene *Reporter News,* 1963.

Amarillo *News,* 1937.

Austin *American.* See Austin *Statesman.*

Austin *American-Statesman.* See Austin *Statesman.*

Austin *Daily Democratic Statesman.* See Austin *Statesman.*

Austin *Daily Journal,* 1871.

Austin *Daily News,* 1892-1903.

Austin *Daily State Journal,* 1871-1874.

Austin *Daily Statesman.* See Austin *Statesman.*

Austin *Daily Texan,* 1947, 1955.

Austin *Statesman,* July 26, 1871-December 30, 1944. Title varies.

Austin *Texas State Gazette,* August 24, 1849-October 19, 1878.

Austin *Tri-Weekly Statesman.* See Austin *Statesman.*

Beaumont *Daily Journal,* 1923.

Beaumont *Enterprise,* 1922, 1956.

Brenham *Daily Banner,* October 5, 1876-June 30, 1913.

Bryan *Brazos Pilot.* See Bryan *Eagle.*

Bryan *Brazos Valley Review,* 1950.

Bryan *Daily Eagle.* See Bryan *Eagle.*

Bryan *Daily Eagle and Pilot.* See *Bryan Eagle.*

Bryan *Eagle,* December 5, 1895-November 20, 1974. Title varies.

Bryan *Morning Eagle.* See Bryan *Eagle.*

Bryan *Enterprise,* 1883.

Bryan *News,* 1934-1952.

Bryan *Weekly Eagle,* October 24, 1889-October 16, 1890; November 15, 1894-September 15, 1937.

Channing *News,* 1926.

College Station *Battalion,* October 1, 1893-April 11, 1973.

College Station *College Journal,* 1889-1893.

College Station *Collegian,* 1890-1891.

College Station *Daily Bulletin* (successor to *The Reveille*), 1918-1926.

College Station *Fortnightly,* 1971-1974.

College Station *Reveille,* October 29, 1918-June 24, 1919. See College Station *Daily Bulletin.*

College Station *Texas A&M System News,* 1958.

College Station *Sparks and Flashes,* 1943-1945.

College Station *Texas Collegian,* 1878-1880.

Corpus Christi *Caller,* 1899.

Corsicana *Sun,* 1937.

Dalhart *Texan,* 1921.

Dallas *Journal.* Undated clipping.

Dallas *Morning News,* 1879-1973.

Dallas *News.* See Dallas *Morning News.*

Dallas *Semi-Weekly Farm News,* 1925.

Dallas *Texas Farmer,* 1880-1912.

Dallas *Times Herald,* 1913-1970.

Denison *Herald,* 1937.

Denton *Record-Chronicle,* 1947.

Fort Worth *Star-Telegram,* 1943-1949.

Galveston *Daily News,* 1865-1900.

Galveston *News.* See Galveston *Daily News.*

Galveston *Tribune,* 1885-1920.

Galveston *Tri-Weekly News,* 1855-1863; 1869-1873.

Honey Grove *Citizen,* 1926.

Houston *Chronicle,* October 14, 1901-.

Houston *Daily Post,* 1913.

Houston *Dispatch,* 1924.

Houston *Harris County News,* 1941.

Houston *Post,* 1880-1910; 1964-1972.

Houston *Press,* 1943.

Houston *Texas Farm and Fireside and Semi-Weekly Post* [1901-1912].

Kansas City (Missouri) *Times,* 1941.

Longview *News,* 1937.

Lufkin *News Daily,* 1947.

Marshall *News,* 1926.

Mexia *Daily News,* 1925.

Midland *Reporter,* 1926.

Nacogdoches *Sentinel,* 1937.

Navasota *Examiner,* 1894-1921.

New York *Times,* 1918-1919; 1941-1945.

Palestine *Herald,* 1925.

San Angelo *Standard Times,* 1970.

San Antonio *Daily Express,* 1908.

San Antonio *Express,* 1865-1970.

San Antonio *Light,* 1924-1958.

Sherman *Democrat,* 1937-1939.

Texarkana *Gazette,* 1937.

Texas City *Sun,* 1947.

Tyler *Journal,* 1926.

Tyler *Times,* 1937.

Vernon *Record,* 1926-1937.

Waco *Daily Examiner,* 1874; October 1-December 31, 1875; 1876-1878; November 12,
  1881-September 30, 1886.

Waco *Daily Times Herald,* 1908.

Waco *News Tribune,* 1947-1958.

Waco *Times,* 1947.

Waco *Times Herald,* 1908.

Waco *Tribune Herald,* 1960.

Wichita *Record News,* 1947.

Wichita Falls *Times,* 1937.

Yoakum *Times,* 1939.

E. *Magazines*

The Agriculturist, 1940-1941; 1946-1972. (Emerged from *The Scientific Review.*)

Alumni Quarterly, April 1916-1921. (Succeeded by the *Texas Aggie.*)

The Architectural Yearbook [c. 1916].

The Commentator, November 1947-May, 1953.

The Countryman, 1933-1934. (Merged with the *Technoscope* to become *The Scientific
  Review.*)

The Engineer, 1940-1941; 1946-April 1972. (Emerged from *The Scientific Review.*)

Farm and Ranch, 1883-1949.

The Student Farmer. [c. 1916].

The Technoscope, 1933-1934. (Merged with *The Countryman* to become *The Scientific
  Review.*)

Texas A&M Review, November 1959-Winter 1972.
The Texas Aggie, 1921-1973.
United States Army. Second Division Association. *The Indian Head,* September, 1954.

F. *Manuscripts*
(in Texas A&M University Archives and Manuscripts Collection unless otherwise indicated)

1. Manuscript Collections
   Alvord, Charles H., Papers.
   Asbury, Samuel E., Papers.
   Astin, Ervin Hugh, Papers.
   Athletics — Baseball File.
   Athletics — Bonfire File.
   Athletics — Football File.
   Austin Mothers' Club Scrapbooks.
   Bizzell, William Bennett, Papers.
   Bolton, Frank C., Papers.
   Brogdon, Stansel T., Papers.
   Coeducation Papers.
   Cole, James Reid, Papers.
   Corps of Cadets — Aggie Band.
   Corregidor Muster File, Association of Former Students Office, Texas A&M University.
   Craik, Rear Admiral James D., USCG (Retired), Galveston, Texas, to Henry C.
      Dethloff, College Station, Texas, undated memorandum, "Training Ship *Texas
      Clipper.*"
   Crane, Charles Judson, Papers.
   Files of the Dean of Admissions and Records, Registrar's Office, Texas A&M
      University.
   Easterwood Airport Papers.
   43rd San Jacinto Day Aggie Scrapbook, April 21, 1946.
   Foy, V. H., Papers.
   Gardiner, C. W., Papers.
   Gartner, George, Papers.
   Gathright, Thomas S., Papers.
   Harrington, Henry Hill, Papers.
   Heaton, Homer Lloyd, Papers, in the possession of the Heaton family, College Station,
      Texas.
   Hill, John E., Papers.
   Holman, Lucius, Papers.
   Honorary Degree File.
   McInnis, Louis L., Papers.
   Milner, Robert T., Milner Administration Papers.
   Morrisey, Robert S., Norman, Oklahoma, to John C. Calhoun, College Station, Texas,
      February 21, 1972.
   Nichols, Joseph F., "Reminiscences of Joseph F. Nichols."
   Pfeuffer, George, Papers.
   Rogan (Judge), Charles, Papers.

Roseborough, William Daniel, Papers.

Ross, Lawrence Sullivan. L. S. Ross Papers, Texas Collection, Baylor University.

Rosser, John. "Journal of a Trip to Texas in 1871."

Russell, Daniel. Scrapbooks.

Sayers, Joseph D., Papers, Texas State Archives, Austin, Texas.

Smith, Robert Franklin. "A Brief Sketch of the Agricultural and Mechanical College of Texas" [1914]. 7 pp.

Sneed, Glenn L., Papers.

Songs — Texas A&M University.

Stark, J. Wayne. Newspaper Clippings.

Steger, Frank D., Papers.

Sterns Football Plaque. Letters regarding the honoring of former A&M athletes, 1952-1953.

Sterns, Josh B. Reminiscences.

Texas A&M College Publicity Department, Press Clippings.

Texas A&M Scrapbooks, 1926-1973.

Texas Agricultural Extension Service Papers.

Texas Agricultural Extension Service, Minutes of the Extension Committee of the Agricultural and Mechanical College of Texas.

Texas Maritime Academy Papers.

Trotter, Ide Peebles, Papers.

TON Program File, Association of Former Students Office, Texas A&M University.

Veterinary Medicine Historical File.

World War II Casualty File, Association of Former Students Office, Texas A&M University.

World War II File.

2. Biographical Papers on:

Allen, Roderick R.

Anderson, David A., letter to Henry C. Dethloff, College Station, Texas, November 23, 1971; "Biographical Sketch of David A. Anderson"; and "Biographical Sketch of Paul R. Kramer."

Armistead, W. W.	Fountain, Charles Perkins.	Keathley, George Dennis.
Banks, William A.	Fowler, Thomas W.	Kiest, Edwin J.
Benson, Fred J.	Francis, Mark.	Kyle, Edwin Jackson.
Bible, Dana X.	Friley, Charles E.	Marsteller, Ross Perry.
Bruce, Andrew D.	Gainer, Charles S.	Morgan, David Hitchens.
Campbell, Charles B.	Giesecke, Frederick Ernst.	Nagle, James C.
Calhoun, John C., Jr.	Gilchrist, Gibb.	Rudder, James Earl.
Connally, James.	Harrell, William G.	Schumacher, Henry C.
Davis, John F.	Hohn, Caesar.	Schmidt, Hubert.
Deware, Charles.	Hughes, Lloyd H.	White, George Rollie.
Dunn, Ralph Clark.	Jones, Jesse Holman.	

G. *Interviews with:*

Brison, Fred R., May 14, 1971, College Station, Texas.

Crawford, Charles W., March 30, 1971, College Station, Texas.

Doak, Clifton C., May 14, 1971, College Station, Texas.

Draper, George H., October 2, 1971, College Station, Texas.

Evans, Edward B., October 11, 1971, Prairie View A&M College, Prairie View, Texas.

Folweiler, Alfred D., November 10, 1971, College Station, Texas.

Geren, Mrs. L. Giesecke, May 14, 1971, College Station, Texas.

Harrington, Marion Thomas, September 13, 1971, College Station, Texas.

Heaton, Homer Lloyd, July 10, 1972, College Station, Texas.

Howell, Eugene Jody, September 18, 1971, Tarleton State College, Stephenville, Texas.

Hutchison, John E., December 15, 1971, College Station, Texas.

Lancaster, Mrs. Robert R., September 9, 1971, Bryan, Texas.

Langford, Ernest, February 24, 1971, College Station, Texas.

Lindsey, James L., October 24, 1972, College Station, Texas.

Merrifield, Robert Glenn, December 1, 1971, College Station, Texas.

McElroy, Henry B., June 26, 1972, College Station, Texas.

McInnis, Miss Malcolm Graham (Scott), January 21, 1971, Bryan, Texas.

Rich, Mrs. Erma Munson, May 14, 1971, College Station, Texas.

Robinson, Elbert L., May 14, 1971, College Station, Texas.

Sherrell, Charles W., May 14, 1971, College Station, Texas.

Smith, Travis L., Jr., May 14, 1971, College Station, Texas.

Spence, Thomas Reese, December 13, 1971, College Station, Texas.

Sterns, Josh B., May 14, 1971, College Station, Texas.

Tate, Marvin, August 29, 1972, College Station, Texas.

Trotter, Ide Peebles, November 17, 1971, College Station, Texas.

Watts, Mrs. Thomas D., September 9, 1971, Bryan, Texas.

Williams, David W., September 15, 1971, College Station, Texas.

Woolfolk, George R., October 11, 1971, Prairie View A&M College, Prairie View, Texas.

II. SECONDARY SOURCES

A. *Books and Monographs*

Adams, Frank Carter (ed.). *Texas Democracy: A Centennial History of Politics and Personalities of the Democratic Party, 1836-1936.* Austin: Democratic Historical Association, 1937. 4 vols.

American Military History, 1607-1958. Headquarters, Department of the Army. ROTC Manual No. 145-20. Washington: 1959. 558 pp.

Atherton, Lewis Eldon. *The Cattle Kings.* Bloomington: Indiana University Press, 1961. 308 pp.

Bailey, Joseph C. *Seaman A. Knapp: Schoolmaster of American Agriculture.* New York: Columbia University Press, 1945. 307 pp.

Bailey, Thomas A. *A Diplomatic History of the American People.* 8th ed. New York: Appleton-Century-Crofts, 1969. 1,015 pp.

Baker, Gladys. *The County Agent.* Chicago: The University of Chicago Press, 1939. 226 pp.

Benedict, Murray R. *Farm Policies of the United States, 1790-1950, A Study of Their Origins and Development.* New York: Twentieth Century Fund, 1953. 548 pp.

Bizzell, William Bennett. *Introduction to the Study of Economics.* New York: Ginn and Company, 1923. 386 pp.

_____. *Rural Texas.* New York: Macmillan Company, 1924. 477 pp.

Block, William J. *The Separation of the Farm Bureau and the Extension Service.* Urbana, Illinois: University of Illinois Press, 1960. 304 pp.

Bradley, Omar. *A Soldier's Story.* New York: Henry Holt & Co., 1951. 618 pp.

Brown, John Henry. *Indian Wars and Pioneers of Texas.* Austin: L. E. Daniell [189-?]. 762 pp.

Buck, Solon Justus. *The Granger Movement: A Study of Agricultural Organization and Its Political, Economic and Social Manifestations, 1870-1880.* Cambridge, Massachusetts: Harvard University Press, 1913. 384 pp.

Burges, Austin E. *A Local History of Texas A. & M. College.* Bryan: 1915. 37 pp.

Casey, Paul D. *The History of the A. & M. College Trouble, 1908.* Waco: J. S. Hill & Co., 1908. 222 pp.

Cofer, David Brooks (ed.). *Early History of Texas A. and M. College through Letters and Papers.* College Station: Association of Former Students, 1952. 143 pp.

———. *First Five Administrators of Texas A. & M. College, 1876-1890.* College Station: Association of Former Students, 1953. 48 pp.

———. *Fragments of Early History of Texas A. & M. College.* College Station: Association of Former Students, 1953. 96 pp.

———. *Second Five Administrators of Texas A. & M. College, 1890-1905.* College Station: Association of Former Students, 1954. 132 pp.

———. *Supplement to First Five Administrators of Texas A. & M. College: James Reid Cole, 1879-1885.* College Station: Association of Former Students, 1955. 49 pp.

Cole, James Reid. *Seven Decades of My Life.* Dallas: James Reid Cole, 1913. 212 pp.

Cook, Robert C. (ed.). *Who's Who in American Education, 1937-1938.* New York: The Robert C. Cook Company, 1938. 737 pp.

Cooper, Lewis B. *The Permanent School Fund of Texas.* Fort Worth: Texas State Teachers Association, 1934. 256 pp.

Davis, J. Thomas (ed.). *John Tarleton, A Memorial to the Founder of Tarleton College.* Stephenville, Texas: Tarleton State College, May 1, 1933. 57 pp.

Dinwiddie, Hardaway H. *Industrial Education in Our Common Schools.* Fort Worth: Loving Printing Co., 1886. 16 pp.

Durden, Robert F. *The Climax of Populism: The Election of 1896.* Lexington: University of Kentucky Press, 1965. 190 pp.

Eaker, Ira C., "Strategic Air Power over Europe," in Nathaniel F. Silsbee, *Bombs Away! Your Air Force in Action.* New York: Wm. H. Wise & Co., Inc., 1948. 386 pp.

Eaton, Clement. *The Growth of Southern Civilization, 1790-1860.* New York: Harper, 1961. 357 pp.

Eby, Frederick (ed.). *Education in Texas: Source Materials.* New York: Macmillan, 1925. 354 pp.

Eddy, Edward D., Jr. *The Land-Grant Movement: A Capsule History of the Educational Revolution Which Established Colleges for All the People.* Land-Grant College Association, 1962. 38 pp.

Fenley, Florence. *Oldtimers of Southwest Texas.* Uvalde, Texas: Hornby Press, 1957. 318 pp.

Galbraith, John Kenneth. *The Great Crash, 1929.* Boston: Houghton Mifflin Company, 1954. 212 pp.

Garvin, William L. *History of the Grand State Farmers' Alliance of Texas.* Jacksboro, Texas: J. N. Rogers, 1885. 84 pp.

Garvin, William L., and S. O. Daws. *History of the National Farmers' Alliance and Cooperative Union of America.* Jacksboro, Texas: J. N. Rogers, 1887. 158 pp.

Gittinger, Roy. *The University of Oklahoma, 1892-1942.* Norman: University of Oklahoma Press, 1942. 282 pp.

Glines, Carroll V. *Doolittle's Tokyo Raiders.* Princeton, New Jersey: Van Nostrand Co., 1964. 447 pp.

Harris, Joseph. *Harris on the Pig: Breeding, Rearing, Management, and Improvement.* New York: Orange Judd Company, 1883. 273 pp.

Hill, Kate Adele. *Home Demonstration Work in Texas.* San Antonio: Naylor Co., 1958. 208 pp.

Hogg, Alexander. *Industrial Education: State Agricultural and Mechanical College of Texas.* Galveston: 1879. 52 pp.

Hohn, Caesar. *Dutchman on the Brazos.* Austin: University of Texas Press, 1963. 194 pp.

Houston, David. *A Critical Study of Nullification in South Carolina.* New York: Longmans, Green, and Co., 1896. 169 pp.

_____. *Eight Years with Wilson's Cabinet, 1913-1920.* Garden City, New York: Doubleday, Page & Co., 1926. 2 vols.

Howell, Eugene J., and Karl Opryshek. *Southern Champions: A Football Treasure.* n.p., n.d. 32 pp.

Jackson, Grace. *Cynthia Ann Parker.* San Antonio: Naylor Press, 1959. 138 pp.

Jennings, Robert. *Cattle and Their Diseases.* Philadelphia: J. E. Potter, 1863. 340 pp.

Johnson, Charles Monroe. *Action with the Seaforths.* New York: Vantage Press, 1954. 342 pp.

Johnson, Frank W. *A History of Texas and Texans.* Edited by Eugene C. Barker and Ernest William Winkler. Chicago: American Historical Society, 1914. 5 vols.

Kahn, E. J., Jr., and Henry McLemore. *Fighting Divisions.* Washington: Infantry Journal Press, 1946. 218 pp.

Lane, John J. *History of the University of Texas.* Austin: Henry Hutchings, 1891. 322 pp.

Langford, Ernest. *First Fifty Years of Architectural Education at the Agricultural and Mechanical College of Texas: A Brief History of the Division of Architecture from September 1, 1905, to August 31, 1956.* College Station: University Archives, 1960. 45 pp.

_____. *Getting the College Under Way.* College Station: University Library, 1970. 62 pp.

_____. *Here We'll Build the College.* College Station: University Archives, 1963. 208 pp.

Lindley, Vick. *The Battalion: Seventy Years of Student Publications at the A&M College of Texas.* College Station: Student Activities Office, 1948. 7 pp.

Little, Van A. *A Brief History of Entomology at the Agricultural and Mechanical College of Texas Prior to the Integration of the Services in 1947.* College Station: College Archives, 1960. 45 pp.

Long, Walter E. *For All Time to Come.* Austin: The Steck Company, 1964. 111 pp.

Martin, Oscar B. *The Demonstration Work: Dr. Seaman A. Knapp's Contribution to Civilization.* 3rd ed. San Antonio: Naylor Co., 1941. 257 pp.

Martin, Roscoe C. *The People's Party in Texas: A Study in Third-Party Politics.* Austin: Texas University, 1933. 280 pp.

McConnell, Grant. *The Decline of Agrarian Democracy.* Berkeley: University of California Press, 1953. 226 pp.

McKay, Seth Shepard. *Debates in the Constitutional Convention of 1875.* Austin: University of Texas Press, 1930. 471 pp.

Miller, Thomas Lloyd. *The Public Lands of Texas, 1519-1970.* Norman: University of Oklahoma Press, 1972. 341 pp.

Mississippi: A Guide to the Magnolia State. Federal Writers' Project of the Works Progress Administration. New York: The Viking Press, 1938. 545 pp.

Nance, Joseph Milton. *The Early History of Bryan and the Surrounding Area.* Bryan: Hood's Brigade-Bryan Centennial Committee, 1962. 64 pp.

Newcomb, Richard F. *Iwo Jima.* New York: Holt, Rinehart and Winston, 1965. 338 pp.

Ousley, Clarence. *History of the Agricultural and Mechanical College of Texas.* Bulletin of the Agri-

cultural and Mechanical College of Texas, 4th ser., vol. 6, no. 8 (December 1, 1935), 172 pp.

Owen, Sir Richard. *On the Anatomy of Vertebrates.* London: Longmans, Green and Co., 1866-1868. 3 vols.

Pasco, John. *Fish Sergeant.* College Station: 1940. 144 pp.

Perry, George Sessions. *The Story of Texas A. and M.* New York: McGraw-Hill, 1951. 264 pp.

Ramsdell, Charles W. *Reconstruction in Texas.* Columbia University Studies in History. New York: Longmans, Green & Co., 1910. 324 pp.

Randall, Henry Stephens. *Sheep Husbandry.* New York: C. M. Saxton, 1863. 338 pp.

Reeder, Russell Potter. *The Story of the Second World War: The Axis Strikes, 1939-1942.* Vol. I. New York: Meredith Press, 1969. 267 pp.

Rice, Lawrence. *The Negro in Texas, 1877-1900.* Baton Rouge: Louisiana State University Press, 1971. 309 pp.

Richardson, Norval Rupert. *Texas: The Lone Star State.* New York: Prentice Hall, 1943. 590 pp.

Robbins, Roy M. *Our Landed Heritage: The Public Domain, 1776-1936.* Princeton: Princeton University Press, 1942. 450 pp.

Rollins, Joseph G., Jr. *Aggies! Y'all Caught That Dam' Ol' Rat Yet?* San Antonio: Naylor Co., 1970. 103 pp.

Rose, Victor M. *Ross' Texas Brigade.* Louisville, Kentucky, 1881. Reprinted by Continental Book Co., Kennesaw, Georgia, 1960. 185 pp.

Saten, Joseph (ed.). *The 1950's: America's "Placid" Decade.* Boston: Houghton Mifflin Company, 1960. 223 pp.

Shepardson, Charles N. *A Study of the Agricultural Graduates of the Agricultural and Mechanical College of Texas. Bulletin of A&M College,* 5th ser., vol. 7 (July 1, 1951), 42 pp.

Schmidt, Hubert. *Eighty Years of Veterinary Medicine: A Brief History of the School of Veterinary Medicine, 1878-1958.* College Station: College Archives, 1958. 40 pp.

Schwettmann, Martin W. *The University of Texas Oil Discovery — Santa Rita.* Austin: The Texas State Historical Association, 1943. 43 pp.

Shannon, David A. (ed.). *The Great Depression.* Englewood Cliffs, New Jersey: Prentice-Hall, Inc., 1960. 171 pp.

Shannon, Fred A. *The Farmer's Last Frontier: Agriculture 1860-1897.* New York: Holt, 1945. 434 pp.

Shuffler, Henderson. *A Man and His College: Frank C. Bolton and the Agricultural and Mechanical College of Texas.* College Station: A. and M. Press, May 27, 1950. 14 pp.

———, (ed.). *Son, Remember . . .* College Station: A&M Press, 1951.

Sims, Edward H. *American Aces in Great Fighter Battles of World War II.* New York: Harper & Row, 1958. 256 pp.

Smith, W. Broaddus. *Brazos County, Texas, Cemetery Inscriptions.* Houston: 1967. 155 pp.

Stephenson, Stanley E. *Interdisciplinary Program in Engineering.* College Station: [1963]. 70 pp.

True, Alfred C. *A History of Agricultural Extension Work in the United States, 1785-1923.* New York: Arno Press, 1969. 436 pp.

Wallace, Ernest. *Charles DeMorse, Pioneer Editor and Statesman.* Lubbock: Texas Tech Press, 1945. 271 pp.

Webb, Walter Prescott, and H. Bailey Carroll (eds.). *The Handbook of Texas.* Austin: Texas State Historical Association, 1952. 2 vols.

Who's Who in America, 1966-1967. Chicago, Illinois: A. N. Marquis Co., 1916. 2,472 pp.

Wilbarger, J. W. *Indian Depredations in Texas.* Austin: 1889. Reprinted by the Steck Company, 1935. 672 pp.

Woolfolk, George Ruble. *Prairie View: A Study in Public Conscience, 1878-1946.* New York:

Pageant Press, 1962. 404 pp.

Wythe, Joseph Henry. *The Microscopist: A Manual of Microscopy and Compendium of the Microscopic Sciences.* Philadelphia: Lindsay & Blakeston, 1877. 259 pp.

Youatt, William. *Youatt's History, Treatment and Diseases of the Horse.* Philadelphia: Lippincott, 1859. 470 pp.

B. *Articles*

Anderson, Frank G., "The Bonfire as It Was," College Station *Battalion,* January 18, 1972.

"The Alumni Memorial Stadium," *Alumni Quarterly,* V (February 1920), pp. 3-4.

Andree, R. A., "With the School of Auto and Motor Truck Mechanics," *Alumni Quarterly,* III (May 1918), pp. 4-5.

Bizzell, William Bennett, "College Appropriations," *Alumni Quarterly,* II (May 1917), pp. 2-3.

_____, "New Agricultural College," *Alumni Quarterly,* II (January 1917), pp. 3-4.

Bolton, Frank C., "With the School of Radio Mechanics," *Alumni Quarterly,* III (May 1918), p. 10.

"Cooperating Their Way through College," *Readers Digest* (June 1939), pp. 43-46.

Dethloff, Henry C., "Missouri Farmers and the New Deal: A Case Study of Farm Policy Formulation on the Local Level," *Agricultural History,* 39 (July 1965), pp. 141-146.

_____, "Rice Revolution in the Southwest, 1880-1910," *Arkansas Historical Quarterly,* XXIX (Spring 1970), pp. 66-75.

"The Dixie Classic," *The Collegiate World,* IV (January-February 1922), pp. 2, 31.

"Dr. Mark Francis," *The Norden News,* X (September-October 1936), p. 6.

Geiser, S. W. "George Washington Curtis and Frank Arthur Gulley: Two Early Agricultural Teachers in Texas," *Field and Laboratory,* XIV (January 1946), pp. 1-13.

Horn, Louis J., "Engineering Research Geared for Immediate Implementation," *Texas A&M Engineer* (May 1969), [1-4].

Heinz, W. C., "I Took My Son to Omaha Beach," *Colliers* (June 11, 1954), pp. 21-27.

Hodenfield, G. K., "I Climbed the Cliffs with the Rangers," *Saturday Evening Post* (August 19, 1944), pp. 18-19, 98.

Humbert, Eugene P., "Report of the Committee on Organization for National Defense," *Alumni Quarterly,* III (February 1918), pp. 18-19.

Jennings, Herbert Spencer, "Stirring Days at A. and M.," *Southwest Review,* XXXI (1946), pp. 341-344.

King, C. Richard, "John Tarleton," *Southwestern Historical Quarterly,* LV (October 1951), pp. 240-253.

Kyle, Edwin J., "The Agricultural Graduates' Part in the War for Democracy," *Alumni Quarterly,* III (February 1918), pp. 10-12.

_____, "The Need for an Agricultural Building at the Agricultural and Mechanical College of Texas," *Alumni Quarterly,* IV (February 1919), pp. 14-15.

"Lawrence Sullivan Ross Statue Unveiled," *Alumni Quarterly,* IV (May 1919), pp. 11-12.

Martin, Roscoe C., "The Grange as a Political Factor in Texas," *Southwestern Political and Social Science Quarterly,* VI (March 1926), pp. 363-383.

"Memorial to Governor Ross," *Alumni Quarterly,* III (February 1918), p. 15.

Pinkard, Tommy, "TTI: Research in All Directions," *Texas Highways* (January 1968), pp. 1-11.

Puryear, Charles, "The War and the College," *Alumni Quarterly,* IV (November 1918), pp. 3-4.

Reynolds, Quentin, "Deep in the Heart," *Colliers* (May 30, 1942), pp. 12, 51-53.

Rosenberg, Charles E., "Science, Technology and Economic Growth: The Case of the Agricultural Experiment Station Scientist, 1875-1914," *Agricultural History,* XLV (January 1971), pp. 1-20.

Sherrod, Robert, "Toughest Guy in the Air Force," *Saturday Evening Post* (March 26, 1955), pp. 38-39, 143-147.

Smith, Ralph A., "The Farmers' Alliance in Texas, 1876-1900," *Southwestern Historical Quarterly,* XLVIII (January 1945), pp. 346-369.

_____, "The Grange Movement in Texas, 1873-1900," *Southwestern Historical Quarterly,* XLII (April 1939), pp. 297-315.

"Two Leaders in Educational Statesmanship," *World's Work,* XII (July 1906), p. 7728.

Walker, B. M., "Henry Hill Harrington," *Journal of Mississippi History,* II (July 1940), pp. 156-158.

C. *Theses, Dissertations, and Unpublished Manuscripts*

"Annual Report of the President Pro Tempore, May 30, 1914," College Station, Texas, unpublished typescript in Texas A&M University Archives. [14 pp.].

[Banks, Mrs. William A.] "College in 1876," unsigned manuscript, presumed to be written by Mrs. William A. Banks, Texas A&M University Archives. [7 pp.].

Brooks, Melvin S., and John R. Bertrand, "Student Attitudes toward Aspects of the A. & M. College of Texas, Spring 1954," College Station, 1954. 78 pp.

Byrnes, Robert Eugene, "Lafayette Lumpkin Foster: A Biography," unpublished master's thesis, Texas A&M University, 1964. 278 pp.

Calhoun, John C., Jr., College Station, to President Jack K. Williams, College Station [memorandum], "Institutes and Centers at Texas A&M University, October 6, 1971" [19 pp.].

Ferguson, Arthur Clinton, "The Provisions for Education in the Texas Constitution of 1876," unpublished Ph.D. dissertation, University of Texas, 1937. 655 pp.

Grosslin, Hiawatha, "The Development of Organization and Administration in the Institutions of Higher Learning in Texas," unpublished Ph.D. dissertation, University of Texas, 1943. 485 pp.

Clarke, Bessie Ross, "S. P. Ross and Sull Ross," Xerox copy of unpublished manuscript by the daughter of Lawrence Sullivan Ross, in Ross Biographical Papers, Texas A&M University Archives. The original is in the L. S. Ross Papers, Texas Collection, Baylor University. 94 pp.

Langford, Ernest, "It's History — Women at A&M," unpublished manuscript in Texas A&M University Archives. 9 pp.

Marshall, Elmer Grady, "The History of Brazos County, Texas," unpublished master's thesis in history, University of Texas, 1937. 234 pp.

Martin, Roscoe C., "The Farmer in Texas Politics, 1875-1900," unpublished master's thesis, University of Texas, 1925. 291 pp.

McGinnis, Francis Kamp, "Reminiscences" (May 1956), Texas A&M University Archives. 8 pp.

Rollins, John Wesley, "The Organization and Administration of the Office of Dean of Men at the Agricultural and Mechanical College of Texas, 1945-1947," unpublished master's thesis in education, East Texas State Teachers College, 1950. 161 pp.

Westbrook, Polly, "A History of Co-education at Texas A&M University," unpublished manuscript in Texas A&M University Archives. 42 pp.

Index

electric trolley, 190
electricity: at A&M, 158-159, 166, 169, 183
Eliot, H. M., 274
Emery, Ambrose Robert, 439
Empire State IV, 602
endowment: enriched by oil, 404, 416. *See also* University Fund
Engineering, Department of, 99, 109
Engineering, School of, 299, 441-442, 537; Gilchrist and, 441-442; Nagle and, 250-251; problems of, 478
engineering, teaching of, 98-99, 118, 121, 246-247; development of, 190, 244-246, 247-253; difficulties of, 243, 247; Pfeuffer on, 114. *See also* classical/technical education conflict; Engineering, Department of; Engineering, School of
Engineering Experiment Station, 254, 537, 604
Engineering Extension Service, 537
engineering library, 57, 441, 573
Engineering Test Laboratory, 593
England: in World War I, 271
English: courses in, 31; Department of, 184, 485
Enlisted Reserve Corps, Army (ERC), 457
enrollment. *See* Texas A&M University, enrollment at
Entomology, Department of, 188, 588
Environmental Design, Department of Architecture and, 573, 582
Environmental Engineering Division, 594
epidemics, 85, 180-181, 202, 288, 406
Estill, Charles Patrick: on faculty, 70-71; firing of, 76-77
Estill, Harry F., 77
Eudaly, Ernest R., 397, 398, 485
Evans, Claude M., 390, 392, 395
Evans, Edward Bertram, 310, 311, 320, 321, 500; and Prairie View A&M University, 323-325, 327, 328
Evans, Robley David, 454
Evans, Sterling C., 395, 568

Evans, Walter W., 205, 210, 216
Ex-Cadets, Association of: organization of, 103, 171
Excellence, 602
Executive Development Program, 592
Experiment Station (building), 267. *See also* Agricultural Experiment Station
Experiment Station Bulletins, 222
Extension, Department of, 383. *See also* Agricultural Extension Service
extension courses, 266, 390, 392, 430, 460
Extension Service. *See* Agricultural Extension Service
extension work, agricultural, 382-403 *passim*

FFFS (Forest Fire Fighters Service), 374
faculty: composition of, 137, 302-303. *See also* Texas A&M University, faculty of
Faculty-Staff-Student Study on Aspirations, 561, 563, 564
Fairleigh, George, 526
Falconer, William, 36
Farm, the College: Board of Directors and, 38, 47, 73, 161; establishment of, 37-38; expansion of, 47, 74; Gorgeson and, 74; problems of, 42, 56-57, 90, 161; superintendent of, 36, 37. *See also* Agricultural Experiment Station
Farm Boys' and Girls' Progressive League, 386
Farm and Ranch Journal, 386
Farm and Ranch Management, Department of, 408
Farmer, James P., 26
"Farmers," 217; Aggies as, 103, 437; first football game of, 501; misnomer, 117
Farmers' Alliance, 14
Farmers' Camp Meeting, 179, 385
Farmers' Congresses, 189, 390; organi-

Printed in the United States
79488LV00004B/7